Drugs and the Neuroscience of Behavior

Second Edition

To Lisa and Joe, for your mentorship and friendship

Sara Miller McCune founded SAGE Publishing in 1965 to support the dissemination of usable knowledge and educate a global community. SAGE publishes more than 1000 journals and over 800 new books each year, spanning a wide range of subject areas. Our growing selection of library products includes archives, data, case studies and video. SAGE remains majority owned by our founder and after her lifetime will become owned by a charitable trust that secures the company's continued independence.

Los Angeles | London | New Delhi | Singapore | Washington DC | Melbourne

Drugs and the Neuroscience of Behavior

An Introduction to Psychopharmacology

Second Edition

Adam Prus
Northern Michigan University

Los Angeles | London | New Delhi
Singapore | Washington DC | Melbourne

FOR INFORMATION:

SAGE Publications, Inc.
2455 Teller Road
Thousand Oaks, California 91320
E-mail: order@sagepub.com

SAGE Publications Ltd.
1 Oliver's Yard
55 City Road
London EC1Y 1SP
United Kingdom

SAGE Publications India Pvt. Ltd.
B 1/I 1 Mohan Cooperative Industrial Area
Mathura Road, New Delhi 110 044
India

SAGE Publications Asia-Pacific Pte. Ltd.
3 Church Street
#10-04 Samsung Hub
Singapore 049483

Printed in the United States of America.

ISBN 978-1-5063-3894-1

Library of Congress Cataloging-in-Publication Data

Names: Prus, Adam J., author.

Title: Drugs and the neuroscience of behavior : an introduction to psychopharmacology / Adam Prus, Northern Michigan University.

Other titles: Introduction to drugs and the neuroscience of behavior

Description: Second edition. | Los Angeles : SAGE, [2018] | Revision of: An introduction to drugs and the neuroscience of behavior. 2014. | Includes bibliographical references and index.

Identifiers: LCCN 2016051143 | ISBN 9781506338941 (pbk. : alk. paper)

Subjects: LCSH: Psychopharmacology. | Psychotropic drugs—Side effects.

Classification: LCC RM315 .P718 2018 | DDC 615.7/8—dc23
LC record available at https://lccn.loc.gov/2016051143

This book is printed on acid-free paper.

Acquisitions Editor: Abbie Rickard
Production Editor: Andrew Olson
Copy Editor: Pam Suwinsky
Typesetter: C&M Digitals (P) Ltd.
Proofreader: Caryne Brown
Indexer: Judy Hunt
Cover Designer: Michael Dubowe
Marketing Manager: Jenna Retana

SUSTAINABLE FORESTRY INITIATIVE
Certified Chain of Custody
Promoting Sustainable Forestry
www.sfiprogram.org
SFI-01268
SFI label applies to text stock

17 18 19 20 21 10 9 8 7 6 5 4 3 2 1

• Brief Contents •

• Detailed Contents •

• Preface •

Drugs and the Neuroscience of Behavior: An Introduction to Psychopharmacology, second edition, provides a broad coverage of the fundamental concepts and principles of psychopharmacology. These include how drugs enter and travel through the body, the various actions psychoactive drugs can have in the brain, and the many types of behavioral and physiological effects brought about by the actions of drugs in the brain. These topics are presented early in the book and show how they can help us to understand the use, actions, and effects of different classes of drugs, including psychostimulants, depressants, cannabis, psychedelics, and drugs used for treating mental disorders.

The first edition of the text came about from my years of teaching and studying psychopharmacology; in particular, I was influenced by my research training, which involved everything from bench-top molecular biology work to assessing behavior in lab rats and mice. The current edition of the textbook continues to emphasize how basic research findings apply to the effects we find in humans. In doing so, students not only learn how drugs act on the nervous system to produce pharmacological effects, but they also learn about the techniques used to study psychoactive drugs.

It's been only a few years since the first edition was released, but the rapid advancement of this field has made a revision to the book absolutely necessary. Here's an example: vaping. Nicotine vaping became popular soon after the release of the first edition and is now a major addition to Chapter 7, "Nicotine and Caffeine." This is one of many major new topics added to the second edition, all of which I note later in this Preface.

How the Materials Are Organized

Like the first edition, the second edition provides a number of features that help to facilitate the delivery of this material to students. Information in the book is provided in a careful, step-by-step presentation of information supplemented by illustrations, figures, boxes, and several unique pedagogical features. These features include the following.

From Actions to Effects Each chapter ends with a section called "From Actions to Effects." These sections cover a topic that brings together information presented in the chapter, providing a way to assemble multiple topics for addressing a single concept. In particular, these topics focus on a concept that requires understanding a drug's actions to account for its effects. These sections aid in the conceptual understanding of chapter material.

Stop & Check Stop & Check questions conclude each section in each chapter. These questions allow students to self-assess their understanding of main points covered in the previous section.

Review! Chapters include important reminders of facts or concepts covered in previous chapters. These help integrate the diverse material covered in this text.

Drug Profiles This a new feature in the second edition that provides important basic information about a key compound. Information in these profiles includes a drug's generic name, trade name, and/or street name and provides a description of its pharmacological actions.

Research Techniques and Methods Chapters include boxes that cover a research technique or method used in psychopharmacology research. These boxes model good working science and provide an easy reference when students come across research findings derived from each technique. These studies are also important in fostering critical thinking habits in students.

Key Terms Each chapter ends with a list of key terms from the chapter. A definition is provided for each key term in a combined glossary and index at the end of the book.

Supplementary Materials The text comes equipped with PowerPoint presentations and a test bank of exam questions organized by chapter.

Changes in the Second Edition

This second edition of *Drugs and the Neuroscience of Behavior: An Introduction to Psychopharmacology* provides major changes throughout book, including the addition of new topics and updated information on past topics.

Major new topics include coverage of:

- Chapter 2: Epigenetics
- Chapter 3: Optogenetics
- Chapter 4: The role of pKa and pH in drug absorption
- Chapter 5: Bulimia nervosa
- Chapter 6: Sex differences in psychostimulant addiction
- Chapter 7: E-cigarettes and vaping
- Chapters 6–15: DSM-5 diagnostic criteria for dependence and mental disorders
- Chapter 8: Kombucha and different types of beer
- Chapter 11: Dabbing and vaping cannabis products
- Chapter 12: Timothy Leary
- Chapter 13: Gliotransmitters, treatments for fibromyalgia
- Chapter 15: Pharmacological treatments for autism spectrum disorder

New findings for topics found in the first edition were provided on:

- Chapter 5: The role of the amygdala in drug addiction
- Chapter 6: Bath salts
- Chapter 7: Tobacco smoke exposure and risk of Alzheimer's disease
- Chapter 8: Changes in glutamate receptor function during chronic alcohol use and alcohol blackout
- Chapter 11: The effectiveness of medical marijuana
- Chapter 12: Effectiveness of ketamine for treating depression
- Chapter 14: The association between cortisol levels and posttraumatic stress disorder

Here is a more detailed overview of what was added for the second edition.

- Chapter 1: Certain safety index, clarifications about study variables, and clinical trial phases.
- Chapter 2: Clarification of information about genetics, new material about neurogenetics and epigenetics, and more information about the autonomic nervous system.
- Chapter 3: An entire box devoted to optogenetics, and new information about turnover, neuromodulation, Down syndrome, and conformational changes to neurotransmitter receptors.
- Chapter 4: Significant content regarding pharmacokinetics, including equations that consider a drug's pKa and the pH levels of the physiological environment, Phase I and II Biotransformation, the term *liberation*, and conjugation and conjugation reaction. Further, new material on allosteric regulation, levodopa, and conditioned tolerance.
- Chapter 5: Consideration of the discordance between state and federal laws regarding medical marijuana, updated material about DSM-5 (as do all subsequent chapters), revised and improved material regarding James Olds and Otto Loewi, role of amygdala in addiction, additional information about 12-step programs, bulimia nervosa, and some helpful information for readers who may need assistance coping with drug addiction.
- Chapter 6: Updated information on bath salts, and other additions included sex differences in psychostimulant addiction, information about use of cocaine for nasal surgeries and severe nose bleeds, and updated statistics on psychostimulant drug use (all subsequent chapter received updated use statistics).
- Chapter 7: Substantially revised material on e-cigarette use and vaping, third-hand smoking, greater mortality rates among African Americans, tobacco flue curing, menthol cigarettes, tobacco smoke exposure and risk of Alzheimer's disease, why some first-time smokers become chronic smokers while others do not, material on how to quit smoking, differences in the success of smoking cessation therapies based on racial and sex differences, pH of caffeine and degree of absorption, and a characterization of adenosine.
- Chapter 8: Descriptions of different alcoholic beverages, polymorphisms and alcohol metabolism, changes in NMDA receptor function from chronic alcohol

consumption, updated statistics on binge drinking, different types of blackout, hormesis, cancer risk from drinking, confabulation, and acamprosate.

- Chapter 9: A note about 1,4-Butanediol being an industrial solvent.
- Chapter 10: The dramatic increase in heroin use was noted, along with information about desomorphine, CYP2D6 activity and metabolism of codeine, definition of opioid overdose, an explanation for why buprenorphine can be prescribed from doctor's offices, and a description of morphine as a potential partial agonist.
- Chapter 11: Updated information on descriptions of different forms of cannabis, THC concentrations if different types of cannabis plants, dabbing, personal vaporizer use of smoking cannabis, relaxed federal regulations on transportation of cannabis, clarified information on THC and weight gain, risk of schizophrenia from cannabis use, major additions to behavioral effects of cannabis use, adverse effects from synthetic cannabis use, and new evidence about effectiveness of medical marijuana.
- Chapter 12: New material, including possibility that Salem witch trials were caused by ergot poisoning, NBOMe drugs, Timothy Leary, effects of chronic hallucinogen use, use of hallucinogens in psychotherapy, multiple organ failure (regarding MDMA), effects of phencyclidine at neuromuscular junctions, out-of-body experience, and effects of dissociative anesthetics on memory.
- Chapter 13: New prevalence data on differences in depression between men and women, greater prevalence of aggression in depressed men, predictors of suicide, higher rates of depression in Alzheimer's disease, role reserpine played in history of psychopharmacology, levodopa and the film *Awakenings*, black box warnings for antidepressants, sexual side effects, emotional blunting, fibromyalgia, issues surrounding placebo effects in antidepressant studies, combining psychotherapy and pharmacotherapy, role of serotonin neurotransmission in antidepressant effects, new material on ketamine and scopolamine, use of diffusion tensor imaging in bipolar disorder, and historical information on lithium.
- In Chapter 14, more information about differences between anxiety and fear, a description of how optogenetics was used to activate fear memories, associations between cortisol levels and PTSD, clarification between sedative and hypnotic, potential for addiction to benzodiazepines, gliotransmitters, endogenous benzodiazepines, Z-drugs, and role of serotonin neurotransmission in effectiveness of drugs for treating anxiety.
- Chapter 15: Now has a description of benzodiazepine use for catatonic schizophrenia, cognitive dysmetria, the long-abandoned theory of the schizophrenogenic mother, the disputes between Laborit and Deniker, antiemetic effects of antipsychotic drugs, antipsychotic depot injections, and the use of antipsychotic drugs for treating autism.

Acknowledgments

I am thrilled to have my second edition developed by SAGE Publishing, which has a strong reputation for high-quality and trusted science textbooks. I am especially thankful for all of the support from the acquisitions editor of this second edition,

Reid Hester, who was always quick to provide guidance, advice, and even a friendly conversation whenever I needed it. Abbie Rickard joined the editorial team overseeing the book's development near of the end of the project and already has provided great advice on the overall scope of this text. Editorial assistants provide a tremendous amount of work behind the scenes, and I am thankful for all of the efforts made by Alex Helmintoller and Morgan Shannon (now an eLearning Editor at SAGE Publishing). I thank the copyeditor, Pam Suwinsky, who spent many long evenings taking this from a rough draft to something presentable. The mad dash to the production finish line was greatly facilitated by the production editor Andrew Olson. I remain grateful for those who were critical to the development and production of the previous edition of this book, and in particular, note Ken King and Jon-David Hague. A number of revisions and corrections suggested for the current edition were provided by psychopharmacology instructors who were kind enough to spend a great deal of time reading and commenting on the first edition. I am grateful for their feedback and, of course, any errors or distortions that may be found in the second edition are entirely my own.

Kristine Bonacchi-Stigi, Brooklyn College, CUNY

Perry W. Buffington, University of Georgia

Deborah Carroll, Southern Connecticut State University

Amy Coren, Northern Virginia Community College, Alexandria Campus

Drew D'Amore, The College of New Jersey

David DeMatteo, Drexel University

Carol Devolder, St. Ambrose University

Karen K. Glendenning, Fort Valley State University

Evan Hill, University of Nebraska at Kearney

William Jenkins, Mercer University, Macon Campus

Chris Jones, College of the Desert

Michael Kerchner, Washington College

Serena King, Hamline University

Lorenz S. Neuwirth, SUNY Old Westbury

Meghan E. Pierce, University of Nevada, Las Vegas

Of course, the test participants for any textbook are one's students. I hesitate a bit in listing those who helped in this regard, since I risk forgetting discussions in the classrooms or hallways that might have prompted me to write something or change something that I otherwise may not have considered. With this caveat stated, I point out Ian Buentello, Sigrid Crowel, Brooke Lewis, and Katelin Matazel as raising very interesting points that helped me in crafting some topics in this book. And finally, I wish to thank my wife Jennifer and my kids Kendell and Daniel who tolerated the many hours I spent shut in our home office tapping away at a laptop. To all: thank you!

Instructor Teaching Site

A password-protected site, available at **www.study.sagepub.com/prus2e**, features resources that have been designed to help instructors plan and teach their course. These resources include an extensive test bank, chapter-specific PowerPoint presentations, lecture notes, discussion questions to facilitate class discussion, and links to SAGE journal articles with accompanying article review questions.

Student Study Site

A Web-based study site is available at **www.study.sagepub.com/prus2e**. This site provides access to several study tools including eFlashcards, web quizzes, and links to full-text SAGE journal articles.

• About the Author •

Dr. Adam Prus is a professor and head of psychology at Northern Michigan University in Marquette, Michigan. He earned his PhD in psychology from Virginia Commonwealth University and a master's degree in psychology from Western Michigan University. While in graduate school, Prus also worked as a research technician at a large pharmaceutical company, where he screened central nervous system drugs using various biological assays. After earning his PhD, Dr. Prus investigated experimental antipsychotic drugs as a postdoctoral fellow in the Psychopharmacology Division of the Department of Psychiatry at Vanderbilt University. Dr. Prus has published numerous original studies on psychoactive drugs, including studies funded by the National Institute on Mental Illness and private foundations. At NMU, he directs the Neuropsychopharmacology Laboratory, where he enjoys mentoring undergraduate and graduate students and spends too much time fixing lab equipment. When he is not teaching, training students, writing books or conducting research, Dr. Prus spends time with his wife and two children, and together they enjoy outdoor activities in Michigan's Upper Peninsula, where NMU is located.

1

Introduction to Psychopharmacology

Psychoactive substances have made an enormous impact on society. Many people regularly drink alcohol or smoke tobacco. Millions of Americans take prescribed drugs for depression or anxiety. As students, scholars, practitioners, and everyday consumers, we may find that learning about psychoactive substances can be invaluable. The chapters in this book provide a thorough overview of the major classes of psychoactive drugs, including their actions in the body and their effects on behavior.

Psychopharmacology

Psychopharmacology
Study of how drugs affect mood, perception, thinking, or behavior

Psychoactive drugs
Drugs that affect mood, perception, thinking, or behavior by acting in the nervous system

Psychopharmacology is the study of how drugs affect mood, perception, thinking, or behavior. Drugs that achieve these effects by acting in the nervous system are called **psychoactive drugs**. The term *psychopharmacology* encompasses two large fields: psychology and pharmacology. Thus, psychopharmacology attempts to relate the actions and effects of drugs to psychological processes.

A psychopharmacologist must have knowledge of the nervous system and how psychoactive drugs alter nervous system functioning. A psychopharmacologist can be a medical practitioner, like a psychiatrist, who specializes in prescribing psychoactive medication, or a scientist who studies psychoactive drugs. This approach defines the structure of this textbook. First, this book provides an overview of brain cells and structures. Second, it covers the basic principles of pharmacology. A psychopharmacologist must also characterize the effects of different types of drugs. We cover this after learning about the basic principles of pharmacology by considering the many different types of psychoactive drugs, beginning with recreational and abused drugs such as cocaine, marijuana, and LSD and ending with therapeutic drugs for treating mental disorders such as depression, anxiety, and schizophrenia.

Psychopharmacology is not the only term used to describe this field (**Table 1.1**). Another term is *behavioral pharmacology*. Many consider behavioral pharmacology as synonymous with psychopharmacology, but others classify *behavioral pharmacology* as part of the subfield of psychology called *behavior analysis*. In this respect, drugs serve as behaviorally relevant stimuli just like other stimuli in behavior analytic models. *Neuropsychopharmacology* is another term for psychopharmacology. The *neuro* prefix represents the nervous system. Although the terms are similar, the neuropsychopharmacology field has a particular emphasis on the nervous system actions of drugs.

TABLE 1.1 ● Names Used to Describe Psychopharmacology	
Field	**Description**
Psychopharmacology	The study of how drugs affect mood, perception, thinking, or behavior.
Behavioral pharmacology	The study of how drugs affect behavior. Sometimes behavioral pharmacologists emphasize principles used in field of behavior analysis.
Neuropsychopharmacology	The study of how drugs affect the nervous system and how these nervous system changes alter behavior.

SOURCE: © Cengage Learning 2014.

Why Read a Book on Psychopharmacology?

Beyond being required reading for a course you're taking, psychopharmacology is an important part of modern psychology. First, psychoactive drug use is highly prevalent.

In the United States, for example, consider the following:

- More than 100 million antidepressant drug prescriptions are written every year.
- More than 80 million anti-anxiety (i.e., anxiolytic), sedative, and hypnotic drugs are prescribed every year.
- More than 200 million pain-relieving drug prescriptions are written every year [Centers for Disease Control and Prevention (CDC), 2008].

When we add recreational drugs to the list, psychoactive drug prevalence in the United States increases further:

- More than 114 million adults consume alcohol on a regular basis (CDC, 2011).
- More than 25 million individuals use marijuana.
- More than 15 million individuals misuse a prescription drug.
- More than 70 million individuals use tobacco products (Substance Abuse and Mental Health Services Administration, 2010).

The World Health Organization (WHO) also reports high rates of psychoactive drug use internationally (WHO, 2012). For us, as students, teachers, researchers, and practitioners in psychology, to understand typical human behavior in the modern world, the sheer prevalence of drug use requires that we understand how drugs affect the way we think and function.

The second reason for reading this text is that the statistics just presented show how nearly all of us are consumers of psychoactive substances; as consumers, we should know about the substances we ingest. Greater knowledge of psychoactive substances improves patient understanding of prescribed medical treatments and health implications of taking recreational and abused substances.

Third, you will come to understand how psychoactive substances provide important tools for understanding human behavior. The actions of antidepressant drugs led to understanding the roles that certain neurotransmitters and brain structures play in depression. Researchers use many experimental psychoactive drugs entirely as pharmacological tools for understanding brain function and behavior.

Fourth, you will see how psychopharmacologists develop psychoactive treatments for psychological disorders. As described later in this chapter, drugs used for treating disorders—referred to as **pharmacotherapeutics**—are not derived only from chemists. Rather, scientists trained in psychology test psychoactive drugs and determine their potential effectiveness for psychological disorders.

Pharmacotherapeutics
Drugs used for treating disorders

Drugs: Administered Substances That Alter Physiological Functions

In a way, you know a drug when you see one. After all, the term *drug* is part of our everyday language. We take drugs for headaches, drugs for infections, drugs for depression or anxiety, and drugs for virtually any other ailment or disorder. We even take drugs to prevent disorders. But what exactly is a drug?

To provide a simple definition, a **drug** is an administered substance that alters physiological functioning. The term *administered* indicates that a person takes or is given the substance. The phrase "alters physiological functioning" implies that the substance must exhibit sufficient efficacy to change physiological processes.

Drug Administered substance that alters physiological functioning

This definition has challenges. The term *administered* excludes substances made naturally in the body. For example, the neurotransmitter dopamine is made in the nervous system and elicits important changes in nervous system functioning. However, hospital physicians may administer dopamine to a patient in order to elevate heart rate. In this context, dopamine is an administered substance that alters physiological functioning. Yet the same dopamine is made in the body—distinguishing the two leads us to call dopamine a drug when a practitioner administers it and call dopamine a neurotransmitter when the brain produces it.

Along the same lines, many of us take vitamins to ward off disease and improve health. We administer vitamins to ourselves. Why not call *vitamins* drugs? We simply describe them as vitamins (**Figure 1.1**). Nor do we describe herbal remedies as drugs despite their physiological effects.

FIGURE 1.1 ● (a) Antidepressants (b) Vitamins (c) Vaping (d) Sniffing glue

(a)

(b)

(c)

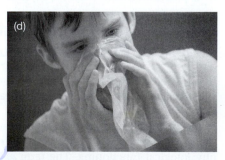
(d)

SOURCE: Clockwise from top left: Copyright iStock Photo/svetikd; Copyright gosphotodesign/Shutterstock.com; Copyright iStock Photo/diego_cervo; Copyright Jan H Andersen/Shutterstock.com.

The term *substance* in the definition of drug also lacks a precise description. The antidepressant in panel A clearly seems to be a drug, but the substances in the other three panels seem less like drugs. Each substance, however, exhibits physiological changes in the body.

The emphasis on physiological functions also has limitations. Certainly drugs produce changes in the body—but is food a drug? After all, food also produces physiological changes in the body.

Do drugs have a certain appearance? Drugs come in a variety of different forms, including pills, liquids, and powders. Most people consider nicotine a drug, although nicotine molecules reside within tar particles inhaled when smoking tobacco. Some teenagers may sniff certain types of glue, the vapors of which contain chemicals such as toluene. In this case, drugs also come in vapor form.

Thus, although *drug* is a common term, we must not restrict our perception of a drug to a specific form or usage in psychopharmacology. Doing so risks excluding nonconforming substances that may have powerful effects for altering behavior. As presented in Chapter 5, for example, thinking of food as a drug provides a useful means of understanding food addiction.

STOP & CHECK

Stop & Check questions provide a quick way to self assess your comprehension of the material. These questions pertain to main points and are provided throughout the chapters of this book.

1. How prevalent is psychoactive drug use?

2. What is the definition of a drug?

1. Both therapeutic and recreational drugs are highly prevalent in society. Alcohol alone is used by more than 114 million adults in the United States, and therapeutic drugs for depression and anxiety are used by as many as one-third of all U.S. adults. 2. A drug is a substance that alters physiological functioning. A more precise term is lacking, but it's helpful to think critically about the limitations of what we consider a drug to be in order to appreciate the forms a psychoactive substance may take and ways a substance might affect us.

Psychoactive Drugs: Described by Manner of Use

Psychoactive drugs broadly fall into two categories: those intended for instrumental use and those intended for recreational use. The major distinction between these categories is a person's intent or motivation for using the substance. **Instrumental drug use** consists of using a drug to address a specific purpose. For example, someone may take an antidepressant drug such as Prozac for the purpose of reducing depression. Further, most adults consume caffeinated beverages like coffee to help them wake up in the morning, another socially acceptable purpose. In psychopharmacology,

Instrumental drug use Using a drug to address a specific purpose

Therapeutic drug Drug used to treat a physical or mental disorder

Recreational drug use Using a drug entirely to experience the drug's effects

instrumental use often occurs with **therapeutic drugs**—drugs used for treating disorders—for treating mental disorders such as depression and schizophrenia.

Recreational drug use refers to using a drug entirely to experience its effects. For example, recreational use of alcohol may consist of drinking alcohol purely to experience its intoxicating effects. Of course, we might describe alcohol use as instrumental if a person were only using it for another purpose such as relieving stress after a long day of work. Again, the intended use distinguishes instrumental use from recreational use. The term *misuse* applies to drugs that are intended for instrumental purposes but are instead used recreationally. For example, cough syrups that contain codeine or dextromethorphan are misused recreationally to achieve mind-altering effects such as euphoria or hallucinations.

Recreational use may lead to dependence. During *drug dependence* a user also experiences a need or urge to continue using a substance and has difficulty reducing use of the substance. Chapter 5 expands upon the clinical characteristics of drug dependence.

Generic Names, Trade Names, Chemical Names, and Street Names for Drugs

Individual drugs have different names. For example, people commonly take Tylenol to treat headaches. Although the name *Tylenol* is the most widely known name, the drug is also known by a different name: acetaminophen. We refer to Tylenol as its *trade name* and acetaminophen as its *generic name*.

Nearly all therapeutic drugs have a generic name and at least one trade name. A pharmaceutical company that develops and markets a drug provides both trade and generic names, each for different purposes. A drug's **trade name** (or **brand name**) is a trademarked name a company provides for a drug. Sometimes a trade name is designed to be memorable or emotion provoking. For example, common sleep aids include Ambien and Lunesta. The name *Lunesta* resembles the word *luna*, meaning "moon," a symbol for night. Plus, the word *Lunesta* is a soft sounding name, giving a relaxing connotation to the drug.

Trade name (or brand name) A trademarked name a company provides for a drug

Generic name A nonproprietary name that indicates the classification for a drug and distinguishes it from others in the same class

↑
do NOT
follow
rules

A drug's **generic name** is a nonproprietary name that indicates the classification for a drug and distinguishes a drug from others in the same class. For example, note the names of the following antipsychotic drugs: chlorpromazine, clozapine, and olanzapine. All three of these drugs end in *a* followed by a consonant and then the suffix *-ine*. We can guess that drugs with *-apine* or *-azine* in their names act as antipsychotic drugs. The names also reflect something about these drugs' chemical structures. The *-ine* suffix corresponds to an amine chemical group in their structures. Moreover, the first two drugs, chlorpromazine and clozapine, have chloride molecules in their structures. Generic names do not follow hard rules and cannot be relied upon entirely to inform us about a drug's classification or important features of its chemical structure. But as shown in this example, they can provide ways to show how drugs organizationally compare to others.

Scientific reports normally refer to a drug's generic name. In these cases, the generic name is sometimes followed by the drug's trade name in parentheses. Moreover, trade names are capitalized. For example, a report might read "Physicians prescribe zolpidem (Ambien) for insomnia." The generic name is zolpidem, and its trade name is Ambien.

Drugs also have chemical names. A drug's **chemical name** details a drug's chemical structure. For example, the chemical name for zolpidem is "N,N-dimethyl-2-[6-methyl-2-(4-methylphenyl)imidazo[1,2-a]pyridin-3-yl]acetamide." It's beyond the scope of this textbook to cover what the many components of this name mean—general chemistry and organic chemistry textbooks can tell you that. For our purposes, we can appreciate that the chemical name tells anyone with sufficient chemistry education what zolpidem's chemical structure looks like. The rules used for writing a drug's chemical name come from the International Union of Pure and Applied Chemistry (or IUPAC for short), an international, independent organization of chemists focused on advancing the chemical sciences.

Recreational drugs are often referred to by **street names**. Street names are given by those who use, sell, or illegally make recreational drugs. Street names can serve as benign-sounding aliases. For example, *ADAM* is a reference to the drug MDMA (an abbreviation of 3,4-methylenedioxymethamphetamine). Street names also reflect the drug's effects. For example, the drug MDMA is also known as *ecstasy*, which describes the drug's pleasurable effects. **Table 1.2** lists common recreational substances and their popular street names.

Chemical name A name that details a drug's chemical structure

do follow hard rules set by IUPAC

Street name An alternative name applied to a recreational or abused substance

TABLE 1.2 ● Street Names for Selected Drugs	
Drug	**Street Name**
Amphetamines	Bennies, black beauties
Benzodiazepines	Candy, downers, sleeping pills
Cocaine	Coke, rock, crack
Dextromethorphan (used in cough syrup)	Robo, triple C
Marijuana	Joint, blunt, weed
Methamphetamine	Meth, ice, crystal
MDMA	Ecstasy, Adam
LSD	Acid, blotter
Phencyclidine	PCP, angel dust

SOURCE: National Institute on Drug Abuse, http://www.drugabuse.gov.

Drug Effects: Determined by Dose

Drug effects depend on the dose of a drug. **Dose** is a ratio of the amount of drug per an organism's body weight. For example, the dose of a drug given to a laboratory rat might be 1.0 gram of drug per kilogram body weight. This is written as 1.0 g/kg.

Dose Ratio of the amount of drug per an organism's body weight

To put this into context, if a rat weighed 1 kg—an incredibly large rat—then it would receive 1 gram of drug. If, instead, a rat weighed 0.3 kg, then it would receive 0.3 grams of drug.

For over-the-counter medications like Tylenol, the dosing instructions assume an average adult's body weight. If the instructions describe something like "Take one to two 325 mg tablets," then the "one to two" range refers to differences in body weight between adults. A larger individual might require two tablets, whereas a smaller individual might only require one tablet. A doctor's office records your weight, in part, to calculate drug dosing. If the doctor prescribes a medication, she needs to know the dose of a drug to prescribe based on your body weight.

Generally, the higher a drug's dose, the greater its effects. Researchers determine the effects of drugs by evaluating a range of different doses. This information is plotted on dose-effect curves. A **dose-effect curve** (or **dose-response curve**) depicts the magnitude of a drug effect by dose. **Figure 1.2** presents two drugs plotted on dose-effect curves.

For each drug in Figure 1.2, lower doses produce weaker effects and higher doses produce stronger effects. Both drugs produce a full 100 percent, effect at a high enough dose. Yet notice that both drugs achieve full effectiveness at different doses. For drug A, 100 percent effectiveness occurs at a 8.0 mg/kg dose, whereas 100 percent effectiveness for drug B occurs at a 16.0 mg/kg dose. In fact, the entire dose-effect curve for drug A is located to the left of drug B (i.e., the curves do not overlap).

Dose-effect curve Depicts the magnitude of a drug effect by dose

FIGURE 1.2   ●   Both drugs shown here achieve 100 percent effectiveness, but at different doses. Drug A is the most potent because it achieves these effects at lower doses than drug B. For drug A, the dose at which 50 percent of the effect occurs (ED_{50}) is 4.0 mg/kg. The ED_{50} for drug B is 10.0 mg/kg.

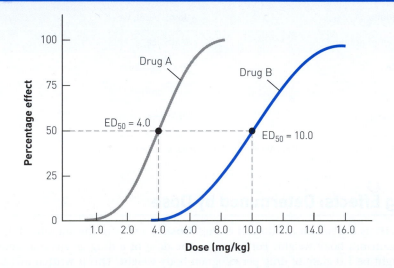

To describe the position of a dose-effect curve, researchers calculate an ED_{50} value. An **ED_{50} value** represents the dose at which 50 percent of an effect was observed.[1] The "ED" stands for "effective dose."

As shown in Figure 1.2, drug A's ED_{50} value is 4.0 mg/kg. This corresponds to a dose that matches with the 50 percent effect point on the dose-effect curve. Nothing prevents a researcher from determining other ED values if she chooses. Perhaps in her particular study, knowing, say, an ED_{75} (i.e., dose at which 75 percent of the effect was observed) or ED_{15} (i.e., dose at which 15 percent of the effect was observed), value would be important. We tend to calculate ED_{50} values because they represent a middle point on the curve and thus are generally more useful for conveying a drug's effective-dose range than other ED values.

ED_{50} values provide a means for comparing the potency of drugs. **Potency** refers to the amount of drug used to produce a certain magnitude of effect. Describing a drug as "highly potent" means that drug effects occur at low doses. The hallucinogen lysergic acid diethylamide, better known as LSD, is considered highly potent, because very small amounts of LSD—as little as 0.02 mg, so small that users may need to lick LSD powder from the glue side of a postage stamp—produce hallucinations (Greiner, Burch, & Edelberg, 1958). Researchers also use potency to compare different drugs that produce similar effects.

Consider again the drugs in Figure 1.2. Drug A produces the same degree of effects as drug B, but drug A does so at lower doses. Thus, drug A has a higher potency than drug B. By representing a dose-effect curve, an ED_{50} value allows a way to calculate the relative level of potency between different drugs. Drug A has an ED_{50} value of 4.0 mg/kg, and drug B has an ED_{50} value of 10.0 mg/kg. The potency difference is calculated from dividing drug B, the compound with the highest ED_{50} value, by drug A, the compound with the lowest ED_{50} value. In this example, we find drug A to be 2.5 times more potent than drug B.

When developing a new therapeutic drug, researchers must determine a drug's dose that causes unacceptable adverse effects. We refer to this dose as a *toxic dose* and can produce toxic dose effect curves using laboratory animals as subjects, just as we can produce therapeutic dose-effect curves. Researchers and regulators understand that no drug is free from a host of potential adverse effects, but certain doses of any drug will produce adverse effects too severe to justify giving to a patient even if the same dose produced therapeutic effects.

As noted previously, toxicity studies also produce dose-effect curves. The ED_{50} for toxic dose-effect curves is referred to as a TD_{50} value (TD stands for *toxic dose*). In this case, we interpret a TD_{50} value as the dose at which 50 percent of the subjects had the particular adverse effect in question (the one too severe to risk producing in humans). TD_{50} values allow for the determination of a therapeutic index.

A **therapeutic index** conveys the distance between toxic and therapeutic doses as a ratio of a drug's toxic dose-effect curve value relative to a therapeutic dose-effect curve value. One way to calculate a therapeutic index is to divide a TD_{50} value by an ED_{50} value. A therapeutic index answers this question: How different is a dose that

ED_{50} value Represents the dose at which 50 percent of an effect was observed

Potency Amount of drug used to produce a certain level of effect

Therapeutic index Ratio of a drug's toxic dose-effect curve value relative to therapeutic dose-effect curve value

---

1 Alternatively, an ED_{50} value can reflect a dose at which 50 percent of the subjects exhibited a full effect.

causes toxic effects in half of the subjects from a dose of the same drug that produces therapeutic effects in half of the subjects?

Although ED_{50} and TD_{50} values provide a means to calculate therapeutic indexes, these values are not ideal for identifying safe drugs. **Figure 1.3** shows a drug's therapeutic dose-effect curve and toxic dose-effect curve. The TD_{50} dose (6.0 mg/kg) is three times greater than the ED_{50} dose (2.0 mg/kg). Is that good? Notice that approximately 15 percent of all subjects experience toxic drug effects at the ED_{50} dose. If you look further, a fully effective therapeutic dose caused toxic effects in half of the subjects. This is clearly not a safe drug!

To avoid any overlapping therapeutic and toxic dose-effect curves, drug developers adopt a far more conservative calculation for a therapeutic index, referred to as a Certain Safety Index. We calculate a **Certain Safety Index** by dividing a toxic dose that caused toxicity in only 1 percent of the subjects—referred to as a TD_1—and divide this by a dose that achieved a 99 percent therapeutic effect—an ED_{99}. Large therapeutic indexes derived from this safer calculation describe very separate therapeutic and toxic dose-effect curves.

Certain Safety Index
A therapeutic index calculated by dividing a TD_1 value by an ED_{99} value

---

FIGURE 1.3 ● Is this drug safe to use? This drug does produce therapeutic effects at doses lower than those that produce lethal effects. In fact, the TD_{50} value (TD_{50} = 6.0 mg/kg) is three times greater than the ED_{50} value (ED_{50} = 2.0 mg/kg). Yet notice that at the ED_{50} dose (2.0 mg/kg), approximately 15 percent of the subjects experienced toxic drug effects. At a dose at which full therapeutic effects were shown (6.0 mg/kg), approximately 50 percent of the subjects experienced toxic drug effects. Thus, although the therapeutically effective doses are lower than the toxic doses, many subjects will experience severe adverse effects—clearly this is not a safe drug to use.

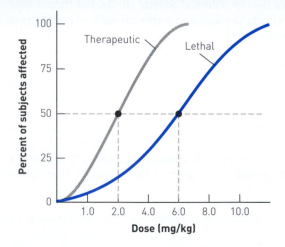

The U.S. Food and Drug Administration (FDA) and similar regulatory bodies in other countries require safe therapeutic indexes for drugs they approve. However, this is not to say that every drug on the market has a large therapeutic index. For example, the mood stabilizer lithium has a lethal dose near the therapeutic dose, and for some individuals, taking only twice the recommended dosage might lead to life-threatening adverse effects.

STOP & CHECK

1. What determines whether a drug is a therapeutic drug or a recreational drug?

2. What are the two different names provided for therapeutic drugs?

3. What is a dose?

4. What is the safest approach for calculating a therapeutic index?

1. The manner of usage. Individuals use therapeutic drugs instrumentally toward treating a disorder or ailment, whereas individuals take recreational drugs entirely to experience the drug's effects. 2. Therapeutic drugs are provided a generic name, which refers to the organizational fit of a drug with similar acting drugs, and a trade name, which is the company's brand name for the drug. 3. A dose is a ratio of the amount of drug per amount of body weight. Most of the instructions provided with over-the-counter drug packages advise taking pills based on an average adult weight. 4. A Certain Safety Index provides the safest approach for calculating a therapeutic index by dividing a toxic dose for 1 percent of subjects, referred to as a TD_1, by a 99 percent effective dose, referred to as an ED_{99} value. When this calculation produces large therapeutic indexes, the toxic doses are much higher than therapeutically effective doses.

Pharmacology: Pharmacodynamics, Pharmacokinetics, and Pharmacogenetics

Pharmacodynamics and pharmacokinetics represent two major areas in pharmacology. **Pharmacodynamics** refer to the physiological actions of drugs. For psychoactive drugs, this includes the drug's actions on the nervous system. Most addictive recreational drugs, for example, act on the brain's reward pathways to produce pleasurable effects. Chapter 4 provides an overview of many pharmacodynamic processes.

Pharmacokinetics refers to how drugs pass through the body. This field considers different ways to administer a drug, how long a drug stays in the body, how well the drug enters the brain, and how it leaves the body. For example, pharmacokinetic properties explain why nicotine reaches the brain more rapidly by smoking tobacco than by chewing tobacco.

Although pharmacodynamics and pharmacokinetics define the classical broad categories in pharmacology, a subfield of pharmacology—pharmacogenetics—affects both categories. **Pharmacogenetics** is the study of how genetic differences influence a drug's pharmacokinetic and pharmacodynamic effects. This field

Pharmacodynamics
The physiological actions of drugs

Pharmacokinetics
A drug's passage through the body

Pharmacogenetics
The study of how genetic differences influence a drug's pharmacokinetic and pharmacodynamic effects

provides the basis for differences in drug response between individuals. As we well know, a single therapeutic drug does not work for everyone. In fact, for psychoactive therapeutic drugs such as antidepressants, a physician may need to switch through several different medications for a patient until finding an effective one.

Genetically related differences in drug responsiveness may affect a drug's actions in the nervous system or passage through the body. In particular, some individuals are "fast metabolizers" for many drugs, meaning that certain drugs are quickly broken down in their livers. When this occurs, less of a drug stays intact in the body, resulting in weaker drug effects. Knowing that a patient is a fast metabolizer for certain drugs enables physicians to alter treatment plans. For example, a physician may prescribe a separate treatment that reduces metabolism of the drug or may prescribe an alternative drug that the person will metabolize more slowly.

Psychoactive Drugs: Objective and Subjective Effects

Objective effects
Pharmacological effects that can be directly observed by others

To characterize the spectrum of a drug's pharmacological effects, researchers must measure the drug's objective and subjective effects. **Objective effects** are pharmacological effects that can be directly observed by others. In other words, a researcher can independently measure the drug's effects. For example, psychostimulant drugs increase heart rate. A researcher can objectively measure an individual's heart rate by taking the person's pulse (**Figure 1.4**).

FIGURE 1.4 ● Objective effects (left) are pharmacological effects that can be directly observed by others, whereas subjective effects (right) are pharmacological effects that cannot be directly observed by others; instead, a study participant may describe a drug's effects to a researcher or rate a drug's effects on a questionnaire.

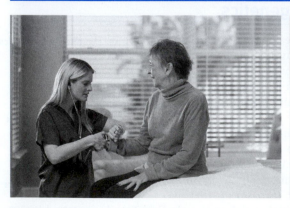

Her pulse is 105 beats per minute.

Rate from strongly disagree to strongly agree: I feel "on edge" after taking this drug.

SOURCE: Left: Copyright iStock Photo/kali9. Right: Copyright iStock Photo/dima_sidelnikov.

Subjective effects are pharmacological effects that cannot be directly observed by others. In other words, we cannot observe or measure another's drug experience. Researchers measure subjective effects by asking study participants to describe a drug's effects as well as using rating scales, such as the Profile of Mood States Questionnaire (POMS). The POMS asks participants to rate the degree of agreement with a word or statement that describes how they might feel, such as "energetic" or "on edge," with rating options ranging from "a little" to "extremely" (McNair, Lorr, & Droppleman, 1971). The inability to independently observe subjective effects has certain scientific limitations. In particular, a drug's subjective effects may vary from person to person. To address this, researchers must develop a consensus about a drug's effects among many individuals and assume that this consensus accurately reflects the drug's effects for anyone else who may take the drug.

Despite some scientific limitations, a psychoactive drug's subjective effects are more important to understand than its objective effects. Subjective effects explain the purpose of recreational and addictive drug use. Subjective effects also explain the therapeutic value of antidepressant, anti-anxiety, and antipsychotic drugs. Only the patient can say whether medications truly help to reduce depressed feelings, anxiety, and paranoid thoughts.

> **Subjective effects**
> Pharmacological effects that cannot be directly observed by others

STOP & CHECK

1. How do pharmacodynamic effects differ from pharmacokinetic effects?

2. How might pharmacogenetic factors alter a person's response to a psychoactive drug?

3. What is the challenge in studying subjective drug effects?

1. Pharmacodynamic effects refer to the biological effects of a drug, whereas pharmacokinetic effects refer to the movement of a drug through the body, including a drug's entry into the nervous system. **2.** One's genetic makeup may alter a drug's passage through the body or alter a drug's actions in the nervous system. **3.** Subjective effects represent an individual's personal and non-publicly observable effects from a drug, including how a person feels after taking the drug. We must rely entirely on self-reported drug effects. Yet for recreational drugs, subjective effects are the most important to characterize and understand.

Study Designs and the Assessment of Psychoactive Drugs

The logic behind study designs provides the means to assess a drug's behavioral effects. Studies attempt to answer scientific questions about drug effects and the nervous system by using dependent and independent variables. A **dependent variable** is a study

> **Dependent variable**
> A study variable measured by a researcher

variable measured by a researcher. In psychology, dependent variables usually consist of behavioral measures, such as how many words an individual recalls from a list or an evaluation of one's level of depression.

Independent variables are study conditions or treatments that may affect a dependent variable. Independent variables for the previous examples might include teaching individuals a memorization technique or providing depressed individuals an antidepressant drug. In each case, study researchers sought to determine whether an independent variable produced changes to a dependent variable.

Research studies fall into two categories: correlational studies and experimental studies (see **Table 1.3**). In a **correlational study**, an investigator does not alter the independent variable.[2] For example, to study the effects of long-term MDMA use on memory, a researcher might recruit participants who used MDMA and then measure each participant's ability to recall words from a list. We could use the duration of MDMA use as the *independent variable*, and each participant's level of memory serves as the *dependent variable*. The investigators did not alter the independent variable, but instead studied duration of MDMA use and memory ability as conditions that already existed. Researchers might infer a relationship between MDMA use and memory if long-term MDMA users exhibited poor word recall and if infrequent MDMA users exhibited good word recall. But it is important that correlational studies do not indicate that a variable *causes* changes to another variable.

Independent variable Study conditions or treatments that may affect a dependent variable

Correlational study Study in which an investigator does not alter the independent variable

TABLE 1.3 ● Correlational and Experimental Studies	
Study Type	**Description**
Correlational study	No alteration of study conditions. Changes in study variables are observed, and relationships are inferred.
Experimental study	Researchers alter a study's independent variable and observe changes in a dependent variable. Experiments can identify causal relationships between an independent variable and a dependent variable.

Experimental study Study in which investigators alter an independent variable to determine whether changes occur to a dependent variable

Placebo Substance identical in appearance to a drug but physiologically inert

In an **experimental study**, investigators alter an independent variable to determine whether changes occur to the dependent variable. For example, many clinical studies use experiments to evaluate drug effects. In a standard experimental study design, individuals sharing a type of disorder are separated into two groups: a control group and a treatment group. The treatment group receives the treatment, and the control group does not. Instead, the control group may be given a **placebo**, or a substance identical in appearance to a drug but physiologically inert. If individuals in the treatment group improve over the course of this study and those in the control group do not, then researchers attribute improvements to the treatment.

---

2 Alternatively, correlational studies can use the term *predictor* instead of *independent variable*.

Experiments such as these indicate that the independent variable *caused* changes to the dependent variable.

Clinical drug studies use other terminology to describe an experiment. Drug experiments in clinical trials describe the number of treatments and doses provided to groups of study participants as **treatment arms**. A two-arm design refers to two experimental groups. Often, one group of participants receives an experimental drug and the other group receives a placebo.

Many times, researchers require more than a dose-versus-placebo comparison. In these cases, researchers may use more arms in a study design. For example, a three-arm design may consist of a high-dose drug group, a low-dose drug group, and a placebo group. Or a treatment arm may include an entirely different drug. Testing an experimental drug in comparison with a standard treatment and placebo provides a valuable assessment of drug efficacy compared to existing medications or no medications, respectively.

Why are study groups called *arms*? Look at the examples of two-arm and three-arm designs in **Figure 1.5**. This is the standard style of illustrating multiple group

Treatment arms
Number of treatments and doses provided to patients described in a clinical study

---

FIGURE 1.5 ● Clinical drug study designs describe treatment conditions as *arms*. In these examples, the left portion of each design shows the total number of participants recruited for the study, and each arm shows the number of participants assigned to each study condition.

Two-arm study

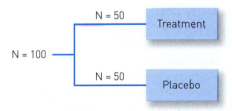

Three-arm study

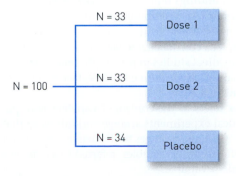

Clinical study reports Detailed summaries of a clinical study's design and results

study designs in **clinical study reports**, the detailed summaries of a clinical study's design and results (International Conference on Harmonization, 1996). As shown in Figure 1.5, the different groups appear on separate lines like arms or branches.

Experiments use random sampling to assign participants to study groups. Through random assignment, researchers seek to achieve groups that have similar characteristics. Many experiments also use blinding procedures to eliminate potential biases by study participants or investigators. In a **single-blind procedure**, researchers do not inform study participants which treatment or placebo they received. To provide informed consent, study investigators provide participants a description of treatments that might be administered, as well as the potential for placebo administration, but they do not identify the assigned treatment to participants during the study.

Single-blind procedure When researchers do not inform study participants which treatment or placebo they received

In a **double-blind procedure**, neither the participants nor the investigators know the treatment assignments during the study. These procedures not only prevent potential biased responses from participants, but also prevent potential biased judgments by study investigators. Although researchers consider blinded procedures important for quality experimental studies, not all experiments allow for blinded procedures.

Double-blind procedure When neither participants nor investigators know the treatment assignments during a study.

In clinical research, **open-label studies** refer to the assignment of study treatments without using blinded procedures. Open-label studies apply to situations in which disguising study medications may have serious ethical consequences or be impractical. For example, many cancer clinical trials use open-label procedures because withholding a potential effective treatment from cancer patients by using a placebo might have serious health consequences.

Open-label studies Assignment of study treatments without using blinded procedures

Validity: Addressing the Quality and Impact of a Study

Say you conducted an experiment and found that a newly developed drug reduced symptoms in depression. Great news, but how good was the experiment? This question addresses the quality of study procedures, the appropriate choice of species tested, the ability to extend these findings to other individuals with the disorder, and many other possible issues. Researchers must address such questions in order to draw *valid inferences* from a study's findings (Elmes, Kantowitz, & Roediger, 2006).

College courses on research methodology and design devote considerable time to discussing valid inferences, and they do so in much greater detail than is considered here. For our interests, let's consider some basic types of validity and think about how the issue of validity can affect studies in psychopharmacology. The types of validity we discuss include internal validity, external validity, face validity, construct validity, and predictive validity (**Table 1.4**).

Internal validity Control of variables with potential to influence a dependent variable

Internal validity refers to the control of variables with potential to influence a dependent variable. Ideal experiments arrange conditions so that only changes to the independent variable will cause changes to the dependent variable. Without appropriately arranging conditions, other variables, referred to as *confound variables*, can cause changes to the dependent variable.

TABLE 1.4 ● Types of Validity	
Validity	**Description**
Internal validity	Adequacy of controlling variables that may influence a dependent variable
External validity	Ability to extend findings beyond study conditions
Face validity	Test appears to measure what a researcher considers it to measure.
Construct validity	How well a study's findings relate to the underlying theory of a study's objectives
Predictive validity	Ability of model to predict treatment effects

For example, a study designed to test new drugs for depression may involve patients checking in with a clinic physician every morning. After several weeks, the study results indicate a reduction in depression. Might this study have confound variables?

The daily clinic visits are a potential confound variable. The act of talking to a physician daily about depressive symptoms in a clinical setting may be sufficient to reduce depression in this study. Without considering potential confound variables such as these study investigators risk wrongly concluding that an experimental drug produces therapeutic effects.

To avoid potential confound variables, researchers blind participants to the study medications, and they may also assign placebo to a participant group. Placebo groups control for many confound variables. If placebo-treated patients also exhibited reduced depression, then we conclude that variables other than the study medication caused reductions in depression.

External validity refers to how well study findings generalize beyond the study conditions. For example, many clinical antidepressant studies examine only adults. Such studies have poor external validity for antidepressant effects in children, because they provide no evidence of an antidepressant's effectiveness in children.

External validity also presents limitations for predicting treatment effects in humans from studies conducted in animals. One example of this occurred with the drug thalidomide in the 1950s. Thalidomide exhibited sedative effects and prevented nausea and vomiting. Without harmful effects to fetuses in pregnant mice, European physicians prescribed thalidomide to pregnant women suffering from morning sickness.

However, thalidomide proved severely harmful to human fetuses. By 1962, nearly 10,000 babies had been born with missing fingers, toes, and limbs after exposure to thalidomide during pregnancy (**Figure 1.6**). In humans, but not in mice, thalidomide was metabolically transformed into a **teratogen**, a substance harmful to a fetus. Had drug developers tested thalidomide in rabbits, which do convert thalidomide into this teratogen, doctors would not have prescribed thalidomide

External validity
Refers to how well study findings generalize beyond the study conditions

Teratogen Substance harmful to a fetus

to pregnant women. Thus, in this case, rabbits, not mice, provide proper external validity for this property of thalidomide (Goldman, 2001). Proper drug screening requires a thorough examination of drugs using many different models and approaches, including a variety of animal species.

Face validity

Appearance of a test measuring what a researcher considers it to measure

Face validity refers to the appearance of a test measuring what a researcher considers it to measure. For example, researchers study drugs for Alzheimer's disease by testing mice with memory deficits. Memory deficits are a prominent symptom of Alzheimer's disease. Thus, testing memory in mice offers face validity for Alzheimer's disease. Sometimes animal models offer no face validity. In particular, testing antipsychotic drugs for treating schizophrenia, a disorder in which individuals can experience auditory hallucinations. among many other symptoms, must often be tested in models lacking face validity. That is, we lack animal models for paranoia and hearing voices.

Construct validity

How well a study's findings relate to the underlying theory of a study's objectives

Construct validity addresses how well a study's findings relate to the underlying theory of a study's objectives. Testing new drugs for Alzheimer's disease in Alzheimer's patients offers high construct validity; that is, the drug is tested in an individual who

---

FIGURE 1.6 ● **Failure to screen thalidomide in rabbits instead of mice led researchers to miss thalidomide's teratogenic effects, leading to babies born with missing digits and limbs.**

SOURCE: Photo by Leonard Mccombe/The LIFE Picture Collection/Getty Images.

has the disease to be treated, including all of the genetic causes of Alzheimer's disease and the resulting damage to cells in the brain. Yet we must first screen experimental drugs in animals to ensure their safety and potential effectiveness before risking testing these drugs in humans.

Testing such drugs in normal mice, which lack genetic and biological features of Alzheimer's disease, leads to construct validity concerns, because normal mice do not have any of the theoretical genetic and biological features of this disease in humans. After all, the objective for such a study would be to find the model most similar to Alzheimer's disease in order to use it for identifying potential treatments. However, researchers have developed genetically altered mice that have certain protein abnormalities similar to those found in Alzheimer's disease. Testing treatments for Alzheimer's disease in these mice provides greater construct validity than testing these treatments in normal mice.

Predictive validity addresses how well a model predicts treatment effects. To continue the preceding example, an experimental drug might improve memory in certain genetically altered mice and later prove to treat Alzheimer's disease. If this were the case, then these mice offer predictive validity for screening Alzheimer's disease medications. At times, an experimental procedure might offer high predictive validity but fail to offer face or construct validity. Many animal models for antipsychotic drugs fail to exhibit features of schizophrenia, yet antipsychotic drugs produce unique behaviors in these models that scientists have learned predicts certain clinical effects in humans. Drug developers rely on models with high predictive validity when screening experimental drugs.

Predictive validity
How well a model predicts treatment affects

STOP & CHECK

1. How is a correlational study different from an experiment?

2. What might a three-arm clinical study consist of?

3. Why is external validity an important concern for animal experimentation?

1. Correlational studies identify potential associations between variables, whereas experiments identify causal relationships between variables. **2.** A three-arm study employs three different participant groups. Although the treatment conditions depend on the disorder and drugs being tested, a three-arm study might employ a placebo group, an experimental drug group, and a comparison drug group. **3.** Important physiological differences exist across all species, and these differences may not accurately reflect a drug's actions in humans.

Animals and Advancing Medical Research

Ethics plays another important role in psychopharmacology research. In particular, experimental treatments may cause serious adverse effects or simply be ineffective for the disorders they were developed for. Thus, participants may be exposed to a dangerous medication, and more than this, may experience no improvement in a disorder they are suffering from. Ethically, and fortunately also legally, researchers engage in years of testing and development before testing a potential treatment is in humans.

To develop drugs for human usage, medical research relies heavily on animal testing. Not only do medical research advances depend on animal models, but governmental regulators, such as the FDA, also require proof of extensive animal research before approving drugs for human testing. Medical advances rely on animal research for two major reasons: a lack of feasible alternatives and the ability to predict drug effects in humans.

A Lack of Feasible Alternatives

Treatment results from studies conducted only on cells and tissues poorly predict treatment efficacy and safety in humans. Although these biological studies provide important steps in medical development, they fail to model the complexity of living organisms. This complexity currently precludes computer simulations or mathematical models from taking the place of animal research. Thus, animal models provide a necessary step in discovery and drug development.

Humans also do not provide a feasible alternative to animal models. Necessary basic research procedures consist of invasive techniques that would be highly unethical to perform in humans. For example, many medical studies require measuring drug-induced changes in cells and tissue by inserting probes into the brain. In addition to invasiveness, experimental drugs that have not been tested in animals carry a risk of severe and possibly irreversible adverse effects in humans. Animal testing prevents dangerous experimental drugs from being tested in humans.

High Predictive Value for Drug Effects in Humans

Beyond having no feasible alternatives, animal models do well in predicting drug effects in humans despite inherent challenges for external validity. During drug development animal models identify effective drugs from the hundreds or thousands synthesized in a drug-development program. The FDA requires that all experimental medications be screened in animal models before testing drugs in humans in order to ensure that there is a reasonable likelihood of improving a disorder in humans. For this same reason, the FDA requires screening for adverse effects in animal models, given that adverse effects occurring in animals may likely occur in humans as well. At the end of this chapter, the "From Actions to Effects" section describes the role that animals play in therapeutic drug development programs.

The Regulation of Animal Research

In developed nations, governmental and private agencies exist to oversee the responsible and humane use of animal subjects for research or teaching purposes. Publishers of journals, in which scientists publish reports of their studies, indirectly regulate nonparticipating countries by insisting that all research described in their journals abide by certain regulations and policies. In short, all legitimate journals publishing scientific studies require high ethical standards for animal care and use in research.

Two government agencies regulate academic and industrial animal research in the United States: the U.S. Department of Agriculture (USDA, 2006) and the Public Health Service (PHS, 2002). The USDA enforces regulations in the Animal Welfare Act, and the Office of Laboratory Animal Welfare enforces polices of the Public Health Service. Failure to comply with federal regulations and policies results in stiff penalties, including institutional fines and withdrawal of federal grant money.

Among the many rules of institutional conduct, both the Animal Welfare Act and the Public Health Policy require that all U.S. institutions conducting federally funded animals research establish an ethics review committee called the Institutional Animal Care and Use Committee (IACUC). The Animal Welfare Act also covers many species regardless of an institution's federal funding status. Federal law not only pertains to academic institutions but also to pharmaceutical companies. The FDA will not approve any treatments resulting from animal studies that have not complied with federal regulations and policies (FDA, 2002).

The IACUC oversees an institution's entire animal care and use program, including quality of housing, veterinary practices, and research practices. All animal experiments require IACUC approval before they begin. To gain approval, researchers must submit animal research proposals to the IACUC. The IACUC then reviews these protocols and determines their abidance with federal and internal policies. Moreover, the IACUC makes ethical judgments according to the "3 Rs."

The 3 Rs stand for "replacement," "reduction," and "refinement," and serve as a basis for determining whether a researcher needs to use animals for a study, and if so, provides a means for refining a study's plan to use animals (National Research Council, 2011; Russell & Burch, 1959). For the first R, replacement, the IACUC assesses the necessity of using animals for a proposed study by asking "Can animals be replaced with something else?" Sometimes equally useful findings may be derived by working only with cells or perhaps with invertebrates (e.g., insects) instead of using animals. An IACUC will reject animal research proposals when such alternatives exist.

The second R, reduction, refers to using the minimum number of animals necessary to achieve the study objectives. Generally, IACUCs use statistics to ensure that researchers use only the minimum number of animals necessary to detect experimental results. For the third R, refinement, the IACUC attempts to minimize any pain and distress experienced by the study animals. These attempts may include changing experimental procedures, requiring analgesic drugs to reduce pain, or using different testing equipment.

IACUCs also weigh the proposed study's ethical costs. **Ethical cost** assessments weigh the value of potential research discoveries against the potential pain and distress experienced by research animals (**Figure 1.7**). For example, IACUC members easily justify painless experiments in animals that aim to develop treatments for lethal illnesses. Essentially, these studies provide tremendous gains with minimal ethical cost. However, IACUC members cannot justify studies with limited potential for discovery that uses highly painful procedures (Carbone, 2000).

During IACUC review, researchers weigh the potential pain or distress experienced by an animal against a study's potential value. In the top panel of Figure 1.7, the scientific value outweighs the minimal pain or distress experienced by animals, whereas the bottom panel shows that the scientific value fails to outweigh considerable pain and distress expected for the animals.

The 3 Rs A review process for animal research that considers "replacement," "reduction," and "refinement" to determine the necessity of using animals, minimum number of animals needed, and procedures to minimize pain and distress

Ethical cost Assessment that weighs the value of potential research discoveries against the potential pain and distress experienced by research subjects

FIGURE 1.7 ●

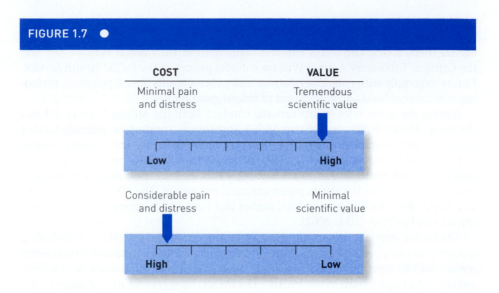

Beyond federally mandated regulations and policies, many U.S. institutions seek private accreditation in order to exceed federal requirements and achieve best practices in the animal care and use. The primary private accreditor for animal care and use in research settings is the Association for Assessment and Accreditation of Laboratory Animal Care (AAALAC). AAALAC inspection teams tour animal facilities, talk to researchers, and oversee how animal research is approved and monitored. AAALAC is an important aid to larger institutions that use thousands of animals for research (AAALAC, 2012).

Animal Rights Activism Seeks to Eliminate Animal Research

The previous section provides information about the use of animals in research and the ethical polices and legal regulations overseeing the humane use of laboratory animals. Animal rights groups such as the People for the Ethical Treatment of Animals (PETA) and the Animal Liberation Front (ALF) have a general goal of actively seeking the complete cessation of animal research, either seeing no value in the work or dismissing any value as ethically unjustified.

Historically, animal rights groups arose from concerns over animal vivisection, a procedure involving surgical procedures on living, and often awake, animals. These concerned individuals formed antivivisection societies in the late nineteenth century, and their efforts led to the Cruelty to Animals Act of 1876 in Great Britain. This act forbade painful procedures in animals unless "absolutely necessary for the due instruction of the persons to save or prolong human life."

In the United States, animal rights groups formed by concerned citizens, including many animal researchers, fought unsuccessfully for national animal research regulations. But the situation changed in the 1960s. In 1966, a *Life* magazine article exposed unethical activities of some animal research dealers, including catching stray dogs or even stealing dogs for the purpose of selling them to animal researchers. An outraged public quickly led federal legislators to pass the Animal Welfare Act in 1966. Among other regulations, the Animal Welfare Act required researchers to obtain animals from federally approved animal dealers.

Modern animal rights activities largely began after publication of philosopher Peter Singer's book *Animal Liberation* (Singer, 1975). Today's animal rights groups are active and well supported. Most take legal actions, but some take illegal actions against animal research.

Legal animal rights activities may include information sessions, public protests, petitions, and advertising. illegally animal rights activities include distributing false information, illegally entering animal facilities, releasing laboratory animals, and damaging laboratory equipment. Recent years have seen terrorist activities directed

FIGURE 1.8 ● Since 1997, illegal animal rights activist activities have occurred in most American states. States colored dark blue in this map have had a high number of incidents, whereas light blue-colored states have had a low numbers of incidents. Gray indicates no reported incidents.

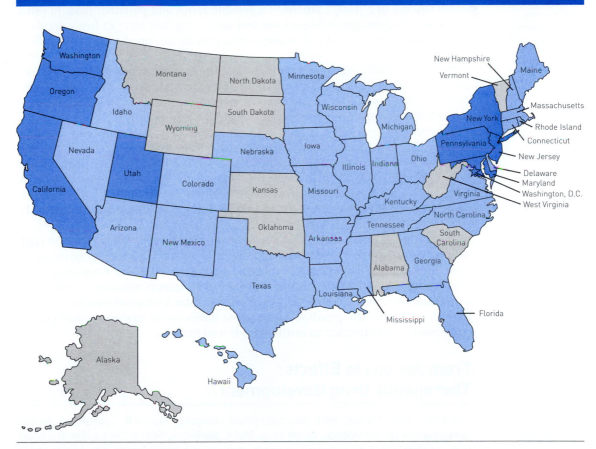

SOURCE: Image provided by the Foundation for Biomedical Research.

at animal researchers ranging from acts of vandalism to attempted murder. A string of incidents of vandalism and fire bombings of vehicles and homes has been linked especially to the ALF over many years (Lewis, 2005). In response to growing threats to researchers and students, groups supporting animal research publicize information on animal research medical discoveries. The Foundation for Biomedical Research, for example, informs the public about illegal animal rights activities (**Figure 1.8**) and produces media describing medical advances from animal research.

Researchers Consider Many Ethical Issues When Conducting Human Research

Informed consent
Consent gained after a participant thoroughly understands a study's procedures, possible gains, and potential risks

Like animal studies, ethics committees review research practices in humans to ensure federal regulatory and policy compliance and to weigh the ethics of proposed human studies. Beyond the obvious species differences, human and animal research differs according in the ability to provide informed consent. **Informed consent** consists of a participant's agreement to enroll in a study after having a thorough understanding of a study's procedures, possible gains, and potential risks. In other words, human participants know what they are getting into and can freely decide to enroll in the study. Animals, of course, cannot provide informed consent (Swerdlow, 2000).

However, some human participants also lack the capacity to provide informed consent. For example, young children lack the ability to understand what may happen during a medical study. Or an adult may be mentally incapable of providing informed consent. In these cases, informed consent is left to a legal guardian.

The informed consent principle is a relatively modern one, and there is a long history of human experimentation conducted either against the will of the participants or with complete dishonesty about what was being studied. The Nuremberg Principles, which arose from the Nuremberg Trials after World War II, consist of some of the first written statements about the ethical conduct of human research. These principles provided the foundation for the Declaration of Helsinki, another set of guidelines for ethical research using humans.

In the United States, the federal Department of Health and Human Services regulates human research. This department assigns the direct responsibility of enforcing these regulations to the Office of Protection from Research Risks. These regulations require that U.S. institutions review and approve all human research in accordance with these federal regulations. U.S. institutions must also file annual reports on human research activities. The penalties for violating government regulations and policies range from fines to freezing an institution's federal funding.

From Actions to Effects: Therapeutic Drug Development

Academic, government, and pharmaceutical company research contributes to the development of therapeutic drugs (e.g., Blake, Barker, & Sobel, 2006). For the most part, academic and government research consists of basic research discoveries about

STOP & CHECK

1. Why are animal models valuable?

2. When evaluating animal research proposals, what considerations are made in an ethical cost assessment?

3. Aside from species differences, what is the major distinction between human research and animal research?

1. Although animal models present important experimental validity challenges, animal models remain the only feasible models because they are effective and provide ways to evaluate drugs under carefully controlled conditions. **2.** By considering ethical costs, an IACUC weighs the benefits of a research proposal against the potential pain and suffering experienced by animal subjects. **3.** Humans can provide informed consent whereas animals cannot.

disorders and the development of theoretical directions for designing new treatments. This work may include characterizing a disorder's effects on the nervous system or developing a theory about chemical structures that mimic chemicals in the nervous system. Although some institutions develop new treatments, the vast majority of new treatments arrive from pharmaceutical companies.

Pharmaceutical drug research and development generally occurs in several stages (Blake et al., 2006; Dingemanse & Appel-Dingemanse, 2007; Jenkins & Hubbard, 1991) (see **Table 1.5**). First, a company usually decides for which disorder to develop a treatment. This decision includes carefully considering opinions from scientists, outside consultants, and business executives. These individuals seek to develop a feasible treatment that yields a reasonable likelihood of making a significant profit.

TABLE 1.5 ● Stages of Therapeutic Drug Development

Stage	Purpose	Description
1	Identify disorder to treat	Decisions include feasibility and profitability concerns.
2	Drug synthesis	Chemists synthesize experimental compounds.
3	Biological experimentation	High-throughput screening methods provide basic biological information about compounds. Results are sent to chemists and guide synthesis of further compounds.
4	Focused screening methods	Focused testing occurs with most promising compounds identified during Stage 3.
5	Safety pharmacology	Tests identify adverse effects and toxic doses.
6	Clinical trials	Most effective and safest compounds tested from previous stages are tested in humans. Regularly approval sought after positive clinical findings.

The likelihood of a profit coincides with a disorder's prevalence and the amount of scientific knowledge available about a disorder. In other words, companies assess the size of the market and the likelihood that research and development efforts can use known information to successfully invent a new drug treatment. In this regard, rare and incurable diseases are often incurable because there is a small market and relatively little scientific knowledge about them. For a rare disease, there must be a high potential of developing a successful treatment, making a research and development program low risk.

Feasibility and profitability often steer a research program into conservative directions, where instead of attempting treatments for currently incurable diseases, companies seek to improve treatments for currently treatable disorders. In fact, many new drugs are derived from active ingredients in natural products (Patridge, Gareiss, Kinch, & Hoyer, 2016). For example, the cough suppressant codeine is an active compound in opium, which is exuded from poppy plants. But occasionally companies will seek a high-risk, high-reward approach. For example, developing a cure for cancer or acquired immunodeficiency syndrome (AIDS) seems an insurmountable challenge, but the profit gained from such a treatment would be tremendous.

Drug synthesis occurs during the second drug-development stage. During this stage, a company's chemists develop experimental compounds. To do so, they may develop variations of existing therapeutic drugs for a disorder or develop drugs based on established theories.

Third, the drugs produced by the chemists during Stage 2 are tested in biological experiments. For example, researchers may assess how well experimental drugs bind to certain proteins in tissue samples. During this stage researchers prefer using **high-throughput screening** methods—rapid testing processes involving a large number of experimental drugs (Garrett, Walton, McDonald, Judson, & Workman, 2003; Szymański, Markowicz, & Mikiciuk-Olasik, 2012). Generally, high-throughput tests provide quick results and can determine whether the experimental drugs appear to be achieving a desired biological effect.

Chemists receive these test results and use the information to develop further experimental drugs. The most on-target drugs from the previous batch of experimental drugs serve as the best directions for synthesizing the next series of drugs. The chemists then send the newest drugs back to the high-throughput screeners. The back-and-forth continues as each new series of drug comes closer to achieving a particular biological effect. When a drug meets the researchers' goal for a biological effect, then drug testing moves to the next stage of development.

Stage 4 represents a shift from high-throughput screening methods to highly focused screening methods. Compared to high-throughput screening methods, these screening methods are slower, but offer greater precision about a drug's effect. In particular, researchers use models that have face, construct, or predictive validity. Often these methods include animal models.

After drugs pass through tests in Stage 4, researchers determine a drug's adverse effects. Thus, Stage 5 consists of **safety pharmacology** testing, screening processes that identify a drug's adverse and toxic effects (Guillon, 2010; Szymański et al., 2012). Adverse effects include mild to serious physiological effects, addiction risks, and changes in mental functioning. As noted in the chapter, we identify adverse effects too

High-throughput screening Rapid testing process involving a large number of experimental drugs

Safety pharmacology The study of a drug's adverse effects

severe to warrant exposing patients to toxic effects. Safety pharmacology tests seek to identify a drug's toxic doses.

Many drugs determined successful in earlier stages of screening reveal a low therapeutic index during safety pharmacology testing—that is, the same doses that produce therapeutic effects are near those that produce toxic effects. For drugs to meet clinical testing approval from governmental regulatory agencies such as the FDA, safety pharmacology tests must demonstrate that a drug's toxic doses are much higher than its therapeutic doses.

Stage 6 of drug development involves human drug testing. Most drugs fail to make it to this stage, having been abandoned because of a lack of efficacy or poor safety. A **clinical trial** is a government-approved therapeutic drug experiment in humans. In the United States and other countries, different phases describe the progression of experimental testing throughout the clinical trial process (**Table 1.6**). Clinical trials begin at Phase 1 and progress through Phases 2 and 3 as long as a drug continues to prove safe and effective. The FDA may request a Phase 4 trial after approving a drug for market in order to further assess the efficacy and safety of the drug (National Institutes of Health, 2012).

Clinical trial
A government-approved therapeutic drug experiment in humans' drug development; a multistep process of developing an effective, safe, and profitable therapeutic drug

TABLE 1.6 ● Clinical Trial Phases			
Clinical Trial Phase	**Goals**	**Dose and Duration of Treatment**	**Participants Involved**
Phase 1	Determine a drug's most likely and frequent adverse effects to occur during treatment	Low dose of the drug given short term	Normally healthy volunteers if feasible
Phase 2	Determination of therapeutic effectiveness; experimental drug may be compared to standard medical treatment; adverse effects continue to be monitored	May be higher dose of drug, but still given short term.	Participants with disorder to be treated
Phase 3	Further determination of therapeutic effectiveness; experimental drug may be compared to standard medical treatment; adverse effects continue to be monitored	Dose selected based on Phase 2 results, but likely given long term	Participants with disorder to be treated, but more inclusive for other populations and those with coexisting conditions
Phase 4	Occurs after FDA approves a drug for the market; might address remaining questions or concerns about the drug; goal is to further determine features of a drug's therapeutic effectiveness and adverse effects.	Dose selected based on Phase 3 results, but likely given long term	Participants with disorder to be treated, might focus on unique effects in different populations or certain other medical conditions; choice of participants may come from results of Phase 3

SOURCE: www.clinicaltrials.gov.

The primary goal of a Phase 1 clinical trial is to determine a drug's safety in humans. Phase 1 clinical trials employ a low dose of drug and provide it to healthy human volunteers if feasible or to a specific patient population for a short period of time. For example, a new pain-relieving drug might first be given to healthy human volunteers, whereas a new cancer-treating drug might need to be given to cancer patients, but perhaps only to those with a specific type of cancer. Clinical treats are terminated for drugs found unsafe in Phase 1.

During Phase 2 clinical trials, researchers primarily seek to measure a drug's therapeutic efficacy by recruiting volunteers with the disorder to be treated. Phase 2 clinical trials tend to use larger doses that are administered for short term, but perhaps longer than Phase 1. These trials often include for comparison an FDA-approved drug that is normally considered to be a standard medical treatment for the disorder. Through using a comparison drug, drug developers determine how well their drug will compete with others on the market. A company may see no benefit to continuing clinical trials for an experimental drug found only as effective as drugs already on the market.

Phase 3 clinical trials provide greater information about the drug's therapeutic effects and potential adverse effects. These trials rely on results from Phase 2 to determine the selection of drug dose (kept the same, or adjusted higher or lower) and normally have a longer duration of drug treatment. Moreover, researchers recruit study participants to have a greater diversity of human populations and health backgrounds than those in previous trials. The FDA grants market approval to drugs deemed safe and effective after Phase 3, although the FDA may request further monitoring after the drug goes to market. Further monitoring occurs during Phase 4 clinical trials, which may be designed to address any remaining questions or concerns from earlier phases. Thus, Phase 4 trials may employ higher doses, use longer durations, or focus on some specific human population or coexisting health condition. For example, a drug for treating tobacco addiction[3] might be further examined in Phase 4 trials in those with tobacco addiction[3] who are also clinically depressed. The approximate cost for bringing a drug through the research and development process and eventually onto the market is $2.6 billion (Mullard, 2014).

STOP & CHECK

1. What most likely happens after the first time drugs are initially screened?

2. Why might an effective and safe drug be removed from clinical trials?

1. Usually, chemists take data from the first screened batch and make further chemical compounds. The interplay between the chemists and the high-throughput screeners continues until the best drugs are made. 2. Sometimes drugs are removed from clinical trials because they fail to be more effective than drugs that are already on the market. A company may decide there's no profit to be made in this case.

---

3 I refrain from using "nicotine addiction" in this book, because there are other psychoactive ingredients in tobacco that make quitting hard to do.

Chapter Summary

Psychopharmacology is the study of how drugs affect mood, perception, thinking, or behavior. The field bridges psychology and pharmacology. Psychoactive drug use is highly prevalent in society. Alcohol, for example, is consumed by the much of the U.S. population, and antidepressant medications are used by close to a third of the Western population. Learning about psychopharmacology provides a greater understanding of behavior and how mental disorders are treated. Defined as substances that alter physiological functioning, drugs are known by generic names, trade names, and street names. Drug amounts used are described as doses, and understanding drug effects and actions requires knowledge of pharmacokinetic and pharmacodynamic actions. Moreover, genetic differences account for varying drug effects among individuals. Drugs fall into two categories: therapeutic drugs and recreational drugs. However, many drugs cross both categories, depending on their usage. Drugs come from three different sources: plants, industry, and clandestine laboratories. Researchers study the objective and subjective effects of drugs in studies that address the importance of drawing valid inferences from study results. Drug studies often employ either animal or human subjects, in abidance with regulatory and ethical guidelines. The drug development process for inventing new drug treatments begins with the decision to pursue a disorder and then proceeds through stages including drug synthesis, tests for efficacy and safety, and finally human clinical trials.

Key Terms

Psychopharmacology 2
Psychoactive drugs 2
Pharmacotherapeutics 3
Drug 3
Instrumental drug use 5
Therapeutic drug 6
Recreational drug use 6
Trade name 6
Generic name 6
Chemical name 7
Street name 7
Dose 7
Dose-effect curve 8
ED_{50} value 9
Potency 9

Therapeutic index 9
Certain Safety Index 10
Pharmacodynamics 11
Pharmacokinetics 11
Pharmacogenetics 11
Objective effects 12
Subjective effects 13
Dependent variable 13
Independent variable 14
Correlational study 14
Experimental study 14
Placebo 14
Treatment arms 15
Clinical study reports 16
Single-blind procedure 16

Double-blind procedure 16
Open-label studies 16
Internal validity 16
External validity 17
Teratogen 17
Face validity 18
Construct validity 18
Predictive validity 19
The 3 Rs 21
Ethical cost 21
Informed consent 24
High-throughput
   screening 26
Safety pharmacology 26
Clinical trial 27

Visit the Student Study Site at **study.sagepub.com/prus2e** to access additional study tools, including eFlashcards, web quizzes, video resources, web resources, SAGE journal articles, and more.

2

The Nervous System

IS THERE MORE TO THE STORY OF PHINEAS GAGE?

Psychology students are familiar with the story of Phineas Gage, a railway construction foreman who, in 1848, survived an accident when a 3-foot tamping iron shot through his skull. As the familiar story goes, his behavior radically transformed from a kind, reliable, and friendly man to one who was "fitful . . . engaging in times in the grossest profanity, [and] manifesting little deference for his fellows" (Harlow, 1868; MacMillan, 2008). The incident shows that one's personality can dramatically change from injury to the brain.

Yet, we may not know the complete story of Phineas Gage (MacMillan, 2008). After recovery from the incident, for example, Gage's mother remarked that he "entertained his little nephews and nieces with the most fabulous recitals" and that he "conceived a great fondness . . . for children, horses and dogs." Moreover, a seemingly industrious Gage had traveled to New York, Boston, and other New England towns to show his injury at medical lectures and at Barnum's American Museum in New York. He also spent 18 months as a

stage coach driver, a job requiring physical stamina, high cognitive functioning, and
social skills in order to prepare horses, keep
to a schedule, collect fares, be polite to hotel
guests, and successfully navigate miles of
winding poor roads.

These characteristics differ dramatically from
popular perceptions of Gage. That Phineas
Gage's personality perhaps did not switch so
abruptly and that his cognitive and social abilities appeared intact is a tacit reminder about
the brain's complexity and adaptability to injury.

The study of psychoactive drugs requires knowledge about how drugs act on
the nervous system. This chapter provides a basic overview of the nervous
system, with an emphasis on cells and structures important for psychoactive
drug effects.

Cells in the Nervous System

Each structure of the brain contains a dense ensemble of neurons and glial cells. **Neurons**
are specialized cells in the nervous system that control behavior, senses, and movement.
Neurons communicate by receiving and transmitting information to other neurons in
the nervous system and other cells in the nervous system and the body. **Glial cells** support the function of neurons. General estimates give the brain approximately 86 billion
neurons and 10 times as many glial cells (Herculano-Houzel, 2012).

Neurons Specialized cells in the nervous system that control behavior, senses, and movement

Glial cells (or glia cells) Cells that support the function of neurons

Neural Communication

Neurons comprise dense communication networks in the brain. These networks support the function of individual brain structures and facilitate communication between
structures. Like other cells in the body, neurons have basic characteristics such as a
membrane, nucleus, ribosomes, and an endoplasmic reticulum (**Figure 2.1**), yet they
have many unique characteristics for cellular communication.

Neurons have four major components: a soma, dendrites, axon, and axon terminal
(**Figure 2.2**). The soma is the body of the neuron. It also contains the nucleus, which
holds DNA. Overall, components within the soma support a neuron's basic physiological processes.

Generally, a neuron has many dendrites that branch off from the soma. The
dendrites of a neuron receive information from other neurons. Small stems called
dendritic spines grow along the length of dendritic branches. The membranes of dendrites and dendritic spines contain proteins called *receptors* that neurotransmitters
can activate. When activated, receptors cause changes in the functioning of the
neuron. The overall coverage of dendrites for a neuron is called the *receptive area*;
the more dendrites a neuron has, the more input it can receive from other neurons.

Dendrites Parts of a neuron that receive information from other neurons

FIGURE 2.1 ● **The soma of a neuron contains the same basic components that other cells of the body have.**

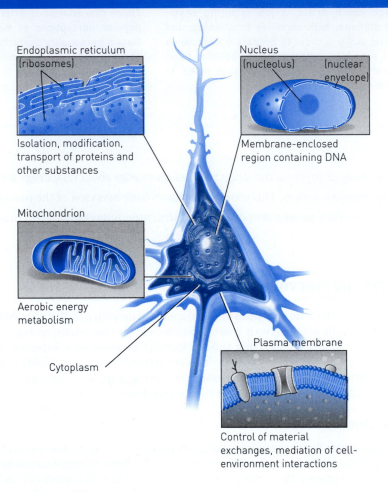

Endoplasmic reticulum (ribosomes)

Isolation, modification, transport of proteins and other substances

Nucleus (nucleolus)   (nuclear envelope)

Membrane-enclosed region containing DNA

Mitochondrion

Aerobic energy metabolism

Cytoplasm

Plasma membrane

Control of material exchanges, mediation of cell-environment interactions

Axons Part of a neuron that sends neurotransmitters to other neurons

Synapse Components that make up a connection between neurons that includes an axon terminal, postsynaptic terminal, and synaptic cleft

Axons send neurotransmitters to other neurons. Most neurons have only one axon, which branches from the soma, usually opposite from the dendrites. An axon begins at a part of the soma called the *axon hillock* and ends with multiple branches containing axon terminals.[1] These branches are called *axon collaterals*. An axon terminal contains and releases neurotransmitters near a part of a dendrite called a *postsynaptic terminal*. The postsynaptic terminal contains receptors for neurotransmitters. The small space between the axon terminal and postsynaptic terminal is called the *synaptic cleft*. The term **synapse** refers to the components that comprise this connection, and these include the axon terminal, postsynaptic terminal, and the synaptic cleft.

---

1 Also referred to as *presynaptic terminals*.

FIGURE 2.2 ● **The four major components of a neuron are the soma, dendrites, an axon, and an axon terminal. Dendrites receive information, and axons send information.**

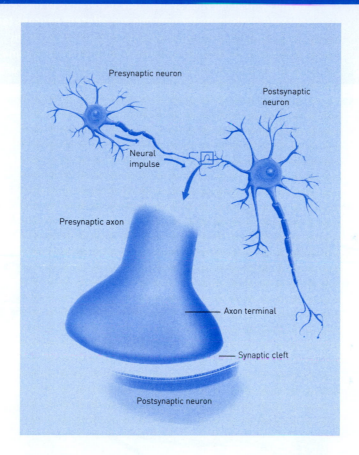

Neuroscientists use different terms to describe the location of a neuron and the direction of its axon. The term **interneuron** describes a neuron with the soma and axon found within the same structure (**Figure 2.3**). An afferent neuron has an axon *going to* another structure. **Sensory neurons**, which convey sensory information via axons to the central nervous system, are considered *afferent* neurons. An *efferent* neuron has an axon *coming from* a structure. **Motor neurons** (or **motoneurons**), which convey motor information via axons from the central nervous system, are considered efferent neurons (Figure 2.3). Thus, the terms *afferent* and *efferent* can refer to any structure being studied. For example, the thalamus, a structure that routes sensory information to different parts of the cerebral cortex, has both types of neurons: afferent neurons send axons *to* the thalamus, and efferent neurons send axons *from* the thalamus.

Interneuron Neuron with the soma and axon found within the same structure

Sensory neuron Neuron that conveys sensory information via axons to the central nervous system

Motor neuron (or motoneuron) Neuron that conveys motor information via axons from the central nervous system

FIGURE 2.3 ● **Motor and Sensory Neurons**
Motor neurons convey movement information to muscles in the body, and sensory neurons convey sensory information to the central nervous system (CNS). Relative to the central nervous system, motor neurons are efferent neurons (going away from the CNS), and sensory neurons are afferent neurons (going to the CNS). Interneurons have the soma, dendrites, and axon all contained within the same structure.

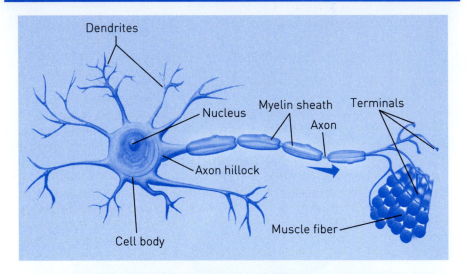

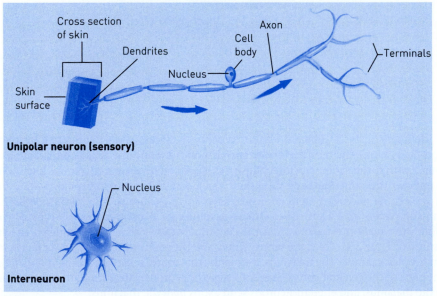

Glial Cells: Facilitating Nervous System Functions

Glial cells consist of three different types: (1) oligodendrocytes, (2) astrocytes, and (3) microglial cells (**Figure 2.4**). **Oligodendrocytes** extend themselves around axons to form a material called *myelin*. Myelin facilitates the movement of electrical impulses down an axon by serving as an insulating material (more on this in Chapter 3). Schwann

Oligodendrocyte
Glial cell that forms a material called myelin around the axons of neurons.

> **FIGURE 2.4** ● Glial cells support neuronal functioning. Oligodendrocytes and Schwann cells provide myelin sheathing for axons. Astrocytes form the blood–brain barrier, break down certain neurotransmitters, and respond to injury in the nervous system. Microglial cells remove cellular waste.

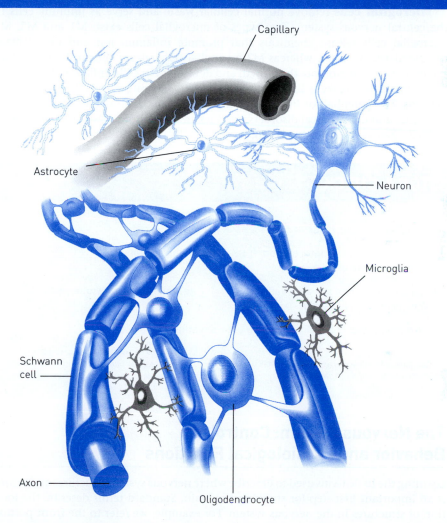

Astrocyte Glial cell that plays a role in the forming the blood-brain barrier, facilitating neuronal function and responding to injury

Gliosis Process involving the swelling of glia cells in response to injury.

Microglial cell Glial cell that removes normal cellular waste and serves as an immune cell in the central nervous system

cells are like oligodendrocytes but are found in the peripheral nervous system. The motor dysregulation, paralysis, and other symptoms of multiple sclerosis result from degeneration of myelin sheaths surrounding axons in the nervous system.

Astrocytes play a role in forming the blood–brain barrier, facilitating neuronal function, and responding to injury. Astrocytes form the blood–brain barrier (discussed in Chapter 5) by forcing endothelial cells to fit tightly together. Astrocytes support neuronal function through acting at synapses during neurotransmission, which we consider in Chapter 3.

Astrocytes respond to injury in the brain through a process called **gliosis**. Gliosis is also referred to as a *glial scar*. During gliosis, glial cells swell in response to injury. By surrounding damaged tissue, glial cells segregate damaged tissue from undamaged tissue. When this occurs, however, gliosis severely limits the ability of regenerated axons to reach healthy tissue and then how well an individual recovers from brain injury.

Microglial cells remove normal cellular waste and serve as immune cells in the central nervous system. Two types of microglial cells exist: M1 and M2. M1 microglial cells release chemicals that promote inflammation and can damage the blood–brain barrier, whereas M2 microglial cells release chemicals that reduce inflammation and promote the growth and development cells. Inflammation caused by M1 microglial weakens the blood–brain barrier, allowing in cells that can damage neurons. The potential for inflammation-induced damage to neurons to contribute to mental and neurological disorders provides an important reason to study microglial cells (Nakagawa & Chiba, 2015).

STOP & CHECK

1. What are the two types of cells found in the brain?

2. _____ receive information from other neurons, and _____ send information to other axons.

3. Sensory neurons are also called _____ neurons because axons go to the central nervous system.

4. Which types of glial cells provide myelin sheathing for axons?

1. Neurons and glial cells 2. Dendrites, axons 3. afferent 4. Oligodendrocytes produce myelin sheathing around axons in the central nervous system, and Schwann cells produce myelin sheathing around axons outside of the central nervous system.

The Nervous System: Control of Behavior and Physiological Functions

Learning the basic terms used to describe where nervous system structures are located is an important first step for studying the brain. Standard terms describe the location of structures in the nervous system. For example, we refer to the front portion of the brain as *anterior* and the back portion of the brain as *posterior*. The bottom of the brain, the side that faces toward the stomach, is referred to as the *ventral* side, and the top of the brain is referred to as the *dorsal* side. We refer to structures near the sides of the brain as *lateral*; structures near the middle of the brain are described as *medial*. **Figure 2.5** presents these and other terms that describe structures in the nervous system.

Looking at structures inside the brain may be accomplished through any of three basic types of dissection planes. Slicing the brain from anterior to posterior produces a *coronal*, or *frontal*, section. We produce horizontal sections by slicing the brain from dorsal to ventral, and sagittal sections provide lateral views of the brain. Dissection planes provide different perspectives of a structure.

FIGURE 2.5 ● The Human Brain
The human brain can be dissected in coronal (i.e., frontal), horizontal, and sagittal sections. We use special terms to describe the location of structures in the brain.

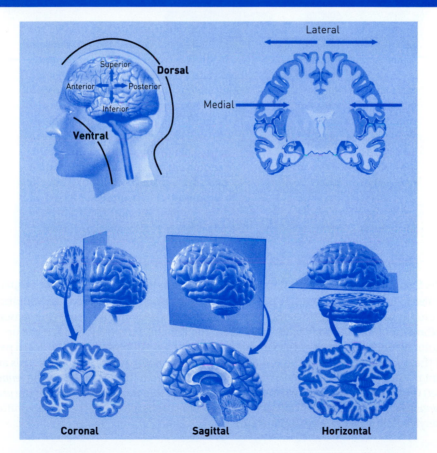

Coronal   Sagittal   Horizontal

The Peripheral Nervous System: Controlling and Responding to Physiological Processes in the Body

The nervous system consists of two systems: (1) the peripheral nervous system and (2) the central nervous system (CNS). Much of what we discuss in this book pertains to the central nervous system, which consists of the brain and spinal cord. Drugs also have many effects on the peripheral nervous system, which contains two subsystems called the *somatic nervous system* and *autonomic nervous system* (**Figure 2.6**).

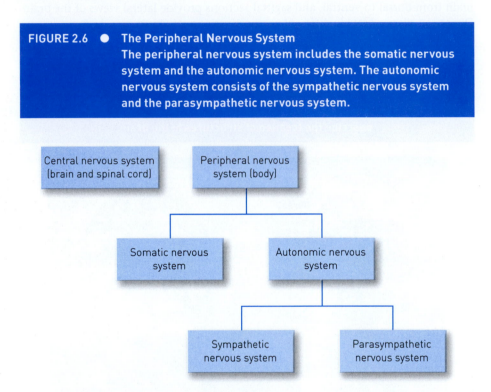

FIGURE 2.6 ● The Peripheral Nervous System
The peripheral nervous system includes the somatic nervous system and the autonomic nervous system. The autonomic nervous system consists of the sympathetic nervous system and the parasympathetic nervous system.

Somatic nervous system System responsible for delivering voluntary motor signals from the central nervous system to muscles throughout the body and for conveying sensory information from the body to the central nervous system

The Somatic Nervous System: Delivering Motor Signals to Muscles and Sensory Signals to the Spinal Cord The **somatic nervous system** is responsible for delivering voluntary motor signals from the CNS to muscles throughout the body and for conveying sensory information from the body to the CNS. Thus, the somatic nervous system is made up of motor neurons and sensory neurons. Sensory neurons send information to the dorsal part of the spinal cord (through the *dorsal root* to the *dorsal horn*), whereas motor signals are sent to muscles from the ventral part of the spinal cord (from the *ventral horn* to the *ventral root*) (**Figure 2.7**). The point where a motor neuron meets a muscle fiber is called the *neuromuscular junction*. Muscles contract when motor neurons release the neurotransmitter acetylcholine at neuromuscular junctions.

FIGURE 2.7 ● Sensory neurons send information to the dorsal part of the spinal cord, whereas motor signals are sent to muscles from the ventral part of the spinal cord. Gray matter appears in the middle portion of the spinal cord forming an H shape. White matter appears in the outermost portions of the spinal cord.

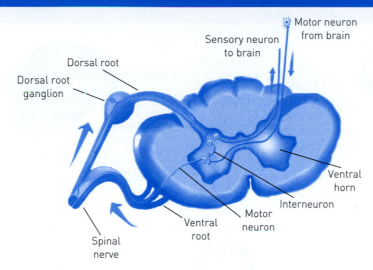

The Autonomic Nervous System: Controlling Vital Functions Whereas the somatic nervous system produces voluntary movement, the **autonomic nervous system** controls involuntary movements for functions such as heartbeat, breathing, swallowing, and sweating by controlling heart muscle, smooth muscle, and exocrine glands. Exocrine glands secrete substances through a duct, such as sweat, saliva, and tears. The autonomic nervous system consists of two systems: (1) the sympathetic nervous system and (2) the parasympathetic nervous system (**Figure 2.8**). The **sympathetic nervous system** prepares the body for rigorous activity by increasing heartbeat, inhibiting digestion, and opening airways, among many other involuntary functions. The **parasympathetic nervous system** is dominant during relaxed states and decreases heartbeat, stimulates digestion, and closes airways.

Both the sympathetic and parasympathetic nervous systems contain ganglia (singular: ganglion). *Ganglia* are clusters of neuron cell bodies for neurons in the sympathetic and parasympathetic nervous system. A ganglion fully contains a neuron's soma and dendrite, while a neuron's axon extends from the ganglion to a muscle or gland. We call this a *postganglionic* neuron because its axon comes after the ganglion and goes to a muscle or gland. A neuron that instead sends an axon from the spinal cord to a ganglion is referred to as a *preganglionic* neuron.

Preganglionic neurons control sympathetic and parasympathetic nervous system neurons by releasing the neurotransmitter acetylcholine at synapses for postganglionic neurons. Through the process of neurotransmission (discussed in Chapter 3)

Autonomic nervous system System that controls involuntary movements for vital functions, such as heartbeat, breathing, and swallowing

Sympathetic nervous system System that prepares the body for rigorous activity by increasing heartbeat, inhibiting digestion, and opening airways, among many other involuntary functions

Parasympathetic nervous system Subsystem of the autonomic system that is dominant during relaxed states, including decreases in heartbeat, stimulation of digestion, and the closing of airways

FIGURE 2.8 ● The autonomic nervous system is made up of of the sympathetic nervous system and the parasympathetic nervous system. The sympathetic nervous system enhances the activity of organs in the body and the parasympathetic nervous system diminishes the activity of these same organs. The activation of each system occurs by preganglionic neurons releasing acetylcholine in ganglia, which binds to receptors on postganglionic neurons.

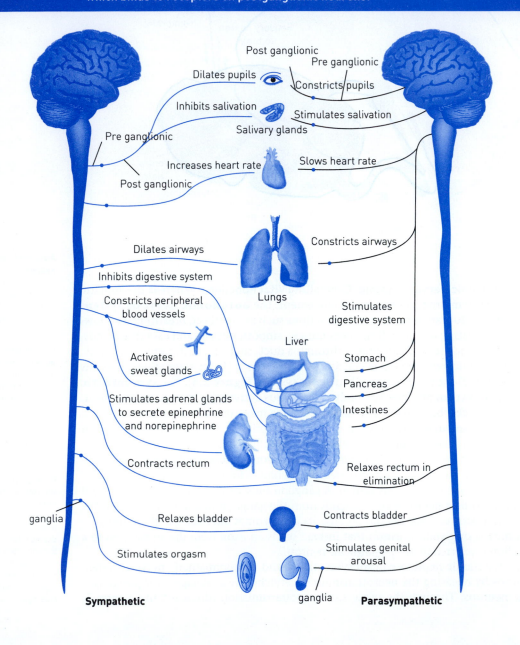

acetylcholine makes these postganglionic neurons more active. Axons for the activated postganglionic neurons then release neurotransmitters at their presynaptic terminals. This leads target muscles or glands to have increased (for sympathetic nervous system neurons) or decreased (for parasympathetic nervous system neurons) activity.

STOP & CHECK

1. Brain sections produced by slicing the brain from anterior to posterior are referred to as _____ sections.

2. The somatic nervous system delivers movement signals to muscles by releasing acetylcholine at _____.

3. The _____ system controls vital functions such as breathing and heartbeat.

1. coronal 2. neuromuscular junctions 3. Autonomic

The Central Nervous System

The brain and spinal cord make up the central nervous system (**Figure 2.9**). The surface of the brain—the **cerebral cortex**—has hills called *gyri* (singular *gyrus*) and crevices called *sulci* (singular *sulcus*). The base of the brain, where the spinal cord meets, is called the *brain stem*. Above the brain stem sits a structure called the *cerebellum*. The brain is divided into two hemispheres, left and right. Structures found in one hemisphere have a matching structure in the other hemisphere.

The brain also contains three different divisions called the *hindbrain, midbrain,* and *forebrain,* also shown in Figure 2.9. The hindbrain is the lower part of the brain stem, and it begins where the spinal cord meets the brain stem at a structure called the *medulla*. The midbrain comprises a region between the hindbrain and forebrain; it includes the *inferior colliculus*, which plays a role in auditory processing, and the *superior colliculus*, which directs eye movement. The forebrain includes the rest of the brain and contains the cerebral cortex and structures beneath the cerebral cortex such as the *corpus callosum, basal ganglia, thalamus,* and *hypothalamus.*

The Medulla and Hypothalamus: Controlling Unlearned Behaviors We previously discussed the autonomic system, which maintains vital functions in the body. The autonomic nervous system is controlled by the medulla (**Figure 2.10**). As already described, the **medulla** rests where the spinal cord meets the hindbrain. In fact, from the surface, the medulla looks like a thicker section of spinal cord. Through controlling the autonomic nervous system, the medulla controls basic autonomic functions such as breathing, heart rate, and vomiting.

Cerebral cortex
The surface of the brain; comprising gyri and sulci

Medulla Structure that controls the autonomic nervous system and is situated where the spinal cord meets the hindbrain

FIGURE 2.9 ● The CNS is divided into three different divisions or regions of the brain called the *hindbrain*, *midbrain*, and *forebrain*.

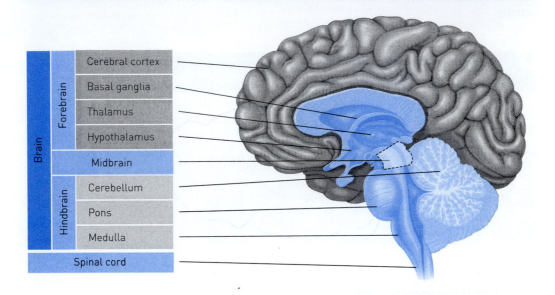

Many of the cranial nerves also come from the medulla. These nerves are devoted to movement and sensations of the head (**Figure 2.10**). There are 12 cranial nerves, each noted by its name and a number. The vagus nerve (roman numeral X) differs from the functions of the other cranial nerves because it controls and receives sensory information from various internal organs in the body, including the heart, liver, and intestines.

Clearly, damaging the medulla can be life threatening, and suppressing its functioning can be just as dangerous. Narcotics and central nervous system depressants suppress medullary functions, which can be fatal at high enough doses. Moreover, mixing two or more CNS depressants at otherwise safe amounts can produce combined suppressant effects on medullary functions.

The **hypothalamus**, a structure found in the forebrain, maintains important physiological conditions (**Figure 2.11**). The hypothalamus maintains many physiological processes by motivating an organism's behavior. When the body requires food, for example, the hypothalamus elicits feelings of hunger. Similarly, the hypothalamus elicits thirst when we become dehydrated. Other processes the hypothalamus regulates include body temperature, sleep, and motivation for sexual activity.

Hypothalamus
Structure found in the forebrain that maintains important physiological conditions, in part by motivating an organism's behavior

FIGURE 2.10 ● The ventral side of the brain reveals many features, including the structures in the brain stem and all 12 of the cranial nerves.

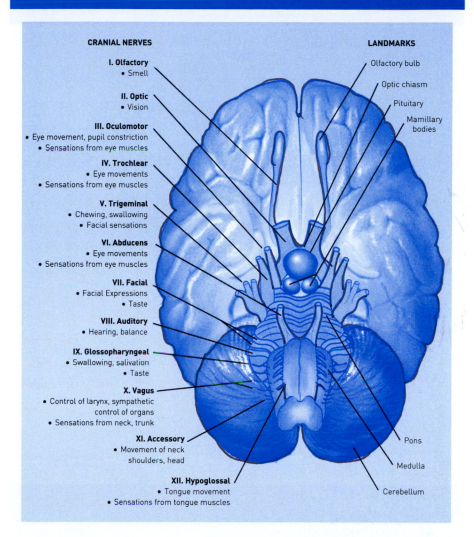

CRANIAL NERVES

I. Olfactory
• Smell

II. Optic
• Vision

III. Oculomotor
• Eye movement, pupil constriction
• Sensations from eye muscles

IV. Trochlear
• Eye movements
• Sensations from eye muscles

V. Trigeminal
• Chewing, swallowing
• Facial sensations

VI. Abducens
• Eye movements
• Sensations from eye muscles

VII. Facial
• Facial Expressions
• Taste

VIII. Auditory
• Hearing, balance

IX. Glossopharyngeal
• Swallowing, salivation
• Taste

X. Vagus
• Control of larynx, sympathetic control of organs
• Sensations from neck, trunk

XI. Accessory
• Movement of neck shoulders, head

XII. Hypoglossal
• Tongue movement
• Sensations from tongue muscles

LANDMARKS

Olfactory bulb

Optic chiasm

Pituitary

Mamillary bodies

Pons

Medulla

Cerebellum

The hypothalamus controls the *pituitary gland*, which sits on the ventral surface of the brain. The pituitary gland releases many hormones into the bloodstream, affecting organ functions in the body. These effects include water absorption into the kidneys, growth, thyroid function, and reproductive functions. The hypothalamus also controls the *pineal gland*, another forebrain structure that is responsible for the release of *melatonin*, a sleep-regulating hormone.

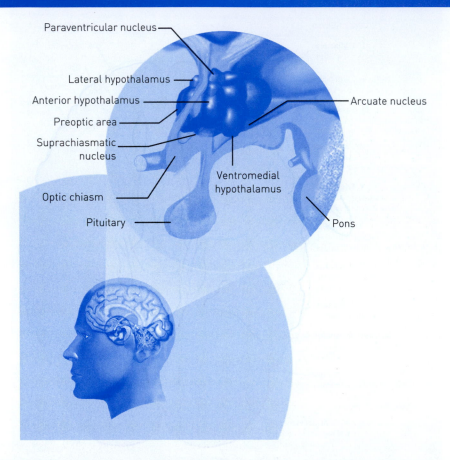

FIGURE 2.11 ● **The hypothalamus plays an important role for homeostasis, partly by eliciting motivation for various physiological activities such as eating and drinking.**

STOP & CHECK

1. The central nervous system contains the brain and _____.

2. What are the lobes of the cerebral cortex?

3. What is the primary structure in the brain for controlling autonomic functions?

4. How does the hypothalamus alter hormone levels in the body?

1. spinal cord **2.** The lobes consist of the frontal, temporal, parietal, and occipital. **3.** The medulla **4.** The hypothalamus controls the pituitary gland, which releases many hormones throughout the body.

FIGURE 2.12 ● The limbic system generally is important for emotion, although the hippocampus also plays an important role in long-term memory.

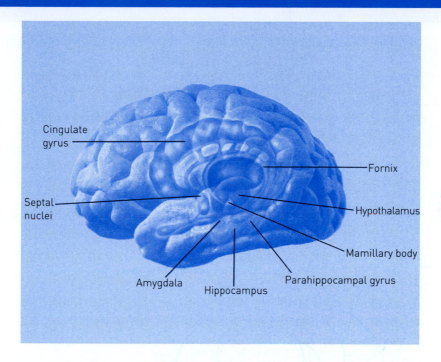

The Limbic System: Controlling Emotional Behaviors The **limbic system** consists of a series of structures that together form a ring around the thalamus and hypothalamus. These limbic system structures include the *cingulate gyrus, hippocampus, amygdala,* and *olfactory bulb* (**Figure 2.12**). Many structures within the limbic system control emotional behavior. The amygdala, for example, facilitates fear and aggression. Many drugs that reduce anxiety decrease the activity of neurons in the amygdala.

The **nucleus accumbens** rests adjacent to the amygdala and facilitates reinforcing effects. For this reason, we refer to the nucleus accumbens as the brain's *reward center*. The nucleus accumbens belongs to a network of other structures referred to as the *reward circuit*. Chapter 5 presents more information on the brain's reward circuitry and the role this circuitry plays in the reinforcing effects of abused substances.

The Cerebral Cortex: Processing Sensory Information, Controlling Cognitive Functions, and Eliciting Movement Four lobes divide the cerebral cortex (**Figure 2.13**). The **occipital lobe** is the most posterior portion of the cerebral cortex and processes visual information. The **temporal lobe** is anterior to the occipital lobe and below the parietal lobe. The temporal lobe processes auditory information and supports language comprehension and production. This area of the cerebral cortex also processes certain

Limbic system
Series of structures that together appear to form a ring around the thalamus and hypothalamus

Nucleus accumbens
Limbic system structure that facilitates reinforcing effects

Occipital lobe Region of the cerebral cortex important for processing visual information

Temporal lobe
Region of the cerebral cortex important for processing auditory information and supporting language comprehension and production

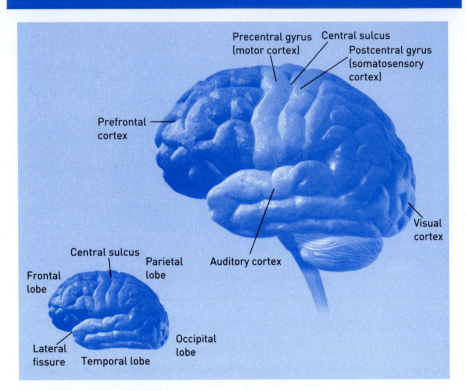

FIGURE 2.13 ● Each lobe of the cerebral cortex processes different types of sensory information. The prefrontal cortex, within the frontal lobe, is an integration center for all types of sensory information.

Parietal lobe Region of the cerebral cortex important for processing touch information

Frontal lobe Region of the cerebral cortex important for decision making and movement

Prefrontal cortex Most anterior part of the frontal cortex; an integration area for all types of sensory input; initiates movements

Thalamus Forebrain structure that routes sensory information from the body to the appropriate lobes

aspects of vision, including shape and color analysis. The **parietal lobe** includes the *somatosensory cortex*, the structure responsible for processing touch information from the body. The parietal lobe also analyzes visual information that contains movement.

The **frontal lobe**, which is at the anterior of the brain, supports decision making and movement. The frontal lobe contains the motor cortex. The most anterior part of the frontal lobe is called the **prefrontal cortex** and is an integration area for all types of sensory input and where the signal to produce movement occurs. Prefrontal cortical function also supports short-term memory and attention.

The **thalamus** routes sensory information from the body to the appropriate lobes. For example, visual information is sent from the eyes through the thalamus and to the occipital lobe, whereas auditory information is sent from the ears through the thalamus and to the temporal lobe. Olfactory information, however, is sent directly to the prefrontal cortex. After processing, all sensory information integrates in the prefrontal cortex.

STOP & CHECK

1. What are the primary functions of the amygdala and nucleus accumbens?

2. Which lobe analyzes sound, including language?

3. What role does the thalamus play in processing sensory information?

1. The amygdala elicits feelings of fear, anxiety, and aggression, whereas the nucleus accumbens elicits reinforcing effects. **2.** Temporal lobe **3.** The thalamus routes sensory information to the appropriate lobes of the cerebral cortex

The Frontal Lobe and Basal Ganglia: Controlling Voluntary Movement After the prefrontal cortex signals a movement to occur, the **motor cortex** sends movement signals to the body the lateral corticospinal tract and the medial corticospinal tract. The lateral corticospinal tract crosses from one hemisphere of the brain to the opposite side of the body. This tract sends motor information to the limbs, hands, and feet. The medial corticospinal tract sends information from each hemisphere mostly to the same side of the body. This tract functions mainly for middle parts of the body, providing for posture and balance.

The **basal ganglia** act to stabilize voluntary movements (**Figure 2.14**). The basal ganglia, also called the *striatum*, have three major structures: the *caudate nucleus*, the *putamen*, and the *globus pallidus*. The *substantia nigra* aids in regulating activity in the basal ganglia. The primary symptoms of Parkinson's disease, a disorder characterized by muscle rigidity, tremor, and resistance to voluntary movement, occurs from the destruction of substantia nigra neurons that go to the basal ganglia. Many of the first drugs to treat schizophrenia, called *antipsychotic drugs*, disrupt these neurons, leading to Parkinson-like symptoms called *extrapyramidal side effects*.

Some other components of the overall motor system must be noted. The **pons**, a structure located just above the medulla in the hindbrain, elicits startle reflexes. The **cerebellum** facilitates balance and the timing of movements.

Learning and Memory Processes in the Brain Psychologists characterize short- and long-term memories in different ways. Most consider short-term memory as working memory. **Working memory** consists of short-term verbal or nonverbal memories employed when carrying out a task. In essence, we are "working" with memory. **Long-term memory** (or **reference memory**), consists of stored verbal and nonverbal information. Long-term memories include information that we can

Motor cortex Part of the frontal lobe that sends movement signals to the body through the pyramidal system

Basal ganglia Aid in the stabilization of movement

Pons A structure that elicits startle reflexes

Cerebellum A structure that facilitates balance and the timing of movements

Working memory Consists of short-term verbal or nonverbal memories employed to carry out a task

Long-term memory (or reference memory) Consists of stored verbal and nonverbal information

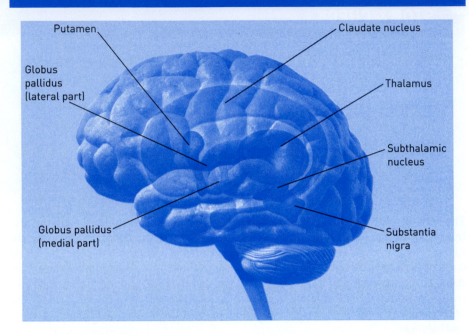

FIGURE 2.14 ● The basal ganglia, which include the globus pallidus, putamen, and caudate nucleus, regulate movement signals sent from the motor cortex.

declare, such as the capital of the United States, or information we can demonstrate, such as how to swing a golf club.

The prefrontal cortex facilitates working memory function. Recall that information from all sensory modalities integrates in the prefrontal cortex. The prefrontal cortex uses this information to control behavior when engaging in a task.

Hippocampus A structure in the limbic system important for long-term memory

Long-term memory formation and retrieval requires the **hippocampus**. The hippocampus then sends information to the prefrontal cortex, possibly for use during working memory function. Damage to the hippocampus in Alzheimer's disease may account for impairments in long-term memory. Long-term motor memories, also referred to as *procedural memories*, may depend on the basal ganglia. Motor memories include skills such as riding a bike.

Reticular activating system System of structures that support arousal in the cerebral cortex

Other parts of the brain indirectly aid memory formation by keeping the brain active. Many of these parts are found in the **reticular activating system**, which includes the *reticular formation, tegmentum, thalamus,* and *hypothalamus.* The activity within these structures ultimately supports arousal in the cerebral cortex. Another structure important for cortical arousal is the basal forebrain area. Drugs that increase cortical arousal include psychostimulant drugs; drugs that depress cortical arousal include benzodiazepines, barbiturates, and alcohol.

STOP & CHECK

1. Which part of the cerebral cortex sends movements signals to the body?

2. What parts of the brain are damaged in Parkinson's disease?

3. Which structures are linked to working memory and long-term memory, respectively?

1. The motor cortex 2. Parkinson's disease arises from damage to neurons that begin in the substantia nigra and end in the basal ganglia 3. The prefrontal cortex is particularly important for working memory, whereas the hippocampus is important for long-term memory.

Cerebral Blood Flow and Cerebrospinal Fluid

Proper blood flow throughout the brain, called **cerebral blood flow**, is critical for neuron and glial cell function. Highly active brain areas require increased blood flow. When you are working hard on a task such as an exam, your prefrontal cortex is very active. Blood flow increases to the prefrontal cortex to sustain this activity. Blood flow changes throughout the brain when blood capillaries dilate and contract. Highly active cells release a chemical called *nitric oxide* that dilates blood capillaries, which in turn delivers more oxygen.

Cerebrospinal fluid is a clear fluid that surrounds cells in the brain. Cerebrospinal fluid provides a medium through which nutrients, a sugar called *glucose*, hormones, and other chemicals access brain cells (**Figure 2.15**). In addition to surrounding cells in the brain, cerebrospinal fluid fills many spaces and canals in the brain. The central canal of the spinal cord is filled with cerebrospinal fluid, and there is a smaller canal-like structure in the brain called the *cerebral aqueduct*. The cerebral aqueduct is surrounded by a small layer of tissue called **periaqueductal gray**. The brain also contains cerebrospinal fluid–filled cavities called **ventricles**.

Cerebrospinal fluid is also found in the *meninges* that surround the brain. Cerebrospinal fluid forms in a layer of the meninges called the *subarachnoid space*. By filling this space, cerebrospinal fluid forms a protective cushion around the brain, protecting it from injury.

Cerebral blood flow Blood flow throughout the brain

Cerebrospinal fluid Fluid that surrounds cells in the brain

Periaqueductal gray Small layer of tissue that surrounds the cerebral aqueduct.

Ventricles Cerebrospinal fluid-filled cavities in the brain.

STOP & CHECK

1. How might thinking be affected if the brain had poor cerebral blood flow?

2. The meninges protect the brain from injury because they contain a clear fluid called _____.

1. Since cells in the brain require oxygen to meet increase energy demands, thinking would certainly be compromised from poor flow. 2. cerebrospinal fluid

FIGURE 2.15   ●   The ventricles are filled with cerebrospinal fluid. The third and fourth ventricles are connected by the cerebral aqueduct. Within the spinal cord, the central canal is filled with cerebral spinal fluid.

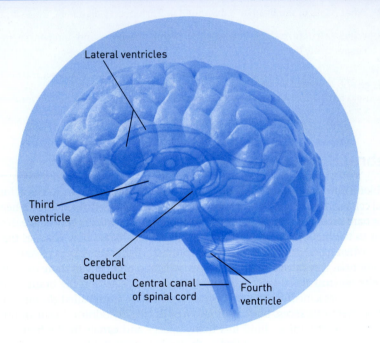

Lateral ventricles

Third ventricle

Cerebral aqueduct

Central canal of spinal cord

Fourth ventricle

Genes and the Physiological Processes of Cells

The blueprints for a cell and its functions reside within the nucleus. The nucleus of every cell for humans contains 46 chromosomes. A child inherits 23 chromosomes from each parent. Two of the 46 chromosomes consist of X and Y chromosomes, which determine an individual's sex. If both of these sex chromosomes are X's, then an individual is genetically female. However, if one of these sex chromosomes is a Y, then the individual is genetically male. All of the other chromosomes are called *autosomal chromosomes*.

Each chromosome contains a strand of *deoxyribonucleic acid* (DNA), which contains the specific coding instructions for the basic functions of cells called **genes**. Genes are encoded with the traits we have (**Figure 2.16**). Within this role, genes contain information to synthesize new proteins. Researchers can alter genetic information in animals to study the nervous system (**Box 2.1**).

Gene Segment of DNA encoded with the traits expressed in an organism

FIGURE 2.16 ● **When a gene is activated, a specific DNA segment is unraveled and transcribed onto ribonucleic acid (RNA), which may then leave the nucleus and carry the transcribed information to ribosomes that synthesize proteins as instructed.**

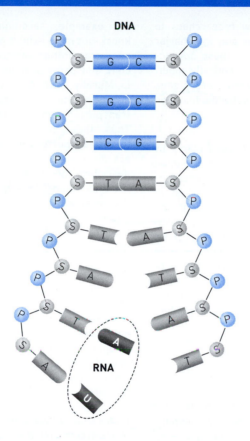

Although genes contain codes to express certain traits such as eye color or production of a particular enzyme, the coding sequence for genes may not be precisely the same from individual to individual. We term these differences *polymorphisms*. A **polymorphism** is a difference in the encoding of a gene compared to the most common sequence in a population. Polymorphisms are common, and determining what type of polymorphism an individual has can aid greatly in understanding a person's response to drug effects. For example, some polymorphisms lead to greater production of certain types of enzymes in the liver. For these individuals, the extra enzymes may break down a drug before it produces any substantial effects.

Activating genes leads to the copying of genetic information, a process referred to as *gene transcription*. A **transcription factor** consists of a substance that increases or decreases gene transcription. During gene transcription, the coding sequence of a gene

Polymorphism A difference in the encoding of a gene compared to the most common sequence in a population

Transcription factor Substance that increases or decreases gene transcription

BOX 2.1 GENETICALLY MODIFIED ORGANISMS

Genetic technologies allow researchers to characterize the role genes play in behavior and physiological functions. These advances led to the creation of genetically modified invertebrate and vertebrate organisms. For vertebrates, most genetic modification research uses mice.

The genetic modification process starts by injecting genetic material into a pregnant mouse. After the mouse has a litter, researchers test the *genotype*, or genetic makeup, of each mouse pup to identify those with the targeted genetic change. Genetically modified mice fall largely into two categories: transgenic animals and *knock-out* animals. A **transgenic animal** has either altered genes or additional genetic information. For example, researchers alter amyloid precursor protein genes in transgenic mice to cause production of amyloid plaques, a key neurobiological characteristic found in Alzheimer's disease. A **knock-out animal** fails to express traits from a particular gene; in essence, the gene is "knocked out."

Scientists use a notation system to describe different genotypes for knock-out animals. A heterozygous genotype is noted by a "–/+," with the "–" sign indicating the removed or deactivated gene on one chromosome and the "+" indicating the unaffected gene on the other chromosome. A +/+ notation, indicating unaffected genes on both chromosomes, describes a nongenetically modified animal, also referred to as a *wildtype*. Animals with a homozygous genotype for a certain trait are noted with a "–/–," indicating a deactivated gene on each chromosome.

For example, serotonin transporter –/– knock-out mice exhibit greater levels of the neurotransmitter serotonin in the synaptic cleft and show anxious behavior (Holmes, Li, Murphy, Gold, & Crawley, 2003). The –/– describes the deactivation of the serotonin transporter gene on both chromosomes. Thus, these mice completely lack serotonin transporters (serotonin transporters are discussed in Chapter 3). A **phenotype** describes the physiological or behavioral changes caused by a genetic alteration. In this example, enhanced serotonin levels and increased anxiety describe the phenotype for a serotonin transporter knock-out mouse.

Although transgenic and knock-out data provide important links between genetics and physiological and behavioral activity, scientists keep in mind that genetic alterations may cause unexpected changes during neurodevelopment. In fact, a study by Zhou, Lesch, and Murphy (2002) demonstrated a unique and unexpected consequence of knocking out the serotonin transporter.

In this study, researchers compared serotonin levels in serotonin transporter knock-out mice and confirmed that greater serotonin levels occurred at serotonin synapses, as described previously. However, these researchers also discovered serotonin neurotransmitters inside of neurons that produce the neurotransmitter dopamine. Exploring further, the team found that dopamine transporters had adapted to allow entry of serotonin into dopamine neurons (Zhou et al., 2002). Thus, instead of having mice with an altered serotonin system, they

FIGURE 1 ● Few neurons reveal the neurotransmitter serotonin in the dopamine-rich ventral tegmental area and substantia nigra in wild-type mice (top panel, a). However, in serotonin transporter knock-out mice (bottom panel, c & d), many dopamine neurons contain serotonin. These findings suggest that removal of serotonin transporters led to the nervous system adapting to the loss of serotonin by using dopamine neurons for synthesizing serotonin instead. VTA = ventral tegmental area; 5-HT = serotonin; 5-HTT = serotonin transporter; ir = immunoreactive; the labeling technique used to identify serotonin; SNc = substantia nigra. From Zhou et al., 2002.

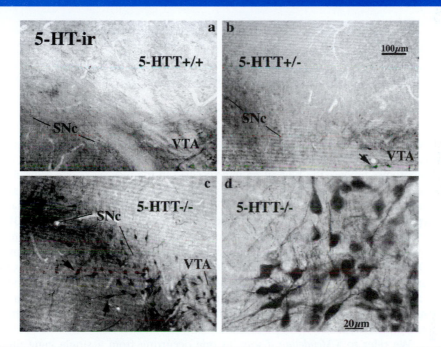

SOURCE: Dr. Feng Zhou/Brain Research/Elsevier.

unintentionally produced mice that also had an altered dopamine system (Figure 1).

For these caveats and other reasons, researchers seek to refine and develop new approaches

(Continued)

(Continued)

for developing genetically modified organisms. In a variation of the knock-out mouse, researchers have developed **conditional knock-out mice** that have normally functioning genes until a researcher administers a type of enzyme that deactivates a gene. Thus, these mice develop normally but still allow researchers to assess the effects of gene deactivation on some physiological or behavior characteristic. During a study, researchers might wait until mice reach an adult age before administering the enzyme. This technology also allows researchers to specify a particular part of the body to alter the gene, such as a structure within the central nervous system. These and other genetic modification procedures have important implications for understanding the nervous system and for characterizing drug actions and their effects.

copies onto ribonucleic acid (RNA). The type of RNA used to trigger protein synthesis is called *messenger RNA* because it leaves the nucleus and binds to ribosomes in the cell. Ribosomes produce the type of protein specified in the message. Gene transcription is one of many areas studied in the field of **epigenetics**, the study of mechanisms of gene expression not involving alterations to DNA sequences. Future drug therapies may target epigenetic mechanisms for treating neurological or mental disorders (Arango, 2015).

The field of **neurogenetics** aims to understand how genes support the function of neurons. In doing so, this field also studies how gene mutations, alterations in the DNA sequence for genes, cause neurological disorders, such as Huntington's disease and Alzheimer's disease. For example, neurogenetics studies revealed a mutation in the Huntington gene that leads to the destruction of neurons and subsequently a host of motor and cognitive disturbances in Huntington's disease. The disease is inheritable and ultimately fatal.

We refer to a *Mendelian disease* as one occurring from a single gene mutation inheritable to offspring. Genetic tests arising from neurogenetic studies provide a means for identifying the risk of contracting a Mendelian disease. For example, one can be tested for a mutated Huntington gene that has near 100% accuracy before the disease's symptoms occur. Other genetic diseases occur from different types of gene mutations. Sometimes a mutation occurs as repeating pattern of nucleotides, the chemical building blocks of DNA, or through an error in replicating or repairing a gene, resulting in *gene duplication*. Many of these diseases can be traced to mutations

Epigenetics
Mechanisms of gene expression not involving alterations to DNA sequences

Neurogenetics How genes support the function of neurons

in multiple genes. For example, *cerebellar ataxia* is a disorder marked by coordination and balance deficits that derives from mutation in over 30 different genes (Jayadev, Smith, & Bird, 2011).

STOP & CHECK

1. How many chromosomes does a human cell contain?

2. A _____ is a protein that activates a gene.

3. Genetic code is copied onto _____, which delivers the code to ribosomes outside the nucleus.

1. 46 2. transcription factor 3. messenger RNA

From Actions to Effects:
Glial Scars and Recovery From Brain Injury

Traumatic brain injury occurs from a severe blow to the head. Mild traumatic brain injury includes a range of potential symptoms including cognitive and mood changes. Moderate and severe traumatic brain injuries also include seizures, vomiting, and sustained headache. Approximately 1.7 million Americans experience a traumatic brain injury each year (Centers for Disease Control [CDC], 2010).

Treatments for traumatic brain injury seldom provide full recovery. The first approach consists of limiting further injury. These efforts may include surgeries to reduce brain swelling or medications to sustain blood flow throughout the brain. Although these approaches may limit further brain injury, they do not restore lost brain function.

An important challenge in brain injury recovery consists of a natural response to injury called a *glial scar* or *gliosis* (Silver & Miller, 2004). A glial scar consists of reactive astrocytes—that is, astrocytes that swell in response to injury. The resulting glial scar from traumatic brain injury segregates damaged tissue from healthy tissue. The action serves to repair the blood–brain barrier. In doing so, however, glial scars prevent neurons in damaged tissue from regaining connections to other structures in the nervous system.

Regaining connectivity after injury involves regenerating severed axons. **Figure 2.17** provides an illustration of regenerating axons near an area of damaged tissue surrounded by a glial scar. Because of the barrier created, the glial scars caused regenerating axon terminals to divert from the damaged tissue. These conditions result in misaligned patterns of growth, including retractions into balls called *dystrophic end bulbs*.

Astrocytes in glial scars prevent axon growth through an **inhibitory extracellular matrix**. The inhibitory extracellular matrix consists of chemicals that inhibit axon growth, including proteoglycans, secreted protein semaphorin 3, and ephrin-B2.

Inhibitory extracellular matrix Part of gliosis consisting of chemicals that inhibit axon growth

FIGURE 2.17 ● **Regenerating axons from dorsal root ganglion (arrow) can grow next to a damaged area (shown in the left side of the image), but cannot penetrate damaged tissue surrounded by gliosis (right side of the image).**

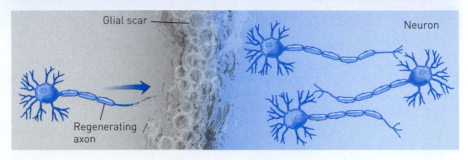

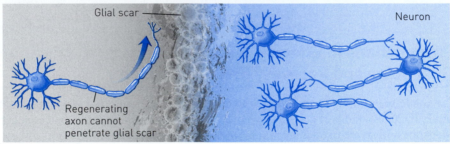

Each molecule prevents the growth or penetration of axons into damaged tissue (Silver & Miller, 2004).

Experimental treatments for traumatic brain injury recovery focus on ways to improve axon regeneration into damaged brain areas. One approach uses the enzyme chondroitinase to break down proteoglycans. Related approaches seek to reduce other inhibitory components in the inhibitory extracellular matrix.

Other treatments focus on improving the availability of growth material for axons. These strategies often involve **neurotrophins**, such as neurotropin-3 and brain-derived neurotrophin factor (commonly abbreviated as BDNF), which promote the growth and development of neurons. The delivery of neural growth factors promotes the growth of axons into damaged tissue.

Finally, researchers have combined both of the preceding strategies to reduce inhibitory extracellular matrix components while promoting the growth of axons. For example, Tropea and colleagues (2003) assessed the effects of each approach on damaged retinal neurons that terminate in the superior colliculus. The application of either chondroitinase or BDNF promoted the regrowth of these neurons into the superior colliculus. Yet far greater neuronal growth was demonstrated by using both chrondroitinase and BDNF.

Neurotrophin
Naturally occurring chemical substance that promotes the growth and development of neurons

STOP & CHECK

1. What functions does a glial scar serve?

2. How does an inhibitory extracellular matrix impair recovery from brain trauma?

3. How might a growth factor such as BDNF aid in neural recovery?

1. Glial scars form from swelled astrocytes in response to injury. Glial scars repair blood–brain barrier damage and separate damaged tissue from healthy tissue. 2. The inhibitory extracellular matrix contains molecules that inhibit the growth of regenerating axons through the glial scar. 3. Neural growth factors promote the growth of axons into damaged brain areas.

Chapter Summary

The cells in the central nervous system consist of glial cells and neurons. Most neurons consist of dendrites, a soma, an axon, and an axon terminal. Signals from other neurons are received through dendrites, and the message is sent to other neurons from the axon terminal. Glial cells play an important role in supporting the function of neurons. Oligodendrocyte and Schwann glial cells form myelin sheathing around the axons of neurons, and astrocytes play an important role in supporting neuronal communication and responding to injury. Microglial cells remove cellular waste from all central nervous system cells.

We divide the brain into subdivisions called the *hindbrain*, *midbrain*, and *forebrain*. The forebrain division is the largest and encompasses the four cortical lobes in the brain called the *occipital lobe* (for vision), the *parietal lobe* (mainly for processing touch information), the *temporal lobe* (for audition and language), and the *frontal lobe*

(for cognition and movement). The limbic system includes the amygdala, hippocampus, cingulate gyrus, thalamus, and hypothalamus. Together these limbic system structures play an important role in emotion. With the exception of olfactory information, which goes directly to the prefrontal cortex, sensory information is received from the head and body and routed through the thalamus to the appropriate lobe for processing. The prefrontal cortex is the most anterior portion of the frontal lobe and the integration center for all sensory information. Motor signals are sent down to the body beginning in the motor cortex. The basal ganglia help to regulate voluntary movements.

The cells in the brain receive important sugars and nutrients from the cerebrospinal fluid surrounding these cells and oxygen from blood vessels. Cerebrospinal fluid exists throughout the central nervous system through the central canal in the spinal cord

(Continued)

(Continued)

and through a network of ventricles and the cerebral aqueduct in the brain. Cerebral blood flow increases in active parts of the brain.

The basic functions and development of cells are directed by genes, which are segments of DNA. Molecules that activate genes are called *transcription factors*. Gene activation causes a copy of the gene to be imprinted on RNA. RNA directs the production of protein synthesis through ribosomes found outside of the cell's nucleus.

Key Terms

Neurons 31
Glial cells (or glia cells) 31
Dendrites 31
Axons 32
Synapse 32
Interneuron 33
Sensory neurons 33
Motor neurons 33
Oligodendrocytes 35
Astrocytes 36
Microglial cells 36
Gliosis 36
Somatic nervous
    system 38
Autonomic nervous
    system 39
Sympathetic nervous
    system 39

Parasympathetic nervous
    system 39
Cerebral cortex 41
Medulla 41
Hypothalamus 42
Limbic system 45
Nucleus accumbens 45
Occipital lobe 45
Temporal lobe 45
Parietal lobe 46
Frontal lobe 46
Prefrontal cortex 46
Thalamus 46
Motor cortex 47
Basal ganglia 47
Pons 47
Cerebellum 47
Working memory 47

Long-term memory (or
    reference memory) 47
Hippocampus 48
Reticular activating
    system 48
Cerebral blood flow 49
Cerebrospinal fluid 49
Periaqueductal gray 49
Ventricles 49
Gene 50
Polymorphism 51
Transcription factor 51
Epigenetics 54
Neurogenetics 54
Inhibitory extracellular
    matrix 55
Neurotrophin 56

Visit the Student Study Site at **study.sagepub.com/prus2e** to access additional study tools, including eFlashcards, web quizzes, video resources, web resources, SAGE journal articles, and more.

Neurotransmission

DRUGS FOR ALZHEIMER'S DISEASE ALTER ACETYLCHOLINE NEUROTRANSMISSION

Jessica's memory loss at age 56 was completely unexpected. In fact, she took pride in having an impeccable memory. Yet now even the simplest memories caused Jessica to struggle. When filling up her car, she would forget if she was going to work or coming from work. Also, on many

(Continued)

(Continued)

occasions she forgot the names of coworkers and even her phone number. Finally, after getting lost in a grocery store and no longer able to hide her memory problems from family, she contacted her doctor.

Jessica's physician diagnosed her with an early onset type of Alzheimer's disease (AD), a neurobiological illness characterized by a progressive decline in cognitive functioning. To slow her cognitive decline, her physician prescribed an acetylcholinesterase inhibitor, a

drug that enhances levels of a neurotransmitter called *acetylcholine* in the brain. Although not a cure, the medication improved cognitive functioning for almost a year before her symptoms no longer improved with treatment.

Many treatments for neurological disorders address neurotransmission abnormalities in the nervous system. Unfortunately, many of these disorders provide daunting challenges for scientists, and there remains a great need for new treatments in neurology.

SOURCE: Story adapted from anonymous personal accounts at www.alz.org.

Neurotransmission
Transmission of information between neurons

Neurotransmission is the transmission of information between neurons. Neurotransmission typically involves a neuron releasing chemicals called *neurotransmitters* into a synapse, which allows these neurotransmitters to act on sites on another neuron. The study of neurotransmission includes looking at events inside the neuron that cause the production and release of neurotransmitters as well as the actions neurotransmitters have on sites situated on other neurons.

Electrical transmission Series of electrical events that begin at an axon hillock and proceed down the length of an axon

Electrical potential Difference between the electrical charge within a neuron versus the electrical charge of the environment immediately outside the neuron

Electrical Events Within a Neuron and the Release of Neurotransmitters

Certain electrical events within a neuron must take place before neurotransmitters can be released. These events are referred to as **electrical transmission**, which is a series of electrical events, called *action potentials* (discussed later in the chapter), that begin at an axon hillock and proceed down the length of an axon. These events depend on electrical potentials.

For a neuron, an **electrical potential** is a difference between the electrical charge within a neuron and the electrical charge of the environment immediately outside the neuron. Normally, the electrical charge within a neuron is negative compared to the outside environment. This characteristic leaves the neuron's membrane polarized, meaning that on one side the charge is negative, but on the other side the charge is positive, similar to the negative and positive poles of a magnet (**Figure 3.1**). The term **depolarization** describes a reduced difference between the positive and negative charges on each side of a membrane. The term **hyperpolarization** describes an increased difference between the positive and negative charges on each side of a membrane.

Review! A neuron has many dendrites and a single axon. A synapse consists of an axon terminal, the synaptic cleft, and the postsynaptic terminal. (Chapter 2.)

Depolarization
Reduced difference between the positive and negative charges on each side of a membrane

Hyperpolarization
Increased difference between the positive and negative charges on each side of a membrane

FIGURE 3.1

During the resting potential, an electrical polarization is maintained because of a concentration of negatively charged ions and negatively charged proteins. Potassium (K⁺) ions can enter and leave the neuron through open K⁺ channels.

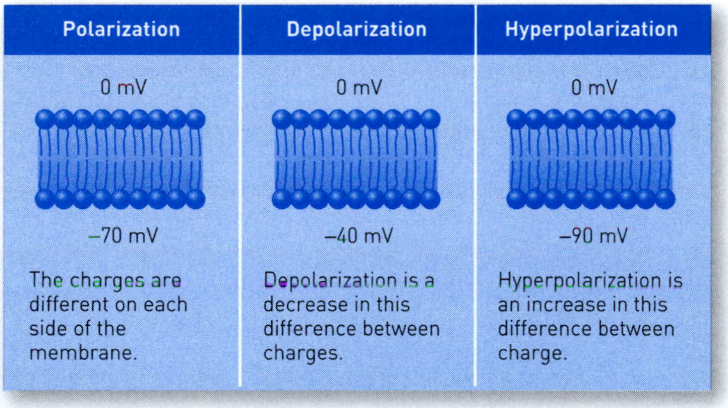

Polarization	Depolarization	Hyperpolarization
0 mV	0 mV	0 mV
−70 mV	−40 mV	−90 mV
The charges are different on each side of the membrane.	Depolarization is a decrease in this difference between charges.	Hyperpolarization is an increase in this difference between charge.

The term **local potential** refers to an electrical potential on a specific part of a neuron. The local potential changes in response to events within a neuron and with communication from other neurons. Local potentials change as charged particles called *ions* move in and out of the neuron through pores called **ion channels**. The influence on local potentials from other neurons occurs as either an excitatory postsynaptic potential or an inhibitory postsynaptic potential. An **excitatory postsynaptic potential (EPSP)** depolarizes a local potential, whereas an **inhibitory postsynaptic potential (IPSP)** hyperpolarizes a local potential. Researchers study local potential changes using electrophysiological procedures as described in Box 3.1.

Local potential
Electrical potential on a specific part of a neuron

Ion channels Pores in a neuronal membrane that allow the passage of ions

Excitatory postsynaptic potential (EPSP)
Stimulus that depolarizes a local potential

Inhibitory postsynaptic potential (IPSP)
Stimulus that hyperpolarizes a local potential

BOX 3.1 ELECTROPHYSIOLOGY AND MICRODIALYSIS

A research technique called *electrophysiology* uses electrodes to measure or stimulate potentials on neuronal membranes. Electrophysiology procedures use either macroelectrodes or microelectrodes. *Macroelectrodes* record the activity of thousands of neurons within a structure. They also can be used as a stimulator to activate thousands of neurons within a structure.

Microelectrodes provide a precise assessment or stimulation of either just a few or even single neurons (**Figure 1, left panel**). The use of a microelectrode to measure potentials within a single neuron is called *intracellular recording*. In particular, researchers use intracellular recording to measure action potentials. This technique allows a neuron's firing rate to be calculated. Although electrophysiological techniques can assess the activity of neurons, they cannot determine the amount of neurotransmitter released from a neuron.

Microdialysis procedures, however, can be used to sample neurotransmitter levels (**Figure 1, right panel**). Microdialysis probes have a semipermeable membrane. When implanted into a structure of the brain, a probe's membrane allows some of the surrounding cerebrospinal fluid to pass through. Researchers then analyze the collected cerebrospinal fluid for levels of certain chemicals such as neurotransmitters. Microdialysis probe size limits neurotransmitter detection to an entire structure rather than a specific neuron. Thus, increases in neurotransmission must be large enough to cause neurotransmitters to cause significant overflow from synapses.

FIGURE 1 ● Researchers can use microelectrodes to both stimulate and record potential changes in neurons (left). Researchers use microdialysis probes to sample cerebrospinal fluid from the brain (right). They then determine the amount of certain chemicals, such as neurotransmitters, in the microdialysis samples.

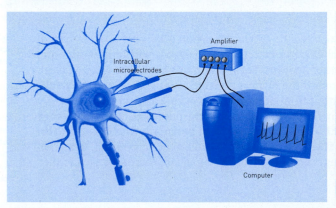

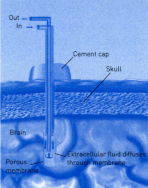

FIGURE 2 ● **Each line on this graph represents the number of action potentials detected over a 10-second period (i.e., spikes/10 sec). The arrows indicate the precise moment when β-PEA (β-phenylethylamine) (followed on the graph by the amount given) was administered. After every administration of β-PEA, a decrease in the firing rate (i.e., the rate of spikes) was shown. Subsequent administrations of β-PEA were given after the firing rate recovered. As greater amounts of β-PEA were administered, greater decreases in the firing rate were observed.**

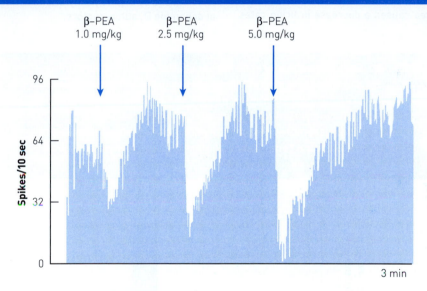

SOURCE: Kota Ishida, Mikio Murata, Nobuyuki Katagiri, Masago Ishikawa, Kenji Abe, Masatoshi Kato, Iku Utsunomiya, and Kyoji Taguchi (2005, August). Effects of β- Phenylethylamine on Dopaminergic Neurons of the Ventral Tegmental Area in the Rat: A Combined Electrophysiological and Microdialysis Study. *Journal of Pharmacology and Experimental Therapeutics, 314*, 916–922.

Microdialysis procedures lack the precision that electrophysiology can achieve, yet microdialysis can answer important questions about neurotransmitter release that electrophysiology cannot. Both procedures complement each other. The

(Continued)

(Continued)

effective use of both procedures together is shown in a study by Ishida and colleagues (2005).

In this study, the effects of b-phenylethylamine (b-PEA) (which is synthesized from phenylalamine) on dopamine neuron firing rates and dopamine release was assessed in rats. The application of b-PEA onto dopamine neurons in the ventral tegmental area caused a decrease in firing rates as determined through electrophysiology **(Figure 3)**. Although a decrease in neuronal firing should be expected to decrease dopamine release from these neurons, microdialysis techniques instead revealed increased dopamine release **(Figure 4)**. Based on these findings and other information known about b-PEA, the authors concluded that increases in dopamine release were caused by b-phenylethylamine acting at dopamine D_2 autoreceptors.

FIGURE 3 ●   Each bar on this graph represents the amount of dopamine sampled from microdialysis probes in the ventral tegmental area during a 60-minute period. The amount of dopamine collected was much higher after administration of a 100-micromole amount of b-phenylethylamine compared to the baseline condition and before b-phenylethylamine was administered.

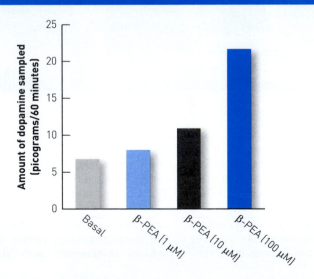

SOURCE: Adapted from Ishida et al. (2005).

Nerve Impulses: Electrical Potential Changes in Neurons

An important way in which neurons release neurotransmitters from the axon terminal is through electrochemical signals called *nerve impulses*. Nerve impulses are made up of changes from resting potentials to action potentials.

Resting Potential

A **resting potential** describes a negatively charged local potential that precedes an action potential. The exact negative charge of the resting potential can vary across species, nervous system structures, and the relative concentration of ions within and outside a neuron (**Figure 3.2**). The resting potential exists because of negatively charged proteins within the neuron and to closed ions channels that prevent the influx of positively charged sodium (Na^+) ions.

We do find some channels open for the positively charged ion potassium (K^+) during the resting potential, however. The negative charge within the neuron attracts positively charged K^+ ions into the neuron, a property called **electrostatic attraction**. Yet at some point, K^+ ions cease entering the neuron because ions of the same type resist being concentrated, a property called a **concentration gradient**. Thus,

Resting potential Negatively charged local potential that precedes an action potential.

Electrostatic attraction Attraction of ions with opposite charges

Concentration gradient Particles of the same type resist being concentrated

---

FIGURE 3.2 ● During the resting potential, an electrical polarization is maintained because of a concentration of negatively charged ions and negatively charged proteins. Potassium (K^+) ions can enter and leave the neuron through open K^+ channels.

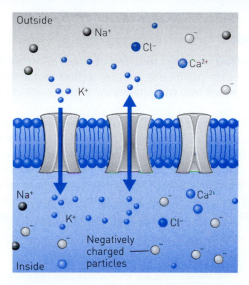

Sodium–potassium pump Neuronal membrane mechanism that brings two K+ ions into the neuron while removing three Na+ ions out of the neuron.

as K+ becomes more concentrated within the neuron, some K+ ions exit the neuron due to a concentration gradient. The balance between the electrostatic attraction and concentration–gradient repulsion facilitates a relatively constant resting potential.

Although Na+ channels are not open during the resting potential, a number of Na+ ions still find their way into the neuron. To prevent these excess Na+ ions from changing the resting potential, neuronal membranes contain sodium–potassium pumps. A **sodium–potassium pump** is a neuronal membrane mechanism that brings two K+ ions into the neuron while removing three Na+ ions out of the neuron (**Figure 3.3**). By removing more Na+ ions than the K+ ions brought in, this pumping activity results in a net negative effect.

Voltage-gated ion channels Channels that open or close, depending on local potential changes

A resting potential changes when Na+ channels open. Na+ channels are **voltage-gated ion channels**, meaning that the opening or closing of these channels depends on local potential changes. Na+ channels open in response to depolarization. When an excitatory postsynaptic potential occurs, depolarization causes local Na+ channels to open, allowing Na+ ions to enter the neuron. If no other EPSPs occur, then depolarization quickly ends and a resting potential resumes. If multiple EPSPs occur in short succession, an action potential will occur.

Action Potential

Action potential Rapid depolarization, causing the potential in the neuron to become temporarily more positive than the outside environment.

An **action potential** is a rapid depolarization that causes the charge in the neuron to become temporarily more positive than the outside environment (**Figure 3.4**). The action potential occurs when all Na+ ion channels open. These Na+ channels remain open for only 1 to 3 milliseconds, and this limits the change in potential to a certain value. As the example shows in Figure 3.5, the action reaches 130 mV. These properties support the **all-or-none law**, which states that the magnitude of an action potential is independent from the magnitude of potential change that elicited the action potential. The action potential ends immediately after the Na+ channels close.

All-or-none law Magnitude of an action potential is independent from the magnitude of potential change that elicited the action potential.

Refractory Periods

Refractory period Period following an action potential when the neuron resists producing another action potential

The **refractory period** is a short duration of time following an action potential when the neuron resists producing another action potential (Figure 3.4). The refractory period is divided into two phases: the *absolute refractory period* and *relative refractory period*.

Absolute refractory period First phase of the refractory period, during which no amount of depolarization can produce another action potential

The **absolute refractory period**, the first of these phases, consists of 1–2 milliseconds during which a neuron is incapable of producing another action potential. During this period, K+ channels are opened, and the concentration of positively charged ions causes K+ ions to rapidly exit the neuron. The rapid exit of K+ ions causes the potential to become negative again. In fact, the negative charge is initially more negative than the resting potential charge. Because the Na+ channels remain closed during the absolute refractory period, no amount of depolarization can produce another action potential.

FIGURE 3.3 ● Sodium–potassium pumps help maintain a resting potential by removing three Na⁺ ions for every two K⁺ ions brought in.

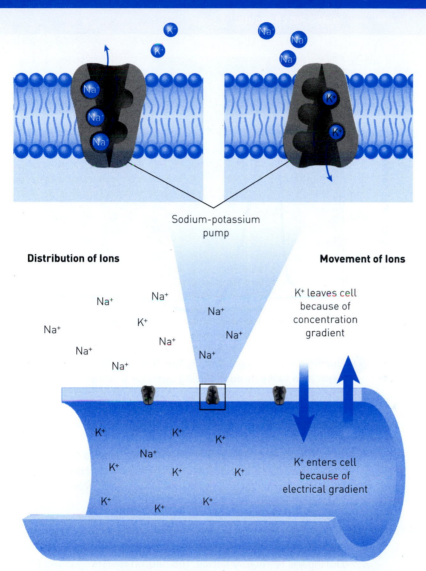

Sodium-potassium pump

Distribution of Ions

Movement of Ions

Na⁺

Na⁺

Na⁺

K⁺

Na⁺

Na⁺

Na⁺

Na⁺

Na⁺

Na⁺

K⁺ leaves cell because of concentration gradient

K⁺

K⁺

K⁺

Na⁺

K⁺

K⁺

K⁺

K⁺

K⁺

K⁺

K⁺ enters cell because of electrical gradient

The **relative refractory period**, the second of these phases, lasts 2–4 milliseconds during which a neuron resists, but is not incapable of, producing an action potential. During this period, Na⁺ channels can be opened, and the local potential remains

Relative refractory period Second phase of the refractory period, during which greater depolarization is necessary to reach threshold and produce another action potential

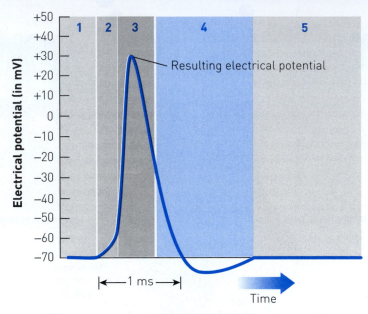

FIGURE 3.4 ● **Electrical impulses within neurons occur in several stages, and each stage depends on the opening or closing of voltage-gated ion channels.**

1 During the resting potential stage, the membrane is only pemeable to K+ through having open K+ channels.

2 As depolarization occurs, the membrane becomes permeable to Na+ ions through opening Na channels.

3 An action potential occurs if polarization meets a specific threshold. During the action potential stage all Na+ channels open, causing rapid Na+ influx. Then Na+ channels reclose.

4 During the refractory period the K+ ions rapidly exit the neuron, returning a negative charge within the neuron. During the refractory period, the neuron resists producing another action potential.

5 After the refractory period, the neuron returns to a resting potential.

hyperpolarized. Because of hyperpolarization, greater depolarization is necessary to reach the threshold and produce another action potential. Unless excitatory postsynaptic potentials occur during the relative refractory period, the membrane returns to a resting potential.

STOP & CHECK

1. Depolarization is a decrease in potential, whereas hyperpolarization is a(n) _____ in potential.

2. To prevent leaked Na^+ from altering a resting potential, a(n) _____ expels Na^+ from the neuron.

3. When membrane depolarization meets a specific threshold value, all Na^+ channels open, resulting in a massive depolarization called a(n) _____.

4. After the action potential, K^+ channels open, causing K^+ to rapidly _____ the neuron.

1. increase 2. sodium–potassium pump 3. action potential 4. Leave

Propagation of Action Potentials Down Axons

The **propagation of action potentials** refers to a series of action potentials occurring in succession down an axon. The propagation of action potentials begins at the axon hillock. Once this begins, each depolarization produced by an action potential causes another action potential to occur further down the axon (**Figure 3.5**). This series of action potentials continues until an action potential occurs at the axon terminal. Action potentials propagate in only one direction because the preceding portion of an axon is in a refractory period.

Myelin sheathing increases the speed of conductance down the axon. Sections of myelin sheaths surround most vertebrate axons. The uncovered sections of axons between myelin sheaths are called **nodes of Ranvier** (pronounced RAHN-vee-ay). Each node contains Na^+ and K^+ channels. When an action potential occurs at one node, depolarization is carried through the myelin sheathing to the next node, where another action potential occurs (Figure 3.5). The jumping of action potentials from one node to another is referred to as *saltatory conduction*. The number of action potentials occurring per unit of time, usually milliseconds, is called a **firing rate**.

Propagation of action potentials
Series of action potentials occurring in succession down an axon

Nodes of Ranvier
Uncovered sections of axons between myelin sheaths

Firing rate
The number of action potentials occurring per unit of time, usually in milliseconds

FIGURE 3.5 ● On myelinated axons, action potentials occur at each node of Ranvier. Action potentials only propagate down the axon because the previous Na⁺ channels remain in a refractory period.

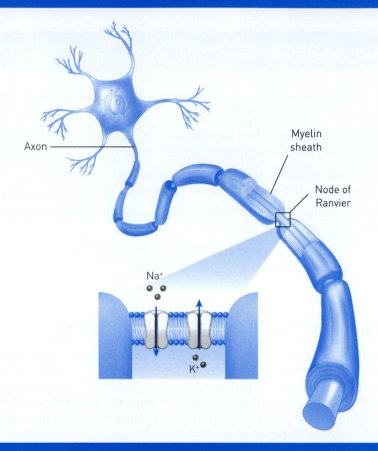

Axon

Myelin sheath

Node of Ranvier

Na⁺

K⁺

STOP & CHECK

1. Sodium and potassium channels are located down the length of an axon, facilitating the propagation of _____ potentials.

2. Axons with _____ sheathing have a greater speed of conductance compared to axons without myelin sheathing.

3. The number of action potentials occurring during a certain period of time is called a(n) _____.

1. action 2. myelin 3. firing rate

Neurotransmitters: Signaling Molecules for Neuronal Communication

When action potentials reach the axon terminal, a series of events occur that ultimately cause the release of neurotransmitters. **Neurotransmitters** are signaling chemicals that are synthesized within neurons, are released from neurons, and have effects on neurons or other cells. Neurotransmission between neurons involves a series of stages, beginning with the synthesis of neurotransmitters and ending with the release of neurotransmitters (**Figure 3.6**).

Neurotransmitters Signaling chemicals that are synthesized within neurons, are released from neurons, and have effects on neurons or other cells

FIGURE 3.6 ● Chemical neurotransmission occurs in many steps, including neurotransmitter synthesis, release, receptor binding, and termination. Please see the text for a description of each stage of this process.

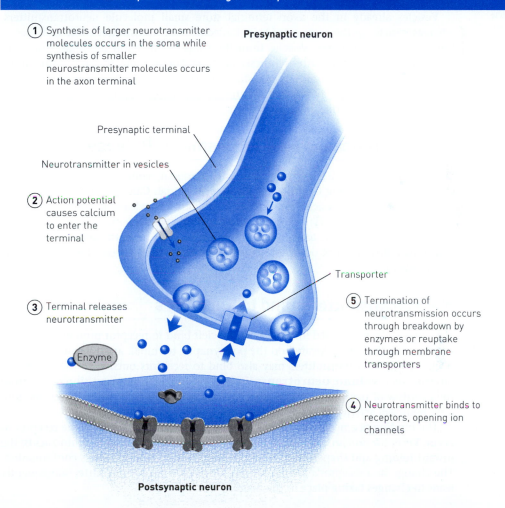

1. Synthesis of larger neurotransmitter molecules occurs in the soma while synthesis of smaller neurostransmitter molecules occurs in the axon terminal

Presynaptic neuron

Presynaptic terminal

Neurotransmitter in vesicles

2. Action potential causes calcium to enter the terminal

Transporter

3. Terminal releases neurotransmitter

5. Termination of neurotransmission occurs through breakdown by enzymes or reuptake through membrane transporters

Enzyme

4. Neurotransmitter binds to receptors, opening ion channels

Postsynaptic neuron

Neurotransmitter Synthesis

Neurotransmitters are synthesized from other molecules with the aid of enzymes. Generally, smaller neurotransmitter molecules such as acetylcholine and dopamine are synthesized in the axon terminal. Larger neurotransmitter molecules such as neuropeptide neurotransmitters are synthesized in the soma.

Neurotransmitter Storage

Synaptic vesicle (or neurotransmitter vesicle) A vesicle that stores and protects neurotransmitters

Vesicular transporter Channel located on a vesicle that allows passage of neurotransmitters

Synaptic vesicles (or **neurotransmitter vesicles**) store and protect neurotransmitters after synthesis. Neurotransmitters enter vesicles through channels called **vesicular transporters** (**Figure 3.6**). Synaptic vesicles protect neurotransmitters from being destroyed by enzymes and prevent neurotransmitters from being released prematurely. Storing neurotransmitters in this manner allows for immediate release during neurotransmission.

Vesicles already in the axon terminal store small molecule neurotransmitters, whereas vesicles in the soma store large molecule neurotransmitters. Microtubules in the axon then transporter vesicles from the soma to the axon terminal. Not every neurotransmitter is stored after synthesis, however. For example, the endocannabinoid neurotransmitter anandamide is not stored in vesicles (Placzek, Okamoto, Ueda, & Barker, 2008). Without a storage mechanism, anandamide escapes from the neuron immediately after synthesis.

Calcium Influx and Neurotransmitter Release

Exocytosis Fusing of synaptic vesicles to the axon membrane and release of stored neurotransmitters into the synaptic cleft

Once an action potential occurs in the axon terminal, voltage-gated calcium (Ca^{2+}) channels open, allowing Ca^{2+} to enter the axon terminal. Calcium causes **exocytosis**, the fusing of synaptic vesicles to the axon membrane and release of stored neurotransmitters into the synaptic cleft (Figure 3.6). After fusing with the membrane, the vesicles are brought back into the terminal and then refilled with neurotransmitters. However, vesicle recycling does not occur for neuropeptide neurotransmitters, they return to the soma instead.

Neurotransmitters Bind to Receptors

Volume neurotransmission Type of neurotransmission involving the binding of neurotransmitters to receptors outside of the synapse

Neurotransmitters released into the synaptic cleft bind to receptor proteins (described shortly), which may be located on the postsynaptic terminal, axon terminal, or both (Figure 3.6). Neurotransmitters may also bind to receptors outside of the synapse, a process called **volume neurotransmission**. Volume neurotransmission occurs from the overflow of neurotransmitters from a synaptic cleft, which generally results from high neuronal activity, normally in the form of a rapid firing rate.

The binding of a neurotransmitter causes a *conformational change* in the receptor to occur. Receptor proteins, like other proteins, comprise long strings of amino acids; the inward folding and shapes produced from the string form a receptor's conformation. The change in a receptor's conformation caused by a neurotransmitter subsequently leads to changes taking place in the neuron.

Termination of Neurotransmission

After a neurotransmitter releases from a receptor, one of a number of processes occurs to prevent the neurotransmitter from binding to other receptors in the synapse (Figure 3.6). These processes serve to end neurotransmission. For one of these processes, enzymes break down a neurotransmitter into different molecules referred to as *metabolites*. This process is called **catabolism**. Because these new molecules do not match to a neurotransmitter's receptor, neurotransmission effectively stops.

We also use the term **turnover** to refer to the conversion of a neurotransmitter to a metabolite. Researchers infer the rate of neurotransmitter release based metabolite levels during from turnover. For example, high levels of the dopamine metabolite DOPAC (stands for "3,4-Dihydroxyphenylacetic acid") in cerebrospinal fluid indicate that neurons produced a large amount of dopamine, since catabolism of dopamine produces DOPAC. Knowing the amount of turnover occurring after administering a drug informs researchers about the levels of neurotransmission that account for the drug's effects.

During another process called **reuptake**, membrane transporters on axon terminals return neurotransmitters to the axon terminal. Vesicles then store the neurotransmitters for later release. In essence, reuptake serves as a recycling program for neurons. Finally, neurotransmitters may be transported from the synaptic cleft into an astrocyte glial cell. Afterward, enzymes within the glial cell catabolize the neurotransmitters.

Catabolism Process involving the enzymatic breakdown of neurotransmitters and other molecules

Turnover of neurotransmitters The conversion of a neurotransmitters to a metabolite

Reuptake Return of neurotransmitters to the axon terminal via membrane transporters

STOP & CHECK

1. After synthesis, a neurotransmitter may be stored in a(n) _____ until released from the neuron.

2. Neurotransmitters are released from a neuron after the influx of _____, which is caused by an action potential.

3. Neurotransmitters bind to and activate _____, which may be on the post-synaptic terminal, axon terminal, or both.

4. Neurotransmission can be terminated through enzymatic breakdown (i.e., catabolism), transportation into a glial cell, or through _____ of neurotransmitters.

1. vesicle 2. calcium 3. receptors 4. reuptake

Neurotransmission: Neurotransmitter Binding to Receptors

Receptors are proteins located in neuron membranes that can be bound to and activated by neurotransmitters. Receptors match to a specific neurotransmitter. Thus, the neurotransmitter dopamine cannot bind to receptors for the neurotransmitter

Receptor Protein located in a neuron membrane that can be bound to and activated by a neurotransmitter

Ligand A molecule that joins with a protein

acetylcholine, and vice versa. Neurotransmitters are **ligands**, a term that refers to a molecule that joins with a protein.

Researchers characterize receptors not only by the neurotransmitter they match to but also by their location within a synapse. The terms *presynaptic* and *postsynaptic* describe the locations for receptors in a synapse. Receptors that are located on the post-synaptic terminal are called *postsynaptic receptors*, and receptors located on the axon terminal are called *presynaptic receptors*.

Autoreceptor Presynaptic receptor that is activated by neurotransmitters released from the same axon terminal

Presynaptic receptors have two types. The first type is an **autoreceptor**, a pre-synaptic receptor that is activated by neurotransmitters released from the same axon terminal (**Figure 3.7**). Activating an autoreceptor usually inhibits neurotransmitter release. This action serves to limit the amount of neurotransmitter released. A recep-tor for the neurotransmitter dopamine functions as an autoreceptor. When released from an axon terminal, dopamine binds to this autoreceptor, reducing the amount of dopamine released.

FIGURE 3.7 ● Receptors on the presynaptic terminal (i.e., axon terminal) influence the amount of neurotransmitter released. Autoreceptors are activated by the neurotransmitter released from the terminal, whereas a heteroceptor is activated by a different neurotransmitter. On the dopamine neuron shown here, the D_2 autoreceptor is activated by dopamine, whereas the α_2 heteroceptor is activated by norepinephrine.

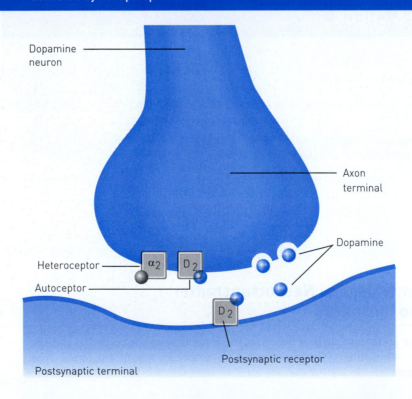

The second type of presynaptic receptor is a **heteroceptor**, a presynaptic receptor that is activated by neurotransmitters different from those released from the axon terminal (Figure 3.7). Heteroceptors may increase or decrease neurotransmitter release. For example, a heteroceptor for the neurotransmitter norepinephrine is located on axon terminals for the neurotransmitter dopamine. Binding to this receptor reduces dopamine release.

Heteroceptor
Presynaptic receptor that is activated by neurotransmitters different from those released from the axon terminal

Receptors: Ionotropic or Metabotropic

In addition to synaptic location, we identify receptors by their structure. We distinguish between two primary types of neurotransmitter receptors based on structure: ionotropic receptors and metabotropic receptors. **Table 3.1** summarizes the differences between these two types of receptors.

Ionotropic receptors are ion channels that open when a matching neurotransmitter binds to a site on the channel (**Figure 3.8**). In this regard, ionotropic receptors act as *ligand-gated* ion channels, with the neurotransmitter serving as the ligand. An ionotropic receptor comprises subunits that span the neuronal membrane. The subunits form a ring that comprises the channel. The shifting of these subunits causes the channel to open or close.

Ionotropic receptor Ion channel that opens when a matching neurotransmitter binds to a site on the channel

A **metabotropic receptor** is physically separated from parts of the neuron where the receptor exerts its effects (**Figure 3.9**). Unlike an ionotropic receptor, which contains an ion channel, many metabotropic receptors rely on a G protein to convey effects to channels or other parts of the neuron. Given this, we also refer to most metabotropic receptors as *G protein-coupled receptors*. Other metabotropic receptors are receptor tyrosine kinases, discussed in "Other Types of Chemical Transmission in the Nervous System" later in this chapter.

Metabotropic receptor Receptor physically separated from parts of the neuron where the receptors exerts its effects

TABLE 3.1 ● Differences Between Ionotropic and Metabotropic Receptors		
	Ionotropic Receptor	**Metabotropic Receptor**
Physical proximity to parts of neuron where effects are exerted	Attached to ion channel	Separated from ion channels and other proteins
Type of effect	Open ion channel	Many use a G protein to activate ion channels and effector enzymes
Duration of effect	Ends when neurotransmitter leaves binding site	Effector enzymes engage a cascade of events that persist after neurotransmitter leaves receptor
Impact on a neuron	Influx of ions changes local potential	Can affect local potentials; also has other effects, including enzyme regulation, gene expression, and protein synthesis

SOURCE: © Cengage Learning 2014.

FIGURE 3.8   ●   An ionotropic receptor consists of an ion channel with a neurotransmitter binding site. The receptor shown here is activated by the neurotransmitter γ-aminobutyric acid (GABA) and is called the GABA$_A$ receptor. GABA$_A$ receptor activation causes an IPSP by allowing negatively charged chloride (Cl^2) ions into the neuron. The GABA$_A$ receptor shown here also has binding sites for different chemical substances, such as benzodiazepines. These other binding sites serve to modify the receptor's function, including how well GABA activates the receptor.

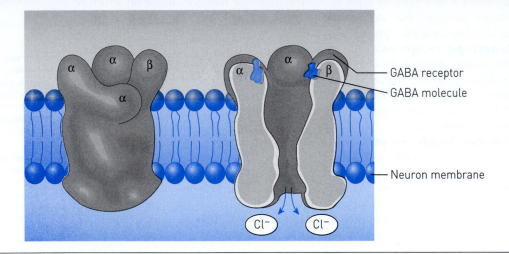

SOURCE: Based on Guidotti et al., 1986.

G protein A three-subunit protein that carries out effects of a metabotropic receptor

A **G protein** resides within the neuron, nearby to the receptor; the three subunits of the G-protein separate to carry out a receptor's effects. The three G proteins subunits are alpha (α), beta (β), and gamma (γ). These subunits remain attached to each other until a neurotransmitter activates the receptor. Activating the receptor causes the G protein to separate into two sections, the α subunit and a βγ combination (referred to as a *dimer*). After a period of time, the subunits return to a three-subunit state, essentially deactivating the receptor. Box 4.1 in Chapter 4 describes a research technique used to characterize the activation and inactivation process for G proteins.

After an activated receptor causes G protein subunits to separate, the separated subunits may cause a variety of effects within a neuron, collectively referred to as *intracellular signaling* (Figure 3.9). First, the free subunits can activate ion channels such as K$^+$ or Ca^{2+} ion channels. Second, the free subunits can activate **effector enzymes**. Common effector enzymes include adenylyl cyclase, phospholipase C, phospholipase A2, and phosphodiesterase.

Effector enzymes Enzyme that usually activates a second messenger

Usually, an effector enzyme activates a *second messenger*. Common second messengers include cyclic adenosine monophosphate (cAMP), cyclic guanosine monophosphate (cGMP), phosphoinositide, and calcium. When using the term second messenger,

FIGURE 3.9 ● **A metabotropic receptor relies on a G protein to carry out effects within the neuron. Through the activation of a G protein (right), a cascade of biological events, collectively referred to as *intracellular signaling*, may occur within the neuron, including the activation (or inhibition) of ion channels, second messengers, protein kinases, and substrate proteins (right).**

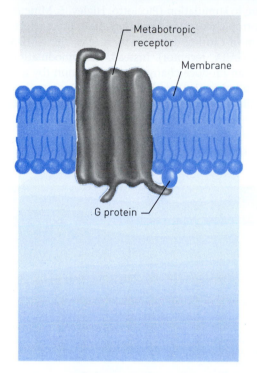

Before activation

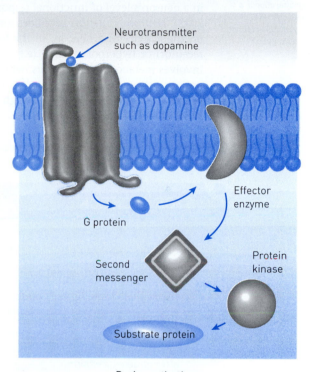

During activation

you can think of the neurotransmitter that activated the receptor as the *first messenger.* Thus, the first messenger (the neurotransmitter) binds to the receptor, leading to the initial activation of a G protein; the second messenger soon after carries out other signaling activities. Specifically, a second messenger activates a protein kinase.

A **protein kinase** is an enzyme that causes phosphorylation of a substrate protein (see below). Phosphorylation is a common process for activating proteins, which involves adding at least one phosphoryl group ($-PO_3^{2-}$) to a protein. Common protein kinases include protein kinase A, protein kinase G, protein kinase C, and calcium/calmodulin kinase.

A protein kinase activates a substrate protein. A **substrate protein** can be an ion channel, an enzyme involved in the making of neurotransmitters, a neurotransmitter receptor, or other proteins within the neuron. A substrate protein also can be a transcription factor. Two common transcription factors for neurons are c-Fos and cAMP

Protein kinase
Enzyme that causes phosphorylation of a substrate protein

Substrate protein
Protein that may consist of an ion channel, enzyme, neurotransmitter receptor, or other proteins involved in neuronal processes

response element-binding (CREB) protein. The activation of genes may lead to the synthesis of proteins within the neuron, including receptors for neurotransmitters and enzymes used in neurotransmitter synthesis. Given that a series of events may occur after activating a metabotropic receptor, effects within a neuron continue after the neurotransmitter leaves the receptor.

The differences between ionotropic receptors and metabotropic receptors have given rise to the concept of neuromodulation. **Neuromodulation** is an alteration in a neuron's level of functional response to stimulation (Picciotto, Higley, & Mineur, 2012). Neuromodulation precludes ionotropic receptors since they have direct effects on the activity of a neuron, in the form of causing depolarization (e.g., the NMDA receptor) or hyperpolarization (e.g., the GABA$_A$ receptor). Instead, neuromodulation involves metabotropic receptors, which can produce changes in polarization (by a G protein acting on an ion channel), by altering the number of receptors present at terminals, or by other ways that might alter a neuron's response to transmission from another another neuron.

Neuromodulation
An alteration in a neuron's level of functional response to stimulation

Review! A transcription factor activates or deactivates a gene (Chapter 2).

STOP & CHECK

1. Where is an autoreceptor located?

2. How does a voltage-gated ion channel differ from a ligand-gated ion channel?

3. Although G proteins may directly activate ion channels, other intracellular effects are carried out by activating _____ such as cAMP or cGMP.

4. After being activated by a second messenger, a protein kinase can affect the functioning of a neuron in a variety of ways, including acting as a _____ to alter gene expression.

1. An autoreceptor is located on an axon terminal and is activated by the neurotransmitters released from the same axon terminal. **2.** A voltage-gated ion channel opens when a certain local potential occurs, whereas a ligand-gated ion channel opens when a neurotransmitter binds to it. **3.** second messengers **4.** transcription factor

Different Types of Neurotransmitters and Communication

Table 3.2 lists the neurotransmitters most important for psychoactive drugs, but this list is only a subset of the dozens of neurotransmitters currently known. Table 3.2 groups neurotransmitters by chemical structure. For example, glutamate and γ-aminobutryic acid (GABA) are both amino acids and thus belong to the amino acids category of neurotransmitters. Dopamine, norepinephrine, and serotonin belong in

TABLE 3.2 ● Neurotransmitter Categories and Selected Neurotransmitters

Amino Acids	Neuropeptides
gamma-aminobutryic acid (GABA)	Endorphins
glutamate	
Acetylcholine	**Gases**
	Nitric oxide
Monoamines	
Catecholamines	
dopamine	
norepinephrine	
epinephrine	
Indoleamines	
serotonin	

the monoamine category because they have a single amine chemical group, $-NH_2$, in their structures.

Glutamate and GABA Are the Most Abundant Neurotransmitters

The amino acids glutamate and GABA are found throughout the nervous system. The amino acid neurotransmitter **glutamate** is the most prominent member of a small amino acid family called *excitatory amino acid neurotransmitters*. The amino acid **GABA** is the most prominent member of a small amino acid family called *inhibitory amino acid neurotransmitters*.

Glutamate Glutamate is synthesized within axon terminals from the amino acid glutamine. The enzyme glutaminase converts glutamine to glutamate (**Figure 3.10**). After synthesis, vesicular transporters carry glutamate into synaptic vesicles, where it resides for later release into the synapse. Glutamate is released from *pyramidal neurons*, so named for the pyramid shape of the soma. The cerebral cortex is rich in pyramidal neurons, and the groupings of pyramidal neurons partly define different layers of the cerebral cortex.

Within the synaptic cleft, glutamate binds to any of four types of receptors (**Table 3.3**). Three of these receptors—NMDA, AMPA, and kainate receptors—are ionotropic. The fourth receptor type, the mGlu receptor, is metabotropic.

When activated, the ionotropic NMDA, AMPA, and kainate receptors allow positively charged ions, such as calcium (Ca^{2+}) and Na^+, to enter a neuron (**Figure 3.11**). The influx of positively charged ions function can cause EPSPs. The names for these receptors come from the chemical substances used to discover them. NMDA stands

Glutamate Excitatory amino acid neurotransmitter

GABA Inhibitory amino acid neurotransmitter

FIGURE 3.10 ● **Glutamate is synthesized from glutamine using the enzyme glutaminase**

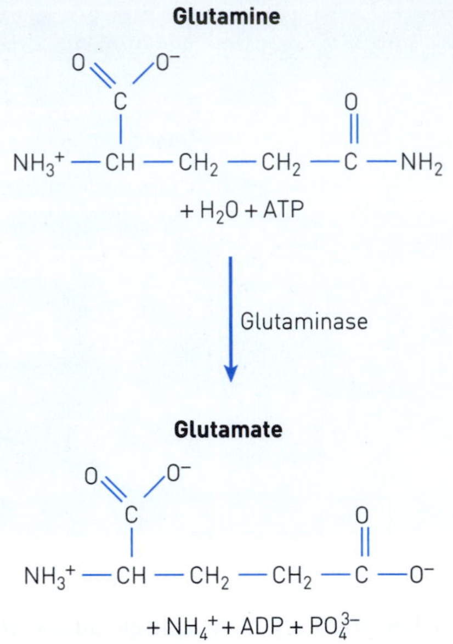

Glutamine

$$NH_3^+ - CH - CH_2 - CH_2 - C - NH_2$$

(with carboxylate group $O = C - O^-$ above the CH, and $C = O$ above the terminal C)

$+ H_2O + ATP$

Glutaminase

Glutamate

$$NH_3^+ - CH - CH_2 - CH_2 - C - O^-$$

(with carboxylate group $O = C - O^-$ above the CH, and $C = O$ above the terminal C)

$+ NH_4^+ + ADP + PO_4^{3-}$

for N-methyl-D-aspartate, an amino acid chemically similar to glutamate that binds to and activates these receptors. AMPA stands for α-amino-3-hydroxy-5-methyl-4-isoxazole propionic acid, a chemical used to discover this receptor. Finally, the kainate receptor is named from the chemical kainic acid.

The subtypes of mGlu receptors include groups I, II, and III receptors. Group I mGlu receptors enhance neuronal activity by activating a G protein, which leads to a cascade of other effects. However, mGlu II and III receptors differ from other glutamate

TABLE 3.3 ● **Glutamate Receptors**

Receptor	Type	Effect on Neuron
NMDA	Ionotropic	Excitatory
AMPA	Ionotropic	Excitatory
Kainate	Ionotropic	Excitatory
mGlu group I	Metabotropic	Excitatory
mGlu group II	Metabotropic	Inhibitory
mGlu group III	Metabotropic	Inhibitory

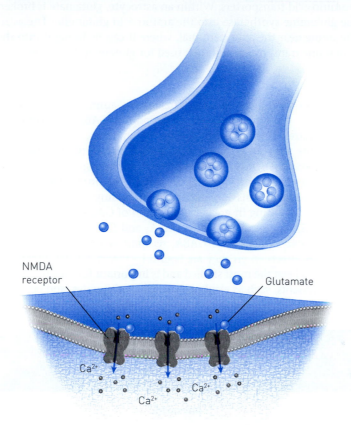

NMDA
receiver

Glutamate

Ca^{2+} Ca^{2+} Ca^{2+}

receptors by activating a G protein that diminishes further signaling inside the neuron (Ferraguti & Shigemoto, 2006).

Glutamate receptors are found not only on neurons but also on glial cells. On astrocytes near the synaptic cleft at glutamate synapses, we find both AMPA receptors and mGlu receptors. Glutamate release from axon terminals, therefore, binds to these receptors on astrocytes as well as to receptors found on neuron terminals.

Activating glutamate receptors on astrocytes results in the Ca^{2+} entering the astrocyte (Shelton & McCarthy, 1999). The influx and build up of Ca^{2+} leads to processes occurring inside astrocytes, which may include the release of glutamate from astrocytes (Parpura, Basarsky, Liu, Jeftinija, Jeftinija, & Haydon, 1994). In these cases, glutamate released from astrocytes binds to glutamate receptors found on neuron terminals (either presynaptic or postsynaptic) in the synaptic cleft, thus having a direct influence on neurotransmission (Auld & Robitaille, 2003).

After glutamate has been released from a receptor, it is removed from the synaptic cleft through any of several *excitatory amino acid transporters*. These transporters for glutamate are found on the axon terminal that released glutamate, effectively recycling glutamate for release at a later time. Astrocytes near the synaptic cleft also have excitatory amino acid transporters. Within an astrocyte, glutamate is broken down by the enzyme glutamine synthetase into the amino acid glutamine. The astrocyte then releases glutamine near the axon terminal, where it can be brought into the terminal through glutamine transporters and then used for glutamate synthesis.

GABA

We find the inhibitory amino acid neurotransmitter γ-aminobutyric acid (again abbreviated as GABA) in most nervous system structures. GABA, like other neurotransmitters, is synthesized from other molecules by enzymes. GABA is converted from glutamate with the enzyme glutamic acid decarboxylase (GAD; also referred to as glutamate decarboxylase). After synthesis, vesicular transporters bring GABA neurotransmitters into synaptic vesicles (**Figure 3.12**). The drug gabapentin (Neurontin) enhances GABA neurotransmission, in part, by increasing the availability of glutamic acid decarboxylase, resulting in greater production of GABA.

There are two GABA receptors, named GABA$_A$ and GABA$_B$ (**Table 3.4**). The GABA$_A$ receptor is ionotropic, whereas the GABA$_B$ receptor is metabotropic. Both receptors produce inhibitory effects when they are bound by GABA. Of these two receptors, the GABA$_A$ receptor has been the most studied and is important for the effects of central nervous system depressants, such as alcohol (ethanol), barbiturates, and benzodiazepines.

FIGURE 3.12 ● The enzyme glutamic acid decarboxylase converts glutamate to GABA by removing the carboxylate group (circled with a dashed line) from glutamate.

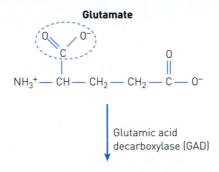

Glutamate

Glutamic acid decarboxylase (GAD)

γ-aminobutyric acid (GABA)

> 💊 **Drug Profile: gabapentin**
>
> *Drug Profile features provide a brief overview of a compound discussed in the text.*

Trade name	Neurontin
Mechanism of action	Increases availability of the enzyme glutamic acid decarboxlyase, which converts glutamate to GABA
Uses	Used for the treatment of pain, convulsions, restless leg syndrome, fibromyalgia, and anxiety
Similar drugs	Pregabalin (Lyrica)

TABLE 3.4 ● GABA Receptors

Receptor	Type	Effect on Neuron
GABA$_A$	Ionotropic	Inhibitory
GABA$_B$	Metabotropic	Inhibitory

Figure 3.8 shows the GABA$_A$ receptor. The GABA$_A$ channel contains a site for GABA$_A$, which opens when GABA binds to this site. Once the channel is open, negatively charged chloride (Cl$^-$) ions enter the neuron, resulting in IPSPs. As previously described, IPSPs cause hyperpolarization to local potentials, reducing the likelihood of action potentials.

After GABA neurotransmitters release from receptors, astrocytes terminate neurotransmission by transporting GABA into astrocytes. Within an astrocyte, the enzyme GABA aminotransferase breaks GABA down to glutamate. In some situations, enzymes further break glutamate down into glutamine, which may be released near GABA neurons and then can be used for the synthesis of GABA.

STOP & CHECK

1. Glutamate is the most common excitatory neurotransmitter in the nervous system, whereas _____ is the most common inhibitory neurotransmitter in the nervous system.

2. Glutamate is synthesized and released from _____ neurons.

3. Of the two types of GABA receptors, the GABA$_A$ receptor is ionotropic, whereas the GABA$_B$ receptor is _____.

4. The inhibitory effects of GABA that occur at GABA$_A$ receptors result from the influx of _____ charged ions such as chloride.

1. GABA 2. pyramidal 3. metabotropic 4. negatively

Monoamine Neurotransmitters: Dopamine, Norepinephrine, Epinephrine, and Serotonin

Chances are that you have already learned something about the neurotransmitters serotonin, dopamine, or norepinephrine in other college courses. Selective serotonin reuptake inhibitors (SSRIs), such as Prozac, for example, treat depression by increasing serotonin levels in synapses. The dopamine system plays an important role in reinforcing the effects of recreational drugs and in the symptoms of schizophrenia. These neurotransmitters belong to the *monoamine* class of neurotransmitters, which includes two subgroups: the catecholamines and the indoleamines.

The catecholamines include the neurotransmitters dopamine, norepinephrine, and epinephrine. Each of these neurotransmitters shares a catechol chemical structure and has a single amine chemical group (**Figure 3.13**). The same synthesis process produced these neurotransmitters, as shown in **Figure 3.14.** This synthesis pathway begins with the amino acid phenylalanine. Phenylalanine is an **essential amino acid**, an amino acid that is not produced in the human body and must come from our diet.

Essential amino acid Amino acid that is not produced in the body and must come from diet

Dopamine

Dopamine is the first monoamine neurotransmitter synthesized in this process. The enzyme phenylalanine hydroxylase converts phenylalanine to the amino acid tyrosine, a nonessential amino acid. Yet tyrosine, like many of the other 20 different amino acids found in the body, also comes from dietary sources. In particular, high-protein foods such as meats, soy, and dairy products contain large amounts of tyrosine (Figure 3.14).

The enzyme tyrosine hydroxylase converts tyrosine to L-3,4-dihydroxyphenylalanine (abbreviated as L-DOPA). The enzyme aromatic L-amino acid decarboxylase then produces dopamine from L-DOPA. In the many synthesis steps for dopamine, tyrosine hydroxylase serves as the **rate-limiting step** because it has the slowest conversion rate. Increasing tyrosine levels is not an effective means of increasing dopamine levels because the relatively slower conversion rate of tyrosine hydroxylase

Rate-limiting step Slowest conversion rate in a synthesis process

---

FIGURE 3.13 ● Every monoamine neurotransmitter has a single amine group in its structure. The catecholamines—including dopamine, norepinephrine, and epinephrine—have a catechol nucleus in their structures.

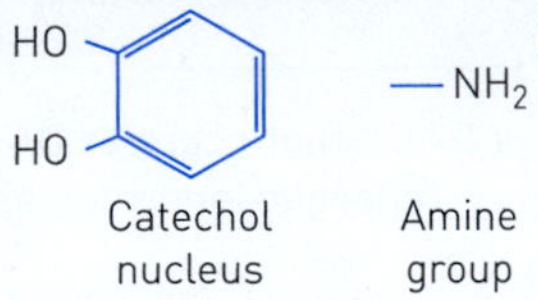

Catechol
nucleus

Amine
group

FIGURE 3.14 ● Monoamine neurotransmitters are synthesized through a series of steps beginning with an amino acid. *Inset:* Dopamine-β-hydroxylase converts dopamine to norepinephrine by adding a hydroxyl group (circled) to dopamine's structure.

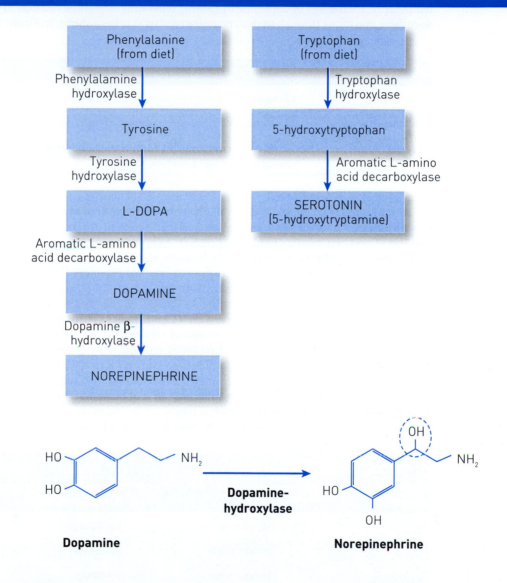

acts as a bottleneck for this synthesis pathway. However, increasing L-DOPA levels will increase dopamine levels because the conversion of L-DOPA to dopamine does not depend on tyrosine hydroxylase. After synthesis, vesicular monoamine transporters (VMATs) deliver dopamine into vesicles for storage.

When prescribed as a drug, we refer to L-DOPA by its generic drug name *levodopa*. Unlike dopamine, levodopa crosses the blood-brain barrier, making this a medication capable of increasing dopamine release in the brain. As such, levodopa remains a primary medication for Parkinson's disease. The symptoms of Parkinson's disease arise from the destruction of dopamine neurons. Levodopa helps to compensate, at least temporarily, for the loss of dopamine by causing remaining dopamine neurons to produce more dopamine through steps in neurotransmitter synthesis shown in Figure 3.14.

⚬ *Drug Profile:* levodopa

Trade name	Larodopa
Mechanism of action	As a monoamine precursor, serves to increase dopamine synthesis
Uses	Treats Parkinson's disease by counteracting dopamine depletion caused by destroyed dopamine neurons

---

Once released from an axon terminal, dopamine may bind to any of several types of **dopamine receptors** that are classified by two families: the D_1 receptor family and the D_2 receptor family (**Table 3.5**). The D_1 receptor family includes the D_1 and D_5 receptors, and the D_2 receptor family includes the D_2, D_3, and D_4 receptors. All dopamine receptors are metabotropic, G protein–coupled receptors. The D_1 family of receptors tend to have excitatory effects on neurons, whereas the D_2 family of receptors have inhibitory effects on neurons.

Once dopamine releases from a dopamine receptor in the synaptic cleft, termination of dopamine transmission occurs in one of two ways. First, dopamine may be catabolized by an enzyme. One type of catabolic enzyme is **monoamine oxidase (MAO)**, which has two types—MAO_A and MAO_B—and is located within the presynaptic neuron. Both types of MAO are capable of breaking down dopamine, as well as norepinephrine and serotonin. Another type of catabolic enzyme is **catechol-O-methyltransferase (COMT)**, which is found on the membrane of the postsynaptic terminal (Karhunen, Tilgmann, Ulmann, & Panul, 1995). COMT catabolizes

Monoamine oxidase (MAO) Enzyme that breaks down dopamine, norepinephrine, and serotonin

Catechol-O-methyltransferase (COMT) Enzyme that breaks down dopamine and norepinephrine

---

TABLE 3.5 ● Dopamine Receptors

Receptor	Type	Effect on Neuron
D_1	Metabotropic	Excitatory
D_2	Metabotropic	Inhibitory
D_3	Metabotropic	Inhibitory
D_4	Metabotropic	Inhibitory
D_5	Metabotropic	Excitatory

catecholamine neurotransmitters, including dopamine, norepinephrine, and epinephrine. Second, dopamine transporters also terminate dopamine neurotransmission by reuptake. After dopamine molecules pass through this transporter, vesicles store dopamine for later release.

Two brain-stem structures—the *ventral tegmental area* and the *substantia nigra*—and the hypothalamus contain most of the brain's dopamine neuron cell bodies (**Figure 3.15**). Bundles of dopamine axons from these structures terminate in other parts of the brain. The dopamine pathways most important for psychoactive drugs are the mesolimbic, mesocortical, nigrostriatal, and tubero-infundibular dopamine pathways.

The **mesolimbic** and **mesocortical dopamine pathways** originate in the ventral tegmental area. The axons in the mesolimbic pathways terminate in the nucleus accumbens as well as other limbic system structures, including the amygdala and hippocampus. The axons in the mesocortical pathways terminate in the frontal cortex, particularly the prefrontal cortex. The **nigrostriatal dopamine pathway** originates in the substantia nigra and terminates in the basal ganglia. These are the dopamine neurons linked to Parkinson's disease, as noted earlier.

The **tubero-infundibular dopamine pathway** originates in the hypothalamus and terminates in the pituitary gland. This pathway plays a role in the secretion

Mesolimbic dopamine pathway
Dopamine neurons with somas in the ventral tegmental area and axons terminating in the limbic system

Mesocortical dopamine pathway
Set of dopamine neurons with somas in the ventral tegmental area and axons terminating in the cerebral cortex, particularly the prefrontal cortex

Nigrostriatal dopamine pathway
Set of dopamine neurons with somas in the substantia nigra and axons terminating in the basal ganglia

Tubero-infundibular dopamine pathway
Set of of dopamine neurons with somas in the hypothalamus and axons terminating in the pituitary gland, where it plays an important role in the secretion of prolactin

---

FIGURE 3.15 ● The Ventral Tegmental Area and the Substantia Nigra Cell Bodies for Dopamine Neurons

Dopamine is released in the (1) cortex from axons in the mesocortical dopamine pathway, (2) limbic system from axons in the mesolimbic dopamine pathway, and (3) the basal ganglia from axons in the nigrostriatal pathway.

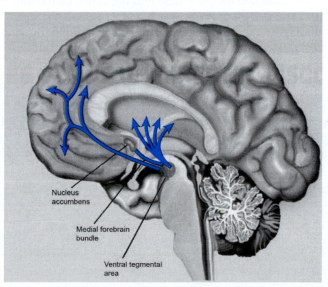

Nucleus accumbens

Medial forebrain bundle

Ventral tegmental area

of *prolactin*, an important hormone for maternal behavior, from the pituitary gland. In the peripheral nervous system, dopamine activates dopamine receptors found in the heart and certain arteries that enhance blood flow from increased cardiac output and dilated arteries.

Norepinephrine and Epinephrine

Norepinephrine represents the next step in the catecholamine synthesis process. Further synthesis leads to epinephrine (Figure 3.14). Epinephrine shares the functions of norepinephrine in the brain but has little unique impact on brain function or psychoactive drug actions of its own. Given this, epinephrine is not further discussed in this book.

Outside of the nervous system, norepinephrine is also known as *noradrenaline*. Thus, the term *norepinephrine* refers to its role as a neurotransmitter, whereas the term *noradrenaline* refers to its role as a hormone. Complicating things further, we use the term *noradrenaline* as the basis for the names of neurons and receptors for norepinephrine. As a result, we call a norepinephrine-releasing neuron a **noradrenergic neuron**; we call receptors for norepinephrine *adrenoceptors*.

Noradrenergic neurons Neurons that synthesize and release norepinephrine

Within noradrenergic neurons, the enzyme dopamine β-hydroxylase converts dopamine to norepinephrine (Figure 3.14). Like dopamine, vesicular monoamine transporters bring norepinephrine into synaptic vesicles for storage. After release from noradrenergic axon terminals, norepinephrine binds to adrenoceptors, which consist of both α and β types (**Table 3.6**). Both types of adrenoceptors are metabotropic receptors. The α adrenoreceptors have two subtypes: α_1 and α_2. The β adrenoceptors have three subtypes: β_1, β_2, and β_3. Depending on the specific receptor, activation of adrenoceptors produce either inhibitory or excitatory effects.

Like dopamine, norepinephrine neurotransmission is terminated by the catabolic enzymes MAO or COMT or through reuptake into the axon terminal. Reuptake occurs through the *norepinephrine transporter*. We find noradrenergic neurons in the *locus coeruleus*, a structure located in the brain stem near dopamine-containing structures. Noradrenergic pathways innervate many structures throughout the brain, including the cerebral cortex, hippocampus, and amygdala (**Figure 3.16**). In the peripheral nervous system, norepinephrine activates cells in the sympathetic nervous system.

TABLE 3.6 ● Noradrenergic Receptors (for the Neurotransmitter Norepinephrine)		
Receptor	**Type**	**Effect on Neuron**
α_1	Metabotropic	Excitatory
α_2	Metabotropic	Inhibitory
β_1	Metabotropic	Excitatory
β_2	Metabotropic	Excitatory
β_3	Metabotropic	Excitatory

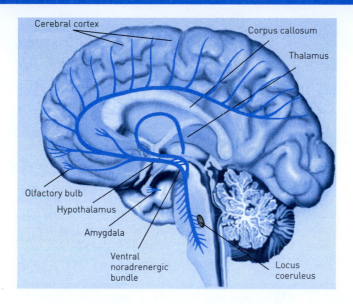

FIGURE 3.16 ● The cell bodies for norepinephrine are mostly found in the locus coeruleus, and axons from these neurons are sent to many areas throughout the brain, including the cortex, amygdala, and structures in the hindbrain.

Cerebral cortex
Corpus callosum
Thalamus
Olfactory bulb
Hypothalamus
Amygdala
Ventral noradrenergic bundle
Locus coeruleus

Serotonin

Serotonin is part of the indoleamine class of monoamines (Table 3.2). Serotonin is also known as *5-hydroxytryptamine*, or *5-HT* for short. Given that serotonin belongs to a different category of monoamines, serotonin's synthesis pathway differs from the catecholamines. The synthesis of serotonin begins with the essential amino acid tryptophan. The enzyme tryptophan hydroxylase converts tryptophan to 5-hydroxytryptophan. From here, the enzyme aromatic L-amino acid decarboxylase—the same enzyme that converts L-DOPA to dopamine—converts 5-hydroxytrypt*ophan* to 5-hydroxytryp*tamine* (Figure 3.14).

Once synthesized, vesicular monoamine transporters (specifically, the $VMAT_2$ transporter), the same vesicular transporters for dopamine and norepinephrine, bring serotonin into synaptic vesicles. The major types of serotonin receptors include 5-HT_1 through 5-HT_7. Each receptor type includes multiple subtypes (e.g., 5-HT_{1A}, 5-HT_{2A}, 5-HT_{2C}, etc.) (**Table 3.7**).

The termination mechanisms for serotonin include enzymatic breakdown and reuptake. Like dopamine and norepinephrine, the enzyme MAO catabolizes serotonin. Otherwise, serotonin neurotransmitters are brought back into the axon terminal through reuptake via the *serotonin transporter*. Like dopamine and norepinephrine, serotonin is then stored in vesicles for later release.

TABLE 3.7 ● 5-HT Receptors (for the Neurotransmitter Serotonin, Abbreviated as "5-HT")

Receptor	Type	Effect on Neuron
5-HT$_1$	Metabotropic	Inhibitory
5-HT$_2$	Metabotropic	Excitatory
5-HT$_3$	Ionotropic	Excitatory
5-HT$_4$	Metabotropic	Excitatory
5-HT$_5$	Metabotropic	Inhibitory
5-HT$_6$	Metabotropic	Excitatory
5-HT$_7$	Metabotropic	Excitatory

The cell bodies for serotonergic neurons are located in the raphe nuclei, which are found in the brain stem near structures for dopaminergic and noradrenergic neurons. Serotonin pathways terminate in structures throughout the brain.

STOP & CHECK

1. The monoamines include the neurotransmitters dopamine, _____, epinephrine, and serotonin.

2. How might one's diet influence dopamine neurotransmission?

3. Unlike dopamine and norepinephrine, serotonin can only be broken down by the enzyme _____.

1. norepinephrine **2.** A poor diet reduces the availability of amino acids important for dopamine synthesis. For example, a protein-impoverished diet reduces tyrosine levels in the body, in turn reducing the amount of dopamine synthesized. **3.** MAO

Acetylcholine

Acetylcholine is listed alone in Table 3.2 for neurotransmitters. Acetylcholine is derived from a single synthesis step by assembling *choline* and *acetyl* coenzyme A using the enzyme *choline acetyltransferase* (**Figure 3.17**). Acetylcholine neurons are referred to as **cholinergic neurons**, owing to choline's role in acetylcholine synthesis. After synthesis, the *vesicular acetylcholine transporter* brings acetylcholine into synaptic vesicles.

Cholinergic neurons Neurons that synthesize and release acetylcholine

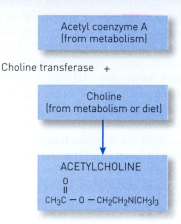

FIGURE 3.17   ●   Acetylcholine is synthesized from acetyl coenzyme A and choline with the enzyme choline acetyltransferase.

Acetyl coenzyme A
(from metabolism)

Choline transferase   +

Choline
(from metabolism or diet)

ACETYLCHOLINE

$$CH_3\overset{\overset{\textstyle O}{\|}}{C} - O - CH_2CH_2N(CH_3)_3$$

The receptors for acetylcholine, called *cholinergic receptors*, have two major classes: *nicotinic receptors* and *muscarinic receptors* (**Table 3.8**). The receptor names come from compounds used to discover them. Nicotine selectively acts on nicotinic receptors. Similarly, muscarine, a toxin found in the mushroom *Amanita muscaria*, was found to act on a separate class of cholinergic receptors.

Nicotinic receptors are ionotropic; when activated, they cause the influx of positively charged sodium (Na^+), potassium (K^+), and Ca^{2+} ions. Five subunit structures make up nicotinic receptors. The names of the primary subunits are the Greek letters α and β. Other subunits include δ and ε. Each subunit has multiple subtypes, which are described by placing a numbered subscript after the subunit name. For example, one type of subunit is α_4. So far researchers have discovered nine α subunits (α_2 through α_{10}) and three β subunits (β_2 through β_4).

TABLE 3.8   ●   Cholinergic Receptors (for the Neurotransmitter Acetylcholine)

Receptor	Type	Effect on Neuron
Muscarinic M_1	Metabotropic	Excitatory
Muscarinic M_2	Metabotropic	Inhibitory
Muscarinic M_3	Metabotropic	Excitatory
Muscarinic M_4	Metabotropic	Inhibitory
Muscarinic M_5	Metabotropic	Excitatory
Nicotinic	Ionotropic	Excitatory

The configuration of nicotinic receptor subunits serves as the receptor's subtype. For example, the receptor comprising α_4 and β_2 subunits is called the $\alpha_4\beta_2$ *nicotinic receptor*, whereas the receptor comprising only α_7 subunits is called the α_7 *nicotinic receptor*. Numerous nicotinic receptor subtypes are based on different subunit configurations.

Muscarinic receptors are metabotropic and coupled to G proteins. There are two families of muscarinic receptors: the M_1 and M_2 families. The subtypes of the M_1 receptor family are M_1, M_3, and M_5, and the subtypes of the M_2 receptor family are M_2 and M_4. In general, activation of M_1 family receptors produces excitatory effects within a neuron by activating second messengers. Activation of M_2 family receptors produce inhibitory effects within a neuron by inhibiting second messengers.

Acetylcholinesterase
Enzyme that catabolizes, or breaks down, acetylcholine

After acetylcholine is released from the receptor, it is broken down into choline and acetic acid by the enzyme **acetylcholinesterase**. There is no reuptake transporter for acetylcholine. However, there is a reuptake transporter for choline. Once choline is transported via the choline transporter into the axon terminal, choline acetyltransferase enzymes facilitate the synthesis of acetylcholine.

Many structures in the brain contain cholinergic neurons, including the *nucleus basalis magnocellularis*, pons, hippocampus, and tegmentum. Cholinergic axons from the nucleus basalis magnocellularis innervate the cerebral cortex. Cholinergic axons from the pons also innervate the cerebral cortex as well as the thalamus. Most cholinergic axons from hippocampal neurons remain in the hippocampus, and tegmental

FIGURE 3.18 ● Acetylcholine cell bodies are located in the basal forebrain, and acetylcholine is released in the cerebral cortex and hippocampus.

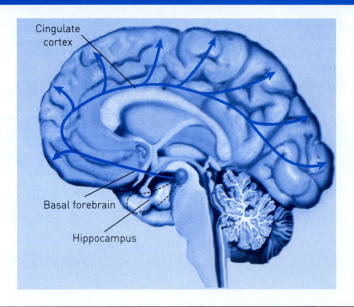

Cingulate cortex

Basal forebrain

Hippocampus

SOURCE: Adapted from Woolf, 1991.

cholinergic axons innervate other brain stem structures, including the dopamine-rich substantia nigra and ventral tegmental area structures (**Figure 3.18**).

Acetylcholine is also the key neurotransmitter released from parasympathetic nervous system neurons. Increased parasympathetic nervous system activation accounts for many of the effects of muscarine poisoning, for example, such as increased salivation, diarrhea, blurred vision (through pupil constriction), and labored breathing. Certain antidepressant drugs impair cholinergic neurotransmission in the parasympathetic nervous system, leading to dry mouth, constipation, and blurred vision (in this case, from dry eyes and pupil dilation).

The cholinergic nervous system is the target of both chemical warfare and therapeutic drugs. The chemical weapon *sarin gas* potently inhibits acetylcholinesterase, causing a massive build-up of acetylcholine. Sarin gas overactivates the parasympathetic nervous system. Inhaling sarin gas causes constriction of the lungs, leading to suffocation and death. This weapon was developed in Nazi Germany in the 1930s and was used by Saddam Hussein during the Iran–Iraq War and on ethnic Kurds in northern Iraq in 1988 (Ganesan, Raza, & Vijayaraghavan, 2010). Sarin was also the agent used in the Japanese subway terrorist attacks in the 1990s (Yanagisawa, Morita, & Nakajima, 2006).

Significantly less potent inhibitors of acetylcholinesterase provide a means to treat some forms of dementia such as Alzheimer's disease. One of the most prescribed *acetylcholinesterase inhibitors* is donepezil (Aricept). These medications compensate for cholinergic loss found in Alzheimer's disease. The "From Actions to Effects" section in this chapter describes the use of these inhibitors and other medications for the treatment of Alzheimer's disease.

Neuropeptides: A Large Class of Neurotransmitters

Neuropeptides make up a large class of neurotransmitters. Opioids are the most studied neuropeptides in psychopharmacology. The opioid system is acted on by opioid drugs such as heroin and morphine, and neurons for opioids terminate in parts of the brain stem and the limbic system. (Chapter 10 covers the opioid system as well as the use and actions of opioid drugs.} Other neuropeptides are often found in neurons that contain another neurotransmitter. For example, dopamine neurons also synthesize and release the neuropeptide neurotensin (Ervin & Nemeroff, 1988).

Nitric Oxide: A Unique Neurotransmitter

Many of the criteria that define a neurotransmitter have changed over the years. Until relatively recently, a neurotransmitter had to be released in a Ca^{2+}-dependent manner and then had to have receptors specific to the neurotransmitter. Fewer criteria exist today, due in no small part to *nitric oxide (NO)*.

NO is a gas that functions as a neurotransmitter. Unlike conventional neurotransmitters, however, NO is not stored in a vesicle; instead, it is immediately released after synthesis. NO synthesis occurs from L-arginine in the presence of the enzyme *nitric oxide synthase*. In this synthesis reaction, the oxidation of L-arginine by nitric oxide synthase causes a nitrogen atom and an oxygen atom to break away and form a NO bond. Although Ca^{2+} does not trigger the release of NO, Ca^{2+} does facilitate nitric oxide synthase activity.

Once synthesized, NO diffuses through the neuronal membrane and permeates the membranes of nearby neurons and glial cells. Furthermore, unlike conventional neurotransmitters, NO does not bind to membrane receptors. Instead it forms bonds with various intracellular proteins, including second messengers and substrate proteins. In addition to effects within neurons, NO causes blood vessels to dilate. NO, therefore, may facilitate increased blood flow to highly active neurons in the brain.

STOP & CHECK

1. The receptor types for acetylcholine are muscarinic receptors, which are metabotropic, and _____, which are ionotropic.

2. Acetylcholine activity in the cortex and _____ has significant effects on cognitive function.

3. _____ neurotransmitters are often in neurons that synthesize another type of neurotransmitter.

4. Although nitric oxide is considered a neurotransmitter, it is neither stored in vesicles released in a calcium-dependent manner nor bound to _____ on the surface of neurons.

1. nicotinic receptors **2.** hippocampus **3.** Neuropeptide **4.** receptors

Other Types of Chemical Transmission in the Nervous System

Neurotrophins

Neurotrophins A family of molecules that promote the survival and plasticity of neurons during development and in adulthood

Receptor tyrosine kinase A family of metabotropic receptors not coupled to a G protein; instead intracellular signaling relies on phosphorylization of a tyrosine kinase molecule located on the intracellular portion of the receptor

Neurotrophins are a family of molecules that promote the survival and plasticity of neurons during development and in adulthood. Neurotrophins include nerve growth factor (typically abbreviated as NGF), brain-derived neurotrophic factor (BDNF), neurotrophin-3, and neurotrophin-4. Neurotrophins are synthesized after expression of a particular gene such as the BDNF gene for BDNF.

Neurotrophins bind to receptor tyrosine kinases, the second family of metabotropic receptors mentioned earlier in this chapter. **Receptor tyrosine kinases** are not coupled to G proteins; instead intracellular signaling relies on phosphorylation of a tyrosine kinase molecule located on the intracellular portion of the receptor. Neurotrophins bind to the "Trk" type of receptor tyrosine kinases. Trk stands for "tyrosine receptor kinase" (a slight rearrangement of the name of this receptor family), and there are three subtypes: TrkA, TrkB, and TrkC.

NGF binds selectively to TrkA receptors, NT-3 binds selectively to TrkC receptors, and both BDNF and neurotrophin-4 bind selectively to TrkB receptors. When a compatible neurotrophin binds to a TrK receptor, phosphorylation of the tyrosine kinase molecule subsequently leads to the activation of other protein kinase and usually then to gene activation. These effects can influence the strength of synaptic connections and may account for the long-term effects of some psychoactive drugs. For example, Trk receptor activation may facilitate hippocampal synaptic changes associated with antidepressant drug treatment (Li et al., 2008).

Hormones

Hormones are signaling molecules derived from cholesterol and released from glands. They differ from neurotransmitters in several ways. First, hormones have widespread effects on target areas, whereas neurotransmitters are often released into tight synaptic junctions to carry out specific effects at postsynaptic terminals. Second, hormones bind not only to membrane receptors but also to intracellular receptors and act as transcription factors. Neurotransmitters primarily bind to receptors located on the surface of a neuron. Third, hormones can be delivered throughout the body via the bloodstream, whereas neurotransmitters generally act on receptors in the close vicinity where the neurotransmitter was released. Neurotransmitters, however, are synthesized and released in the nervous system.

The central nervous system uses hormones to regulate the endocrine system. The hypothalamus directly controls the pituitary gland. The pituitary gland is sometimes referred to as the *master gland* because it releases a number of different hormones into the bloodstream that control the release of hormones from other endocrine system glands.

Review! The hypothalamus regulates body temperature, thirst, hunger, and other internal regulatory functions (Chapter 2).

Neurons from the hypothalamus release two hormones into the pituitary gland: vasopressin and oxytocin. Through the pituitary gland, these two hormones enter the bloodstream and are delivered throughout the body. **Oxytocin** is particularly important for uterine contraction during childbirth, and it also contributes to milk letdown during breast-feeding. **Vasopressin** is an antidiuretic hormone that causes the kidneys to absorb more water from the bloodstream. Alcohol suppresses vasopressin release, partly accounting for the frequent urination associated with alcohol consumption (Meier & Mendoza, 1976).

The hypothalamus also has control over the pineal gland. The pineal gland releases melatonin, which is synthesized from serotonin. **Melatonin** is a sleep-inducing hormone that plays an important role in circadian rhythm, our natural sleep cycle (Marczynski, Yamaguchi, Ling, & Grodzinska, 1964). The sleep aid ramelteon (Rozerum) exerts its sleep-inducing effects by activating receptors for melatonin (Buysse, Bate, & Kirkpatrick, 2005; Miyamoto, Nishikawa, Doken, Hirai, Uchikawa, & Ohkawa, 2004).

Hormones Signaling molecules derived from cholesterol and released from glands

Oxytocin Pituitary hormone important for uterine contraction during childbirth; also contributes to milk letdown during breast-feeding

Vasopressin Antidiuretic hormone that causes the kidneys to absorb water from the bloodstream

Melatonin Sleep-inducing hormone that plays an important role in circadian rhythm, our natural sleep cycle

STOP & CHECK

1. Both NGF and BDNF are types of _____, which promote the survival and plasticity of neurons.

2. _____ receptors may account for the hippocampal plasticity changes caused by chronic antidepressant treatment.

3. In addition to neurotransmitters, the other major messaging chemicals in the body are _____.

1. neurotrophins 2. Trk 3. hormones

From Actions to Effects: Treating Alzheimer's Disease

Alzheimer's disease
A progressive neurological disorder characterized by severe impairments in memory, decision making, attention, motivation, language production and comprehension, and mood regulation

Alzheimer's disease is a progressive neurological disorder characterized by severe impairments in memory, decision making, attention, motivation, language production and comprehension, and mood regulation. Alzheimer's disease affects approximately 5 million individuals in the United States. Within this estimate, Alzheimer's disease affects approximately 5 percent of men and women between ages 65 and 74 and 50 percent of men and women 85 and older (Hebert, Scherr, Bienias, Bennett, & Evans, 2003).

Alzheimer's disease progresses through different stages, beginning with mild cognitive impairment. *Mild cognitive impairment* is defined as exhibiting more than age-appropriate declines in cognitive functioning. Examples of mild cognitive impairment include forgetting important appointments and difficulty following conversations. For an individual showing early signs of Alzheimer's disease, mild cognitive impairment eventually leads to early stage Alzheimer's disease. *Early stage Alzheimer's disease* represents a worsening of mild cognitive impairment symptoms. In addition, an individual with early stage Alzheimer's disease may experience changes in mood such as irritability or depression, as well as forgetfulness about one's personal history, including the names of friends or family members or places worked. *Late stage Alzheimer's disease* represents severe impairments in cognitive impairment—to the extent that individuals lose touch with their environment. During late stage, a person cannot follow conversations or control his or her movements. These individuals need assistance for personal daily care needs.

During the course of this disease, patients commonly develop other illnesses that contribute to declining health and a shortened life span. Patients normally live for 8 to 10 years after diagnosis. In most cases, an individual with Alzheimer's disease dies from pneumonia, often because they are not swallowing correctly, which leads to food entering the trachea rather than the esophagus. This, in turn, inflames the lungs, leading to risk of pneumonia.

Alzheimer's disease causes damage to the brain. The cerebral cortex shrinks in size, as shown in **Figure 3.19**. Further, the brain's lateral ventricles become enlarged by encroaching in areas of degenerated brain tissue. At the cellular level, dying and degenerated neurons form aberrant cellular formations called *senile plaques* (**Figure 3.20**).

Senile plaques
Degenerated neurons formed from overproduction of amyloid β 42 peptides, causing cell death

Senile plaques form from the overproduction of *amyloid β 42* (abbreviated at *Aβ42) peptides* that impair neuronal function and cause cell death. The production

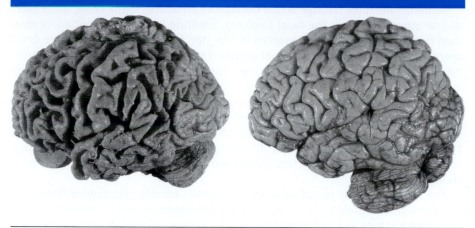

FIGURE 3.19 ● The volume of cerebral cortex is reduced in Alzheimer's disease (left). Compare this to the brain of an individual without Alzheimer's disease on the right.

SOURCE: Photos courtesy of Dr. Robert D. Terry.

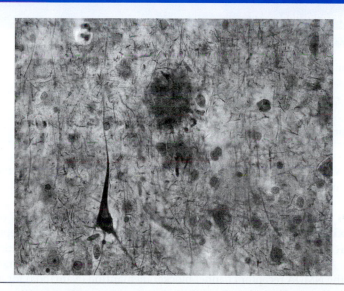

FIGURE 3.20 ● Dying and dysfunctional neurons form senile plaques in Alzheimer's disease

SOURCE: Shutterstock/Jose Luis Calvo.

of *Aβ42* comes from a gene from chromosome 21 that produces *amyloid precursor protein*. Extra partial or complete chromosome 21 DNA is found in Down syndrome, a physical and neurological developmental disorder, most characterized by certain facial features and cognitive impairment. Those with Down syndrome have a far greater risk of developing Alzheimer's disease compared to the normal population. This may be because of greater production of amyloid precursor protein, leading to subsequent production Aβ42 and senile plaques.

Although neuronal damage occurs throughout structures in the brain, Alzheimer's disease especially affects the basal forebrain, resulting in the degeneration of more than two-thirds of cholinergic neurons in this structure. Because of this, drug developers have targeted the destruction of cholinergic neurons for pharmacological treatment strategy. Such strategies do not cure this disease, but they can delay, to some extent, cognitive decline.

The brain's cholinergic system contributes to normal cognitive functioning. Drugs such as scopolamine that impair cholinergic functions selectively impair memory and other domains of attention. Currently, the first-line treatments for AD consist of **acetylcholinesterase inhibitors**. By inhibiting acetylcholinesterase, these drugs raise acetylcholine levels, counteracting diminished acetylcholine levels from the loss of cholinergic neurons.

Acetylcholinesterase inhibitors Drugs that raise acetylcholine levels by inhibiting acetylcholinesterase

The most commonly prescribed include donepezil (Aricept), galantamine (Razadyne), and rivastigmine (Exelon). As a class, acetylcholinesterase inhibitors stabilize cognitive function for as long as 3 to 6 months when given during the mild cognitive impairment or early AD stages. However, these medications fail to alter disease progression. Further, greater acetylcholine levels results enhance parasympathetic nervous system functioning, leading to risk of nausea, diarrhea, and vomiting. These risks prevent physicians from increasing drug doses as cognitive impairment worsens during the disease's progression.

🔗 *Drug Profile:* **donepezil**	
Trade name	Aricept
Mechanism of action	acetylcholinesterase inhibitor
Uses	Treats Alzheimer's disease by counteracting acetylcholine depletion caused by destroyed cholinergic neurons
Similar compounds	galantamine (Razadyne) rivastigmine (Exelon)

Optogenetics A research technique that uses light to alter the firing rate of specific types of neurons

Review! Within the autonomic nervous system, the parasympathetic nervous system reduces heart rate, digestion, and other autonomic functions (Chapter 2).

Another pharmacological strategy addresses excitotoxic destruction of neurons. **Excitotoxicity** derives from overstimulation of glutamate NMDA receptors. Given this, researchers have studied drugs that prevent NMDA receptor activation as treatments for Alzheimer's disease. The federal Food and Drug Administration (FDA) approved the NMDA receptor channel blocker memantine (Namanda) for all stages of Alzheimer's disease. Clinical studies vary in the effectiveness of memantine for preventing cognitive decline in this disease, with some studies revealing significant treatment response and other studies reporting no perceived benefits. In a systematic review of dozens of clinical studies using memantine for AD and other dementias, McShane and colleagues (2006) found that only modest cognitive effects occurred overall.

Drug Profile: memantine

Trade name	Namanda
Mechanism of action	NMDA receptor channel blocker
Uses	Treats Alzheimer's disease by possibly by slowing down destruction by excitotoxicity

Important scientific discoveries in neuroscience, genetics, and pharmacology will continue to improve on existing treatments. We hope that newer medications can sustain cognitive functioning not only for months but also for years. Although a cure for AD would be wonderful, simply restoring years of normal mental health would tremendously improve the quality of life for those with this disease.

STOP & CHECK

1. What parts of the brain are affected in Alzheimer's disease?

2. What are the first-line treatments for AD and how do they work?

1. Key anatomical abnormalities in Alzheimer's disease consist of shrunken cerebral cortex and enlarged ventricles. Further, this disease selectively destroys cholinergic neurons in the basal forebrain. 2. Acetylcholinesterase inhibitors. By elevating acetylcholinesterase, these drugs compensate for cholinergic neuron loss by elevating acetylcholine levels. Elevated acetylcholine levels help maintain normal cognitive functioning.

Chapter Summary

Neurotransmission is a neuronal communication process that uses signaling molecules called *neurotransmitters*. Both electrical and chemical processes within a neuron facilitate neurotransmitter release. Electrical transmission conveys a signal from the soma to the axon terminal to release neurotransmitters. The nature of this transmission is a series of action potentials that first begin at the axon hillock and propagate down to the axon terminal.

Neurotransmission consists of several steps, including neurotransmitter synthesis, storage, release, receptor binding, and termination. Receptors are proteins activated by a matching neurotransmitter. There are two types of neurotransmitter receptors: ionotropic and metabotropic. Ionotropic receptors contain an ion channel, whereas metabotropic receptors utilize other proteins to convey effects. The two most common neurotransmitters in the brain are glutamate, an excitatory neurotransmitter, and GABA, an inhibitory neurotransmitter. Monoamine neurotransmitters include serotonin, dopamine, norepinephrine, and epinephrine. Monoamine oxidase enzymes break down all monoamine neurotransmitters, whereas COMT breaks down dopamine, norepinephrine, and epinephrine. Acetylcholine is synthesized and released from cholinergic

(Continued)

(Continued)

neurons. The enzyme acetylcholinesterase breaks down acetylcholine. Neurotrophins are a family of molecules that promote the survival and plasticity of neurons during development and adulthood. The class of neurotrophins includes nerve growth factor (NGF), brain-derived neurotrophic factor (BDNF), neurotrophin-3, and neurotrophin-4. Hormones are chemical messengers derived from cholesterol and released from endocrine glands. The hypothalamus controls parts of the endocrine system through controlling the release of hormones from the pituitary gland. The hypothalamus also elicits melatonin secretion from the pineal gland. Alzheimer's disease results from the degeneration of neurons, as shown by senile plaques and neurofibrillary tangles. Acetylcholinesterase inhibitors can temporarily improve cognitive functioning, although these treatments fail to slow progression of the disease.

Key Terms

Neurotransmission 60
Electrical transmission 60
Electrical potential 60
Depolarization 61
Hyperpolarization 61
Local potential 61
Ion channels 61
Excitatory postsynaptic potential (EPSP) 61
Inhibitory postsynaptic potential (IPSP) 61
Macroelectrodes 62
Microelectrodes 62
Intracellular recording 62
Microdialysis 62
Resting potential 65
Electrostatic attraction 65
Concentration gradient 65
Sodium–potassium pump 66
Voltage-gated ion channels 66
Action potential 66
All-or-none law 66
Refractory period 66
Absolute refractory period 66
Relative refractory period 67
Propagation of action potentials 69

Nodes of Ranvier 69
Firing rate 69
Neurotransmitters 71
Synaptic vesicle 72
Vesicular transporter 72
Exocytosis 72
Volume neurotransmission 72
Catabolism 73
Turnover of neurotransmitters 73
Reuptake 73
Receptor 73
Ligand 74
Autoreceptor 74
Heteroceptor 75
Ionotropic receptors 75
Metabotropic receptor 75
G protein 76
Effector enzymes 76
Protein kinase 77
Substrate protein 77
Neuromodulation 78
Glutamate 79
GABA 79
Essential amino acid 84
Rate-limiting step 84
Dopamine receptors 86

Monoamine oxidase (MAO) 86
Catechol-O-methyltransferase (COMT) 86
Mesolimbic dopamine pathways 87
Mesocortical dopamine pathway 87
Nigrostriatal dopamine pathway 87
Tubero-infundibular dopamine pathway 87
Noradrenergic neurons 88
Cholinergic neurons 90
Acetylcholinesterase 92
Neurotrophins 94
Receptor tyrosine kinase 94
Nitric oxide (NO) 60
Hormones 95
Oxytocin 95
Vasopressin 95
Melatonin 95
Alzheimer's disease 96
Senile plaques 96
Acetylcholinesterase inhibitors 98
Optogenetics 98

Visit the Student Study Site at **study.sagepub.com/prus2e** to access additional study tools, including eFlashcards, web quizzes, video resources, web resources, SAGE journal articles, and more.

Properties of Drugs

DO ENVIRONMENTAL STIMULI CONTRIBUTE TO HEROIN TOLERANCE?

In 1984, Shepard Siegel published a summary of interviews he conducted with heroin-addicted individuals who had survived an accidental heroin overdose (Siegel, 1984). Given the frequency of heroin use, one might expect heroin users to accidentally overdose from time to time. Yet chronic heroin users have significant experience using heroin and thus exhibit an appreciable tolerance for the drug. In this respect, accidental heroin overdose may seem unlikely. Siegel's interviews sought to determine the conditions under which experienced heroin users overdosed.

Of the 10 addicts he interviewed, seven reported using their normal amount of heroin, but under *atypical* circumstances. These circumstances included a change in how they injected the drug or using the drug in a different location than normal. Although seemingly benign, an earlier animal experiment reported by Siegel suggested that, in fact, these condition changes may partly account for heroin overdose in experienced users. We present the details of this prior study and the implications for human heroin addiction later in this chapter.

I n previous chapters you learned about parts of the nervous system that are important for understanding drug effects. In this chapter, our attention turns to drugs themselves. We focus on how drugs move through the body and how they produce their actions.

As first noted in Chapter 1, pharmacology consists of two subfields called *pharmacokinetics* and *pharmacodynamics*. Pharmacokinetics refers to how drugs move throughout the body, and pharmacodynamics refers to how drugs cause biological changes in the body. Because the focus of this textbook is on how drugs produce behavioral effects by acting in the brain, most of the material in this book concerns the pharmacodynamic effects of drugs.

Pharmacokinetic properties, however, have a lot to do with how people use drugs. For example, cocaine users prefer to smoke or snort the drug rather than consume it orally. These different methods of use do not change how cocaine acts in the brain, but they do determine how quickly cocaine reaches the brain. Thus, pharmacokinetic issues explain the common administration methods for cocaine. Chapter 6 presents an overview of cocaine use, including details about cocaine's pharmacokinetic and pharmacodynamic effects.

Pharmacokinetic Properties and Drug Passage Through the Body

As first stated in Chapter 1, pharmacokinetics is the study of how drugs pass through the body. This process involves factors concerning how a drug is administered and how it is absorbed into the bloodstream, permeates different body parts, and is eliminated from the body. Designing drugs to pass through the body is a painstaking area of drug development. In fact, many therapeutic drugs fail in clinical testing because they inadequately reach the areas of the body necessary for the drug's actions. A treatment is useless if the drug cannot reach its site of action. This section of this chapter provides an overview of the four primary stages of a drug's pharmacokinetic properties: absorption, distribution, biotransformation, and elimination (**Figure 4.1**).

Absorption

Absorption Passage of a drug from the site of administration to the bloodstream

The process of **absorption** refers to the passage of a drug from the site of administration to the bloodstream. To do so, a drug must pass through different membranes such as the mucous membranes in the mouth or the walls of the intestines. The particular membrane that a drug must pass through depends on the drug's *route of administration*. **Figure 4.2** shows examples of absorption for different administration routes, and **Table 4.1** describes the characteristics of different administration routes.

For the vast majority of drugs, absorption relies on a drug's ability to passively diffuse through membranes. Diffusion works best for *non-ionized* drug molecules, which have a neutral *pH* (i.e., pH = 7; recall that positively charged ions, called *bases*, have pH

FIGURE 4.1 ● The life cycle of a drug in the body begins with the administration of the drug and its absorption into the bloodstream. After entering the bloodstream, drugs diffuse through membranes and into organs. Drugs are usually metabolized by enzymes, a process that most often occurs in the liver. Finally, any remaining drug or its metabolites are eliminated from the body.

PHARMACOKINETICS

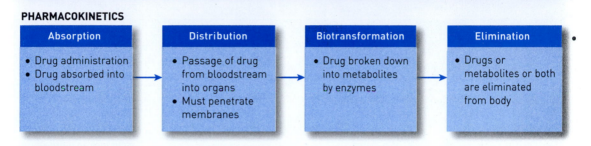

Absorption	Distribution	Biotransformation	Elimination
• Drug administration • Drug absorbed into bloodstream	• Passage of drug from bloodstream into organs • Must penetrate membranes	• Drug broken down into metabolites by enzymes	• Drugs or metabolites or both are eliminated from body

FIGURE 4.2 ● The route of administration is an important determinant for how much drug reaches the bloodstream (vertical axis) and the length of time needed for drug absorption (horizontal axis). This figure shows different administration routes for a fictional drug. The time needed for elimination will vary from drug to drug, but the general pattern tends to be the same.

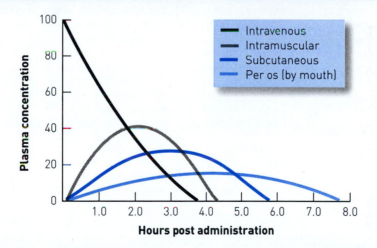

values above 7 and that negatively charged ions, called *acids*, have pH values below 7). Drugs have both non-ionized and ionized drug molecules produced after administration to an organism.

The ratio of non-ionized molecules to ionized molecules, which is calculated by the *Henderson-Hasselbalch equation*, depends upon the pH of the local environment and a

TABLE 4.1 ● Common Routes of Administration				
Route	**Form**	**Absorption Amount**	**Time for Absorption**	**Other**
Inhalation	Inhaled into lungs	High rate of absorption	Rapid	Convenient for patients and common for many drugs of abuse
Intramuscular	Injection into skeletal muscle	Variable, but generally more stable than oral administration	Quicker and more even than oral administration but not as rapid as intravenous injection	Not convenient for patients and not common for drug abusers
Intravenous	Injection into vein	100 percent	Immediate	Patients cannot administer drugs themselves; drug effects occur too rapidly to counteract prescribing errors or drug overdose
Oral	Pill	Variable; affected by food in stomach and digestive rates	Variable, but usually at least several minutes	Convenient for patients; most preferred and common route of administration
Nasal and mucosal membrane	Absorbed through membranes in nasal passage or mouth	Variable but generally more stable than oral administration	Quicker and more even than oral administration but not as rapid as intravenous injection	Convenient for patients and common for drug abusers
Subcutaneous	Injected under skin	Variable but generally more stable than oral administration	Quicker and more even than oral administration but not as rapid as intravenous injection	Individuals can administer themselves, but not convenient to do so
Sublingual	Dissolved under tongue	Variable but generally more stable than oral administration	Quicker and more even than oral administration but not as rapid as intravenous injection	Can be used for individuals who may not want to take a medication (e.g., children or patients with schizophrenia)
Transdermal	Absorbed through skin, commonly through a skin patch	Variable but generally more stable than oral administration	Quicker and more even than oral administration but not as rapid as intravenous injection	Convenient and provides an even, sustained release of drug into bloodstream

drug's pKa. *pKa* refers to the strength of an acid; the lower the pKa value, the stronger the acid. Drugs with a pKa close to the local pH will have more non-ionized molecules than those with a pKa further away from the local pH.

For example, a drug with a pKa of 3 will have far more non-ionized molecules in the stomach, which has a pH of 1, than a drug with a pKa of 8. In this case, the drug with a pKa of 3 will have molecules that can diffuse through cell membranes lining the stomach. However, the drug with a pKa of 8 will absorb more readily in the intestines where the pH is 7 (**Figure 4.3**).

FIGURE 4.3 ● A drug's pKa and the local pH impact a drug's ability to form non-ionized molecules, which diffuse most easily through cell membranes. The first example shows a drug with a pKa = 3.0 passes well through cell membranes when the local pH is 1.0, whereas the drug with a pKa = 8 does not. The opposite is shown below, where the local pH is 7. Thus, the closer a pKa value is to the pH, the more non-ionized molecules are formed and penetrate through cell membranes.

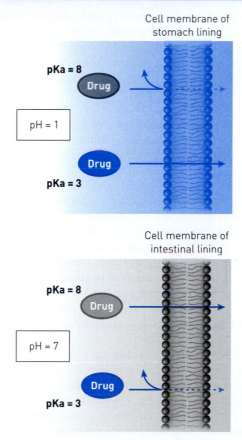

Although pKa-pH issues do affect a drug's ability to absorb into the bloodstream, the surface area of tissue matters as well. The drug with a pKa of 3 will not have many non-ionized molecules in the intestine, yet the enormous surface area of the intestines means that much of this drug will still absorb into the bloodstream. Later in this book, in Chapter 7, we consider a similar case with smoked tobacco—the pH of the lungs is not ideal for nicotine, but the large surface area of the lungs still provides significant absorption for nicotine.

Most therapeutic drugs are orally administered. As consumers, we prefer this administration route because it is much easier than giving ourselves an injection (and less painful!). After swallowing a pill or drinking a liquid, a drug passes through the stomach and into the intestines. We use the term **liberation** to describe the process of drug molecules separating from the pill or solution it was delivered in. When a drug liberates from a pill or solution, the orally administered drug may absorb through stomach or intestinal walls as it passes through the digestive system. Generally, most drug absorption occurs in the small intestine.

Liberation Process of drug molecules separating from the pill or solution in which it was delivered

The oral administration route creates a difficult challenge for drug developers, who generally aim to have drugs absorbed in the intestines. To orally administer a new drug, developers must find ways to protect the drug from digestive acids in the stomach. Encasing a drug within a tablet or capsule will manage this. At the same time, however, stomach acids must dissolve enough of the tablet or capsule to free drug molecules for absorption in the intestines. This delicate balance often reduces the amount of drug that actually reaches the bloodstream.

The duration of time needed for an orally administered drug to pass through the digestive system largely determines when drug effects occur. Although these delays also depend on unique chemical properties of the drug and the substance it is delivered in, most drugs take at least several minutes to reach the bloodstream; for intestinal absorption, it might take between 15 minutes and one hour. The *analgesic*—that is, pain-relieving—drug acetaminophen (Tylenol) requires about 30 minutes to provide sufficient headache relief for most people.

Users also inhale many substances, including medications such as albuterol for treating asthma or addictive substances such as tobacco. Through the inhalation route, drugs enter the circulatory system primarily through the lungs and to some degree through membranes in the nose, mouth, and throat. Therapeutically for asthma and other lung disorders, inhalation brings a drug directly to the area needing treatment. For example, albuterol treats asthma by relaxing air passages in the lungs.

Similar to oral administration, not all of an inhaled substance absorbs through tissue to reach the bloodstream. Yet inhaled substances absorb more quickly than orally administered drugs. For example, when tobacco is smoked, nicotine reaches the user's brain within 7 seconds.

Many administration methods require an injection. Intravenous injection involves drug delivery into a vein through a hypodermic needle. This route provides for rapid drug effects and avoids absorption limitations. Intravenous injections may be used in emergency medicine if physicians need a rapid drug effect. A physician may give, for example, an intravenous injection of naloxone to a patient experiencing a heroin overdose (Sporer, 1999). Users of abused drugs may also prefer intravenous injections because of their speed of onset and full absorption of the drug.

Noncompliance to a medication provides another reason for delivering drugs by injection. These circumstances occur for some patients in psychiatric care. A patient with schizophrenia may refuse to swallow an antipsychotic medication out of suspicions about the motives of the medical care staff. To provide treatment to the patient, a nurse may provide an antipsychotic drug through an intramuscular injection in the arm or leg. To help psychiatric medical care staff with this particular patient noncompliance issue, many drug developers have pursued delivering antipsychotic drugs for sublingual administration—that is, a pill dissolves on or under the tongue—or intranasally by using a nasal spray (Miller, Ashford, Archer, Rudy, & Wermeling, 2008; Potkin, Cohen, & Panagides, 2007).

Many other administration methods for drugs exist, each differing by speed of onset and amount of absorption. Later in this section, discussion of another issue, first-pass metabolism, presents further differences between drug injection routes.

STOP & CHECK

1. What are the four primary phases of drug pharmacokinetics?

2. The administration route for a drug is important for the _____ phase of pharmacokinetics.

1. Absorption, distribution, biotransformation, and elimination 2. Absorption

Distribution

Distribution, the passage of a drug from the bloodstream to sites in the body, is the second stage of pharmacokinetics. After absorption of the drug into the bloodstream, the drug may need to cross certain membranes in order to reach its site of drug action. The distribution phase of pharmacokinetics affects a drug's **bioavailability**, the ability of a drug to reach a site of action. For psychoactive drugs, bioavailability depends on the drug reaching the central nervous system. To enter the brain, drugs must possess sufficient properties to permeate the blood–brain barrier.

The **blood–brain barrier** prevents substances in the blood from entering the brain by surrounding capillaries and other small vessels (**Figure 4.4**). Astrocytes form the blood–brain barrier by forcing *endothelial cells* making up capillary and vessel walls to fit tightly together (Janzer & Raff, 1987). These tight junctions prevent pathogens, hormones, and other substances from entering the brain. Nutrients and other important molecules pass through this barrier through either *passive diffusion* or *active transport*.

Distribution The passage of a drug from the bloodstream to sites in the body

Bioavailability Ability of a drug to reach a site of action

Blood–brain barrier Barrier that surrounds the blood capillaries and vessels in the brain and prevents substances in blood from entering the brain.

FIGURE 4.4 ● **Tight junctions between endothelial cells surrounding blood vessels in the brain prevent substances from entering the brain unless the substances possess the properties for passive diffusion or have an active transport mechanism.**

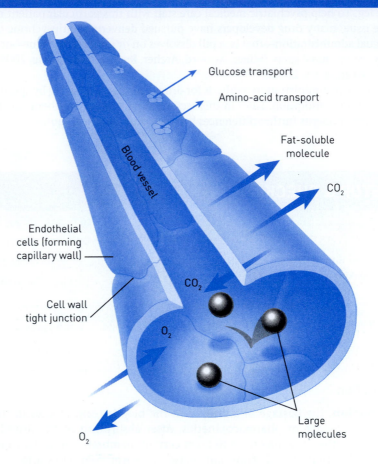

Glucose transport

Amino-acid transport

Fat-soluble molecule

CO_2

Blood vessel

Endothelial cells (forming capillary wall)

CO_2

Cell wall tight junction

O_2

Large molecules

O_2

Passive diffusion through the blood-brain barrier
Blood–brain barrier penetration by lipid-soluble, uncharged, small substances

Passive diffusion through the blood-brain barrier occurs for drug (and other substances) that possess three properties (Figure 4.4). First, the drugs should be lipid (or fat) soluble, meaning that it can pass through cell membranes (Oldendorf, 1974). Second, the drug should be uncharged, which is an important reason why many neurochemicals cannot pass from the bloodstream into the brain (Butt, Jones, & Abbott, 1990). Instead, neurochemicals must be made within cells in the brain. Third, the drug should be relatively small (van de Waterbeemd, Camenisch, Folkers, Chretien, & Raevsky, 1998).

Many nutrients needed for cells in the brain lack the necessary properties for passive diffusion. Instead, nutrients enter the brain through active transport. Mechanisms for **active transport through the blood-brain barrier** consist of channels or other types proteins that transport chemicals through endothelial cell membranes (Figure 4.4). For example, the sugar glucose, which is an energy source for cells, passes through a channel in the blood–brain barrier in order to access cells within the brain.

The placental barrier is also important to consider for drug effects. However, unlike with the blood–brain barrier, virtually all drugs taken by the mother can permeate the placental barrier and enter the placenta. Thus, the ease of drug permeability through this barrier may allow for harmful effects to a fetus.

Another factor for drug distribution is **nonspecific binding**, or the binding of the drug to sites that are not the intended target for drug effects (**Figure 4.5**). This may occur in the form of *protein binding*, which means that the drug binds to proteins in the bloodstream. By remaining bound to proteins in the bloodstream, drugs cannot

Active transport through the blood–brain barrier Mechanisms consisting of channels or other types proteins that transport chemicals through endothelial cell membranes

Nonspecific binding Binding of a drug to sites that are not the intended target for a drug's effects

FIGURE 4.5 ● Several factors reduce the amount of drug available at the site of action. After absorption, a drug may bind to nonspecific sites in the bloodstream or body (nonspecific binding), and orally administrated drugs are susceptible to first-pass metabolism. Membrane barriers, such as the blood–brain barrier, may further reduce the amount of drug reaching the site of action.

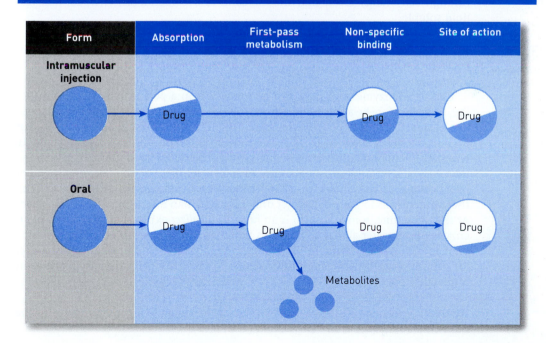

cross the blood–brain barrier. Another form of nonspecific binding is depot binding, which is the binding of drugs to receptors or other parts of the body that the drug does not affect.

Biotransformation

Biotransformation (or drug metabolism)
Process of converting a drug into one or more metabolites

Metabolite
Product resulting from enzymatic transformation of a drug

Phase I biotransformation
First biotransformation phase for a drug that normally involves P450 enzymes and produces a water-soluble metabolite

Phase II biotransformation
Second biotransformation phase occurring through conjugation of a drug's metabolites, making them resistant to passive diffusion

Biotransformation (or **drug metabolism**) is the process of converting a drug into one or more other products called **metabolites**. Drugs are broken down, or catabolized, by enzymes, which most often takes place in the liver but may also occur in other areas such as the stomach. Biotransformation of substances may also take place within cells.

We identify two phases for biotransformation. **Phase I biotransformation** occurs first for a drug and produces a metabolite that is water soluble and easily excreted. Phase I biotransformation mostly occurs by members of the CYP-1, CYP-2, and CYP-3 cytochrome P450 enzymes. Metabolites produced in Phase I may have pharmacological properties, which we refer to as *active metabolites* (discussed later in this section).

Phase II biotransformation occurs from catabolism by enzymes through the process of *conjugation*, and normally occurs for metabolites produced in Phase I. Some drugs, however, may bypass Phase I biotransformation and be catabolized by Phase II biotransformation processes instead. The term *conjugation* refers to a *conjugation reaction*, involving the attachment of another molecule onto the metabolite. This normally results in the metabolite becoming less able to passively diffuse through cell brains, given that the metabolites become larger, charged, and less lipid soluble.

Review! Catabolism refers to enzymes breaking down a substance into other molecules (Chapter 2).

Catabolic enzymes can play an important role in a person's ability to metabolize, and therefore be affected by, drugs. For example, some individuals have a poor rate of transformation for antidepressant drugs (Tiwari, Souza, & Muller, 2009). For these individuals, referred to as *poor metabolizers* in this context, the appropriate enzymes for an antidepressant drug may either be too few or, because of gene polymorphisms, have a diminished ability to transform these drugs. For poor metabolizers certain drugs remain for a longer duration in unmetabolized form, leading these individuals to have a stronger drug response than may otherwise be expected. At the same time, someone who is an *rapid metabolizer* exhibits greater levels of an enzyme or a greater ability of enzymes to metabolize antidepressant drugs. Unlike poor metabolizers, ultrarapid metabolizers tend to have a weaker drug response, for certain drugs because the drug remains in the body for a shorter duration in unmetabolized form.

Review! A polymorphism is a difference in the encoding of a gene compared to the most common sequence in a population (Chapter 2).

Learning whether someone exhibits a difference in speed of drug metabolism can aid in prescribing drugs. For example, if an individual exhibits ultrarapid metabolism for antidepressant drugs metabolized by CYP2C19 enzymes, then a physician might prescribe an antidepressant drug not metabolized by CYP2C19 enzymes, such as fluoxetine (Prozac). Blood testing for these enzymatic activities provides an important approach for **personalized medicine**, a method of prescribing treatments most appropriate for a patient's unique biological makeup.

Drug biotransformation may occur before a drug circulates to the entire body, a process referred to as **first-pass metabolism**. First-pass metabolism occurs for drugs absorbed through the gut, which includes drugs administered orally. Drugs entering blood circulation enter the liver before being distributed to other parts of the body. Thus, liver enzymes may convert many drug molecules to metabolites before drug molecules ever enter the bloodstream (Figure 4.5). Biotransformation may also occur in the stomach, which is the case for the anti-anxiety drug (i.e., an anxiolytic) buspirone (BuSpar). Depending on the pill's formulation, up to approximately 90 percent of buspirone can be transformed into metabolites in the stomach after oral administration (Sakr and Andheria, 2013).

Because of biotransformation processes, physicians treating Parkinson's disease typically administer the drug levodopa with another drug called *carbidopa*. Carbidopa prevents aromatic L-amino acid decarboxylase from converting levodopa to dopamine while outside of the brain. Levodopa can cross the blood–brain barrier, but dopamine and carbidopa cannot. Thus, carbidopa helps keep levodopa molecules intact, allowing more of these molecules to reach the brain (Nutt, Woodward, & Anderson, 1985).

A drug's metabolites may help to explain its effects. First, metabolites may act in the body. These actions could be harmful, or they may interact with another drug a patient is taking. Second, the metabolites of a drug may offer physiological effects of their own. In this case, the metabolite is referred to as an **active metabolite**. For example, enzymes convert the antipsychotic drug quetiapine (Seroquel) to the metabolite N-desalkylquetiapine, which functions as an antidepressant drug (Jensen et al., 2007).

We use the term **prodrug** to describe a compound transformed in the body to produce the active drug. Thus, the active drug in this case is actually the prodrug's active metabolite. The prodrug itself is either pharmacologically inactive or has far fewer effects than its active metabolite (Ortiz de Montellano, 2013).

Drug developers may use a prodrug as tool for a variety of reasons, particularly for pharmacokinetic processes that may otherwise limit the bioavailability of the active drug (Rautio et al., 2008). The prodrug may bypass any absorption limitations that the active drug might have had, for example. We can also think of levodopa as a prodrug; in this case, the active "drug" is dopamine. Because dopamine cannot cross the blood–brain barrier, this limitation is overcome by using levodopa to cross the blood–brain barrier instead. The biotransformation process then takes place in dopamine neurons to produce dopamine, as previously discussed.

Third, metabolites reveal the substances a person used. For example, many employers require employees to undergo drug-screening tests, which detect metabolites of

Personalized medicine Method of prescribing treatments most appropriate for a patient's unique biological makeup

First-pass metabolism Drug metabolism that occurs prior to absorption into the bloodstream

Active metabolite A drug's metabolite that has physiological effects

Prodrug A physiologically weak or inactive compound metabolized in the body to produce an active drug

controlled substances. Probation programs also employ drug tests that assess metabolites as indicators of illicit substance use. For example, the opioid drug heroin will be transformed by liver enzymes to the metabolite monoacetylmorphine, although enzymes subsequently convert this enzyme to another metabolite (Rook, Hillebrand, Rosing, van Ree, & Beijnen, 2005; see Chapter 10). Drug testers may need to look for multiple metabolites to determine the actual substance taken.

Elimination

Elimination Process for how a drug leaves the body

Elimination rate Amount of drug eliminated from the body over time

Half-life Duration of time necessary for the body to eliminate half of a drug

First-order kinetics The elimination of a drug in half-lives

Elimination is the last stage of pharmacokinetics. **Elimination** is the process by which a drug leaves the body. The body eliminates drugs through urine, feces, sweat, saliva, and breath, although the particular route of elimination depends on the drug. For example, the body eliminates alcohol partly through breath. Given this, law enforcement officials use breathalyzers to determine whether an individual consumed alcohol.

Drugs have an **elimination rate**—that is, the amount of drug eliminated from the body over time. Physicians rely on drug elimination rates when prescribing how frequently a patient should take a medication. The elimination rate for most drugs occurs in half-lives. A **half-life** is the duration of time necessary for the body to eliminate half of a drug, usually based on measuring drug concentration in blood. A drug eliminated in half-lives is referred to as having **first-order kinetics**.

Figure 4.6 provides an illustration of a drug eliminated in half-lives. For the drug in the left panel, half of the drug leaves the body every 2 hours, as determined by concentration in blood plasma. The amount of drug eliminated differs for every half-life. After the first half-life shown, 2.0 milliequivalents of blood per liter (mEq/L) of drug was eliminated during the first 2 hours. Two hours later, 1.0 mEq/L of drug was eliminated, half of the amount of the previous half-life. Two hours after this, only 0.5 mEq/L of drug was eliminated.

Zero-order kinetics The elimination of a drug in non-half-lives

However, not all drugs follow first-order kinetics for elimination. For other drugs, the elimination rate will consist of a set amount of drug per unit time, referred to as **zero-order kinetics**. For example, the body eliminates approximately 10 to 14 milliliters (ml) of alcohol per hour. Thus, if someone ingested 20 milliliters of alcohol, the body would eliminate all of the alcohol after about 2 hours. The graph on the right in Figure 4.5 shows a fictional drug eliminated according to zero-order kinetics.

A drug's elimination rate determines how long effects will last. Physicians use elimination rate information when prescribing how frequently a patient should take a medication. In doing so, they can have patients take the next dose of medication at a time when the effects from the previous treatment begin to subside. In this way, drug effects reach a *steady state*.

A steady state is a sustained level of drug in the body. This is why a doctor may prescribe a drug to be taken, for example, three times a day: The drug's half-life might be about 6–8 hours. Thus, as approximately half of the drug is still in the body 6–8 hours later, the next administration of the drug would boost the drug

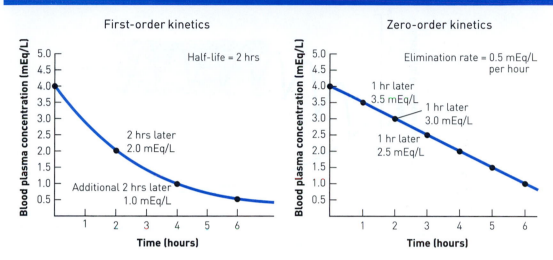

concentrations back to therapeutically effective levels. **Figure 4.7** provides an illustration of a dosing schedule that achieves a steady state for drug concentration in blood.

Pharmacodynamics: Describing the Actions of Drugs

Pharmacodynamics refers to the mechanisms of action for a drug. For many psychoactive drugs, particularly those covered in this text, pharmacodynamics deal largely with the actions of a drug at synapses. Psychoactive drugs alter neurotransmission at the synapses.

Pharmacodynamics Mechanisms of action for a drug

Depending on a drug's unique characteristics, it may alter any stage of neurotransmission. As presented in Chapter 3, neurotransmission consists of synaptic events that include action potentials reaching the axon terminal, the influx of calcium, the fusing of vesicles to membrane walls, and the emptying of stored neurotransmitters into the synaptic cleft. Within the synaptic cleft, neurotransmitters may bind to receptors. Then neurotransmission terminates. The following paragraphs provide examples of drug actions occurring at different stages of neurotransmission.

FIGURE 4.7 ● The half-life of a drug can be used to determine when later administrations of the drug should be given. Eventually, a steady state can develop between the rate of drug elimination from a previous administration and the rate of drug absorption from the next administration.

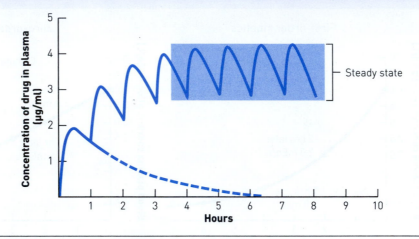

SOURCE: Poling, A. D., & Byrne, T. (2000).

STOP & CHECK

1. What is bioavailability?

2. What type of enzymes metabolize most drugs?

3. How might first-pass metabolism affect a drug's pharmacological effects?

4. Why is a steady state important for therapeutic drug effects?

1. Bioavailability describes a drug's ability to reach its site of action. 2. Cytochrome P450 enzymes 3. First-pass metabolism consists of the conversion of drug molecules to metabolites, causing less of a drug to be available for reaching its site of action. 4. As a medical treatment, sustained drug effects are usually necessary to combat a particular illness. Thus, physicians derive a treatment schedule to achieve a steady state for drug effects.

Review! Termination of neurotransmission occurs when enzymes convert a neurotransmitter into metabolites, membrane transporters return neurotransmitters to the axon terminal, or transporters draw neurotransmitters into astrocytes (Chapter 3).

First, certain substances can interfere with the propagation of action potentials. For example, a toxin called *tetrodotoxin*, found in the puffer fish, prevents action potentials from occurring. Tetrodotoxin does so by blocking Na^+ channels (Narahashi, Moore, & Scott, 1964). Through these actions, puffer fish paralyze any prey they successfully inject. For nervous system research, neuroscientists administer tetrodotoxin to different brain structures in animals to temporarily disable a structure's functioning. This allows neuroscientists to learn about a structure's effects on the functioning of other structures in the brain as well as the importance a structure has for behavior.

Review! Action potentials consist of the rapid influx of Na^+ ions through open Na^+ channels (Chapter 3).

Figure 4.8 provides examples of drug actions on dopamine neurotransmission. Many substances can alter the synthesis for dopamine. The precursor molecule for dopamine, L-DOPA, also serves as a drug for the treatment of Parkinson's disease (we referred to this as "levodopa" in previous chapters). By increasing the number of L-DOPA molecules within dopamine neurons, increased production of dopamine occurs.

Drugs also may interfere with neurotransmitter storage in vesicles. The drug *tetrabenazine (Xenazine)* prevents dopamine storage by blocking transport of dopamine into vesicles. Subsequently, dopamine molecules become catabolized by enzymes leading to depletion of dopamine (Pettibone, Totaro, & Pflueger, 1984). The dopamine-depleting effects of tetrabenazine diminish the degree of writhing, facial tics, and other abnormal movements seen in Huntington's disease (Paleacu, 2007).

Drugs may also interfere with the binding of a neurotransmitter to a receptor. Figure 4.8 shows an antipsychotic drug called haloperidol binding to a dopamine D_2 receptor. Haloperidol acts through a basic receptor mechanism called *receptor antagonism* (described later in this chapter). As a receptor antagonist, haloperidol binds to the D_2 receptor and prevents dopamine from binding to and activating the D_2 receptor. Through this action, haloperidol prevents dopamine neurotransmission through the D_2 receptors (Seeman, Chau-Wong, Tedesco, & Wong, 1975). The next section of this chapter describes drug actions at receptors in greater detail.

Drugs can alter the activity of enzymes that break down neurotransmitters. Figure 4.8 shows a drug bound to both the monoamine oxidase (MAO) and catechol-O-methyltransferase (COMT) enzymes. For MAO, an antidepressant drug called *moclobemide* binds to and prevents MAO from breaking down dopamine (Stefanis, Alevizos, & Papadimitriou, 1982). As described in greater detail in Chapter 14, MAO inhibitors such as moclobemide may reduce depressive symptoms by enhancing neurotransmission of dopamine, as well as the neurotransmitters serotonin and norepinephrine.

Figure 4.8 also shows a drug called *entacapone* acting on the enzyme COMT. Entacapone belongs to a class of drugs called COMT inhibitors. Like MAO inhibitors, COMT

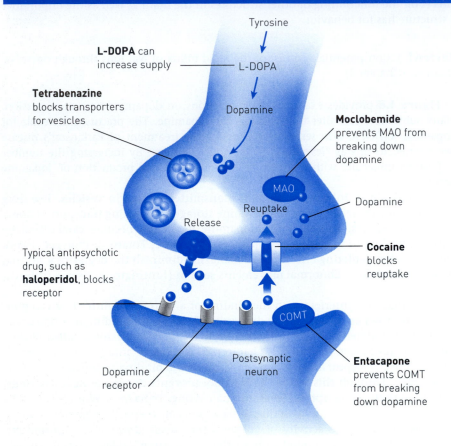

FIGURE 4.8 ● Drugs can alter any step in neurotransmission, including synthesis of a neurotransmitter, storage of a neurotransmission, synaptic release of a neurotransmission, enzymatic breakdown of a neurotransmitter, and reuptake of a neurotransmitter. Drugs may also act on receptors for neurotransmitters.

inhibitors increase dopamine levels. COMT inhibitors serve as another treatment option for Parkinson's disease (Guttman et al., 1993).

Many drugs also interfere with the reuptake of neurotransmitters. Figure 4.8 shows the psychostimulant drug cocaine bound to the dopamine transporter. Cocaine blocks the dopamine transporter, preventing dopamine from entering the axon terminal. This action results in increased dopamine levels in the synaptic cleft and the continuation of dopamine neurotransmission.

Drug Profile: tetrabenazine	
Trade name:	Xenazine
Mechanism of action	Inhibits transport of dopamine into vesicles
Uses	Reduces degree of abnormal movements occurring in Huntington's disease

Review! The dopamine transporter sends dopamine from the synaptic cleft into a dopamine axon terminal (Chapter 3).

STOP & CHECK

1. How might a drug, by acting on a neurotransmitter storage vesicle, diminish levels of the neurotransmitter?

2. How does a drug inhibiting the enzyme MAO increase dopamine levels?

1. as with tetrabenazine, an inability for a neuron to store a neurotransmitters leaves neurotransmitters susceptible to breakdown by enzymes. **2.** MAO catabolizes, or breaks down, dopamine; thus, preventing MAO from doing so will increase dopamine levels.

Psychoactive Drugs and Receptors

As one of the many ways that a drug can alter neurotransmission, most psychoactive drugs act on receptors for neurotransmitters. The actions of a drug at a receptor depend on how well a drug binds to the receptor and the effects a drug has on the receptor. Researchers describe these two considerations as binding affinity and receptor efficacy. **Binding affinity** refers to a drug's strength of binding to a receptor, and **receptor efficacy** refers to a drug's ability to activate a receptor.

Researchers measure a drug's binding affinity using techniques described in **Box 4.1.** These techniques result in a value for drug called a *dissociation constant*, generally noted as K_d, or an inhibition constant, noted as K_i. These values derive from the level of drug concentration necessary to bind to receptors. For both constants, *the lower the value, the greater a drug's binding affinity*.

The previous section, which presented the different ways a drug can alter neurotransmission, used the antipsychotic drug haloperidol as an example of a drug binding

Binding affinity
Drug's strength of binding to a receptor

Receptor efficacy
Drug's ability to alter the activity of receptor

BOX 4.1 RADIOLIGAND BINDING FOR MEASURING RECEPTOR AFFINITY

Radioligand binding is an important technique for studying the affinity and efficacy that drugs have for receptors. The term *ligand* refers to a chemical substance that binds to a receptor, as noted in an earlier chapter. A radioligand is produced by adding a radioactive element to a ligand. As another reminder, affinity refers to a drug's strength of binding to a receptor.

Researchers conduct most radioligand experiments using dissected brain tissue that was mixed together with a chemical solution called a *buffer*, forming a homogenized solution of brain tissue and buffer. Another approach uses a large collection of cells grown in culture, referred to as *cell lines*, for radioligand experiments. After preparing the brain tissue using either method, researchers apply the radioligand to the tissue solution.

Afterward, the tissue solution, which contains both brain tissue and the radioligand, is passed through a filter. These filters allow the buffer solution to pass through but not brain tissue to pass through. After filtering, the filter contains brain tissue along with any of the radioligand bound to receptors in the brain tissue.

Researchers then use radioactivity counters on the filters. If the drug successfully binds to receptors in the brain tissue, then the researchers will find high radioactivity counts in the filters. However, if the radioligand bound to few receptors in the tissue, then the radioligand would have passed through the filter with the rest of the solution. In this case, researchers would detect low radioactivity counts from the filter.

Figure 1 shows an example of results from a radioligand binding experiment. This example shows, using a percentage, how many receptors the drug occupied. The *y*-axis of this graph shows the percentage of receptors occupied. The *x*-axis shows the different amounts of radioligand used, shown as the drug concentration expressed as molality. *Molality*, a term used in chemistry, refers to the number of moles (mol) per volume of solution. A *mole* refers to the number of grams of a substance divided by the molecular weight of the substance—think of this as the amount of substance.

The term called B_{max}, the abbreviation for *maximum binding potential*, refers to the amount of drug that fully binds to a population of receptors. In Figure 1, the B_{max} value of the radioligand is 10^{-3} moles/liter (or 0.001 moles/liter), the concentration that occupies 100 percent of the population of receptors. The K_d value, or *dissociation constant*, refers to the amount of drug that occupies 50 percent of receptors. Drugs with low K_d values can achieve 50 percent receptor occupancy at lower drug concentrations than drugs with higher K_d values. For interpreting these data, think of it this way: the lower the K_d value, the greater a drug's receptor affinity.

An alternative approach for assessing receptor affinities produces an inhibition constant, or K_i value. This approach uses similar radioligand experimental procedures, except that K_i values are derived by assessing the competition between two different drugs. Only one of the drugs serves as the radioligand; the other drug is not radioactive.

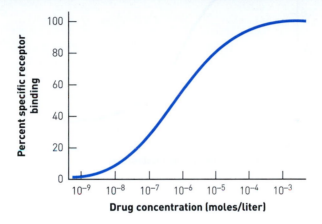

For this procedure, a researcher places both the radioligand and the nonradioactive drug into the same brain tissue solution. In this way, the researcher assesses the affinity of the nonradioactive drug by how well it binds to these receptors in the presence of the radioligand. The compound with the higher receptor affinity binds to receptors in place of the the compound with the lower receptor affinity. In this case, fewer radioactivity counts indicate that the nonradioactive compound had a greater receptor affinity than the radioligand.

Figure 2 shows an example of results from a K_i experiment. Like Figure 1, this graph provides the concentration of a drug—in this case, the nonradioactive drug—on the *x*-axis. In this figure, however, the *y*-axis refers to the percentage of receptors bound by the radioligand. According to the figure, greater receptor occupancy by the radioligand occurred with the lowest concentration of the nonradioactive drug, whereas lower receptor occupancy by the radioligand occurred with the highest concentration of the nonradioactive drug. The K_i value represents the concentration of the nonradioactive compound that caused the radioactive compound to provide 50 percent receptor occupancy. Similar to K_d, the lower the K_i value the greater the compound's affinity (in this case, the nonradioactive drug) for the receptor.

(Continued)

(Continued)

FIGURE 2 ● This figure shows a K_i experiment. The *y*-axis shows radioactivity counts, and the *x*-axis shows the concentration for the nonradioactive drug.

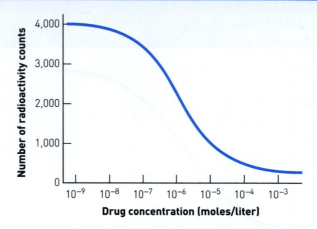

to a dopamine D_2 receptor. **Table 4.2** shows haloperidol's binding affinity, along with related compounds, for the D_2 receptor as well as the binding affinity of dopamine for the D_2 receptor. You may be surprised to see that haloperidol has a far greater affinity for the dopamine D_2 receptor than dopamine does. This is another important point about drugs: They can outcompete a receptor's natural neurotransmitter.

TABLE 4.2 ● The Dissociation Constant (K_d) in nM* for Dopamine and Selected Antipsychotic Drugs at the Dopamine D_2 Receptor	
Substance	**K_d (in nM)**
Chlorpromazine	4.8
Haloperidol	2.6
Chlorprothixene	8.0
Dopamine	544

*n = nano, M = molality

SOURCE: Richelson and Nelson, 1984; Richelson and Souder, 2000; Seeman 2001; and Sokoloff et al., 1992.

Drugs may produce a variety of different effects on receptors. The primary receptor actions include *agonism, antagonism, partial agonism*, and *allosteric regulation*.[1] We refer to many metabotropic receptor theory models as *ternary receptor models* (*ternary* means "threefold") (Brink, Harvey, Bodenstein, Venter, & Oliver, 2004). These models characterize receptor actions by considering the interactions between a drug, receptor, and G-protein activity. **Box 4.2** presents a method researchers use to determine a drug's efficacy at a metabotropic receptor.

Figure 4.9 presents the basic features of ternary models used to describe the effects of drugs acting as agonists, antagonists, and partial agonists at metabotropic receptors. The "Before" column in Figure 4.8 refers to the receptor state before a drug binds to it. The "Briefly" column illustrates a transition process that occurs when a drug first binds to the receptor, and the "After" column illustrates the subsequent changes to the active of a receptor's G protein.

Review! Metabotropic receptors can cause change within neurons by activating G proteins (Chapter 3).

An **agonist** refers to a drug that activates a neurotransmitter receptor. Researchers also refer to agonists as *full agonists* to contrast these drugs with partial agonists, described

Agonist Drug that activates a neurotransmitter receptor

1 Another function is *inverse agonism*, but that is beyond the scope of this book.

BOX 4.2 THE [^{35}S]GTP$_\gamma$S BINDING ASSAY ASSESSES G-PROTEIN ACTIVATION

The process of activating and deactivating G proteins depends on two biochemicals: guanosine diphosphate (GDP) and guanosine triphosphate (GTP). Before receptor activation by a neurotransmitter, GDP is bound to the inactive alpha subunit of a G protein. When a neurotransmitter or agonist activates a receptor, GTP replaces GDP on the alpha subunit, and this switch from GDP to GTP characterizes an active G-protein state (**Figure 1**). This active G-protein state ends when the alpha subunit hydrolyzes GTP, causing a conversion from GTP to GDP. With GDP attached to the alpha subunit, the G protein returns to an inactive state, just as it was before the receptor was activated by a neurotransmitter.

The [^{35}S]GTP$_\gamma$S binding assay employs a radioactivity compound to assess the ability of drugs to activate G proteins. Because this is a binding assay, the procedure used involves tissue and radioactivity counting procedures similar to those described in Box 4.1. [^{35}S] GTP$_\gamma$S is an analogue of GTP, and as an analogue it can replace GTP when the G protein is activated. However, unlike with GTP, researchers can measure [^{35}S]GTP$_\gamma$S using radioactivity counters. Another advantage of [^{35}S]GTP$_\gamma$S is that the alpha subunit cannot convert it into GDP. Thus, the label of an active G protein does not vanish before researchers can measure radioactivity counts.

Figure 2 shows a graph providing the ability of three drugs to bind to a receptor (left) and the ability to activate the receptor as measured using [^{35}S]GTP$_\gamma$S (right). As shown in the left graph, each drug fully occupies the population

FIGURE 1 ● During an inactive state for a G-protein coupled metabotropic receptor, GDP is bound to G-protein's α subunit (left). When an agonist activates the receptor, GTP replaces GDP on the α subunit, leading to a separation of the α subunit from the βγ subunit (right); these subunits go on to carry out intracellular signaling processes, as described in Chapter 3. GDP = guanosine diphosphate; GTP = guanosine triphosphate.

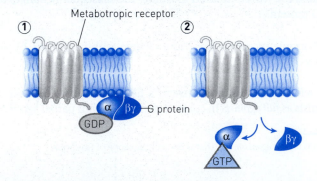

of receptors and does so at similar dosages. Yet the [³⁵S]GTPγS assay demonstrates that these drugs have different abilities to activate the receptor. At high enough concentrations, drug A exhibits full radioactivity counts, demonstrating full activation of the receptors' G proteins.

Drug B achieves no more than half of drug A's radioactivity counts. Finally, drug C results in no radioactivity counts from [³⁵S]GTPγS. Try to identify the receptor actions of these drugs based on their results in the [³⁵S]GTPγS assay. Refer to Figure 4.9 and Box 4.1 for this.

FIGURE 2 ● The graph on the left shows the percentage of a receptor population occupied by three different drugs. The graph on the right shows the number of [³⁵S]GTPγS radioactivity counts. The *x*-axis for both figures refers to the concentration of drug expressed in molality (i.e., moles per liter). The illustration (right panel) reveals that drug A functions as a full agonist because it fully activates G proteins. Drug B functions as a partial agonist because, within a population of receptors, drug B fails to activate all of the G proteins. Finally, drug C acts as an antagonist—it lacks the capacity to activate receptors.

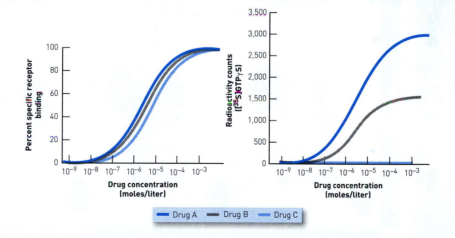

FIGURE 4.9 ● Drugs can have different types of action at receptors. An agonist (first row) will bind to a receptor (second column) and cause the receptor to shift into an active state (third column). The strong preference for the active state is indicated by the thick arrow. An antagonist (second row) will bind to a receptor but fail to shift the receptor's conformation into an active state (i.e., no effect). A partial agonist (third row) will bind to a receptor but is weaker, compared to an agonist, for shifting the receptor's conformation into an active state, as shown by the dashed line.

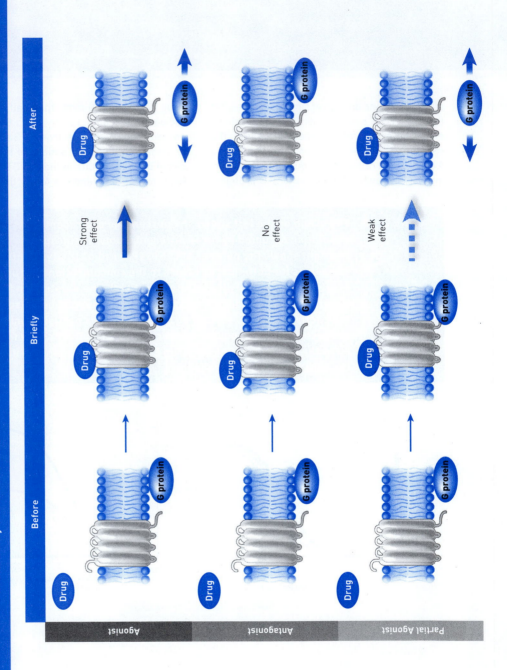

shortly. For the first line of Figure 4.8, a drug acting as an agonist approaches an inactive receptor. The Before column represents the inactivity of the receptor by showing a stationary G protein adjacent to the receptor. When the agonist binds to the receptor, the G protein draws close to the receptor, as shown in the Briefly column. The Briefly column for an agonist shows a ternary complex consisting of both a drug and a G protein bound to the receptor. Afterward, as shown in the After column, the G protein separates from the receptor and elicits biological actions within the neuron.

Review! When activated, G proteins separate into α and βγ subunits leading to activation of ion channels or enzymes (Chapter 3).

The second row of Figure 4.9 shows a drug action as an antagonist. Unlike an agonist, an **antagonist** refers to a drug that fails to activate a receptor. Referring to the model shown in Figure 4.9, an antagonist fails to produce a ternary complex, meaning that an antagonist fails to cause a G protein to temporarily bind to the receptor. Without the G protein being activated, no other changes within the neuron occur.

> **Antagonist** Drug that fails to activate a receptor

The third line of Figure 4.9 presents a drug acting as a **partial agonist**—that is, it possesses a weaker efficacy for activating receptors than a full agonist. These weaker effects mean that a partial agonist may or may not be able to activate a receptor. In figure 4.9, a partial agonist causes a G protein to shift toward the receptor in the Briefly column. After this, the G protein may separate and elicit effects within a neuron, or it may remain bound to the receptor, thereby producing no effects.

> **Partial agonist** Drug that possesses a weaker efficacy for activating receptors than a full agonist

Although these examples concerned metabotropic receptors, similar drug effects occur at ionotropic receptors. For an ionotropic receptor, an agonist causes the attached channel to open, allowing ions to pass in or out of the neuron **(Figure 4.10)**. In contrast, an antagonist binds to an ionotropic receptor but fails to open the channel.

Antagonists for ionotropic receptors may be *competitive* or *noncompetitive antagonists*. **Competitive antagonists** bind to the same site as a neurotransmitter, preventing a neurotransmitter from binding to the receptor. Bicuculline acts as a competitive antagonist for $GABA_A$ ionotropic receptors. By preventing GABA-mediated inhibition of nervous system functioning, bicuculline results in greater activity in the nervous system. In fact, researchers study bicuculline-induced seizures in laboratory animals to study *epilepsy* (Johnston, 2013).

> **Competitive antagonist** Drug that binds to the same site as a neurotransmitter, preventing a neurotransmitter from binding to the receptor

A **noncompetitive antagonist** does not bind to the same site as a neurotransmitter, but it does prevent the neurotransmitter from activating the receptor (Figure 4.10). For example, *phencyclidine (PCP)*, a drug of abuse (discussed in Chapter 12), functions as a noncompetitive antagonist for glutamate NMDA receptors. Glutamate can bind to an NMDA receptor, but PCP prevents ions from passing through the receptor.

> **Noncompetitive antagonist** Drug that does not prevent a neurotransmitter from binding to the receptor but does prevent the neurotransmitter from activating the receptor

For an ionotropic receptor, the term *partial agonist* describes a drug that occupies a receptor but does not fully activate the receptor (Figure 4.10). In this case, the ion channel partially opens, allowing fewer ions to flow through than if the ion channel were fully open. For example, the compound kainate functions as a partial agonist for

FIGURE 4.10 ● Although an agonist will fully activate an ionotropic receptor, causing the channel to fully open, a partial agonist may only partially activate an ionotropic receptor and the channel will only partially open. In these cases, more ions can flow through the fully open channel than can flow through a partially open channel. A competitive antagonist fails to change the channel configuration by preventing neurotransmitters from binding to neurotransmitter sites on the receptor. A noncompetitive antagonist also fails to change the channel configuration, but does so by preventing ions from flowing through the receptor, rather than by preventing a neurotransmitter from binding to sites on the receptor.

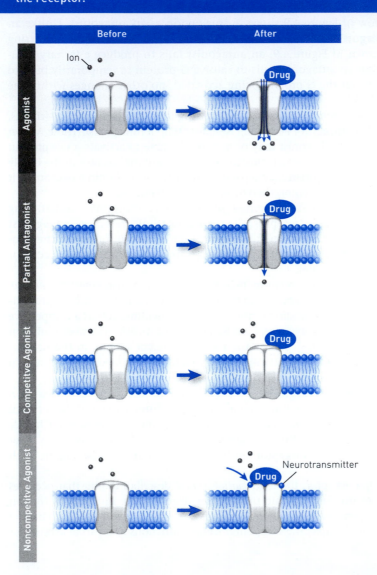

⚕ *Drug Profile:* bicuculline	
Trade name:	None; only used as a research compound
Mechanism of action	Competitive antagonist for GABA$_A$ receptors
Uses	Used in research to learn about GABA neurotransmission and to study seizures

the glutamate AMPA receptor because kainate causes a weaker flow of ions through the AMPA receptor channel than a full agonist produces (Arinaminpathy, Sansom, & Biggin, 2002; Armstrong & Gouaux, 2000).

Drugs may also act as allosteric regulators. An **allosteric regulator** is a substance that binds to site on a protein and causes a conformational change in the protein, but neither activates nor prevents activation of the protein. For our purposes, an allosteric regulator changes the conformation of a receptor, but does not activate a receptor. An allosteric regulator binds to a different place on the receptor than the neurotransmitter does; therefore it doesn't prevent a neurotransmitter from binding to a receptor like a competitive antagonist does.

Allosteric regulators may augment or diminish a receptor's response to a neurotransmitter. We identify such substances as either *positive* or *negative modulators*. A **positive modulator** is a chemical substance that binds to an allosteric site on a receptor and increases the ability of a neurotransmitter to bind to and/or activate the receptor. A **negative modulator** decreases the ability of a neurotransmitter to bind to and/or activate a receptor.

Many drugs act as positive or negative modulators for GABA$_A$ receptors. For example, a benzodiazepine drug such as alprazolam (Xanax) binds to an allosteric site, named the *benzodiazepine site*. When a benzodiazepine drug binds to this site, the receptor undergoes a change that enhances its affinity for binding to GABA. This ultimately leads to more activation of GABA$_A$ receptors. In this way, a benzodiazepine drug serves as a positive modulator for GABA$_A$ receptors. The drug sarmazenil also binds to benzodiazepine sites but serves as a negative modulator[2]. Through causing a conformational change in the receptor, sarmazenil causes fewer Cl⁻ ions to flow through the GABA$_A$ channel when it is activated by GABA (Yakushiji, Fukuda, Oyama, & Akaike, 1989).

Allosteric regulator
A substance that binds to site on a protein and causes a conformational change in the protein, but neither activates nor prevents activation of the protein

Positive modulator
A chemical substance that binds to an allosteric site on a receptor and increases the ability of a neurotransmitter to bind to and/or activate the receptor

Negative modulator
A chemical substance that binds to an allosteric site on a receptor and decreases the ability of a neurotransmitter to bind to and/or activate the receptor

STOP & CHECK

1. A drug that prevents the activation of a receptor but does not bind to the same site as a neurotransmitter is called a _____.

2. A drug that increases the ability of an ionotropic receptor to be activated by a neurotransmitter is called a _____.

1. noncompetitive antagonist 2. positive modulator

2 Sometimes the term *inverse agonist* is used instead.

Neurotoxins and Damage to the Nervous System

Neurotoxins
Substances that damage or destroy parts of the nervous system

Although this chapter pertains to the properties of psychoactive drugs, many toxins also alter nervous system functioning. **Neurotoxins** are substances that damage or destroy parts of the nervous system. Some of these toxins are found in venoms. Mentioned in this chapter, the toxin released from puffer fish called *tetrodotoxin* prevents neurotransmission by blocking Na$^+$ channels. Another venom called *alpha-bungarotoxin*, which is found in the Taiwanese banded krait and other types of snakes, blocks cholinergic nicotinic receptors at neuromuscular junctions. Through interfering with neurotransmission, these toxins induce paralysis to make it easy for the predator to consume its prey.

Environmental neurotoxicology A field devoted to the study of neurotoxins in the environment

Environmental neurotoxicology is a field devoted to the study of neurotoxins in the environment. Many toxins are found in our everyday environment. Chemicals classified as *endocrine disruptors*—named for their interference with the endocrine system, including dysfunctions in the reproductive system, nervous system, and immune system—are commonly found in pesticides, plastics, flame retardants, and many types of building materials. In particular, many household plastics contain the endocrine disruptor bisphenol-A (BPA), one of the better-known *endocrine disruptors*.

Environmental neurotoxins also include heavy metals such as lead and mercury. Lead exposure in particular may damage neurons and can contribute to learning problems in children. We encounter lead more than we think. Aside from the lead found in computer monitors or other electronics, buildings built before the 1980s likely contain lead-based paints, and lead dust can be released in air, particularly when renovating older buildings.

Researchers study neurotoxins in the same ways that pharmacologists study psychoactive drugs. Neurotoxins may cause *neuronopathy* (the destruction of neurons), *myelinopathy* (the destruction of myelin sheathing), *axonopathy* (the destruction of axons), and *transmission toxicities*. Transmission toxicities consist of damage to processes involved in neurotransmission. Toxins for neurotransmission may destroy storage vesicles for neurotransmitters, irreversibly block receptors, or block enzymes that break down neurotransmitters.

STOP & CHECK

1. How might a neurotoxin disrupt neurotransmission?

1. A neurotoxin can affect neurotransmission in a variety of ways, including irreversibly binding to enzymes or destroying synaptic vesicles.

Adaptations to Chronic Drug Use

Chronic drug use is the repeated, usually daily, use of a drug. The body may react differently to a drug when administered chronically compared to an acute administration. Three unique features of chronic drug use include tolerance, sensitization, and dependence (**Table 4.3**).

Tolerance refers to an adaption that requires a user to take greater doses of a drug to achieve the same desired drug effects. Tolerance most often occurs as a result of chronic administration, which occurred for the example of heroin noted previously. Some drugs cause tolerance after acute administration. Acute administration of nicotine, for example, causes an immediate change to nicotinic receptors that results in a temporary tolerance to nicotine's effects (Ochoa & McNamee, 1990).

Three forms of tolerance may occur from drug treatment: pharmacokinetic, pharmacodynamic, and behavioral. In the first form, **pharmacokinetic tolerance** (or **drug dispositional tolerance**), pharmacokinetic actions reduce the amount of drug reaching its site of action. Often pharmacokinetic tolerance causes an increased rate of drug conversion to metabolites. For example, a

> **Tolerance** Occurs when a user must take greater doses of a drug to achieve desired effects
>
> **Pharmacokinetic tolerance** (or **drug dispositional tolerance**) Pharmacokinetic actions that reduce the amount of drug reaching its site of action

TABLE 4.3 ● Dependence, Tolerance, and Sensitization		
Function	**Type**	**Characteristics**
Tolerance		Drug adaptations require escalating drug doses to achieve desired effects
	Pharmacokinetic	Reduces the amount of drug reaching its site of action
	Pharmacodynamic	Reduced responsiveness at a drug's site of action
	Behavioral	Decreased behavioral responsiveness
	Conditioned	Environmental stimuli elicit physiological compensatory effects to a drug's effect
	Cross tolerance	Tolerance to other drugs in the same class
Sensitization		Increased responsiveness to a drug's effects
Dependence		Presence of withdrawal symptoms after a period of drug cessation
	Physical	Physiological withdrawal symptoms such as nausea
	Psychological	Psychological withdrawal symptoms such as drug cravings or mood changes

pharmacokinetic tolerance to alcohol occurs when increased levels of an enzyme, *alcohol dehydrogenase*, causes increased conversion of alcohol to its metabolite. By increasing the conversion of alcohol, alcohol dehydrogenase causes less alcohol to reach the brain.

The second form of tolerance, **pharmacodynamic tolerance**, consists of a reduced responsiveness to a drug at the drug's site of action. Chronic administration of the anti-anxiety drug buspirone causes lower levels of serotonin receptors (Taylor & Hyslop, 1991). For buspirone, fewer serotonin receptors lead to weaker drug effects.

The third form of tolerance, **behavioral tolerance**, produces a decreased behavioral responsiveness to a drug's effects. Alcohol use provides a good example here as well. Studies show that moderate drinkers perform certain behavioral tasks under the effects of alcohol better than those who seldom drink alcohol do while under the effects of alcohol (Goodwin, Powell, & Stern, 1971; Sdao-Jarvie & Vogel-Sprott, 1991).

Another form of tolerance is conditioned tolerance. **Conditioned** (or **contingent**) **tolerance** occurs as a physiological response to stimuli associated with substance use that serves to counteract a drug's physiological actions. The physiological response might inhibit a drug's pharmacokinetic or pharmacodynamic actions, but this response will either not occur or be weaker when certain drug-associated stimuli are absent. When absent, the dependent organism will experience significantly greater effects, potentially including drug overdose. The From Actions to Effects section at the end of this chapter provides an example of conditioned tolerance.

The tolerance effects for a drug may carry over to drugs with similar biological actions. For example, heroin addicts can tolerate a much higher dose of the opioid replacement drug methadone than those not addicted to heroin. This form of tolerance is called **cross tolerance.**

Chronic drug administration may also cause **sensitization**, an increased responsiveness to a drug's effects. Researchers study sensitization in animal models. Nicotine, which is characterized as a psychostimulant drug, first causes inhibitory effects on activity in laboratory rats. However, after several days of administration, nicotine induces excitatory effects on activity in rats (Rosecrans, Stimler, Hendry, & Meltzer, 1989).

A drug **dependence** consists of a user needing a drug to function normally. During dependence, the absence of a drug leads to withdrawal symptoms. The term **withdrawal syndrome** refers to the collection of withdrawal symptoms for a drug. The nature of withdrawal symptoms defines the type of drug dependence.

Physical dependence is defined by the presence of physical withdrawal symptoms. For example, physical withdrawal symptoms occurring from abrupt withdrawal of an antidepressant drug may consist of dizziness, nausea, as well as sensations of buzzing or electric shock. **Psychological dependence** is defined by the presence of psychological withdrawal symptoms, which can include drug cravings or changes in mood or behavior.

Withdrawal symptoms often result from the body's compensatory adaptive changes to drug actions. When a sufficient period of time without a drug administration occurs, the body's compensatory effects become evident and manifest themselves as withdrawal symptoms. For example, heroin initially produces euphoria, constipation,

Pharmacodynamic tolerance Reduced responsiveness to a drug at the drug's site of action

Behavioral tolerance Decreased behavioral responsiveness to a drug's effects

Conditioned (or contingent tolerance) Occurs as a physiological response to stimuli associated with substance use that serves to counteract a drug's physiological actions

Cross tolerance Tolerance for other drugs with similar biological actions

Sensitization Increased responsiveness to a drug's effects

Dependence Needing a drug to be able to function normally

Withdrawal syndrome The collection of withdrawal symptoms for a drug

Physical dependence Presence of physical withdrawal symptoms when a drug is not taken

Psychological dependence Presence of psychological withdrawal symptoms when a drug is not taken

and pain relief, but after some period of chronic usage, the body develops a tolerance to these effects. Once a tolerance to heroin occurs, cessation of heroin use produces withdrawal symptoms that include depression, diarrhea, and exaggerated sensitivity to pain. Thus, the compensatory actions become withdrawal symptoms.

STOP & CHECK

1. A defining feature of drug dependence is the presence of _____.

2. Adaptation to chronic drug administration, as indicated by a dose of drug no longer producing the same magnitude of effects, is called _____.

1. withdrawal symptoms 2. tolerance

From Actions to Effects: Heroin Tolerance and Overdose

The beginning of this chapter described Siegel's questions about why heroin users experienced an overdose to their usual amount of heroin. Why would a chronic user's normal heroin dose cause an overdose that he apparently should have a tolerance for? From these interviews, Siegel found that most overdose victims reported a significant change in the usual drug injection routine before experiencing an overdose. Siegel suspected that a previous heroin study he conducted in rats might explain this issue.

Siegel and colleagues (1982) had given two groups of rats incrementally increasing doses of heroin during the course of a month, so that at the end of this month, rats tolerated a relatively high dose of heroin (8.0 mg/kg). However, each group of rats received these heroin injections in different environments. The first group received injections in the animal colony room in which the animals were normally housed. The other group received its injections only in a different room that contained a speaker used to generate constant white noise (like radio static).

After completing one month of daily heroin injections in these animals, the researchers conducted an overdose test by giving each rat nearly double (15.0 mg/kg) the tolerated dose. In addition, the researchers switched the injection environments for half of the animals; that is, on the overdose test, half of the animals were treated in the same injection room, whereas the other half of the animals were treated in the different injection room.

Figure 4.11 shows the results of this experiment. The researchers found that a significantly greater number of rats died after receiving heroin in a different environment compared to rats receiving heroin in the same environment. Apparently, environmental stimuli facilitated a tolerance to heroin; when these environmental stimuli were removed, the rats demonstrated a weaker tolerance for heroin.

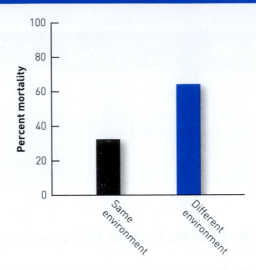

FIGURE 4.11 ● More heroin-tolerant rats died when injected with high doses of heroin when they were in environments that were different from the ones in which they previously received injections.

SOURCE: Based on Siegel et al., 1992.

STOP & CHECK

1. What type of tolerance may have been demonstrated in the study by Siegel and colleagues (1982)?

2. How might environmental stimuli changes increase the likelihood of heroin overdose?

1. The study authors suggested that pharmacokinetic tolerance may have been weakened when the rats were injected in a different environment. 2. If tolerance failed to sufficiently occur after heroin injection as a result of changes in environment, then the body exhibits a greater sensitivity to heroin's effects. If these differences resulted from pharmacokinetic tolerance, then greater heroin amounts were more available than usual to act within the body.

A link between environmental factors and conditioned tolerance may explain these findings. The researchers suggested that long-term treatment with heroin resulted in pharmacokinetic effects because of increased enzyme activity to break down heroin. By keeping the injection conditions constant, environmental stimuli occasioned the increased activity of these enzymes, providing for the creation of tolerance.

Changing the injection environment removed the stimuli associated with heroin, which possibly failed to elicit increased activation of these enzymes. With enzymes for heroin less active, less heroin was converted. Then, because much of the heroin remained in nonmetabolized form in the body, the effects were similar to taking an even higher overdose of heroin. Essentially, a routine dose of heroin could in fact be an overdose of heroin without sufficient activity of these enzymes. The results suggest that heroin users who have a typical place and routine for using heroin have developed a tolerance that is promoted by these environment stimuli, a form of conditioned tolerance. Removing these stimuli may result in greater drug effects, possibly accounting for the overdose cases that Siegel observed.

Chapter Summary

The field of pharmacology is largely divided into two general areas: pharmacokinetics and pharmacodynamics. Pharmacokinetics concerns the passage of the drug through the body in four phases: absorption, distribution, biotransformation, and elimination. Absorption is the ability of a drug to enter the bloodstream, and this depends on the administration route used. Distribution refers to drug passage through the bloodstream to target sites. Drugs must possess certain properties to passively diffuse through the blood–brain barrier. Biotransformation refers to the process of enzymatically converting a drug into metabolites. Elimination is the process of expelling drugs from the body.

Pharmacodynamics are the mechanisms of action for a drug. The pharmacodynamics of a psychoactive drug consist of altering neurotransmission, including changes in neurotransmitter synthesis, storage, release, receptor binding, and conversion to metabolites. Drugs have the ability to activate receptors or to prevent the activation of receptors. Further, drugs can alter how well a neurotransmitter binds to and activates a receptor.

Chronic drug use can lead to dependence, tolerance, or sensitization. Drug dependence is shown when abstention from a drug causes withdrawal effects. Dependence occurs as either physiological dependence or psychological dependence. Users exhibit tolerance when they require higher doses to achieve similar effects. Tolerance occurs as pharmacokinetic tolerance, pharmacodynamic tolerance, or behavioral tolerance. Sensitization consists of an increase in responsiveness to a drug over time.

Key Terms

Absorption 102
Liberation 106
Distribution 107
Bioavailability 107
Blood–brain barrier 107
Passive diffusion through
blood–brain barrier 108
Active transport through
blood–brain barrier 109
Nonspecific
binding 109
Biotransformation 110
Metabolite 110
Phase I biotransformation 110
Phase II biotransformation 110
Personalized medicine 111
First-pass metabolism 111
Active metabolite 111
Prodrug 111

Elimination 112
Elimination rate 112
Half-life 112
First-order kinetics 112
Zero-order kinetics 112
Pharmacodynamics 113
Binding affinity 117
Receptor efficacy 117
Agonist 121
Antagonist 125
Partial agonist 125
Competitive
antagonist 125
Noncompetitive
antagonist 125
Allosteric regulator 127
Positive modulator 127
Negative modulator 127
Neurotoxins 128

Environmental
neurotoxicology 128
Tolerance 129
Pharmacokinetic tolerance
(or drug dispositional
tolerance) 129
Pharmacodynamic
tolerance 130
Behavioral tolerance 130
Conditioned (or contingent)
tolerance 130
Cross tolerance 130
Sensitization 130
Dependence 130
Withdrawal syndrome 130
Physical dependence 130
Psychological
dependence 130

Visit the Student Study Site at **study.sagepub.com/prus2e** to access additional study tools, including eFlashcards, web quizzes, video resources, web resources, SAGE journal articles, and more.

Drugs of Abuse

JAMES OLDS'S UNEXPECTED DISCOVERY

James Olds was firmly convinced when he received a PhD in psychology from Harvard University in 1952 that all valid psychological theories could be successfully linked to nervous system functioning. To further his already promising career, Olds believed he needed only to expand his experimental skill set in order to evaluate nervous system processes. Toward this end, Olds gained a postdoctoral fellowship to study under famed psychologist Donald Hebb at McGill University in Montreal. This work would lead to a critical discovery in the field of neuroscience.

(Continued)

(Continued)

Under Hebb, Olds endeavored to study the reticular activating system by quickly contriving a rudimentary brain electrode out of wire and surgically installing it into the brain of a laboratory rat. After the rat recovered from the surgery, Olds allowed the rat to wander around a box as he toggled the connected electrode on and off. Then Olds noticed something curious. The rat had developed a preference for areas of the box associated with the activated electrode. In fact, Olds found that he could purposely attract the rat to different areas of the box with this device.

Olds's electrode had missed the reticular activating system, but instead led to the discovery of the brain's *reward center*. This accidental finding led to a fundamental understanding of a key motivational process for behavior and identified an important biological property for drugs of abuse.

SOURCE: From Olds, 1956, and Thompson, 1999.

As first presented in Chapter 1, psychoactive drugs broadly fall into two categories: those intended for instrumental use and those intended for recreational use. If you recall, the major distinction between such drugs is a person's intent or motivation for using the substance. This chapter expands on the use of recreational drugs to consider problem drug use leading to abuse and dependence.

Review! A person uses a drug *instrumentally* for a socially acceptable purpose, but uses a drug *recreationally* entirely to experience the drug's effects. (Chapter 1.)

Regulatory Agencies and Drug Classification

Harrison Narcotics Act U.S. federal law passed in 1915 that restricted the sale of narcotics

Controlled Substances Act U.S. federal law passed in 1970 that regulates sale and possession of drugs identified as controlled substances

In addition to describing drugs based on their intended use, we also characterize drugs by their legal status. Laws at the state and national levels limit the availability of drugs deemed to have a significant risk of abuse. One of the first national regulations on drugs of abuse was the **Harrison Narcotics Act** passed in 1915, which restricted the sale of narcotics, primarily opioid drugs, to medical uses. More important, law enforcement officials interpreted these medical uses to exclude treating withdrawal symptoms in opioid dependence.

In 1970, the **Controlled Substances Act** first described drugs of abuse as *controlled substances*. The act required the legal regulation of certain drugs with abuse potential, and it led to a classification system of **controlled substances schedules** for ranking drugs by abuse potential and proven medical use. This act led to a classification system that still exists today. **Table 5.1** shows a list of selected drugs of abuse, and their schedules, regulated in the United States.

The U.S. Drug Enforcement Administration (DEA) uses five schedules to categorize drugs of abuse. Lower schedule numbers indicate greater abuse potential than higher schedule numbers, based on the DEA's assessment of these drugs. All drugs scheduled II through V have established medical uses. For example, the DEA assigned schedule V to codeine, an opioid drug considered to have less abuse potential than drugs in other categories. Codeine is a key ingredient in prescription strength cough syrups.

According to the DEA, schedule II controlled substances have high abuse potential, but also have legitimate medical uses. For example, the DEA assigns cocaine as schedule II because of its legitimate medical uses, such as acting as a local anaesthetic. Schedule I controlled substances are classified as having high abuse potential and no legitimate medical uses. For example, the DEA scheduled the hallucinogenic drug lysergic acid diethylamide (LSD) as schedule I, based on the agency's view of LSD's high abuse potential and lack of medical usefulness. For similar reasons, the DEA also lists cannabis as a schedule I controlled substance.

Other countries use different scheduling systems for controlled substances. For example, the United Kingdom assesses the harm caused by abused drugs according

Controlled substances schedules A scheduling system mandated by the Controlled Substances Act that classifies a drug according to its drug abuse potential and medical use potential

TABLE 5.1 ● Selected Controlled Substances

Schedule	Controlled Substance
I	Heroin
	LSD
	Marijuana (cannabis)
II	Cocaine
	Morphine
	Phencyclidine (PCP)
III	Ketamine
IV	Alprazolam (Xanax)
V	Codeine

SOURCE: Adapted from the DEA Controlled Substances Schedules, www.deadiversion.usdoj.gov/schedules/index.html.

to three classification levels. Class A drugs cause the most harm and carry the stiffest penalties for possession and drug dealing. These drugs include MDMA (Ecstasy), cocaine, and psychedelic mushrooms. Class C drugs cause the least harm and carry the lightest penalties for possession and drug dealing. This class includes barbiturates, ketamine, and gamma-hydroxybutyric acid (GHB). Class B drugs have a moderate potential for harm. Although marijuana regulations have relaxed in most countries, including many states in the United States, the United Kingdom elevated marijuana from class C to class B in 2009.

The United Kingdom presents different considerations for certain drugs than the United States. For example, the United Kingdom classified GHB as a class C compound, whereas the United States classified GHB as a schedule I controlled substance. Further, the United Kingdom classified marijuana as a class B compound, but the United States classified marijuana as a schedule I controlled substance.

Although the controlled substances schedules represent a standard labeling system for drug-use risk, disagreements for drugs schedules occur among practitioners and researchers. A well-known example of this is cannabis, which we commonly refer to as marijuana. According to the U.S. government, marijuana is a schedule I substance, indicating high abuse potential with no established medical uses. Yet many states allow the use of marijuana for medical uses, placing state laws in conflict with federal law. Thus, many states would not agree with classifying marijuana as a schedule I substance.

Critics also question the methods used for scheduling drugs. One area of concern regards a slow response to new drugs of abuse. In particular, many potentially dangerous so-called *club drugs* are not currently scheduled substances. The DEA schedules drugs only after accumulating sufficient scientific evidence and law enforcement drug-use statistics. Thus, drug scheduling can take years. Adding to this, clandestine drug suppliers develop designer drugs, substances designed to circumvent existing drug schedules. Consider the designer drug 1,4-butanediol, also known as *one comma four*—this compound is a prodrug for GHB (Carai et al., 2002; Satta, Dimitrijevic, & Manev, 2003). The DEA lists GHB as a schedule I substance but doesn't list 1,4-butanediol.

Review! A prodrug is a physiologically weak or inactive compound metabolized in the body to produce an active drug. (Chapter 4.)

Nutt and colleagues (2007) offered an alternative approach for drug scheduling. They defined *harm* as consisting of physical harm, addiction, or societal harm. *Physical harm*, in their approach, included damage to the body, such as impairment of heart or liver function. *Addiction* consisted of an inability to stop taking a drug, along with other factors used in the clinical diagnosis of substance dependence. *Societal harm* ranged from harm to family and other social relationships to costs associated with health care and law enforcement. After developing these definitions, an expert panel rated 20 abused drugs according to harm subgroupings. **Table 5.2** shows ratings from this study for selected drugs.

The harm assessment by Nutt and colleagues reveals many discrepancies with regulatory scheduling. Although the drugs heroin and cocaine rated highly for harm, the drugs GHB and MDMA (Ecstasy) rated low. In contrast, the United States classifies GHB and MDMA as schedule I substances, and the United Kingdom classifies MDMA as class A, but GHB as class C. Two noncontrolled substances, alcohol and tobacco, also made the list. The harm-assessment study rated alcohol as the fourth most harmful substance and tobacco, which includes nicotine, as the ninth most harmful substance. Studies such as these have the potential to guide regulatory changes for controlling drugs of abuse.

TABLE 5.2 ● Harm Ratings for Selected Drugs of Abuse

Drug	Physical Harm	Addiction	Societal Harm
Heroin	2.8	3.0	2.5
Cocaine	2.3	2.8	2.2
Alcohol	1.4	1.9	2.2
Tobacco	1.2	2.2	1.4
Inhaled solvents	1.3	1.0	1.5
LSD	1.1	1.2	1.3
GHB	0.9	1.2	1.3
MDMA (Ecstasy)	1.1	1.1	1.1

NOTE: Higher scores = most harmful.

SOURCE: Based on data from Nutt et al., 2007

STOP & CHECK

1. How might the DEA schedule a drug with high abuse potential and no perceived medical uses?

2. How does the harm scheduling for MDMA offered by Nutt and colleagues (2007) differ from the DEA's controlled substances scheduling?

1. The DEA schedules drugs with these characteristics as schedule I. **2.** Although the DEA considers MDMA a schedule I controlled substance, MDMA rated low for harm according to the study by Nutt and colleagues.

Clinical Definitions and the Diagnosis of Drug Addiction

Although regulatory agencies classify substances based on abuse potential and potential medical uses, clinicians use precise criteria to define and diagnose drug addiction. Early clinical definitions of addiction focused on the development of tolerance, physical dependence, and craving (National Institute on Alcohol Abuse and Alcoholism, 1995). **Craving** consists of a strong urge to use a drug. These early definitions describe an addiction to some drugs but not others. They clearly apply to heroin and alcohol, which produce tolerance, manifest physical withdrawal symptoms, and elicit powerful cravings. Yet these definitions may fail to classify a drug such as cocaine as addictive substances because it causes few physical withdrawal symptoms. Clinicians consider addiction as a chronically relapsing disorder that may require years of treatment. **Relapse** consists of a return to a chronic drug use state that meets the clinical features of a substance use disorder.

CravingA strong urge to use a drug

RelapseReturn to a chronic drug use state that meets the clinical features of a substance use disorder

Review! Tolerance is an adaptation to a drug that requires a user to take escalating doses to achieve desired drug effects. (Chapter 4.)

Review! A person demonstrates a dependence when he or she needs the drug to function normally and when removal of the drug causes withdrawal symptoms. (Chapter 4.)

More recent clinical definitions of drug addiction are provided in the fifth edition of the American Psychiatric Association's *Diagnostic and Statistical Manual of Mental Disorders* (DSM-5) (2013) and the World Health Organization's *International Statistical Classification of Diseases and Related Health Problems* (ICD-10) (2011). The definitions described in these diagnostic manuals are similar, so only the DSM criteria are described here.

The DSM refers to addiction as a *substance use disorder*, which is defined as "a cluster of cognitive, behavioral, and physiological symptoms indicating that the individual continues using the substance despite significant substance-related problems" (p. 483). These symptoms include tolerance, withdrawal, a persistent desire to reduce use of the substance, significant time spent in drug seeking and taking, replacing important activities with substance use, and continued use despite knowledge of social, physical, or psychological problems.

It is important to note that the DSM differs from earlier clinical definitions because it considers drug use that persists despite a strong desire to stop. Furthermore, the DSM recognizes that drug use may continue despite the user's knowledge of physical or psychological harm to oneself and the toll that drug use takes on valuable social relationships and occupational activities.

According to the DSM's definition, both cocaine and cannabis can produce substance use disorders. Cocaine has the ability to produce strong cravings, produce tolerance, and compete with valuable social and occupational activities and other important natural reinforcers. Users who develop a dependence on cannabis most often report "persistent desire or unsuccessful efforts to reduce or cease use" along with other DSM symptoms such as continued use despite health problems and craving cannabis during withdrawal (Coffey et al., 2002).

The DSM addresses remission according to different categories after a diagnosis for a substance use disorder. These remission categories consist of "'in early remission,' 'in sustained remission,' 'on maintenance therapy,' and 'in a controlled environment'" (p. 484). In general, *early remission* corresponds to an individual meeting none of the criteria for a substance use disorder for a period of a few months to less than a year. *Sustained remission* refers to meeting none of these criteria for a year or longer. *Maintenance therapy* indicates that the individual does not meet the criteria for a substance use disorder while the individual is participating in a treatment program. In particular, maintenance therapy can refer to a medication intended to address drug craving or ward off withdrawal symptoms, such as an opioid medication like buprenorphine. Remission might also be occurring in a *controlled environment*, such as living in an environment where drugs are not available. The last two remission types caution that an individual might relapse without taking a particular medication or after leaving a treatment facility.

Theoretical Models and the Features of Drug Addiction

Theoretical **models of drug addiction** attempt to characterize and explain compulsive drug use. They derive from scientific research and can be used to form scientific hypotheses for conducting further studies to learn more about drug addiction. The characteristics and theoretical reasons for addiction derived from addiction models may differ from those described by clinical definitions, such as those described above from the DSM-5. Though we can learn about drug addiction from the DSM-5, the primary purpose of the DSM-5 or any other diagnostic manual is to develop a correct diagnosis for the disorder. Correctly diagnosing a disorder means that a clinician can design a treatment plan for his or her patient. By developing models, researchers attempt to understand the causes and factors for facilitating addictive behavior.

Models of drug addiction Scientific attempts to characterize and explain compulsive drug use

Disease Model of Drug Addiction

The **disease model** characterizes drug addiction as a disease (**Table 5.3**). To put this in perspective, consider the definition for a disease offered by *Stedman's Medical Dictionary* (Stedman, 1999): "An interruption, cessation, or disorder of body function, system, or organ." When considering drug addiction as a disease, one may thus determine how drugs of abuse may interrupt, cease, or disrupt functions in the body. Diseases also have causes, such as a pathogen, and the degree of susceptibility to disease may depend on one's potential to have a predisposition for the disease.

Disease model Model that characterizes drug addiction as a disease

Those who advocate this model affirm that the substance serves as the cause of the disease that leads to long-lasting changes to biological processes. Thus, just as a disease may disrupt physiological processes, drugs also can disrupt neurobiological

TABLE 5.3 ● Addiction Model Characteristics	
Addiction Model	**Characteristics**
Disease	Drug addiction fits the medical definition of a disease.
Drive theory	Drugs elicit powerful positive reinforcing effects that drive individuals to seek and use drugs.
Opponent-process theory	Individuals seek drugs to avoid or remove withdrawal effects.
Incentive salience	Stimuli associated with drug use receive salient incentive value. These stimuli then command a user's attention and produce a motivational state for drug seeking.

SOURCE: © Cengage Learning 2014.

processes causing addictive behaviors. From this viewpoint, we can think of relapse as the reemergence of the biological processes underlying addiction that result an abstinent individual's beginning substance use again.

Further, one may possess a predisposition for drug addiction, just as one may have a predisposition for other diseases. In addition to drawing connections between a disease's characteristics and addictive behavior, advocates of this model argue that defining addiction as a disease allows medical treatment of the disease. The goal of treatment, then, is to manage the disease. The disease model is also a central perspective for abstinence-based 12-step recovery programs such as Alcoholics Anonymous and Narcotics Anonymous, which are discussed later in this chapter.

Associative Learning
Principles Used in Addiction Models

Other drug-addiction models focus on associative learning principles to characterize the behavioral features of drug use. **Associative learning** is the process by which an organism learns associations between stimuli or between behaviors and stimuli. Much of associative learning theory comes from principles of operant conditioning and classical conditioning.

During operant conditioning, consequences modify the occurrence and form of behavior (Skinner, 1938). The term **reinforcement** refers to a process in which the resulting consequence from a response increases the frequency of future responses. Said another way, reinforcing outcomes strengthen behavioral tendencies.

We also use the terms *negative* and *positive* when discussing reinforcers. In this usage, *negative* refers to the removal of a stimulus, and *positive* refers to the addition of a stimulus. An example of a positive reinforcement context is a hungry rat pressing

Associative learning Process by which an organism learns associations between stimuli or between behaviors and stimuli

Reinforcement Process in which the resulting consequence from a response increases the frequency of future responses

a lever to earn food pellets. The food pellets serve as positive reinforcers. An example of a negative reinforcement context is a rat pressing a lever to remove some of type of aversive stimulation such as a bright light. Removal of the bright light serves as a negative reinforcer. *Extinction* refers to a decline in responding as the result of failing to achieve reinforcers.

A **conditioned stimulus** may develop from presenting stimuli in the presence of a stimulus involved in an associative learning process. Using one of the previous examples, a tone might acquire reinforcing properties if the tone repeatedly occurs in the presence of food. If a hungry rat then emits responses in order to activate the tone, we refer to the tone as a *conditioned reinforcer*. Conditioning also takes place in classical conditioning procedures, which are described following.

Associative learning may occur during certain conditions or in environmental contexts. We describe one type of condition as a **discriminative stimulus**, which is a stimulus that, when present, signals the availability of reinforcement. Reinforcers are unavailable when the discriminative stimulus is absent. For the hungry rat just described, a discriminative stimulus might consist of a soft tone during experimental procedures. Lever presses result in food reinforcers when the tone is on but not when the tone is off.

Classical conditioning procedures describe how stimuli can elicit behavioral responses. The behaviors occur reflexively, whereas operant conditioned behaviors occur as a result of meeting past consequences. Described another way, classical conditioning consists of stimuli eliciting responses, whereas operant conditioning consists of responses producing stimulus outcomes.

Russian physiologist Ivan Pavlov (Pavlov & Anrep, 1927) first described behavior in terms of classical conditioning relationships. First, we recognize that many unlearned behaviors exist, such as Pavlov's description of food in the mouth eliciting salivation. We do not learn to salivate when food is in mouth; this is simply a natural reflex. Second, Pavlov found that associations can develop, through conditioning, between other stimuli and those that produce natural reflexes. This work led to the following terms to define stimulus–response relationships.

An *unconditioned stimulus* (UCS) consists of a stimulus that elicits a reflexive response, which is referred to as an *unconditioned response* (UCR). Food in the mouth serves as a UCS, and salivation serves as a UCR. A stimulus not part of this association, such as a light or tone, will not naturally elicit salivation; given this lack of association, we refer to such stimuli as *neutral stimuli*. By repeatedly pairing a neutral stimulus with a UCS, the neutral stimulus may incur associative properties that enable the stimulus alone to elicit salivation. When this occurs, the stimulus serves as a *conditioned stimulus* (CS); to describe salivation as elicited in this conditioned associative process, salivation is identified as a *conditioned response* (CR).

The ability to condition a stimulus is subject to the principle of latent inhibition. **Latent inhibition** consists of a resistant or slower conditioning process that occurs from using a familiar stimulus as the neutral stimulus in an associative learning process. In this case, *familiar* suggests that the stimulus already belongs to at least one other associative learning process. Incorporating a familiar stimulus into a new associative learning process tends to be comparatively slower than incorporating an entirely novel stimulus into an associative learning process.

Conditioned stimulus A stimulus that acquires the behavioral controlling properties of another stimulus that is involved in an associated learning process

Discriminative stimulus A stimulus that, when present, signals the availability of reinforcement

Latent inhibition A resistant or slower conditioning process that occurs from using a familiar stimulus as the neutral stimulus in an associative learning process

Incentive salience
Attribution of salient motivational value to otherwise neutral stimuli

Conditioning may also occur for motivational states. In particular, a motivational concept called **incentive salience** serves as an important part of modern drug-addiction theory: it is the attribution of salient motivational value to otherwise neutral stimuli. These attributions can occur through associations of neutral stimuli with rewarding stimuli. When presented, incentivized stimuli command an individual's attention and elicit a motivation to pursue these and associated stimuli. The incentive-salience model for drug addiction, described later, utilizes this concept to explain compulsive drug use, where the presentation of stimuli incentivized through associations with drug use may motivate users to engage in drug seeking. The incentive-salience model also relates incentive-salience function to neural systems (Robinson & Berridge, 2003).

Goal-directed behavior Behavior that occurs when an organism engages in learned behaviors in order to achieve a desired goal.

We also have goal-directed behaviors, which may play an important role in decision making. **Goal-directed behavior** occurs when an organism engages in learned behaviors in order to achieve a desired goal. The topic of goal-directed behavior encompasses a large area of study approached from different areas of psychology, including cognitive and social psychology. Many frameworks for explaining and characterizing goal-directed behavior use associative learning principles, particularly in reference to drug-seeking behavior.

Many theorists use associative learning principles to characterize goal-directed behavior, particularly when describing this behavior during drug seeking. In this context, conditioned associations between responses and outcomes govern goal-directed behavior (de Wit & Dickinson, 2009). Neuroscientists tend to relate goal-directed behavior to the brain's reward system and the involvement of these pathways with the brain's learning and memory systems (Goto & Grace, 2005; Pennartz, Ito, Verschure, Battaglia, & Robbins, 2011).

Drive, Opponent-Process Theory, and Incentive-Salience Models of Drug Addiction

Drive theory of drug addiction Repeated drug use causes a motivation, or drive, to engage in seeking a drug's positive reinforcing effects

In 1952, Abraham Wikler provided one of the first drug-addiction models to consider drug effects as behavioral variables. Based on studies with individuals addicted to opioid drugs, Wikler stated that drug-addicted individuals developed a drive to achieve a drug's positive reinforcing effects (Table 5.3). We refer to this as the **drive theory of drug addiction**. This drive consists of a motivation to seek a drug's effects. Moreover, the withdrawal effects from a drug serve to strengthen an individual's motivation to obtain and use the drug.

Opponent-process theory of drug addiction The effects of a drug are automatically counteracted by opposing actions in the body

Solomon and Corbit (1974) offered the opponent-process theory as another explanation for drug use during addiction (Table 5.3). According to the **opponent-process theory of drug addiction**, the effects of a drug are automatically counteracted by opposing actions in the body. These opposing actions may serve to attain homeostasis or return the brain to normal functioning. During addiction, the brain may, for example, elicit anhedonic effects to counteract a drug's hedonic (i.e., pleasurable) effects.

As illustrated in **Figure 5.1**, the sum of a drug's effects and its opposing processes defines an individual's subjective experience. If a drug's effects outweigh those from opposing processes, then an individual will experience the drug's effects. However, if effects generated from opposing processes significantly outweigh drug effects, then an individual will experience withdrawal effects. A normalized state occurs when drug effects equally balance against opponent-process effects.

The type of reinforcement governing addictive behavior also distinguishes between Wikler's drive model and Solomon and Corbit's opponent-process theory. Unlike drive theory, the opponent-process theory considers that addictive drug use occurs partly to remove or prevent withdrawal symptoms. Thus, during the development of addiction,

FIGURE 5.1 ● According to the opponent-process theory of drug addiction, opposing processes counter the effects of an abused drug. Before addiction occurs (left panel), few if any processes counteract a drug's effects. During addiction, opponent processes counteract a drug's effects. Equally balancing drug effects and opposing processes lead to a normal state (top, right panel), whereas overpowering drug effects can overcome opponent processes (middle, right panel). Withdrawal effects occur when opposing processes occur in the absence of drug effects (bottom, right panel). See text for further information.

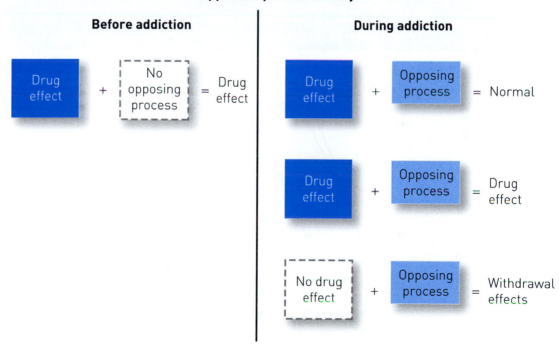

SOURCE: © Cengage Learning 2014.

BOX 5.1 SELF-ADMINISTRATION

Self-administration procedures use drugs as reinforcers for operant responding in animals. In a typical self-administration procedure, an animal learns to respond to an operandum such as a lever to receive an injection of the drug. The drug is usually delivered intravenously through a surgically implanted intravenous catheter. When drugs serve as positive reinforcing stimuli, drug injections alone are entirely capable of initiating self-administration responses. For example, if a cocaine injection occurred whenever a rat pressed a lever, then cocaine's reinforcing effects would occasion further lever pressing.

The self-administration procedure provides an important analogue for human drug use. As reviewed in this chapter, chronic use of an abused drug incorporates brain systems important for learning. In the self-administration

FIGURE 1 ● Break points consist of the maximum number of lever presses an animal will emit for a drug injection. The *y*-axis shows the final reinforcement ratio, defined as the total number of lever presses needed to earn a reinforcer, and the *x*-axis shows the dosage of drug administered per injection.

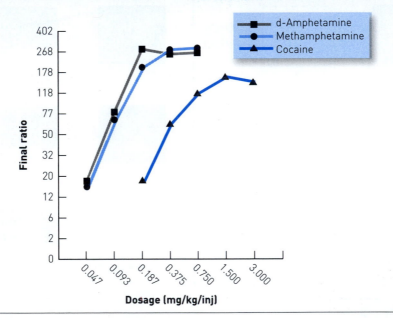

SOURCE: Adapted from Richardson & Roberts, 1996.

procedures, animals also learn to take drugs of abuse. Beyond this, self-administration procedures provide measurements of a drug's reinforcing strength. In doing so, self-administration procedures provide an indication of a drug's potential for causing addiction.

We measure a drug's reinforcing strength by determining its *break point,* the maximum amount of response effort an organism will devote toward receiving an administration of drug. Break-point studies normally employ *progressive-ratio reinforcement schedules*, which gradually increase the number of responses necessary to achieve a drug administration.

Figure 1 shows data from rats that self-administered any of several psychostimulant drugs on a progressive-ratio schedule (Richardson & Roberts, 1996). For d-amphetamine and methamphetamine, rats pressed the lever as many as 268 times to receive an injection. For cocaine, rats pressed the lever as many as 178 times to receive a drug injection. These maximum numbers of lever presses define each drug's break point at a given dose.

Researchers also employ other drugs to modify self-administration. For example, Maric and colleagues (2012) administered the hunger-stimulating hormone *ghrelin* to rats

FIGURE 2 ● The hunger-stimulating hormone ghrelin increased the break point for self-administered heroin. The *y*-axis shows the break-point value compared to baseline responding, and the *x*-axis shows the amount of ghrelin provided to the rats.

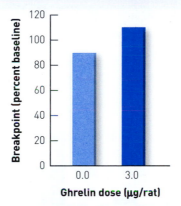

SOURCE: Adapted from Maric, T., Sedki, F., Ronfard, B., Chafetz, D. and Shalev, U. (2012), A limited role for ghrelin in heroin self-administration and food deprivation-induced reinstatement of heroin seeking in rats. *Addiction Biology*, 17: 613–622. doi: 10.1111/j.1369-1600.2011.00396.x.

(Continued)

(Continued)

trained to self-administer heroin (Figure 2). In this study, ghrelin administration increased the break point for heroin, suggesting that ghrelin enhanced heroin's reinforcing effects.

Researchers also use self-administration procedures to assess **reinstatement**, the recurrence of drug self-administration responding after a period of extinction. Reinstatement may provide an analogue of drug relapse in humans. The general procedure for reinstatement goes as follows. After animals learn to self-administer a drug, researchers disable the operandum, resulting in an extinction period when responding no longer achieves a drug infusion. Over time, responding reduces substantially. At this point, a researcher may cause responding to occur by giving the animal an injection of drug (drug-induced reinstatement), eliciting a stimulus previously paired with drug delivery (cue-induced reinstatement), or delivering a brief shock or other aversive stimulus (stress-induced reinstatement).

In one of the first demonstrations of drug-induced reinstatement, Gerber and Stretch (Gerber & Stretch, 1975) extinguished self-administration responding for cocaine by replacing cocaine with saline in the chamber's infusion syringe. After responding decreased to a low level, these researchers gave the monkeys an infusion of the psychostimulant drug d-amphetamine, which resulted in a return to self-administration responding, despite having still having saline in the syringe. Figure 3 provides the findings from this experiment.

FIGURE 3 ● A presession infusion of d-amphetamine caused monkeys trained to self-administer cocaine to resume self-administration responding. For the data shown, the infusion syringe contained only saline. The left bar shows self-administration responding, and the right bar shows self-administration responding after an injection of d-amphetamine (1.0 mg/kg).

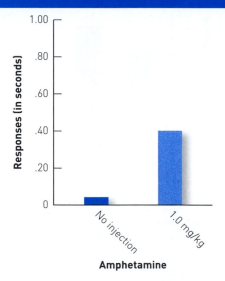

SOURCE: Data from Gerber and Stretch, 1975.

motivations for drug use can shift from achieving reinforcing effects, in a positive reinforcement context, to ridding or avoiding withdrawal symptoms, in a negative reinforcement context.

The **incentive-salience model** states that drug addiction occurs after a shift from *liking* the effects of a drug to *wanting* the effects of a drug. *Wanting* occurs in an incentive-salience context, whereby stimuli associated with drug use command attention and elicit a salient motivational state toward pursuing the drug (Robinson & Berridge, 2003). In a technical sense, *wanting* in this model represents the process of developing and expressing incentive salience, whereas the term *craving*, in a basic sense, simply refers to a desire to use a drug (Sayette et al., 2000). *Liking* refers to the enjoyment of a drug's effects, which, according to this model, fails to uniquely explain drug addiction. In fact, the incentive-salience model may explain why addicted users may *want* a drug more while, as tolerance develops, *liking* the drug less (Robinson & Berridge, 2003).

Incentive salience may also offer an explanation for relapse in drug addiction. Through conditioning, such incentivized stimuli may serve as reminders of former drug use; when encountered, they may implicitly engage motivational states for drug use. As described in **Box 5.1**, researchers study conditions that reinstate drug self-administration responses in animals in an effort to better understand why relapse occurs.

Incentive-salience model Drug addiction occurs after a shift from "liking" the effects of a drug to "wanting" the effects

STOP & CHECK

1. Compare the clinical definitions for addiction for cocaine.

2. How does the opponent-process theory of drug addiction account for drug withdrawal?

3. According to the incentive-salience model, what are the characteristics of drug wanting?

1. Early definitions for addiction may fail to consider cocaine as addictive because it has few physical withdrawal symptoms. However, the modern DSM definition for substance dependence incorporates other features of cocaine use, including an inability to quit despite wanting to. **2.** During drug addiction, the body automatically elicits opposing processes to regain homeostasis and normal brain functioning. When a drug is absent, effects resulting from these unchecked opposing processes occur as withdrawal effects. **3.** Drug wanting consists of a motivational state elicited by stimuli incentivized through associations with drug use.

Drugs of Abuse and Reward Circuitry

Drugs of abuse act directly or indirectly on the brain's reward circuitry (**Figure 5.2**). The key structures along this circuit consist of the ventral tegmental area and the nucleus accumbens. Mesolimbic dopamine neurons largely make up this circuit.

FIGURE 5.2 ● The *reward circuit* is made up of mesolimbic dopamine neurons that originate from the ventral tegmental area and terminate in the nucleus accumbens. The release of dopamine in the nucleus accumbens leads to rewarding effects. GABA neurons inhibit the activity of these dopamine neurons via the activation of inhibitory GABA receptors on these dopamine neurons. Some GABA neurons form a negative feedback loop from the nucleus accumbens to the ventral tegmental area.

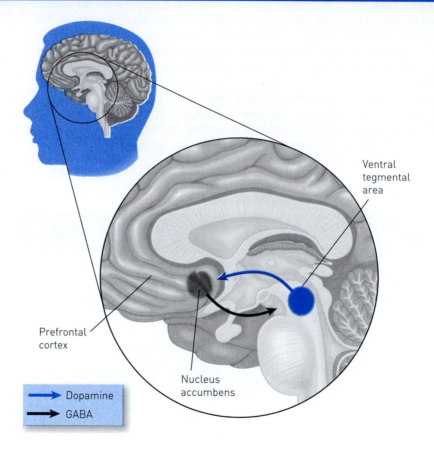

Ventral
tegmental
area

Prefrontal
cortex

Nucleus
accumbens

→ Dopamine
→ GABA

Review! The axons in the mesolimbic dopamine pathway terminate in the nucleus accumbens as well as other limbic system structures, including the amygdala and hippocampus. (Chapter 3.)

As described in the chapter opening, we attribute the discovery of the brain reward circuit to James Olds. In collaboration with Peter Milner, a graduate student also working in this lab, Olds published his discovery in 1954 (Olds & Milner, 1954). The report they published provided an assessment of electrodes placed in different parts of the septal forebrain area.

To demonstrate these reinforcing effects, Olds and Milner designed an operant chamber equipped with a lever; when pressed, the lever activated the brain electrode. In this way, the researchers provided an apparatus by which rats governed the number of times they received electrical stimulation (**Figure 5.3**). We now use the term **intracranial self-stimulation** to describe a procedure in which an organism's responses activate a brain electrode, with the assumption that responding continues because the electrode produces reinforcing effects.

Intracranial self-stimulation A procedure in which an organism's responses activate a brain electrode

FIGURE 5.3 ● In the seminal experiment by Olds and Milner, a rat learned to press a lever at a high rate to achieve the reinforcing effects produced by the electrodes. This electrode placement likely activated dopamine axons along the brain's reward circuit.

Since this original study, Olds and many other researchers further investigated this newly discovered system of reward in the brain, including studies in a host of different organisms, including humans. Olds wrote a paper reviewing the constellation of findings about this system some years later, in 1962, after his discovery (Olds, 1962). Taking a look at all of these findings, Olds noted that greater reinforcing effects occurred from electrodes placed between the *medial forebrain bundle* and an area found around the midbrain and hindbrain. We now know that mesolimbic dopamine axons traveling to the nucleus accumbens pass through the medial forebrain bundle.

The discovery by Olds and Milner revealed a system or circuit for producing rewarding effects, but the researchers lacked sufficient information to understand the nature of along this circuit. In fact, the notion that chemical molecules, rather than electricity, were the basis for communication between neurons was only recently settled. In biological psychology textbooks (e.g., Garrett, 2015), we learn about Otto Loewi's 1921 experiment to demonstrate chemical transmission from neurons. Otto Loewi took two frogs, exposed the chest cavity in each, and in only one of the frogs electrically stimulated the vagus nerve that runs to the heart. Vagus nerve stimulation decreased the frog's heart rate; when the heart rate decreased, Loewi collected fluid around the heart and applied the fluid around the other frog's heart. The other frog's heart rate also decreased—thus, he concluded that chemical molecules, rather than simply ions in an electrical sense, must be the mode of communication between neurons.[1]

Yet we don't typically learn from biological psychology textbooks that Loewi failed to replicate this experiment, at least at first, and that others failed as well. His methods were criticized, and the discovery was written off as an anomaly. A key chemical in the substance he had transferred was eventually identified as acetylcholine, a chemical known at the time to rapidly degrade in the presence of acetylcholinesterase.

This finding led to a hypothesis concerning the irreproducibility of Loewi's frog experiment, and the confirmation finally came years later. In 1926, Loewi added an acetylcholinesterase inhibitor to his experiment. This prevented the catabolism of acetylcholine and finally led to the same inhibition of heart rate upon transfer of the substance surrounding the heart of the frog who received stimulation of the vagus nerve (Loewi & Navratil, 1926; Rubin, 2007). We now regard this discovery as critical in determining that chemical neurotransmitters, not electrical conductance, were the messengers of neuronal communication. However, studies purporting electrical conductance as this mode of communication still persisted into the late 1940s (e.g., Eccles, 1948), but the issue was finally settled in the mid-1950s (e.g., Eccles, Fatt, & Koketsu, 1954; Rubin, 2007).

Thus, the discovery by Olds and Milner in 1954 came at a time when the study of modern theories on neurotransmission were in their infancy. A few years after this discovery, Kathleen Montagu reported the existence of dopamine in the brain (Montagu, 1957). In 1958, Arvid Carlsson first reported that dopamine likely had some functional significance for brain function as it was affected by treatment with the drug reserpine (Carlsson, Lindqvist, Magnusson, & Waldeck, 1958). Then, during the 1960s and early 1970s, new research techniques revealed the brain's major dopamine pathways.

---

1 We now know that some synapses are in fact electrical, but most are chemical.

Today we know that reinforcing effects can occur from increased dopamine release in the nucleus accumbens. Under natural conditions, nucleus accumbens dopamine levels elevate in the presence of stimuli that predict positive outcomes. Such stimuli include food and sex as well as complex social or cultural reinforcers.

For example, Hajnal, Smith, and Norgren (2004) used a microdialysis procedure to assess nucleus accumbens dopamine level changes elicited by food. At times during the procedure, rats consumed a sweet-tasting sucrose liquid food mix. When the sucrose mix was consumed, nucleus accumbens dopamine levels increased; dopamine levels returned to baseline levels after consumption of the food ceased (**Figure 5.4**).

We should also note that increased dopamine concentrations in the nucleus do more than elicit reinforcing effects. One perspective suggests that enhanced dopamine signaling is related to latent inhibition effects. De Leonibus, Verheij, Mele, and Cools (2006) used microdialysis to examine nucleus accumbens dopamine levels in rats before and after introducing a novel or a familiar rat into the testing chamber. When the introduced rat was novel—that is, the experimental rat previously never met the introduced rat—dopamine levels increased in the nucleus accumbens. However, dopamine levels did not increase when familiar rats were introduced (**Figure 5.5**).

Many drugs of abuse activate reward circuits, achieving dopamine elevations far above those produced by natural reinforcers. For example, the psychostimulant drugs cocaine and amphetamine directly enhance dopamine release from axon terminals in the nucleus accumbens. In doing so, they can elevate nucleus accumbens dopamine levels many times greater than those achieved by natural reinforcers and novel stimuli (Carboni, Imperato, Perezzani, & Di Chiara, 1989; De Leonibus et al., 2006; Hajnal et al., 2004; Sharp, Zetterstrom, Ljungberg, & Ungerstedt, 1987). Other abused substances may indirectly alter the activity of these dopamine pathways, such as by

FIGURE 5.4 ● Sucrose consumption elicited significant dopamine level increases in the nucleus accumbens in rats as revealed by microdialysis. M = molality, an index of concentration.

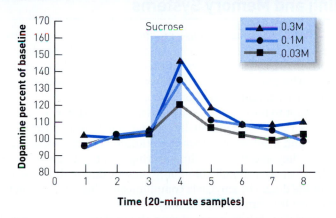

SOURCE: Adapted from Hajnal, Smith, & Norgren, 2004.

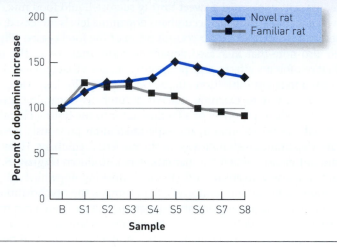

FIGURE 5.5 ● The presentation of novel rats led to significant increases in nucleus accumbens dopamine levels, whereas the presentation of familiar rats did not increase nucleus accumbens dopamine levels.

SOURCE: Adapted from De Leonibus, Verheij, Mele, & Cools (2006).

reducing GABA's inhibitory effects on mesolimbic dopamine neurons, as is the case with opioid drugs (van Zessen, Phillips, Budygin, & Stuber, 2012; Xiao & Ye, 2008) (more on this in Chapter 9). Rewarding effects may also be produced by activating glutamate receptors in the nucleus accumbens (Koob & Volkow, 2009; LaLumiere & Kalivas, 2008).

Drug Abuse and Changes to Learning and Memory Systems

Acute administration of a drug of abuse produces reinforcing effects by activating reward circuitry, as described in the previous section. Chronic administration of an abused drug leads to changes in other brain systems, especially those involved in learning and memory. The interconnected structures that facilitate learning and memory include the amygdala, thalamus, prefrontal cortex, and the hippocampus. Each of these structures adapt to the chronic use of abused drugs (**Figure 5.6**).

The amygdala is a structure traditionally associated with fear and anxiety, yet it also supports learning and memory by associating stimuli with emotional events, such as experiencing rewarding effects from a drug. During chronic drug use, the **amygdala** forms associations between stimuli commonly present during drug use and the reinforcing effects of the drug. The amygdala communicates this information to two other structures important for learning and memory.

First, the amygdala is interconnected with the thalamus, a structure that routes sensory information to the cerebral cortex. Second, the amygdala interconnects

Amygdala (role in drug addiction)
During chronic use of an abused substance, it associates stimuli commonly present during drug use with the reinforcing effects of the drug; elicits physical withdrawal symptoms and a negative emotional state when drug is absent

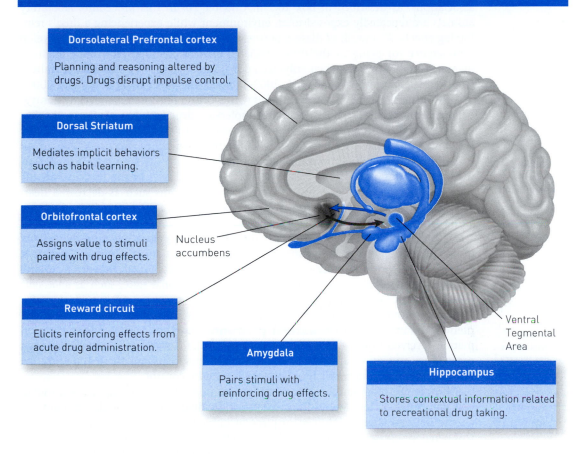

FIGURE 5.6 ● Chronic administration of abused drugs affects many brain structures beyond the reward circuit. Through incorporating these structures, chronic drug administration leads to pairing stimuli with drug effects, associating an environmental context with drug effects, and inhibiting impulse control and reasoning.

Dorsolateral Prefrontal cortex

Planning and reasoning altered by drugs. Drugs disrupt impulse control.

Dorsal Striatum

Mediates implicit behaviors such as habit learning.

Orbitofrontal cortex

Assigns value to stimuli paired with drug effects.

Nucleus accumbens

Reward circuit

Elicits reinforcing effects from acute drug administration.

Amygdala

Pairs stimuli with reinforcing drug effects.

Hippocampus

Stores contextual information related to recreational drug taking.

Ventral Tegmental Area

with the prefrontal cortex, the brain's executive center where stimuli are processed and motor responses are initiated. These structures together form the *thalamo-cortical-amygdala pathway*.

The prefrontal cortex contains substructures important for normal learning processes, and these structures adapt to chronic drug use. The **orbitofrontal cortex**, a structure within the prefrontal cortex, receives input from the amygdala and may enhance the incentive value of stimuli associated with drug use. The orbitofrontal cortex may also elicit drug cravings when the drug is absent (Koob & Volkow, 2009).

The thalamo-cortical-amygdala pathway also has connections with the hippocampus. During chronic administration of a drug of abuse, the hippocampus provides

Orbitofrontal cortex (role in drug addiction) A structure within the prefrontal cortex that receives input from the amygdala and may enhance the incentive value of stimuli associated with drug use; may elicit cravings when the drug is absent

contextual information linked with drug taking. Examples of context include the physical environment where drugs are normally taken or the types of individuals a user interacts with when obtaining and administering drugs.

The structures described above play an important role in associating stimuli with drug effects and assigning value to these associated stimuli, such as conditioned reinforcing properties. *Conditioned place preference procedures* demonstrate these stimulus associations, as described in Box 10.1 in Chapter 10. In this procedure, laboratory animals are repeatedly exposed to an environment while experiencing a drug's reinforcing effects. As a result of these exposures, animals, when given the choice, develop a preference for being in the drug-associated environment. In fact, these environmental stimuli alone can elicit enhanced dopamine levels in the nucleus accumbens (Duvauchelle, Ikegami, Asami, et al., 2000; Duvauchelle, Ikegami, & Castaneda, 2000).

In addition to a role in pairing stimuli with a drug's reinforcing effects, the amygdala-thalamo-cortical circuitry facilitates unpleasant drug withdrawal effects. Physical withdrawal effects manifest from the involvement of this circuitry with autonomic systems, particularly those involved with internal regulatory processes. The amygdala influences these functions through connections with the **hypothalamus**. During repeated administration, these systems adapt to a drug in the body; when the drug is absent, they elicit physical withdrawal symptoms such as decreased heart rate, gastrointestinal dysfunction, sweating, and breathing irregularities, among a variety of effects.

During withdrawal from a drug, we also find the amygdala reducing the activity of dopamine neurons in the ventral tegmental area (Belujon, Jakobowski, Dollish, & Grace, 2016). These inhibitory effects, in turn, reduce one's ability to experience rewarding effects. Thus, the amygdala elicits a negative emotional state, such as *anhedonia* (a lack of joy), as a form of psychological withdrawal.

Chronic administration of abused drugs also alters functioning of the dorsolateral prefrontal cortex. The **dorsolateral prefrontal cortex** integrates sensory information received from other cortical areas and mediates working memory, planning, organizing, and other upper-level cognitive activities. Through these activities, the dorsolateral prefrontal cortex is important for impulse control.

Chronic use of an abused drug compromises normal functioning of the dorsolateral prefrontal cortex. Many drug-addicted individuals exhibit a reduced ability to choose delayed larger reinforcers in place of immediate smaller reinforcers. Overall, this behavior creates a problem for drug-addiction therapy because delayed outcomes associated with being drug free may weigh poorly against immediate gratification from taking a drug of abuse. Other drugs such as depressant drugs (e.g., alcohol) or psychedelic drugs (e.g., phencyclidine) significantly impair memory function, partly through acting on the dorsolateral prefrontal cortex (Aura & Riekkinen, 1999; Mao, Arnsten, & Li, 1999; Paulus, Tapert, Pulido, & Schuckit, 2006).

Review! Working memory consists of short-term verbal or nonverbal memories employed when carrying out a task. (Chapter 2.)

Chronic treatment with an abused drug may recruit procedural memory systems involving dorsal parts of the basal ganglia—also referred to as the *dorsal striatum*—and

Hypothalamus (role in drug withdrawal) Elicits autonomic system effects associated with physiological withdrawal symptoms

Dorsolateral prefrontal cortex Integrates sensory information received from other cortical areas and mediates working memory, planning, organizing, and other upper-level cognitive activities; important for impulse control

interconnections between this structure and the nucleus accumbens and thalamus. As Robinson and Berridge (2003) describe, tying shoelaces involves procedural memory because once lace tying starts, the behavior basically continues automatically until the lace is tied. During situations in which a user commonly smokes a cigarette, such as talking on the phone or having a cup of coffee, the user may engage in an automated series of behaviors involving removing a cigarette from a pack and lighting it. In other words, a user may obtain, light, and smoke a cigarette without giving it much thought.

STOP & CHECK

1. What effects does dopamine release in the nucleus accumbens have?

2. What role does GABA play in the reward circuit?

3. What role does the amygdala play in chronic drug actions in the brain?

4. How might altered dorsolateral prefrontal cortex functioning interfere with treating addiction?

1. Enhanced dopamine concentrations in the nucleus accumbens are linked to reinforcing effects and may facilitate certain associative learning processes involving novel stimuli. 2. GABA neurons produce inhibitory effects on dopamine neurons in the reward circuit 3. The amygdala pairs stimuli with a drug's reinforcing effects. 4. Compromised dorsolateral prefrontal cortex functioning impairs impulse control, which may prevent drug-addicted individuals from abstaining from immediate drug use in place of delayed benefits from being drug free.

Neurobiology and the Stages of Drug Addiction

Leading authorities in drug-addiction research describe addiction as a cycle involving three primary stages (Kalivas, 2002; Koob & Volkow, 2009). The first stage of addiction is **intoxication**, a drug's effects after acute administration that produce a maladaptive and impaired state. The second stage is withdrawal, and the third stage consists of preoccupation and anticipation. These stages relate to important concepts developed from drug-addiction models and their association with drug actions in the brain (**Table 5.4**).

Drug intoxication is a necessary first stage in the development of drug addiction. Drug use during this stage occurs for the purpose of achieving a drug's intoxicating and, in particular, rewarding effects. In this way, the intoxication stage resembles the primary feature of Wikler's drive model as previously described. The actions of drugs on the brain's reward circuitry sufficiently explain drug use at this stage.

The next stage of this cycle consists of the *development of dependence during chronic use*. As drug use continues, the reasons for using the drug shift from purely seeking a drug's positive reinforcing effects to avoiding withdrawal effects. The opponent-process model characterizes this change in motivation for drug seeking. Neurobiologically, withdrawal effects depend largely on the amygdala. As previously described, the

Intoxication A drug's effects after acute administration that overall produce an abnormal and impaired state

TABLE 5.4 ● Drug-Addiction Cycle		
Addiction stage	**Characteristics**	**Neurobiology**
Intoxication	Acute drug effects that produce a maladaptive and impaired state	Reward circuitry
Withdrawal	Repeated drug use results in physical or psychological withdrawal effects (or both)	Amygdala, hypothalamus, and autonomic nervous system
Preoccupation and anticipation	Behavior orients from seeking natural reinforcers to seeking drug reinforcers	Prefrontal cortex, amygdala, thalamus, and hippocampus

SOURCE: © Cengage Learning 2014.

amygdala functions to pair stimuli with a drug's effects. When these drug effects cease, the amygdala, through connections with the hypothalamus and autonomic nervous system control centers such as the medulla, triggers an array of physical withdrawal symptoms. These physical withdrawal symptoms can include gastrointestinal effects, heart-rate changes, breathing-rate changes, body temperature dysregulation, and sleep disturbances. Further, the amygdala facilitates negative affective symptoms such as fear, anxiety, and dread. Although the amygdala is capable of producing a wide array of withdrawal effects, the specific withdrawal effects produced depend on the particular drug a person has been using.

As the chronic use of abused drugs continues, addiction enters a *preoccupation and anticipation stage*. During this stage, a person is preoccupied with seeking and using drugs. Drug use at this stage is more than simply seeking a drug for positive reinforcing effects or avoiding aversive withdrawal effects. Rather, this stage reflects a learning pattern of drug seeking that can conflict with learning patterns important for normal everyday activities. Incentivization of stimuli that promote drug "wanting" may develop through the intercommunication of brain reward circuitry with learning systems, including the thalamo-cortical-amygdala pathway and the hippocampus. Overall, this circuitry facilitates associating drug effects with stimuli, especially in assigning value to these stimuli. Through changes in the prefrontal cortex, chronic drug use affects planning and decision making, thereby facilitating a preoccupation with drug seeking and use.

Relapse represents another important feature of this third addiction stage. In a neurobiological context, relapse occurs as a result of the drug's changes to the brain's learning systems. In particular, encountering stimuli once strongly paired with drug use may elicit the desire for a drug by reengaging systems that facilitated drug seeking. Studies by Kalivas and colleagues show that such stimuli activate glutamate neurons that innervate the nucleus accumbens and ventral tegmental area (Kalivas, 2009; LaLumiere & Kalivas, 2008). These glutamate signals may reengage neural associations that gave incentive value to these stimuli, essentially eliciting a wanting state. Such stimuli can include a friend the individual used drugs with in the past or physical environments similar to those in which the individual routinely used drugs. Another reminder is the drug itself. Administering only a small amount of the drug, such as a drink of alcohol, may lead to further drug use. Box 5.1 provides an example of drug-induced reinstatement in the self-administration procedure.

Mortality and Drug Addiction

Once established, a drug addiction is long lasting and challenging to treat. Individuals who fail to respond to treatment have a high mortality rate compared to individuals who responded to treatment and remained drug free. A longitudinal study conducted by Mützell (1998) provides an assessment of mortality rates among treated and non-treated drug-addicted patients. In this study, Mützell conducted a 20-year longitudinal study of 284 heroin-addicted individuals. The study began with the presentation of an individual to an emergency room, usually the result of a heroin overdose. After receiving emergency care, medical staff invited these patients into a drug-addiction treatment program. Unfortunately, more than half of those attempting treatment absconded soon after.

Twenty years later, more than two-thirds of the heroin-addicted individuals had died—regardless of whether or not they had attempted treatment at the hospital. The most frequent causes of death were pneumonia, suicide, physical assault, alcohol intoxication, heroin overdose, and cirrhosis of the liver. During those 20 years, two-thirds of the individuals had also committed various crimes. Only approximately 10 percent of the heroin-addicted individuals remained drug free. These results are similar to a longitudinal study conducted in the United States among individuals addicted to heroin or other opioid drugs. That study reported only a 22 percent abstinence rate after a 30-year follow-up (Hser, Hoffman, Grella, & Anglin, 2001).

High mortality rates associated with drug addiction applies to legally available drugs as well. Long-term tobacco use is the greatest cause of deaths from lung cancer, chronic obstructive pulmonary disease, and heart disease annually in the United States. Alcohol causes thousands of U.S. deaths each year from liver diseases and alcohol overdose. Moreover, alcohol is a significant contributor to lethal car accidents and violence-related deaths each year.

Psychological and Pharmacological Therapies for Treating Drug Dependence

Drug-addiction treatment options include psychotherapy, medications, or a combination of both. These forms of treatment address drug detoxification, prevention of and coping with withdrawal symptoms, and the prevention of relapse. Detoxification is the first step in any addiction treatment.

Detoxification consists of a process aimed at ceasing drug intoxication and reducing withdrawal symptoms. Detoxification uses two key approaches: medication and prevention of drug use. Medications provide the means to reduce or

Detoxification
Process aimed at ceasing drug intoxication and reducing withdrawal symptoms

eliminate short-term withdrawal symptoms. Otherwise, a drug-addicted individual may simply refrain from using a drug or be denied access to the drug. For a treatment program, detoxification from illicit substances usually occurs in a hospital setting or an in-house treatment facility.

After the completion of drug detoxification, treatment options seek to reduce further withdrawal symptoms and prevent relapse. Both medication and psychotherapy provide approaches for remaining drug free. Medications for treating drug addiction include those that directly address drug withdrawal symptoms and medications that treat comorbid disorders such as depression and anxiety. One medicinal approach is drug-replacement therapy.

Drug-replacement therapy Exchanging the addictive drug with a similar but less harmful drug

Drug-replacement therapy exchanges the addictive drug with a similar but less harmful drug. For treating a heroin addiction, for example, medications can include substitute heroin-like drugs (such as buprenorphine or methadone) to prevent physical and psychological withdrawal symptoms. Replacement therapies for tobacco include nicotine patches, nicotine gums, and nicotine-like drugs such as *varenicline (Chantix)*. Treating drug dependence using the drug-replacement approach requires that an individual slowly reduce the amount of replacement substance used until the individual can successfully quit without the occurrence of appreciable withdrawal symptoms.

Another approach consists of psychotherapy. For drug addiction, *psychotherapy* includes behavioral therapies and cognitive–behavioral therapies. Each therapy type seeks to eliminate maladaptive behavior surrounding drug use. Toward this goal, therapy aims to reduce addictive drug use to manageable levels or to eliminate drug use altogether.

Behavioral therapies Therapies that use the principles of applied behavior analysis to analyze and develop strategies for treating drug addiction

Behavioral therapies use applied behavior analysis principles to analyze and develop strategies for treating drug addiction. According to behavioral analyses, drugs serve as powerful reinforcing stimuli that maintain drug-seeking behavior. Behavioral therapies attempt to provide alternative reinforcers for behaviors in this drug-seeking and using process.

Behavioral therapy can include contingency-management approaches, which seek to provide healthy alternative reinforcers to those associated with addictive drug seeking. Alternative reinforcers include community reinforcers, monetary reinforcers, and voucher reinforcers. Community reinforcers include engagement in valuable and rewarding activities such as employment, volunteering, and recreational activities. Monetary and voucher reinforcers are incentives for remaining drug free. In this context, a voucher is exchangeable for a tangible good in the community.

Cognitive–behavioral therapies Therapies that teach drug-addicted individuals to identify and reduce urges to use a substance

Cognitive–behavioral therapies teach drug-addicted individuals to identify and reduce their urges to use a substance. Once trained, individuals learn to avoid stimuli or situations that precipitate drug cravings and learn strategies for coping with drug cravings. For legal substances such as tobacco and alcohol, cognitive–behavioral therapy goals may consist of reduced and responsible drug use rather than completely ending drug use. In this perspective, addictive drug use is a manageable behavior, not an incurable disease.

Twelve-step recovery programs such as Alcoholics Anonymous and Narcotics Anonymous are common social therapies for drug addiction. Although they are conducted in a group setting, we do not consider these programs to be group psychotherapy because the group leader may not be a trained or licensed therapist and psychotherapy techniques are not used. Instead the group leader is generally an individual who has succeeded in the 12-step program and can use his or her knowledge and experiences in the program to run group meetings. Thus, the "therapy" in this context consists of individuals sharing with others their struggles and successes in a supportive group setting.

These programs tend to characterize drug addiction similar to a disease model; that is, drug addiction is something inherent and lifelong. These programs advocate complete abstention from substance use to prevent drug addiction from recurring. From this perspective, we term someone successfully abstaining from substance use for a long period of time as "in recovery," similar to someone in recovery from a disease. The term used in this context also highlights the belief that no one can ever be "cured" of drug addiction, that a relapse is always possible.

Twelve-step anonymous programs guide members, known only on a first-name basis, through 12 recovery steps, beginning with an admission that drug use is out of control. The 12 steps further include acceptance of weaknesses in control of drug use as well as other parts of their life. Ultimately, these weaknesses are addressed through moral and social support by group members, a program sponsor, and family and friends. Twelve-step programs also encourage members to accept a greater moral purpose or power beyond themselves, which contributes to a heightened sense of spirituality.

Twelve-step anonymous programs A type of substance addiction program where anonymous members give testimonies in group settings and follow an outline of 12 steps toward recovery

Although a variety of treatment options exist, all have relatively low success rates. A nationwide assessment of treatment effectiveness called the Drug Abuse Treatment Outcomes Study provides one of best surveys of long-term outcomes of drug-addiction treatment. This study assessed the effectiveness of four primary treatment programs for patients who abused heroin, cocaine, marijuana, or alcohol. The programs included outpatient methadone treatment, long-term residential treatment, outpatient drug-free treatment, and short-term inpatient treatment. Both long-term residential and short-term inpatient treatments employed some type of medication to address cravings or physiological withdrawal effects. Outpatient drug-free treatment programs provided any variety of therapeutic approaches, including 12-step programs or one-on-one therapy. Short-term inpatient programs provided some type of medical treatment to address symptoms derived from abrupt withdrawal of a drug.

Although most patients reported declines in substance use 1 year later, a follow-up with patients 5 years later revealed increased trends in substance use (Hubbard, Craddock, & Anderson, 2003) (**Figure 5.7**). More individuals previously enrolled in methadone outpatient and long-term residential treatment programs for heroin abuse reported using heroin at a 5-year follow-up compared to a 1-year follow-up. The number of individuals previously enrolled in a long-term residential treatment or outpatient program for heroin or cocaine use also increased when surveyed 5 years after treatment compared to 1 year after treatment. Fortunately, not every program saw increased relapse rates. While five-year follow-ups found a slight increase in heroin use for a short-term inpatient program, there was also as slight decrease in cocaine for short-term inpatient programs.

FIGURE 5.7 ● One-year (dark-blue) and 5-year follow-ups (light blue) in patients seeking a treatment for heroin (left) or cocaine (right) addiction. The bars report the percentage of patients still using a substance for each program.

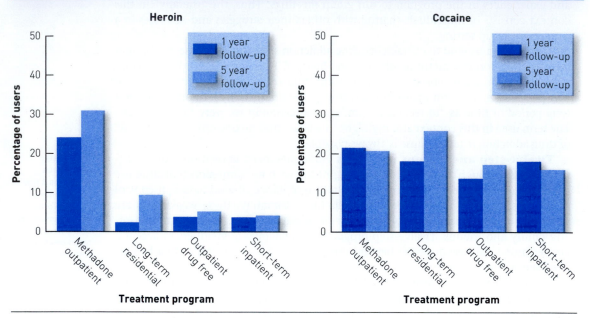

SOURCE: Adapted from Hubbard et al., 2003.

Although increased substance use was reported for two programs shown in Figure 5.7, many patients had relapsed and then sought treatment again during this 5-year period. Relapse is not unusual after a successful abstention from substance use. As discussed previously in this chapter, learning how to prevent relapse is an important part of drug-addiction research. To determine why some patients sought treatment again after relapse but others did not in the Drug Abuse Treatment Outcomes Study, Grella, Hser, and Hsieh (2003) conducted an analysis of the reasons patients expressed for reseeking treatment.

For this analysis, Grella and colleagues (2003) focused on cocaine-addicted users who relapsed during this study. By assessing the data gathered on these users, this research team used correlational study procedures to determine the impact of certain personal or environmental characteristics on the decision to reseek treatment. The investigators found that users reseeking treatment after relapse had an increased likelihood of being married and had past experiences with drug-treatment programs. Among these prior treatment programs, most users who resought treatment had participated in a 12-step recovery program. Finally, those reseeking treatment expressed a desire for help and a readiness to accept treatment. Findings such as these provide researchers and therapists directions for improving successful treatment approaches.

STOP & CHECK

1. Which neurobiological systems mediate rewarding effects during the intoxication of drug use?

2. How do withdrawal symptoms occur when a chronically administered drug is absent from the body?

3. What is the first step in addiction treatment?

4. What is the key difference between behavioral or cognitive–behavioral therapies and 12-step programs such as Alcoholics Anonymous?

1. The reward circuit structures, which consist of the ventral tegmental area and the nucleus accumbens **2.** When an addicted drug is absent, the amygdala elicits a negative affective state and elicits the hypothalamus to produce autonomic nervous system effects, leading to withdrawal symptoms. **3.** Detoxification **4.** Behavioral and cognitive–behavioral therapies seek to reduce drug use to a manageable level. Anonymous programs seek the complete abstinence of the addicted drug's use.

From Actions to Effects: Food Addiction

Food addiction shares many features with drug addiction. Food addiction appears to be relatively prevalent among maladaptive disorders. Although we lack precise numbers on the prevalence of food addiction, currently one-third of U.S. adults have body mass index (BMI) values over 30, which is the medical definition for *obesity*. Obesity in the United States accounted for more than $200 billion in health care expenses between 1998 and 2000, and obesity contributes to more than 300,000 deaths in the United States each year. Although obesity occurs from many factors, including physical inactivity, types of foods consumed, and genetic predispositions, the rewarding effects of highly palatable foods are likely contributors.

However, overeating in food addiction may not necessarily equate to obesity. Bulimia nervosa is an eating disorder characterized as binge eating followed by a compensatory response to avoid gaining weight. The compensatory response may consist of vomiting, using laxatives, overexercising, or any of a variety of different methods to prevent gaining weight from overeating. Binge eating typically involves sweet-tasting, high-calorie foods, which suggests that bulimia nervosa can be considered a form of food addiction (Hadad & Knackstedt, 2014).

Food addiction is an emerging focus for mental health professionals. The current DSM fails to characterize food addiction as a disorder, although clinicians who work with food-addicted individuals tend to follow criteria used for diagnosing a substance use disorder (Davis et al., 2011; Ifland et al., 2009). Further, we find growing scientific interest in considering habitual overeating to be similar to substance use disorders (Ifland et al., 2009; Volkow & O'Brien, 2007; Volkow & Wise, 2005). Here we consider some of the features that food addiction that shares with substance dependence.

A study by Pretlow (2011) provides an illustration for how obesity might satisfy DSM criteria for a substance use disorder. This study relied upon the earlier edition of the DSM, the DSM IV-TR, but the major features of substance use disorders relevant to their study are the same for the most current DSM, the DSM-5. This study included a survey of anonymous qualitative statements provided by nearly 30,000 individuals ranging from age 8 to 21. All participants had BMI levels 30 or higher and were, on average, at the 96th percentile for BMI.

From reviewing statements posted on the study's website, Pretlow wrote that "the majority of posts exhibited at least three criteria [for substance dependence], particularly: (a) large amounts of substance consumed over a long period, (b) unsuccessful efforts to cut down, and (c) continued use despite adverse consequences." Further, participants described food use that shared many characteristics of drug tolerance, which consisted of progressively increasing food consumption over time, and drug withdrawal, as characterized by urges to overeat when attempting to diet. Among those who reported urges, nearly half described them as "intense cravings."

Overeating shares many of the neurobiological features of drug addiction (Hadad & Knackstedt, 2014; Volkow, Wang, Fowler, Tomasi, & Baler, 2012). Like drugs of abuse, foods can produce reinforcing effects by acting on brain reward circuitry. As described previously, sugary liquid food consumed by rats causes large elevations in nucleus accumbens dopamine levels (Figure 5.3). Appetite hormones also regulate dopamine neurons in the reward pathway. The hunger-stimulating hormone ghrelin greatly enhances food-elicited increases in mesolimbic dopamine neuron activity, and research also shows that ghrelin enhances self-administration responding for heroin (Box 5.1). The hunger-reducing hormone leptin diminishes food-elicited increases in dopamine neuron activity. Thus, hunger enhances food's reinforcing effects, whereas satiety reduces foods' reinforcing effects. Research is ongoing to determine how addictive food use may interact with learning and memory systems in ways similar to addictive drug use.

Some food-addiction therapies resemble drug-addiction therapies, but others do not. Behavioral therapies, for example, may provide alternative reinforcers to overeating. Cognitive–behavioral approaches attempt to alter a person's view of food and then develop strategies to cope with food cravings. Just as 12-Step programs include Alcoholics Anonymous and Narcotics Anonymous, 12-Step groups exist for overeating include Overeaters Anonymous and Food Addicts Anonymous (Johnson & Sansone, 1993; Russell-Mayhew, von Ranson, & Masson, 2010).

Medically, however, most therapies address the physical impact of food addiction rather than treating the addiction itself. For example, medical obesity treatments include appetite-reducing medications, medications that impair food absorption, and surgical procedures (Powell, Apovian, & Aronne, 2011; Stefater, Wilson-Perez, Chambers, Sandoval, & Seeley, 2012). Surgical procedures include liposuction, a fat-extracting procedure; stomach bands or staples, which reduce the size of the stomach; and temporarily wiring a patient's jaw shut to enforce a liquid diet.

Otherwise, the DSM considers overeating, or *compulsive eating*, as a symptom of another disorder such as anxiety or depression. Thus, to reduce overeating, one must treat the disorder causing overeating. For example, if overeating is a way of coping with stress or anxiety, then directly treating stress or anxiety will reduce overeating.

Similarly, if overeating allows one to cope with depression, then treating depression will reduce overeating.

Thus, although psychologists and other mental health therapy providers treat overeating either as substance dependence or as a symptom of another disorder, the lack of a clear clinical definition for food addiction leaves food-addictive behaviors largely in the realm of medical symptoms for other disorders. An agreement among mental health professionals about food addiction would help clarify this diagnosis and aid in the development of appropriate treatment strategies.

STOP & CHECK

1. How do highly palatable foods elicit reinforcing effects?

2. How do therapists diagnose food addiction?

1. Like drugs of abuse, foods elicit increased dopamine release in the nucleus accumbens. **2.** The DSM does not include food addiction among psychological disorders. However, therapists find that the general DSM definition for substance dependence applies as well to food addiction. Moreover, some therapeutic approaches for drug addiction, such as 12-step programs, also apply well to food addiction.

Chapter Summary

Regulatory agencies regulate the availability and use of drugs with abuse potential. In the United States, the Drug Enforcement Administration categorizes such drugs according to abuse potential and medical utility on a controlled substances schedule. Drug scheduling occurs in other countries, but their methods and category systems sometimes differ. Although drug scheduling provides a regulatory rating for the abuse potential of drugs, these ratings do not necessarily coincide with scientific ratings of abuse potential. Clinical definitions of drug addiction include harmful effects from drug use and consider addiction as a chronically relapsing disorder.

To understand addictive behavior better, researchers use drug-addiction models. These models include considering addiction as a disease or as behavior controlled by drug-elicited variables. Drugs of abuse derive their effects through acting on the brain's reward circuit, which was first discovered by James Olds. Drugs that elicit positive reinforcing effects cause dopamine neurons in the reward circuit to release dopamine into the nucleus accumbens. Chronic usage of drugs of abuse affect brain structures for learning and memory.

We have many treatment strategies for addiction, including detoxification, medicines, and therapy—unfortunately, these strategies offer limited success. Many of the features of drug abuse and addiction relate to other addictions as well. For example, food addiction engages many of the same brain systems involved in drug addiction, satisfies clinical definitions for drug addiction, and can be treated by many approaches used for drug addiction.

Key Terms

Harrison Narcotics Act 136
Controlled Substances Act 136
Controlled substances
  schedules 137
Craving 140
Relapse 140
Models of drug addiction 141
Disease model 141
Associative learning 142
Reinforcement 142
Conditioned stimulus 143
Discriminative stimulus 143
Latent inhibition 143

Incentive salience 144
Goal-directed behavior 144
Drive theory of drug
  addiction 144
Opponent-process theory of
  drug addiction 144
Incentive-salience model 149
Intracranial self-
  stimulation 151
Amygdala (role in drug
  addiction) 154
Orbitofrontal cortex (role in
  drug addiction) 155

Hypothalamus (role in drug
  withdrawal) 156
Dorsolateral prefrontal
  cortex 156
Intoxication 157
Detoxification 159
Drug-replacement therapy 160
Behavioral therapies 160
Cognitive–behavioral
  therapies 160
Twelve-steps anonymous
  programs 161

A Final Note About Drug Addiction

If you or someone you know may be struggling with addiction, please consider looking into any of the following resources.

1. Most colleges can refer students to addiction services. Consider contacting your institution's health center or contacting a substance abuse awareness office on your campus. You might find a listing of resources on your college's website as well.

2. The National Council on Alcoholism and Drug Dependence offers a free online self-assessment to help you determine if you might have a drug addiction. You can find the test here: https://ncadd.org/get-help/take-the-test/am-i-drug-addicted. For seeking help with addiction, this organization's phone number (U.S.) is 800-622-2255

3. The U.S. Substance Abuse and Mental Health Services Administration offers a source for locating treatment services. You can called their helpline at (U.S.) 800-662-4357 or visit online treatment services locator at https://findtreatment.samhsa.gov.

4. Contact your county's department of health. Most can refer you to drug addiction treatment services.

5. Searching for a particular 12-step program (e.g., Alcoholics Anonymous) in your town on an Internet search engine is a quick way to find where and when these groups meet.

Visit the Student Study Site at **study.sagepub.com/prus2e** to access additional study tools, including eFlashcards, web quizzes, video resources, web resources, SAGE journal articles, and more.

Psychostimulants

FLEISCHL AND THE NEUROLOGIST

Dr. Fleischl-Marxow was a desperate man. He had painful tumors down his spine; in search of relief, he developed an addiction to morphine. Fleischl sought the help of his hospital colleagues, including a motivated young neurologist known for unique thinking and big ideas.

The neurologist visited Fleischl-Marxow on many occasions and offered what advice he could. During these visits, Fleischl obsessed over suicidal thoughts, and the neurologist became convinced that unless he did something, Fleischl would kill himself. Although the neurologist was unable to treat the disease, he perhaps could rid Fleischl of his morphine addiction. In May 1884, the neurologist administered his experimental treatment: cocaine.

(Continued)

(Continued)

At the beginning of treatment, Fleischl experienced his first pain-free days without morphine in years. But only one week later his pain returned in force. Then, instead of an addiction to morphine, Fleischl developed an addiction to cocaine. The neurologist wrote that Fleischl clung to cocaine "like a drowning man," and

the neurologist was horrified by the enormous doses Fleischl used and paid a fortune for.

Fleischl survived for 6 more agonizing years, dying at age 45. Fleischl's suffering and cocaine addiction made a tremendous impact on the life of this young neurologist, Sigmund Freud.

SOURCE: Based on Byck (1974) and Jones (1953).

Throughout the day, all of us experience moments of high alertness and arousal. You might experience this after realizing you slept through your alarm clock and have to rush out the door to avoid being late. Or you might be jolted to alertness if a car swerves in front of you and you quickly slam on the brakes. You may become more attentive if your instructor begins randomly choosing students in class to answer questions about the lecture she just gave.

Think about how you feel in these situations. Your heart rate probably becomes rapid. Your mind is racing to meet the challenge you face. You are in a state of high alertness. You might even find the experience exhilarating. All of these states activate arousal processes in the central and peripheral nervous systems. Psychostimulant drugs act on these same nervous system processes.

Psychostimulants: A Large Variety of Substances

Psychostimulants
Drugs that increase psychomotor and sympathetic nervous system activity as well as improve alertness and positive mood

Psychostimulant drugs increase psychomotor and sympathetic nervous system activity as well as improve alertness and positive mood. **Psychostimulants** are also referred to as *sympathomimetics,* because they increase sympathetic nervous system activity. Common psychostimulants include amphetamines, methylphenidate, cathinones, and cocaine. Amphetamines represent a class of drugs, among which include amphetamine and methamphetamine. Cathinones include many drugs, such as cathinones and pyrovalerone, as well as synthetic cathinones such as methcathinone and mephedrone.

Although psychostimulants are common drugs of abuse, many psychostimulant drugs have legitimate therapeutic purposes. Some amphetamines have legitimate uses for the treatment of *attention deficit hyperactivity disorder* (ADHD), narcolepsy, and obesity. Cocaine was once commonly used as a local anesthetic for nasal and tear duct surgery. Given these medical uses, the U.S. Drug Enforcement Administration (DEA) assigns most psychostimulant drugs above schedule I (see **Table 6.1**). However, the level of regulatory control for these drugs varies among countries. Canada, for example, assigns methamphetamine to schedule I, thereby preventing medicinal use of methamphetamine.

Psychostimulants are well known as drugs of abuse. According to the National Institute on Drug Abuse, approximately 0.4% of Americans used methamphetamine in 2009. In schools, 3.4% of 12th graders abused methylphenidate in 2008 (Substance Abuse and Mental Health Services Administration, 2010). In 2014, approximately 0.5% of Americans used cocaine, including 0.1% individuals who used *crack* cocaine Nonmedical use of psychostimulants such as methylphenidate, amphetamine, and methamphetamine was reported by 1.6 million Americans, including 569,000 who used methamphetamine (Center for Behavioral Health Statistics and Quality, 2015). In Europe, approximately 5% of those 15 and older used cocaine in their lifetimes (European Monitoring Centre for Drugs and Drug Addiction, 2009).

Few studies have evaluated the prevalence of synthetically produced cathinones, commonly known as *bath salts*. Cathinones make up approximately 25% of all new psychoactive drugs (United Nations Office of Drugs and Crime, 2014). Bath salts can contain any variety of synthetic cathinones, including methcathinone,

TABLE 6.1 ● Drug Enforcement Administration Controlled Substances Schedules for Psychostimulant Drugs

Psychostimulant	Schedule
Amphetamine	III
Cathinone	I
Cathine (norpseudoephedrine)	IV
Cocaine	II
Methamphetamine	II
Methcathinone	I
Methylphenidate	II
Pyrovalerone	V

SOURCE: Adapted from the DEA Controlled Substances Schedules, www.deadiversion.usdoj.gov/schedules/index.html.

methylenedioxypyrovalerone, methylone, and mephedrone. Reports of bath salt use and overdose began appearing in 2010 and 2011 (CDC, 2011b; James et al., 2011; Wood, Greene, & Dargan, 2011), and in September 2011, the DEA used its emergency scheduling authority to temporarily classify suspected psychoactive bath salt ingredients as schedule I controlled substances (Drug Enforcement Administration, 2011). The schedule I classification for synthetic cathinones known as bath salts became permanent thereafter.

Psychostimulants: Herbal Products, Prescription Drugs, and Substances of Abuse

Ephedra

Ephedra An extract of the plant *Ephedra sinica* that contains ephedrine and pseudoephedrine

The first amphetamines were derived from **ephedra**, an extract of the plant *Ephedra sinica* found in dry climates in North and South America, southern Europe, central Asia, and northern Africa (**Figure 6.1**). Ephedra contains two psychostimulants: *ephedrine* and *pseudoephedrine* (**Table 6.2**). Many cold remedies contain these stimulants, but since 2006, U.S. pharmacies limit the number of products sold in a single purchase. By regulating the sale of ephedrine and pseudoephedrine, state law enforcement agencies hope to reduce the clandestine production of methamphetamine and other illicit psychostimulant drugs.

Amphetamines

Amphetamines Class of psychostimulant drugs that share a similar structure

Racemic A mixture containing equal amounts of both optical isomers of a compound

Amphetamines represent a class of psychostimulant drugs that share a similar structure. The drug amphetamine has two *optical isomers*—that is, the chemical structure occurs in two different forms that are *mirror images* of each other—designated as *d* or *l*.[1] *The drug amphetamine* (Benzedrine) refers to **racemic** amphetamine, a mixture containing equal amounts of both d and l optical isomers. The d-amphetamine isomer is sold as the medication Dexedrine, and the drug Adderall contains a 3:1 ratio of d-amphetamine and l-amphetamine. At one time, both racemic and d-amphetamine were approved by the Food and Drug Administration (FDA) for the treatment of attention hyperactivity disorder and narcolepsy, but currently these drugs have been pulled from the market. Adderall, however, remains on the market and has been approved by the FDA for the treatment of attention hyperactivity disorder and narcolepsy (Food and Drug Administration, 2007).

Although methamphetamine is notoriously known as a drug of abuse, the FDA approves its use for the treatment of ADHD, marketed under the trade name Desoxyn. The illicit production of methamphetamine occurring in a "meth lab" uses household chemicals along with either ephedrine or pseudoephedrine. In addition, meth labs may use the chemical phenylacetone in place of either ephedrine or pseudoephedrine.

---

1 The *d* and *l* designations refer to *dextrorotatory* and *levorotary*, meaning the molecules turn to the right or left in a plane of polarized light.

FIGURE 6.1 ● *Ephedra sinica* plants are native to dry climates in North and South America, southern Europe, central Asia, and northern Africa.

SOURCE: Copyright iStockphoto/Renphoto.

Meth lab synthesis methods produce a crystallized form of methamphetamine referred to as *crystal meth, crystal, speed, crank,* and other street names (**Figure 6.2**). Synthesizing methamphetamine from these methods produces toxic and flammable solvent vapors and gases, which account for a large number of third-degree burn victims in emergency care every year.

German chemists developed amphetamine, in 1887, in an effort to develop a mass-producible form of ephedra. In the 1920s, physicians used amphetamine as a drug for raising blood pressure; in 1937, amphetamine was first used to treat ADHD (Bradley, 1937; Brecher, 1972). Amphetamine's stimulant effects provided the first effective treatment for *narcolepsy*, a neurological sleep disorder characterized by

TABLE 6.2 ● Psychostimulants

Psychostimulant	Related psychostimulants	Origin
Ephedrine		Both ephedrine and pseudoephedrine derive from *Ephedra*
	Pseudoephedrine	
Amphetamine		Laboratory synthesis
	Methamphetamine	From ephedrine or pseudoephedrine
Methylphenidate		Laboratory synthesis
Cathinone		The *khat* plant
	Mephedrone	Synthesized from cathinone
	Methylone	Synthesized from cathinone
	Methylenedioxypyrovalerone	Synthesized from cathinone

FIGURE 6.2 ● Methamphetamine crystals are clandestinely made in meth labs from ephedrine, pseudoephedrine, or the organic solvent phenylacetone.

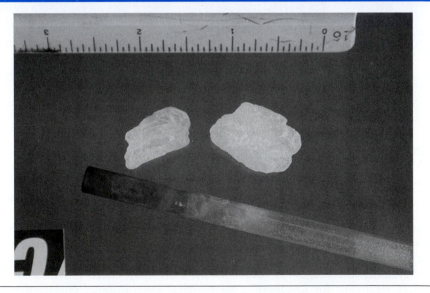

SOURCE: Department of Justice.

extreme fatigue and excessive daytime sleep. During World War II, the U.S. military used amphetamine to improve alertness and reduce fatigue. After the war, leftover amphetamine supplies released to the general population led to a brief amphetamine abuse epidemic in Japan (Brecher, 1972; Brill & Hirose, 1969).

In 1919, a Japanese chemist discovered methamphetamine after testing different synthesis methods that employed either ephedrine or pseudoephedrine. Another method was later developed for synthesizing methamphetamine from the organic solvent phenylacetone. In an attempt to reduce illicit methamphetamine production, the U.S. Drug Enforcement Administration first regulated the sale of phenylacetone, but this led illicit meth labs to synthesize methamphetamine from ephedrine or pseudoephedrine instead. In response to this, in 2006 the DEA began regulating the sale of ephedrine and pseudoephedrine, which, as described earlier, are common ingredients in over-the-counter cold medications (Vearrier, Greenberg, Miller, Okaneku, & Haggerty, 2012).

Methylphenidate

Methylphenidate is a prescription psychostimulant drug used for the treatment of ADHD. Methylphenidate structurally differs from the amphetamines and cocaine and is available only in prescription form. We generally regard methylphenidate as a relatively weaker psychostimulant drug. To use methylphenidate as a drug of abuse, users may often obtain methylphenidate from instrumental users, that is, those who were prescribed methylphenidate for a legitimate medical use. Those who are prescribed methylphenidate may choose to recreationally use the drug by grinding it up and snorting it. Because of its use for treating attention hyperactivity disorder in children, a common street name for methylphenidate is *kiddie coke*.

Methylphenidate was discovered in 1944 by Leandro Panizzon, a chemist working for the Ciba Pharmaceutical Company. Panizzon named the drug *Ritaline* after this wife Rita. After identifying the drug's psychostimulant effects, physicians began prescribing methylphenidate for the treatment of ADHD in the 1960s. However, ADHD was not universally accepted as a disorder until the 1980s, and as ADHD diagnoses subsequently increased, so did methylphenidate prescriptions. Today, methylphenidate is prescribed to more than two-thirds of the approximately 5 million U.S. children with ADHD (Mayes, Bagwell, & Erkulwater, 2008).

Cathinones

The psychostimulant **cathinone** comes from the leaves of *Catha edulis*, which is also referred to as *khat*. It is found in east Africa and the Arabian Peninsula, and the traditional use of khat involves chewing the leaves or using the leaves in tea. Fresh khat leaves produce the most potent psychostimulant effects, which limits khat use to local inhabitants. A number of synthetic cathinone compounds are used as drugs of abuse, including methcathinone, mephedrone, and pyrovalerones.

Clandestine laboratories produce cathinone derivatives such as methcathinone from cathinone, as well as other chemicals including the ephedra extract pseudoephedrine. As discussed previously, bath salts have recently emerged as

Cathinone
Psychostimulant derived from the leaves of *Catha edulis*

psychostimulant drugs, which include mephedrone, methylone, and the meth-cathinone-like substance methylenedioxypyrovalerone (Baumann, Ayestas, Dersch, & Rothman, 2012). Bath salts are known by many names, including *Starry Nights*, *Vanilla*, *Sky*, and *White Rush* (**Figure 6.3**).

Inhabitants of Arabia, Ethiopia, and east Africa have used khat, the source of cathinone, for centuries. The first cultivation of khat was documented in the early 1300s by King Sabr ad-Din of Ifat, who ordered its planting in the town of Marad. Europeans first discovered khat during an expedition in 1760 to Arabia ordered by King Frederick V of Denmark. During this expedition, physician and botanist Peter Forsskål discovered khat and named the plant *Catha edulis* (Al-Hebshi & Skaug, 2005; Gebissa, 2010).

Methcathinone was synthesized in the Soviet Union in 1928 and has been recreationally used since the late 1970s. Reports of methcathinone abuse began in the early 1990s (Emerson & Cisek, 1993; Glennon, 2014).

FIGURE 6.3 ● We find synthetic cathinones sold as "bath salts," which are sold by many names including *Starry Nights*, *Vanilla*, *Sky*, and *White Rush*.

SOURCE: Department of Justice.

Cocaine

Leaves of the *Erythroxylon coca* plant, which is found in the higher elevations of South America, provide a direct source of **cocaine** (**Figure 6.4**). The separation of cocaine from *coca* leaves occurs through multiple steps. The process begins by breaking down and mixing coca leaves into a liquid to form a **coca paste**. The coca paste, which contains between 30 and 80 percent of cocaine base, is then dried and sold for recreational use as is or transported to a *crystal lab* for further processing (Casale & Klein, 1993).

Crystal labs convert cocaine from a base into a salt, which puts cocaine in a powdered form. The salt form is produced for two reasons. First, it is a purer cocaine product than the cocaine in extracted base form. Second, the salt form allows for either *insufflating* (snorting) or intravenously injecting cocaine.

Many cocaine users, however, prefer the base form, which can be smoked because it has a lower vaporization point. Vaporization of the salt form of cocaine occurs at a very high temperature: 195°C (383°F). This method makes it hard not only to reach these temperatures with an ignition source but also for users to safely inhale the vapors without burning themselves. However, the base form of cocaine has a lower vaporization point, 98°C (208°F), allowing users to easily smoke it by heating the crystals over a flame.

Given that the smugglers often transport the salt form of cocaine, smoking cocaine requires transforming the salt form into a base form, also called a **free-base**.[2] This process consists of removing a hydrochloride molecule (the salt) from the cocaine molecule. When cocaine salt is heated with a mixture of baking soda and water, the hydrochloride molecule separates from cocaine, "freeing" the base from the salt. The *freebase* form of cocaine is called *crack* cocaine because of the

Cocaine
Psychostimulant derived from the leaves of *erythroxylon coca*

Coca paste Liquid paste made from the breaking and mixing of coca leaves

Freebase A base form of a compound converted from a salt from of the compound

---

FIGURE 6.4 ● Cocaine is a constituent in the leaves of the *Erythroxylon* coca plant, which is found at higher elevations in South America. Workers cultivate coca plants (left) in order to make a coca paste (right), a first step in extracting cocaine from coca leaves.

 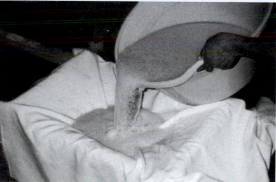

SOURCE: Left: Getty Images/Piero Pomponi. Right: Department of Justice.

---

2 Technically, a freebase must include an amine (NH$_2$) group, which cocaine does.

crackling sound these freebase crystals make when heated (**Figure 6.5**). The term *freebasing* refers to the process of converting a drug from a salt form of to a base form and can also refer to using the freebase form of a substance. The term mostly applies to processing an illicit substance.

Erythroxylon coca was long used by indigenous people for religious purposes, appetite suppression, and enhanced vigor and stamina. In the mid-1500s, Spanish conquistadors first discovered the plant during their conquest of the Incan empire in Peru. Cocaine was first extracted from coca leaves in 1844. In 1883, Theodor Aschenbrandt, a German Army physician, reported the anti-fatiguing properties of cocaine in soldiers. This report inspired a young physician, Sigmund Freud, to study cocaine's behavioral effects (Freud, 1974).

In 1884, Freud was fresh out of medical school and serving as a physician and lecturer at the Psychiatric Institute of the General Hospital of Vienna. Freud already had achieved a distinguished series of accomplishments in research on the nervous system. In fact, he wrote extensively in letters to his fiancé, Martha Bernays, about his desire for a career in research, but practicing medicine seemed his only option for making a living. He first chose to practice surgery because this required the least amount of interaction with his patients. A few months later, Freud obtained a psychiatric institute position, which held possibilities for research. A major discovery, he hoped, would lead to a profitable research career.

With this in mind, Freud sought a major discovery. He was intrigued by Aschenbrandt's reports on cocaine and decided to study it. In April 1884, Freud requested 1 gram of cocaine from Merck pharmaceuticals, and on June 18, 1884, less than 2 months later, he had completed both his research and a full manuscript on his findings.

In this manuscript, *Über Coca* ("On Coca"), Freud provided the most in-depth review of cocaine at the time, which included information on coca plants, ancient human use,

FIGURE 6.5 ● **Cocaine is used in both a powdered salt form (left) and a crystal or *crack* form (right).**

SOURCE: Department of Justice.

effects observed in animals, and his own self-reports (**Figure 6.6**). Freud lauded the benefits of cocaine and pressed its usage at every opportunity. Yet Freud's interest in cocaine eventually waned. Years later Freud declared cocaine a "scourge" of humanity.

His first misgivings arose from a suffering friend, Dr. von Fleischl-Marxow, who suffered from severe pain caused by tumors along his peripheral nerves. Freud suggested that the anesthetic properties of cocaine might help, and soon Fleischl had escalated his daily dose to 1000 mg per day—approximately 20 times the amount Freud occasionally gave to himself. Event ually, Fleischl developed hallucinations, and on one occasion he saw "white snakes creeping over his skin." As the adverse effects of cocaine became known, cocaine use declined in Europe and North America (Freud, 1974; Jones, 1953).

Cocaine served as a key ingredient in Coca-Cola between 1886 and 1904 (**Figure 6.7**), along with another important ingredient, caffeine. The result of this combination, as displayed in the Coca-Cola advertisement in Figure 6.7, was a drink that reduced headache and relieved exhaustion. Although not a narcotic, which is defined as a sleep-inducing

FIGURE 6.6 ● Sigmund Freud provided some of the earliest characterizations of cocaine's pharmacological effects in *Über Coca*.

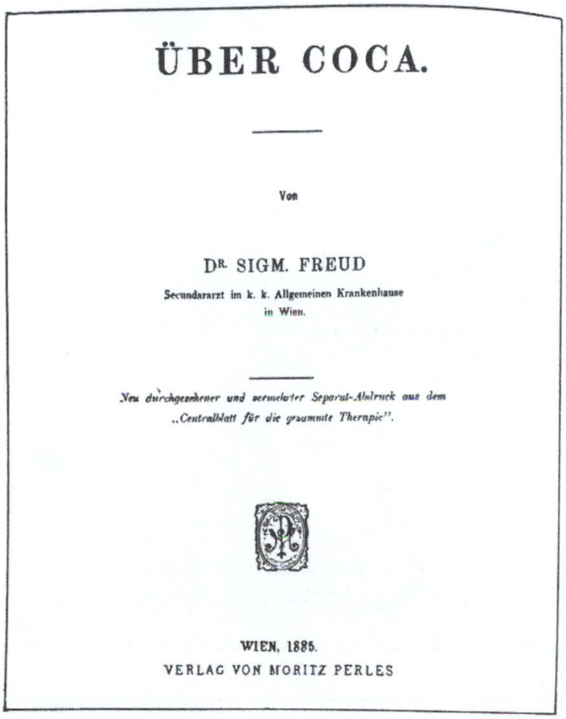

ÜBER COCA.

Von

DR. SIGM. FREUD

Secundararzt im k. k. Allgemeinen Krankenhause
in Wien.

Neu durchgesehener und vermehrter Separat-Abdruck aus dem „Centralblatt für die gesammte Therapie".

WIEN, 1885.
VERLAG VON MORITZ PERLES

SOURCE: Über Coca (Wein: 1885).

drug, the sale and distribution of "coca leaves, their salts, derivatives, or preparations" were regulated under the Harrison Narcotics Act of 1914. The act dealt primarily with the sale and distribution of opioids, which are narcotic drugs, but also listed cocaine among the drugs to be regulated. The association of cocaine with opioids led to cocaine's common designation as a narcotic, although this label doesn't accurately represent cocaine's pharmacological effects (Schultz, 1983). Cocaine remains classified as a narcotic by the U.S. Drug Enforcement Administration, despite other psychostimulant drugs, like methamphetamine, that do not have this designation.

FIGURE 6.7 ● Cocaine was a key ingredient in Coca-Cola between 1886 and 1904. The drink was advertised as a tonic that reduced headache and relieved exhaustion.

SOURCE: Copyright Coca-Cola 1897.

STOP & CHECK

1. What are the primary psychoactive ingredients in ephedra?

2. The sale of ephedrine and pseudoephedrine is regulated in the United States and other countries because of the clandestine production of _____.

3. Why have bath salts become a concern for law enforcement agencies?

4. Which form of cocaine can be smoked? Why?

1. Ephedrine and pseudoephedrine **2.** methamphetamine **3.** Drugs sold as bath salts contain synthetic cathinone compounds that elicit psychostimulant effects. **4.** The freebase form, which is referred to as *crack* cocaine. The boiling point for freebase cocaine allows it to be smoked in a pipe, whereas the vaporization point for the salt form of cocaine is too high to reach without special laboratory equipment.

Pharmacokinetics of Psychostimulants

Routes and Forms of Psychostimulant Administration

The selected route of psychostimulant drug administration depends on the user's desired purpose for taking the drug. For achieving therapeutic effects, physicians prescribe psychostimulant drugs such as amphetamine and methylphenidate for oral administration in pill form. Methylphenidate is also available in liquid and skin-patch form. For achieving rewarding effects, users prefer administration routes that provide rapid drug absorption, including intravenous injection, insufflation, and inhalation.

The salt forms of psychostimulant drugs tend to allow for intravenous injections. To prepare amphetamine pills or methamphetamine crystals in salt form, the substance is first ground into a fine powder. Then it is mixed with a household chemical, which could be a chemical base or an organic solvent, to place the drug in a salt form. Because prescribed methylphenidate tablets contain the salt form of methylphenidate, recreational users crush the tablets in a fine powder. The cathinone drugs in bath salts already exist in salt form. Users dissolve the drug in salt form into water, making a drug solution that can be injected.

The salt forms of these drugs also allow for insufflation or *snorting*. Users typically insufflate psychostimulant drugs by sharply inhaling lines of powder into a nostril through a short tube. This method places a substance into contact with membranes in the nose, throat, and lungs. The salt form is necessary for this route because drugs must be water soluble for proper absorption into these membranes.

The base forms of these drugs allow for inhalation. This is usually accomplished by heating the drug on a foil or plate or by heating the drug in a glass bulb or pipe. A *crack pipe* is a glass pipe used to smoke the freebase or crack form of cocaine. Smoking freebase cocaine can cause the release of **methylecgonidine**, a by-product of the freebase synthesis process that is harmful to the heart, lungs, and liver.

Methylecgonidine
By-product of the freebase synthesis process for cocaine that is harmful to the heart, lungs, and liver

Although intravenous injection, insufflation, and inhalation all provide quick absorption, the time courses among these routes vary. For example, Volkow and colleagues (2000) studied the peak drug effect onset times for a "high" for different routes of cocaine in cocaine-addicted individuals. Through the inhalation route, cocaine's peak subjective effects occurred after only 1.4 minutes. The intravenous route took twice as long to achieve peak effects, at 3.1 minutes, and insufflation produced the longest onset time for peak subjective effects, at 14.6 minutes (**Figure 6.8**). A drug's onset times can affect its addiction liability. Hatsukami and Fischman (1996), for example, found that cocaine addiction occurred more often for users who preferred inhalation and intravenous routes compared to users who preferred insufflation routes.

Other administration routes result in poorer absorption. Inhabitants of coca plant regions have long chewed coca leaves for their rejuvenating effects and for oral pain-relieving effects. Because the base form poorly penetrates mucous membranes, the leaves are often chewed with lime to improve water solubility. This in turn improves mucous-membrane absorption. Even with lime, only a small portion of cocaine absorbs through the mucous membranes. This isn't the case for all stimulants found in plants, however. Chewing khat leaves leads to 60 percent of cathinone absorption into mucous membranes (Toennes, Harder, Schramm, Niess, & Kauert, 2003).

Biotransformation of Psychostimulants

Some psychostimulant drugs produce active metabolites in the liver, and many times these metabolites exhibit effects similar to the parent drug. For example, liver enzymes

FIGURE 6.8 ● The time peak for research participants to feel a "high" from cocaine varies by administration route. Among these most common routes, inhalation provides a quicker onset time than either insufflation or intravenous injection.

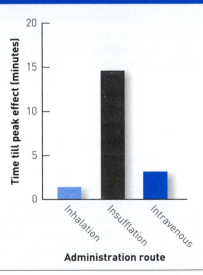

SOURCE: Adapted from Volkow et al., 2000.

convert methamphetamine to amphetamine. By serving as a parent drug for amphetamine, methamphetamine administration produces psychostimulant effects from both methamphetamine and amphetamine. Other drugs that produce amphetamine as an active metabolite include the amphetamines *prenylamine* (*Segontin*) and *selegiline* (*Anipryl*).

We find active metabolites for cathinone and cocaine as well. Cathinone metabolism in the liver produces the active metabolite norephedrine, the *d* optical isomer of pseudoephedrine. Thus, cathinone administration leads to psychostimulant effects produced by itself *and* pseudoephedrine. Cocaine's active metabolite benzoylecgonine functions to constrict blood vessels as cocaine does (Madden, Konkol, Keller, & Alvarez, 1995).

Drug combinations may also interact to produce active metabolites. Combining cocaine with alcohol produces, through metabolism in the liver, the active metabolite cocaethylene, a compound with psychostimulant properties (Bradberry et al., 1993; McCance, Price, Kosten, & Jatlow, 1995; Rafla & Epstein, 1979). Through producing this psychostimulant, combined cocaine and alcohol use—an example of **polydrug use**—may provide greater rewarding effects than those produced by either drug alone (McCance et al., 1995). A similar reaction occurs after ingesting methylphenidate and alcohol, which results in the formation of the psychostimulant ethylphenidate. The production of such active metabolites suggests that polydrug use may increase the likelihood of abuse (Grant & Harford, 1990).

Polydrug use The use of multiple substances, normally with the intention of achieving a specific effect

Elimination of Psychostimulants

Amphetamine and methamphetamine have longer elimination rates than cocaine. The half-life for amphetamine is approximately 10 hours; similarly, the half-life of methamphetamine is approximately 11 hours. In comparison, cocaine's half-life is approximately 1 hour, which accounts for shorter duration of psychostimulant effects than amphetamine and methamphetamine. Studies find a 1.5-hour half-life for cathinone, although we need pharmacokinetic information on the rapidly emerging synthetic cathinones (Toennes et al., 2003). Methylphenidate's half-life is approximately 2 hours, requiring additional administrations during a day for a steady drug effect. Given this, a physician may prescribe amphetamine (Adderall) for ADHD to school-age children in order to avoid having the medication wear off during a school day. Researchers are also developing new formulations of the methylphenidate to prolong its effects (Childress, Sallee, & Berry, 2011).

STOP & CHECK

1. Why might a user prefer to inhale psychostimulant drugs instead of resorting to other administration methods?

2. Why are knowing a drug's metabolites important for learning about psychostimulant effects?

1. The inhalation route offers quicker absorption than insufflation or even intravenous administration. 2. Many psychostimulant drugs alone or in combination with alcohol produce active metabolites, including those acting as psychostimulant drugs.

Psychostimulants and Monoamine Neurotransmitters

Amphetamines

Amphetamines cause an increase in synaptic dopamine levels through two mechanisms of action (**Figure 6.9**). First, amphetamine expels dopamine from the neuron through dopamine membrane transporters. Amphetamine does this by causing a reversal in the direction of the dopamine transporter. Second, at high doses, amphetamine drugs

FIGURE 6.9 ● Amphetamine and methamphetamine cause an increase in synaptic dopamine levels through (1) displacing dopamine from dopamine storage vesicles and (2) reversing the direction of the dopamine transporter. MAO enzymes can break down unstored dopamine in the axon terminal as well.

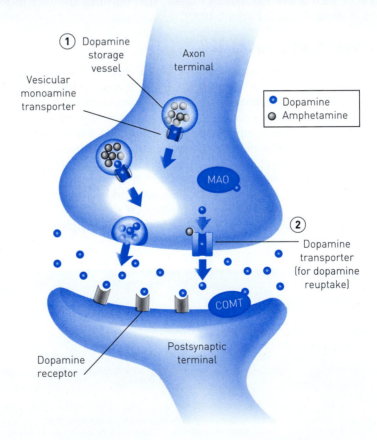

prevent dopamine storage. Amphetamine and methamphetamine do this by entering dopamine storage vesicles through the vesicular transporter and displacing dopamine from the vesicle (Pifl, Drobny, Reither, Hornykiewicz, & Singer, 1995). Dopamine not stored in vesicles can be expelled into the cleft by membrane transporters—those with a reverse flow due to amphetamine—or will be broken down by enzymes.

Review! Dopamine enters vesicles through a vesicular transporter. After release, dopamine molecules reenter the terminal through dopamine membrane transporters. (Chapter 3.)

Review! The enzyme MAO (monoamine oxidase) catabolizes (i.e., breaks down) dopamine and other monoamine neurons inside an axon terminal. (Chapter 3.)

Amphetamine and methamphetamine also enhance serotonin and norepinephrine levels through acting at axonal terminals, but do so to a lesser extent than dopamine. Amphetamine and methamphetamine also prevent both serotonin and norepinephrine storage, and they reverse the direction of the membrane transporter for these neurotransmitters (Seidel et al., 2005).

Methylphenidate and Cathinones

The pharmacological actions of methylphenidate resemble those of amphetamine. These drugs prevent reuptake of dopamine, serotonin, and norepinephrine but do so with less efficacy than amphetamine. Also like amphetamine, methylphenidate prevents the storage of dopamine in synaptic vesicles (Pan et al., 1994).

Given the dramatic increase in use of cathinone and synthetic cathinones, there has been an increased focus on evaluating the pharmacological actions of these drugs. Recent findings suggest that these drugs inhibit reuptake of dopamine, norepinephrine, and serotonin. Baumann and colleagues (2012) conducted radioligand binding experiments with two synthetic cathinones—mephedrone and methylone—to determining their binding affinity for dopamine, norepinephrine, and serotonin membrane transporters (see Box 4.1 for an overview of radioligand binding experiments). They next used microdialysis procedures to sample neurotransmitter levels in the nucleus accumbens of rats after administration of these drugs, in addition to testing methamphetamine for comparison. Both mephedrone and methylone increased levels of dopamine, although less so than levels produced by methamphetamine (**Figure 6.10**). Mephedrone and methylone also exhibited increased serotonin levels and were similar to serotonin levels produced by methamphetamine.

Cocaine

The primary mechanisms of action for cocaine involve prevention of monoamine reuptake by blocking the membrane transporters for dopamine, norepinephrine, and serotonin (Chen, Sachpatzidis, & Rudnick, 1997; Jones, Garris, & Wightman, 1995; Ritz, Cone, & Kuhar, 1990) (**Figure 6.11**). Further, cocaine *increases* transport of dopamine into synaptic vesicles, which may provide more stored dopamine for

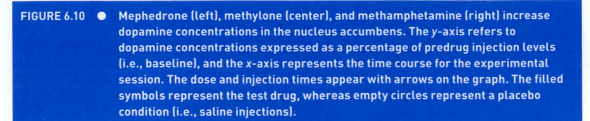

FIGURE 6.10 ● Mephedrone (left), methylone (center), and methamphetamine (right) increase dopamine concentrations in the nucleus accumbens. The *y*-axis refers to dopamine concentrations expressed as a percentage of predrug injection levels (i.e., baseline), and the *x*-axis represents the time course for the experimental session. The dose and injection times appear with arrows on the graph. The filled symbols represent the test drug, whereas empty circles represent a placebo condition (i.e., saline injections).

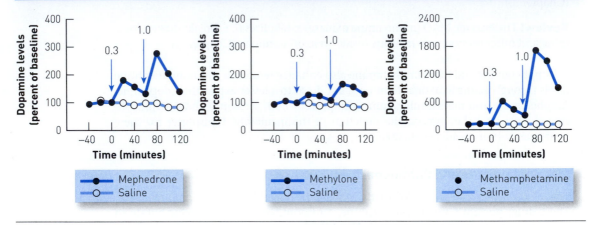

SOURCE: Adapted from Baumann, et al., 2012. "The Designer Methcathinone Analogs, Mephedrone and Methylone, are Substrates for Monoamine Transporters in Brain Tissue." *Neuropsychopharmacology* 37, 1192–1203, Nature Publishing Group.

release (Brown, Hanson, and Fleckenstein, 2001). The active metabolite cocaethylene, produced after ingesting both cocaine and alcohol, also functions as a dopamine reuptake inhibitor (McCance et al., 1995). In high concentrations, cocaine acts as a Na^{2+} channel blocker. This concentration far exceeds those necessary for producing the psychoactive effects just described, and actually will cause serious adverse effects and possibly death. However, these adverse effects can be avoided by applying cocaine locally; in doing so, cocaine serves as a local anesthetic. In fact, the discovery of these properties revolutionized ophthalmic surgery, because cocaine not only numbs the eye but also temporarily stops bleeding during surgery due to its vasoconstricting properties (i.e., constricts blood vessels) (dos Reis, 2009). These same vasoconstriction properties make cocaine still useful today as a treatment for stopping severe nose bleeds and as a local anesthetic for intranasal surgeries (e.g., Yung, Sharma, Jablenska, & Yung, 2015).

Cocaine- and amphetamine-regulated transcript (CART) Peptide neurotransmitter that is produced after psycho-stimulant administration

Cocaine- and Amphetamine-Regulated Transcript

The **cocaine- and amphetamine-regulated transcript (CART)** is a peptide neurotransmitter that is produced after psychostimulant administration. Acute administration of a psychostimulant drug causes the activation of the gene for CART, leading to the synthesis of the CART peptide, which is then stored in vesicles within axon

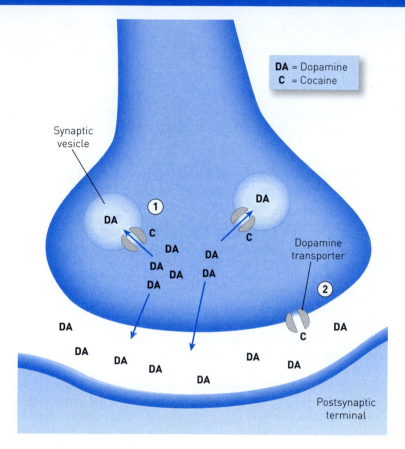

FIGURE 6.11 ● Cocaine causes an increase in synaptic dopamine levels by 1) blocking the dopamine transporter and 2) reducing reuptake. Cocaine exhibits similar effects for norepinephrine and serotonin membrane transporters (not shown). Cocaine also increases dopamine's entry into vesicles.

terminals. CART peptides are found in the hypothalamus and mesolimbic dopamine system, where they increase dopamine release, although the precise mechanisms responsible for these actions remain unknown. CART peptides produce psychostimulant-like increases in locomotor activity. Yet CART peptides also prevent psychostimulant-induced increases and dopamine-induced increases in locomotor activity (Jaworski, Kozel, Philpot, & Kuhar, 2003). Thus, CART alone produces psychostimulant-like effects, but CART in combination with a psychostimulant drug appears to counteract a psychostimulant's effects (Hubert, Jones, Moffett, Rogge, & Kuhar, 2008). In this way, CART might act to regulate the degree to which psychostimulant- and dopamine-induced effects can occur.

STOP & CHECK

1. Through similar mechanisms, the amphetamines, methylphenidate, cathinones, and cocaine all enhance synaptic levels of the neurotransmitters _____, _____, and _____.

2. Unlike the other psychostimulants, what other actions does cocaine have?

3. What peptide neurotransmitter is released on acute administration of certain psychostimulant drugs?

1. dopamine, norepinephrine, serotonin (in any order) **2.** At high doses, cocaine acts as a Na²⁺ channel blocker, which accounts for its local anesthetizing properties. **3.** CART, which stands for *cocaine- and amphetamine-regulated transcript.*

Pharmacological Effects of Psychostimulants

Physiological Effects

Psychostimulant drugs produce most of their physiological effects by activating the sympathetic nervous system. Activation of the sympathetic nervous system increases heart rate, constricts blood vessels, relaxes airways, dilates pupils, inhibits salivation, inhibits digestion, and produces various other effects described in Chapter 2 (see **Table 6.3**). We find some suggestions of these effects in Sigmund Freud's *Über Coca*, mentioned previously in this chapter. Freud described a moderate increase in pulse rate that was "often accompanied by a rumbling . . . from high up in the intestine," an effect observed in two other individuals. These two individuals had also reported "an intense feeling of heat in the head," and Freud added, "I noticed this in myself" (Freud, 1974).[3]

Activation of the sympathetic nervous system accounts for many of the uses and risks associated with psychostimulants. Psychostimulants ease nasal congestion by constricting swollen blood vessels in the sinuses and nasal passages. They also open airways in the lungs. These actions explain why ephedra is an effective herbal remedy for colds and why its main constituents, ephedrine and pseudoephedrine, serve as effective ingredients in cold medications.

Psychostimulants can cause hyperthermia, especially when used during strenuous physical exertion. Indeed, amphetamines contributed to the hyperthermia-related deaths of several athletes in the 1960s and 1970s (Wyndham 1977). Wide public attention was given to ephedra after it contributed to the heat-stroke–related death of Baltimore Orioles pitcher Steve Bechler in 2003.

Anorectics Appetite-suppressant drugs

Psychostimulants also reduce appetite. As stated previously, psycho-stimulants served as appetite suppressant drugs called **anorectics** during the 1950s and 1960s. In the

---

3 This reference refers to an English translation of Freud's cocaine papers, including *Über Coca*. Freud's actual manuscript was published in 1885.

TABLE 6.3 ● Selected Objective and Subjective Psychostimulant Effects		
Objective Effects		
Physiological Effects	**Behavioral Effects**	**Subjective Effects**
Increased heart rate	Psychosis, including hallucinations	Increased energy
Blood-vessel constriction (high blood pressure)	Increased motor activity	Increased alertness
		Improved sense of well-being
Airway relaxation		Euphoria
Pupil dilation		Anxiousness
Dry mouth (reduced salivation)		Agitation
Inhibited digestion		
Increased body temperature		
Tooth decay with chronic use		

SOURCE: © Cengage Learning 2014.

1990s, a combination therapy of the amphetamines fenfluramine and phentermine, together referred to as *fen-phen*, proved remarkably effective for weight loss. Another amphetamine, dexfenfluramine (Redux), was also used in combination with phentermine. Severe adverse cardiovascular effects resulting in heart valve damage and some deaths led to an abrupt decline of fen-phen treatments for obesity (Wadden et al., 1998).

Psychostimulants reduce hunger through actions in the hypothalamus, a key structure for the regulation of appetite. Within this structure, enhanced dopamine release contributes to appetite suppression. CART also plays a role in hunger. In the hypothalamus, CART is activated by the appetite-suppressing hormone leptin. Correlational studies suggest that impaired CART functioning, because of polymorphisms of the CART gene, is associated with obesity (Vicentic & Jones, 2007).

Behavioral Effects

Increased behavioral activity is a key feature of psychostimulant drugs. These effects are dose dependent and affect both purposeful and purposeless behavior. At lower doses, psychostimulants produce an increase in **purposeful behavior**—that is, it appears to be goal directed. For example, a laboratory rat pressing a lever to receive food reinforcers is engaging in purposeful behavior. Relatively low doses of psychostimulants can cause *faster* lever pressing. In humans, an increase in purposeful behavior may result in fast speech or faster completion of various tasks. Increased purposeful behavior occurs from increased dopamine concentrations in the nucleus accumbens (Ellinwood, King, & Lee, 2000).

Purposeful behavior (for psychostimulant use) Behavior that is goal directed; increased by lower doses of psychostimulants

Rate-dependent effects Differing effects of a drug depending on the rate of behavior prior to drug administration

Purposeless behavior (for psychostimulant use) Non-goal-directed behavior; may appear as habits; increased by higher doses of psychostimulants

Stereotypy Psychostimulant-produced purposeless behavior

Punding Psychostimulant-induced stereotypy in humans

These activity changes in purposeful behavior also have rate-dependent effects. For drugs, **rate-dependent effects** reflect differences in a drug's behavioral effects as a function of predrug administration response rates (Ginsburg, Pinkston, & Lamb, 2011). Psychostimulant drugs increase low rates of baseline behavioral activity. At the same time, psychostimulant drugs decrease high rates of baseline behavioral activity. As shown in **Figure 6.12**, for example, amphetamine increased activity in rats that had relatively low rates of lever pressing. However, amphetamine *decreased* activity in rats that had a relatively high rate of lever pressing (MacPhail & Gollub, 1975). These properties may explain why amphetamine and methylphenidate are effective for treating ADHD.

At higher doses, psychostimulants produce an increase in **purposeless behavior**, which occurs as non-goal-directed behavior that appears habitual. In nonhuman animals, this increase in purposeless behavior is called **stereotypy**. Stereotypy in rodents is characterized by repetitive grooming, head swaying, gnawing, or licking. In humans, we refer to stereotypic effects as **punding**. Punding may consist of repetitive teeth grinding, tapping, skin picking, or nail biting. Increased dopamine concentrations in dorsal portions of the basal ganglia, particularly the caudate nucleus, appear most associated with purposeless behavior (Ellinwood et al., 2000).

Subjective Effects

In humans, low doses of psychostimulants provide feelings of increased energy, alertness, a sense of well-being, enthusiasm, and other positive emotional effects

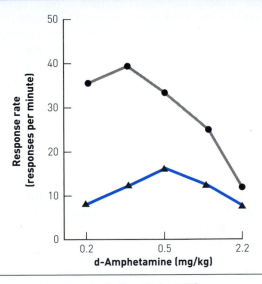

FIGURE 6.12   ●   D-amphetamine reduces high response rates (circles) and increases low response rates (triangles) at an appropriate dose—0.5 mg/kg—in rats.

SOURCE: Adapted from a paper, data from MacPhail and Gollub, 1975.

(Smith & Davis, 1977). Such doses are used to combat fatigue and reduce the symptoms of narcolepsy. Higher doses of psychostimulants, when administered through a route that offers rapid absorption, produce a "rush" and euphoria. Active metabolites that function as psychostimulants enhance these effects.

Review! Subjective effects are uniquely experienced by the individual and cannot be directly observed by others. Objective effects can be measured by recording overt behavior or physiological events. (Chapter 1.)

Drug discrimination procedures measure the subjective effects of psychostimulants (**see Box 6.1**). For example, Johanson, Lundahl, Lockhart, and Schubiner (2006) used a drug-discrimination procedure to determine whether human participants experience the same subjective effects for cocaine as they do for methamphetamine. During training, the participants were rewarded with money for correctly identifying a cocaine-like effect or non-cocaine-like effect. After learning to accurately discriminate between these two conditions, the participants were administered methamphetamine instead of cocaine. Most of the participants indicated that they had received cocaine in this procedure. We infer from these results that the subjective effects of cocaine and methamphetamine are similar.

As presented in Chapter 5 (Box 5.1), break points also assess the strength of positive mood effects of psychostimulant drugs. For example, **Figure 6.13** (page 192) shows the results of break-point studies conducted in rats using d-amphetamine, methamphetamine, cocaine, and other psychostimulants. In these studies, the break points for the highest doses of d-amphetamine and methamphetamine are both found at 268 responses per reinforcer. The break point for cocaine was 178 responses, lower than either d-amphetamine or methamphetamine. Thus, rats were willing to work harder for d-amphetamine and methamphetamine than for cocaine (Richardson & Roberts, 1996).

Review! A break point is the maximum level of responding a subject is willing to do in order to receive a drug injection. (Chapter 5.)

Adverse Effects

Psychostimulants produce many adverse physiological effects. Among the most prominent are cardiovascular dysfunction, pulmonary dysfunction, abnormal fetal development, and tooth decay. Adverse effects also occur from the conditions of drug use. Drug administration in unclean environments or through shared needles exposes users to a high risk of infection. Among the most common diseases associated with abuse of intravenously administered drugs are human immunodeficiency virus (HIV), hepatitis, and tuberculosis (Brecher, 1972; Cadet & Krasnova, 2007; Ellinwood et al., 2000).

Cardiovascular effects represent the greatest risk of psychostimulant use. Enhanced sympathetic nervous system activation taxes the cardiovascular system by constricting blood vessels and increasing heart rate. These actions lead to an increased risk of hypertension, stroke, aortic rupture, and heart attack. Hypertension during psychostimulant use is an important cause of abnormal fetal development. Through blood-vessel constriction, total blood flow to the fetus is reduced, causing limited oxygen availability

BOX 6.1 DRUG DISCRIMINATION

A *drug-discrimination procedure* trains an organism to recognize or discriminate between the subjective effects of a particular drug compared to noticeably different effects. This procedure is used in other animals and humans to assess the subjective effects of both recreational and therapeutic drugs.

Drug-discrimination procedures often are conducted in rats, pigeons, or monkeys using operant chambers. In a typical design, researchers select a *training drug*, which is a psychoactive of interest for the study. The training drug is also called a *discriminative stimulus*, because it signals an opportunity for reinforcement. After administration of the training drug, the animal is placed into the operant chamber containing two levers: buttons (often referred to as *keys*), or some other type of operandi. Only responses on one operandum will be reinforced, usually by delivery of a food pellet or small water cup. On a different day, the organism is administered the training drug vehicle, the inert solution in which the drug was dissolved, and only responses on the other operandum will be reinforced. After extensive training, an organism learns to associate one operandum with the training drug's subjective effects and the other operandum with the absence of the training drug's effects.

Note that *drug discrimination* and *self-administration* procedures are different. In a self-administration procedure, which is used for break-point studies, animals produce a behavioral response to *receive a drug injection*.

In a drug-discrimination procedure, animals must attend to a drug's subjective effects in order to receive food, water, or other type of reinforcer.

To place the drug discrimination procedure into context, consider the following study by de la Garza and Johanson (1985) using pigeons. The operandi used in this study were two response keys. One key was associated with cocaine and other was associated with *saline*—that is, the absence of cocaine's stimulus effects. These cocaine or saline training conditions alternated in daily sessions until the pigeons correctly responded to each condition with greater than 90-percent accuracy.

After training, the pigeons were administered different drugs to determine whether the pigeons responded on the cocaine key, indicating cocaine-like stimulus effects, or the saline key, indicating *non*-cocaine like stimulus effects. Figure 1 shows these study results.

These figures show the percentage of pecking that occurred on the cocaine key during test sessions for each drug and dose tested. At 1.0 mg/kg and 2.0 mg/kg doses, d-amphetamine caused almost all of the key pecks to occur on the cocaine lever. Similarly, the highest dose of cathinone produced nearly all pecks on the cocaine key. Both d-amphetamine and cathinone are psychostimulant drugs that have similar subjective effects as cocaine and

FIGURE 1 ● The psychostimulant drugs d-amphetamine (left) and cathinone (middle), but not the barbiturate pentobarbital (right), engendered cocaine key responding in a cocaine drug-discrimination task in pigeons. These findings suggest that d-amphetamine and cathinone produce subjective effects similar to those of cocaine. The y-axis refers to the percentage of key pecks occurring on the cocaine key, and the x-axis refers to the dose of the drug.

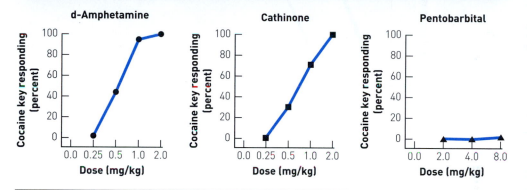

SOURCE: Data from de la Garza & Johanson, 1985.

may represent the stimulus effects of cocaine in this task. However, pentobarbital, a barbiturate that exhibits very different subjective effects than cocaine, resulted in few pecks on the cocaine key.

Human drug-discrimination procedures are similar to animal drug-discrimination procedures. In place of an operant chamber, human participants emit responses on a computer mouse; clicks usually substitute for key pecks or lever presses. Money usually serves in place of food pellets.

There are many variations on the typical drug-discrimination design. For example, two or more training drugs may be used in the same procedure, or there may be more than two operandi used in an operant chamber. These design variations can provide a further resolution of the biological actions supporting a drug's subjective effects.

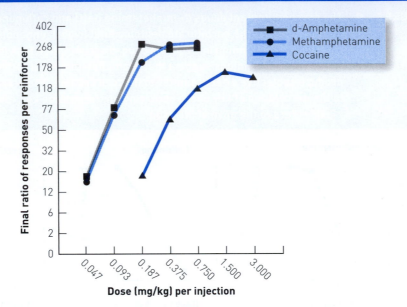

FIGURE 6.13 ● The break point for three psychostimulant drugs is shown as the highest "final ratio" completed. On the bottom (x-axis) is the amount of drug delivered per injection. Cocaine, shown by the triangles, had a lower break point than both d-amphetamine (squares) and methamphetamine (circles).

and nutrient delivery. These effects, in turn, contribute to lower fetal growth and the risk of severe injury to the fetus, including hemorrhage, ischemia, and neuronal death.

The adverse effects on pulmonary function include injury during inhalation, hemorrhaging, edema, and tissue inflammation. Normal pulmonary function is compromised when sympathetic nervous system activity is significantly enhanced as well as when the lungs are exposed to vapor from inhaled methamphetamine or crack cocaine. Smoking these drugs exposes the lungs to the drug as well as any harmful by-products produced during the drug's synthesis (Ellinwood et al., 2000; Lineberry & Bostwick, 2006).

Among the psychostimulant drugs, methamphetamine use is most associated with tooth decay, a condition referred to as "**meth mouth**." The American Dental Association describes these teeth as "blackened, stained, rotting, crumbling, or falling apart" (American Dental Association, 2005). Meth mouth occurs even when methamphetamine does not contact the teeth.

Meth mouth Tooth decay caused by methamphetamine use

Important contributing factors for meth mouth include poor dental hygiene, such as brushing and flossing, as well as damaged gums due to contact with inhaled chemicals during drug use. Two other contributing factors for meth mouth occur from activation of the sympathetic nervous system. First, methamphetamine's activation of the sympathetic nervous system reduces salivation, which has important protective properties for preventing tooth decay. Second, reduced saliva causes *dry mouth*, which motivates a methamphetamine user to drink fluids. Methamphetamine users tend to consume sugary soft drinks, and exposing teeth to sugar, particularly in the absence of saliva's tooth protective properties, leads to cavities and tooth decay (Klasser & Epstein, 2005).

Psychostimulants also produce psychosis at high doses. **Psychostimulant-induced psychosis** is similar to symptoms of schizophrenia, including paranoia, agitation, and auditory hallucinations. Given that psychostimulants enhance brain dopamine levels, psychostimulant-induced psychosis suggests that abnormally high dopamine levels exist in schizophrenia. Yet psychostimulant-induced psychosis differs from psychosis in schizophrenia. First, many psychostimulant hallucinations are tactile. High psychostimulant doses cause **formication**, a tactile hallucination described as feeling like insects or worms crawling under the skin. Such tactile hallucinations are less common for schizophrenia. Second, psychostimulant-induced psychosis often includes visual hallucinations and occasional olfactory hallucinations. Psychosis in schizophrenia mainly includes auditory hallucinations.

Psychostimulant-induced psychosis Psychotic behavior caused by psychostimulant use

Formication A tactile hallucination described as feeling like insects or worms crawling under the skin

STOP & CHECK

1. Activation of the _____ nervous system accounts for many of the physiological objective effects of psychostimulant drugs.

2. Appetite-suppressant effects are the reason why psychostimulant drugs have been used to treat _____.

3. Although low psychostimulant doses may increase purposeful behavior, high psychostimulant doses may increase _____ behavior.

4. How do subjective effects of cocaine compare to methamphetamine?

1. sympathetic **2.** obesity **3.** purposeless **4.** Both drugs produce euphoria and other positive mood effects. Moreover, humans trained to recognize the subjective effects of cocaine misidentify methamphetamine as cocaine.

Psychostimulant Drugs Produce Sensitization and Tolerance

Either sensitization or tolerance can occur from repeated use of psychostimulants. Sensitization tends to occur for *purposeless* behavior. In rats, sensitization presents as an increase in stereotypic behaviors such as sniffing and head movements (Robinson & Becker, 1986). Repeated administration of psychostimulant drugs may also lead to incentive sensitization, which may play an important role in the development of psychostimulant addiction (Robinson & Berridge, 2003).

Review! Incentive salience describes the heightened neurobiological and behavioral responses to stimuli associated with drug use. (Chapter 5.)

Tolerance occurs to the positive subjective effects of psychostimulants by creating a need to use higher doses of a psychostimulant drug to achieve these effects. However, the initial "high" first felt from a psychostimulant drug can be hard to achieve. Cocaine users, for example, seldom experience the same rush they felt on first using cocaine, and efforts to achieve this same intense rush is a driving force in cocaine addiction.

We find that a key form of psychostimulant tolerance is *pharmacodynamic tolerance*. Although many pharmacological actions may play a role, pharmacodynamic tolerance relies in part on changes in dopamine D_2 receptor sensitivity. Barrett, White, and Caul (1992) demonstrated a link between D_2 receptors and repeated psychostimulant administration using a drug-discrimination procedure. In this study, rats learned to discriminate the D_2 receptor antagonist haloperidol[4] versus the psychostimulant drug d-amphetamine. The latter causes D_2 receptor activation by enhancing synaptic dopamine levels. After learning this discrimination, a chronic treatment regimen was employed. During this regimen, animals were treated either with haloperidol or with d-amphetamine for 10 consecutive days. On the day after treatment ended, the rats were placed in the operant chamber without a drug injection and were free to choose the appropriate lever, either haloperidol or amphetamine. Rats chronically treated with haloperidol chose the amphetamine lever, whereas rats chronically treated with d-amphetamine chose the haloperidol lever (**Figure 6.14**). This happened because pharmacodynamic tolerance developed over the course of the treatment regimen.

The study authors speculated that synaptic sites adapted to haloperidol's repeated blockade of D_2 receptors by increasing the sensitivity of D_2 receptors. Similarly, the synaptic sites adapted to repeated activation of D_2 receptors by d-amphetamine by decreasing the sensitivity of D_2 receptors. When they returned the rats to the operant chamber for a drug-discrimination test, chronically treated haloperidol rats had an oversensitive dopamine state; these effects resembled d-amphetamine–like stimulus effects. Similarly, the chronically treated d-amphetamine rats had an undersensitive dopamine state; these effects resembled haloperidol-like stimulus effects.

Cross tolerance also occurs between psychostimulant drugs. In an early characterization of psychostimulant cross tolerance, Woolverton, Kandel, and Schuster (1978) demonstrated that rats tolerant to cocaine-induced reductions in milk intake exhibit this same tolerance when treated with amphetamine. The same was true when amphetamine-tolerant rats were treated with cocaine.

A psychostimulant drug's dosing frequency—intermittent or continuous—plays an important role in determining whether sensitization or tolerance will occur. Sensitization occurs after a period of intermittent dosing of psychostimulants, whereas tolerance occurs after continuous dosing of psychostimulants. Generally, intermittent dosing consists of using a drug after all of the drug, as well as similarly acting metabolites, from past use has been eliminated from the body. Given the half-life of amphetamine in humans, two or three amphetamine administrations per week might qualify as intermittent drug administration. Continuous dosing consists of a user administering a drug while drug molecules (or similarly acting metabolites) from a previous administration remain in the body. Depending on the particular drug, continuous administration might consist of one or multiple administrations per day (Ellinwood et al., 2000).

---

4 Also an antipsychotic drug

FIGURE 6.14 ● In rats trained to discriminate haloperidol versus amphetamine in a two-lever drug-discrimination task, a test session conducted after chronic administration of haloperidol (left) led to increased amphetamine-lever responding, whereas a test session conducted after chronic administration of amphetamine (right) led to decreased amphetamine-lever responding (see text for further details). The *y*-axis refers to percent of responses occurring on the amphetamine lever.

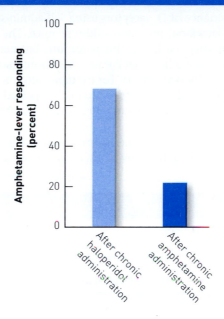

SOURCE: Data from Barrett et al., 1992.

STOP & CHECK

1. In addition to sensitization for purposeless behavior, what other type of sensitization occurs during long-term use of psychostimulant drugs?

2. Reduced D_2 receptor sensitivity after prolonged administration of a psychostimulant drug is an important mechanism of _____ tolerance.

3. Cross tolerance implies that an individual who tolerates high doses of cocaine would tolerate _____ doses of amphetamine.

1. In addition to sensitization to purposeless behavior, incentive sensitization may also occur. 2. pharmacodynamic 3. high

Psychostimulant Addiction

Linking Pharmacological Actions to Reinforcing Effects Increased dopamine neurotransmission in the nucleus accumbens mostly accounts for the reinforcing effects of psychostimulant drugs. In particular, these actions rely on dopamine D_2 receptors. The positive subjective effects of d-amphetamine, for example, can be blocked by D_2 receptor antagonists such as the antipsychotic drug haloperidol.

For cocaine, reinforcing effects also depend on the activation of dopamine D_1 receptors and serotonin neurotransmission. Greater activation of D_1 receptors occurs because of cocaine-induced elevations in dopamine levels. Caine and colleagues (2007) demonstrated the importance of D_1 receptors using self-administration procedures in dopamine D_1 receptor knock-out mice and wild-type mice. The wild-type mice readily learned to self-administer cocaine in this procedure, but none of the D_1 receptor knock-out mice learned to self-administer cocaine. Serotonin transporter blockade also contributes to cocaine's subjective effects. For example, serotonin transporter knock-out rats exhibit enhanced cocaine self-administration, hyperactivity, and conditioned place preference compared to wild-type rats (Homberg et al., 2008).

Review! Receptor knock-out mice lack certain receptors as a result of genetic modification. Wild-type mice are not genetically modified. (Chapter 2.)

🔗 *Drug Profile:* modafinil	
Trade name:	Provigil
Mechanism of action	Elevates dopamine levels in the nucleus accumbens
Uses	Psychostimulant detoxification and relapse prevention

The withdrawal symptoms associated with psychostimulants primarily occur from psychological dependence rather than physical dependence. Just as psychostimulants produce increases in activity, enjoyment, and euphoria, withdrawal from psychostimulants produces lethargy, lack of joy, and *dysphoria*, which is characterized as feelings of hopelessness, unhappiness, and discomfort.

Genetics Influence the Susceptibility to Psychostimulant Addiction Genetic animal studies provide a framework for identifying possible links between human genetic differences and susceptibility to psychostimulant addiction. There are three primary ways that genetic differences alter psychostimulant drug effects.

First, genetic differences can alter the rate of drug metabolism. If an individual's genetic expression of P450 enzymes leads to a quicker metabolism of a psychostimulant drug, this will shorten the duration of the drug's effects. Shorter drug effects may lead to more frequent drug use. Second, a genetic predisposition can enhance the subjective effects of psychostimulant drugs. Individuals have a greater risk of drug addiction if they experience powerful reinforcing effects. Third, a genetic predisposition can alter the negative effects of psychostimulant drugs. Drug addiction is unlikely to develop for an individual who experiences adverse effects or negative subjective effects after acute use (Haile, Kosten, & Kosten, 2009).

The **C-1021T polymorphism** has received much attention by psychostimu-lant addiction researchers. This polymorphism causes low expression of dopamine β-hydroxylase, the enzyme that converts dopamine to norepinephrine. Based on animal research that evaluated inhibitors of dopamine β-hydroxylase, psychostimulants likely exhibit lower norepinephrine release for those with lower dopamine β-hydroxylase expression compared to those exhibiting normal dopamine β-hydroxylase expression (Schroeder et al., 2010).

Through these actions, the C-1021T polymorphism may increase the negative sub-jective effects of psychostimulants. Kalayasiri and colleagues (2007) studied the rela-tionship between the C-1021T polymorphism and cocaine's subjective effects. This study used a cocaine self-administration experiment in humans with the C-1021T polymorphism. A greater degree of paranoia was observed in participants homozygous for the C-1021T polymorphism compared to other study participants. Cocaine users consider paranoia an aversive effect; some individuals experience and report paranoia and other features of psychosis and cite these as reasons for seeking addiction treat-ment (Brady, Lydiard, Malcolm, & Ballenger, 1991).

Sex Differences in Psychostimulant Addiction For all illicit substances, including psy-chostimulants, we find rates of use higher for men than women (Center for Behavioral Health Statistics and Quality, 2014). However, a number of findings suggest that women are particularly at risk for developing a psychostimulant addiction. Compared to men, women start using cocaine and amphetamine at an earlier age (Griffin, Weiss, & Lange, 1989; Mendelson et al., 1991). Women are also more likely to engage in binge cocaine use, use cocaine more frequently, and matriculate from first cocaine use to dependent use at a faster rate (Chen & Kandel, 2002; McCance-Katz, Carroll, & Rounsaville, 1999).

The potential reasons for a greater risk of cocaine addiction in women include estra-diol and progesterone levels and susceptibility to stress (Becker & Hu, 2008). During the follicular phase of the menstrual cycle, when estradiol slowly rises from low levels during the phase and progesterone levels are low, women report enhanced positive subjective effects from d-amphetamine use compared to use during the luteal phase, characterized by moderate estradiol and high progesterone levels. In female rats, administration of estrogen enhances the dopamine release produced by cocaine and appears necessary for CART-induced dopamine turnover in the nucleus accumbens (Shieh & Yang, 2008; Tobiansky et al., 2016). Studies also suggest that progesterone may weaken the subjective effects of psychostimulants (Becker & Hu, 2008).

Women who become psychostimulant dependent may have stronger reactions to stressors. For example, Back, Brady, Jackson, Salstrom, and Zinzow (2005) found that cocaine-dependent women reported greater feelings of stress than cocaine dependent men after completing stressful tasks in a laboratory setting. Sinha and colleagues (2007) found that cocaine-dependent women studied during the luteal phase reported feeling lower stress and less craving for cocaine than cocaine-depen-dent women studied during the follicular phase. Stress may also affect dopamine levels and pattern of drug administration in males versus females, based on studies

C-1021T polymorphism Polymorphism that causes low expression of dopamine β-hydroxylase, the enzyme that converts dopamine to norepinephrine in rats. Holly, Shimamoto, DeBold, and Miczek (2012) applied stressors to male and female rats, finding that stressed females (a) exhibited a greater duration of enhanced

FIGURE 6.15 ● Cocaine administration causes stressed female rats to exhibit a longer duration of elevated dopamine levels in the nucleus accumbens compared to stressed male rats (left). The *y*-axis shows the percentage of dopamine levels compared to pre-cocaine adminsitration. The *x*-axis shows time points when the samples were taken. Stressed female rats also exhibit a greater duration of cocaine self-administration binges compared to stressed male rats (right).

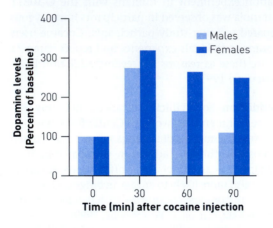
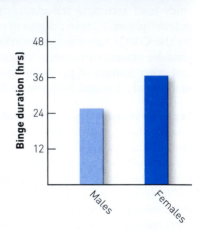

STOP & CHECK

1. Which dopamine receptors are important for the reinforcing effects of psycho-stimulant drugs, like cocaine and amphetamine?

2. How might the C-1021T polymorphism affect norepinephrine levels after cocaine use?

3. What role might estradiol play in the subjective effects of psychostimulants?

1. Dopamine D_2 and D_1 receptors. **2.** Given that people with the C-1021T polymorphism have a poorer ability of synthesizing norepinephrine from dopamine, which may lead to lower norepinephrine levels. **3.** Estradiol increases cocaine-induced elevations in nucleus accumbens dopamine release, which might be expected to enhance the positive subjective effects of cocaine.

dopamine levels in the nucleus accumbens, and (b) engaged in a greater overall duration of "binge" (a period of frequent self-administration) cocaine self-administration episodes compared to stressed males when given free access to cocaine over a 48-hour period (**Figure 6.15**).

From Actions to Effects:
Treatments for Psychostimulant Addiction

The therapies for psychostimulant addiction address two primary phases of recovery: abstinence and relapse. Abstinence begins with detoxification from a drug and then consists of a state of no drug use. During detoxification (*detox*), the withdrawal effects of psychostimulant use are most prominent. Treatment for detoxification typically involves hospitalization and medical treatment.

One treatment is **disulfiram**, a medication used to treat alcohol addiction. Disulfiram is an inhibitor of aldehyde dehydrogenase, an enzyme involved in alcohol metabolism, as well as an inhibitor of dopamine β-hydroxylase, an enzyme that converts dopamine to norepinephrine. Several clinical studies have evaluated disulfiram after cocaine administration, generally finding reduced positive subjective effects, including a reduced high or rush, and enhanced negative subjective effects, including paranoia, agitation, and nervousness (Baker, Jatlow, & McCance-Katz, 2007; Hameedi et al., 1995). Individuals with a C-1021T polymorphism are even more susceptible to negative subjective effects from disulfiram and cocaine administration (Haile et al., 2009). However, the ability of disulfiram to reduce positive subjective effects may depend on dosage. For example, Oliveto and colleagues (2011) found that lower doses of disulfiram increased the frequency of cocaine use over several weeks of treatment in cocaine-addicted users.

Many studies have evaluated *modafinil (Provigil)* for aiding psychostimulant detoxification. Modafinil engenders mild psychostimulant effects and has approved therapeutic uses for narcolepsy. Like other psychostimulants, modafinil elevates dopamine levels in the nucleus accumbens, yet these elevations are lower and longer lasting compared to other psychostimulant drugs (Zolkowska et al., 2009). Modafinil also increases glutamate levels in the nucleus accumbens after chronic cocaine use (Mahler et al., 2014). These actions may make modafinil a safe substitute for abused psychostimulant drugs.

Disulfiram
Medication used for treating alcohol addiction that inhibits aldehyde dehydrogenase and dopamine β-hydroxylase

🔎 Drug Profile: modafinil	
Trade name:	Provigil
Mechanism of action	Elevates dopamine levels in the nucleus accumbens
Uses	Psychostimulant detoxification and relapse prevention

Review! Rewarding effects can be produced by activating glutamate receptors in the nucleus accumbens. (Chapter 5.)

To investigate modafinil as a treatment for psychostimulant addiction, Dackis, Kampman, Lynch, Pettinati, and O'Brien (2004) evaluated 8 weeks of modafinil treatment, combined with psychotherapy, in cocaine-addicted individuals enrolled in an outpatient treatment program. Researchers collected and tested urine samples each week to determine abstinence from cocaine. During the course of the study, modafinil significantly increased the number of patients remaining abstinent from cocaine. Although these study results show promise, another study using modafinil failed to show changes in the frequency of cocaine use in addicted users (Anderson et al., 2009). Thus, modafinil for psychostimulant addiction requires further investigation.

Tricyclic antidepressant drugs such as imipramine effectively reduce craving, depression, and other withdrawal symptoms during psychostimulant detoxification. Chronic tricyclic antidepressant treatment elevates dopamine, norepinephrine, and serotonin levels, which may address a deficiency in these neurotransmitters during

FIGURE 6.16 ● Effects of a cocaine vaccine in cocaine-dependent subjects. No differences were shown between the groups during the first 8 weeks after injection of the vaccine, which was the time neccesary for sufficient antibody levels to develop. Some participants produced high levels of antibodies (labeled the "High antibody group"), and some produced low levels of antibodies (labeled the "Low antibody group"). The *y*-axis shows the percentage of users testing negative for cocaine in the body; the *x*-axis shows each week following injection of the vaccine. The dashed vertical line shows the time point (8 weeks) at which enough antibodies should have been sufficiently produced to act on cocaine molecules.

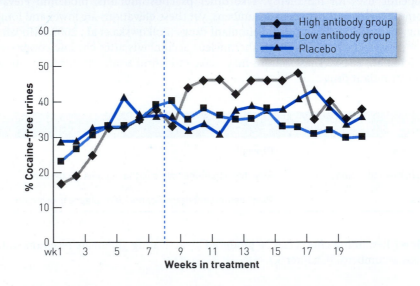

psychostimulant withdrawal. Addressing these deficiencies can aid in relapse prevention. For example, in an assessment of methamphetamine relapse rates, imipramine treatment was associated with significantly longer stays in a free drug-addiction clinic (Galloway, Newmeyer, Knapp, Stalcup, & Smith, 1996).

Drugs that facilitate GABA neurotransmission also demonstrate clinical efficacy for preventing psychostimulant relapse. For example, the anticonvulsant drug topiramate (Topamax) is commonly used for cocaine relapse prevention. In one clinical study, 60 percent of former cocaine-dependent patients treated with topiramate were completely abstinent for more than 3 weeks, compared to 26 percent of those treated with placebo (Kampman et al., 2004). Another anticonvulsant drug, vigabatrin (Sabril), provided similar improvements in treatment outcomes for cocaine-addicted patients (Kampman, 2010). Drugs that facilitate GABA neurotransmission may interrupt associative learning processes important during the preoccupation and anticipation stage of addiction. By interrupting these processes, these treatments may weaken sensitized incentive processes for drug seeking and use (Koob & Volkow, 2009).

Finally, researchers have developed approaches for vaccinating against psychostimulant effects as a way to prevent or eliminate abuse (Shen, Orson, & Kosten, 2012). The general approach consists of the production of antibodies that bind to a psychostimulant drug and prevent the drug from crossing the blood–brain barrier. Kosten and colleagues have evaluated a potential cocaine in cocaine-dependent users. In one of these studies the researchers found more cocaine-free urine samples for those with high antibody levels than compared to those with low antibody levels or placebo. These results were evident following 8 weeks, the amount of time needed for antibodies to reach sufficient levels (Figure 6.16). Yet even in the high antibody group, researchers found that less than 50 percent of patients were ultimately cocaine free; further, fewer cocaine-abstinent users were found a few weeks later (Martell et al., 2009). A later study from the group reported similar results (Kosten et al., 2014). Thus, although this approach may have appeal, further vaccine development is needed.

STOP & CHECK

1. What are the two primary aims of pharmacological treatment for psychostimulant addiction?

2. For the treatment of psychostimulant addiction, how might disulfiram drug therapy be related to the C-1021T polymorphism?

3. What are the shared pharmacological mechanisms for modafinil and tricyclic antidepressants that may be important for treating psychostimulant addiction?

1. To treat withdrawal symptoms during abstinence and prevent relapse. **2.** Like individuals with the C-1021T polymorphism, disulfiram lowers the expression of dopamine b-hydroxylase, causing unpleasant subjective effects to occur when a psychostimulant is administered. **3.** Modafinil and tricyclic antidepressants increase dopamine, norepinephrine, and serotonin concentrations just as amphetamine and cocaine do. In this way, these drugs may provide a replacement of these elevated neurotransmitters during psychostimulant use.

Chapter Summary

Psychostimulant drugs, also called *sympathomimetics*, increase psychomotor and sympathetic nervous system activity and promote alertness and positive mood. Common psychostimulant drugs include amphetamine drugs, cathinones, and cocaine. Many psychostimulant drugs are derived from plants and are produced legally or illegally. Traditionally, the plants containing psychostimulants were used by humans, often through chewing leaves. Psychostimulants such as methamphetamine and cocaine also are prepared in a base form that can be smoked. The salt forms of these drugs can be insufflated or injected. Psychostimulant drugs are administered in many forms, including insufflation, intravenous injection, and inhalation. Among these administration routes, inhalation provides the quickest drug effects. Many psychostimulant drugs have active metabolites that also exhibit psychostimulant effects.

Elevated dopamine levels in the nucleus accumbens account for the reinforcing effects of psychostimulant drugs, and elevated peripheral dopamine and norepinephrine levels account for increased sympathetic nervous system activity. Psychostimulants increase heart rate, blood pressure, body temperature, and other sympathetic nervous system functions. Behaviorally, psychostimulants increase purposeful activity at lower doses and purposeless activity at higher doses. High doses can produce psychotic behavior that resembles positive symptoms in schizophrenia. The subjective effects of psychostimulants include positive mood effects such as increased energy, alertness, and euphoria—and negative mood effects such as anxiousness, agitation, and paranoia. Sensitization occurs for purposeless behavior and for the incentive value of conditioned stimuli during prolonged use of psychostimulants, whereas tolerance occurs for the subjective effects of psychostimulants. Although more men use psychostimulants than women, women may be more likely to become addicted, possibly because of estrogen levels and reactivity to stress.

Pharmacological treatments for psychostimulant addiction either address withdrawal symptoms during abstinence or attempt to prevent relapse. These treatments act on the same sites of actions as psychostimulants such as the tricyclic antidepressant drugs or act through other mechanisms such as the anticonvulsant drug topiramate. Researchers have also investigated vaccination strategies for preventing psychostimulant effects.

Key Terms

Psychostimulant 168
Ephedra 170
Amphetamines 170
Racemic 170
Cathinone 173
Cocaine 175
Coca paste 175
Freebase 175
Methylecgonidine 179
Polydrug use 181

Cocaine- and amphetamine-
  regulated transcript
  (CART) 184
Anoretics 186
Purposeful behavior (for
  psychostimulant use) 187
Rate dependent effects 188
Purposeless behavior (for
  psychostimulant use) 188
Stereotypy 188

Punding 188
Meth mouth 192
Psychostimulant-induced
  psychosis 193
Formication 193
C-1021T polymorphism 197
Disulfiram 199

Visit the Student Study Site at **study.sagepub.com/prus2e** to access additional study tools, including eFlashcards, web quizzes, video resources, web resources, SAGE journal articles, and more.

Nicotine and Caffeine

IS NICOTINE NOT ADDICTIVE?

On April 14, 1994, a House subcommittee met to discuss the health concerns of tobacco use. Before the committee were seven corporate executive officers of large U.S.-based tobacco companies. In his opening remarks, the subcommittee chair reviewed the risks of tobacco use: high mortality rate, cancer, heart disease, and lung disease. Then Rep. Ron Wyden

(Continued)

(Continued)

(D–Oregon) asked the first question: "Yes or no, do you believe nicotine is not addictive?"

The executives' responses made this hearing famous. Down the line, every CEO made

a clear, simple answer to Wyden's answer: Nicotine is not addictive.

Did these CEOs have a defensible position? As presented later in this chapter, the CEOs' answers depend on how addiction is defined.

n Chapter 6, we considered the most powerful psychostimulants: amphetamines, cathinones, and cocaine. The current chapter covers two less powerful but more often used psychostimulant drugs: nicotine and caffeine.

Nicotine: Key Psychoactive Ingredient in Tobacco

Nicotine Central psychoactive ingredient in tobacco

Nicotine is the central psychoactive ingredient in tobacco. Tobacco consists of leaves from plants in the genus *Nicotiana* of which the primary nicotine-containing species grow in South and North America (**Figure 7.1**). The most popular plant used commercially is *Nicotiana tabacum*, leading to the name "tobacco." This plant species produces greater amounts of nicotine than other *Nicotiana* species (Saitoh, Noma, & Kawashima, 1985). Traditional forms of tobacco consisted of rolled tobacco leaves, and modern versions consist of cigars and cigarettes. When tobacco is chewed or smoked, small nicotine-containing tobacco particles called *tar* and other tobacco chemicals enter the body.

Cigarette A tobacco blend rolled in a thin sheet of paper

Cigarettes are the most commonly used tobacco product. A **cigarette** is composed of a tobacco blend rolled in a thin sheet of paper. Many cigarettes contain a filter of cellulose acetate that reduces the amount of tobacco tar inhaled. The tobacco portion of a regular cigarette is approximately 60 mm (2.25 in.) in length, and filtered cigarettes have a 25 mm (~1 in.) filter and usually shorter length of tobacco. Depending on the size and blend, a cigarette contains 1–2 mg of nicotine. Some brands of cigarettes have a flavoring added, the most popular of which is menthol. Menthol cigarettes, in particular, are almost exclusively used by African Americans, and more women tend to use menthol cigarettes than men (Muscat, Richie, & Stellman, 2002).

Cigar Tightly rolled bundle of dried tobacco leaves wrapped in a leaf

Cigars consist of tightly rolled bundles of dried tobacco leaves wrapped in a leaf. Cigars vary widely in diameter, length, and nicotine content. For example, a Winchester Little Cigar is 8 mm (~ ⅓ in.) in diameter and 60 mm (2⅓ in.) long, whereas a Cuesta-Rey No. 1 is 20 mm (~ ¾ in.) in diameter and 211 mm (8⅓ in.) in length. A Winchester Little Cigar contains 5.9 mg of nicotine, and a Cuesta-Rey No. 1 cigar contains 335.2 mg of nicotine (Henningfield, Fant, Radzius, & Frost, 1999).

SOURCE: iStockphoto/Praiwun.

Pipe smoking consists of inhaling smoke from a tobacco blend. Water pipes consist of inhaling smoke that has passed through a container of water. Hookah water pipe smoking is increasingly prevalent among younger Western adults, although it has been a common method of smoking in the Middle East for centuries (Neergaard, Singh, Job, & Montgomery, 2007) (**Figure 7.2**). A typical **hookah** is an ornately shaped and decorated water pipe assembly consisting of a charcoal-heated tobacco-holding chamber pipe connected through the water jar mouth and into the water; smokers inhale tobacco smoke from a hose projecting from the top of the jar. Inhaled tobacco smoke first passes through a bowl of water. Many users believe that this method reduces the harmful effects of tobacco, although studies of water-pipe tobacco exposure state otherwise (Ahmed, Jacob, Allen, & Benowitz, 2011; Jacob et al., 2011).

Smokeless tobacco products consist of any tobacco form intended for absorption in the mouth. Products called *chew*, *snuff*, and *dipping tobacco* consist of a tobacco blend that a user either chews or pockets in his or her cheek. When the product is spent, users spit the tobacco out. *Dissolvable tobacco* is another type of smokeless tobacco. These products come in the form of sweetened strips, sticks, or pellets that dissolve in the mouth. Dissolvable tobacco products contain amounts of nicotine similar to those found in cigarettes. For example, a strip contains 0.6 mg of nicotine, and a stick contains 3.1 mg of nicotine. The resemblance of these products to candy recently led to redesigning the appearance of these products (Connolly et al., 2010).

Hookah An ornately shaped and decorated water pipe assembly consisting of a charcoal-heated tobacco-holding chamber pipe connected through the water jar mouth and into the water, with tubes from the jar allowing for tobacco smoke inhalation

Smokeless tobacco A tobacco form intended for absorption in the mouth

FIGURE 7.2 ● A water pipe or *hookah* is traditionally used for smoking tobacco and is increasingly used among young Western adults.

Charcoal placed here

Bowl

Hose

Water jug (base)

Mouthpiece

SOURCE: Copyright iStockphoto/spilman.

E-cigarettes (or electronic nicotine delivery systems) Electronic nicotine vaporizers often shaped like a cigarettes

Finally, **e-cigarettes** (or **electronic nicotine delivery systems**), electronic nicotine vaporizers often shaped like a cigarettes, have emerged as another popular form of nicotine delivery. Modern e-cigarettes contain a battery that powers a heater attached to an *atomizer*, a component that reduces liquid into a fine spray. A liquid cartridge containing nicotine and propylene glycol plugs into the atomizer, which vaporizes the liquid when a sensor detects airflow passage or the user presses a button (Trtchounian, Willams, & Talbot, 2010) (**Figure 7.3**). Thus, a user inhales a nicotine vapor solution through an e-cigarette.

E-cigarettes once were used as a cigarette cessation approach—that is, they somewhat had the feel of a cigarette, but the user inhaled vaporized nicotine rather than tar particles from tobacco. These first-generation e-cigarettes closely resembled traditional cigarettes. Thus, we could describe those e-cigarette users as "smokers" who

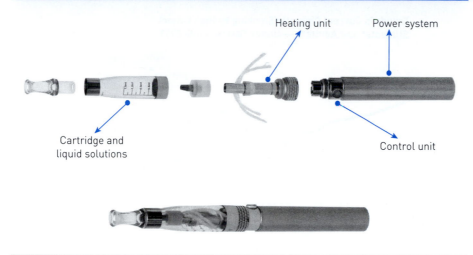

SOURCE: Copyright iStockphoto/-zlaki-.

were attempting to quit smoking traditional cigarettes. Today, many e-cigarette liquid cartridges also include flavorings, such as fruit and candy flavors, and users can assemble their e-cigarettes using customized components (or "mods"). For example, a user can add a mod to adjust the level of power to the heater, with greater heat leading to more e-liquid vaporized, and vice versa (Farsalinos et al., 2014). The amount of nicotine found in most e-cigarette liquid cartridges varies from 20 to 40 mg/ml (Davis, Dang, Kim, & Talbot, 2015). These second-generation e-cigarettes seldom resemble actual cigarettes; instead they have metallic, sleek-looking designs (Farsalinos et al., 2014). These devices tend to be referred to as *personal vaporizers*, *"vape pens,"* or similar names. Further, users of these devices may not be current or former tobacco smokers, leading us to identify them as "vapers" rather than smokers. Thus, a person using a nicotine vaporizer is "**vaping**" rather than smoking (Fagerstrom, Etter, & Unger, 2015).

Vaping Inhaling vapor from an e-cigarette

Tobacco use is widespread. In 2009, 70 million Americans ages 12 and older—a little less than 25 percent of the U.S. population—had used tobacco products within the preceding month. However, tobacco use is declining in the United States. Cigarette use in the United States peaked during the 1960s and has steadily decreased since (**Figure 7.4**).

According to the World Health Organization, tobacco use is high in many parts of Europe and Asia and throughout Central and South America (**Figure 7.5**).

FIGURE 7.4 ● Cigarettes are widely consumed, but their use has declined since the 1960s as tobacco's adverse health effects have become more publicly known in the United States. The y-axis shows the percentage of U.S. adults and high school students. The x-axis shows each year residents were surveyed.

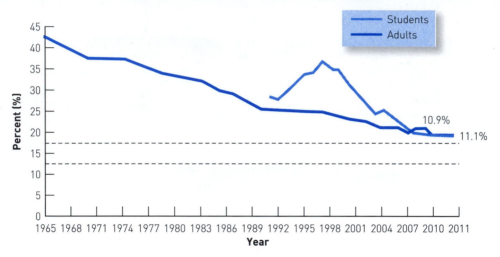

Trends in Current Cigarette Smoking by High School Students* and Adults** — United States, 1965-2011

*Percentage of high school students who smoked cigarettes on 1 or more of the 30 days preceding the survey (Youth Risk Behavior Survey, 1991-2011).

**Percentage of adults who are current cigarette smokers (National Health Interview Survey, 1965–2011).

Asia includes the highest rates. More than 60 percent of males in the Russian Federation and China use tobacco products. Males generally use tobacco products more than females, but these differences vary across countries. For example, equal smoking rates occur among males and females in Norway and Sweden, whereas less than 10 percent of females smoke in the Russian Federation and China (Mackay & Eriksen, 2002).

Vaping e-cigarette products is still a relatively new practice at the time of writing this book, but there are a number of trends suggesting increased use of these products and a likelihood of later using traditional tobacco products. The percentage of a large sample of U.S. adults who ever used an e-cigarette rose from 3.3 percent in 2010 to 8.5 percent in 2013; among a large sample of chronic smokers, reported recent e-cigarette use had risen from 1.1 percent in 2010 to 18.4 percent in 2013 (King, Patel, Nguyen, & Dube, 2014; Rigotti et al., 2015). 6.1 percent of middle and high school students had reported ever using e-cigarettes between the years 2011 and 2013 (Bunnell et al. 2015).

> **FIGURE 7.5** ● **The highest rates of tobacco use are found in many parts of Europe and Asia.**

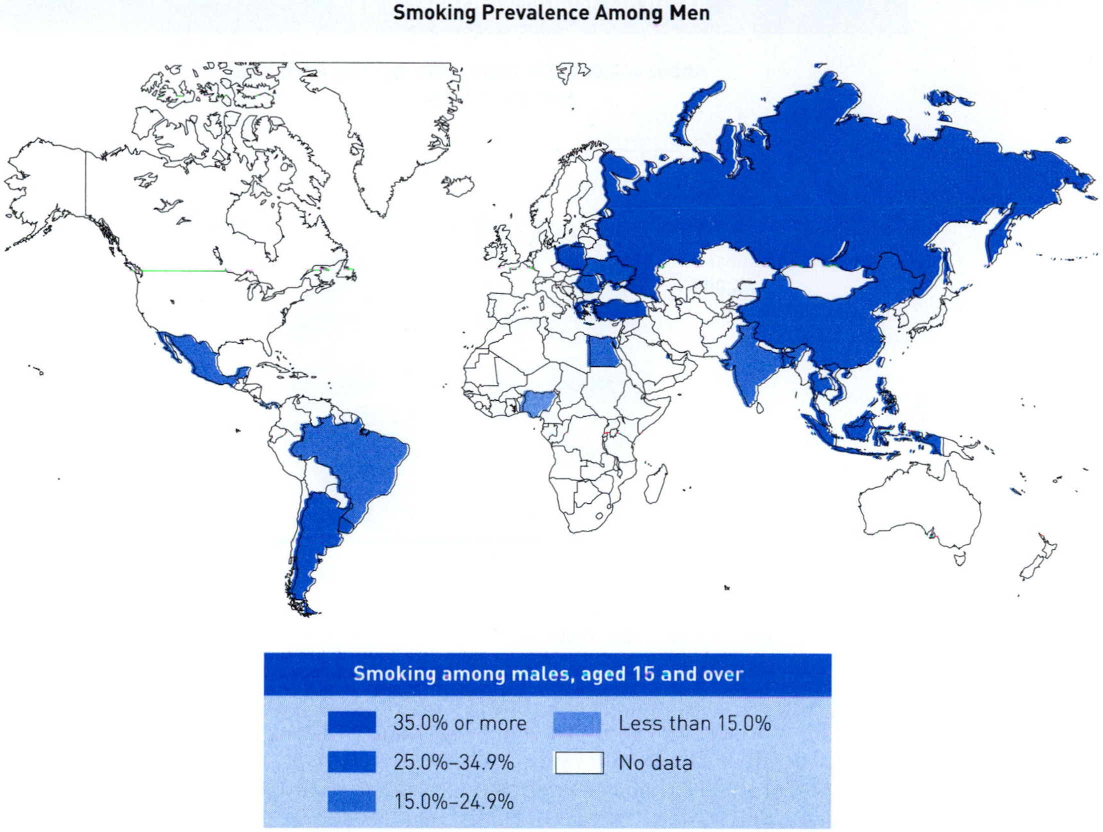

Smoking Prevalence Among Men

Smoking among males, aged 15 and over

- 35.0% or more
- 25.0%–34.9%
- 15.0%–24.9%
- Less than 15.0%
- No data

SOURCE: Based on data from CDC Foundation, World Health organization, World Lung Foundation. (2015). *The GATS Atlas: Global adult tobacco survey.* Retrieved from http://www.who.int/tobacco/publications/surveillance/gatstlas/en/.

Tobacco use has serious health effects. The three primary causes of tobacco-related death each year are cancer, pulmonary disease, and cardiovascular disease. According to the U.S. Centers for Disease Control and Prevention, 443,000 tobacco-related deaths occurred each year between 2000 and 2004. Of those deaths, more than 75 percent resulted from at least one of these three conditions, with lung cancer being the leading cause of tobacco-related deaths (**Figure 7.6**). African Americans have greater mortality rates from smoking, despite smoking less than European Americans, because of greater incidents of these smoking-related diseases (Fiore et al., 1989).

Evidence of adverse effects from e-cigarette use varies across scientific studies. The most consistent finding is that most e-cigarette vapors contain volatile organic compounds, including toluene and xylene. Otherwise, conflicting studies have been shown for a variety of potential health effects, including presence of organic compounds

FIGURE 7.6 ● **Lung cancer, chronic obstructive pulmonary disease such as emphysema, and heart disease are the greatest causes of death associated with tobacco use.**

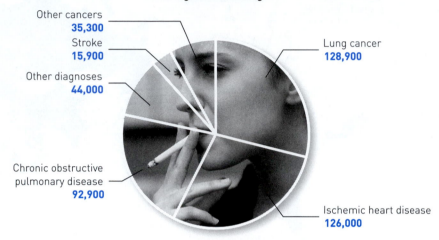

About 443,000 U.S. Deaths Attributable Each Year to Cigarette Smoking*

Other cancers
35,300

Stroke
15,900

Other diagnoses
44,000

Lung cancer
128,900

Chronic obstructive
pulmonary disease
92,900

Ischemic heart disease
126,000

* Average annual number of deaths, 2000–2004.

SOURCE: MMWR 2008;1226–1228. Photo: Copyright iStockphoto/Kuzma.

(e.g., formaldehyde, acetaldehyde) and particulate matter in e-cigarette vapor and the potential of vapor exposure to cause cytotoxity (i.e., damage to cells). In a comprehensive review of studies that evaluated potential negative health effects from e-cigarette use, Pisinger and Døssing (2014) concluded that inconsistent results across studies and lack of long-term data preclude making firm conclusions about e-cigarette use, except that using them appears safer than smoking cigarettes.

Secondhand smoke exposure also increases one's risk to negative health effects. **Secondhand smoke** consists of smoke exhaled from a smoker or smoke released from a burning tobacco product (i.e., a lit cigarette or cigar). In 2005, this form of tobacco exposure accounted for 3,000 deaths from lung cancer and 46,000 deaths related to coronary heart disease. Secondhand smoke exposure also accounted for 430 sudden infant death syndrome incidents in that same year (CDC, 2008). We also link secondhand smoke to health effects in children, where we find greater incidents of asthma, bronchitis, pneumonia, and ear infections (U.S. Department of Health and Human Services, 2006).

A nonsmoker may also be exposed to thirdhand smoke. **Thirdhand smoke** consists of remnants from tobacco smoking gathered on material in the smoker's local environment after smoking has finished (Winickoff et al., 2009). A nonsmoker may be exposed to tobacco products that cling to hair, skin, or clothing, and these products can remain on fabrics for months after smoking ceases (Bahl et al., 2016). Tobacco products from smoke gather on walls, flooring, and various objects in the setting, making these other sources of exposure for nonsmokers. Young children, in particular, may ingest this material from

Secondhand smoke
Smoke exhaled from a smoker or smoke released from a burning tobacco product

Thirdhand smoke
Remnants from tobacco smoking gathered on material in the smoker's local environment after smoking has finished

playing on the floor or putting objects on their mouths. Thirdhand smoke effects is a relatively new area of research, and potential health effects from this exposure have yet to be found. So far, researchers have found cytotoxic chemicals deposited from thirdhand smoke as well as chemicals that inhibit cell proliferation (Bahl et al., 2016). These findings suggest that a risk of adverse effects occur from exposure to thirdhand smoke.

Discovery of Tobacco

The discovery of fossilized leaves of *Nicotiana tabacum* in Peru suggests that tobacco existed at least 2.5 million years ago. Indigenous peoples in the Americas, including the Mayas, Incans, Toltecs, and Aztecs, smoked tobacco as part of their religious practices. In religious ceremonies, tobacco was smoked to achieve a trancelike state (**Figure 7.7**).

FIGURE 7.7 ● **Tobacco was smoked by ancient Mayan priests for ceremonial purposes.**

SOURCE: Shutterstock/Jef Thompson.

Religious practices remained the primary use of tobacco until Europeans discovered tobacco during Columbus's 1492 expedition. After Columbus landed in the Bahamas, the native Arawak gave dried tobacco leaves as a gift to the explorer. Not realizing the significance of the tobacco leaves to the Arawak, Columbus simply discarded them. A few days later, however, Columbus noted that the leaves had "high value among [the Arawak]" (Brecher, 1972; Gately, 2001).

Rodrigo de Jerez, a member of Columbus's expedition, participated in the native practice of rolling tobacco leaves and smoking them. Thus, Jerez became the first European to smoke tobacco. In fact, he became a habitual user and brought back a large personal tobacco supply to Spain. Yet the frightening site of tobacco smoke coming from his mouth and nose brought him to judgment by the holy inquisitors, who imprisoned him for 7 years (Gately, 2001).

Use of tobacco in Europe soon grew. By the mid-16th century, tobacco was a widely traded commodity. Complaints against tobacco also grew. The first medical concern against using tobacco was published in the early 17th century, which compared the deleterious health effects of chimneysweeps to those of tobacco smokers. In 1610, Sir Francis Bacon noted the difficulty in quitting tobacco use. In 1634, Russian Tsar Michael I decreed that a first offense for tobacco use was punishment by whipping and transport to Siberia; the second offense was death (Brecher, 1972).

In 1612 Jamestown, John Rolfe raised the first European tobacco crop for commercial use, marking the beginning of a thriving American industry that remains active today. Nearly 200 years later, in 1809, Louis Nicolas Vanquelin isolated nicotine as a key ingredient in tobacco.

The beginning of the 20th century marked a renewed study of tobacco's health effects. Early in this century, scientists studied the effects of tobacco and cancer in animals, and biologist Davis Jordan publicly stated, "The boy who smokes cigarettes need not be anxious about his future—he has none." In 1938, a study by Raymond Pearl reported that heavy smokers lived a shorter life than nonsmokers (Gately, 2001).

By the 1990s, the health risks of tobacco were well characterized and widely publicized. As presented at the beginning of this chapter, the 1994 tobacco hearings included the testimony of seven tobacco company CEOs who denied any knowledge of tobacco's adverse effects. Today, tobacco products must include special health warning labels, but the product is still sold legally throughout the world.

STOP & CHECK

1. What is the key psychoactive ingredient in tobacco?

2. Among the many forms of tobacco, which product remains the most used?

3. What is the greatest cause of death from smoking?

4. In which American colony was the first tobacco crop grown?

1. Nicotine 2. Cigarettes 3. Lung cancer 4. Jamestown

Tobacco Use and Pharmacokinetic Properties

Tobacco Use and Nicotine Absorption

Tobacco use consists of inhaling or chewing tobacco blends or other products. Smoked tobacco was seldom inhaled into the lungs prior to common practice of flue-curing tobacco blends in cigarettes in the early 1900s. **Flue curing** consists of venting heat through a metal flue onto tobacco leaves. The process reduces the pH of smoke toward neutral (i.e., closer to pH = 7.0) by converting starches to sugars, making the smoke less harsh and irritating to inhale. Cigars instead use air-dried tobacco leaves, retaining an alkaline pH and having less sugars. As a result, cigar smokers may be less likely to inhale tobacco smoke into their lungs than cigarette smokers. Cigarette smokers who also smoke cigars, however, do tend to fully inhale cigar smoke into their lungs (Turner, Sillett, McNicol, 1977).

Flue curing Venting heat through a metal flue onto tobacco leaves

Nicotine Absorption Through Lung and Oral Tissues

A typical cigarette user consumes 13 cigarettes per day, although smokers who repeatedly attempt to quit smoking tend to smoke between 20 and 40 cigarettes per day (Shiffman, 1989). In general, though cigarette smokers tend to inhale smoke into their lungs more often than cigar smokers do, cigar smokers absorb more nicotine than cigarette smokers. Greater nicotine absorption from cigars likely occurs from nicotine absorption though mucous membranes in the mouth (Turner, Sillett, & McNicol, 1977). For e-cigarettes, Farsalinos and colleagues (2014) found that newer devices lead to 70 percent greater nicotine levels in plasma than first-generation devices, and that nicotine absorbed from new-generation devices reaches levels similar to traditional cigarettes.

When smoking tobacco, **tar**, the particulate matter produced from burning tobacco, adheres to tissues in the mouth, nose, throat, and, if fully inhaled, the lungs. When exhaled, tar also adheres to the skin. Nicotine and many other chemicals leach from the tar and onto tissue the tar makes contact with. All tissue sites provide a means of absorption. Given the large surface area of the lungs, inhaled tobacco smoke provides the most effective route of nicotine administration.

Tar Particles released from burning tobacco

The freebase form of nicotine is lipid soluble, allowing for absorption through mucous membranes in the mouth. The greatest amount of freebase nicotine that can be absorbed is 50 percent, which occurs at a pH of 8.02. As pH levels deviate from 8.02, the percentage of freebase nicotine decreases. Many smokeless and dissolvable tobacco products offer pH values close to 8.02, as shown for dissolvable nicotine products in **Table 7.1** (Djordjevic, Hoffman, Glynn, & Connolly, 1995; Henningfield, Radzius, & Cone, 1995; Rainey, Conder, & Goodpaster, 2011). The majority of e-cigarette liquids have pH values between 7.0 to 9.0, leading to greater than 50 percent of freebase nicotine for many of these products (Lisko, Tran, Stanfill, Blount, & Watson, 2014).

When inhaling tobacco smoke, the acidity of smoke from a cigarette reduces saliva to a pH less than 6.0, reducing the amount of freebase nicotine available for absorption in the mouth (Armitage & Turner, 1970). However, tobacco companies do add ammonia-forming compounds to tobacco blends, which increases the amount of freebase nicotine (Pankow et al., 1997). Smoke from cigars tends to have pH levels closer to 7.0, although the pH levels vary considerably, depending on the size of the

TABLE 7.1 ● pH and Percentage Free Nicotine in Selected Dissolvable Camel Tobacco Products		
Camel Brand	**pH**	**Percentage Free Nicotine**
Mellow Orb	7.82	38.5
Fresh Orb	7.1	28.0
Mellow Stick	7.51	23.5
Fresh Strip	8.02	50.2

SOURCE: Adapted from Rainey et al., 2011.

cigar and part of the cigar smoked (Henningfield et al., 1999). The pH levels for cigars therefore favor greater nicotine absorption in the mouth. This can mean significant nicotine absorption for many cigar smokers who do not fully inhale tobacco smoke, as noted earlier.

Most tobacco products result in blood nicotine concentrations of 12 to 16 nanograms[1] per milliliter, although absorption times vary. Peak absorption for nicotine from cigarettes occurs after approximately 7 minutes. Nicotine absorption times through oral mucous membranes tend to peak between 20 and 30 minutes after introduction (Vansickel et al. 2010; Henningfield & Keenan, 1993). Peak nicotine absorption from e-cigarettes, from either first- or new-generation devices, occurs after 30 minutes, suggesting that most nicotine absorption occurs through mucous membranes in the mouth, rather than the lungs (Farsalinos et al. 2014).

In addition to the speed of nicotine delivery, tobacco smoking or vaping provides users the ability to adjust the amount of nicotine absorbed. A smoker accomplishes these adjustments by varying the number of inhalations, duration of an inhalation, completeness of inhalation, and the number of cigarettes smoked (Frederiksen, Martin, & Webster, 1979). Vapers also can adjust a nicotine vaporizer's heating level to alter the amount of nicotine inhaled.

Distribution and Biotransformation of Nicotine

Once absorbed, nicotine readily passes through the blood–brain barrier. In the liver, CYP-2A6 enzymes metabolize 80 percent to 90 percent of nicotine, producing the active metabolite **cotinine**, which exhibits pharmacological actions similar to nicotine. Slower metabolism occurs for mentholated versus non-mentholated cigarettes (Benowitz, Herrera, & Jacob, 2004).

Cotinine Metabolite of nicotine

Genetic polymorphisms influence CYP-2A6 activity levels. CYP-2A6*4, *7 and *9 polymorphisms exhibit reduced CYP-2A6 activity, causing slower metabolism of nicotine to cotinine. In other words, nicotine levels remain higher in the body because of

1 A nanogram is one billionth, or 10^{-9}, of a gram.

reduced metabolism. These polymorphisms are prevalent within Asian populations. Individuals who exhibit homogenous mutant forms of these gene polymorphisms or heterogeneous mutant forms that have a combination of the *4, 7*, or *9 polymorphisms, tend to be light smokers and have a lower risk of tobacco-related health effects (Ariyoshi et al., 2002; Minematsu et al., 2006; Yusof & Gan, 2009). African Americans exhibit a slower metabolism of nicotine, engendering a longer period of time for intact nicotine to exert pharmacological effects (Pérez-Stable, Herrera, Jacob, & Benowitz, 1998). This may be due to a preference by African American smokers for using mentholated cigarettes.

Elimination of Nicotine

The half-life for nicotine is approximately 2 hours, but this clearance time depends on a smoker's status. Chronic smokers have a 30-percent faster elimination rate of nicotine than nonsmokers. These findings suggest that chronic tobacco use sensitizes pharmacokinetic processes for nicotine (Perkins et al., 1994). The half-life for cotinine is approximately 17 hours (Pérez-Stable et al., 1998). Both nicotine and cotinine are primarily eliminated from the body through urine, and so a simple urine analysis for cotinine can reveal tobacco use more than a day later.

STOP & CHECK

1. Why is inhalation the most effective route for absorbing nicotine from tobacco tar?

2. What factors influence nicotine's ability to be absorbed in the mouth?

3. What is the active metabolite for nicotine?

1. The lungs have a large surface area that helps speed delivery of nicotine to the brain after blood absorption. The large surface area also overcomes the poor absorption of nicotine when delivered in tobacco smoke, which has a less-than-ideal pH of approximately 6. 2. The freebase from of nicotine absorbs through mucous membranes in the mouth. The most ideal pH for absorption in the mouth is 8.02. Thus, nicotine producing products producing similar pH levels will be conducive to nicotine absorption through mucous membranes. 3. Cotinine

Nicotine and Nervous System Functioning

Nicotine functions as an agonist for cholinergic nicotinic receptors (**Figure 7.8**). Cotinine, the active metabolite of nicotine, serves as a weak agonist for nicotine receptors. When a nicotinic receptor agonist binds to these receptors, a conformational change takes place, opening a channel for positively charged ions, such as Ca^{2+}, Na^+, and K^+. Some ions pass more readily through nicotinic receptor channels than others. For examples, α_7 receptors are most permeable for Ca^{2+} ions (Séguéla, Wadiche, Dineley-Miller, Dani, & Patrick, 1993).

FIGURE 7.8 ● **Each nicotinic ionotropic receptor comprises a configuration of α and β subunits.**

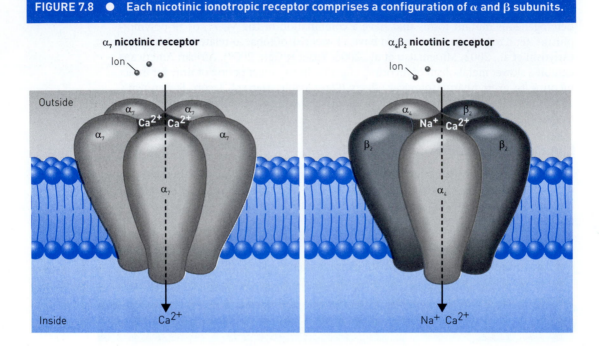

α₇ nicotinic receptor

$\alpha_4\beta_2$ nicotinic receptor

Ion

Outside

Ca^{2+} Ca^{2+}

α_7 α_7 α_7 α_7 α_7

α_4 β_2 Na^+ Ca^{2+} β_2 β_2 α_4

Inside Ca^{2+}

Na^+ Ca^{2+}

Review! Nicotinic receptors are ionotropic and comprise α and β subunits. Nicotinic receptors can include other subunit types as well, which are denoted by different Greek symbols. The configuration of these subunits defines each receptor's name. (Chapter 3.)

A short time after nicotine (or another agonist) activates a nicotinic receptor, the receptor enters a desensitized state, which limits the duration of action for nicotine's acute pharmacological effects (**Figure 7.9**) (Hsu, Amin, Weiss, & Wecker, 1995; Fenster, Rains, Noerager, Quick, & Lester, 1997). During the desensitized state, the channels close and the receptors cannot be activated. These receptors enter this desensitized state even when the receptors remain bound by an agonist. After a period of time, the desensitized state ends and the receptors can again be activated by an agonist.

Because of desensitization, agonists cause nicotinic-receptor channels to remain closed *longer* than they are open. In this way, nicotinic-receptor agonists also produce **functional antagonism**, meaning that nicotine causes these receptors to have a longer inactivated state than an activated state. Thinking of nicotine as a *functional antagonist* is useful for understanding changes in nicotinic receptors during chronic nicotine administration. During such administration, the brain compensates for the repeated closing of nicotinic-receptor channels by *upregulating* nicotinic receptors (Schwartz & Kellar, 1985; Wonnacott, 1990). **Upregulation** refers to an increased production of proteins.

Functional antagonism An indirect or atypical means of inhibiting a receptor's activity, such as when the net effects of a receptor agonist consist of a longer inactivated receptor state and a shorter activated receptor state

Upregulation Increased production of proteins

FIGURE 7.9 ● **When bound to by an agonist, nicotinic receptors undergo an active state and then a desensitized state. The receptor cannot be activated during the desensitized state, and the desensitized state occurs for a longer period of time than the active state.**

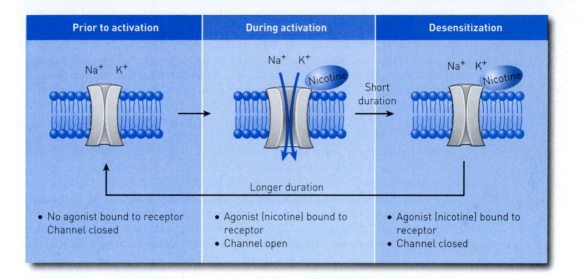

Both the central and peripheral nervous systems contain nicotinic receptors. Peripherally, nicotinic receptors are located postsynaptically on neuromuscular junctions in the somatic nervous system. Within neuromuscular junctions, the activation of $\alpha_1\beta_1\delta\gamma$ nicotinic receptors on muscle fibers causes muscles to contract.

Nicotinic receptors are located in ganglia of the autonomic system, including both the sympathetic and the parasympathetic nervous systems. Of these two systems, the activation of nicotinic receptors primarily increases sympathetic nervous system activity (Li, LaCroix, & Freeling, 2009). Different subtypes of nicotinic receptors are likely involved in the sympathetic and parasympathetic systems. For cardiovascular effects, Li and colleagues (2009) discovered that α_7 receptors activate the parasympathetic nervous system, whereas $\alpha_4\beta_2$ receptors activate the sympathetic nervous system.

Review! The autonomic nervous system includes the sympathetic nervous system, which increases physiological activity, and the parasympathetic nervous system, which decreases physiological activity. (Chapter 2.)

Nicotinic receptors are found throughout the central nervous system and play an important role in many nervous system processes. The cerebral cortex and hippocampus, two brain areas important for cognitive functioning, highly express both $\alpha_4\beta_2$ and

α_7 nicotinic receptors. High amounts of $\alpha_4\beta_2$ nicotinic receptors are also found in the basal ganglia, an area important for regulating movement, and the substantia nigra, the source of dopamine neurons that terminate in the basal ganglia. In the dopamine reward pathway, the ventral tegmental area contains $\alpha_4\beta_2$ and $\alpha_6\beta_2$ receptors, and the nucleus accumbens also contains $\alpha_4\beta_2$ receptors (Brunzell, 2012; Yang et al., 2011; Zhao-Shea et al., 2011).

The activation of nicotinic receptors in either the ventral tegmental area or the nucleus accumbens increases dopamine release in the nucleus accumbens. Researchers discovered these effects using microdialysis techniques in animals (see Box 3.1). For example, Nisell and colleagues (1994) infused nicotine into either the ventral tegmental area or the nucleus accumbens in rats. Microdialysis probes in these structures collected cerebrospinal fluid samples for dopamine analysis. The infusion of nicotine in the ventral tegmental area produced a large, sustained increase in dopamine levels in the nucleus accumbens. When infused into the nucleus accumbens, nicotine produced a much shorter increase in dopamine levels in the nucleus accumbens (**Figure 7.10**). Based on these findings, nicotine acts in both areas to elevate dopamine levels in the nucleus accumbens, but nicotine's actions in the ventral tegmental area are especially effective for inducing dopamine release in the nucleus accumbens.

In addition to enhancing the release of dopamine in the brain, the activation of nicotinic receptors influences many other neurotransmitters in the brain, including acetylcholine, glutamate, GABA, norepinephrine, serotonin, and the hormone vasopressin. These widespread interactions preclude identifying highly specific roles

FIGURE 7.10 ● Infusion of nicotine into either the ventral tegmental area (empty circles) or the nucleus accumbens (filled circles) increases dopamine release in the nucleus accumbens.

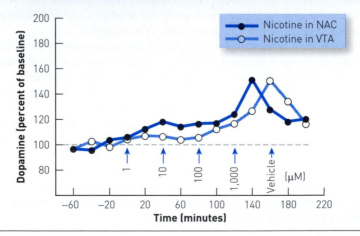

SOURCE: Nisell, M., Nomikos, G. G. and Svensson, T. H. (1994), Infusion of Nicotine in the Ventral Tegmental Area or the Nucleus Accumbens of the Rat Differentially Affects Accumbal Dopamine Release. *Pharmacology & Toxicology*, 75: 348–352. doi: 10.1111/j.1600-0773.1994.tb00373.x. John Wiley & Sons Ltd.

that nicotinic receptors have on behavior. Clearly, by acting on nicotinic receptors, nicotine and other nicotinic-receptor agonists have diverse effects on the central nervous system.

Beyond nicotine, other compounds in tobacco may act in the nervous system, possibly enhancing nicotine's effects. In particular, many chemicals in tobacco inhibit MAO_A and MAO_B activities, including the compounds 2,3,6-trimethyl-1,4-naphthoquinone, 2-naphthylamine, harman, and norharman (Hauptmann & Shih, 2001; Herraiz & Chaparro, 2005; Khalil, Steyn, & Castagnoli, 2000).

These actions may explain why long-term smokers exhibit a decreased activity of MAO_A and MAO_B enzymes (Fowler et al., 1996a, 1996b). MAO inhibition also enhances the effects of nicotine on dopamine levels in the nucleus accumbens. In a microdialysis study conducted by Lotfipour and colleagues (2011), rats treated with both nicotine and tranylcypromine, an $MAO_{A/B}$ reuptake inhibitor, exhibited a substantially greater increase in nucleus accumbens dopamine levels than rats treated with either drug alone (**Figure 7.11**).

Review! Monoamine oxidase (MAO) is an enzyme that breaks down, or catabolizes, dopamine, norepinephrine, and serotonin. (Chapter 3.)

FIGURE 7.11 ● Rats treated with both nicotine and tranylcypromine, an MAO reuptake inhibitor, exhibited a substantially greater increase in nucleus accumbens dopamine levels than rats treated with either drug alone.

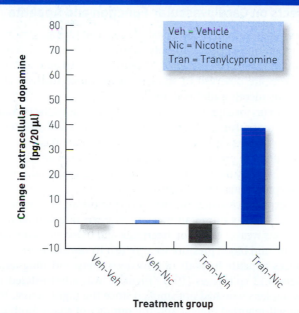

SOURCE: Data from Lotfipour et al., 2011.

Nicotine's Potent Pharmacological Effects

Nicotine produces physiological, behavioral, and subjective effects, and tobacco, the main source of nicotine, produces a host of adverse effects. When characterizing the pharmacological effects of nicotine, researchers understand that the length of nicotine use is important. Because upregulation of nicotinic receptors occurs during repeated administration, the acute effects of nicotine can differ from the chronic effects of nicotine. Thus, the effects of nicotine on a first-time smoker can differ greatly from the effects of nicotine on a long-time smoker.

Nicotine's Effects on Cardiovascular Function and Appetite

Nicotine produces widespread physiological effects. The two most notable are on the cardiovascular system and appetite. In both smokers and nonsmokers, nicotine produces cardiovascular effects consisting of increases in heart rate and blood pressure. Because these effects are observed in smokers, a tolerance to these effects does not occur during chronic nicotine administration.

Acute tolerance
Decreased responsiveness to a drug's effects after single administration of drug

Acute tolerance occurs for a number of nicotine physiological effects. **Acute tolerance** refers to a decreased responsive to a drug's effects after single administration of drug. Acute tolerance to nicotine's effects on heart rate and blood pressure happens when nicotine is administered soon after the previous administration (Perkins et al., 1994) (**Figure 7.12**). Acute tolerance occurs partly because the subsequent nicotine administration occurs while many nicotinic receptors remain in a desensitized state.

Most smokers experience acute tolerance every morning. Nicotine delivered from the first cigarette of the day causes an increase in heart rate and blood pressure. The next cigarette exhibits weaker effects on heart rate and blood pressure. Because of acute tolerance, heart rate and blood pressure soon return to normal levels.

Nicotine reduces appetite in both non-tobacco users and long-term smokers. In a study by Perkins and colleagues (1991) nicotine was administered to either non-tobacco users or smokers who had not smoked since the night before. In both groups, nicotine reduced self-reported hunger and the number of snack foods consumed during the testing sessions (**Figure 7.13**). The appetite-suppressing effects of nicotine

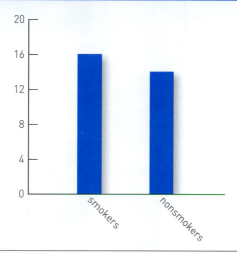

SOURCE: Data from Perkins et al., 1994.

FIGURE 7.12 ● Smokers exhibit acute tolerance to nicotine's increase in heart rate. When smokers are given nicotine placebo prior to nicotine administration, an increase in heart rates occurs. However, after several administrations of nicotine, a subsequent administration of nicotine leads to weaker effect on heart rate.

contribute to weight loss in many tobacco users, and tobacco users often cite potential weight gain as a reason not to quit.

Nicotine Affects Movement and Cognitive Functioning

Nicotine's behavioral effects include alterations in movement and cognitive function. These effects differ between naïve and chronic tobacco users. Nicotine produces effects on motor stability, which are particularly noticeable in the hands. Hand tremor and reduced hand steadiness occur after nicotine administration to non-tobacco users. Tolerance occurs with these effects in tobacco users (Perkins et al., 1994).

Nicotine's effects on psychomotor function also differ between acute and chronic administration. Acute administration of nicotine in nicotine-naïve users causes a decrease in psychomotor activity. However, sensitization to these effects occurs during chronic administration. Thus, in chronic tobacco users, nicotine increases psychomotor function. For example, Perkins and colleagues (1994) reported that nicotine administration increases the rate of finger tapping in chronic smokers, but decreases the rate of finger tapping in nonsmokers.

Animal studies also find differences between acute and chronic nicotine administration. For example, Pehrson and colleagues (2008) studied locomotor activity in rats during 14 days of nicotine administration using an open field-apparatus

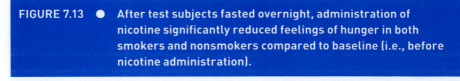

FIGURE 7.13 ● After test subjects fasted overnight, administration of nicotine significantly reduced feelings of hunger in both smokers and nonsmokers compared to baseline (i.e., before nicotine administration).

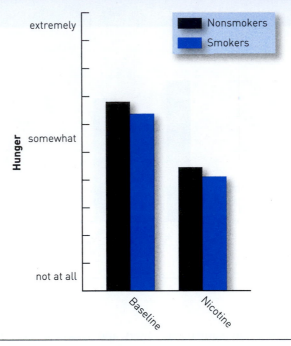

SOURCE: Data from Perkins et al., 1991.

(**Figure 7.14**). An *open-field apparatus*, when used for rodents, consists of a box constructed from plastic or metal with walls high enough to prevent escape and an open top to allow for observation; open fields typically have grid lines drawn on the bottom. The grid lines allow researchers to count line-crosses an animal makes as an index of overall movement. In place of grid lines, many open fields can emit photo beams instead; that is, researchers count photo beam breaks rather than line crosses. On the first day of treatment, nicotine suppressed locomotor activity as indicated by fewer photo beam breaks in an open-field apparatus. However, on the 7th and 14th days of treatment, nicotine enhanced locomotor activity.

Although public attitudes toward nicotine are generally negative, nicotine may show some benefits for cognitive functioning. Studies show that nicotine improves attention, particularly when reorienting attention toward another stimulus (Thiel, Zilles, & Fink, 2005), and improves information processing (Juliano, Fucito, & Harrell, 2011; Wesnes & Warburton, 1984).

In attention tasks, nicotine improves information processing by shortening times to detect stimuli. Wesnes and Warburton (1984) first demonstrated these effects, finding

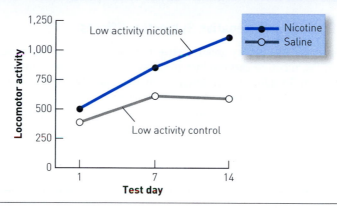

FIGURE 7.14 ● Nicotine-treated rats (solid symbols) exhibited increased locomotor activity on the 7th and 14th days of treatment compared to saline-treated rats. The *y*-axis shows locomotor activity as an expression of number of photo beams rats crossed within a test chamber. The *x*-axis refers to the number of days of treatment.

SOURCE: Data from Pehrson et al., 2008.

that nicotine improved the detection of targets during an 80-minute vigilance task consisting of identifying number of sequences from numbers scrolling across a display. David Warburton later reflected that this seminal study was first rejected from a journal because the editor refused to publish "anything good about nicotine" (Warburton, 2002).

Nicotine's improvements in attention occur after chronic administration as well. For example, Perkins and colleagues (1994) used a *Stroop test*—a standard test of processing speed used for neuropsychological assessments that evaluates reaction times to mismatched stimulus presentations (Lansbergen & Kenemans, 2008)—to assess attention after nicotine administration in both nonsmokers and smokers. Nicotine improved reaction times in both test subjects, both nonsmokers and smokers.

Aside from information processing and attention, the effects of nicotine on memory are unclear. In the study by Perkins and colleagues (1994), nicotine also improved memory in a word list recall test, which required participants to remember words presented to them in a list. Nicotine's memory improvements were greater in nonsmokers than in smokers, suggesting that smokers develop a tolerance to these effects. Yet many studies also fail to show improvements in memory after nicotine treatment, and some studies show that nicotine worsens memory in chronic smokers (Ernst et al., 2001; Myers, Taylor, Moolchan, & Heishman, 2007; Park, Knopick, McGurk, & Meltzer, 2000).

Many studies have evaluated nicotine for the treatment of Alzheimer's disease. Biologically, nicotine reduces the destructive effects of amyloid β42 proteins in the hippocampus, an important characteristic of this disease. However, Deng and colleagues (2010) demonstrated that nicotine worsens the memory-inducing impairments caused by amyloid β42 proteins in rats. Further, in a transgenic mouse model of Alzheimer's disease, exposure to cigarette smoke caused greater production amyloid β42 proteins and other abnormalities in Alzheimer's disease (Moreno-Gonzalez, Estrada, Sanchez-Mejias, & Soto, 2013). In humans, some studies report a decreased risk of Alzheimer's disease in smokers, whereas other studies report an increased risk (Ulrich, Johannson-Locher, Seiler, & Stahelin, 1997; Ott et al., 1998). Heavy smoking, at least, is not beneficial for Alzheimer's disease; in fact, Rusanen and colleagues (2011) found that heavy smoking increases the risk of Alzheimer's disease by 157 percent.

Nicotine's Positive and Negative Subjective Effects

Nicotine's subjective effects vary greatly between acute and chronic administration. In non-tobacco users, nicotine can produce negative subjective effects, including nausea and disequilibrium. In addition, as described in the study by Perkins and colleagues (1994), nicotine produces feelings of jitteriness, tension, and confusion in nonsmokers. Yet acute tolerance to these negative subjective effects occurs after subsequent nicotine administrations. Further, many users instead feel relaxed after smoking for the first time. Researchers find a much greater risk of continued smoking for those feeling relaxed compared to those who experienced negative subjective effects (DiFranza et al., 2004).

A conditioned taste-aversion procedure can demonstrate nicotine's aversive effects as well as acute tolerance to these aversive effects. The conditioned taste-aversion procedure is described in Box 7.1. Prus and colleagues (2007) used this procedure to link the timing of nicotine administration with the time course of nicotinic-receptor changes (**Figure 7.15**). For rats treated with nicotine 5 minutes before a pairing session with saccharin, less saccharin was consumed on the following day. This pairing session took place during the activated nicotinic-receptor state.

In this same study, another group of rats was treated with nicotine 90 minutes before the pairing session and given a second treatment of nicotine 5 minutes before the session. These rats drank more of the saccharin solution on the following day. For these rats, the second injection of nicotine occurred when the nicotinic receptors were desensitized, thus reducing aversive effects from occurring during or after the pairing session.

Long-term treatment with nicotine also causes tolerance to these negative subjective effects. Without negative subjective effects, chronic tobacco users experience only positive subjective effects from nicotine. In chronic smokers, nicotine administration produces feelings of vigor, arousal, and reduced fatigue (Perkins et al., 1994). Chronic smokers report that the effects of nicotine are pleasant and enjoyed and produce a positive mood (Myers et al., 2007). These smokers can detect a distinct rewarding effect with each puff of cigarette smoke.

The positive subjective effects of nicotine can be difficult to establish in animals. In a standard self-administration procedure (see Box 5.1), rats will not learn to self-administer nicotine because of the initial adverse effects experienced on first exposure to nicotine. In other words, if the effects are negative, an animal will avoid those effects rather than seek to achieve them. To observe the reinforcing effects of nicotine in this procedure, researchers use a variation on the standard self-administration design.

For example, Boules and colleagues (2011) used a common design variation to study nicotine self-administration in rats. First, these researchers trained rats to press a lever

FIGURE 7.15 ● Nicotine failed to exhibit a conditioned taste aversion (NIC/NIC group) when it was administered during the nicotine receptor desensitized state. See text for further details.

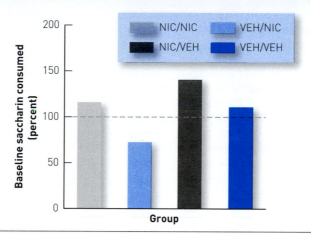

SOURCE: Prus, A. J., Maxwell, A. T., Baker, K. M., Rosecrans, J. A., & James, J. R. (2007). Acute behavioral tolerance to nicotine in the conditioned taste aversion paradigm. *Drug Development Research, 68*(8), 522–528. doi: 10.1002/ddr.20219. Reproduced with permission of Wiley Inc.

for sucrose food pellets. Then the researchers changed the consequence for pressing a lever from the sucrose food pellet to an intravenous nicotine injection. Because the rats had learned to repeatedly press the lever for sucrose pellets in the past, they persisted in pressing the lever, resulting in further nicotine injections. Through this process, tolerance quickly developed to nicotine's negative effects. After a tolerance developed to the negative effects, the reinforcing effects of nicotine administration were sufficient to maintain lever pressing.

Other components in tobacco may contribute to the reinforcing effects of nicotine. In particular, MAO inhibitors found in tobacco enhance nicotine-induced effects on nucleus accumbens dopamine levels. Self-administration of nicotine is enhanced by MAO inhibition (Guillem et al., 2005; Villégier, Lotfipour, McQuown, Belluzzi, & Leslie, 2007). For example, in a study by Villégier and colleagues (2007), the MAO inhibitor tranylcypromine facilitated self-administration for nicotine in rats. This facilitation avoided the need to have a prior training history, allowing the researchers to use a standard self-administration procedure. Rats that did not receive the MAO inhibitor were unable to self-administer nicotine without altering the standard procedure. These findings suggest that an addiction to tobacco may develop more rapidly than an addiction to only nicotine.

Adverse Effects of Tobacco Use

Many of the severely adverse effects associated with nicotine are the result of its vehicle: tobacco. Tobacco contains thousands of chemicals, including carcinogens such

BOX 7.1 CONDITIONED TASTE AVERSION

A *conditioned taste aversion* is the result of a pairing process between a noxious stimulus and a novel-tasting substance. This procedure also is called the *Garcia effect* in recognition of a discovery by John Garcia in 1955 (Garcia, Kimeldorf, & Koellino, 1955). Garcia discovered that rats ingested less of a saccharin solution after an occasion in which prior consumption of the solution was followed by gastrointestinal pain. Conditioned taste aversion is a process resembling classical, or Pavlovian, conditioning procedures.

Many psychoactive drugs function as noxious stimuli, allowing them to be studied in a conditioned taste-aversion procedure. In a typical procedure, researchers give water-deprived rats access to two water bottles. One bottle contains the usual tap water, whereas the other bottle contains a novel, and often sweet-tasting, solution. After overcoming a *neophobic reaction*—that is, a rat's natural fear response to ingesting novel substances—rats consume the novel solution.

After a session in which rats consume the novel-tasting substance, researchers conduct one or multiple pairing sessions with a drug or its placebo. The timing of a drug injection is set to produce noxious effects after a session when subjects consume the novel substance. We refer to this type of session as a *pairing session*. A conditioned taste aversion is demonstrated if significantly less solution is consumed during subsequent sessions.

For example, nicotine produces a robust conditioned taste aversion. In one of the earliest characterizations of nicotine in this procedure, Stolerman (1983) conducted repeated pairings over several sessions with nicotine and a flavored solution consisting of either saccharin or sodium chloride. Selected results from this study are shown in **Figure 1**. Over the course of several trials, the nicotine-paired solutions were consumed less, whereas saline-paired solutions were consumed at the normal level.

Although conditioned taste aversion appears to be only a measure of adverse effects, this

Nitrosamines
Chemicals shown to produce cancerous tumor growth

as nitrosamines. **Nitrosamines** are chemicals shown to produce cancerous tumor growth. The release and inhalation of tar from smoked tobacco provides direct contact of these carcinogens with tissue in the mouth, throat, esophagus, and lungs. E-liquids used for e-cigarettes tend to have low to no levels of nitrosamines (Pisinger & Døssing, 2014). Although safer in this regard, e-cigarette vapors include chemicals with potential to damage cells in the lungs, including aldehydes, which provide different flavorings for e-liquids, and formaldehyde (Pisinger & Døssing, 2014; Rowell & Tarran, 2015). The content of these and other chemicals varies considerably, however, across different e-liquid brands, as noted earlier.

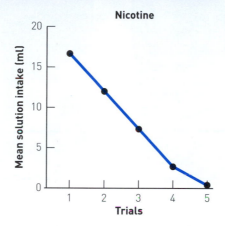

FIGURE 1 ● **Less consumption of a flavored solution occurred after pairing the solution with the effects of nicotine in rats. The *x*-axis represents the number of consecutive pairing sessions, and the *y*-axis represents the volume of solution consumed. Data adapted from Stolerman et al., 1983.**

is not necessarily the case. For many recreational drugs, the doses used to achieve positive subjective effects are the same doses effective for producing conditioned taste aversions (Wise, Yokel, & Wit, 1976).

Smoked tobacco is a cause of pulmonary diseases such as **emphysema**, a type of *chronic obstructive pulmonary disease* (typically abbreviated as COPD) caused by irreversible lung damage (**Figure 7.16**). The symptoms of emphysema include shortness of breath, wheezing, chronic cough, and fatigue. Emphysema patients are treated with a bronchodilator inhaler such as *albuterol* to open lung passages.

Tobacco use also increases the risk of cardiovascular disease. Nicotine in tobacco causes arteries and blood vessels to narrow and constrict, increasing heart rate. Together, these effects increase the risk of heart attack, stroke, and diseases associated with impoverished blood to flow to other organs.

Emphysema Type of chronic obstructive pulmonary disease caused by irreversible lung damage

FIGURE 7.16 ● Emphysema, shown in the lung on the right, is a smoking-related irreversible lung damage. A healthy lung is shown on the left.

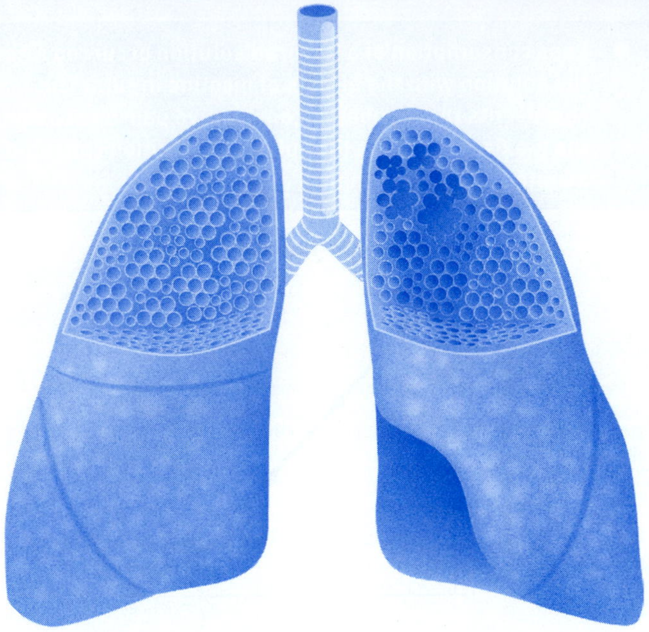

Healthy lung   *Emphysema*

SOURCE: Copyright iStockphoto/ttsz.

💊 *Drug Profile:* albuterol	
Trade name:	Salbutamol
Mechanism of action	β_2 adrenoceptor agonist
Uses	Addresses a poor ability to breathe common in disorders like asthma and COPD by dilating bronchi and bronchioles in the lungs (i.e., opening air passages)

During pregnancy, tobacco causes slower gestational development, preterm births, and low birth weight. Any number of chemicals in smoked tobacco can interfere with prenatal development, but reduced oxygen to the fetus is a significant contributor. Women who smoke also have an increased risk of breast cancer and may begin menopause at an earlier age than women who don't smoke (Perkins, 2001).

Nicotine and Psychological Dependence

As noted at the beginning of this chapter, seven tobacco company CEOs famously testified that nicotine is non-addictive. This opinion, of course, lies in the best interest of tobacco companies, which seek to minimize tobacco regulation. Beyond this conflict of interest, the basis for their opinion depends on the different ways drug addiction has been defined.

As described in Chapter 5, traditional notions of drug addiction were largely based on opioids and alcohol. For drugs like these, addiction appears as intense motivation to seek and use a substance, often at the expense losing one's career or jeopardizing relationships with friends or family. When considering addiction as only this, the CEOs likely felt comfortable asserting the non-addictive nature of nicotine.

The American Psychiatric Association's *Diagnostic and Statistical Manual* (DSM-5), however, offers other features of *substance use disorders*; namely, that individuals express difficulty quitting or reducing use. When nicotine use discontinues, chronic users may experience a collection of psychological withdrawal symptoms called the **nicotine abstinence syndrome**, which is characterized by craving, irritability, anxiety, hostility, concentration difficulties, impatience, and insomnia. Avoidance of nicotine's withdrawal effects is an important contributor to tobacco usage. Based on the dependence criteria described in the DSM, nicotine is an addictive substance. Further, as described previously in this chapter, nicotine exhibits a rapid tolerance to both

Nicotine abstinence syndrome Nicotine withdrawal symptoms characterized by craving, irritability, anxiety, hostility, concentration difficulties, impatience, and insomnia

---

STOP & CHECK

1. During sustained use, nicotine produces a(n) _____ in locomotor activity.

2. Nicotine improves two particular aspects of attention: orientation to a stimulus and _____.

3. On first using nicotine, the positive subjective effects are overshadowed by _____ effects.

4. How might the reinforcing effects of tobacco differ in magnitude from the reinforcing effects of nicotine?

5. Many of the adverse effects associated with nicotine actually result from _____, the nicotine vehicle.

6. Repeated nicotine use causes an upregulation of nicotinic receptors, which is the result of _____ of nicotinic receptors

1. increase. However, the first administration of nicotine causes a decrease in locomotor activity. The increase in locomotor activity during sustained nicotine use is described as *sensitization*. **2.** information processing. **3.** aversive. **4.** Tobacco smoke contains many chemicals that may enhance nicotine's reinforcing effects. Therefore, smoking may produce a greater reinforcing effect than nicotine alone. **5.** tobacco. **6.** desensitization

physical and psychological effects during chronic use. Given our modern conceptions of substance dependence, few people would agree with a tobacco company's claims that their products do not cause addiction.

Environmental, Genetic, and Receptor Differences Between Light and Heavy Tobacco Users

Chippers Smokers who fail to develop an addiction to tobacco

Humans vary in their susceptibility to nicotine addiction. People who are the most resistant to nicotine addiction are called *chippers*. These are light smokers who fail to develop an addiction to tobacco. **Chippers** are long-term smokers, but they typically smoke only a few cigarettes a day. They make up approximately one-third of all smokers (Shiffman, 1989). The term *chipper* can also be applied, as a slang term, to any occasional user of abused drugs.

Chippers smoke cigarettes the same way as normal smokers—that is, they fully inhale tobacco smoke, have the same puff duration, and have the same interval times between puffs (Brauer, Hatsukami, Hanson, & Shiffman, 1996). Chippers and regular smokers have similar abilities to absorb and metabolize nicotine. However, chippers fail to show significant pharmacological effects from tobacco, and they fail to exhibit withdrawal symptoms when deprived of tobacco.

Exactly how chippers resist nicotine addiction is unknown. Two possible explanations concern environmental and genetic factors. For an environmental explanation, Shiffman (1989) found that chippers, more often than smokers, had greater coping skills, less stress, and better social support structures. These psychosocial factors may reduce an individual's risk of developing a substance addiction.

Genetically, chippers and chronic smokers differ in gene expression for α_5, α_3, and β_4 receptor subunits, which are found on chromosome 15 (Saccone et al., 2007). Of these, the single nucleotide polymorphism Chrna4 for the α_5 unit is particularly associated with greater risk of nicotine dependence. Although this subunit has not been directly implicated in the reinforcing effects of nicotine, this subunit alters state changes from active to desensitized in α_4 subunit-containing nicotinic receptors (Ramirez-Latorre et al., 1996). As noted already in this chapter, $\alpha_4\beta_2$ receptors facilitate the reinforcing effects of nicotine.

These genetic variations suggest that differences in nicotinic receptors may facilitate the resistance of chippers for nicotine addiction. In particular, chippers may have weaker acute tolerance to the effects of nicotine because of diminished desensitization of nicotinic receptors. Reduced acute tolerance to nicotine would produce longer-lasting effects (Rosecrans, 1995).

To better understand nicotine tolerance in chippers, animal studies have assessed the association between nicotinic receptor desensitization and acute tolerance. For example, rats that differed in nicotinic receptor desensitization were studied in the conditioned taste-aversion procedure study by Prus and colleagues (2007) described previously. As in the earlier experiment, rats were injected with nicotine both 90 minutes and 5 minutes before a pairing session. The rats used for this experiment were either normal or had diminished nicotinic receptor desensitization. In the normal rats, saccharin consumption increased the following day because the injection of nicotine 5 minutes before the pairing session occurred during the nicotine receptors' desensitized state, preventing aversive effects. However, in the rats with diminished nicotinic receptor desensitization, saccharin consumption decreased the following day because the receptors were not desensitized and thus did not prevent aversive effects (**Figure 7.17**).

These data suggest that differences in nicotinic receptor desensitization differ between individuals and that these differences significantly alter acute tolerance to nicotine.

FIGURE 7.17 ● **Nicotine administered during the desensitized nicotinic-receptor state produces a conditioned taste aversion in rats that exhibit reduced nicotinic-receptor desensitization. See text for further details.**

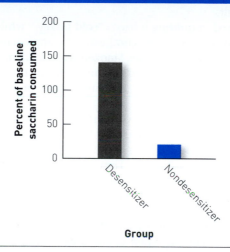

SOURCE: Prus, A. J., Maxwell, A. T., Baker, K. M., Rosecrans, J. A., & James, J. R. (2007). Acute behavioral tolerance to nicotine in the conditioned taste aversion paradigm. *Drug Development Research, 68*(8), 522–528. doi: 10.1002/ddr.20219. Reproduced with permission of Wiley Inc.

STOP & CHECK

1. Chippers smoke without developing a nicotine addiction, possibly because they exhibit weaker _____ tolerance to nicotine.

2. Which subunit of the nicotinic receptor appears most related to reduced sensitization of nicotinic receptors?

1. acute 2. The α_5 subunit

From Actions to Effects:
Why People Smoke and How They Quit

Humans learn to use tobacco for many reasons. Many people begin smoking because their friends smoke. Smoking may also be common in an individual's family or culture. Tobacco advertisers market cigarettes as fun, cool, sexy, and rebellious. Not too long ago, workers who smoked were allowed frequent short smoke breaks, whereas non-smokers had to continue working.

As smoking persists, an addiction to nicotine develops, serving as the primary reason for tobacco use. For frequent smokers, the effects of nicotine become associated with routine, everyday activities such as talking on a phone, watching TV, or working on a computer. Associative learning processes incentivize these conditioned responses, leading to the preoccupation and anticipation features of addiction as described in Chapter 5. Without having a cigarette, these stimuli lead to craving tobacco, which makes quitting difficult.

Many people succeed in quitting tobacco "cold turkey," while others need to participate in a treatment plan. Many psychotherapeutic approaches address the behavioral cues that trigger a craving to smoke. Smokers learn to identify the causes of these cravings and make attempts to diminish the influence of these cravings. No matter the method, studies generally show that reaching 2 weeks of tobacco abstinence most strongly predicts long-term success.

Looking into the 2-week success correlation, Lussier and colleagues (2005) examined smokers using choice comparisons between desire to smoke versus earning small amounts of money among those who successfully or unsuccessfully abstained from smoking after 2 weeks. They found that far fewer of the abstinent smokers selected a desire to smoke over an option to earn money when given the choice. However, those still smoking after 2 weeks more often selected the desire to smoke option. Thus, the rewarding value of tobacco appears to weaken after reaching 2 weeks of tobacco abstinence. We also learn that 2 weeks of tobacco abstinence leads to less craving when exposed to stimuli associated with former tobacco use (Bradstreet et al., 2014).

Many treatment plans also employ pharmacological strategies in order to address the absence of nicotine in the body. As described previously, nicotinic receptors are upregulated during chronic nicotine administration, creating a need for nicotine to maintain this sensitized state. An abrupt drop in nicotine levels leaves these extra receptors inactivated, leading to withdrawal symptoms. Therefore, pharmacological treatments mostly fall into one of three categories: nicotine-replacement therapy, nicotinic-receptor agonism, and antidepressant drugs (Polosa & Benowitz, 2011).

Nicotine replacement therapy consists of using a non-tobacco nicotine product to minimize or prevent withdrawal symptoms. Nicotine replacement therapy products include nicotine skin patches, gum, nasal spray, and inhalers. To reduce their dependence on nicotine, users gradually reduce the dose of nicotine used until they reach a point where few withdrawal symptoms occur in the absence of nicotine. This approach may take weeks or or prevent withdrawal months.

Yet even with regard to use of nicotine-replacement products, studies show that long-term smoking success relies on complete cessation of smoking. Kenford and colleagues

Nicotine replacement therapy Therapy that consists of using a nontobacco nicotine product to minimize symptoms

(1994) evaluated smoking abstinence success among participants using a nicotine patch. In one of their experiments, they found that the 41 percent who were not smoking after 2 weeks from using the patch were still abstinent at a 6-month follow-up. These findings contrast dramatically with those using a patch but still smoking after 2 weeks using the patch: at a 6-month follow-up, 97 percent were still smoking. These and subsequent studies reveal that reaching 2 weeks of tobacco abstinence strongly predicts long-term success.

Nicotinic-receptor agonist medications also reduce withdrawal symptoms. The first drug approved from this class approved by the Food and Drug Administration is *varenicline (Chantix)*, a partial agonist for nicotinic receptors (Coe et al., 2005). By acting as a partial agonist, less activation of nicotinic receptors occurs compared to a full agonist like nicotine. Verenicline also binds to the nicotine receptors that nicotine would normally bind to, preventing nicotine's effects. This may reduce the amount of dopamine released compared to nicotine, but some dopamine release also serves to substitute for nicotine's effects, which may help with nicotine withdrawal. When varenicline is taken, users report that smoking becomes less enjoyable and overall produces weaker effects (Gonzales et al., 2006; Polosa & Benowitz, 2011). However, these pharmacological actions tend to reduce smoking in fewer than half of all smokers (Gonzales et al., 2006).

💊 *Drug Profile:* **varenicline**	
Trade name:	Chantix
Mechanism of action	Partial agonist for nicotinic receptors
Uses	Reduces withdrawal symptoms from nicotine dependence

Antidepressant drugs reduce smoking by addressing nicotine's effects on dopamine by acting as dopamine reuptake inhibitors. The most commonly prescribed antidepressant drug for nicotine cessation is *bupropion (Zyban* or *Wellbutrin)*. By blocking reuptake of dopamine, bupropion elevates dopamine levels within synapses. Researchers hypothesize that when this occurs in the nucleus accumbens, the elevated dopamine levels compensate for dopamine elevations normally produced by nicotine. Although this drug produces pharmacological actions suggestive of reducing smoking, fewer than one-third of patients in clinical studies have successfully abstained from smoking when taking bupropion (Gonzales et al., 2006).

💊 *Drug Profile:* **bupropion**	
Trade name:	Zyban or Wellbutrin
Mechanism of action	Blocks reuptake of dopamine
Uses	Reduces withdrawal symptoms from nicotine dependence by substituting for nicotine's rewarding effects

No matter the cessation treatment, rates of successful abstinence remain poor overall. There appear to be trends depending on gender, race, and socioeconomic status. In one study, Piper and colleagues (2010) evaluated 2,850 smokers enrolled in different types of cessation trials, including nicotine replacement therapies, bupropion, or a combination of bupropion and a nicotine replacement strategy. The smokers group consisted of men and women of either African or European American descent as well as different levels of socioeconomic status. After 6 months, the researchers found greater abstinence among men (vs. women), European Americans (vs. African Americans), and those with higher socioeconomic status (vs. low socioeconomic status). A combination of bupropion with a nicotine replacement product was most effective in men, whereas none of the therapies appeared ideal for African Americans. No matter the demographic characteristics or therapy used, none of the groups achieved greater than approximately 50 percent smoking abstinence at a 6-month follow-up.

In another examination of sex differences in smoking, Cosgrove and colleagues (2012) examined sex steroid hormone levels and used single-photon emission tomography (typically abbreviated as SPECT) to examine β_2-containing nicotinic receptor levels in smoking and nonsmoking men and women. They found that men who smoke express up-regulation of β_2 nicotinic receptors compared to men who do not smoke, while no upregulation was observed in women who smoke. Further, during the luteal phase when progesterone levels are high, women who smoked expressed greater cravings to smoke and more symptoms or nicotine withdrawal compared to the follicular phase when estradiol slowly rises from low levels during the phase and progesterone levels are low. These findings might suggest why nicotine replacement products appear less effective in women (i.e., no change in β_2 nicotinic receptor levels) and why women appear less susceptible to smoking relapse if therapy begins during the luteal phase of the menstrual cycle (Allen, Allen, Lunos, & Hatsukami, 2009). Overall, there remains much to learn about tobacco addiction and a great need for improved treatment approaches.

STOP & CHECK

1. Given that the first use of nicotine causes aversive effects, why does tobacco use continue?

2. Why are nicotine replacement therapies helpful for tobacco cessation programs?

1. Behavioral reasons account for the persistent use of tobacco until tolerance to adverse effects develop. **2.** Nicotine replacement therapies address changes that chronic nicotine use causes to the nicotinic-receptor system. A nicotine replacement therapy provides a gradual reduction in physiological nicotine levels, allowing this receptor system to slowly adapt to a nicotine-free state, thereby reducing withdrawal symptoms.

Caffeine

Caffeine is a psychostimulant compound and a member of the xanthine chemical class. Other xanthines, including theobromine and theophylline, also exhibit psychostimulant effects. Caffeine is by far the most used. Approximately 90 percent of Americans consume caffeine on a regular basis and average about 227 milligrams (mg) of caffeine per person each day (Frary, Johnson, & Wang, 2005). Best estimates indicate that children consume about half the caffeine as adults, although data on young children are generally lacking (Temple, 2009). In one study, average caffeine intake consisted of 52 mg in 5–7 year olds and 109 mg in 8–12-year-olds (Warzak, Evans, Floress, Gross, & Stoolman, 2011).

Caffeine and Related Compounds in Plants

Caffeine, and to a lesser extent other xanthine compounds, exist in many plants grown naturally in the environment. Caffeine, theobromine, and theophylline are found in kola nuts and cocoa tree nuts, which we use for cola soft drinks and chocolate, respectively. Colas contain caffeine from kola nuts, and chocolate has caffeine from cocoa nuts. A large variety of tea leaves also contain caffeine, theobromine, and theophylline. Coffee beans, which are brewed for coffee drinks, are a significant source of caffeine. Because caffeine represents the most-used and strongest-acting compound among naturally occurring xanthines, this section of the chapter focuses on the use and properties of caffeine.

The caffeine content among products varies. A 10-ounce (oz.) cup of regular coffee contains approximately 200 mg of caffeine, and a 16-oz. coffee contains approximately 320 mg of caffeine. For coffee, the caffeine content varies, in part, with roasting time. Darker roast coffees, which are roasted longer, tend to have less caffeine content than lighter roast coffees.

A 10-oz. cup of tea contains approximately 100 mg of caffeine, or half as much caffeine as coffee. A 1-oz. piece of chocolate contains approximately 25 mg of caffeine. **Figure 7.18** lists the caffeine content of other popular substances.

Energy drinks are rapidly growing in popularity because of their invigorating properties. They contain a large amount of caffeine, often around 200 mg. Beyond describing energy-enhancing effects, advertisers also promote energy drinks for weight loss, physical stamina, and athletic performance. Individuals 25 years and younger, including a significant portion of children 12 and younger, consume nearly half of all energy drinks. College students report that between 39 percent and 57 percent had consumed energy drinks within the previous month (Malinauskas, Aeby, Overton, Carpenter-Aeby, & Barber-Heidal, 2007; Miller, 2008). Energy drinks are the fastest-growing beverage in the United States, accounting for $9 billion in sales in the United States in 2011 (Arria & O'Brien, 2011).

Energy drinks include not only caffeine as a direct ingredient but also may include caffeinated products such as kola nut, yerba maté, and cocoa. They often include other xanthines such as theobromine and theophylline. Many other chemicals in energy drinks, including sugar and a variety of herbs, amino acids, and plant extracts, promote energy-enhancing effects (Arria & O'Brien, 2011).

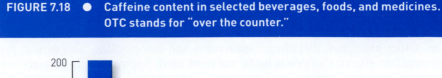

FIGURE 7.18 ● Caffeine content in selected beverages, foods, and medicines. OTC stands for "over the counter."

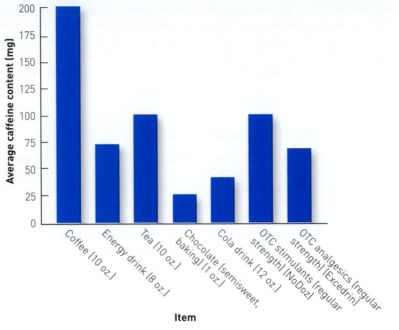

SOURCE: Mayo Foundation, 2011; Reissig et al., 2009.

Caffeinated alcoholic beverage
Beverage made by mixing energy drinks with alcohol.

Alcoholic beverages have become a source of caffeine. These beverages, referred to as **caffeinated alcoholic beverages**, consist of mixing energy drinks such as Red Bull with alcohols such as vodka. Many concoctions are now sold this way, including Four Loko, a popular alcohol and energy drink beverage now banned in many states. The energy drink component of these beverages can temporarily counter alcohol's intoxicating effects, thus facilitating excessive drinking and an increased risk of alcohol poisoning.

Caffeine Has an Ancient History

The plant products just listed were consumed long before the Europeans discovered them. Teas were used in China for thousands of years, and coffee beans were brewed in Arabia since at least A.D. 1000. In South and Central America, the Olmec, Maya, Toltec, and Aztec cultures consumed cocoa beans. European explorers subsequently brought cocoa seeds to Europe, and Europeans harvested the seeds and commonly prepared cocoa with sugars and milk to make chocolate drinks and candies.

The very first human discoveries of the invigorating properties of these plants are shrouded in stories passed through an oral history, as reviewed by Fredholm (2011). For example, scholars often report a story about an Ethiopian named Kaldi as the discoverer of coffee. Kaldi observed that his goats became excited after consuming berries from a coffee bush, which he confirmed on trying the berries himself.

Before A.D. 1000, people normally consumed coffee by eating coffee beans, but around A.D. 1000, brewed coffee became popular. Brewed coffee became a social drink in Arabia, and students and scholars consumed coffee in intellectual centers. In fact, a type of coffee bar consumed in intellectual centers in Turkey was given the name *mekteb-i-irfan*, meaning "the school of the wise."

Coffee was not immediately accepted in Europe, and an attempt to persuade Pope Clement VIII (reign 1592 to 1605) to officially ban this "Muslim drink" led him to state, "This satanic drink is in truth so good that it would be a pity if only nonbelievers were allowed to drink it. We will fool Satan and baptize it so that it becomes a Christian drink, with no danger for the soul." Thus, any social barriers to coffee consumption in Europe soon fell.

The first European cafés appeared in the early 1700s. These cafés were male-only establishments that not only served coffee but also sold newspapers and cultural reviews. The British, however, preferred tea, possibly because of the influence of the British East India Company, which facilitated a strong tea trade with India. Russia also preferred tea over coffee, possibly because of that nation's ties with China.

Friedlieb Runge first extracted caffeine in 1819, and Emil Fischer identified caffeine's chemical properties in 1881. Other xanthene discoveries came later. Theobromine was first extracted in 1841, and Fischer discovered its chemical structures in 1882. Soon after this, Fischer discovered theophylline, another xanthine.

STOP & CHECK

1. In addition to coffee, teas, and soda, energy drinks are a major source of _____.

2. Coffee beans have been brewed since at least A.D. 1000 in _____.

1. caffeine 2. Arabia

Caffeine Absorption, Duration, and Interaction With Other Psychoactive Drugs

Caffeine products are administered orally, in the form of beverages, food, or pills. Coffee contains a number of acids, called *chlorogenic acids*, that lower the pH of coffee to generally between from 5 to 6 with caffeine itself a weak base (Fujioka & Shibamoto, 2008). Once ingested, 100% percent of caffeine is absorbed through intestinal walls, reaching peak blood levels after approximately 40 minutes (Blanchard & Sawers, 1983; Liguori, Hughes, & Grass, 1997). Caffeine penetrates both brain and placental blood barriers. The liver metabolizes caffeine primarily by the enzyme CYP-1A2 and, to a lesser extent, by the enzyme CYP-2E1. Most individuals metabolize approximately 90 percent of caffeine, although the amount of caffeine metabolized depends on the activity of these enzymes. For example, individuals with reduced CYP-1A2 enzymatic activity metabolize less caffeine, subsequently prolonging caffeine's pharmacological effects.

Enzymatic involvement with other drugs also may alter the metabolism rate for caffeine. For example, many antidepressant drugs are CYP-1A2 enzyme inhibitors. Thus, individuals who take these antidepressant drugs metabolize less caffeine. Given that caffeine can produce anxiousness (see "Pharmacological Effects" later in chapter), this interaction effect may weaken an antidepressant drug's effectiveness if caffeine intake is not monitored (Fredholm & Arnaud, 2011). At the same time, smoking enhances CYP-1A2 activity, resulting in increased metabolism of caffeine (Begas, Kouvaras, Tsakalof, Papakosta, & Asprodini, 2007; Joeres et al., 1988).

The metabolism of caffeine produces active metabolites that, like caffeine, belong to the xanthene class of drugs (**Figure 7.19**). In particular, these metabolites include theophylline, theobromine, and another xanthine compound with related psychoactive effects, paraxanthine. Unlike theophylline and theobromine—which, as stated earlier, occur naturally in plants—paraxanthine occurs only when metabolically converted from caffeine. The relative distribution of metabolites produced from caffeine consists of 70–80 percent paraxanthine, 7–8 percent theophylline, and 7–8 percent theobromine (Begas et al., 2007).

FIGURE 7.19 ● The liver enzymes CYP-1A2 and CYP-2E1 convert caffeine into xanthine metabolites, including theophylline and theobromine. The dashed arrow indicates that less conversion occurs from CYP-1A2 to theophylline and theobromine.

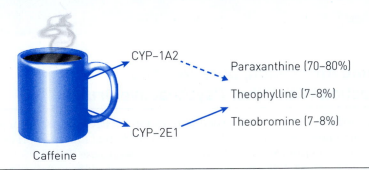

Caffeine

CYP-1A2 ⇢ Paraxanthine (70–80%)

Theophylline (7–8%)

Theobromine (7–8%)

CYP-2E1

SOURCE: © Cengage Learning 2014.

The body primarily eliminates caffeine through the kidneys. The rate of elimination varies widely from approximately 3 to 10 hours (Blanchard & Sawers, 1983). The range in elimination rates may explain why some individuals have difficulty sleeping at night if they drink coffee in the afternoon, whereas other individuals have no difficulty sleeping at night after drinking coffee in the evening. Cigar or cigarette smoking doubles the rate of caffeine elimination because of the previously mentioned increased metabolic activity (Joeres et al., 1988). Because of this increased elimination rate, smokers may drink more coffee to maintain caffeine's effects.

Caffeine: Antagonist for Adenosine Receptors

Caffeine's primary mechanism of action is antagonism of adenosine A1 and A2 receptors. **Adenosine** is a neuromodulator that has inhibitory effects on neurons throughout the central and peripheral nervous system. In particular, adenosine has inhibitory effects on cholinergic neurons in the cerebral cortex and on dopamine neurons in the basal ganglia. Through these actions, we know adenosine as a chemical that contributes to sleepiness. By blocking adenosine receptors, caffeine prevents the inhibitory influence of adenosine within these parts of the brain, thus promoting alertness (Fisone, Borgkvist, & Usiello, 2004).

Adenosine A neuromodular that has inhibitory effects on neurons throughout the central and peripheral nervous system

STOP & CHECK

1. How can enzymatic activity in the liver influence caffeine's effects?

2. Caffeine is an antagonist for _____ receptors.

1. The behavioral effects of caffeine will persist longer in individuals who are slower metabolizers of caffeine. In a slow metabolizer, caffeine's effects may persist into nighttime and interfere with sleep. In addition, drugs may interact with CYP-1A2 enzymes, potentially slowing the metabolism of caffeine. 2. adenosine

Caffeine: Mild Psychostimulant Effects

Caffeine exhibits many physiological, behavioral, and subjective effects, including increased heart rate, blood vessel constriction, breathing rate, reduced appetite, attention, alertness, and positive mood. Caffeinated products usually are consumed for their fatigue-fighting properties and are commonly consumed by people in the morning after waking up (Brecher, 1972) and when attempting to stay alert at work (Ker, Edwards, Felix, Blackhall, & Roberts, 2010).

Consuming high doses of caffeine leads to **caffeinism**, a condition characterized by agitation, anxiety, insomnia, and negative mood as well as rapid heart rate and high blood pressure. This condition can occur at doses of 500 to 1,000 mg of caffeine, although tolerance to caffeine may require higher doses before a person exhibits caffeinism.

Caffeinism Condition characterized by agitation, anxiety, insomnia, and negative mood as well as rapid heart rate and high blood pressure

Based on the high caffeine content and the presence of other stimulant chemicals, the risk of adverse effects for energy drinks may be greater than for coffee, tea, and other traditional caffeinated products. In addition to caffeine's adverse effects, energy drink ingredients can cause hypertension, abdominal pain, and seizures when administered at high enough quantities. Moreover, the chemical ingredients in energy drinks can interact with psychoactive medications. For example, two ingredients found in many energy drinks—5-hydroxytryptophan and yohimbine—can strengthen the adverse effects of antidepressant drugs (Arria & O'Brien, 2011).

Tolerance and Dependence During Sustained Caffeine Use

Tolerance occurs with many of caffeine's acute subjective effects, including positive mood, improved alertness, and anxiousness, whereas tolerance may not occur with caffeine's physiological effects, including changes in cardiovascular activity and blood vessel constriction (Hughes, Oliveto, Liguori, Carpenter, & Howard, 1998; Sigmon, Herning, Better, Cadet, & Griffiths, 2009). Daily consumption also leads to features of dependence, as demonstrated by the occurrence of withdrawal symptoms when first discontinuing use. In one survey, Juliano and colleagues (2012) recorded the prevalence of withdrawal symptoms among adult respondents who expressed interest in reducing or quitting caffeine use (**Figure 7.20**). These individuals reported an average of

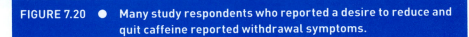

FIGURE 7.20 ● **Many study respondents who reported a desire to reduce and quit caffeine reported withdrawal symptoms.**

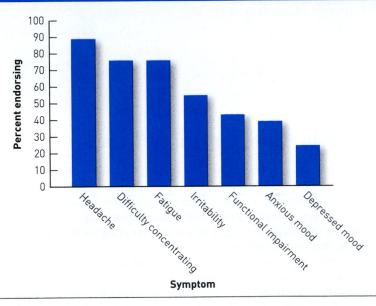

SOURCE: Data from Juliano et al., 2012.

548 mg of caffeine per day, approximately double the normal daily average intake for U.S. adults (Frary et al., 2005). Nearly 90 percent experienced headaches, and approximately 85 percent experienced cravings for caffeine. Other common withdrawal symptoms included difficulty in concentrating, fatigue, irritability, and anxious or depressed mood. The study authors also noted that more than 40 percent of participants felt functionally impaired without caffeine. These symptoms are also described for *caffeine withdrawal* in the DSM-5 (American Psychiatric Association, 2013).

STOP & CHECK

1. An increase in positive mood is one of the many _____ effects of caffeine.

2. Excessive doses of caffeine can produce _____, which is characterized by agitation, anxiety, insomnia, and other symptoms.

3. Other chemicals in energy drinks may interact with _____ drugs, causing an increase in adverse effects.

4. In the absence of caffeine, hostility, fatigue, and negative mood are indications of _____ on caffeine.

1. psychostimulant 2. caffeinism 3. antidepressant 4. dependence

From Actions to Effects:
Why People Consume Caffeinated Products

Improvements in mood and alertness are common reasons for seeking caffeinated products such as coffee, tea, and other caffeinated beverages. Moreover, these and other products, such as chocolate, taste good, which adds to their appeal. Yet during the course of repeated use, a dependence on caffeine, as indicated by withdrawal symptoms, may facilitate consumption of caffeinated products.

Given the prevalence of caffeine use, most readers of this text probably consume caffeinated products on a daily basis. In particular, you may use coffee, a soft drink, or an energy drink to help wake up in the morning. If this describes you, then consider this: Is the tiredness you feel in the morning natural—or is it caffeine withdrawal?

Assuming that you do not consume a caffeinated product within several hours before bedtime, sleeping 6–8 hours may provide for a total caffeine abstinence period of about 10–12 hours. This abstinence period exceeds caffeine's elimination half-life, suggesting that your body's caffeine levels will be low or absent by morning. Indeed, many studies describe morning as an early withdrawal state for chronic caffeine users (James & Rogers, 2005). Thus, for most people, caffeine's ability to fight morning sleepiness may have a lot to do with removing caffeine's withdrawal symptoms.

The DSM-5 considers *caffeine intoxication*, generally similar to caffeinism presented earlier, and *caffeine withdrawal* as two potential disruptive features of caffeine use.

Although the DSM-5 does not consider caffeine as generating a specific substance-use disorder, some clinical studies characterized problem caffeine use as meeting the general features of a disorder (Bernstein, Carroll, Thuras, Cosgrove, & Roth, 2002; Griffiths & Chausmer, 2000). In an assessment of caffeine dependence, Bernstein and colleagues (2002) evaluated caffeine use among a sample of U.S. teenagers. Among the 36 teenagers assessed, 22.2 percent exhibited a sufficient number of symptoms to meet the DSM diagnostic criteria for a substance use disorder. The most commonly observed symptoms included tolerance, withdrawal symptoms, desire to quit or unsuccessful efforts to control use, and continued use despite physical or psychological problems. The total group of teenagers studied reported 244 mg of caffeine per day, with values ranging from as little as 49 mg to as much as 767 mg of caffeine per day.

Although some researchers support applying substance use disorder criteria to caffeine use, others are unconvinced. In a review of scientific studies that assessed caffeine use, Satel (2006) concluded that caffeine does not meet substance dependence criteria. Key points in Satel's study consist of weak or inconsistent reporting of withdrawal effects and a failure to demonstrate strong compulsions to use caffeine. Given that caffeine appears neither irresistible nor a cause of social disruption, Satel argues that caffeine fails a common-sense test as an addictive substance.

Chapter Summary

This chapter has covered two widely used psychostimulant drugs: nicotine and caffeine. Tobacco products are the key source of nicotine. Cigarette smoking is the most common form of nicotine administration, but other forms of tobacco such as smokeless tobacco and e-cigarettes are popular as well. Tobacco use has a long history, dating back to the ancient uses in the Americas and then reaching Europe after Columbus's expedition to the New World.

Nicotine is delivered to the body from tobacco or e-liquids and is absorbed through tissues in the lungs, throat, mouth, and skin. Inhalation is the most efficient route for nicotine delivery. Nicotine is metabolized in the liver, producing cotinine, an active metabolite.

Nicotine produces an increase in nucleus accumbens dopamine levels by activating nicotinic cholinergic receptors in the nucleus accumbens and ventral tegmental area.

Continine also is an agonist for these receptors, but it has a much weaker affinity than nicotine. Nicotine increases sympathetic nervous activity and increases locomotor activity during repeated administration. Nicotine also improves attention. Subjectively, nicotine produces adverse effects on first usage, but tolerance to the effects soon subsides to reveal positive subjective effects. Most of nicotine's adverse effects are the result of tobacco, which contains many known cancer-causing agents. In addition to cancer, tobacco increases the risk of cardiovascular disease and lung disease. Because of desensitization at nicotinic receptors, upregulation of nicotinic receptors occurs during chronic use. Upregulation leads to a sensitized behavioral state.

Nicotine addiction accounts for chronic, habitual tobacco use. Quitting nicotine is difficult in part because of the association of tobacco use with everyday activities. Further, upregulation of nicotinic receptors facilitates a physiological dependent state, requiring sustained elevated nicotine levels for normal functioning.

Caffeine is a xanthine psychostimulant drug found naturally in kola nuts, cocoa tree nuts, and tea leaves. The most common caffeine sources include coffee, tea, and energy drinks. Caffeine-containing leaves and nuts were long used in China and Arabia, and teas and coffee were used throughout Europe beginning in the 1700s.

Caffeine is orally administered and is metabolized in the liver. Caffeine's elimination rate varies, depending on liver enzymatic activity. Caffeine's effects are derived through antagonism of adenosine receptors, not only producing an improvement in alertness, mood, and energy, but also a facilitation of dopamine's effects on the sympathetic nervous system. Excessive caffeine intake produces caffeinism, which is characterized by agitation, anxiety, and negative mood. Tolerance soon develops to caffeine's effects during chronic use, and continued caffeine use is mostly maintained by avoidance of caffeine-withdrawal symptoms.

Key Terms

Nicotine 204
Cigarette 204
Cigar 204
Hookah 205
Smokeless tobacco 206
E-cigarette 207
Vaping 208
Secondhand smoke 210
Thirdhand smoke 210
Flue curing 213

Tar 213
Cotinine 214
Functional antagonism 216
Upregulation 216
Acute tolerance 220
Nitrosamines 226
Emphysema 227
Nicotine abstinence syndrome 229

Chippers 230
Nicotine replacement therapy 232
Caffeine 235
Caffeinated alcoholic beverages 236
Caffeinism 239
Adenosine 239

Visit the Student Study Site at **study.sagepub.com/prus2e** to access additional study tools, including eFlashcards, web quizzes, video resources, web resources, SAGE journal articles, and more.

8

Alcohol

"HALFWAY TO CONCORD" AND "TAKING HIPPOCRATES'S GRAND ELIXIR"

We all know colloquial phrases for over-drinking alcohol such as "getting drunk." Such terms are nothing new, as evidenced by a letter titled "The Drinker's Dictionary," that appeared in *The Pennsylvania Gazette* on January 13, 1737. As the author of that letter noted, drunkenness "bears no kind of similitude with any sort of virtue, from which it might possibly borrow a name; and is therefore reduc'd to the wretched necessity of being express'd by distant round-about phrases as they come to be well understood to signify plainly that A MAN IS DRUNK." The letter included a comprehensive alphabetized listing of terms and phrases for drunkenness. A couple of the terms, such as *tipsy*, are still used today. Most seem obscure, though, such as "He sees the bears," "loaded his cart," and "He's eat a toad & half for breakfast." Although this compilation provides an amusing perspective on terms and phrases for drunkenness in the 18th century, we also regard this letter as an interesting work in American history, one of the many early American writings by the author Benjamin Franklin.

Alcohol: The Most Commonly Used Depressant Substance

Beverage alcohol consists of any drink containing **ethyl alcohol**, also known as **ethanol**, a central nervous system (CNS) depressant. We regularly contact other forms of alcohol, but these types are not safe to drink. One of these types is *isopropyl alcohol*, or *isopropanol*, which is commonly known as *rubbing alcohol*. Another type is *methyl alcohol*, or *methanol*. **Methyl alcohol**, or **methanol**, is an industrial solvent used in many products, including antifreeze. Methyl alcohol acts as a toxin for optic nerves and can be produced during distillation process for *moonshine;* if consumed, it causes blindness.

Beverage alcohol is widely consumed across the world, second only to caffeine. According to the World Health Organization, approximately 2 billion people a year consume alcoholic beverages, and approximately 76 million individuals have an alcohol use disorder such as alcohol addiction. As shown in **Figure 8.1**, alcohol consumption per capita varies across countries. The highest alcohol consumptions levels occur in Europe, the Russian Federation and former Soviet states, North America, South America, and Australia. The Middle East reports the lowest levels of alcohol consumption (World Health Organization, 2014).

According to a 2014 survey conducted by the Substance Abuse and Mental Health Services Administration (SAMHSA), more than half of all U.S. individuals 12 and older reported being current consumers of alcohol, and 81.5 percent report ever consuming alcohol. We tend to find current alcohol use slightly higher for men (57.3 percent) than women (48.4 percent). The youngest of those surveyed, 12- to 17-year-olds, represent approximately 11.5 percent of alcohol consumers (Center for Behavioral Health Statistics and Quality, 2014b).

Ethyl alcohol (or ethanol) An alcohol that functions as a central nervous system depressant

Methyl alcohol (or methanol) An industrial solvent that acts as a toxin for optic nerves and can be produced during distillation process for *moonshine*

Alcohol Production Through Fermentation and Distillation

Beer, wine, and spirits serve as the primary sources of beverage alcohol. As presented in Chapter 7, certain energy drink mixes such as Four Loko also contain alcohol. Small amounts of alcohol are also found in vinegar, leftover from the production of acetic acid from ethanol, and certain liquid medications such as cough syrups.

The amount of alcohol in a beverage is labeled in two ways: by percentage and by proof. **Percentage alcohol**, also known as **alcohol by volume**, refers to the number of grams of alcohol found in 100 milliliters of solution. For example, 50 g of alcohol in 100 ml of solution equates to 50 percent. The **proof of alcohol** is a numerical value that is double the actual percentage of alcohol. For example, a beverage with 50 percent alcohol is 100 proof.

Recreational alcoholic beverages vary in percent alcohol content, depending on whether brewers used a fermentation method or a distillation method. **Fermentation** is a process of alcohol production using yeast cells and some type of starch such as grain or fruit. During fermentation, yeast interacts with sugars from starches, creating alcohol. The longer that yeasts have to metabolize these sugars, the greater the percentage of alcohol produced. The approximate upper limit for alcohol production

FIGURE 8.1 ●   Alcohol Consumption per Capita per Year in Liters of Pure Alcohol.

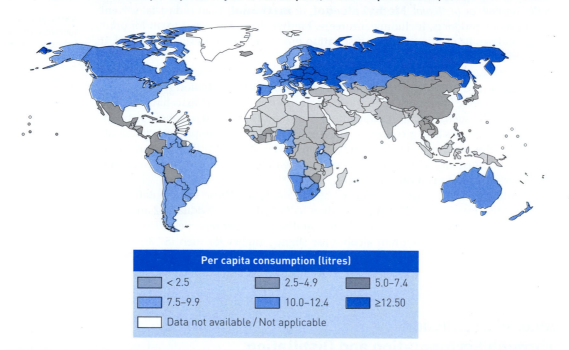

Total alcohol per capita (15+ years) consumption, in litres of pure alcohol, 2010

Per capita consumption (litres)

< 2.5	2.5–4.9	5.0–7.4
7.5–9.9	10.0–12.4	≥12.50
Data not available / Not applicable		

SOURCE: Reprinted from Global Status Report on Alcohol and Health, 2014, Vladimir Poznyak and Dag Rekve (eds.), *Alcohol Consumption*, pp 28–43, Copyright (2014). Map accessed 1/30/17 from the following URL: http://gamapserver.who.int/mapLibrary/Files/Maps/Global_consumption_percapita_2010.png

using fermentation is 15 percent. Higher alcohol percentages kill yeast cells, causing fermentation to end.

Most beers and wines contain less than 15 percent alcohol. **Beer** is an alcoholic beverage, usually with 5 percent or less alcohol content, made through fermentation of certain types of starch such as barely, wheat, or rice. During the fermentation process, brewers add other ingredients such as hops and fruit to further promote fermentation and provide flavoring. *Indian pale ales* (typically referred to as IPAs) are noted for strong hops flavorings. Most commercial domestic beers are made from barley and hops and contain about 5 percent alcohol. *Malt liquor*, although actually beer, comes from malted barely and contains more than 5 percent alcohol due to having more sugars added to enable further alcohol production from fermentation. Some countries are known for unique varieties of beer. Belgium, for example, produces fruitier beers, and Japan produces rice beers, such as *Saké*.

Wine is an alcoholic beverage, usually with 12–15 percent alcohol content, made through fermentation of fruit. Most wine makers use grapes, which provide a sugar source, along with certain acids, enzymes, and nutrients during the fermentation process. Beyond grapes, some winemakers use other fruits such as strawberries or cherries. Wines made from fruits other than grapes are called *fruit wines*.

Another alcoholic beverage is kombucha. *Kombucha* blends consist of brewed teas that contain alcohol. Alcohol fermentation occurs by adding yeast to the tea. This typically produces a 1 percent alcohol beverage, although longer brewing times and increase this to 3 percent (Mayser, Fromme, Leitzmann, & Gründer, 1995).

Distilled alcoholic beverages (also referred to as *liquors* or *spirits*) are produced through distillation and have a higher alcohol content than beers and wines. Distillation is a method that separates alcohol from a fermented mixture. During this process, distillers heat a fermented mixture until it exceeds alcohol's boiling point. At this boiling point, alcohol evaporates; the alcohol vapors are routed through tubes into a cooler compartment where the alcohol returns to a liquid form, making a highly concentrated alcoholic solution.

Distilled alcoholic beverages tend to contain at least 20 percent alcohol and come in many different varieties such as brandy, gin, rum, tequila, vodka, and whiskey. The different flavors born from distillation depend on the starch used in fermentation, the filtration methods used to purify the alcohol collected during distillation, and the method of storage. In other words, along with the distilled alcohol, other chemicals collect in the fermented brew, and the desired flavor in part depends on the filtration of these chemicals from the distilled solution and the type of container in which the end product is aged or stored.

One of the purest distilled spirits is a grain-based alcohol marketed as Everclear. Everclear is highly filtered so that it contains a high concentration of alcohol with few other chemicals. The varieties of Everclear vary from 75 percent to 95 percent alcohol. The highest concentration version is illegal to sell in some U.S. states. Vodka consists of another highly filtered distilled spirit that may be based on grains or other starch sources. Although many vodkas contain around 50 percent alcohol, other varieties of vodka may contain as much as 95 percent. Brandy, whiskey, and rum typically contain 40–60 percent alcohol and vary in bitterness and flavor.

Beer An alcoholic beverage, usually with 5 percent or less alcohol content, made through fermentation from certain starches such as barely, wheat, or rice

Wine An alcoholic beverage, usually with 12–15 percent alcohol content, made through fermentation of fruit

Distilled alcoholic beverages Alcoholic beverages produced through distillation that have a higher alcohol content than beer and wine

FIGURE 8.2   ●   Standard Drink Comparisons Between Whiskey and Domestic Beer

Source: Fig 8.2: ©iStockphoto.com/EHStock.

Home distillation is illegal in most U.S. states. These methods produce a beverage often referred to as *moonshine*. Home-distillation methods, however, are notorious for dangerous impurities, including methanol as noted earlier.

Given the enormous variety of alcohol concentrations among beverages, health officials compare beverages according to standard drink units. A **standard drink** contains 14 grams of 100 percent alcohol, which is equivalent to about 2/3 of a fluid ounce. To put this in perspective, a small shot glass holds about 1½ fluid ounces. A standard drink equivalent of 190-proof Everclear (95 percent alcohol) fills about half of a small shot glass. A standard drink equivalent of whisky is approximately 1½ fluid ounces and fills a small shot glass. For a typical domestic beer, the standard drink equivalent consists of 16 ounces or one pint (National Institute on Alcohol Abuse and Alcoholism, 2012) (**Figure 8.2**).

Standard drink
Drink that contains 14 grams of 100-percent alcohol; equivalent to about 2/3 fluid ounces

STOP & CHECK

1. Of the many types of alcohol, which is safe to drink (in moderation)?

2. If an alcoholic drink is 40 percent alcohol, what is the proof?

3. Although fermentation can produce as much as 15 percent alcohol, higher concentrations can be achieved using_____.

4. Alcoholic beverages are compared for alcohol content by referring to _____ drinks, which are equivalent to 14 grams of 100-percent alcohol.

1. Ethyl alcohol, also known as *ethanol* **2.** The proof of an alcoholic beverage is double the percentage of alcohol. A 40-percent alcoholic drink is 80 proof. **3.** distillation **4.** Standard

The History of Alcohol Consumption

Scholars hypothesize that early Neolithic peoples raised and fermented grapes as early as 6000 B.C. The recorded history of alcohol dates to Sumerian writings in 3200 B.C. During this period, early taverns in Samaria and Egypt sold alcohol, and traders transported alcohol throughout the known world.

Both wine and beers were described during this age. Wine was a limited commodity and considered a drink of luxury for consumption by ruling figures. Sumerian writings describe a beer made from barley. Egyptian writings describe many types of beers made from barley as well as a beer called *hek* made from honey. In both Samaria and Egypt, beer making was common in households, and the recreational use of beer was a normal part of everyday life.

Opposition to alcohol also existed during this time. In 2000 B.C., an Egyptian priest wrote a letter to one of his pupils, stating "I forbid thee to go to the tavern. . . . Thou are degraded like the beasts." The Code of Hammurabi, written around 1750 B.C., regulated drinking establishments called "wine shops" to prevent riotous gatherings.

Aside from recreational purposes, the Sumerians also used alcohol as a vehicle for many medicines. Around 800 B.C., Greeks used wine in religious ceremonies and to treat pain. Moderate drinking occurred soon after Rome's founding around 750 B.C. However, rampant drinking occurred around 200 B.C. and was a hallmark of Roman culture through its fall around A.D. 200. By this time, alcohol consumption was a normal part of European life.

Distilled alcohol arrived around A.D. 1250, mostly as an expensive medicine, and its lauded benefits led to the term *aqua vitae*, the water of life. The sense of youth, vitality, and physical well-being led to describing distilled alcohol as a *spirit*. Brandy was the primary spirit consumed until around the late 1400s, when a Scottish publication described a recipe for whiskey made from malted barley rather than wine. In 1550, a publication in Holland described the first recipe for gin. Rum was popular in colonial America because of its low production cost and the triangle trade that brought inexpensive sugar cane to the colonies.

Many alcohol-related adages have their origins in this period. In England, public houses—*pubs*—served alcoholic drinks in pints and quarts. The oldest pub in English history is Ye Olde Fighting Cocks, which was established sometime in the 12th century and still operates today. The phrase "Mind your p's and q's," meaning "Be careful of your behavior," was derived from the practice of publicans (pub keepers) who recorded the number of drinks in pints or quarts served to each customer. A publican "minded his p's and q's" if he didn't lose money, and a customer "minded his p's and q's" if he did not get drunk (Austin, 1985; Carson-Dewitt, 2003).

In the early 1800s, a powerful alcohol prohibition movement began in the United States. Many groups contributed to this movement, including the American Temperance Union and the Washingtonians. Joining them were Protestants, Catholics, and other religious organizations.

These political forces achieved many local and state bans on alcohol sales and consumption. After overcoming a pause in these efforts during the American Civil War, they eventually were influential enough to help pass the National Prohibition

18th Amendment
Amendment to U.S. Constitution that banned the sale and distribution of alcohol

21st Amendment
Repealed the 18th amendment

Act, which became the **18th Amendment** to the U.S. Constitution in 1920. This amendment did not ban alcohol consumption, but it did ban the sale and distribution of alcohol. The 18th Amendment failed to eliminate alcohol use. In many communities, the ban on sale of alcohol was virtually ignored, and *bootleggers*, those who illegally transported alcohol in the United States, were often regarded as celebrities. In 1933, the **21st Amendment** repealed the 18th Amendment. Still, although the federal government no longer prohibits the sale of alcohol, some towns and counties remain "dry" to this day. One of the most famous dry counties is Moore County, Tennessee—ironically, the home of Jack Daniel's distillery, a well-known whiskey producer (Carson-Dewitt, 2003; Hall, 2010).

STOP & CHECK

1. The _____ provided the first written evidence of alcoholic beverages.

2. Other than recreational use, what were the first spirits used for?

3. Which U.S. constitutional amendment prohibited the sale and distribution of alcohol?

1. Sumerians 2. Dating back to A.D. 1250, the first spirits were used as medicines. 3. The 18th Amendment

Pharmacokinetic Factors and Alcohol's Effects

Alcohol is highly soluble in water and fat, allowing for easy absorption in tissue. Users consume alcohol orally, and after ingestion alcohol absorbs into the bloodstream through the gastrointestinal tract. Most alcohol absorbs through the upper intestine because of its large surface area. In the intestine, alcohol also impairs thiamine transporter function, also known as Vitamin B1, reducing thiamine availability for critical cellular functions in the body (Subramanya, Subramanian, & Said, 2010). Thiamine deficiency occurs in Wernicke-Korsakoff Syndrome, discussed later in this chapter.

Blood alcohol concentration (BAC)
Number of grams of alcohol in a 100 ml volume of blood

Alcohol dehydrogenase
Enzyme that metabolizes alcohol

We measure the amount of alcohol in the body by blood alcohol concentration. **Blood alcohol concentration** (or **BAC**) refers to the number of grams of alcohol in a 100 ml volume of blood. For example, 1 gram of alcohol in 100 ml of blood equates to a BAC of 1.0. This is an extremely high and fatal concentration of alcohol. A drink or two may produce a BAC of only 0.04. The maximum BAC from an alcoholic drink occurs after approximately 45 minutes (Dubowski, 1985).

Enzymes in the stomach, liver, and other parts of the body metabolize alcohol. The enzyme **alcohol dehydrogenase** metabolizes 95 percent of alcohol. It

converts it to **acetaldehyde**, a chemical that produces noxious effects (Zimatkin, Liopo, & Deitrich, 1998). In addition to alcohol dehydrogenase, other metabolic processes in tissues throughout the body, including the brain, convert alcohol to acetaldehyde. Acetaldehyde converts to acetic acid and acetate by different forms of the enzyme aldehyde dehydrogenase (Chinnawirotpisan et al., 2003). Another process converts acetic acid and acetate to carbon dioxide and water (**Figure 8.3**).

Acetaldehyde
Metabolite produced from enzymatic conversion of alcohol with alcohol dehydrogenase

FIGURE 8.3 ● The metabolic process for alcohol consists of conversion to acetaldehyde and then conversion of acetaldehyde to acetic and acetate. Other metabolic process cause acetic acid and acetate to convert to water and carbon dioxide.

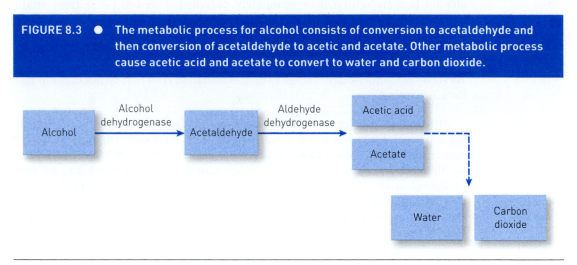

SOURCE: © Cengage Learning 2014.

Researchers have found different polymorphisms that can affect the rate of alcohol metabolism. Those with the *alcohol dehydrogenase 1C*1 allele* polymorphism more quickly convert alcohol to acetaldehyde, leading to greater accumulation of acetaldehyde compared to those without this polymorphism (Coutelle et al., 2004). The *acetaldehyde H2*2 allele* polymorphism, which is found in approximately half of those of Asian descent, also causes a greater accumulation of acetaldehyde, but does so via slower catabolism of acetaldehyde by aldehyde dehydrogenase (Wall et al., 1997). As noted later in this chapter, we associate acetaldehyde with noxious effects, potentially related to the symptoms of hangover.

Both the stomach and liver contain alcohol dehydrogenase enzymes. Little alcohol metabolism takes place in an empty stomach because alcohol is quickly digested to the intestines in the absence of food. However, on a full stomach, alcohol remains in the stomach longer, giving alcohol greater exposures to alcohol dehydrogenase enzymes. In this case, some of the alcohol metabolizes before reaching the intestines for absorption. We also find that metabolism of alcohol in the stomach occurs 20 percent less in women (Frezza et al., 1990). After absorption, alcohol dehydrogenase enzymes in the liver metabolize most of the remaining alcohol.

As described in Chapter 4, the rate of alcohol elimination follows zero-order kinetics. Most individuals eliminate approximately 10 to 14 mL, or about ½ ounce, of 100-percent alcohol per hour. The general concept for alcohol elimination indicates that this elimination rate remains the same regardless of the amount of alcohol consumed. However, a truer picture of alcohol elimination presents a mix of zero-order and first-order kinetics, depending on the dose of alcohol ingested and the amount of enzymes available for metabolizing alcohol. Zero-order kinetics apply to alcohol's elimination rate until all available enzymes for metabolizing alcohol become saturated or completely occupied. This can occur from attaining and maintaining high BACs. After saturating alcohol metabolic enzymes, the elimination rate of alcohol approximates reductions in half-lives, which resembles first-order kinetics (Dubowski, 1985).

Review! Zero-order kinetics refers to drug-elimination rates that do not occur in half-lives. (Chapter 4.)

Although 95 percent of alcohol is metabolized, the body eliminates the remaining 5 percent percent of alcohol, unchanged, from the lungs. The ratio of alcohol concentration in expelled air to blood is 1:2,300 (Dubowski, 1985). *Breathalyzer tests* use this ratio to accurately determine the amount of alcohol in blood. The amounts of alcohol analyzed are expressed as BAC. For example, saying someone "blew a 0.11" means that the individual had a BAC of 0.11. Researchers correlate blood alcohol's pharmacological effects, and law enforcement uses BACs to determine if someone is legally intoxicated.

STOP & CHECK

1. The percentage of alcohol in blood is referred to as the _____.

2. The enzyme alcohol dehydrogenase converts alcohol to _____.

3. Because a set rate of 10 to 14 ml of alcohol are eliminated per hour, alcohol is eliminated following _____ kinetics.

1. blood alcohol concentration 2. acetaldehyde 3. zero-order

Alcohol and Central Nervous System Functioning

The pharmacological actions of alcohol in the body involve many different neurotransmitter systems and depend on the amount of alcohol consumed. These pharmacological actions involve GABA, glutamate, endogenous opioid, dopamine, serotonin, and endocannabinoid systems.

Alcohol and GABA$_A$ Receptors

Alcohol acts directly on ionotropic GABA$_A$ receptors, which produce inhibitory effects on neurons (Mihic et al., 1997). When GABA activates GABA$_A$ receptors, the associated channels open and cause negatively charged chloride ions to enter the neuron. Negatively charged ions in turn hyperpolarize the neuron, inhibiting the neuron's activity.

Alcohol binds to and functions as a positive modulator for GABA$_A$ receptors (Ticku, Burch, & Davis, 1983). Positive modulation of GABA$_A$ receptors increases the length of receptor activation and increases the flow of chloride ions into the neuron. These two actions enhance the inhibitory effects of GABA$_A$ receptors.

Review! Positive modulators facilitate neurotransmitter effects at a receptor. (Chapter 4.)

The location of GABA$_A$ receptors determines the effects of alcohol. Although many brain structures contain GABA$_A$ receptors, those most relevant to alcohol's CNS depressing effects include the cerebral cortex, hippocampus, and thalamus. These three structures are important for information processing, memory, and other cognitive activities.

GABA$_A$ receptors also mediate alcohol's reinforcing effects (**Figure 8.4**). First, alcohol facilitates GABA$_A$ receptor activation in the nucleus accumbens, a known receptor action that produces reinforcing effects. Second, alcohol activates GABA$_A$ receptors located on GABA neurons in the ventral tegmental area. The activation of these receptors causes reduced GABA release, in turn decreasing the inhibition of dopamine neurons (Xiao, Zhou, Li, & Ye, 2007). Reduced inhibition of dopamine neurons results in enhanced dopamine release in the nucleus accumbens, a known rewarding action (Yoshimoto, McBride, Lumeng, & Li, 1992).

In addition to acting on GABA$_A$ receptors in the ventral tegmental area, alcohol indirectly inhibits GABA neurons by increasing levels of the endogenous opioid β-endorphin (Schulz, Wüster, Duka, & Herz, 1980). In the ventral tegmental area, β-endorphin activates inhibitory opioid receptors on these GABA neurons, further contributing to diminished GABA release (Figure 8.4) (Xiao & Ye, 2008).

Chronic administration of alcohol causes several changes in alcohol's effects on GABA neurons. First, chronic administration reduces the number of GABA$_A$ receptors. Second, GABA$_A$ receptors become less affected by alcohol (Montpied et al., 1991). Third, alcohol produces a lower increase in β-endorphin levels, resulting in less inhibition of GABA neurons (Schulz et al., 1980). As noted following, reduced levels of GABA$_A$ receptors contribute to dangerous withdrawal symptoms.

Alcohol and Glutamate Receptors

Alcohol also produces depressant effects by inhibiting excitatory glutamate NMDA receptors. NMDA receptors produce excitatory effects and facilitate learning and memory processes. Like GABA$_A$ receptors, alcohol binds noncompetitively to NMDA

FIGURE 8.4 ● Alcohol produces reinforcing effects through GABA neurotransmission in three ways: (1) Alcohol enhances endogenous opioid release (β-endorphin), which inhibits GABA neuron activity. (2) Alcohol enhances the inhibitory effects of GABA$_A$ receptors on ventral tegmental GABA neurons. These two mechanisms prevent GABA's inhibition of dopamine neurons and cause increased nucleus accumbens dopamine release. (3) Alcohol also produces reinforcing effect by facilitating GABA$_A$ inhibition of GABA neurons in the nucleus accumbens.

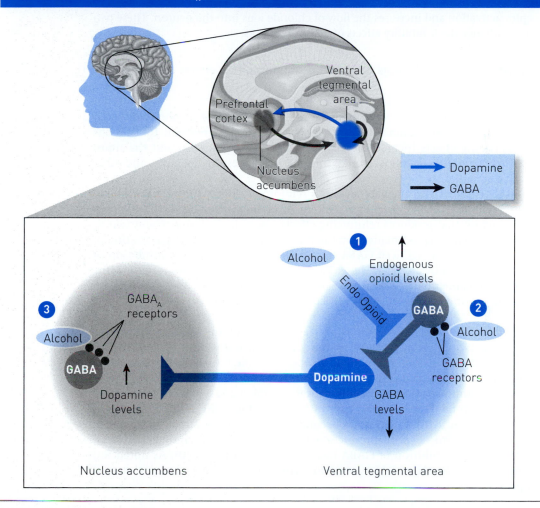

receptors, but not at a clearly identified site (Krystal, Petrakis, Mason, Trevisan, & D'Souza, 2003). After binding to the receptor, alcohol inhibits ion passage through the NMDA receptor channel.

Chronic alcohol administration increases the number of NMDA receptors. During withdrawal from alcohol, the enhanced levels of NMDA receptors allow glutamate to exhibit greater excitatory effects on neurons. These greater excitatory effects, combined with lower $GABA_A$ receptor levels, increase the risk of seizures, a serious alcohol withdrawal symptom (Grant, Valverius, Hudspith, & Tabakoff, 1990; Hillbom, Pieninkeroinen, & Leone, 2003).

Enhanced NMDA receptor function may occur during chronic alcohol use. The enhanced activity occurs by from interfering with a negative feedback loop, involving a type of potassium (K^+) channel called SK2, for the NMDA receptor. Chronic alcohol use inhibits the function of SK2 channels, which likely diminishes the effectiveness of negative feedback (Mulholland, Becker, Woodward, & Chandler, 2011).

Alcohol and Calcium

Voltage-gated calcium channels facilitate neurotransmitter release and many other functions, including gene expression and enzyme regulation. Not only does the nervous system contain voltage-gated calcium channels, but also so does the heart, smooth muscle, kidneys, and pancreas. There are six known types of voltage-gated calcium channels; these are classified by the letters L, N, P, Q, R, and T. Among these, alcohol inhibits the L-type calcium channel.

Because of the widespread expression of L-type calcium channels in the brain, alcohol's inhibitory actions through these channels cause generalized effects. Overall, acute administration of alcohol reduces neurotransmitter release from axon terminals containing these channels. However, alcohol inhibition of L-type calcium channels specifically inhibits vasopressin release. By inhibiting vasopressin levels, alcohol causes increased urination. In addition, diminished vasopressin activity impairs cognition, disrupts circadian rhythm, lowers blood pressure, and enhances aggression (Walter & Messing, 1999).

Calcium may also play a role in negative feedback pathways for NMDA receptors. As noted above, SK2 channels provide negatively affect the activity of NMDA receptors, and chronic alcohol use diminishes SK2 channel function. Calcium activates SK2 channels. In the hippocampus, calcium enters neurons through the R-type calcium channel, providing a source of calcium within neurons to activate SK2 channels, thereby facilitating negative feedback for NMDA receptors (Mulholland et al., 2011).

Review! Vasopressin is an antidiuretic hormone, meaning that it causes the kidneys to absorb more water from the bloodstream. (Chapter 3.)

Alcohol and Serotonin Receptors

In addition to the other mechanisms described so far, alcohol also increases serotonin concentrations in the nucleus accumbens (Yoshimoto et al., 1992). As reviewed in Chapter 6, increased serotonin concentrations in the nucleus accumbens contribute to the reinforcing effects of cocaine and amphetamine, suggesting that increased

serotonin levels may contribute to alcohol's reinforcing effects as well. Alcohol also appears to exhibit specific actions on serotonin ionotropic 5-HT_3 receptors and metabotropic 5-HT_{2A} receptors.

Review! An ionotropic receptor contains an ion channel, and a metabotropic receptor uses a G-protein to carry out intracellular effects. (Chapter 3.)

Alcohol causes the activation of 5HT_3 receptors through either of two ways. First, alcohol enhances serotonin levels, leading to greater activation of 5HT_3 receptors. In the nucleus accumbens, for example, alcohol-induced increases in serotonin levels causes the activation of 5-HT_3 receptors, as well as any other serotonin receptors in the vicinity. Second, alcohol increases the flow of positively charged ions through the 5-HT_3 ion channel (Machu & Harris, 1994).

The involvement of 5HT_3 receptors in alcohol-induced dopamine release can be assessed pharmacologically. Campbell and McBride (1995) used a microdialysis procedure in rats to assess alcohol administration with a 5-HT_3 receptor antagonist on dopamine release in the nucleus accumbens (**Figure 8.5**). In rats treated only with alcohol, dopamine levels significantly increased. Yet in rats administered the 5HT_3 receptor antagonist ICS 205-930 into the nucleus accumbens, alcohol failed to increase dopamine levels (Ding et al., 2011). These findings suggest that 5-HT_3 may

FIGURE 8.5 ● The serotonin $(5\text{-HT})_3$ receptor antagonist ICS 205-930 prevented alcohol from increasing nucleus accumbens dopamine levels in rats, as indicated by the bar for the combination of ethanol and the 5-HT_3 receptor antagonist being near the 100 percent mark. The *y*-axis refers to dopamine levels as expressed as a percentage of baseline levels (i.e., 100 percent equals baseline levels of responding).

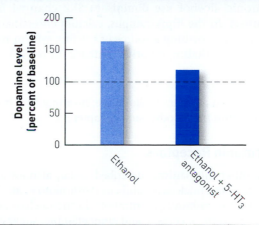

SOURCE: Based on data from Campbell & McBride, 1995.

be important for alcohol's ability to increase dopamine concentration in the nucleus accumbens.

In addition to 5-HT$_3$ receptors, 5-HT$_{2A}$ receptors in the ventral tegmental area also contribute to alcohol effects on nucleus accumbens dopamine levels. As demonstrated in a study by Ding and colleagues (2009), the direct infusion of a 5-HT$_{2A}$ receptor antagonist into the ventral tegmental area reduced self-administration of alcohol in rats. The researchers attributed reduced self-administration to diminished dopamine release in the nucleus accumbens.

Alcohol and the Endocannabinoid System

The endocannabinoid system may contribute to alcohol's reinforcing and other pharmacological effects. These interactions may depend partly on the role of the cannabinoid CB$_1$ receptor, which, as described in Chapter 11, influences the activity of dopamine neurons within the reward circuit. In a microdialysis study by Cohen, Perrault, Voltz, Steinberg, and Soubrie (2002), administration of the CB$_1$ receptor antagonist rimonabant prevented alcohol from increasing dopamine levels in the nucleus accumbens of rats. In another microdialysis study, alcohol failed to increase nucleus accumbens dopamine levels in CB$_1$ receptor knock-out mice (Hungund, Szakall, Adam, Basavarajappa, & Vadasz, 2003).

STOP & CHECK

1. Alcohol functions as a positive modulator for _____ receptors.

2. Alcohol inhibits ion passage through glutamate _____ receptors.

3. Alcohol's actions on L-type calcium channels have specific effects on the hormone _____.

4. Alcohol acts on the serotonin receptors 5-HT$_{2A}$ and _____.

1. GABA$_A$, 2. NMDA 3. vasopressin 4. 5-HT$_3$

Pharmacological Effects of Alcohol

Alcohol's pharmacological effects vary, depending on alcohol's concentration in the body. In general, higher concentrations yield depressant effects on physiological and psychological functions, whereas lower concentrations yield excitatory effects for certain physiological and psychological functions. In addition, some of alcohol's effects change during chronic usage.

Types of Drinking and Number of Drinks Consumed

Health officials apply certain terms to describe amounts of alcohol consumed. Studies use these terms to relate alcohol consumption to pharmacological effects. *Moderate*

drinking consists of about two standard drinks per day for men and one standard drink per day for women (**Table 8.1**). By this definition, *light drinking* is less than these amounts. *Heavy drinking* consists of more than four drinks per day for men and three drinks per day for women (Dufour, 1999). Further, heavy drinking can also consist of at least 14 drinks per week for men and 7 drinks per week for women. In 2014, an estimated 9.3 percent of men and 3.2 percent of women in the U.S. had reported recently engaging in heavy alcohol consumption (Center for Behavioral Health Statistics and Quality, 2014b).

Heavy drinking during a short period of time is given a unique term: **binge drinking**. It consists of drinking at least five standard drinks for men and four standard drinks for women during one occasion. This definition is also called the "5/4 rule," referring to the drink definitions for men and women, respectively (Wechsler et al., 2002). These sessions can achieve BACs of 0.08 and higher. We find more adults stating that they engage in binge drinking sessions rather than in patterns of general heavy drinking (i.e., a session of drinking rather than days of heavy drinking in close succession). In 2014, an estimated 30.0 percent of men and 16.4 percent of women in the United States had reported recently engaging in binge alcohol drinking (Center for Behavioral Health Statistics and Quality, 2014b).

Extreme drinking consists of consuming two to three times more alcohol than in binge drinking. It is not uncommon among young adults. In a survey conducted among freshmen after their first two weeks in college, White, Kraus and Swartzwelder (2006) found that nearly 30 percent of men and 10 percent of women had already engaged in extreme drinking.

Extreme drinking is especially prominent during 21st birthday celebrations in the United States. According to surveys conducted by Rutledge, Park, and Sher (2008), most individuals reported binge drinking at their 21st birthday. Approximately 12 percent engaged in a type of extreme drinking called "21 for 21," meaning drinking 21 drinks on their 21st birthday. The involvement in 21 for 21 was similar between men and women in this survey. The estimated BAC levels among these drinkers exceeded 0.26.

Binge drinking
Consumption of at least five standard drinks for men and four standard drinks for women during one occasion

Extreme drinking
Consuming two to three times more alcohol than in binge drinking

TABLE 8.1 ● Different Types of Drinking

Type of Drinking	Standard Drinks Consumed
Light drinking	Less than 2 drinks per day for men; less than 1 drink per day for women
Moderate drinking	Two drinks per day for men; one drink per day for women
Heavy drinking	At least 4 drinks per day for men; at least 3 drinks per day for women
Binge drinking	Drinking occurs in short time period consisting of at least 5 drinks per day for men and at least 4 drinks per day for women.
Extreme drinking	Two or three times the number of drinks considered as binge drinking

SOURCE: © Cengage Learning 2014.

Acute Alcohol Consumption and Cardiovascular and Respiratory Functioning

The physiological effects of light to moderate alcohol consumption primarily involve the respiratory and cardiovascular systems. Alcohol's respiratory effects depend on the concentration level. At lower alcohol concentrations, such as a BAC around 0.03, alcohol increases respiration. Beyond these concentrations, alcohol inhibits respiration, and this inhibition increases as the alcohol concentration increases. Respiratory inhibition is a key factor in alcohol poisoning.

Alcohol produces concentration-related effects on the cardiovascular system. Alcohol causes blood vessels to dilate, improving blood flow throughout the body. By increasing blood flow in the skin and extremities, alcohol provides feelings of warmth and contributes to a false but common belief that alcohol warms the body. In truth, the diversion of blood flow to the skin and extremities diminishes blood flow to core body organs. This actually makes the body colder (Oscar-Berman & Marinkovic, 2007).

Alcohol's cardiovascular effects at low alcohol concentrations can promote cardiovascular health. Some of these health benefits include a reduced risk of ischemia, stroke, and vascular-related dementias. The health benefits of daily low alcohol use result from four primary effects (see **Table 8.2**).

Review! Ischemia is a reduced blood supply, and it often results from constricted blood vessels. (Chapter 2.)

First, chronic light daily alcohol use increases high-density lipoprotein (HDL) levels, also referred to as "good cholesterol." HDLs reduce other cholesterols in the circulatory system. Second, chronic light daily use of alcohol reduces pro-inflammatory cellular signaling that contributes to the thickening of artery walls. Third, acute alcohol administration disrupts blood platelets from bonding together to form clots, the immediate cause of heart attacks and stroke. Fourth, acute alcohol administration causes blood clots to separate by causing the activation of *plasmin*, the enzyme responsible for degrading the bonding components between platelets in blood clots (Zakhari, 1997).

TABLE 8.2 ● Effects of Light and Heavy Alcohol Consumption on Cardiovascular Health	
Light Chronic Consumption (1–2 drinks per day)	**Heavy Chronic Consumption (several drinks per day)**
Decreased risk of ischemia	Increased risk of ischemia
Decreased risk of heart disorders	Increased risk of heart disorders
Decreased risk of heart attack	Increased risk of heart attack
Decreased risk of stroke	Increased risk of stroke

SOURCE: © Cengage Learning 2014.

Although we find that light alcohol consumption provides health benefits for cardiovascular functioning, individuals with certain genetic traits may experience harm to the cardiovascular system from light consumption. For example, individuals with a polymorphism for the *alcohol dehydrogenase type 3 enzyme* may exhibit a reduced rate of alcohol metabolism and subsequently have an increased risk of heart attack associated with moderate alcohol consumption (Hines et al., 2001). In this regard, alcohol serves as an example of **hormesis**, beneficial effects produced by low doses of a toxic substance (Cook & Calabrese, 2006). Later in this chapter, we discuss that adverse effects of alcohol that can occur even from moderate or light use.

Hormesis Beneficial effects produced by low doses of a toxic substance

Alcohol's Depressive Effects on Behavior and Cognitive Functioning

Alcohol's depressant effects affect behavior and cognitive processing. Beginning at low BACs, alcohol impairs balance and equilibrium (**Figure 8.6**). Impaired equilibrium occurs at BACs as low as 0.05 (Liguori, D'Agostino, Dworkin, Edwards, & Robinson, 1999). This BAC falls below the legal limit for U.S. states, but it serves as the legal driving limit for many European countries. During field sobriety testing, which is conducted when a police officer suspects an individual is driving intoxicated, equilibrium is assessed by having an individual walk on a straight line, walk and then turn, or attempt to balance on one leg.

Alcohol use also causes poor judgment as a result of **disinhibition**, a weakening of behavioral control that manifests as poor risk assessment, engagement in dangerous behavior, and impulsivity. Disinhibition with alcohol use can cause

Disinhibition Weakening of behavioral control

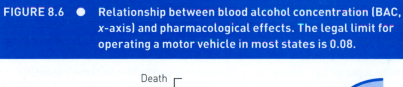

FIGURE 8.6 ● Relationship between blood alcohol concentration (BAC, *x*-axis) and pharmacological effects. The legal limit for operating a motor vehicle in most states is 0.08.

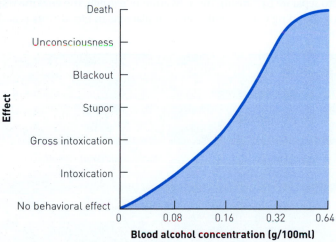

SOURCES: Adapted from the Center for Disease Control, 2011, and Loyola Marymount University, 2006.

socially unconventional behavior such as loud outbursts or aggressive behavior (Oscar-Berman & Marinkovic, 2007).

A specific disinhibition trait in alcohol use is **impulsivity**, or decision making without reflecting adequately on the consequences of those decisions. Researchers use delay-discounting designs to measure impulsivity. These procedures present a participant with a choice between an immediate small reward or a delayed larger reward. Both acutely alcohol-treated participants and former alcohol-addicted participants exhibit impulsivity deficits in such tasks (Bjork, Hommer, Grant, & Danube, 2004).

After consuming one or two drinks of alcohol, users develop an urge to consume more alcohol, a phenomenon described as **alcohol priming**. The phenomenon may be partly the result of alcohol's ability to disinhibit behavior and to increase impulsive decision making. Priming occurs in non-addicted alcohol users, irrespective of drinking patterns, as shown in **Figure 8.7** (Rose & Grunsell, 2008).

Alcohol markedly reduces reaction time. These slower reaction times can occur at relatively low BACs and are especially dangerous when driving. Researchers use simulators to measure alcohol's effects on driving. In a study conducted by Liguori and colleagues (1999), placebo- and alcohol-treated participants operated a simulator to drive on a straight road at 50 miles per hour. During the simulation, yellow barricades appeared at random intervals, requiring participants to immediately press on the brake pedal. The reaction time consisted of the time between the presentation of the barricade and the pressing of the brake pedal.

Impulsivity Decision making without reflecting adequately on the consequences of those decisions

Alcohol priming Tendency of users to develop an urge to consume more alcohol after having one or two drinks of alcohol

FIGURE 8.7 ● An urge to consume more alcohol occurred 30 minutes after consuming an alcoholic drink, as shown by the triangles. Baseline represents the urge to drink before consuming the first alcoholic drink. The *y*-axis represents the level of urge to consume alcohol.

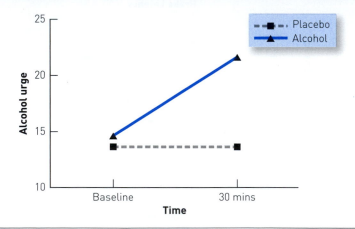

SOURCE: Rose, A. K., & Grunsell, L. (2008). The Subjective, Rather Than the Disinhibiting, Effects of Alcohol Are Related to Binge Drinking. *Alcoholism: Clinical and Experimental Research, 32*(6), 1096–1104. doi: 10.1111/j.1530–0277.2008.00672.x. Reproduced with permission of John Wiley & Sons Ltd.

Figure 8.8 shows the results from this driving simulator study. Compared to placebo-treated participants, alcohol-treated participants reacted more slowly to the yellow barricades. These reaction deficits occurred for BACs as low as 0.05, and they were especially pronounced at a 0.08 BAC, a legal limit for operating motor vehicles in most states.

Reductions in reaction time extend to prenatally exposed infants as well. Jacobson, Jacobson, and Sokol (1994) tested the reaction time of infants from mothers who reportedly consumed small amounts of alcohol throughout their pregnancies. None of the infants was diagnosed with fetal alcohol syndrome. Despite this, these infants exhibited significantly reduced reaction times compared to those whose mothers did not consume alcohol during pregnancy.

Divided attention
Sustained attention on a stimulus despite the presence of distracters

In addition to reaction time, alcohol significantly impairs **divided attention**, sustained attention on a stimulus despite the presence of distracters. Schulte, Müller-Oehring, Strasburger, Warzel, and Sabel (2001) demonstrated alcohol-associated deficits in divided attention. Using the grid shown in **Figure 8.9**, the researchers asked individuals to identify square patterns formed by X's in a rapid series of differently patterned screens. On this task, alcohol-treated participants who had a BAC of 0.05 or higher produced more errors than placebo-treated patients.

Divided attention deficits, in particular, may help explain some of the characteristics of alcohol-related vehicle crashes. Johnston (1982) suggested that most crashes occur during obstructed road conditions such as maneuvering a vehicle around a tight curve. Such conditions rely on focused divided attention in order to successfully steer the vehicle amid a variety of road conditions.

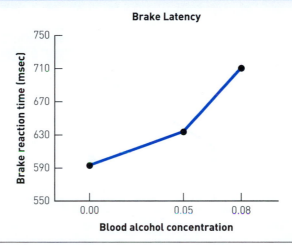

FIGURE 8.8 ● BACs as low as 0.05, shown on the *x*-axis, significantly impair brake reaction time (*y*-axis) in a driving simulator.

Brake Latency

SOURCE: Liguori, A., D'Agostino, R. B., Dworkin, S. I., Edwards, D., & Robinson, J. H. (1999). Alcohol Effects on Mood, Equilibrium, and Simulated Driving. *Alcoholism: Clinical and Experimental Research, 23*(5), 815–821. doi: 10.1111/j.1530-0277.1999.tb04188.x. Reproduced with permission of John Wiley & Sons Ltd.

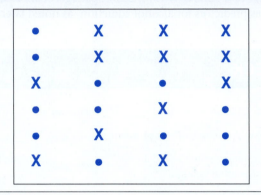

FIGURE 8.9   ● One type of divided attention task requires participants to identify square patterns with X's in an array such as this. Each array is shown only briefly.

SOURCE: With kind permission from Springer Science+Business Media: Schulte, T., Müller-Oehring, E. M., Strasburger, H., Warzel, H., & Sabel, B. A. (2001). Acute effects of alcohol on divided and covert attention in men. *Psychopharmacology*, *154*(1), 61–69. doi: 10.1007/s002130000603, Fig 1.

Alcohol does not affect all types of attention equally. Light to moderate alcohol consumption does not affect **vigilance**, a state of readiness for detecting and responding to unpredictable events. Nor does light to moderate alcohol consumption disrupt sustained attention, which is demonstrated by having someone focus intently on a single stimulus.

Vigilance A state of readiness for detecting and responding to unpredictable events

Alcohol produces deficits in memory, particularly at BACs of approximately 0.08 and higher. In a study of human volunteers with BACs of 0.04 and 0.08, those with BACs of 0.08 exhibited significant deficits in *episodic memory*, the conscious memory of a personally experienced event, and *semantic memory*, the memory of verbal or written information (Kleykamp, Griffiths, & Mintzer, 2010). However, BACs of 0.08 do not significantly affect working memory unless the working memory task is especially difficult (Grattan-Miscio & Vogel-Sprott, 2005; Gundersen, Specht, Grüner, Ersland, & Hugdahl, 2008; Kleykamp et al., 2010). Deficits in memory appear worse during inclining BACs than during declining BACs (Schweizer & Vogel-Sprott, 2008).

Alcohol and Positive Subjective Effects

After consuming alcohol, individuals usually report an improvement in mood. These effects increase as alcohol concentrations increase. Human study participants can detect clear drug effects at BACs of 0.05 consisting of a high and mild dizziness (Liguori et al., 1999). Alcohol users with BACs of 0.08 and higher report feelings of intense well-being.

Alcohol also produces relaxing effects, and many users consume alcohol to reduce feelings of stress. This appears to occur with lower amounts of alcohol, generally in conjunction with positive subjective effects (Brabant, Guarnieri, & Quertemont, 2014). In fact, Conger (1956) developed a **tension reduction hypothesis**, which holds that

Tension reduction hypothesis Drinking alcohol reduces stress

drinking alcohol reduces stress, to explain habitual alcohol use. An important part of this hypothesis is that anxiety sufferers have a greater likelihood of drinking. Although this hypothesis is difficult to confirm in humans, animals identified with anxious traits have a greater likelihood to self-administer alcohol compared to non-anxious animals (Primeaux, Wilson, Gray, York, & Wilson, 2006; Spanagel et al., 1995). Moreover, stress and anxiety serve as predictors for alcohol addiction, as noted later in this chapter.

STOP & CHECK

1. The game 21 for 21 is an example of _____ drinking.

2. How does alcohol produce feelings of warmth?

3. A specific disinhibitory effect of alcohol is _____, which can be measured using delay-discounting tasks.

4. Alcohol also impairs _____, which may explain why alcohol-related crashes occur during obstructed driving conditions.

5. Two key subjective effects of alcohol are an improvement in mood and a reduction in _____.

1. extreme **2.** Alcohol dilates blood vessels, increasing blood flow to the skin and extremities. This provides a feeling of warmth. **3.** impulsivity **4.** divided attention **5.** stress or anxiety

Severe Adverse Effects of High BAC

Alcohol stupor (or drunken stupor) Dulled senses and poor cognitive functioning caused by overconsumption of alcohol; also known as drunken stupor

Acute alcohol consumption generates severe adverse effects above a 0.20 BAC (see Figure 8.6). At these BACs, drinkers develop an **alcohol stupor**, or **drunken stupor**, that is characterized by disorientation, dulled senses, and poor cognitive function. Someone described as *drunk*, *smashed*, or *hammered* exhibits many of the signs of stupor.

Reversible drug-induced dementia Reversible drug-induced dementia characterized by stupor and anterograde amnesia

At BACs of 0.25 and higher, drinkers can develop a reversible drug-induced dementia. **Reversible drug-induced dementia** is characterized by stupor and anterograde amnesia, better known as **blackout**. Anterograde amnesia is the inability to form new memories. This type of dementia is called *reversible* because the effects subside as BAC levels decline (Oscar-Berman & Marinkovic, 2007).

Blackout Term used to describe anterograde amnesia due to alcohol use

Blackout from alcohol occurs as either of two types, *En bloc* or *fragmentary*. **En bloc blackout** consists of a total inability to recall events during a set period of time of alcohol intoxication. These blackouts reflect a disruption in converting short-term memories into long-term memories. This means that during the drinking session, the user maintains short-term memory function, allowing the person to carry on conversations and engage in other behaviors, but an ability to convert these experiences into long-term memory precludes any later recollection of those events. As indicated earlier, a high BAC, such as 0.25, is needed to produce the en bloc type of blackout (Rose & Grant, 2010).

En bloc blackout A total inability to recall events during a set period of time of alcohol intoxication

Fragmentary blackout (sometimes referred to as a **brownout**) consists of incomplete memories from a period of alcohol intoxication. Prompting by others can make users aware of forgetting certain events from that period. Unlike en bloc blackouts, fragmentary blackouts can occur at lower BACs, even as low as 0.06 for some users. These blackouts might occur from impaired encoding for long-term memories, as opposed to the en bloc type (Rose & Grant, 2010).

At higher BACs, drinkers may pass out. Unconsciousness occurs when alcohol in the brain reaches sufficient concentrations to dampen cortical functioning and cortical arousal areas in the forebrain and brainstem. As BACs rise further, so does the inhibition of CNS functioning.

A particular risk of high BACs is the suppression of function in the hindbrain, which includes the medulla, a structure critical for autonomic processes such as breathing. BACs of approximately 0.25 and higher can cause **alcohol poisoning**, an alcohol-induced inhibition of autonomic system functions, including breathing, heart functioning, and the gag reflex. During alcohol poisoning, most deaths occur from depressed respiration (Adinoff, Bone, & Linnoila, 1988).

Binge and extreme drinking carry a significant risk of alcohol poisoning. The number of drinks consumed during these forms of drinking reach these high BACs, yet the speed of alcohol consumption is the most critical determinant for alcohol poisoning. As stated previously, although users feel alcohol's effects within minutes, the maximum absorption of alcohol occurs after 30 minutes. This means that a quick succession of alcoholic drinks, like drinking a line of shots, during a binge causes a dramatic increase in BAC levels.

Chronic Alcohol Consumption and Adverse Cardiovascular and CNS Effects

Although chronic light alcohol consumption may provide positive benefits for the cardiovascular system, chronic exposure to alcohol, no matter the drinking level, can expose users to other risks. One of these risks, as discussed earlier, is *alcohol priming*, which increases the likelihood of consuming more alcohol than was originally intended. Another is cancer risk. Alcohol use is associated with increased rates of a variety of cancers, including cancers of the liver, gastrointestinal tract, and breast (Cogliano et al., 2011). Moreover, we also link the metabolic product from alcohol metabolism, acetaldehyde, with cancer risk, particularly for breast cancer. The risk increases for those with the alcohol dehydrogenase 1C*1 allele (ADH1C*1 allele) polymorphism, because these individuals more quickly convert alcohol to acetaldehyde a create greater levels of acetaldehyde compared to those without this polymorphism (Coutelle et al., 2004).

Chronic heavy alcohol consumption causes many negative effects: increased risks of ischemia, stroke, and heart attack. One of these adverse effects is cardiomyopathy, which consists of any number of specific disorders that affect the heart muscle. Chronic heavy alcohol use can cause **alcoholic cardiomyopathy**, which is characterized by low cardiac output because of enlargement of the heart and dilation of the heart chambers. This disorder leads to congestive heart failure, the inability to adequately supply blood to the body.

Heavy acute or chronic alcohol consumption can cause *cardiac arrhythmias*, which are characterized by abnormal or rapid heartbeats. Cardiac arrhythmias that occur after

Fragmentary blackout (or brownout) Incomplete memories from a period of alcohol intoxication

Alcohol poisoning Alcohol-induced inhibition of autonomic system functions, including breathing, heart functioning, and the gag reflex

Alcoholic cardiomyopathy Low cardiac output from enlargement of the heart and dilation of heart chambers caused by heavy and chronic alcohol use

Holiday heart syndrome Cardiac arrhythmias occurring after an acute heavy drinking episode

an acute heavy drinking episode constitute what is referred to as a **holiday heart syndrome**. These effects range in severity and account for approximately 5 percent of alcohol-related deaths (Zakhari, 1997).

Unlike the dilating effects of light alcohol consumption, heavy alcohol consumption constricts blood vessels. This hypertensive state is particularly dangerous for individuals suffering from cardiomyopathy, because the ability to pump blood is already diminished. Hypertension requires increased heart output to deliver blood through the high-pressure system (Zakhari, 1997).

Chronic alcohol consumption also taxes the liver. The alcohol metabolic process causes oxidation of liver cells over time, resulting in cellular damage and the development of **cirrhosis**, a chronic liver disease characterized by tissue scarring and poor liver functioning. Poor liver functioning impairs metabolism of nutrients from foods, protein synthesis, and other vital processes (Lieber, 1997).

Cirrhosis A chronic liver disease characterized by tissue scarring and poor liver functioning

Fetal alcohol syndrome Disorder characterized by physical and neurological abnormal development

Alcohol use during pregnancy can cause **fetal alcohol syndrome**, a disorder characterized by physical and neurological abnormal development. Babies with fetal alcohol syndrome have characteristic facial abnormalities, such as a widened distance between the eyes, and risk of a variety of other physiological effects, such as congenital heart defects and abnormal development of the eyes and ears (**Figure 8.10**). These babies develop more slowly intellectually and cognitively and maintain deficiencies in these areas.

The full onset of fetal alcohol syndrome is most associated with heavy alcohol use, particularly from pregnant mothers who engaged in binge drinking. Lesser amounts

FIGURE 8.10 ● Alcohol use during pregnancy can cause fetal alcohol syndrome, a disorder noted for physical facial abnormalities, as shown in the photograph, and other physical and neurological abnormalities.

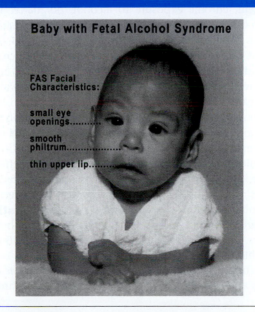

SOURCE: Courtesy of Teresa Kellerman.

STOP & CHECK

1. Chronic heavy alcohol use can produce _____, an enlargement of the heart and dilation of heart chambers.

2. Alcohol use during pregnancy can cause _____.

3. Chronic heavy alcohol use diminishes absorption of thiamine, which can cause a central nervous system disorder called _____.

1. alcoholic cardiomyopathy 2. fetal alcohol syndrome 3. Wernicke-Korsakoff's syndrome

of alcohol consumed during pregnancy can produce a weaker fetal alcohol syndrome, referred to as *alcohol-related neurodevelopmental disorder*. A child born without the full spectrum of fetal alcohol disorder symptoms will have fewer physiological, behavior, and cognitive deficits (Sokol, Delaney-Black, & Nordstrom, 2003).

How much alcohol is safe to drink during pregnancy? The specific limit of alcohol consumption during pregnancy is a moving target. Most physicians recommend no consumption during pregnancy, whereas some advise only occasional consumption (Anderson et al., 2010). In 2005, U.S. Surgeon General Richard Carmona stated in an advisory on fetal alcohol syndrome risk that "it is now clear that no amount of alcohol can be considered safe [during pregnancy]" (Carmona, 2005). This remains the recommendation from the U.S. surgeon general as well as the Centers for Disease Control and Prevention and the National Institute on Alcohol Abuse and Alcoholism.

Long-term, heavy use of alcohol may cause a serious central nervous system disorder called **Wernicke-Korsakoff's syndrome**, a condition characterized by memory loss, false memories, poor insight, apathy, and tremor. We refer to false memories as part of *confabulation* when the individual confidently purports false memories without the intention to deceive. Coma can also occur in Wernicke-Korsakoff's syndrome. This disorder manifests from the destruction of nervous system tissue resulting from thiamine, or vitamin B1, deficiency. Thiamine is deficient because alcohol inhibits thiamine absorption from the intestinal tract, as described previously (Kopelman, Thomson, Guerrini, & Marshall, 2009). A less severe form of Wernicke-Korsakoff's syndrome is called *alcohol dementia*, which consists primarily of deficits in cognitive functioning (Moriyama, Mimura, Kato, & Kashima, 2006).

Wernicke-Korsakoff's syndrome Condition caused by heavy, long-term alcohol use resulting in memory loss, false memories, poor insight, apathy, and tremor

Alcohol: Tolerance and Sensitization

Acute tolerance to alcohol occurs when alcohol's behavioral effects are weaker for declining BACs than for inclining BACs. The term **acute tolerance** refers to the development of tolerance during the same session (Fillmore, Marczinski, & Bowman, 2005). The chart in **Figure 8.11** illustrates this condition.

In figure 8.11, alcohol administration caused BACs to steadily increase until a maximum BAC of 0.12 was reached. Behavior was significantly impaired when BACs first reached 0.08. After the peak BAC, a BAC of 0.08 was again reached as BACs were declining later in the session. The second 0.08 BAC on the *declining* BAC curve, however, was less impairing than the first 0.08 BAC on the *inclining* BAC curve. In other words, tolerance developed to the effects of a 0.08 BAC.

Acute tolerance (to alcohol) Tolerance that occurs when alcohol's behavioral effects are weaker for declining BACs than for inclining BACs

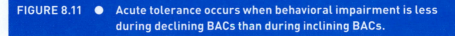

FIGURE 8.11 ● Acute tolerance occurs when behavioral impairment is less during declining BACs than during inclining BACs.

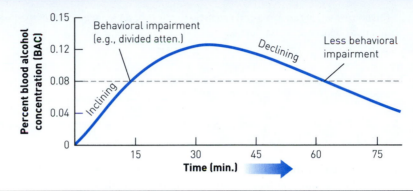

SOURCE: © Cengage Learning 2014.

Metabolic tolerance (to alcohol) Increase in liver alcohol dehydrogenase enzymes resulting in an increased rate of alcohol metabolism

Other forms of tolerance develop through chronic administration. One of these forms is **metabolic tolerance to alcohol**, which consists of an increase in liver alcohol dehydrogenase enzymes and results in an increased rate of alcohol metabolism. The increased rate of alcohol metabolism diminishes BAC levels (Israel et al., 1979).

Pharmacodynamic tolerance (to alcohol) Reduced physiological responsiveness to alcohol's pharmacological actions

Another form of chronic tolerance is **pharmacodynamic tolerance to alcohol**, or reduced physiological responsiveness to alcohol's pharmacological actions. Pharmacodynamic tolerance is known to occur with glutamate NMDA receptors. As described previously, alcohol inhibits the function of NMDA receptors. During chronic administration, NMDA receptors are upregulated in order to compensate for alcohol's inhibitory actions at NMDA receptors (Gulya, Grant, Valverius, Hoffman, & Tabakoff, 1991).

Behavioral tolerance (to alcohol) Reduced behavioral impairment to alcohol

Chronic alcohol administration also produces **behavioral tolerance to alcohol**, which is defined as a reduced behavioral impairment to alcohol. For example, Goodwin, Powell, and Stern colleagues (1971) demonstrated that experienced drinkers performed better on a simple motor task than novice drinkers after the administration of alcohol.

Sensitization (to alcohol) Increase in alcohol's efficacy, especially its reinforcing effects

In addition to tolerance, sensitization occurs to some of alcohol's pharmacological effects. **Sensitization to alcohol** consists of an increase in alcohol's efficacy. In particular, sensitization occurs to alcohol's reinforcing effects. In animals, chronic alcohol administration produces an increase in alcohol self-administration, locomotor activity, and sexual behavior. Chronic alcohol administration also produces greater increases in dopamine levels in the nucleus accumbens compared to acute alcohol administration (for review, see Fish, DeBold, & Miczek, 2002).

Alcohol Addiction and Withdrawal

Chronic heavy alcohol use often leads to an alcohol use disorder. The *Diagnostic and Statistical Manual* (DSM-5) identifies an addiction to alcohol as *alcohol use disorder*. Alcohol use disorder is generally synonymous with the term *alcoholism*, although alcoholism lends itself more to a disease concept of alcohol dependence. An individual diagnosed with alcohol use disorder may meet all of the general DSM criteria for a substance use disorder as described in Chapter 5.

Experts generally agree on two subtypes of alcohol addiction—type I and type II—although neither is included in the DSM-5 per se. The DSM-5 makes mention of environment and genetic factors, but refrains from type I or type II designations. In 1987, Claude Cloninger first described the characteristics of these two types of alcohol addiction (Cloninger, 1987). Cloninger characterized **Type I alcohol addiction** as occurring with those 25 and older and having low genetic risk but high psychosocial risk. Environmental variables such as stressful interpersonal situations or psychological disorders primarily account for type I alcohol addiction. Cloninger characterized **type II alcohol addiction** as occurring with those younger than 25 and exhibiting high genetic risk and traits associated with poor impulse control. Type II alcohol-addicted individuals often have a parent who was a chronic alcohol user, and they tend to engage in heavy drinking at a young adult age (**Table 8.3**).

A physiological dependence develops during alcohol addiction and leads to severe and potentially life-threatening withdrawal symptoms. *Seizures* are the primary withdrawal symptoms of concern. Seizure risk develops as the brain adapts to alcohol's chronic actions in the brain. In particular, chronic alcohol use is associated with increased levels of glutamate NMDA receptors and decreased levels of $GABA_A$ receptors. The result of having more excitatory receptors and fewer inhibitory receptors, respectively, is a hyperactivated state in many brain regions. This state sets the occasion for seizures. Because of this, anticonvulsant drugs should be provided during the first days of alcohol-cessation therapy (Hall & Zador, 1997).

Repeated alcohol withdrawals, which may occur with someone who repeatedly quits and relapses, can increase the risk and severity of withdrawal seizures. An increased seizure risk from repeated withdrawals is called **kindling** (Ballenger & Post, 1978). Beyond seizure risk, alcohol withdrawal can produce an **alcohol withdrawal syndrome**, also

Type I alcohol addiction Alcohol addiction that occurs at age 25 or older, has low genetic risk, and exhibits high psychosocial risk

Type II alcohol addiction Alcohol addiction that occurs before age 25, exhibits high genetic risk, and has traits associated with poor impulse control

Kindling An increased seizure risk from repeated withdrawals from alcohol

Alcohol withdrawal syndrome (delirium tremens) Alcohol withdrawal syndrome characterized by hallucinations, trembling, confusion, disorientation, and agitation

TABLE 8.3 ● Types of Alcohol Addiction

Types of Alcohol Addiction	Description
Type I	Occurs at age 25 and older; has low genetic risk and high psychosocial risk
Type II	Occurs at less than age 25; has high genetic risk and poor impulse control

SOURCE: © Cengage Learning 2014.

STOP & CHECK

1. How is acute alcohol tolerance shown?
2. Between the two types of alcohol addiction, which has the greatest genetic risk?
3. Which alcohol withdrawal symptom is the greatest concern?

1. Acute alcohol tolerance is shown when declining BACs exhibit weaker effects than inclining BACs. 2. Type II alcohol addiction 3. seizures

referred to as *delirium tremens* (often referred to as "DTs"), that is characterized by hallucinations, trembling, confusion, disorientation, and agitation (Hall & Zador, 1997).

Treating Alcohol Addiction

A variety of therapeutic strategies exist for treating alcohol addiction. The ultimate goal of treatment is to eliminate the behavioral, social, and physical harm caused by alcohol use. To achieve this goal, most therapeutic approaches seek complete abstention from alcohol use. However, some therapeutic approaches seek to transform problem alcohol use into controllable alcohol use.

Alcoholics Anonymous A 12-step program for alcohol addiction that provides extensive social support to encourage drinking abstinence for its anonymous members

The 12-step recovery program **Alcoholics Anonymous (AA)** represents the most- recognized approach for alcohol addiction. Although numbers are difficult to determine because of the protected identities of participants, AA estimates it has 1.2 million members in the United States and 800,000 members elsewhere in the world (Alcoholics Anonymous, 2012). During AA meetings, a member shares personal stories about his or her struggles with alcohol use and connects with a sponsor who is normally a longtime AA member in recovery from alcohol addiction. AA programs provide extensive social support to encourage abstinence from drinking. Those who optimally respond to AA therapy have frequent meeting attendance, actively seek advice from AA sources, and strongly adhere to 12-step beliefs (Morgenstern, Kahler, Frey, & Labouvie, 1996).

Cognitive-behavioral therapies (for alcohol dependence) Therapies that seek to improve an individual's cognitive and behavioral skills toward changing problem alcohol use

Cognitive-behavioral therapies for alcohol dependence seek to improve an individual's cognitive and behavioral skills toward changing problem alcohol use. This approach views alcohol dependence as a maladaptive learning pattern that can be adjusted by replacing maladaptive responses with adaptive responses (Longabaugh & Morgenstern, 1999). These approaches have users learn to identify and cope with conditions that facilitate problem alcohol use such as stress and alcohol-related stimuli (Witteman et al., 2015). By addressing alcohol use as maladaptive behavior, complete cessation of alcohol use is not the ultimate therapeutic goal per se. Rather, therapists seek to eliminate the problems associated with alcohol use, which may or may not require abstinence. These therapies are sometimes referred to as *controlled drinking therapies* because a user may learn to avoid excessive alcohol use and accompanying problems without completely abstaining from alcohol (Longabaugh & Morgenstern, 1999).

Pharmacological treatments for alcohol addiction attempt to reduce alcohol intake by *(1) producing aversive effects, (2) weakening effects, or (3) reducing cravings. Disulfiram (Antabuse)* has been used since 1949 to treat alcohol addiction. Disulfiram discourages alcohol use by generating aversive effects through disrupting alcohol's metabolic process in the body. Disulfiram inhibits acetaldehyde dehydrogenase enzyme activity, the enzyme that breaks acetaldehyde down into inactive metabolites. After consuming alcohol, disulfiram, through inhibiting this enzyme, causes a buildup of acetaldehyde. Acetaldehyde, in turn, causes a number of adverse physiological effects, including nausea, sweatiness, and facial flushing (**Figure 8.12**). By producing these adverse effects, disulfiram deters alcohol consumption (Heather, 1989).

Disulfiram appears most effective at reducing alcohol consumption when patients are willing to participate in cessation programs and when disulfiram compliance is supervised. Otherwise, alcohol-addicted individuals who are coerced, often through court-mandated treatment, into taking disulfiram either fail to take the medications

🕮 *Drug Profile:* disulfiram

Trade name:	Antabuse
Mechanism of action	Inhibits acetaldehyde dehydrogenase
Uses	Reduces alcohol consumption by producing a buildup of the noxious substance acetaldehyde

FIGURE 8.12 ● Disulfiram inhibits the metabolism of acetaldehyde, causing acetaldehyde buildup and aversive effects after alcohol consumption.

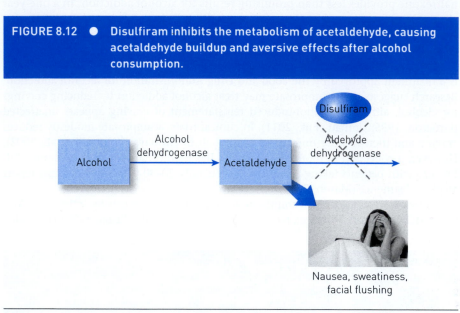

Nausea, sweatiness, facial flushing

SOURCE: © Cengage Learning 2014. Photo: Copyright iStockphoto/michaelpuche

regularly or switch to alternative drugs of abuse (Heather, 1989). Only one in five patients treated with disulfiram remain abstinent one year later (Miller, Walters, & Bennett, 2001).

Although disulfiram treatment generates aversive effects, naltrexone treatment may reduce alcohol's reinforcing effects. *Naltrexone* is an opioid receptor antagonist approved in Canada, Europe, and the United States for treating alcohol addiction. By blocking opioid receptors, naltrexone may interfere with endogenous opioid mediation of alcohol's reinforcing effects, as described previously in this chapter (Volpicelli, Sarin-Krishnan, & O'Malley, 2002).

🕮 *Drug Profile:* naltrexone

Trade name:	Vivitrol, Revia, Depade
Mechanism of action	Opioid receptor antagonist.
Uses	Reduces reinforcing effects of alcohol by blocking contribution of endogenous opioids for alcohol-induced dopamine release in the nucleus accumbens

Gonzales and Weiss (1998) demonstrated naltrexone's reduction of alcohol's reinforcing effects in rats using both self-administration and microdialysis procedures. In this study, rats self-administered less alcohol after naltrexone administration. Moreover, naltrexone caused a weaker elevation of nucleus accumbens dopamine levels after alcohol administration (**Figure 8.13**). In humans, naltrexone prevents alcohol-addicted individuals from consuming alcohol to dangerously high BACs (Volpicelli, Alterman, Hayashida, & O'Brien, 1992). Beyond this, however, naltrexone provides less than promising results for alcohol addiction. In a one-year clinical study conducted by Krystal, Cramer, Krol, Kirk, and Rosenheck (2001), naltrexone, in combination with psychosocial therapy, failed to increase the number of alcohol-free days compared to placebo.

Acamprosate (Campral) (the chemical name is *calcium*-bis[N-acetylhomotaurinate]) is a treatment approved by the Food and Drug Administration for alcohol addiction. Research suggests that acamprosate may treat alcohol addiction by reducing cravings for alcohol, although alcohol-induced reinstatement of craving appears unaffected (Littleton, 1995; Umhau et al., 2011). In clinical trials, acamprosate modestly reduces craving and increases the number of alcohol-abstinent days (Volpicelli et al., 2002). However, a collection of more recent studies has found that at 6- and 12-month follow-ups with patients taking acamprosate, generally 20–40 percent of patients report alcohol abstinence (Mason, 2001).

For years, we considered acamprosate to engender these effects by acting on GABA and NMDA receptors. However, recent work by Spanagel and colleagues (2014) revealed

FIGURE 8.13 ● The opioid receptor antagonist naltrexone reduces alcohol's elevation of nucleus accumbens dopamine concentrations. The *y*-axis shows the amount of dopamine contained in each collected sample, as measured in nanomolar concentrations.

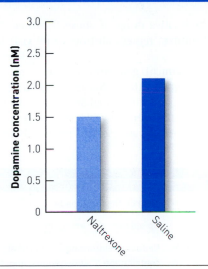

SOURCE: Data from Gonzales & Weiss, 1998.

that N-acetylhomotaurinate without calcium (i.e., they separated calcium from the acamprosate molecule) lacked any activity at NMDA or GABA receptors. This left one possible explanation for acamprosate's effect: calcium.

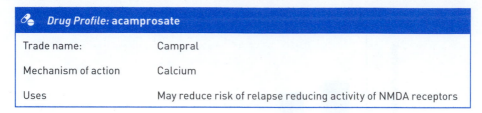

💊 *Drug Profile:* **acamprosate**	
Trade name:	Campral
Mechanism of action	Calcium
Uses	May reduce risk of relapse reducing activity of NMDA receptors

As noted earlier in this chapter, alcohol inhibits calcium channels, preventing calcium from entering neurons. Calcium may provide a means for restoring negative feedback of NMDA receptors. In this way, calcium might contribute to reduce relapse by counteracting the increased activity of NMDA receptors caused by chronic alcohol use (Mulholland et al. 2001). Looking further, Spanagel and colleagues (2014) sought to determine why some patients fare better with acamprosate while others do not. They found that greater calcium levels in blood plasma correlated with longer times before relapse and with more time spent abstinent from alcohol. In fact, calcium therapy, referred to as *Calmonose*, had been used successfully in the past to reduce alcohol relapse (O'Brien, 1964).

STOP & CHECK

1. Among the psychotherapies for alcohol addiction, which approach may not have alcohol abstinence as a goal?

2. How does disulfiram cause aversive effects after alcohol consumption?

1. Cognitive–behavioral strategies seek to reduce maladaptive behavior associated with alcohol. These strategies may succeed in reducing such maladaptive behavior without alcohol abstinence. For this reason, these approaches are often referred to as *controlled-drinking therapies*. 2. Disulfiram inhibits breakdown of the alcohol metabolite acetaldehyde, a noxious chemical.

From Actions to Effects: Hangover

Hangover is an unpleasant experience that occurs after alcohol consumption. Its symptoms include headache, a poor sense of overall well-being, diarrhea, fatigue, and nausea. Headache is the most common symptom (Harburg, 1981) (**Figure 8.14**). There is no set limit of drinks that will trigger hangover symptoms. The risk of hangover varies from individual to individual because of such factors as alcohol tolerance, enzymatic breakdown, medication interactions, and overall physical health. Other factors are addressed in the following text (Prat, Adan, & Sanchez-Turet, 2009).

Hangovers not only are unpleasant but also are associated with cognitive deficits. These deficits occur even when BAC reaches zero. In a study by Howland and

Hangover
Unpleasant experience that may occur after alcohol consumption

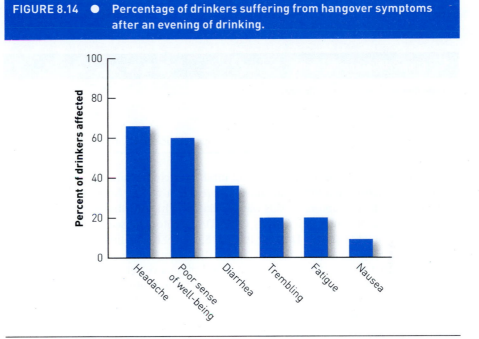

FIGURE 8.14 ● **Percentage of drinkers suffering from hangover symptoms after an evening of drinking.**

SOURCE: Data from Harburg et al., 1981.

colleagues (2010), those experiencing hangover with no BAC levels exhibited significant deficits in reaction time and attention. The severity of the hangover relates to the magnitude of these deficits.

Hangover is highly prevalent in the general population. Based on survey information, nearly 75 percent of those drinking to intoxication have experienced a hangover, and about half of these drinkers experienced hangover within the last year. The prevalence of these debilitating effects present a high economic burden from worker absenteeism, low productivity, and accidents. Absenteeism, in particular, accounts for billions in lost wages each year (Wiese, Shlipak, & Browner, 2000).

Hangover symptoms appear around 6–8 hours after drinking ceases. These symptoms begin to occur as the BAC approaches 0, and they worsen when the BAC reaches 0. Once hangover symptoms occur, they remain for as long as 14–16 hours. The cause of hangover is not entirely understood. Currently, there are thought to be five possible contributors to hangover.

The first contributor to hangover may be acute alcohol withdrawal. Many of the features of hangover match the DSM-IV characteristics for alcohol withdrawal. Moreover, alcohol consumption reduces hangover symptoms (Swift & Davidson, 1998). Unlike alcohol addiction, however, hangover symptoms do not develop into further stages of alcohol withdrawal such as seizures.

A second possible contributor to hangover is the buildup of acetaldehyde after alcohol consumption. As previously described, alcohol dehydrogenase converts alcohol to acetaldehyde. Acetaldehyde produces aversive hangover-like effects.

However, alcohol consumption must be very high to produce sufficient buildup of acetaldehyde to produce aversive symptoms. Further, hangover symptoms occur when the body no longer contains acetaldehyde.

A third possible contributor for hangover may be acetate accumulation. A metabolite of acetaldehyde, acetate accumulates to much greater levels in the body than acetaldehyde and may be present in the body when hangover symptoms begin. Acetate causes other effects in the body, such as increased levels of adenosine, and causes headaches in humans and laboratory animals. Adenosine produces increased pain sensitivity and fatigue. Thus, acetate together with its production of adenosine may contribute to many hangover symptoms. In a demonstration of acetate's effects, Maxwell, Spangenberg, Hoek, Silberstein, and Oshinsky (2010) assessed the effects of acetate on headache in laboratory animals. The resulting headache from acetate was substantially reduced with treatment by caffeine, an adenosine receptor antagonist.

A fourth possible contributor to hangover is direct action by alcohol. Alcohol consumption causes dehydration, electrolyte imbalance, low blood sugar, vasodilatation, and gastric irritation. All of these effects could support the symptoms of hangover. However, studies indicate that these specific effects are most related to *severe* hangover.

The fifth possible contributor for hangover is overconsumption of other chemicals in alcoholic drinks. These other chemicals can include acetones, polyphenols, and methanol. Methanol, in particular, is known to produce aversive effects similar to hangover. Moreover, hangover symptoms are worse for drinks with a high number of fermentation by-products, referred to as *congeners*, than those with less congener content. In a study conducted by Chapman (1970), more participants exhibited hangover after consuming bourbon, a drink with high congener content, than those who consumed vodka, a drink with low congener content.

Is there a treatment for hangover? All of the possible explanations for hangover just given are suggestive for potential treatment avenues. In practice, however, research addressing these explanations has yet to provide scientifically proven treatments. There still remains only one way to completely prevent hangover: Do not overindulge.

STOP & CHECK

1. What is the most common hangover symptom?

2. Hangover symptoms worsen as the BAC approaches _____.

3. One of the possible explanations for hangover is that there is a buildup of _____, similar to how disulfiram reduces alcohol consumption.

4. Why might coffee reduce hangover symptoms?

1. Headache **2.** zero **3.** acetaldehyde **4.** Coffee contains caffeine, an adenosine receptor antagonist. Adenosine antagonism can counteract elevated adenosine levels, which cause elevated pain sensitivity and fatigue.

Chapter Summary

Central nervous system depressants produce reinforcing and relaxing effects. By far the most used CNS depressant is alcohol, chemically known as *ethyl alcohol*. Although alcohol has been used for thousands of years, U.S. alcohol sales were prohibited during the 1920s.

Alcohol drink concentrations are measured as percentages or by proof, and we compare alcoholic drinks according to *standard drink* units. We also relate alcohol pharmacological effects to blood alcohol concentrations (BACs). Multiple steps occur for alcohol metabolism, and the alcohol elimination rate follows zero-order kinetics. Alcohol exhibits diverse pharmacological actions involving facilitation of GABA receptors, inhibition of NMDA receptors,

activation of serotonin receptors, inhibition of calcium channels, and indirect actions involving endogenous opioids and endocannabinoids. These actions lead to reinforcing effects as well as impairing effects on cognition and behavior-reinforcing effects. Acute alcohol use can produce hangover, an overall sense of poor well-being marked by symptoms such as headache and nausea. Other adverse alcohol effects relate to long-term chronic usage, including damage to the heart and central nervous system. Several forms of tolerance develop for alcohol, and heavy chronic alcohol usage elicits severe withdrawal symptoms, including seizures. Alcohol is highly addictive and is addressed by both psychotherapeutic and pharmacological treatment strategies.

Key Terms

Ethyl alcohol 245
Methyl alcohol 245
Percentage alcohol (or alcohol by volume) 246
Proof of alcohol 246
Fermentation 246
Beer 247
Wine 247
Distilled alcoholic beverages 247
Standard drink 248
18th Amendment 250
21st Amendment 250
Blood alcohol concentration (BAC) 250
Alcohol dehydrogenase 250
Acetaldehyde 251
Binge drinking 258
Extreme Drinking 258
Hormesis 260

Disinhibition 260
Impulsivity 261
Alcohol priming 261
Divided attention 262
Vigilance 263
Tension reduction hypothesis 263
Alcohol stupor (or drunken stupor) 264
Reversible drug-induced dementia 264
Blackout 264
En bloc blackout 264
Fragmentary blackout (or brownout) 265
Alcohol poisoning 265
Alcoholic cardiomyopathy 265
Holiday heart syndrome 266
Cirrhosis 266
Fetal alcohol syndrome 266

Wernicke-Korsakoff's syndrome 267
Acute tolerance (to alcohol) 267
Metabolic tolerance (to alcohol) 268
Pharmacodynamic tolerance (to alcohol) 268
Behavioral tolerance (to alcohol) 268
Sensitization (to alcohol) 268
Type I alcohol addiction 269
Type II alcohol addiction 269
Kindling 269
Alcohol withdrawal syndrome (delirium tremens) 269
Alcoholics Anonymous 270
Cognitive-behavioral therapies 270
Hangover 273

Visit the Student Study Site at **study.sagepub.com/prus2e** to access additional study tools, including eFlashcards, web quizzes, video resources, web resources, SAGE journal articles, and more.

9

GHB and Inhalants

DID THE REVELATIONS OF ANCIENT GREEK ORACLES COME FROM CHEMICAL INHALANTS?

On the slope of Mount Parnassus, ancient Greeks sought the advice of their gods by communicating with the Pythia at the Temple of Apollo. The Pythia, local women who served as mediums for the gods, received their messages by entering a small, enclosed basement chamber filled with a vapor arising from exposed chasms or springs of water in the temple floor.

(Continued)

(Continued)

Most modern scholars, having failed to verify any such gas emissions, long considered such stories about the Pythia as either mistaken or fraudulent. Yet in 2001, de Boer, Hale, and Chanton (2001) discovered that the temple's small chasms and springs contained minerals capable of producing ethylene, a known intoxicating agent that causes delirium, disinhibition, euphoria, and even feelings of disembodiment. To the Pythia of ancient Greece, this mind-altering experience served as their connection with the gods.

SOURCE: From de Boer, Hale, and Chanton, 2001.

C hapter 8 dealt with alcohol, the most widely consumed depressant substance. This chapter considers other depressant substances found within our society: the substance GHB and agents administered in vaporous form called *inhalants*.

Gamma-Hydroxybutyrate

Gamma-hydroxy butyrate (GHB)
Substance that serves as both a drug and a neurotransmitter that produces CNS depressant effects

Gamma-hydroxybutyrate (GHB) is both a drug and a neurotransmitter that has depressant effects on the central nervous system (CNS). GHB is a white, tasteless powder that dissolves easily in water. Depending on the formulation, GHB has both recreational and instrumental uses. As a club drug, GHB goes by many street names, including "Gamma-OH," "Georgia Home Boy," and "Liquid E" (Drug Enforcement Administration, 2012a). GHB earned a negative reputation in the late 1990s as a substance used in sexual assault (ElSohly & Salamone, 1999). The media most often refers to GHB-associated sexual assault as *date rape*, although many of these assaults do not occur during a date and often the victim fails to even recall meeting the assailant. Because of its use as a club drug and in sexual assaults, the Drug Enforcement Administration (DEA) categorized GHB as a schedule I controlled substance in 2000 (Drug Enforcement Administration, 2012b).

Narcolepsy
A disorder characterized by sudden bouts of daytime heavy sleepiness

Physicians use another formulation of GHB, *sodium* gammahydroxybutyrate, as a treatment approved by the Food and Drug Administration (FDA) for **narcolepsy**, a disorder characterized by sudden bouts of daytime heavy sleepiness ("FDA-Approved Labeling for Xyrem Oral Solution," 2005). This formulation, which the DEA assigns as schedule III, goes by the generic name *sodium oxybate* and the trade name *Xyrem*. Although prescribing a depressant to relieve daytime sleepiness may

seem strange, researchers find that GHB addresses some of the neuropathological features of narcolepsy, leading to a reduction in its symptoms. More on this later in the chapter.

Recreational users obtain GHB either purchasing GHB from illicit sources or by synthesizing GHB from **gamma-butyrolactone (GBL)**. Because GBL serves as an immediate precursor to GHB, the DEA categorizes GBL as a schedule I controlled substance. However, given the legitimate uses of GBL in many household products, such as in stain and paint removers, the DEA exempts products containing less than 70 percent of GBL (Drug Enforcement Administration, 2010). We also find small amounts of GHB and GBL in certain red and white wines, vinegar, beer, and coffee (Elliott & Burgess, 2005). As described later in the chapter, GBL serves as a prodrug by metabolically converting to GHB in the body.

Gamma-butyrolactone (GBL) Chemical used in household products that is converted by enzymes to GHB in the body

Approximately 1 percent or fewer of U.S. individuals 12 and older abuse GHB (Substance Abuse and Mental Health Services Administration, 2010). Although this rate seems low overall, some areas of the country see more prevalent use. Twenty percent of local and state law enforcement agencies report moderate to high GHB availability (National Drug Intelligence Center, 2004). Together, these data suggest that either users underreport GHB abuse or that GHB is being used for nonrecreational uses such as drug-facilitated sexual assaults.

History of GHB

Researchers first synthesized GHB in 1960 as part of an effort to develop compounds with a chemical structure similar to the neurotransmitter GABA. After its discovery, physicians used GHB as an anesthetic agent. In the late 1970s, researchers discovered that the body naturally synthesizes GHB in the central nervous system. In the 1980s, GHB was widely available as a potential supplement for enhancing muscle growth among weight lifters, although no evidence supports the beneficial use of GHB for this purpose (Andresen, Aydin, Mueller, & Iwersen-Bergmann, 2011; Volpi et al., 1997). Because of concerns over GHB-induced adverse effects, including intoxication and deep unconsciousness, the FDA banned the over-the-counter sale of GHB in 1990 (Woodworth, 1999).

During the 1990s, GHB began to be used in clubs and at parties for its euphoric effects. Along with the recreational use of GHB, law enforcement agencies began investigating increasing charges of GHB use in sexual assault. In particular, reports stated that assailants secretly added GHB to alcoholic drinks, strengthening alcohol's and GHB's depressant effects.

As the association of GHB with clubs and sexual assaults strengthened, local and state governments passed laws regulating and banning its possession and use. During this period, the U.S. Drug Enforcement Agency monitored GHB as a substance of concern; in 2000, the DEA placed GHB on the controlled substances schedule (Drug Enforcement Administration, 2012a). According to law enforcement agencies, the availability and use of GHB has declined significantly since these regulations went into effect (**Figure 9.1**) (Carter, Pardi, Gorsline, & Griffiths, 2009).

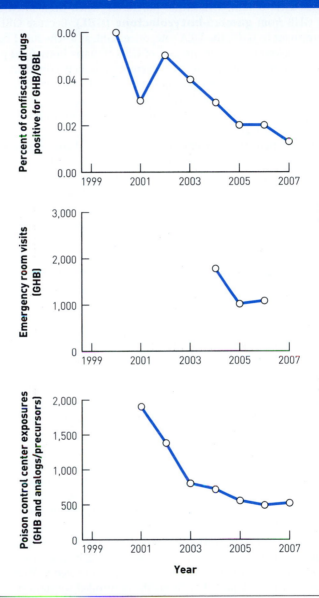

FIGURE 9.1 ● GHB use has declined sharply since its schedule I categorization in 2000, according to measures of illicit GHB seizure, emergency room visits, and poison control reports.

SOURCE: From Carter, L. P., Pardi, D., Gorsline, J., & Griffiths, R. R. (2009). Illicit gamma-hydroxybutyrate (GHB) and pharmaceutical sodium oxybate (Xyrem®): differences in characteristics and misuse. *Drug & Alcohol Dependence, 104*, 1–10. doi: 10.1016/j.drugalcdep.2009.04.012.

STOP & CHECK

1. GHB, gamma-hydroxybutyrate, is not only a drug but also a _____.

2. To obtain GHB for recreational purposes, what other substances might a user seek?

3. What factors led to the banning of GHB possession and use?

1. neurotransmitter 2. Because GHB is a controlled substance, users may seek compounds such as GBL that serve as prodrugs for GHB. 3. GHB became known for its adverse effects and its use in sexual assaults.

GHB: Natural and Synthetic

As noted earlier, GHB is both a naturally occurring substance in the CNS and a synthetically produced drug. In the body, GHB is a metabolite of the neurotransmitter GABA. The metabolic process begins when the enzyme *GABA transaminase* converts GABA to its metabolite *succinic semi-aldehyde*. The enzyme *succinic semialdehyde reductase* transforms succinic semialdehyde to GHB (**Figure 9.2**) (Andresen et al., 2011).

As previously stated, certain substances serve as prodrugs for GHB. Figure 9.2 shows the process of these metabolic reactions for producing GHB. Its primary prodrugs consist of the chemicals GBL and another substance named *1,4-butanediol*. 1,4-butanediol is an industrial solvent used in types of plastics and other materials. GBL and 1,4-butanediol are biotransformed in the alcohol metabolic pathway to produce GHB. First, when 1,4-butanediol enters the liver or the stomach, alcohol dehydrogenase converts 1,4-butanediol to GBL. Second, in the liver, the enzyme aldehyde dehydrogenase converts GBL to GHB (**Figure 9.3**).

1,4-butanediol
Industrial solvent that produces GBL in the body; GBL subsequently transforms into GHB

Review! The enzyme alcohol dehydrogenase converts alcohol to acetaldehyde, which is in turn converted to acetic acid by the enzyme aldehyde dehydrogenase. (Chapter 8.)

As a salt, the drug GHB easily dissolves in liquid. The liquid form of GHB, or GHB's chemical precursors, are colorless and tasteless. The oral delivery of GHB is most common for recreational use and as the form of exposure used in sexual assault cases. The prescription form of GHB, sodium oxybate, is also administered orally, in pill form. Although GHB can be delivered intravenously, this administration route is seldom used. GHB readily penetrates the blood–brain barrier after absorption from the gastrointestinal tract (Andresen et al., 2011). After oral administration in humans, GHB reaches peak levels in blood after 15–45 minutes, and pharmacological effects

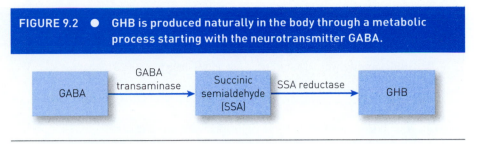

FIGURE 9.2 ● **GHB is produced naturally in the body through a metabolic process starting with the neurotransmitter GABA.**

SOURCE: © Cengage Learning 2014.

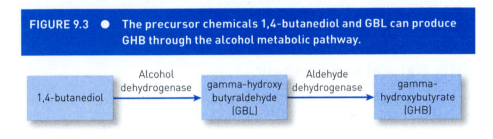

FIGURE 9.3 ● **The precursor chemicals 1,4-butanediol and GBL can produce GHB through the alcohol metabolic pathway.**

SOURCE: © Cengage Learning 2014.

first occur within 15–20 minutes and last approximately 2 hours (Carter et al., 2009; Mason & Kerns, 2002).

In the liver and brain, the enzyme GHB dehydrogenase transforms GHB into its own precursor chemical, succinic semialdehyde, which then converts to the neurotransmitter GABA. The elimination half-life for GHB from the body is only 30 minutes. It can remain at detectable levels in blood for only 4–8 hours and in urine for only 8–12 hours. These short elimination periods make determining GHB's use in sexual assault difficult (LeBeau et al., 1999). Although tests confirm GHB use in 1–5 percent of sexual assaults, the majority of suspected drug-facilitated sexual assault victims present themselves to authorities too late for GHB detection (Zvosec & Smith, 2009). Moreover, standard blood tests conducted after sexual assault do not detect GHB. Instead, victims must notify health professionals that they suspect the use of GHB so that proper tests will be conducted (National Drug Intelligence Center, 2004).

Pharmacological Actions of GHB

As stated previously, GHB is not only a drug but also a neurotransmitter. The neurotransmitter GHB is found throughout the brain. After synthesis, GHB accumulates within vesicles used for storing GABA. Given that GABA facilitates GHB synthesis and that the same vesicles store both GABA and GHB, many GABA neurons likely release both GABA and GHB (**Figure 9.4**) (Muller et al., 2002).

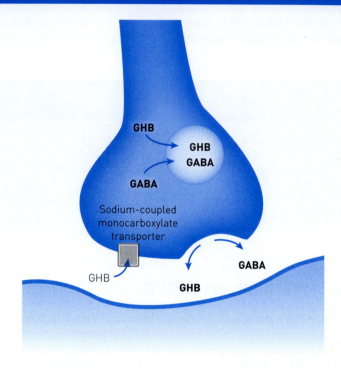

SOURCE: © Cengage Learning 2014.

Currently, researchers have confirmed only one type of GHB receptor, but evidence suggests the existence of a second GHB receptor. The GHB receptor is a G-protein–coupled receptor that causes inhibitory effects on neurons. The GHB receptor is found throughout the brain, but is highly concentrated in the hippocampus. The cerebral cortex and basal ganglia also exhibit high GHB receptor concentrations (Maitre, 1997). Beyond the GHB receptor, studies indicate that GHB functions as an agonist for the GABA$_B$ receptor (Diana et al., 1991; Pistis et al., 2005).

GHB reenters neurons through a *sodium-coupled monocarboxylate transporter* (Figure 9.4) and then rapidly degrades to form GABA, as described previously (Cui & Morris, 2009; Roiko, Felmlee, & Morris, 2012). In fact, although GHB eliminates from the body in 30-minute half-lives, GHB degrades in the brain in 5-minute half-lives (Doherty, Stout, & Roth, 1975). Thus, given the rapid degradation to

GABA, many of GHB's pharmacological effects may be accounted for by GABA neurotransmission (Wu et al., 2003).

GHB has complex effects on the regulation of dopamine. At low doses in animals, GHB inhibits the firing of dopamine neurons and the release of dopamine from these neurons. High doses of GHB in animals initially produce this same effect, but afterward we find increased dopamine concentrations in the nucleus accumbens and other parts of the basal ganglia (Maitre, 1997). Thus, high doses of GHB exhibit changes in dopamine levels predictive of generating reinforcing effects.

STOP & CHECK

1. GHB is synthesized from the neurotransmitter _____.

2. GHB is an endogenous neurotransmitter that activates GHB and _____ receptors.

1. GABA 2. GABA

Pharmacological Effects of GHB

Studies find that GHB has a complex series of pharmacological effects. Early pharmacological studies found that GHB elicits a unique sleeping pattern that is characterized by growth-hormone release during the first two hours of sleep and longer periods of deep sleep (**Box 9.1**). The combination of enhanced growth-hormone release and deep sleep made GHB an attractive substance for many bodybuilders seeking a substance to enhance muscle repair and growth as well as enhancing restorative sleep. However, these purported benefits have never been substantiated (Okun, Boothby, Bartfield, & Doering, 2001).

GHB's effects on growth hormones and deep sleep may have important benefits for narcolepsy. Although narcolepsy is generally considered a disorder of daytime sleepiness, it also consists of fragmented and nonrestorative sleep. These disruptions to nighttime sleeping also lead to deficiencies in growth hormone, which researchers speculate could contribute to this disorder. When given at nighttime, sodium oxybate, the FDA-approved form of GHB, restores growth-hormone deficits and increases the length of nighttime sleeping in narcolepsy patients. As a result of improved nighttime sleeping, patients have reduced episodes of sleeping during the day (Donjacour et al., 2011; Okun et al., 2001).

Recreational users characterize three general ranges for orally used GHB doses: "light" doses ranging from 6 to 17 mg/kg, "common" doses ranging from 11 to

28 mg/kg, and "strong" doses ranging from 22 to 51 mg/kg (Oliveto et al., 2010).[1] Studies in controlled laboratory conditions report that GHB increases blood pressure at strong doses; no other appreciable physiological effects occur within these dose ranges (Abanades et al., 2006; Oliveto et al., 2010).

GHB's behavioral and subjective effects depend on the dose and the time course. Studies find that strong doses of GHB cause confusion and induce drowsiness (Oliveto et al., 2010). Survey data among GHB users and anecdotal reports suggest that memory loss most often occurs after finishing GHB use, as opposed to during GHB use, for about half of GHB users. Anecdotal reports describe memory-impairing effects seldom occurring for doses as low as 10 mg/kg (Mamelak, 1989; Miotto et al., 2001). Strong doses produce significant impairments in balance as demonstrated when study participants attempt to stand on one foot or perform other motor tasks. Peak effects for these motor effects occur 1 hour after administration (Abanades et al., 2006). The effects described for GHB in many ways resemble those produced by alcohol; in fact, clinical trials have shown GHB to reduce withdrawal symptoms in alcohol-addicted patients (Addolorato et al., 1999; Gallimberti et al., 1989). When sexual predators use GHB in combination with alcohol the victim appears inebriated and the dual effects of both depressant compounds induce memory loss (i.e., blackout) of the assault (Varela, Nogue, Oros, & Miro, 2004).

Those attending bars and clubs can help prevent a drug added to an alcoholic drink by keeping an eye on one's beverage and also by carrying *drink test kits*, which come in the form of small paper strips that can detect GHB and many other substances added to a drink. However, in a study on drink test kits, researchers did not find 100 percent reliability of these test kits; results depended greatly on the type of alcoholic drink used (Beyton, Sumnall, McVeigh, Cole, & Bellis, 2006). Thus, test kits can be useful, but relying on them completely provides a false sense of security.

GHB users report positive subjective experiences from GHB use. In a survey conducted by Miotto and colleagues (2001), the majority of regular GHB users reported experiencing euphoria, happiness, increased sexuality, optimism, and other positive subjective effects during GHB use. However, this study did not identify the doses used or provide information on the time course for these effects.

GHB studies conducted in laboratory conditions have attempted to relate subjective effects to doses and time course. Stimulant-like subjective effects tend to occur for common doses early in GHB's time course, peaking around 45 minutes. During this stimulant phase, study participants report feeling stimulated, experiencing amphetamine-like effects, and having feelings of greater energy. They also reported liking the drug's effects. Depressant-like subjective effects tend to occur later in GHB's time course for common and strong doses, peaking at around 1.5 hours. During the depressant phase of this time course, participants report feeling

---

1 Amounts converted to mg/kg based on mean weight for U.S. male adults.

BOX 9.1 ELECTROENCEPHALOGRAPHY

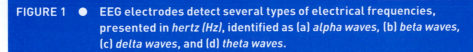

FIGURE 1 ● EEG electrodes detect several types of electrical frequencies, presented in *hertz (Hz)*, identified as (a) *alpha waves*, (b) *beta waves*, (c) *delta waves*, and (d) *theta waves*.

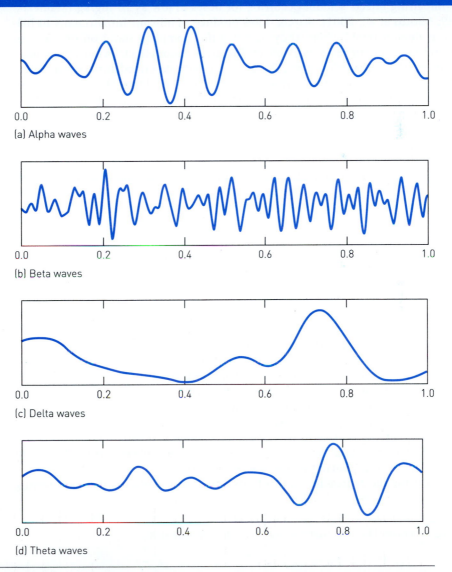

SOURCE: Adapted from Metcalf et al., 1966.

Electroencephalography (EEG) is a method for recording the electrical activity of brain areas through electrodes placed on the scalp. Brain electrical activity is recorded when electrons on the metal of the electrodes on the scalp are moved by electrical changes occurring beneath the electrodes. These electrical changes occur because of exchanges of ions within neurons, particularly ion passage in neuronal axons. Ion passage occurs on neuronal axons during the resting potential when potassium (K^+) ions enter and sodium (Na^+) ions exit a neuron, during action potentials when Na^+ ions rapidly enter a neuron, and during refractory periods when K^+ ions exit a neuron. When these electrical events occur among thousands of neurons in a part of the brain at the same time, then these overall

FIGURE 2 ● In awake participants, GHB produced slow wave bursts characteristic of delta and theta waves (circled; compare to Figure 1). Delta and theta waves normally occur during deep sleep.

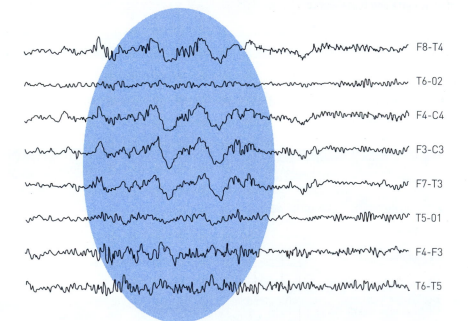

F8-T4

T6-02

F4-C4

F3-C3

F7-T3

T5-01

F4-F3

T6-T5

SOURCE: © Cengage Learning 2014.

(Continued)

(Continued)

electrical changes are detected on EEG electrodes.

EEG electrodes detect several types of electrical frequencies **(Figure 1)** presented in *hertz (Hz)*, a value that represents the number of waves produced within a second of time. The *alpha frequency* consists of 8–12 Hz. Alpha waves become larger—that is, have greater amplitude—during relaxation and when eyes are closed. They are prominent during the early stages of sleep. The *beta frequency* is characterized by 12–30 Hz and is low amplitude and irregular during thinking, concentration, movement, and when eyes are opened. Other frequencies, which include *delta* and *theta*, are most often studied during the stages of sleep. Deep sleep, in particular, consists of slow delta and theta waves.

During research or clinical assessment, EEG recordings are made when participants are exposed to some type of stimulus or engaging in a task. An *evoked potential* is an EEG recording during a specific stimulus presentation. An *event-related potential* is an EEG recording during a behavioral or cognitive activity.

Researchers use EEG to study drug effects, such as those produced by CNS depressant drugs. For example, in a study conducted by Metcalf and colleagues (1966), GHB produced a synchronized, slow wave characteristic of a deep sleep. Yet these slow wave patterns were seen in awake participants. These findings suggest that GHB inhibits cortical arousal centers such as the reticular formation **(Figure 2)**.

drunk, dizzy, drowsy, confused, and sedated (Abanades et al., 2006; Oliveto et al., 2010) (**Table 9.1**).

TABLE 9.1 ● Time-Dependent Subjective Effects of GHB	
~ 45 minutes	1½ hours
Stimulated	Drunk
Amphetamine-like effects	Dizzy
Greater energy	Drowsy
Enjoy the drug effects	Confused
	Sedated

SOURCE: © Cengage Learning 2014.

STOP & CHECK

1. Why have some weight lifters used GHB?

2. During GHB use, when might a user experience stimulant or depressant effects?

1. GHB elicits increases in growth hormone and increased deep sleep, leading weight lifters to believe that GHB may promote muscle repair and growth as well as enhance restorative sleep. 2. Some of GHB's subjective effects depend on time course. Studies show that stimulant effects occur earlier in GHB's time course than do depressant effects.

GHB Overdose and Risk of Addiction

Many of GHB's adverse effects arise from overdose or GHB withdrawal. GHB overdose presents as nausea, unconsciousness, reduced blood pressure, and lowered heart rate. However, most emergency room visits related to GHB, particularly those involving cardiovascular effects, involve the use of other substances, including alcohol or other depressant drugs (Chin, Sporer, Cullison, Dyer, & Wu, 1998). In particular, emergency room admissions because of combined use of GHB or GBL and alcohol tend to involve a nonreactive coma (Liechti, Kunz, Greminger, Speich, & Kupferschmidt, 2006). An acute withdrawal period follows an episode of GHB use. Most regular users report exhaustion, memory loss, confusion, and clumsiness after GHB use. Some users also report anxiety, insomnia, depression, and dizziness (Miotto et al., 2001).

Although the effects of GHB on nucleus accumbens dopamine levels and the production of pharmacological effects similar in many ways to alcohol indicate that GHB produces positive subjective experiences, GHB is uncommon as an addictive substance. In fact, GHB use seldom meets the *Diagnostic and Statistical Manual* (DSM) criteria for a substance use disorder. Yet this likely has much to do with the short half-life of GHB.

When GHB use meets the general DSM criteria, the use pattern consists of individuals taking GHB around the clock, about every 1–3 hours. This manner of use creates a physical dependency that results in the appearance of severe withdrawal symptoms occurring within 2–6 hours after using GHB. **GHB withdrawal** symptoms include tremor, seizures, memory loss, anxiety, and confusion (Andresen et al., 2011).

GHB withdrawal
Withdrawal symptoms occurring within hours of last using GHB that include tremor, seizures, memory loss, anxiety, and confusion

STOP & CHECK

1. Why might it be difficult to isolate GHB's overdose effects during an emergency room visit?

1. Users seldom take GHB alone. When overdose occurs, physicians often suspect an interaction between GHB and another substance such as alcohol, which, in particular, may interact with GHB to impair cardiovascular function.

Inhalants

Inhalants are vaporous chemicals that elicit psychoactive effects. Inhalants represent a large class of compounds that include volatile alkyl nitrites, nitrous oxide, and volatile solvents, fuels, and anesthetics (Balster, 1998; Williams & Storck, 2007). The most representative alkyl nitrite consists of **amyl nitrite**, a compound abused in the 1960s and 1970s for its ability to provide feelings of warmth, throbbing sensations, light-headedness, and enhanced sexual experiences (Balster, 1998; Everett, 1972). Users also refer to amyl nitrite as *poppers* in reference to the sound made when users broke open the small glass ampoules, or vials, containing this compound.

Nitrous oxide, also known as *laughing gas*, represents another recreationally used inhalant largely because of its euphoric effects, along with a mixture of depressant and hallucinogenic effects (Balster, 1998). The most common source for abuse of nitrous oxide consists of aerosol sprays. In particular, many users inhale nitrous oxide from aero-solized whipped cream containers, which release a puff of nitrous oxide just before releasing whipped cream; users refer to these containers as *whippets* (Howard & Perron, 2009).

By far, the majority of abused inhalants consists of volatile solvents, fuels, and gas anesthetics. The most frequently used compound in this category is *toluene*, but others include gasoline, butane, xylene, and acetone. Many of these chemicals are hydrocarbons, referring to their composition of entirely carbon and hydrogen atoms (**Figure 9.5**). These chemicals exist among many household products or in products readily available at hardware stores. Many glues such as model airplane cement contain toluene, and aerosol cans and cigarette lighters contain butane. We find xylene

FIGURE 9.5 ● **Many inhalants are hydrocarbon chemicals, which consist entirely of carbon (C) and hydrogen (H) atoms.**

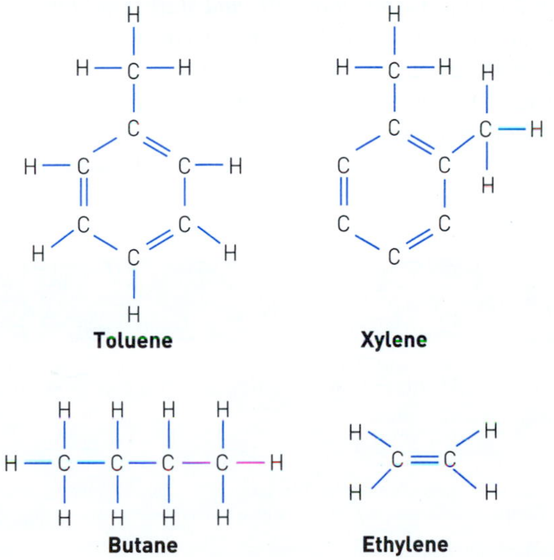

Toluene

Xylene

Butane

Ethylene

in certain cleaning solutions and in solvents for dissolving oil-based paints. Solutions for dissolving nail polish and paint often contain acetone (Lubman, Hides, & Yucel, 2006). Mentioned at the beginning of this chapter, researchers discovered that another hydrocarbon compound, *ethylene*, may have been emitted from beneath the Temple of Apollo, possibly accounting for the experiences of the Pythia when in small, enclosed spaces (de Boer et al., 2001).

Adolescents represent the largest portion of inhalant users. Approximately 2 million adolescents use inhalants, with most inhalant use occurring at age 14. They are the most widely abused drugs for U.S. adolescents below 8th grade, and 12th graders report lower rates of inhalant use, suggesting that inhalant use decreases as adolescents grow up (Johnston, O'Malley, & Bachman, 2003). Researchers find that geographical isolation, poverty, and unemployment represent important risk factors for inhalant abuse, although inhalant abuse is less likely to occur with African American children, children from two-parent households, and children with strong academic performance (Cairney, Maruff, Burns, & Currie, 2002; Nonnemaker, Crankshaw, Shive, Hussin, & Farrelly, 2011).

Beyond the pharmacological effects of inhalants, users find two significant practical aspects that make inhalant abuse relatively easy. First, none of the products containing commonly abused inhalants is illegal to purchase. Second, the intoxication users achieve from inhalants wears off quickly, allowing an inhalant to be used after school and then go home sober soon afterward (Cohen, 1977; Kurtzman, Otsuka, & Wahl, 2001).

STOP & CHECK

1. What is the most commonly abused inhalant?

2. In addition to ease of access, what is another practical reason why adolescents abuse toluene?

1. Toluene, which is found in many types of glue. 2. The effects of toluene wear off quickly, allowing for an adolescent, for example, to sniff glue after school and then go home sober soon after.

History of Inhalants

The opening of this chapter provided an intriguing finding about ethylene gases likely contributing to the spiritual experiences of ancient Greek oracles (de Boer et al., 2001). Even though ancient human history has scattered tales of ritualistic inhalation of vapors, most of our history of inhalant use comes during the age of modern chemistry. Two of the oldest known psychoactive inhalants include nitrous oxide and ether. After Joseph Priestley discovered nitrous oxide in 1776, Sir Humphrey Davy in the same year discovered that it produced an excited state, hence the name *laughing gas*. Davy gathered together many people for nitrous oxide parties. We attribute the discovery of nitrous oxide's anesthetic effects to Horace Wells, who observed an individual's apparent lack of pain while intoxicated with nitrous oxide and decided to try it out for pulling teeth,

albeit with limited success. However, other dentists and physicians perfected its use, and nitrous oxide remains a common anesthetic gas today (Brecher, 1972).

Some of the first reports of inhalant sniffing occurred immediately after World War II (Kerner, 1988). The first scientific report on glue sniffing came out in the *Journal of the American Medical Association* in 1959, which reported on arrests for glue sniffing made in Arizona and Colorado (Glaser & Massengale, 1962). The first major indication of an epidemic came from a report by Bass (1970), who reported 110 cases of sudden death occurring from inhalant abuse. Today, although these remain legal substances because of their use in everyday products, many states and localities have laws banning glue sniffing and the abuse of other inhalants (Brecher, 1972; Williams & Storck, 2007).

STOP & CHECK

1. Although nitrous oxide first gained notoriety as laughing gas, what was an important therapeutic use of this inhalant?

1. Nitrous oxide exhibits anesthetic effects and eventually became an important anesthetic gas for dental procedures.

Inhalants: Rapid Absorption and Elimination

Users generally administer inhalants by taking a series of inhalations over 15–20 minutes, briefly achieving inhalant concentrations of more than 6,000 parts per million. Three common approaches to inhaling solvents are called *sniffing, huffing,* and *bagging.* Sniffing involves directly inhaling vapors emitted from a small container or a soaked cloth. Huffing involves placing a soaked cloth directly over the mouth or nose, usually to increase the amount of compound inhaled. Bagging consists of a user placing a compound in a small paper or plastic bag and then inhaling the contained vapors (Kurtzman et al., 2001; Lubman, Yucel, & Lawrence, 2008).

Most inhalants offer high lipid solubility, making for rapid absorption and penetration through tissues, including the brain. In animals, intravenous delivery of toluene achieves peak levels in the brain within 1–3 minutes, and these brain levels of toluene reduce by half after approximately 20 minutes. However, toluene eliminates more slowly from white matter in the brain and reduces by half after 30 minutes (Gerasimov, 2004). As described previously, the rapid elimination of inhalants offers an important practical appeal to adolescents who seek to sober up before going home after school.

Pharmacological Actions of Inhalable Solvents

As already noted, inhalants represent a large class of diverse compounds that lead to a variety of different pharmacological actions. This chapter focuses on the actions of toluene and related inhalable chemicals because these are the most commonly abused

inhalants. Toluene and most other inhalants elicit depressant effects through mechanisms shared with alcohol, including antagonism of NMDA receptors and positive modulation of $GABA_A$ receptors.

Review! Positive modulators increase the ability of a neurotransmitter to bind to and activate a receptor. (Chapter 4.)

Like alcohol, acute toluene administration acts as a noncompetitive antagonist for NMDA receptors, eliminating the flow of ions through the NMDA channel (Cruz, Mirshahi, Thomas, Balster, & Woodward, 1998). Several days of repeated toluene exposure leads to an increase in NMDA receptors, suggesting a potential mechanism for pharmacodynamic tolerance (Bale, Tu, Carpenter-Hyland, Chandler, & Woodward, 2005). Also like alcohol, acute toluene administration increases the activation of $GABA_A$ receptors by serving as a positive modulator, and repeated toluene administration results in decreased activation of $GABA_A$ receptors (Bale et al., 2005; Beckstead, Weiner, Eger, Gong, & Mihic, 2000). Beyond NMDA and $GABA_A$ receptors, toluene may also function as an antagonist for serotonin 5-HT_3 receptors and nicotinic receptors (Lopreato, Phelan, Borghese, Beckstead, & Mihic, 2003).

Microdialysis studies evaluating toluene's ability to enhance nucleus accumbens dopamine levels, an action usually predictive of a drug's reinforcing effects, provide mixed results. Gerasimov and colleagues (2002) failed to find changes in dopamine concentrations in the nucleus accumbens in rats exposed to 3,000 parts per million toluene. However, Riegel, Zapata, Shippenberg, and French (2007) found increased dopamine concentrations in the nucleus accumbens in rats after administration of toluene directly into the ventral tegmental area. Yet these authors found that dopamine occurred at a specific dose of toluene; above or below this level, doses failed to increase dopamine concentrations in the nucleus accumbens.

Inhalants: Pharmacological Effects and Interference with Oxygen Intake

Like many other depressant drugs, toluene and other inhalants initially exhibit stimulant-like effects and later exhibit depressant-like effects. From reviewing numerous clinical studies on acute inhalant effects, Kurtzman and colleagues (2001) describe four general stages of inhalant effects (**Table 9.2**). The *first stage* begins within a few minutes after inhalation. During the first stage, an inhalant elicits stimulant-like positive subjective effects, including excitation, euphoria, and exhilaration. As these researchers report, this stage resembles the initial effects of alcohol for most users. In studies examining mice, we find increased locomotor activity in an open field after administration of lower concentrations of an inhalant (Bowen & Balster, 1998).

The *second stage* consists of many behavioral effects that resemble alcohol intoxication. The behavioral effects include disorientation, slurred speech, and confusion. However, unlike general alcohol intoxication, toluene may also produce hallucinations, particularly during frequent use (Cruz & Dominguez, 2011). The *third stage* of inhalant intoxication consists of further depressant effects, including a blunting of sensations

Stage	Effects
1	Stimulant-like positive subjective effects, including excitation, euphoria, and exhilaration
2	Behavioral effects resembling alcohol intoxication, including disorientation, slurred speech, and confusion; hallucinations may occur
3	Enhanced depressant effects, including blunted sensations and impaired motor coordination
4	Overdose consisting of stupor, unconsciousness, seizures, breathing cessation, and cardiac arrest

TABLE 9.2 ● Stages of Inhalant Effects

SOURCE: © Cengage Learning 2014.

Inhalant overdose
Overdose from inhalant use characterized by a series of adverse effects that can include stupor, seizure, unconsciousness, cessation of breathing, and cardiac arrest

Sudden sniffing death syndrome
Death occurring from inhalant overdose

and poor motor coordination. In mice, we find that higher concentrations of inhalants lead to suppressed locomotor activity in an open field (Bowen & Balster, 1998).

Depending on the amount of inhalant administered, users may also experience a *fourth stage* of intoxication that consists of **inhalant overdose**, a condition characterized by a series of adverse effects including stupor, seizure, unconsciousness, cessation of breathing, and cardiac arrest. Cardiac arrest serves as the primary cause of **sudden sniffing death syndrome**. Poor oxygen availability occurs when inhalant vapors compete with the inhalation and absorption of oxygen. Low oxygen levels significantly impair brain and cardiovascular function. Sudden sniffing death syndrome can occur when someone is startled while highly intoxicated with an inhalant. In particular, this may occur if an adolescent sniffing glue is caught by a parent. Oxygen delivery serves as the primary treatment for treating inhalant overdose (Alper et al., 2008; Kurtzman et al., 2001).

Chronic heavy use of inhalants can produce severe neural damage, including cortical white matter degeneration and ventricle enlargement, an indicator of brain tissue loss (Rosenberg, Grigsby, Dreisbach, Busenbark, & Grigsby, 2002). This damage is consistent with a study conducted by Hormes, Filley, and Rosenberg (1986) in inhalant users. These researchers assessed individuals who used high concentration of toluene chronically for more than 2 years. Most of these individuals exhibited severe cognitive impairment, muscle weakness, tremor, poor eye tracking, poor hearing, and a poor sense of smell.

Yuncu and colleagues (2015) conducted a series of neurological assessments in adolescents (generally defined as ages 10 to 19) who used inhalants nearly every day for at least 6 months. Using *diffusion tensor imaging*, an MRI method used to assess the structural orientation of cells based on water diffusion, they found reduced integrity of white matter tissue in the parietal, occipital, and temporal lobes. Further, these users performed poorly on a Wisconsin Card Sorting Task, a test of executive functioning, and a Stroop test, a test of processing speed, compared to a control group of noninhalant users.

According to the DSM-5, chronic inhalant use may also develop into an inhalant use disorder. A user with an inhalant use disorder may exhibit tolerance as defined by requiring greater amounts of an inhalant to achieve the same effect. Although the DSM defines inhalant use disorder as being similar to most substance dependence disorders, it states that withdrawal symptoms either do not occur or are generally mild and not clinically significant (American Psychiatric Association, 2013). In a study by Ridenour, Bray, and Cottler (2007), however, 11 percent of inhalant-dependent users described experiencing headaches, nausea, hallucinations, craving for an inhalant, depressed mood, and fast heartbeat as time passed after inhalant use. However, these authors did note that unlike most substance dependencies, withdrawal symptoms most likely occur after a binge with inhalants and tend to occur for only 1 or 2 days.

STOP & CHECK

1. What is the primary pharmacological action of inhalable solvents?

2. The primary adverse physiological effects of inhalable solvents result from competition with _____.

3. What types of brain damage occur during long-term inhalant use?

1. Inhalable solvents facilitate activation of GABA receptors. **2.** Oxygen **3.** Researchers find degeneration of cortical white matter and enlarged ventricles.

From Actions to Effects:
Stimulus Properties of GHB and Toluene

As first presented in Box 6.1, drug-discrimination procedures provide the ability to determine similarities among the subjective effects of different drugs. Researchers also use this procedure to determine the role different receptor actions may play in a drug's subjective effects. Drug-discrimination procedures provide important information on the receptor actions for depressant drugs, as illustrated in the section on the discriminative stimulus properties of GHB and toluene.

Cook, Biddlestone, Coop, and Beardsley (2006) conducted a drug-discrimination study using mice trained to discriminate a dose of GHB versus saline—that is, a placebo. After the mice learned to perform this discrimination accurately, the researchers gave the mice doses of alcohol to determine which lever the mice would choose. When given alcohol, some mice responded on the GHB lever, but others responded on the saline lever, suggesting to these researchers that alcohol's subjective effects do not closely resemble GHB's subjective effects.

As an important next step in this research area, Baker, Searcy, Pynnonen, and Poling (2008) conducted a three-lever drug-discrimination procedure that required rats to discriminate alcohol for one lever, versus GHB for another lever, versus saline for the

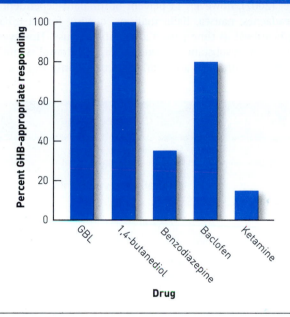

FIGURE 9.6 ● **Drug-discrimination experiments reveal receptor actions important for GHB's subjective effects. For simplicity, this figure only shows the percentage of responses occurring on the GHB-appropriate lever (y-axis). See text for further details on this study.**

SOURCE: Data from Baker et al., 2008.

third lever. In this way, rats had to attend to the different subjective effects between alcohol and GHB to accurately learn this procedure. After the rats achieved a high accuracy of performance, these researchers conducted a series of tests to determine the receptors important for the discriminative stimulus effects for these compounds.

The study by Baker and colleagues (2008) provided several interesting findings about the discriminative stimulus effects of GHB (**Figure 9.6**). *First*, both GBL and 1,4-butanediol led animals to respond on the GHB-appropriate lever, probably because GBL and 1,4-butanediol convert to GHB in the body through metabolic processes. *Second*, a benzodiazepine drug, which functions as a GABA$_A$ positive modulator, led to more responses on the alcohol lever and few responses on the GHB lever, suggesting that, consistent with GHB's known pharmacological actions, GABA$_A$ receptor actions do not contribute to GHB's subjective effects. *Third*, administration of the GABA$_B$ receptor agonist baclofen led animals to press the GHB lever, which supports pharmacological evidence that GHB acts as a GABA$_B$ receptor agonist. *Finally*, when the researchers administered the NMDA receptor antagonist ketamine, rats mostly responded on the alcohol lever rather than the GHB lever. This also supports known pharmacological evidence, because alcohol serves as an antagonist at NMDA receptors, whereas GHB appears devoid of NMDA receptor effects.

Drug-discrimination findings also correspond with the pharmacological actions of toluene. For example, Rees, Knisely, Jordan, and Balster (1987) trained mice to discriminate toluene, which was injected as a liquid solution, from the drug's vehicle. They first verified that mice would press the toluene lever and administered toluene via inhalation. After verifying this, they found that administration of the GABA$_A$ receptor positive modulator pentobarbital led to toluene lever responding. This finding coincides with toluene's positive modulation of GABA$_A$ receptors.

In a separate study, Shelton and Balster (2004) trained mice to discriminate an NMDA receptor antagonist, dizocilpine, from saline in a drug-discrimination task. Although toluene exhibits antagonism of NMDA receptors, the mice failed to choose the dizocilpine lever after toluene administration. The researchers concluded that NMDA receptor antagonism may not be important for toluene's subjective effects.

STOP & CHECK

1. What do drug-discrimination procedures tell us about the subjective effects of GHB?

2. What mediates the stimulus properties of toluene?

1. Although pharmacological procedures determine the receptor actions of psychoactive drugs, drug-discrimination procedures link these receptor actions to a drug's subjective effects. For GHB, we learn that activation of GABA$_B$ receptors contribute to its subjective effects. We also learn that the prodrugs GBL and 1,4-butanediol also produce GHB-like subjective effects, likely by producing GHB through metabolism. 2. Based on drug-discrimination procedures, positive modulation GABA$_A$ receptors elicit toluene-like stimulus properties.

Chapter Summary

Gamma-hydroxybutyrate (GHB) is both a drug and a neurotransmitter that produces depressant effects. The drug is colorless and tasteless and is used as a recreational substance, sexual assault drug, and therapeutically to treat narcolepsy. Because GHB is a controlled substance, many users instead seek one of GHB's prodrugs, GBL or 1,4-butanediol. Neurotransmitter synthesis of GHB begins with the inhibitory neurotransmitter GABA. GHB is stored in vesicles with GABA; when released, it binds to and activates GHB receptors and GABA$_B$ receptors. The pharmacological effects of GHB include prolonged deep sleep, confusion, drowsiness, memory impairment as well as positive subjective effects such as euphoria and optimism.

Inhalants include volatile alkyl nitrites, nitrous oxide and volatile solvents, fuels,

(Continued)

(Continued)

and anesthetics, among which toluene is the most used. Adolescents serve as the majority of inhalant users. Inhalants absorb rapidly, readily penetrate tissues, and have short-lasting effects. Their pharmacological actions depend on antagonism of NMDA receptors and positive modulation of $GABA_A$ receptors. Inhalants produce a time-dependent course of stimulant and depressant effects. Inhalant overdose may lead to sudden sniffing death syndrome, and long-term inhalant abuse may damage parts of the brain.

Key Terms

Gamma-hydroxybutyrate
   (GHB) 278
Narcolepsy 278
Gamma-butyrolactone
   (GBL) 279

1,4-butanediol 281
GHB withdrawal 289
Inhalants 290
Amyl nitrite
   (or poppers) 290

Nitrous oxide
   (or laughing gas) 290
Inhalant overdose 294
Sudden sniffing death
   syndrome 294

Visit the Student Study Site at **study.sagepub.com/prus2e** to access additional study tools, including eFlashcards, web quizzes, video resources, web resources, SAGE journal articles, and more.

10

Opioids

A "TREATMENT" FOR MORPHINE ADDICTION?

At the turn of the 19th century, Americans had an epidemic of morphine use. The drug's powerful analgesic effects made it a popular medicine for a variety of ailments, but around this time morphine's withdrawal effects became a concern. This led to a medical dilemma: Maintaining morphine treatment led to tolerance and the emergence of withdrawal symptoms if physicians did not increase the dose. At the same time, removing morphine led not only to withdrawal symptoms but also the natural reemergence of symptoms the drug was meant to treat. Searching for answers, physicians took an unfortunate turn toward a "treatment" that was said to prevent morphine withdrawal and any subsequent problems emerging from removing morphine. Unfortunately, the cure—heroin—turned out to be worse.

SOURCE: From Duarte, 2005.

Opioids consist of psychoactive substances that elicit pharmacological effects by acting on opioid receptors in the central nervous system (CNS) and other parts of the body. They are among the most effective pain-relieving medications today and among the most sought-after substances for abuse. The term **narcotic**, from the Latin *narcoticus,* which means "sleep-inducing," refers to the sedative effects of drugs and generally serves as a synonym for opioids. However, we find *narcotic* used incorrectly to describe many other types of controlled substances, including psychostimulant drugs such as cocaine. Overall, the term *narcotic* is used commonly by laypersons, lawmakers, and law enforcement but holds little value as a precise term for use by scientists.

Opioids serve as major drugs of abuse in the United States. The prevalence of opioid abuse occurs not only because of its reinforcing effects but also because of its ease of access. We find increased heroin use in the United States. Lipari and Hughes (2015) examined heroin use trends in the United States between 2002 and 2013, finding more users switching from prescription opioids to heroin, increased reports of heroin overdose deaths, and an overall increase of heroin use for the first time among users 12 and older of 117,000 in 2002 and 169,000 in the United States in 2013. Although heroin use occurs mostly in men, rates of use among women doubled during that period of time. Further, we find use spreading from urban to suburban areas, and it has more than doubled among non-Hispanic white Americans, with use slightly lower for other racial or ethnic groups. The most recent estimate of those 12 and older using heroin for the first time in the past year is 212,000. An estimated 435,000 people in the United States report being current heroin users (Center for Behavioral Health Statistics and Quality, 2015).

Prescription opioid drugs such as *hydrocodone (Vicodin)* and *oxycodone (OxyContin)* are also popular because they produce powerful reinforcing effects and are easy to obtain. In 2014, an estimated 2.6 percent of adolescent U.S. adolescents had used a prescription opioid in the past year (Center for Behavioral Health Statistics and Quality, 2015). Of particular concern, 75 percent of heroin users report using prescription opioids first before switching to heroin. Among these users, the reasons for switching to heroin not only included seeking a stronger high but also finding heroin more affordable than prescription opioids (Cicero, Ellis, Surratt, & Kurtz, 2014).

Many individuals also obtain opioids by drinking over-the-counter cough syrups that contain the opioid drug *dextromethorphan*. Dextromethorphan represents the "DM" in the brand-name cough syrup Robitussin DM. The slang term *robo-tripping* refers to psychedelic drug effects achieved from drinking large quantities of cough syrups for recreational opioid use. Recreational cough syrup use was reported in 6.3 percent of 12th-grade high school students in 2009 (Substance Abuse and Mental Health Services Administration, 2010). Dextromethorphan exhibits some effects beyond those of traditional opioids (more on this substance in Chapter 12).

Opioids: Natural and Synthetic

There are two main types of opioid compounds: those produced naturally in the environment and those produced through chemical synthesis in a laboratory. Natural opioids are found in opium exudate from poppy plants, *Papaver somniferum*. *Papaver somniferum* is an annual flowering plant that stands 3 to 4 feet high and has a vibrant pink, red, white, or violet flower (**Figure 10.1**).

A large seedpod, as shown in Figure 10.1, is revealed after the flower petals fall off only 2–4 days after flowering. After scoring the pod with a knife, a white substance emerges that turns red when exposed to air. This reddish resin is raw opium, and opium scraped from the seedpod can be used "as is" or further refined and processed, as described later in the chapter (Booth, 1998). Most opium cultivation occurs in Afghanistan, and it also occurs in Pakistan, Myanmar, Colombia, and Mexico (United Nations Office of Drugs and Crime, 2010).

We refer to opioids found within opium as **naturally occurring opioids**. The primary naturally occurring opioids are morphine and codeine (Wu & Wittick, 1977). The U.S. Drug Enforcement Administration (DEA) categorizes morphine and codeine as controlled substances, but they are not schedule I substances because of their legitimate medical uses. Morphine is a schedule II drug and is only available in hospitals, and codeine is a schedule III or IV product, depending on the quantity, and is used in prescription cough suppressants (Drug Enforcement Administration, 2012b) (**Table 10.1**). *Thebaine* is another component of opium but is a relatively minor component (Wu & Wittick, 1977).

FIGURE 10.1 ● *Papaver somniferum* is an annual flowering plant that reveals an opium-containing seedpod after its petals fall off.

SOURCE: Copyright iStockphoto/phodo.

| TABLE 10.1 ● DEA Schedules for Selected Opioids ||
Drug	Schedule
Buprenorphine	III
Codeine for cough syrup preparations	V
Diacetylmorphine (heroin)	I
Desomorphine	I
Fentanyl	II
Hydrocodone	II
Morphine	II
Methadone	II
Opium extract	II
Thebaine	II

SOURCE: Adapted from the DEA Controlled Substances Schedules, http://www.deadiversion.usdoj.gov /schedules/ index.html.

Semisynthetic opioids Opioid drugs synthesized from morphine or codeine

All other opioids are synthetically produced (**Table 10.2**). **Semisynthetic opioids** are synthesized from morphine or codeine. Semisynthetic opioids include *diacetylmorphine (heroin), desomorphine (krokodil), buprenorphine (Subutex), hydrocodone,* and *oxycodone (OxyContin). Percocet* is a combination of oxycodone and *acetaminophen (Tylenol),* and *Vicodin* is a combination of hydrocodone and

TABLE 10.2 ● Opioids	
Naturally occurring	Morphine Codeine
Semisynthetic	Buprenorphine (Subutex) Diacetylmorphine (Heroin) Hydrocodone (Vicodin) Oxycodone (Oxycontin)
Fully synthetic	Fentanyl (Duragesic) Levacetylmethadyl (LAAM) Methadone (Dolophine)

acetaminophen. Acetaminophen is not an opioid drug; instead, acetaminophen is a *nonsteroidal anti-inflammatory drug* (or NSAID for short) used for pain relief, which may result from reduced inflammation. Other NSAIDs include aspirin and *ibuprofen (Motrin)*.

🔗 *Drug Profile:* **oxycodone + acetaminophen**

Trade name:	Percocet
Properties:	Oxycodone acts as an opioid analgesic and acetaminophen acts as a *nonsteroidal anti-inflammatory drug*
Uses:	Reduces pain by acting on opioid receptors and reducing inflammation

---

Desomorphine, which goes by the street name *krokodil* (Russian for "crocodile"), is still a popularly abused opioid in Russia, despite harmful by-products made during its synthesis from codeine that causes severe toxicity to skin, muscle, and other tissues, particularly near injection sites but throughout the rest of the body as well. The by-products have given krokodil a reputation as a flesh-eating drug, which is not technically true (i.e., it's from toxic damage from chemical by-products) but the description serves well to describe the physical appearance of long-term krokodil users nonetheless (Grund, Latypov, & Harris, 2013). The **fully synthetic opioids** are not derived from morphine, codeine, or any other naturally occurring opioids. Fully synthetic opioids include *fentanyl (Duragesic), methadone (Dolophine)*, and *levacetylmethadyl (LAAM)*.

Naturally occurring opioids and synthetic opioids were developed for medicinal purposes. However, many opioids such as heroin offer powerful reinforcing effects, precluding their medical use because of their addiction risk. Producers illegally synthesize heroin from morphine through a process that begins with extracting morphine from opium and then applying industrial chemical agents to synthesize heroin. After synthesis, heroin is packed and illegally shipped throughout the world (Hosztafi, 2001).

Fully synthetic opioids Opioids not derived from morphine, codeine, or any other naturally occurring opioid

---

STOP & CHECK

1. Why are opioid drugs easy to access?

2. What are the two primary opioids in poppy plants?

3. Morphine is used in the clandestine production of _____, a commonly abused opioid drug.

1. Although known illicit drugs such as heroin remain available, many users abuse prescription and over-the-counter medications that contain opioids. 2. Morphine and codeine 3. Heroin

History of Opium Use

Opium has been used since prehistoric times. Archeological research revealed evidence of *Papaver somniferum* plants in Neolithic villages in Switzerland. Historical records indicate opium cultivation in Egypt and Asia Minor in 3000 B.C., and ancient medical texts throughout Europe, the Middle East, and northern Africa list numerous medical uses for opium. Greek physician Hippocrates (460–357 B.C.) detailed the sleep-inducing and pain-relieving effects of opium and dismissed the magical interpretation of these effects by priests. Theophrastus (371–287 B.C.), a philosopher, referred to poppy juices as *opion*, which is now translated as *opium* (Duarte, 2005).

Soon after Rome conquered Greece, opium became intertwined with Roman culture and was purported as a treatment for a virtually endless list of maladies, including deafness, poisoning, and leprosy. The Romans regarded the poppy plant as a symbol of pain and death and regarded it as a convenient lethal poison. Arabs during this time cultivated and sold opium as a trading commodity. Moreover, they advanced the medical study of opium. Arab physician Avicenna (A.D. 980–1037) medically used opium for dysentery, diarrhea, and eye diseases as part of his 14-volume *Canon of Medicine*.

In the 16th century, Europeans developed and popularized a number of opium-containing medical potions, including **laudanum**. In the 1660s, English physician Thomas Sydenham developed the most common variety of laudanum. In this version, Sydenham made a drink containing opium, cinnamon, saffron, and fortified wine from the Canary Islands.

During the 19th century, drug stores legally sold opium products such as morphine. In addition to selling morphine or another opioid as is, various elixirs for treating illnesses and pain contained morphine. Near the end of the 19th century, the addictive effects of opioids received greater focus, and the beginning of the 20th century marks the religious and political movements leading up to the Harrison Act of 1914 (Booth, 1998; Duarte, 2005).

The Harrison Act did not directly ban opioid use, but rather limited the prescribing and sale of opioids to medical uses. Law enforcement interpreted this law as a means to prevent physicians from prescribing opioids to reduce opioid withdrawal symptoms. The enforcement of this law triggered an epidemic of addicted individuals leading to, according to a New York medical journal editorial on May 15, 1915, "crimes of violence . . . due usually to desperate effects by addicts to obtain drugs, but occasionally to a delirious state induced by sudden withdrawal" (Brecher, 1972). Many other controlled substances acts followed. Today, opioids are among the most highly regulated medicines.

The terminology for opioids has changed over the years. Originally, the term *opiate* referred only to opium-derived compounds, and the term *opioids* referred to other opioid drugs. For example, under this distinction, morphine is an *opiate*, whereas heroin is an *opioid* (Steinberg & Sykes, 1985). However, these conventions are seldom followed, and in general the term *opioid* describes all types of opioid and opiate compounds,

Laudanum An opium-containing drink intended for medical purposes

and less often vice versa. Thus, *opioid* is the term used throughout this chapter. For researching material on opioids, one should use both terms in database searches to avoid missing any critical work.

Pharmacokinetic Properties and Opioid Abuse

In general, users administer opioids through inhalation, oral administration, or intravenous administration. The preferred routes of opioid administration depend on the particular drug and the purpose for using it. To achieve reinforcing effects, users prefer intravenous injection or inhalation for a rapid speed of onset. The intravenous route also provides rapid relief from pain. Physicians prescribe codeine for oral administration to suppress coughing (Farré & Camí, 1991).

After absorption, opioids permeate the blood–brain barrier and enter the brain. Opioids differ in lipid solubility, affecting the time it takes them to reach the brain. For example, heroin crosses through the blood–brain barrier faster than morphine, which may explain why users prefer heroin over morphine for achieving reinforcing effects (Oldendorf, Hyman, Braun, & Oldendorf, 1972) (**Figure 10.2**).

Opioids are primarily metabolized in the liver, often producing metabolites that have biological effects. Morphine, for example, produces the biologically active metabolite *morphine-6-glucoronide*, a potent analgesic that may account for many of morphine's analgesic effects (Christrup, 1997). We also find morphine as a metabolite of codeine and a secondary metabolite of heroin. For codeine, the cytochrome P450 enzyme CYP2D6 is responsible for converting approximately 5 percent of codeine to morphine. We find more metabolic production morphine taking place for those with high CYP2D6 activity, however, suggesting that some individuals, particularly children, are prone to overdose from codeine (Ortiz de Montellano, 2013).

Opioid metabolites provide key indicators of opioid use and are detectable in urine samples. However, the presence of opioid metabolites may not identify the exact opioid used. For example, morphine is a metabolite of codeine and a secondary

FIGURE 10.2 ● Because of its greater lipid solubility, heroin enters the brain, through the blood-brain barrier, more readily than morphine.

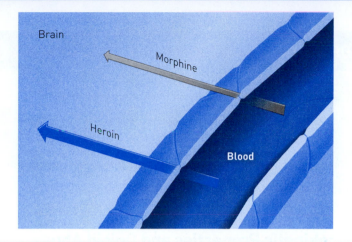

SOURCE: © Cengage Learning 2014.

metabolite of heroin (Rook, Hillebrand, Rosing, van Ree, & Beijnen, 2005; Yeh & Woods, 1970) (**Figure 10.3**). Thus, the presence of morphine in a urine sample could suggest morphine, codeine, or heroin use, but not the exact drug used.

If a technician needs to identify the precise opioid used, then she or he must test for other metabolites. For example, heroin is metabolized to *monoacetylmorphine*, which

FIGURE 10.3 ● Many opioid drugs have active metabolites, often including morphine. The active metabolites appear in bold.

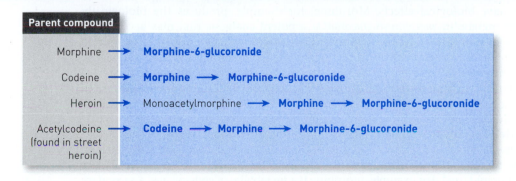

SOURCE: © Cengage Learning 2014.

is then converted to morphine. The presence of both monoacetylmorphine and morphine might suggest heroin use. In addition, street heroin often includes acetylcodeine, which is metabolized to codeine. The added presence of codeine in a urine analysis would further indicate heroin use.

The elimination rate of opioids varies from drug to drug. Many heroin cessation programs prescribe patients methadone, partly because of methadone's long elimination rate. Methadone levels peak in the body several hours after administration and remain at biologically active levels 24 hours after administration (Vos, Ufkes, Wilgenburg, Geerlings, & Brink, 1995). Although methadone remains in the body, it functions to prevent heroin withdrawal symptoms from occurring. The semisynthetic opioid buprenorphine also exhibits a weak euphoric effect and offers long elimination rate. Given these traits, opioid-cessation programs also use buprenorphine as a substitute for an addictive opioid drug (Comer, Collins, & Fischman, 2001).

STOP & CHECK

1. Opioids are usually administered orally, intravenously, or through _____.

2. What is a common active metabolite of many opioid drugs?

1. Inhalation 2. Morphine and morphine-6-glucuronide

Opioid Drug Interactions With the Endogenous Opioid System

The endogenous opioid system includes opioid neurotransmitters and receptors. Endogenous opioids are neuropeptide neurotransmitters. The amino acids linked together to make up each neuropeptide is part of a large chain of amino acids referred to as a **propeptide**. We use the term *cleavage* to refer to the separation of a peptide segment from a longer propeptide.

Propeptide Chain of amino acids containing one or more peptides

The endogenous opioid neuropeptides consist of β-endorphin, met-enkephalin, leu-enkephalin, dynorphin A, dynorphin B, and neoendorphin. These endogenous opioid neuropeptides derive from three propeptides: proopiomelanocortin, proenkephalin, and prodynorphin. Cleavage of proopiomelanocortin produces β-endorphin (**Figures 10.4** and **10.5**). Met-enkephalin and leu-enkephalin come from proenkephalin, and cleavage of prodynorphin produces dynorphin A, dynorphin B, and neoendorphins (Chavkin, James, & Goldstein, 1982; Comb, Seeburg, Adelman, Eiden, & Herbert, 1982; Hughes, Smith, Morgan, & Fothergill, 1975).

FIGURE 10.4 ● The endogenous opioid β-endorphin comprises 31 amino acids. A strand of amino acids is called a peptide, and shorter *peptides* such as β-endorphin are "cleaved" from longer peptides called *propeptides.* To better illustrate the origin of opioid peptides, the schematics shown in Figure 10.5 are used.

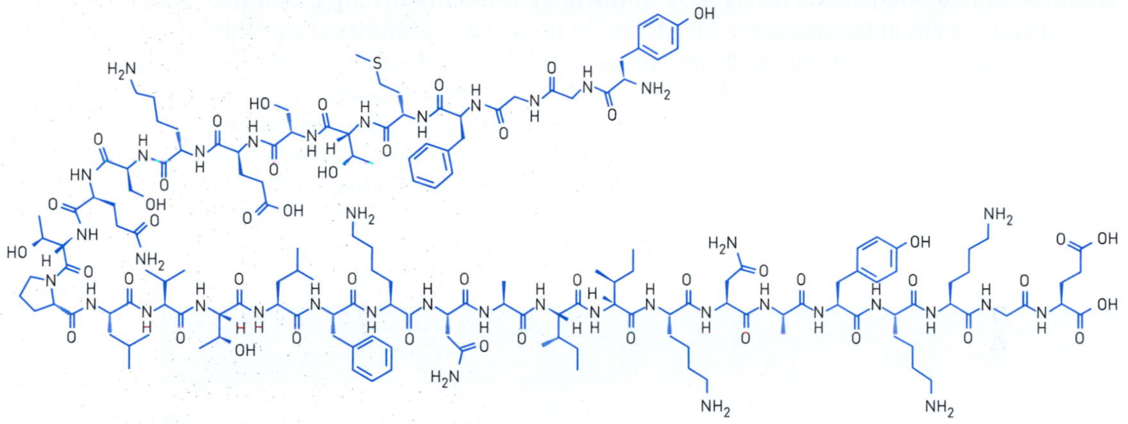

FIGURE 10.5 ● These schematics illustrate propeptides and constituent peptides. The dynorphin A and B peptides are represented as a segment of the propeptide prodynorphin. There are multiple leu- and met-enkaphalin peptides found on proenkephalin, and β-endorphin is a peptide found on proopiomelanocortin. OFQ=orphanin FQ, NE =neoendorphin, DynA = dynorphin A, DynB=Dynorphin B, and M=met-enkephalin, L=leu-enkephalin.

Pronociceptin

Prodynorphin

Proenkephalin

Proopiomelanocortin

SOURCE: © Cengage Learning 2014.

The endogenous opioids bind to three types of opioid receptors: μ (pronounced "mu"), δ ("delta"), and κ ("kappa") receptors. β-endorphin, met-enkephalin, and leu-enkephalin bind to μ and δ opioid receptors. The dynorphin and neoendorphin neurotransmitters selectively bind to κ ("kappa") receptors (**Table 10.3**). Most of the pharmacological effects associated with opioids are derived through activating μ and δ receptors (Mansour, Hoversten, Taylor, Watson, & Akil, 1995; Trigo, Martin-García, Berrendero, Robledo, & Maldonado, 2010). Kappa receptors, however, elicit hallucinogenic effects (Roth et al., 2002). A kappa receptor drug called *salvinorin A* is discussed in Chapter 12.

The endogenous opioid system may also include the neuropeptide *nociceptin*. Nociceptin, also known as *orphanin FQ*, is produced from prepronociceptin and binds to the opioid receptorlike-1 (ORL-1) receptor. The ORL-1 receptor is also called the *nociceptin receptor*. The structure of the ORL-1 receptor is similar to other opioid receptors, supporting the case that nociceptin is another opioid neurotransmitter.

Beyond these structural similarities, the ORL-1 receptor exhibits pharmacological effects that oppose those of other opioid receptors. In particular, the activation of ORL-1 receptors can limit the analgesic effects produced by μ opioid receptor agonists such as morphine. The location of ORL-1 receptors may account for these and other opposing effects. ORL-1 receptors are either located on different neurons than other opioid receptors or found on a different part of the neuron where other opioid receptors are located (Meunier, 1997).

Opioid receptors, including the ORL-1 receptor, are G-protein–coupled metabotropic receptors. Through activation of G proteins, these receptors *reduce* metabolic activity within neurons. As a result, neurons that have opioid receptors tend have reduced neurotransmission after administration of an opioid receptor agonist. The

TABLE 10.3 ● Endogenous Opioid Neurotransmitters and Their Matching Receptors	
Endogenous Opioid Neurotransmitter	**Receptor Activated**
β-endorphin	μ (mu) δ (delta)
Met-enkephalin and leu-enkephalin	μ δ
Dynorphin A & B	κ (kappa)
Neoendorphins	κ (kappa)
Nociceptin	ORL-1

SOURCE: © Cengage Learning 2014.

G-protein–coupled inwardly rectifying K+ channel (GIRK) A K+ channel that causes the influx of K+ when a neuron is hyperpolarized and less K+ influx when a neuron is depolarized

internal neuronal mechanisms involved in these inhibitory effects are complex and not entirely identified. One known inhibitory mechanism consists of the activation of inwardly rectifying K+ channels. A **G-protein–coupled inwardly rectifying K+ channel (GIRK)**, causes the influx of K+ when a neuron is hyperpolarized and diminished K+ influx when a neuron is depolarized. Through these properties, GIRKs help maintain a neuron's resting potential. When these membrane channels are activated, which happens from activation of ORL-1 receptors, a neuron's membrane potential approaches a resting potential (Meunier, 1997; Trigo et al., 2010).

Review! A resting potential describes a negatively charged local potential that precedes an action potential. (Chapter 3.)

Adaptation occurs to opioids during repeated administration. One of these processes involves a reduction in sodium–potassium pump activity. By reducing this activity, a neuron membrane adapts to the inhibitory effects of opioids by depolarizing the membrane. This increases the excitability of a neuron, which serves to counteract an opioid drug's inhibitory effects. When an opioid drug is not present, this state of depolarization increases a neuron's activity, accounting for certain withdrawal effects noted later in this chapter (Trigo et al., 2010).

Review! The sodium–potassium pump maintains a negative resting state potential by expelling three Na^+ ions for every two K^+ ions brought into a neuron. (Chapter 3.).

STOP & CHECK

1. Endogenous opioids are cleaved from four different _____.

2. Opioid receptors are G-protein–coupled receptors that produce _____ effects on neurons.

1. propeptides 2. inhibitory

Opioid Drugs: Classification by Receptor Action

Pure opioid receptor agonists Drugs that act as full receptor agonists at μ opioid receptors

Most of the opioid drugs used, either recreationally or instrumentally, act on μ opioid receptors. We also find that opioid drugs can have different actions at opioid receptors, and this in turn accounts for different pharmacological effects across compounds. Given this, opioids also are classified by their receptor actions. Drugs identified as **pure opioid receptor agonists** produce full agonist actions at μ opioid receptors. Many of these drugs also act as full agonists at other opioid receptors too. Fentanyl and morphine are examples of pure opioid receptor agonists (DeWire et al., 2013; Hughes,

Kosterlitz, & Leslie, 1975). In some experiments on the pharmacodynamic actions of opioids, morphine produces weaker effects compared to synthetic drugs, such as fentanyl, causing some to label morphine as a partial agonist instead (DeWire et al., 2013). Yet, compared to other classifications for receptor agonists considered here, morphine fits far better in the pure opioid receptor agonist category than as a partial opioid receptor agonist.

Partial opioid receptor agonists produce partial agonist actions at μ opioid receptors and therefore a smaller magnitude of pharmacological effects compared to pure opioid receptor agonists. Buprenorphine is classified as a partial opioid receptor agonist and exhibits weaker pharmacological effects compared to morphine (Virk, Arttamangkul, Birdsong, & Williams, 2009). For example, Dahan and colleagues (2006) found that even though buprenorphine exhibited gains in pain-relieving effects as they raised the dose in human volunteers, a ceiling effect was reached for respiratory depressant effects. Thus, they concluded that buprenorphine serves as an analgesic opioid drug that fails to cause significant impairments in breathing.

Review! Partial agonists have a lower efficacy for activating receptors than full agonists do. (Chapter 4.)

Pure opioid receptor antagonists act as full-receptor antagonists at μ opioid receptors. These drugs not only fail to produce opioid pharmacological effects but also inhibit opioid system activity by preventing endogenous opioids from binding to opioid receptors. They also counteract the effects produced by drugs acting as full or partial opioid receptor agonists. Physicians prescribe pure opioid receptor antagonists for treating opioid addiction (Fudala & Woody, 2002). The "From Actions to Effects" section describes this and other approaches for treating opioid addition.

The final type of an opioid drug is a mixed opioid receptor agonist–antagonist. **Mixed opioid receptor agonist–antagonists** exhibit agonist actions at some opioid receptors while exhibiting antagonist actions at other opioid receptors. Together, these actions limit the magnitude of opioid pharmacological effects. For example, the mixed opioid receptor agonist–antagonist *pentazocine (Talwin)* exhibits a ceiling effect for reducing pain (Shu et al., 2011). Many opioids were once classified as mixed receptor agonist–antagonists but have since been found to act through other mechanisms such as partial agonism or other receptors such as the recently discovered ORL-1 opioid receptor.

Buprenorphine is an opioid drug found to act through many mechanisms. First, as stated earlier, buprenorphine acts as a partial agonist for at μ opioid receptors. Second, buprenorphine is an antagonist for δ receptors. Third, it has as an active metabolite, norbuprenorphine, which acts as a full agonist for both μ and δ receptors.

A fourth mechanism may contribute to buprenorphine's ceiling effects for pain. Buprenorphine is an agonist for the ORL-1 receptor. Activation of the ORL-1 receptor counteracts the pharmacological effects produced by the activation of other opioid receptor types. Thus, ORL-1 receptor activation opposes the effects produced through μ and δ receptor activation, accounting for buprenorphine's limiting effects for pain (Lufty & Cowan, 2004).

Partial opioid receptor agonists Drugs that produce partial agonist actions at μ opioid receptors

Pure opioid receptor antagonists Drugs that act as full receptor antagonists at μ opioid receptors

Mixed opioid receptor agonist–antagonists Drugs that exhibit agonist actions at some opioid receptors while exhibiting antagonist actions at other opioid receptors

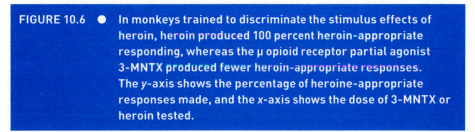

🔖 **Drug Profile: buprenorphine**	
Trade name:	Subutex
Mechanisms of action:	1. partial agonist for μ receptors
	2. antagonist for δ receptors
	3. active metabolite, norbuprenorphine, acts as agonist for μ and δ receptors
	4. agonist for ORL-1 receptors
Uses:	Used for treating opioid addiction and for pain

Different mechanisms of action produced by opioid receptors produce different discriminative stimulus effects (see Box 6.1 to review the drug-discrimination procedure). This was demonstrated in a study by Platt, Rowlett, Izenwasser, and Spealman (2004) using rhesus monkeys trained to discriminate the stimulus effects of heroin, a pure opioid receptor agonist (**Figure 10.6**). In these monkeys, full opioid receptor agonists produced heroin-like stimulus effects, whereas an experimental μ opioid receptor partial agonist called 3-MNTX produced weak heroin-like stimulus effects.

FIGURE 10.6 ● **In monkeys trained to discriminate the stimulus effects of heroin, heroin produced 100 percent heroin-appropriate responding, whereas the μ opioid receptor partial agonist 3-MNTX produced fewer heroin-appropriate responses. The *y*-axis shows the percentage of heroine-appropriate responses made, and the *x*-axis shows the dose of 3-MNTX or heroin tested.**

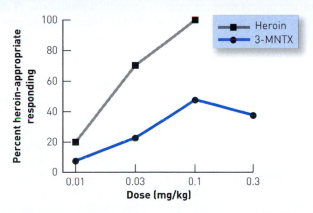

SOURCE: Data from Platt et al., 2004.

STOP & CHECK

1. An opioid drug with a ceiling effect for pain relief is likely a(n) _____.

2. Opioid receptors are G-protein–coupled receptors that produce _____ effects on neurons.

3. Should buprenorphine still be considered a representative drug for partial opioid receptor agonists?

1. partial opioid receptor agonist **2.** inhibitory **3.** Although buprenorphine is still classified as a representative of the partial opioid receptor agonist class of drugs, it exhibits many other actions that may alternatively account for its pharmacological effects. In particular, buprenorphine's ceiling effect can be accounted for not only through partial opioid receptor agonism but also through antagonism of δ receptors and activation of ORL-1 receptors.

Opioid System Interactions With Reward, Pain, and Stress Systems

Endogenous and exogenous opioids produce reinforcing effects by affecting dopamine and GABA neurotransmission. Opioids increase dopamine release primarily by binding to μ opioid receptors on GABA neurons in the ventral tegmental area. **Figure 10.7** shows the series of actions involved in this reward circuitry.

Review! The ventral tegmental area contains dopamine neurons, which send axons to the nucleus accumbens, other parts of the limbic system, and the cerebral cortex. (Chapter 3.)

First, opioids inhibit the activity of GABA neurons in the ventral tegmental area. By doing so, there is less GABA released in the ventral tegmental area to activate inhibitory GABA receptors on mesolimbic dopamine neurons. By removing this inhibition on dopamine neurons, the activity of dopamine neurons increases, leading to greater dopamine release in the nucleus accumbens (McBride, Murphy, & Ikemoto, 1999; Omelchenko & Sesack, 2010; Wise, 1989).

Second, opioids produce reinforcing effects through activating μ opioid receptors in the nucleus accumbens. The majority of μ opioid receptors in the nucleus accumbens are found on GABA neurons. Drugs that act as opioid agonists activate inhibitory opioid receptors, leading to an inhibition of these GABA neurons. Many of these GABA neurons project to the ventral tegmental area, where they may contribute to the inhibition of dopamine neurons as just described (Kalivas, Churchill, & Klitenick, 1993; McBride et al., 1999; Svingos, Moriwaki, Wang, Uhl, & Pickel, 1997; Wise, 1989).

Due to these interactions with reward pathways, antagonists for opioid receptors have been evaluated as treatments for substance addictions. For example, in amphetamine-addicted users, naltrexone has been shown to reduce cravings for amphetamine and decrease amphetamine use compared to placebo (Jayaram-Lindström, Hammarberg,

FIGURE 10.7 ● Opioids produce reinforcing effects by acting on dopamine and GABA neurons in either the ventral tegmental area or the nucleus accumbens. (1) This occurs through an opioid's activation of opioid receptors on GABA neurons in the ventral tegmental area, causing reduced GABA release and reduced activation of GABA receptors on dopamine neurons. (2) This in turn increases the activity of dopamine neurons. (3) This causes increased dopamine release in the nucleus accumbens, an action that increases reinforcing effects. (4) An opioid's activation of opioid receptors on nucleus accumbens GABA neurons causes a reduction in GABA neuron activity, an action associated with increased reinforcing effects.

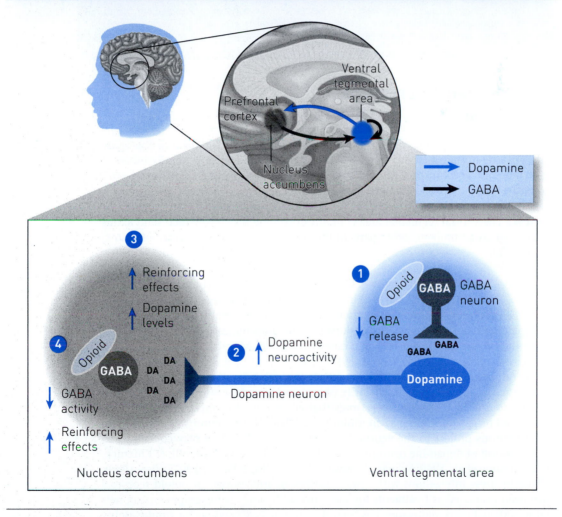

Beck, & Franck, 2008). We find similar data for naltrexone for tobacco smokers. In one study, during 12 weeks of naltrexone treatment, study participants reported fewer cravings to smoke and many quit smoking completely. Upon discontinuing naloxone treatment, smoking returned to pre-naloxone treatment levels (King et al., 2012).

Opioids also closely interact with pain signaling pathways to the brain, as shown in **Figure 10.8**. We can think of the communication of pain sensations in the nervous system, referred to as **nociception**, as a relay involving two pathways. The first pathway includes two types of axons, referred to as *Aδ fibers* and *C fibers,* that communicate nociceptive information from the source of a painful stimulus to the dorsal horn of the spinal cord. Within the dorsal horn, these pathways release the neurotransmitters glutamate and *substance P* at postsynaptic terminals on spinothalamic neurons. During inflammation or after suffering a trauma, enhanced pain sensitivity—called *hyperalgesia*—may occur because of a process of synaptic strengthening called *long-term potentiation*

Nociception
Communication of pain sensations in the nervous system

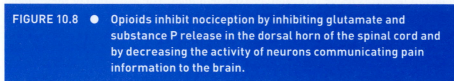

FIGURE 10.8 ● **Opioids inhibit nociception by inhibiting glutamate and substance P release in the dorsal horn of the spinal cord and by decreasing the activity of neurons communicating pain information to the brain.**

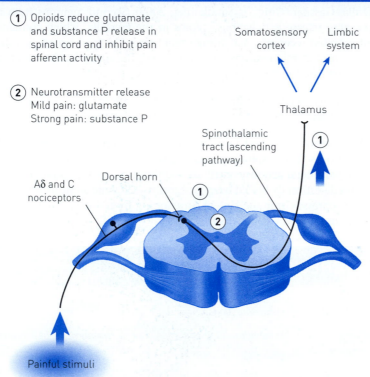

(1) Opioids reduce glutamate and substance P release in spinal cord and inhibit pain afferent activity

(2) Neurotransmitter release
Mild pain: glutamate
Strong pain: substance P

Somatosensory cortex

Limbic system

Thalamus

Spinothalamic tract (ascending pathway)

Aδ and C nociceptors

Dorsal horn

Painful stimuli

SOURCE: © Cengage Learning 2014.

(described in detail in Chapter 12) (Ikeda et al., 2006). This process results in greater pain signaling between the as Aδ and C fibers and the spinothalamic neurons.

Second, spinothalamic neurons send nociceptive information via an *ascending pathway* to the thalamus. The thalamus, in turn, distributes the information to the somatosensory cortex and two structures in the limbic system: the cingulate cortex and the amygdala. The somatosensory cortex processes the nociceptive information, while the cingulate cortex and amygdala produce emotional responses to pain and play a role in approach and avoidance behavior (Watkins, Milligan, & Maier, 2001; Willis & Westlund, 1997).

Review! The peripheral nervous system sends sensory information to the dorsal horn of the spinal cord, whereas motor information comes from the ventral horn of the spinal cord. (Chapter 2.)

Opioids weaken neurotransmission within these pain pathways. First, all four types of opioid receptors reside on C and Aδ axon terminals. The activation of these opioid receptors causes a reduction in glutamate and substance P release, thereby reducing pain signaling (Chen & Sommer, 2006; Ossipov et al., 2004). Chronic administration of opioids appears to produce long-term potentiation as a compensatory action for these inhibitory effects. Similar to long-term potentiation seen with inflammation and trauma, long-term potentiation causes enhanced pain sensitivity when opioid use ceases (Drdla, Gassner, Gingl, & Sandkuhler, 2009). Second, neurons from the periaqueductal gray release endogenous opioids in the medulla, which contains a high density of μ opioid receptors. Activating opioid receptors in the medulla inhibits the activity of spinothalamic neurons passing through the medulla, thus reducing nociceptive information flow to the thalamus (Ossipov et al., 2004).

Review! Periaqueductal gray surrounds the cerebral aqueduct, a conduit for cerebrospinal fluid connecting the third and fourth ventricles in the brain. (Chapter 2.)

Opioid receptors are found outside the nervous system as well, including the immune, cardiovascular, respiratory, and digestive systems (Stein, Schafer, & Hassan, 1995). These peripheral actions contribute to inhibition of respiration, cardiovascular function, and digestion by opioid receptor agonists. Chronic administration of an opioid agonist suppresses immune system functioning by reducing the reproduction of immune system cells (Roy & Loh, 1996).

STOP & CHECK

1. What effect do opioids have on GABA neurons?

2. What effect do opioids have on Aδ fibers and C fibers, which relay pain signals to the spinal cord?

1. We find inhibitory opioid receptors on GABA neurons; when the opioids bind to these receptors, the activity of GABA neurons decreases (i.e., inhibitory effects). **2.** Opioids bind to inhibitory opioid receptors on these neurons, which reduces pain signaling in the form of reduced glutamate and substance P release from these neurons.

Opioid Reinforcing and Analgesic Effects

Opioid Receptor Agonists and Reinforcing Effects

The subjective effects of an opioid receptor agonist occur during four phases (**Table 10.4**). The *rush* phase is the initial and rapid onset of euphoria that occurs within seconds of an intravenous injection of heroin or other opioid that readily crosses the blood-brain barrier. The rush is a key achievement for opioid recreational use. As the rush subsides, a second phase called the *high* sets in, which is generally characterized by feelings of joy and ease. A third phase is occasionally referred to as a *nod* and is characterized by calm, disinterest, and unawareness of surroundings. During the nod phase, anxiety is lifted and users may doze in a light sleep. Although the nod is different from euphoria, many users find this relaxed state to be quite enjoyable. Finally, the fourth phase is referred to as *straight* and consists of a period of normalcy between craving an opioid and feeling the euphoric or other positive effects of an opioid (Agar, 1974).

Based on surveys in humans, users report a number of positive subjective effects from opioid receptor agonists. In one such study, Preston, Bigelow, and Liebson (1988) assessed the subjective effects of the opioid receptor agonist hydromorphone by using questionnaires to rate the degree of *liking*, *high*, *good effects*, and other terms associated with a positive subjective experience in study participants currently taking methadone for opioid addiction. When asked to rate these effects some minutes after hydromorphone administration, all participants rated hydromorphone as highly enjoyable, according to these scales. The participants also were surveyed after receiving an injection of the opioid receptor antagonist naloxone. After this treatment combination, the participants no longer recorded increases in liking, high, or good effects; instead they reported bad effects, likely because of naloxone triggering opioid withdrawal effects (**Figure 10.9**).

Self-administration procedures in animals also indicate that opioid receptor agonists produce potent reinforcing effects. Further, the duration of these reinforcing effects alters drug-seeking behavior. A self-administration study conducted by Panlilio and Schindler (2000) demonstrated these properties (**Figure 10.10**). In this study, rats were assessed on a progressive ratio schedule for intravenous injections of an opioid. In one group of rats, the opioid was heroin; in another group of rats, the opioid was

Phase	Description
rush	initial and rapid onset of euphoria
high	feelings of joy and ease
nod	calm, disinterest, and unawareness of surroundings
straight	period of normalcy between craving an opioid and feeling the euphoric or other positive effects of an opioid

TABLE 10.4 ● Subjective Effects of Opioid Agonists

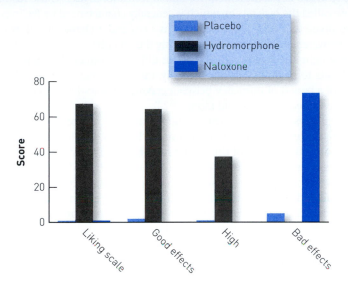

FIGURE 10.9 ● Study participants currently in treatment for opioid addiction were asked to a rate the subjective effects (liking the effects, good effects, feeling a high, or bad effects) of the opioid agonist hydromorphone, the opioid antagonist naloxone, and placebo conditions. Respondents endorsed positive effects for hydromorphone and bad effects for naloxone.

remifentanil (Ultiva). Remifentanil exhibits similar actions to heroin, except that remifentanil has an elimination half-life of only 40 seconds!

Both heroin and remifentanil achieved similar break points in this study, but the remifentanil rats reached the break point much sooner than the heroin rats because of a much shorter post-reinforcement pause during responding for remifentanil. Because the reinforcing effect of remifentanil was short lived, the rats quickly returned to lever pressing after every injection, thus shortening the post-reinforcement pause. Heroin-treated rats had longer periods of time between receiving an injection and when they resumed lever pressing.

The subjective effects of opioids readily pair with environmental stimuli, which researchers demonstrate using a conditioned place preference procedure (see **Box 10.1**). This procedure is often used to study the reinforcing effects of opioids, such as heroin. For example, Spyraki, Fibiger, and Phillips (1983) used a conditioned place preference procedure to study the effects of heroin administration in rats. A single dose of heroin was paired with one compartment of a shuttle box, and the heroin vehicle was paired with the opposite compartment for 4 days each. After pairing, rats spent significantly more time in the heroin-paired environment than the vehicle-paired environment (**Figure 10.11**). A preference for the drug compartment implies an association between the compartment and heroin's reinforcing effects.

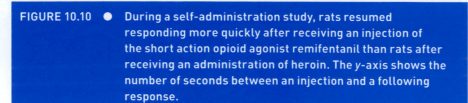

FIGURE 10.10 ● During a self-administration study, rats resumed responding more quickly after receiving an injection of the short action opioid agonist remifentanil than rats after receiving an administration of heroin. The y-axis shows the number of seconds between an injection and a following response.

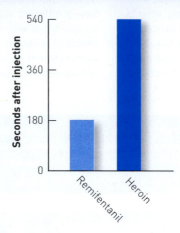

SOURCE: Data from Panlilio & Schindler, 2000.

Review! A *vehicle* is the solvent in which a drug is dissolved. Functionally, a vehicle is a placebo. (Chapter 1.)

Researchers have also found a role for glutamate NMDA receptors in the reinforcing effects of opioids using the conditioned place preference procedure. In a study conducted by Popik and Kolasiewicz (1999) a conditioned place preference for morphine was established in rats (**Figure 10.12**). In the test session, in which rats were given the choice to move freely between the morphine- and vehicle-paired compartments, these researchers treated rats with a glutamate NMDA receptor antagonist called NPC17742. NPC17742 caused rats to have a significantly lower preference for the morphine-paired compartment. This reduction in preference for the morphine-paired compartment also occurred when NPC17742 was directly injected into the ventral tegmental area or the nucleus accumbens. Because this compound functioned as an antagonist for NMDA receptors, these researchers concluded that NMDA receptor agonism may, therefore, facilitate morphine's reinforcing effects. These findings coincide with neurobiological models of addiction described in Chapter 5.

Review! During drug addiction, glutamate levels are elevated in mesolimbic dopamine structures, including the nucleus accumbens and ventral tegmental area. Increased glutamate levels lead to increased activation of glutamate NMDA receptors. (Chapter 5.)

BOX 10.1 CONDITIONED PLACE PREFERENCE

During a *conditioned place preference* procedure, an organism associates a unique environment with a drug's reinforcing effects. Researchers typically conduct this procedure with rats or mice using a shuttle box. Most shuttle boxes have two or three connected compartments with doorways between each compartment, as shown in Figure 1. Researchers design each compartment to have a different appearance (e.g., white walls versus black walls), floor texture (e.g., horizontal bars versus a wire grid), and odor in the compartment waste pans (e.g., pine shavings versus cellulose bedding).

FIGURE 1 ● After pairing different parts of a shuttle box with either drug or vehicle (top row), researchers test for a conditioned place preference by placing a subject in a neutral part of the box and allowing the subject to freely explore the shuttle-box chambers.

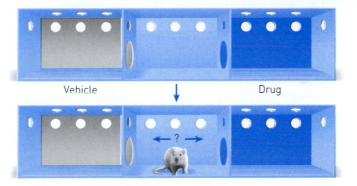

Vehicle   Drug

SOURCE: © Cengage Learning 2014.

A conditioned place preference develops over the course of several pairings with a reinforcing drug. Generally, researchers devote three to five pairing sessions with a drug's reinforcing effects and a specific shuttle-box compartment. Other pairing sessions occur with the drug's vehicle and the opposite compartment. After drug- and vehicle-pairing sessions, researchers place a trained animal into the shuttle box with all compartment doors raised, allowing the animal free access to any compartment. A conditioned place preference is shown when rats spend significantly more time in the drug-paired compartment than in the vehicle-paired compartment (Prus, James, & Rosecrans, 2009).

To demonstrate the process of conditioned place preference, Mucha, van der Kooy, O'Shaughnessy, and Bucenieks (1982) conducted four pairing sessions with an intravenous morphine or saline injection given 4 minutes before the session. Each compartment contained different environment stimuli. After conducting four daily sessions each with morphine and saline, rats were placed in the chamber without an injection and allowed to explore both compartments. Rats spent significantly more time in the morphine-associated compartment than the saline-associated compartment (**Figure 2**).

Next, Mucha and colleagues (1982) conducted the same procedure with the noxious substance lithium chloride. After several pairings, rats spent significantly more time in the saline-paired compartment (**Figure 3**). In this case, the researchers demonstrated a *conditioned place aversion*. During a conditioned place aversion procedure, an organism associates a unique environment with a drug's aversive effects. In this case, animals avoid the drug-paired side.

FIGURE 2 ● **Rats spent significantly more time in a morphine-paired compartment than a saline-paired compartment, demonstrating a conditioned place preference. The *y*-axis represents time spent in a compartment, and the *x*-axis represents the dose of morphine administered. Light blue bars refer to the morphine compartment.**

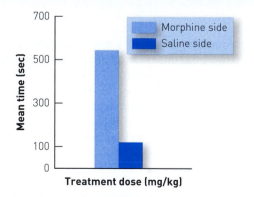

SOURCE: Mucha et al., 1982.

(Continued)

(Continued)

> **FIGURE 3** ● Rats spent significantly more time in a saline-paired compartment than a lithium-chloride–paired compartment, demonstrating a conditioned place aversion. The *y*-axis represents time spent in a compartment. Light blue bars refer to the lithium-chloride compartment.

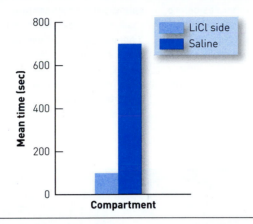

SOURCE: Mucha et al., 1982.

Self-administration studies also reveal a role for glutamate in the reinforcing effects of an opioid. For example, LaLumiere and Kalivas (2008) assessed the effects of a reinstatement period in rats that learned to self-administer heroin. After initiating reinstatement with an administration of heroin, microdialysis procedures revealed that nucleus accumbens concentrations of glutamate increased. After finding these changes in glutamate levels, these researchers next found that inhibiting glutamate neurons that innervate the nucleus accumbens prevented heroin reinstatement. Interpreting these findings in the context of drug addiction models presented in chapter 5, inhibition of glutamate neurotransmission may reduce a wanting state for heroin.

Review! Reinstatement consists of a return to drug self-administration responding that usually occurs after an administration of the drug, presentation of a stimulus associated with the drug, or the causation of stress. (Chapter 5.)

Review! Wanting occurs when stimuli associated with drug use command attention and elicit a salient motivational state toward pursuing the drug. The most salient stimulus is the drug itself. (Chapter 5.)

FIGURE 10.11 ●   After pairing sessions were completed in a conditioned place preference procedure, rats preferred the shuttle-box compartment associated with heroin's pharmacological effects compared to the compartment not associated with these effects. The *y*-axis shows the percentage of time spent in the heroin-paired compartment. The *x*-axis shows the doses of heroin tested; a zero (0) dose refers to vehicle.

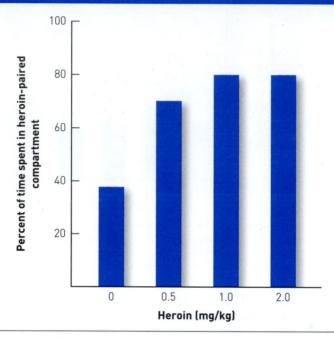

SOURCE: Adapted from Springer Science+Business Media: Spyraki, C., Fibiger, H. C., & Phillips, A. G. (1983). Attenuation of heroin reward in rats by disruption of the mesolimbic dopamine system. *Psychopharmacology*, 79(2), 278–283. doi: 10.1007/bf00427827, p. 6.

Opioid Analgesic Effects

As noted previously, opioids have traditionally been used for treating pain. Today they remain the most effective medications for this purpose. Morphine, the key constituent in opium, as described previously, represents the gold standard for opioid analgesics, although physicians frequently prescribe other μ opioid receptor agonists, including oxycodone and fentanyl, for severe pain management (Gomes et al., 2011). However, studies find that opioid analgesics lack significant efficacy for *neuropathic pain*, which is derived from damage to pain-signaling neurons, or *idiopathic pain*, which consists of pain derived from an unknown organic cause (Arnér & Meyerson, 1988).

Opioid Drugs and Other Therapeutic Effects

Beyond analgesia, the medicinal value of opioids is derived from other effects in the body. The inhibitory effects of opioid receptors in the intestinal tract produce constipation and provide an effective and important treatment for diarrhea. This has long been

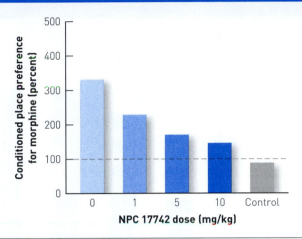

FIGURE 10.12 ● Blockade of glutamate NMDA receptors using the NMDA receptor antagonist NPC 17742 prevents the recall of the morphine preference for one side of a shuttle-box compartment. Glutamate release is an important contributor to opioid addiction.

SOURCE: Adapted from Springer Science+Business Media: Popik, P., & Kolasiewicz, W. (1999). Mesolimbic NMDA receptors are implicated in the expression of conditioned morphine reward. *Naunyn-Schmiedeberg's Archives of Pharmacology, 359*(4), 288–294. doi: 10.1007/pl00005354, p. 7.

a key therapeutic use of opium, and opioid drugs are still used for this purpose today. For example, morphine is used in hospitals to reduce diarrhea associated with severe flu or other diseases (De Schepper, Cremonini, Park, & Camilleri, 2004; Shook, Lemcke, Gehrig, Hruby, & Burks, 1989).

By activating inhibitory opioid receptors in the medulla, opioids also suppress the cough reflex. Therapeutically, opioids remain a highly effective cough suppressant. The natural opioid codeine is still used in prescription-strength cough syrups (Bolser, 2006). Opioids also constrict pupils, which occurs even in low light conditions. This effect, called **miosis**, is a direct effect of opioid receptor activation and occurs at analgesic doses (Ravnborg, Jensen, Jensen, & Holk, 1987).

Opioid Overdose and Respiratory Function

Opioid overdose comes in the form of severe respiratory depression, accompanied by weakness, weak pulse, bluish color to lips and skin, inability to talk, and, potentially, unconsciousness. Much of these overdose effects derive from impaired oxygen delivery to body because of inhibited breathing. In the United States in 2014, we find approximately 25,000 deaths occurring because of opioid overdose, a nearly threefold increase since 2001 (National Center for Health Statistics, 2015).

Some respiratory depression also occurs at therapeutically effective doses for prescribed opioids, but is not dangerous unless an individual suffers from a respiratory disorder such as emphysema. We also find these effects magnified by other depressant drugs such as

Miosis Pupil constriction that can occur after opioid administration

Opioid overdose Overdose from opioid use in the form of severe respiratory depression, accompanied by weakness, weak pulse, bluish color to lips and skin, inability to talk, and, potentially, unconsciousness

alcohol and benzodiazepines (Horlocker et al., 2009). Respiratory depression results from inhibitory effects in the medulla, the same area responsible for cough suppression (Etches, Sandler, & Daley, 1989). The typical emergency treatment for opioid overdose begins by determining whether ventilation support will suffice in restoring proper breathing; if not, medical staff will next administer an opioid receptor antagonist, such as naloxone or naltrexone, in an effort to counteract the effects of the opioid (Sporer, 1999).

Tolerance and Dependence With Chronic Opioid Use

Tolerance occurs with all opioid pharmacological effects during repeated opioid use. During chronic administration, users develop a physiological dependence that arises from compensatory actions that counteract an opioid drug's acute effects. These compensatory effects account for the physical withdrawal symptoms from opioids. For example, because opioids produce constipation, the related withdrawal effect is diarrhea. Opioids reduce pain, so the related withdrawal effect is increased pain sensitivity (Gossop, Bradley, & Phillips, 1987; Ossipov et al., 2004). Users also develop a tolerance for the reinforcing effects of opioids, resulting in the use of escalating doses to achieve desirable effects. Psychological withdrawal effects can include drug cravings and depressed mood (Gossop et al., 1987). **Table 10.5** lists these and other withdrawal effects from opioid use.

STOP & CHECK

1. The initial and rapid euphoria produced by an opioid is referred to as a(n) _____ .

2. Which neurotransmitter plays a role in addictive features of opioid use such as reinstatement and relapse?

3. In ancient times, opium was considered effective for many different ailments. Why do you suppose this was the case?

1. rush **2.** Glutamate. **3.** Opium improved many symptoms associated with severe illness, including pain relief, diarrhea, and cough.

TABLE 10.5 ● Opioid Pharmacological Effects and Withdrawal Symptoms

Acute Pharmacological Effect	Withdrawal Symptom
Analgesia	Pain sensitivity
Constipation	Diarrhea
Decreased blood pressure	Increased blood pressure
Euphoria	Dysphoria and depression
Hypothermia	Hyperthermia
Relaxation	Restlessness
Respiratory depression	Hyperventilation

SOURCE: Based on Brecher, 1972.

From Actions to Effects: Pharmacological Approaches for Treating Opioid Addiction

Detoxification (or detoxication)
Process that uses an opioid agonist or antagonist to reduce withdrawal symptoms

Long-term opioid detoxification
Detoxification process that lasts approximately 180 days and occurs by prescribing an opioid receptor agonist or a partial opioid receptor agonist to replace the illicit opioid drug.

Methadone clinics
Specialized clinics that prescribe and dispense methadone to patients in treatment for opioid addiction

Pharmacological treatments for opioid addiction include detoxification and the management of comorbid disorders. **Detoxification** (also referred as *detoxication* or "detox") is the first step of an opioid cessation program. Detoxification typically involves using an opioid agonist or antagonist to reduce withdrawal symptoms. Detoxification procedures vary in time course, ranging from long-term detoxification to ultra rapid detoxification (**Table 10.6**).

Long-term opioid detoxification lasts approximately 180 days and occurs by prescribing an opioid receptor agonist (such as methadone or LAAM) or a partial opioid receptor agonist (such as buprenorphine) to replace the illicit opioid drug. These therapeutic opioid drugs prevent serious withdrawal symptoms, have long-lasting effects, and engender weak or no euphoria and other positive subjective effects (Gossop et al., 1987). Long-term detoxification occurs outside of hospital settings.

In the United States the Drug Addiction Treatment Act allows doctors to prescribe schedule III, IV, and V narcotic drugs to treat opioid addiction. Thus, doctors can prescribe buprenorphine, a schedule III drug, from their offices, meaning that pharmacies can dispense this medication to a patient. This makes buprenorphine more available to patients that methadone, a schedule II drug. Instead, prescribing and dispensing of methadone occurs in specialized clinics, generally referred to as **methadone clinics**. Methadone clinics must abide by regulations the FDA and the DEA for handling and dispensing methadone. These regulations include drug-testing clients for illicit substance use and requiring that clients have frequent contact with medical staff, counselors, and social workers.

Short-term detoxification programs last as long as 30 days and usually use opioid receptor agonists such as methadone and LAAM. Short-term detoxification

TABLE 10.6 ● Detoxification Programs

Detoxification Type	Opioid Receptor Treatment	Approximate Length	Facility	Withdrawal Symptoms
Long-term	Agonist or partial agonist	180 days	Outpatient clinic; methadone clinic	Mild
Short-term	Agonist or partial agonist	30 days	Inpatient	Moderate. May require treatment.
Rapid	Antagonist	10 days	Inpatient	Severe. Requires treatment.
Ultra-rapid	Antagonist	2 days	Inpatient hospital setting	Severe. Requires anesthesia.

SOURCE: © Cengage Learning 2014.

is more aggressive than long-term detoxification and includes moderate withdrawal symptoms. These programs may be entirely conducted in an in-patient treatment facility.

Rapid detoxification lasts as long as 10 days, and ultra-rapid detoxification lasts as many as 2 days. Rapid detoxification is conducted in hospital or in-patient treatment facilities, and ultra-rapid detoxification is conducted in hospital settings. Both programs utilize an opioid receptor antagonist such as *naltrexone* or *naloxone*. Naltrexone and naloxone provide long-lasting occupancy of μ opioid receptors, preventing activation of these receptors by opioid receptor agonists such as heroin. These antagonist actions increase the severity of withdrawal symptoms but also shorten the total duration of withdrawal symptoms (Loimer, Schmid, Presslich, & Lenz, 1989).

Ultra-rapid detoxification uses high doses of an opioid receptor antagonist that further worsens and shortens withdrawal symptoms. Patients must be anesthetized during the most severe withdrawal effects, which occur during the first several hours of treatment. After this, the withdrawal symptoms taper off over the course of 1–2 days.

By blocking opioid receptors, the body quickly adapts to the lack of opioid receptor activation. Thus, even though withdrawal symptoms are severe during rapid or ultra rapid detoxification, they do not last as long as normal withdrawal symptoms. Moreover, many withdrawal symptoms such as diarrhea and pain sensitization are treated by medications such as *Imodium*, an antidiarrheal medication that has a small amount of the opioid agonist loperamide, or acetaminophen, an analgesic (Dupont et al. 1990). Drugs that act as α_2 adrenoceptor agonists, such as *clonidine*, can be used to reduce hypertension, restlessness, insomnia, hostility, and other peripheral withdrawal symptoms. *Benzodiazepine* drugs can also reduce anxiety, hostility, and restlessness during opioid detoxification.

Individuals addicted to opioids may have other psychological disorders to treat, including depression or another addiction. In particular, the majority of individuals addicted to opioids have an antisocial personality disorder, and many also have borderline personality disorder (Darke, Williamson, Ross, Teesson, & Lynskey, 2004). Other common comorbid conditions include HIV infection, hepatitis B and other medical conditions related to shared needle use or unprotected sex (Shapatava, Nelson, Tsertsvadze, & Del Rio, 2006). The risk of these medical conditions is a major rationale for "harm reduction" programs, which provide safe alternatives to risky health choices associated with illicit opioid use, including clean needle access, medical testing, and medical treatment.

As described in previous chapters, opioid and other drug addiction treatment programs offer limited success. During detoxification, many patients either discontinue treatment or return to drug use after treatment ends. As presented in Chapter 5, follow-ups 5 years later of patients who underwent methadone treatment revealed that most patients had resumed regular use of an opioid drug (Hubbard, Craddock, & Anderson, 2003). Other follow-up studies revealed that those who remain drug free tend to be married, better employed, better educated, and psychologically healthy (Simpson & Marsh, 1986). Although a pharmacological treatment may weaken withdrawal symptoms, medications alone may be insufficient for providing improvements in these areas of social adjustment.

Short-term opioid detoxification
Detoxification process that lasts as long as 30 days and usually uses opioid receptor agonists.

Rapid detoxification
Detoxification process lasting as long as 10 days and using opioid antagonist administration in a treatment facility

Ultra-rapid opioid detoxification
Detoxification process lasting as long as 2 days and using opioid antagonist administration in a hospital setting

STOP & CHECK

1. During long- or short-term opioid detoxification programs, medications are provided into order to reduce the severity of _____ symptoms.

2. What type of drug is used during rapid opioid detoxification?

1. withdrawal 2. Opioid antagonist.

Chapter Summary

Opioid drugs are powerful pain-relieving and reinforcing substances used for medical and recreational purposes. Opioids are found naturally in poppy plants and can be synthesized in laboratories. Opioid drugs can be inhaled, ingested orally, or injected intravenously. Endogenous opioid neurotransmitters are peptides that bind to μ, δ, κ, and nociceptin receptors.

The reinforcing effects of opioids derive from elevating dopamine levels and reducing GABA neuron activity in the nucleus accumbens. Opioids inhibit pain sensation by reducing glutamate and substance P neurotransmitter release in the spinal cord and by inhibiting pain

afferents to the brain. Tolerance develops quickly to opioid pharmacological effects, preventing long-term therapeutic use and requiring greater doses for recreational use.

Opioid addiction is maintained by avoiding withdrawal symptoms and achieving reinforcing effects. Detoxification programs address these components of addiction by reducing withdrawal symptoms. Long-term detoxification programs utilize a safer replacement for the illicit opioid drug, whereas rapid detoxification programs shorten withdrawal symptoms by using an opioid receptor antagonist. Treatment programs also address comorbid medical conditions.

Key Terms

Opioids 300
Narcotic 300
Naturally occurring
    opioids 301
Semisynthetic opioids 302
Fully synthetic opioids 303
Laudanum 304
propeptide 307
G-protein–coupled inwardly
    rectifying K⁺ channel
    (GIRK) 310

Pure opioid receptor
    agonists 310
Partial opioid receptor
    agonists 311
Pure opioid receptor
    antagonists 311
Mixed opioid receptor agonist-
    antagonists 311
Nociception 315
Miosis 324
Opioid overdose 324

Detoxification
    (or detoxication) 326
Long-term opioid
    detoxification 326
Methadone clinics 326
Short-term opioid
    detoxification 327
Rapid detoxification 327
Ultra-rapid opioid
    detoxification 327

Visit the Student Study Site at **study.sagepub.com/prus2e** to access additional study tools, including eFlashcards, web quizzes, video resources, web resources, SAGE journal articles, and more.

11

Cannabinoids

SHOULD MEDICAL MARIJUANA BE LEGAL?

Both opponents and proponents of legalized medical marijuana have strong opinions. Those who favor medical marijuana argue that, as an herbal remedy, marijuana offers therapeutic benefits for many chronic conditions, including pain, glaucoma, and even cancer. At the same time, opponents argue that patients should instead take medications approved by the Food and Drug Administration, such as Marinol, that act like key pharmacologically active compounds found in marijuana.

Most patients prefer marijuana to drugs such as Marinol, suggesting that marijuana may be

(Continued)

(Continued)

more effective and better tolerated. However, opponents argue that medical marijuana is just a means of getting high. Given the increasing trend by U.S. states to legalize medical marijuana, this debate will not likely end anytime soon. This chapter considers both the recreational and medical uses of marijuana, including considerations about the tolerability of marijuana-like drugs such as Marinol.

SOURCE: From Marmor, 1998, and Clark, Capuzzi, and Fick, 2011.

Cannabinoids
Substances that act on cannabinoid receptors

Cannabis Three varieties of plants that contain naturally occurring psychoactive cannabinoids

Cannabinoids consist of drugs that act on cannabinoid receptors in the nervous system and elsewhere in the body. The term *cannabinoid* comes from cannabis plants, which contain the naturally occurring types of cannabinoid compounds. **Cannabis** plants come in three varieties: (1) *Cannabis sativa,* the most commonly used; (2) *Cannabis indica*; and (3) *Cannabis ruderalis.* These plants are also referred to as *hemp,* although the name refers technically to fibers of a plant and thus can describe many different types of plants.

Phytocannabinoids
Cannabinoids derived from cannabis plants

Δ⁹-tetrahydro cannabinol (Δ⁹-THC)
Key psychoactive substance in cannabis

The flowers and leaves of cannabis plants contain *trichomes,* small hair-like structures with glands that release a resin containing cannabinoids referred to as **phytocannabinoids**. Phytocannabinoids include cannabis's key psychoactive ingredient, **Δ^9-tetrahydrocannabinol (Δ^9-THC)**, as well as other compounds such as Δ^8-tetrahydrocannabinol (Δ^8-THC), *cannabidiol,* cannabinol, N-alklamide, and B-caryophyllene (Gertsch, Pertwee, & Di Marzo, 2010).

The composition of the compounds in cannabis varies, depending on the variety of cannabis, the region in which it is grown, the plant's level of maturation, and the part of the plant sampled. *Cannabis sativa* plants contain the greatest concentrations of Δ^9-THC relative to other varieties, and *Cannabis indica* tends to have a relatively greater concentration of cannabidiol compared to Δ^9-THC, although Δ^9-THC concentrations can vary considerably (Hillig & Mahlberg, 2004). Trichomes appear mostly on the leaves and flowers of cannabis plants, yielding relatively higher concentrations of Δ^9-THC than other phytocannabinoids. As shown in **Table 11.1**, the concentration of Δ^9-THC in *Cannabis sativa* increases with the maturation of the plant (Bruci et al., 2012).

Marijuana (or marihuana) Consists of dried cannabis flowers, leaves, and stems compressed and rolled for smoking

Marijuana (or **marihuana**) consists of dried cannabis flowers, leaves, and stems compressed and rolled into cigarettes for smoking. Slang terms for marijuana include *weed, pot, reefer,* and *grass.* The most commonly known term for cannabis, *pot,* may derive from a Mexican slang term for marijuana, *potiguaya* (Booth, 2005).

TABLE 11.1 ● Phytocannabinoid Composition of *Cannabis Sativa* Leaves at Different Stages of Maturation

Phytocannabinoid	Δ^9-THC (%)	Cannabidiol (%)	Cannabinol (%)
June	0.2	0.1	0.1
August	7.1	1.0	0.7

SOURCE: Data from Bruci et al., 2012.

The Δ^9-THC content in marijuana cigarettes has increased from 1 to 3% during the 1960s and 1970s for traditional cigarettes (referred to as *reefer*) to 6 to 20 percent for modern cigarettes (referred to as *joints*) (Ashton, 2001; Cascini, Aiello, & Di Tanna, 2012) (see **Table 11.2** for Δ^9-THC content in common cannabis products). The greater Δ^9-THC content in modern marijuana cigarettes comes as a result of different cultivation methods and using types and subspecies more potent in Δ^9-THC content, including *sinsemilla* (a nonpollinated female cannabis plant) and *skunk weed* (selectively bred strains of cannabis), along with using hydroponics to facilitate plant growth (Ashton, 2001).

E-cigarette technologies provide a modern means for using cannabis (see Chapter 7 for an overview of e-cigarette components). Unlike nicotine e-cigarettes, the liquid cartridge in this case includes Δ^9-THC and possibly other components found in cannabis, such as *cannabidiol*. Cannabis e-cigarettes may provide a less toxic means of using cannabis because of reduced exposure to other chemicals released from burning cannabis plant material (Giroud, de Cesare, Berthet, Varlet, Concha-Lozano, & Favrat, 2015).

Another form of cannabis use is referred to as *dabbing*. **Dabbing** consists of inhaling vapors emitted from a flame-heated hashish oil and butane mixture (the "dab") that was dabbed onto the end of a glass or titanium rod. The user normally

Dabbing Inhaling vapors emitted from a flame-heated hashish oil and butane mixture (the "dab") that was dabbed onto the end of a glass or titanium rod

TABLE 11.2 ● THC Content in Cannabis Products

Product	THC Content
Marijuana reefer (1960s–1970s)	1–3%
Marijuana joint	6–20%
Hashish	10–20%
Hashish oil	15–30%

SOURCE: Ashton, 2001.

heats the dab using a blow torch. The vapors release from the dab, after heating, include Δ^9-THC and other products from mixture or heated metal (Loflin & Earleywine, 2014).

Hashish Condensed preparation of cannabis that primarily contains the trichome resins from the plant

Hashish consists of a condensed, hardened preparation of cannabis that primarily contains the dried trichome resins and other parts of the plant. Given this, hashish provides a higher concentration of Δ^9-THC, ranging from 10 to 20 percent. Even higher concentrations occur in oil extracted from hashish, typically referred to as *hash oil*, which can range from 15 to 30 percent and occasionally as high as 65 percent (Adams & Martin, 1996; Ashton, 2001).

Herbal marijuana alternatives (or synthetic marijuana) Laboratory-synthesized cannabinoid drugs

In addition to the forms of cannabis just described, we find a recent emergence of herbal marijuana alternatives, which are commonly referred to as *synthetic marijuana*. **Herbal marijuana alternatives** (or **synthetic marijuana**) such as K2 and Spice contain synthesized cannabinoid drugs, such as the compounds *WIN52212-2*, JWH-018, and JWH-073 (Logan, Reinhold, Xu & Diamond, 2012; Seely et al. 2013). We also find, however, these terms for herbal marijuana alternatives applied to a substance to which a user adds THC. A popular type of herbal marijuana alternative involves spraying a synthetic cannabinoid compound on herbs, referred to an *herbal incense*, that a user then smokes like marijuana. A user may apply the substance on tobacco to smoke as well (Hu, Primack, Barnett, & Cook, 2011). Users may also inhale vapors from an herbal marijuana alternative via an e-cigarette, as described for cannabis and referred to in this case as a **liquid incense** or **cannabinoid-enhanced electronic liquid** (Giroud et al. 2015).

Herbal incense Herbal marijuana alternative that involves smoking herbs or tobacco sprayed with a synthetic cannabinoid

🔖 *Drug Profile:* WIN52212-2	
Street name	K2, Spice (names applied to others as well)
Properties	WIN52212-2 is a synthetic cannabinoid receptor agonist
Uses	Developed by researchers to study cannabinoid system, but now also used as a substance of abuse

Liquid incense (or cannabinoid-enhanced electronic liquid) Vapors emitting from a synthetic cannabinoid liquid using an e-cigarette

Much like bath salts (see Chapter 6), sellers market herbal marijuana alternatives for seemingly benign purposes such as potpourri or incense. Herbal marijuana alternatives acting as ligands for cannabinoid receptors emerged from scientific research endeavoring to develop highly selective drugs to serve as tools for learning about the brain's endocannabinoid system (discussed later in this chapter). Because these are experimental compounds, there remain a paucity of findings about their pharmacological effects, although many reports suggest that herbal marijuana alternatives exhibit different properties, such as psychostimulant or hallucinogenic effects, than traditional cannabis preparations (Rosenbaum, Carreiro, & Babu, 2012).

In the United States, as previously noted, the Drug Enforcement Administration (DEA) has classified cannabis products and herbal marijuana alternatives as schedule

I controlled substances. The DEA also classifies Δ^9-THC as a schedule I substance, although it classifies the prescription Δ^9-THC, known as *dronabinol (Marinol)*, as a schedule III controlled substance. The DEA permanently added herbal marijuana alternatives as schedule I controlled substances in 2012 (**Table 11.3**).

🕭 **Drug Profile: dronabinol**	
Trade name	Marinol
Properties	Agonist for cannabinoid CB1 receptors
Uses	Approved for treating nausea and vomiting during chemotherapy

TABLE 11.3 ● Controlled Substances Schedule for Selected Cannabinoid Compounds

Drug	Controlled Substance Schedule
Cannabis	I
Dronabinol (Marinol; synthetic Δ^9-THC)	III
Tetrahydrocannabinol (any form of THC, including Δ^9-THC and Δ^8-THC)	I
Herbal marijuana alternatives (e.g., WIN52212-2)	I

SOURCE: Adapted from the Controlled Substances Schedule found at the DEA site, http://www.deadiversion.usdoj.gov/schedules/index.html.

Marijuana is one of the most commonly used illicit substances in the world. According to the World Health Organization (2012), approximately 2.5 percent of the world's population consumes cannabis on a regular basis. In 2014, an estimated 22.2 million Americans age 12 and older reported being current marijuana users, making this the most illicitly used substance in the United States. This also represents an increase from past years, primarily because of greater use among those 26 and older (Center for Behavioral Health Statistics and Quality, 2015). These rates do include those purportedly using marijuana for medical purposes, which is not recognized in surveys conducted by the U.S. government. Based on surveys currently available (Lynne-Landsman, Livingston, & Wagenaar, 2013) medical marijuana laws do not appear to have caused increased marijuana use among adolescents.

Solid data on prevalence rates of herbal marijuana alternatives use is presently lacking. In a survey of college students in 2010, Hu and colleagues (2011) estimated

that 8 percent have tried an herbal marijuana alternative. Based on surveys conducted in 2014, an estimated 5 percent of 12th graders have used an herbal marijuana alternative in the past year (National Institute on Drug Abuse, 2015). Some evidence suggests an increased use of these substances. For example, over a 3-day period, 41 individuals "experienced serious medical reactions" to herbal marijuana alternative products described as 'Bubblegum Flavor' or 'Smacked!' in Manchester, New Hampshire, causing the state governor to declare a state of emergency (Hassan, 2014). In addition, during a 2-week period in 2015, New York state hospitals reported 160 patients brought in for poisoning from products identified as Spice or K2 (New York State, 2015).

STOP & CHECK

1. A preparation of *cannabis sativa* consisting mostly of dried leaves and stems is called _____.

2. The primary psychoactive ingredient in cannabis is _____.

3. _____ is a condensed form of cannabis consisting mainly of trichome resins.

1. marijuana 2. Δ⁹-THC 3. Hashish

Historical Use of Cannabis

Like other psychoactive plants, cannabis has an ancient history. Some of the earliest records find cannabis used for medical purposes in ancient China. In 2737 B.C., Emperor Shen-Nung is said to have recommended cannabis resin for "female weakness, gout, rheumatism, malaria, beriberi [*sic*] [a nervous system disorder caused by thiamine deficiency], constipation, and absent mindedness." Later in China, physician Hua-T'o wrote of a mixture of cannabis resins and wine to use as a surgical anesthetic (Emboden, 1972).

In Arabia, cannabis was commonly smoked for its mood-enhancing effects. Hashish also began to be used in this region in approximately A.D. 1100. Hashish played a critical role in a religious cult formed by Hashishin ibn al-Sabbah, who commonly went by the name al-Hasan ibn al-Sabbah (ca. A.D. 1124). During his purported travels, Marco Polo remarked in his journal about the practices al-Hasan used for recruiting men into his sect:

Now no man was allowed to enter the Garden save those whom he intended to be his ASHISHIN. There was a fortress at the entrance to the Garden, strong enough to resist all the world, and there was no other way to get in. He kept

at his Court a number of the youths of the country, from twelve to twenty years of age, such as had a taste for soldiering, and to these he used to tell tales about Paradise, just as Mahommet had been wont to do, and they believed in him just as the Saracens believe in Mahommet. Then he would introduce them into his Garden, some four, or six, or ten at a time, having first made them drink a certain potion which cast them into a deep sleep, and then causing them to be lifted and carried in. So when they awoke they found themselves in the Garden.

When therefore they awoke, and found themselves in a place so charming, they deemed that it was Paradise in very truth. And the ladies and damsels dallied with them to their heart's content, so that they had what young men would have; and with their own good will they never would have quitted the place. (Polo, 1871, pp. 132–134)

Marco Polo expanded on his description of al-Hasan's followers and deadly tactics, writing, "When the Old Man would have any prince slain, he would say to such a youth: 'Go thou and slay So and So; and when thou returnest my Angels shall bear thee into Paradise. And shouldst thou die, natheless even so will I send my Angels to carry thee back into Paradise'" (Polo, 1871, p. 135). We better know the term *hashinin* by its Anglicized version *assassin*.

The use of cannabis in modern medicine largely began from the efforts of William O'Shaughnessy, a British physician working as a professor in Calcutta, India, in 1839. During his time in India, O'Shaughnessy experimented with the medical potential of cannabis, discovering that its sedative and anticonvulsant properties improved some of the symptoms of rabies, tetanus, and cholera (Kalant, 2001). This led Western physicians to consider cannabis as a legitimate medicine.

The Pharmacopoeia of the United States of America lists cannabis as a medicine in volumes published from 1851 to 1942. The United States criminalized nonmedical use of cannabis in 1937 (Aggarwal et al., 2009). Even though marijuana remained legal for medical use, the Marihuana Tax Act of 1937 required patients to pay $1 per ounce of marijuana, which largely limited its medicinal use. Possibly because of this tax and declining use, later editions of the pharmacopoeia excluded cannabis from its compilation of medicines (Aggarwal et al., 2009; Kalant, 2001).

Cannabis abuse increased in the late 1950s, and by the 1960s millions of Americans had smoked cannabis. In 1969, the U.S. government under President Richard Nixon began search-and-seizure operations at the U.S.–Mexico border primarily aimed at cannabis smugglers (Brecher, 1972). The first controlled substances schedule in the United States in 1970 included cannabis under schedule I. Since then, the DEA has approved lower scheduling for cannabinoid-based medicines such as dronabinol. The lower scheduling of these medications, together with the recent emergence of medical marijuana approval in many U.S. states, has led to petitions to the DEA to lower the scheduling level of cannabis. The response to one petition came in 2011 when DEA Administrator Michele M. Leonhart rejected the request because of marijuana's "high potential for abuse," "no currently accepted medical use in treatment in the United States," and lack of "accepted safety for

use under medical supervision" (Leonhart, 2011). Yet, in 2015 the administration of President Barack Obama requested that the U.S. Supreme Court not take up a lawsuit case regarding the transportation of cannabis across state lines, suggesting a relaxing of federal oversight regarding the production and sale of cannabis (Hughes, 2015).

STOP & CHECK

1. To which country do we trace the earliest medical uses of cannabis?

2. What is the connection between cannabis and the term assassin?

1. China 2. *Assassin* is the anglicized form of *hashishin*, cult members who used hashish in their religious and recruiting practices.

Methods of Cannabis Preparation and Use

For both recreational and instrumental purposes, users most often administer cannabis by inhalation. To smoke cannabis, users roll a cannabis preparation in cigarette paper and then light and smoke it like a cigarette. As noted earlier, we refer to modern cannabis cigarettes as *joints*. Users may also inhale vapors from hash oil by dabbing, as described earlier (Loflin & Earleywine, 2014). Inhalation is also the preferred method for using herbal marijuana alternatives, which tend to be added to herbs or tobacco for smoking (Ashton, 2001; Hu, Primack, Barnett, & Cook, 2011). Further, applying synthetic cannabinoids to e-liquid solutions allows for inhaling vapors using e-cigarettes.

Users also smoke cannabis using a water-pipe device called a *hookah* or through a less elaborate pipe referred to as a *bong*. As first described in Chapter 7, water pipes entail inhaling smoke from a plant substance through water. Users deeply inhale smoke from cannabis, allowing for absorption of cannabinoids through lung tissue (Ashton, 2001).

Contact high
Positive subjective effects from secondhand exposure to cannabis smoke

We also find that secondhand smoke exposure to cannabis smoke causes a **contact high**, pharmacological effects from secondhand cannabis smoke. To determine the legitimacy of contact highs, Cone and Johnson (1986) evaluated subjective effects and blood plasma levels of Δ^9-THC in volunteers who inhaled secondhand cannabis smoke for an hour a session. The researchers found positive subjective effect scores in the secondhand smokers as well as plasma Δ^9-THC levels close to those found from actually smoking cannabis.

For oral administration, users may eat the *hashish* form of cannabis or prepare cannabis by baking it into some type of dessert, such as brownies or cookies. Hash oil also may be applied to foods for consumption or may be applied to herbs

or tobacco for smoking. Another manner of consuming cannabis orally consists of heating it with water to make a tea (Hazekamp, Bastola, Rashidi, Bender, & Verpoorte, 2007). Pharmaceutical companies sell prescription dronabinol in a capsule for oral administration.

Fifty percent of Δ^9-THC releases into smoke from lit cannabis. From e-cigarette liquid preparations, up to 80 percent of Δ^9-THC might be inhaled from vaporized e-liquids (Giroud et al., 2015). Most of the Δ^9-THC reaching the lungs absorbs into the bloodstream. Via inhalation, effects from cannabis first occur within seconds and significant effects are observed within minutes. Via oral administration, effects first occur between 30 minutes and 2 hours, but slower absorption leads to a prolonged duration of effects compared to smoking cannabis (Ashton, 2001).

Approximately 25 to 30 percent of Δ^9-THC reaches the bloodstream after oral administration, mainly due to first-pass metabolism in the liver (**Figure 11.1**). As are most compounds, we find Δ^9-THC metabolized in the liver by P450 enzymes, and these metabolites themselves produce effects within the body. The primary metabolite of Δ^9-THC is 11-hydroxy-Δ^9-THC, which produces psychoactive effects similar to those of Δ^9-THC (Takeda et al., 2010). Δ^9-THC exhibits high lipid solubility, leading to rapid distribution into tissues in the body, including the brain, as well as an accumulation in fat. Δ^9-THC in fat releases slowly over time, leading to long-term pharmacological actions (**Figure 11.2**) (Adams & Martin, 1996; Ashton, 2001).

Because of the accumulation of Δ^9-THC in fats, there is a long elimination rate of Δ^9-THC during sustained use. After 4–5 days, Δ^9-THC reaches a peak concentration in fat, which then releases Δ^9-THC slowly with a half-life of 7 days. This half-life makes Δ^9-THC detectable for as long as 30 days after ceasing repeated use (Ashton, 2001).

FIGURE 11.1 ● First-pass metabolism occurring after oral consumption of a Δ^9-THC product leads to significant reduction in Δ^9-THC that reaches the brain.

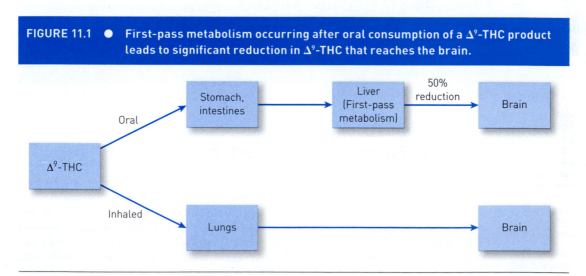

SOURCE: © Cengage Learning 2014.

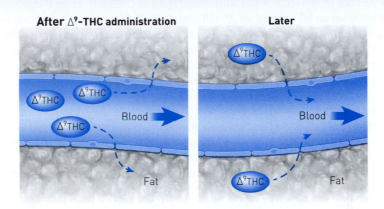

FIGURE 11.2 ● Δ^9-THC molecules accumulate in fat after administration (left), leading to a later release of Δ^9-THC into the bloodstream.

After Δ^9-THC administration   Later

SOURCE: © Cengage Learning 2014.

STOP & CHECK

1. What are the two common administration routes for cannabis?

2. Assuming the same content of Δ^9-THC, why might someone experience greater potency from inhalation than from oral administration?

1. *Inhalation* through smoking and *oral* through eating or drinking. 2. The oral administration routes subjects Δ^9-THC to first-pass metabolism, which limits the amount of Δ^9-THC that reaches the brain.

Endocannabinoids
Endogenous (derived internally) neurotransmitters that activate cannabinoid receptors

Anandamide
Endocannabinoid neurotransmitter

2-arachidonoyl-glycerol (2-AG)
Endocannabinoid neurotransmitter

Cannabinoid Compounds and the Endocannabinoid System

The effects of Δ^9-THC and other psychoactive cannabinoid compounds occur by their actions on the endocannabinoid neurotransmitter system. **Endocannabinoids** are endogenous (derived internally) neurotransmitters that activate cannabinoid receptors. Two endocannabinoids—**anandamide** and **2-arachidonoylglycerol (2-AG)**—serve as the most biologically active neurotransmitters for these cannabinoid receptors. Several other endocannabinoid neurotransmitters exist but are significantly less active, and their functional relevance has yet to be clearly determined (Battista, Di Tommaso, Bari, & Maccarrone, 2012; Brown, 2007; Felder et al., 1993).

The enzyme phospholipase D converts N-arachidonoyl-phosphatidylethanolamine (NAPE) into anandamide. Unlike other neurotransmitters described in this text, storage vesicles do not store anandamide; instead we find anandamide released from neurons immediately after synthesis. Anandamide returns to a neuron via an anandamide transporter; thereafter, the enzyme fatty acid amide hydrolase (FAAH) breaks anandamide down into inactive components (**Figure 11.3**) (Battista et al., 2012; Beltramo et al., 1997).

The enzyme sn-1-diacylglycerol lipase converts a diacylglycerol containing 2-arachidonate to 2-AG. Just like anandamide, this enzyme is activated by calcium; furthermore, like anandamide, 2-AG is not stored in vesicles. After release, 2-AG returns to the neuron through the same transporters used for anandamide. The enzyme monoacylglycerol lipase breaks down 2-AG into inactive components (Figure 11.3) (Blankman, Simon, & Cravatt, 2007; Cravatt et al., 1996).

Cannabinoids and CB$_1$ and CB$_2$ Receptors

The various behavioral and physiological effects described for cannabinoids (e.g., Δ^9-THC) and endocannabinoids (e.g., anandamide) result from actions at **cannabinoid receptors**. Two such receptors have been confirmed and thoroughly studied: the

Cannabinoid receptors G-protein–coupled receptors consisting of CB$_1$ and CB$_2$ activated by cannabinoids

FIGURE 11.3 ● Anandamide (left) is synthesized from NAPE through a NAPE-phospholipase D enzyme. The enzyme FAAH converts anandamide into inactive components. 2-AG (right) is synthesized from a diaglycerol, such sn-1-acyl-2-arachidonyl-glycerol, by the enzyme sn-1-diacylglycerol lipase. Monoacyglycerol lipase converts 2-AG into inactive components.

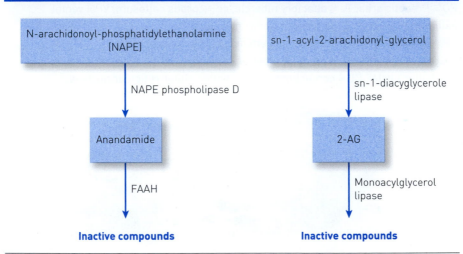

cannabinoid CB$_1$ and CB$_2$ receptors. Both receptors are G-protein–coupled receptors that exhibit inhibitory effects. Researchers have discovered other possible cannabinoid receptors, but these appear less important for explaining the effects of known cannabinoid compounds, so we will not cover these receptors in this text (Brown, 2007).

In the brain, CB$_1$ receptors densely occur in the basal ganglia, nucleus accumbens, substantia nigra, cerebellum, hippocampus, and cerebral cortex. CB$_1$ receptors also are found in the hypothalamus, thalamus, and throughout the brainstem (**Figure 11.4**) (Herkenham et al., 1990). A dense population of CB$_1$ receptors also exist in the eye, which may potentially play a role in cannabis-induced reductions of intraocular pressure, discussed later in this chapter (Porcella, Casellas, Gessa, & Pani, 1998; Porcella, Maxia, Gessa, & Pani, 2000). Outside the brain, CB$_1$ receptors can be found in the heart, kidneys, liver, spleen, and intestines. With the exception of glial cells, CB$_2$ receptors reside outside of the brain, particularly in the immune system on macrophages (i.e., white blood cells), leukocytes (including B cells, natural killer cells, and T cells), and mast cells (important for injury response) (Brown, 2007; Munro, Thomas, & Abu-Shaar, 1993).

Cannabinoid compounds vary in their affinity for CB$_1$ receptors, which can account for their different potencies for eliciting pharmacological effects. **Table 11.4** shows

---

FIGURE 11.4 ● Shown in a sagittal section of a rat brain, the darker portions are the result of higher levels of radioactivity from radiolabeled CB$_1$ receptors. Thus, the darker portion represents higher densities of CB$_1$ receptors, and the lighter portion represents lower densities of CB$_1$ receptors.

KEY (anterior to posterior): Fr = frontal cortex, FrPaM = motor cortex area, PO = Preoptic area, Tu = olfactory tubercle, cc = corpus callosum, VP = vental pallidum, fi = fibria of the hippocampus, ic = internal capsule, GP = globus pallidus, EP = exterior pallidus, Me = median eminence, Hi = hippcampus, LP = lateral posterior thalamic nucleus, SC = superior colliculus, SNR = substantia nigra, CbN = cerebellar nuclei, Cb = cerebellum, PCRt = parvicellular reticular nucleus.

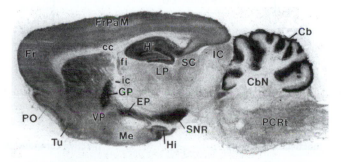

SOURCE: Miles Herkenham, NIMH.

TABLE 11.4 ● CB1 Receptor Binding Affinities for Selected Cannabinoid Compounds		
Compound	**Source**	**Binding Affinity Expressed as Ki (nM Concentration)***
Δ^9-THC (delta-9-tetrahydrocannabinol)	Main psychoactive component in cannabis	37
Cannabinol	Component in cannabis	247
Cannabidiol	Component in cannabis	2283
JWH-018	Synthetic CB_1 receptor agonist used for research purposes and abused as an herbal marijuana alternative	1.22
JWH-073	Synthetic CB_1 receptor agonist used for research purposes and abused as an herbal marijuana alternative	12.9
WIN55212-2	Synthetic CB_1 receptor agonist used for research purposes and abused as an herbal marijuana alternative	2
Anandamide	Endocannabinoid neurotransmitter	30
2-AG	Endocannabinoid neurotransmitter	1750

*Recall that lower values represent high affinities.

SOURCE: Data from Brents et al. 2011; Brents et al., 2012; Shoemaker et al., 2005; Thomas et al., 1998.

the receptor affinities for selected cannabinoid compounds (see Box 2.1 for a review of receptor-binding procedures). Both Δ^9-THC and the endocannabinoid anandamide exhibit high affinities for the CB_1 receptor (Thomas, Gilliam, Burch, Roche, & Seltzman, 1998). The endocannabinoid 2-AG weakly binds to CB_1 receptors (Shoemaker, Joseph, Ruckle, Mayeux, & Prather, 2005). Cannabinol and cannabidiol also have weaker affinities for CB_1 receptors, likely accounting for their weaker potencies compared to Δ^9-THC. The synthetically produced CB_1 agonist WIN55212-2, which users abuse as an herbal marijuana alternative, exhibits at least a tenfold greater affinity than either Δ^9-THC or anandamide (Thomas et al., 1998).

Activation of CB_1 receptors leads to increased dopamine concentrations in the nucleus accumbens. In a study by Polissidis and colleagues (2012), administration of the CB_1 receptor agonist WIN55212-2 led to a significant increase in nucleus accumbens dopamine concentrations. Researchers have yet to determine exactly how activation of CB_1 receptors increases dopamine concentrations. The authors of this study

speculated that CB_1 receptor agonists may act on CB_1 receptors on dopamine neurons in the ventral tegmental area or indirectly influence dopamine neuron activity by acting on CB_1 receptors located on glutamate or GABA neurons.

STOP & CHECK

1. What are the two primary endocannabinoid neurotransmitters?

2. What effect might a FAAH inhibitor have if someone also was using cannabis?

3. Activation of CB_1 receptors causes _____ effects on the activity of a neuron.

1. Anandamide and 2-AG **2.** The FAAH inhibitor would likely enhance the effects of cannabis through increasing levels of the endocannabinoid anandamide. **3.** inhibitory

Physiological Effects of Cannabinoids

Given the wide reach of the endocannabinoid system, cannabinoid compounds exhibit many physiological effects. Acute administration of a cannabinoid containing Δ^9-THC causes a significant elevation in heart rate, and acute cannabis use is associated with hypotension and heart palpitations (Malit et al., 1975). Cannabis also produces a reddening of *conjunctivae*, the membrane covering the front of the eye and lining the inside of the eyelids. Redness comes from swelling of small blood vessels, which include the small blood vessels found at the bottom of the eye and membranes around the eye. Thus, we find cannabis associated with red eyes or bloodshot eyes. Δ^9-THC itself appears to exhibit minimal effects on respiration at the usual amounts administered. Many of the respiratory problems associated with cannabinoids occur from smoked preparations, as described later in the chapter (Battista et al., 2012).

Cannabis use produces an increase in appetite, which recreational users refer to as having the "munchies." This is not a uniquely human phenomenon. For example, increased food intake is observed in *Hydra*, a tubular freshwater species that measures only a few millimeters long, after administration of the endocannabinoid anandamide (De Petrocellis, Melck, Bisogno, Milone, & Di Marzo, 1999). In rats, administration of anandamide leads to increased overnight food intake (Willams & Kirkam, 1999).

The endogenous cannabinoid system may be important for normal regulation of food intake. This inference is based on the effects that leptin, a *satiety hormone* (i.e., reduces hunger), has on anandamide and 2-AG release. After fat cells release leptin, leptin reduces anandamide and 2-AG concentrations in the hypothalamus (**Figure 11.5**). When comparing obese versus lean laboratory mice, obese mice exhibit greater levels of anandamide and 2-AG in the hypothalamus, suggesting that lower endocannabinoid levels reduce food intake and greater endocannabinoid levels increase food intake. We find CB_1 receptors important for these effects, given

that administration of a CB_1 receptor antagonist, SR141716A, reduces food intake in mice and that CB_1 receptor knockout mice consume less food than wild type mice (**Figure 11.6**) (Di Marzo et al., 2001).

Review! The hypothalamus maintains many physiological processes through motivating an organism's behavior, such as producing hunger to motivate feeding. (Chapter 2.)

FIGURE 11.5 ● **The psychological and physiological effects of cannabinoids depend on the locations and function impact of CB_1 and CB_2.**

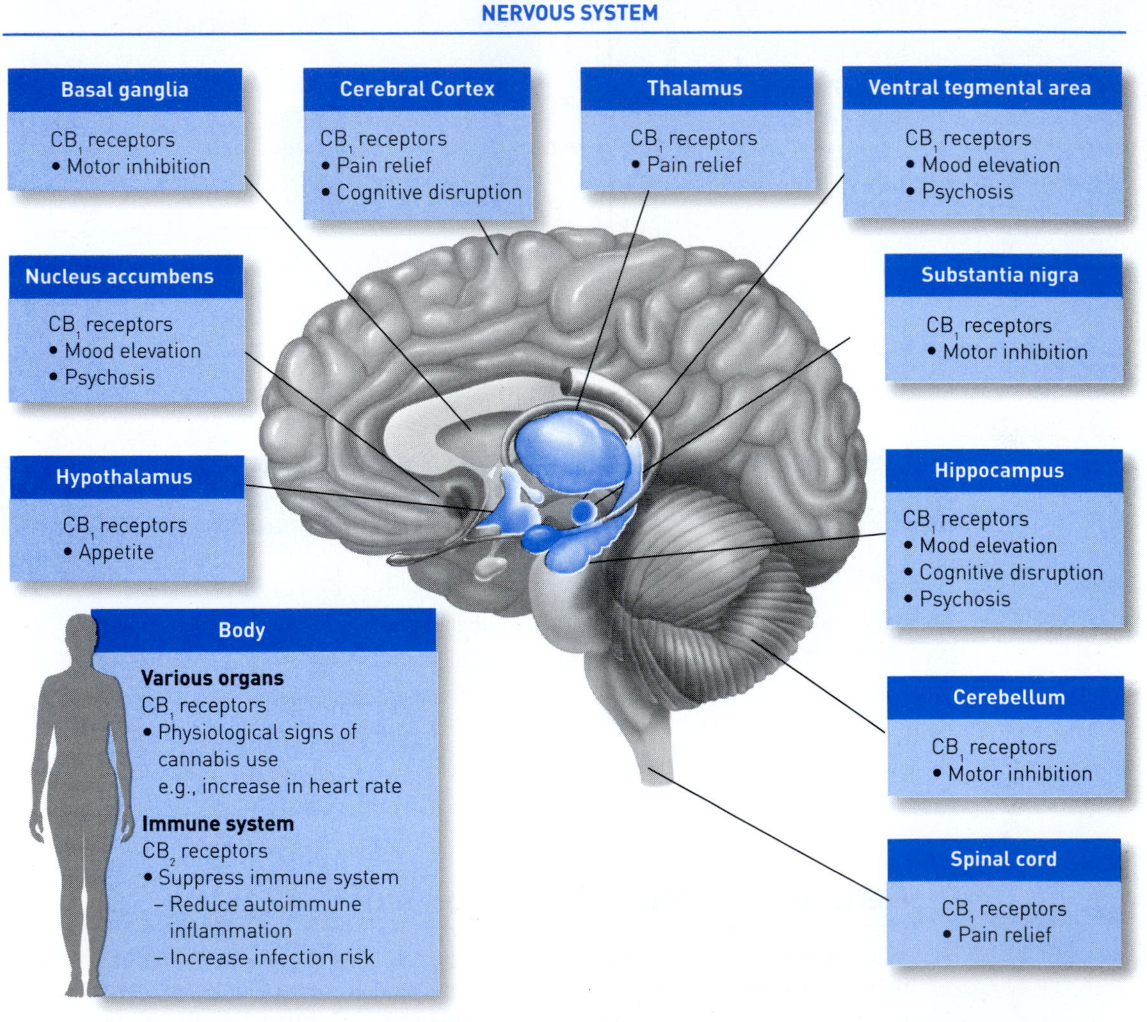

NERVOUS SYSTEM

Basal ganglia
CB_1 receptors
• Motor inhibition

Cerebral Cortex
CB_1 receptors
• Pain relief
• Cognitive disruption

Thalamus
CB_1 receptors
• Pain relief

Ventral tegmental area
CB_1 receptors
• Mood elevation
• Psychosis

Nucleus accumbens
CB_1 receptors
• Mood elevation
• Psychosis

Substantia nigra
CB_1 receptors
• Motor inhibition

Hypothalamus
CB_1 receptors
• Appetite

Hippocampus
CB_1 receptors
• Mood elevation
• Cognitive disruption
• Psychosis

Body

Various organs
CB_1 receptors
• Physiological signs of cannabis use
e.g., increase in heart rate

Immune system
CB_2 receptors
• Suppress immune system
– Reduce autoimmune inflammation
– Increase infection risk

Cerebellum
CB_1 receptors
• Motor inhibition

Spinal cord
CB_1 receptors
• Pain relief

SOURCE: © Cengage Learning 2014.

FIGURE 11.6 ● Reduced food intake occurs in CB$_1$ receptor knock-out mice (i.e., mice devoid of CB$_1$ receptors) compared to wildtype mice (i.e., mice with normal expression of CB$_1$ receptors) following 18 hours of food deprivation.

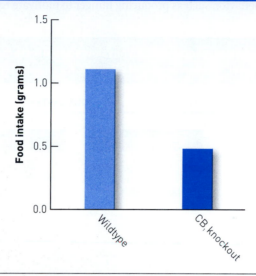

SOURCE: Adapted from DiMarzo et al., 2001.

STOP & CHECK

1. What causes red eyes from cannabis use?

2. Given that cannabis is an appetite enhancer, what therapeutic uses might the cannabinoid receptor antagonist offer?

1. Cannabis causes small blood vessels in the conjunctivae of the eye to swell, giving a red appearance. 2. If cannabis, which acts as an agonist for cannabinoid receptors increases appetite, then a cannabinoid receptor antagonist might decrease appetite. In fact, researchers have assessed cannabinoid receptor antagonists as weight-loss medications.

Behavioral Effects of Cannabinoids

Many studies find mild memory deficits occurring after acute administration with cannabis or Δ⁹-THC. For example, Weil, Zinberg, and Nelsen (1968) found that, among human volunteers, cannabis use impaired memory performance while failing to impair attention performance. Curran, Brignell, Fletcher, Middleton, and Henry (2002) found

that a 15 mg/kg dose of Δ^9-THC reduced the number of words that study participants could recall from a list. Like the study by Weil and colleagues (1968), this study failed to find deficits in attention. However, at concentrations of Δ^9-THC found after smoking cannabis, users exhibit impairments in memory, reasoning, and attention.

In an attempt trace neurobiological changes from cannabis use and effects on memory, Jager and colleagues (2006) fMRI scans in frequent cannabis users revealed lower activity in the hippocampus and dorsolateral prefrontal cortex, two structures linked to memory function, compared to control participants. Preclinical studies reveal extensive interactions of CB_1 receptor activation with firing rates, inhibition of long-term potentiation and depression formation (two processes important for memory; see Chapter 12), and decreased concentrations of the neurotransmitters acetylcholine and GABA in the hippocampus. Further, glutamate neurons from the hippocampus release less glutamate in other structures (Sullivan, 2000). The neurobiological findings overall suggest a disruption in hippocampal functioning that may lead to impaired memory.

These concentrations also increase suspiciousness and paranoia, although the degree of these behaviors varies across individual users (Morrison et al., 2009). Yet, among those who have paranoia thoughts from time to time, cannabis is especially likely to induce paranoia, something that Freeman and colleagues (2015) found by having study participants rate their perceptions of computerized characters they engaged with in a virtual environment. Psychotic effects also occur from use of herbal marijuana alternatives (e.g., Every-Palmer, 2011).

Given the ability of cannabis produce paranoia and suspiciousness has given rise to the notion that cannabis uses causes schizophrenia. Propaganda media, like the movie (and cult favorite) *Reefer Madness* have claimed risks for psychosis from cannabis use for decades. Correlational studies have led to a general consensus that repeated cannabis use during adolescence is a risk factor, not a causal factor, for schizophrenia (Andréasson, Engström, Allebeck, & Ryberg, 1987; Manrique-Garcia et al., 2011). Determining the nature of this risk, however, involves deciphering complex interactions between a genetic risk for schizophrenia (see Chapter 15), brain maturation during adolescence, and psychological factors, such as a stress.

Cannabis tends to impair motor coordination and muscle tone. These effects, coupled with cannabis-induced impairments in reaction, likely contribute to impaired driving ability and an increased number of auto accidents (Ramaekers, Berghaus, van Laar, & Drummer, 2004). These effects directly relate to the concentration of Δ^9-THC and coincide with the subjective effects described as being *stoned* (Chesher, Bird, Jackson, Perrignon, & Starmer, 1990). Animal studies suggest that motor effects may change depending on the dose. In laboratory rats, low doses of CB_1 receptor agonists increase locomotor activity, whereas higher doses decrease locomotor activity (Polissidis et al., 2012).

McGlothlin and West (1968) first proposed an **amotivational syndrome** occurring in cannabis users. They characterized an amotivational syndrome as a persisting lack of motivation to engage in productive activities. Individuals with amotivational syndrome exhibit apathy, lethargy, and passivity that are manifested as a failure to follow through on long-term plans, an indulgence in childlike thinking, and an engagement in introversive behavior.

Amotivational syndrome Lack of motivation to engage in productive activities possibly related to cannabis use

Despite these observations, many researchers have failed to confirm an amotivational syndrome in controlled laboratory settings. Several studies have tested the hypothesis that cannabis use should reduce the effectiveness of reinforcers if it reduces motivation. For example, if an individual loses interest in working, then one may reason that the individual has less motivation to earn money.

Published studies that investigated this hypothesis either reveal no effects on motivation or, in fact, find an increase in motivation. For example, Foltin and colleagues (1990) asked volunteers to live in a laboratory environment for 2 weeks and engage in various activities of low or high effort to earn reinforcers. In this study, a *reinforcer* was an opportunity to conduct a task an individual preferred more than the one he or she was currently conducting. On certain days, participants smoked cannabis cigarettes, but they smoked placebo cigarettes, which lacked Δ^9-THC, on other days. The researchers reasoned that study participants would express amotivation by choosing less-effortful tasks. Yet when participants smoked the cannabis cigarettes, they actually chose the tasks requiring more effort. Thus, an amotivational syndrome was not apparent. The researchers instead concluded that smoking cannabis made effortful tasks seem less effortful.

STOP & CHECK

1. What effects does cannabis use have on memory?

2. What is the hypothesis that many researchers test when investigating a potential amotivation syndrome for cannabis use?

1. Cannabis tends to impair memory. **2.** Researchers sometimes assess the effectiveness of reinforcers, reasoning that a user finding a goal less reinforcing would therefore demonstrate reduced motivation.

Subjective Effects of Cannabinoids

The subjective effects of cannabinoids are dose dependent. After a few puffs of marijuana, a user may experience a light-headed, dizzy feeling referred to as a *buzz*. A person with a buzz may also experience tingling sensations in the body. A *high* occurs after additional inhalations and is defined as a euphoric and exhilarating feeling. Increased agitation or anxiety is occasionally reported during the buzz and high phases as well. The *stoned* phase occurs with further usage and is described as a calm and relaxed state. This stage is also consistently characterized by **accelerated time**, a perceived faster passage of time, as described previously (Abood & Martin, 1992).

Accelerated time (cannabis use) Perceived faster passage of time associated with cannabis use

Accelerated time appears to be related to the effects of cannabis on the cerebellum. In a positron emission tomography (PET) imaging study, Mathew and colleagues (1998) used PET to image cerebral blood flow following the administration of Δ^9-THC in human participants. Although findings varied among the participants, those who overestimated time passage exhibited reductions in blood flow to the cerebellum.

Review! The cerebellum facilitates balance and the timing of movements. (Chapter 2.)

To carefully assess the subjective effects of cannabis in humans in a laboratory environment, Curran and colleagues (2002) recruited 50 volunteers who had used cannabis in the past to rate how they felt after oral administration of Δ^9-THC. The investigators chose both a low dose (7.5 mg/kg) and a high dose (15.0 mg/kg) of Δ^9-THC to study, along with a placebo. Researchers employed a double-blind design so that neither the investigators nor the participants knew who received treatments during the study. The participants reported the strongest drug effect when given the highest dose of Δ^9-THC. They liked both the low and high dose of Δ^9-THC equally well, and they liked both more than placebo. Similarly, they indicated a desire for more of the drug. The highest dose caused the most reports of being stoned, and the participants indicated difficulty remembering things.

Although this study employed oral administration of Δ^9-THC, rather than smoked cannabis, the effects are likely similar. In a study conducted by Hart and colleagues (2002), experienced cannabis smokers reported similar subjective effects, including similar "high" and "stoned" effects between smoked cannabis and oral Δ^9-THC. These findings further implicate Δ^9-THC in the subjective effects of cannabis.

Drug-discrimination studies can be used to study subjective effects in humans as well. In a study conducted by Lile, Kelly, Pinsky, and Hays (2009), the ability to discriminate

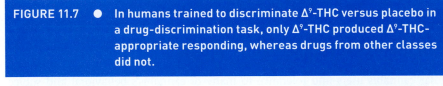

FIGURE 11.7 ● **In humans trained to discriminate Δ^9-THC versus placebo in a drug-discrimination task, only Δ^9-THC produced Δ^9-THC-appropriate responding, whereas drugs from other classes did not.**

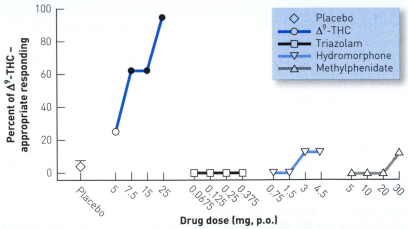

SOURCE: With kind permission from Springer Science+Business Media: Lile, J. A., Kelly, T. H., Pinsky, D. J., & Hays, L. R. (2009). Substitution profile of Delta9-tetrahydrocannabinol, triazolam, hydromorphone, and methylphenidate in humans discriminating Delta9- tetrahydrocannabinol. *Psychopharmacology* (Berl), *203*(2), 241, p. 10.

between a specific dose of a training drug—in this case, 25 mg of Δ⁹-THC—and a compound with no drug effects (i.e., a placebo) were assessed in experienced cannabis users. The participants were given the drug or placebo orally, using pills that were identical in both appearance and taste. In fact, the participants were not even told that the training drug was Δ⁹-THC; rather, they were told to closely attend to effects experienced after taking "drug X." The human participants then rated, by repeatedly clicking "drug" or "no drug" on a computer screen, their certainty that they had received drug X. After attaining a high level of accuracy, researchers administered a different test substance to the participants. **Figure 11.7** shows the results from this study. Participants clicked for drug X after Δ⁹-THC administration and they seldom clicked for drug X after administration of a benzodiazepine, opioid, or psychostimulant drug. Thus, the stimulus effects of Δ⁹-THC appear different from those produced by these other drug classes.

STOP & CHECK

1. What are the dose-dependent phases of the subjective effects of cannabis?

2. Which brain structure may be responsible for the perception of accelerated time during cannabis use?

1. As the dose increases, an individual will experience buzzed, high, and stoned phases. 2. Cerebellum.

Cannabinoid Tolerance and Dependence

Regular cannabis users find tolerance to many of cannabis's behavioral and subjective effects, including memory impairment, motor coordination, and accelerated time passage (Abood & Martin, 1992). A study by Georgotas and Zeidenberg (1979) demonstrated both the development of tolerance and the demonstration of dependence. These researchers recruited 5 healthy male volunteers who agreed to remain in an institutional setting for 8 weeks. During the first 4 weeks, participants had free access to cannabis cigarettes (i.e., joints). **Figure 11.8** shows the frequency of cannabis smoking during this study.

On the first day of study, each participant smoked one cannabis cigarette of his own choosing. During the last day of these first 4 weeks, each participant smoked an average of 19 cannabis cigarettes (Figure 11.7). Over the course of the study, they each smoked an average of 292 cannabis cigarettes. As the amount of cannabis consumed increased, participants became suspicious, paranoid, agitated, apathetic, withdrawn, and depressed.

During these first 4 weeks, participants complained that the cannabis cigarettes became weak and that the stoned phase was less salient. To overcome this, the participants smoked escalating amounts of cannabis to achieve a desired effect, a classic indication of tolerance. On the day after these 4 weeks, the research team withheld cannabis from study participants. At this point, the participants were described as "very irritable, uncooperative, resistant, and at times hostile." The participants also lacked an appetite

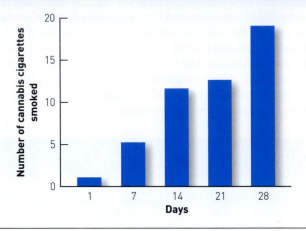

FIGURE 11.8 ● Institutionalized participants with free access to cannabis cigarettes (e.g., joints), steadily increased the number of cigarettes smoked per day during a 4-week study. The participants indicated a need to smoke more cigarettes in order to achieve the same subjective effects.

SOURCE: Data from Georgotas and Zeidenberg, 1976.

and had difficulty sleeping. These withdrawal effects subsided after about a week, and the participants' mood progressively improved during the final three weeks of the study.

Although this study is an extreme example of cannabis use, withdrawal effects were quite apparent and appeared to be counter to those effects elicited by cannabis use. Thus, as cannabis produces a relaxed state, the participants experienced agitation and restlessness. The appetite-enhancing effects of cannabis gave way to appetite suppression during withdrawal.

The *Diagnostic and Statistical Manual* (DSM-5) describes a **cannabis use disorder** as meeting the general criteria for substance use disorder, as first presented in Chapter 5 (American Psychiatric Association, 2013). Features include using more cannabis than originally intended, cravings, and replacing normal healthy activities with cannabis use among others. Further, the DSM-5 recognizes tolerance developing during cannabis use and describes a **cannabis withdrawal syndrome** as including irritability, anger, aggression, anxiety, difficulty sleeping, decreased appetite, and depressed mood as well as any physical withdrawal symptoms such as stomach pain, tremor, sweating, headache, or fever.

Cannabis and Health Risk

Although cannabis presents some possible medical benefits for cancer, cannabis cigarettes share a number of carcinogens with tobacco cigarettes. These carcinogens include benzanthracene and benzpyrene compounds. In fact, cannabis cigarettes contain

Cannabis use disorder Defined by the DSM-5 as cannabis use meeting the criteria for a substance use disorder

Cannabis withdrawal disorder Occurrence of physical and psychological withdrawal symptoms in the absence of cannabis

greater amounts of these chemicals than do tobacco cigarettes. Compared to tobacco, cannabis smoking results in greater amounts of tar in the lungs (Ashton, 2001).

Despite sharing similar carcinogen content with tobacco, cannabis smoke also yields different chemicals that may limit a user's risk for lung cancer. This may explain why correlational studies fail to find increased risk of lung cancer among cannabis smokers (Hashibe et al., 2005; Mehra, Moore, Crothers, Tetrault, & Fiellin, 2006). Moreover, cannabis contains compounds shown to reduce cancers of the skin, breast, and prostate, suggesting that these compounds may counteract the carcinogens found in cannabis (Melamede, 2005). Aside from cancer risk, cannabis smoking may increase the risk of respiratory diseases such as bronchitis and emphysema, although this risk increases most for users who smoke both cannabis and tobacco (Ashton, 2001; Tan et al., 2009). Other adverse effects may derive from the preparation of the cannabinoid or its manner of use. One of the more common significant adverse effects reported from use of herbal marijuana alternatives is damage to kidneys (Centers for Disease Control and Prevention, 2013).

STOP & CHECK

1. How are some withdrawal effects from cannabis related to the drug effects of cannabis?

2. Although smoke cannabis tar contains carcinogens, why might cancer risk not be evident in correlational studies?

1. Some withdrawal effects appear as compensatory effects from cannabis use. Thus, the withdrawal effect of *reduced appetite* is the result of compensating for the *appetite enhancement* of cannabis. Other withdrawal effects can be linked to the drug effects of cannabis in this way. **2.** Unlike tobacco tar, cannabis tar includes chemicals that might reduce cancer risk, potentially compensating for the effects of carcinogens in some way. Still, there's much to learn about cancer risk and cannabis smoking before one can state with certainty the safety of cannabis products in this regard.

From Actions to Effects: Medical Marijuana

Although marijuana is a popular drug of abuse, it is also emerging as a medical treatment. Despite the federal classification as a schedule I controlled substance, 23 states in the United States, as well as Washington, D.C., allow licensed cannabis use for medical purposes (ProCon, 2016). Canada also allows medical marijuana. When investigating the scientific validity of using marijuana as a medical treatment, researchers study both the effects of cannabis and the effects of phytocannabinoids, including not only Δ^9-THC but also cannabidiol and cannabinol. Amid a number of purported uses, evidence mainly supports **medicinal cannabis** for managing cancer medications, unhealthy weight loss, pain, intraocular pressure, and autoimmune diseases (**Table 11.5**) (Alexander, 2016).

For the treatment of cancer, cannabis may help patients cope with adverse side effects of *chemotherapy*, the use of medicines that kill rapidly dividing cells. In 1985, the Food and Drug Administration (FDA) approved the prescription of Δ^9-THC, again

Medicinal cannabis Cannabis used for treating medical conditions such as cancer, weight gain, pain, intraocular pressure, and autoimmune diseases

TABLE 11.5 ● Medical Uses for Cannabis	
Cancer	Reduces nausea and vomiting associated with chemotherapy; limited evidence showing reduced tumor growth in patients
Weight	Promotes weight gain in disorders that diminish appetite
Pain	Reduces neuropathic pain from trauma or surgery
Glaucoma	Relieves intraocular eye pressure
Autoimmune disease	Inhibits immune system functioning; appears effective for multiple sclerosis

SOURCE: © Cengage Learning 2014.

known as dronabinol (Marinol), for the reduction of nausea and vomiting during chemotherapy. However, with the development of other medications for treating chemotherapy-induced nausea and vomiting, physicians usually do not prescribe dronabinol as a first-line treatment (Todaro, 2012). Cannabinoids have repeatedly demonstrated appetite-enhancing effects in clinical studies. This property may help promote weight gain conditions that diminish appetite, including cancer, chemotherapy treatment, and HIV infection. Another drug that is chemically similar to THC, *nabilone* (*Cesamet*), has been approved for similar uses. Because Δ^9-THC is the central psychoactive ingredient in cannabis, it is likely that cannabis use (e.g., smoking cannabis) has similar benefits (Haney et al., 2007).

Only tentative evidence exists in clinical trials to suggest that medical marijuana may effectively treat cancer. In one study, physicians injected Δ^9-THC directly into glioblastoma multiforme tumors (a type of brain tumor) and found evidence of temporary reductions in tumor progression (Guzmán et al., 2006). Other than this, most evidence for using cannabinoids as cancer treatment comes from studies in animals and using tumor cells (Massi, Solinas, Conquina, & Parolaro, 2013).

Ellis and colleagues (2009) found that smoked cannabis significantly reduces neuropathic pain in HIV-infected patients compared to placebo control. These findings coincided with findings by Ware and colleagues (2010) that smoked cannabis reduces neuropathic pain in patients after suffering a trauma or when recovering from surgery. The pain-relieving properties of cannabinoids may result from activation of CB_1 receptors in the thalamus, brain stem, and cerebral cortex. Moreover, CB_1 receptors are located on neurons within the spinal cord where cannabinoids may reduce pain signaling to the brain (Pertwee, 2001).

Cannabis and phytocannabinoids may offer therapeutic benefits for glaucoma, a disease characterized by damage to the optic nerve from increased fluid pressure in the eye. Hepler and Frank (1971) first reported that smoking cannabis cigarettes led to a significant reduction in intraocular pressure. Several studies reported that Δ^9-THC engendered similar effects (Merritt, Crawford, Alexander, Anduze, & Gelbart, 1980; Purnell & Gregg, 1975). Porcella, Maxia, Gessa, and Pani (2001) also found that a selective CB_1 receptor agonist WIN55212-2 significantly reduced intraocular pressure in

patients, concluding that CB_1 receptors play a direct role in mediating fluid pressure in the eye.

Cannabinoids also suppress immune system functioning. These actions are illustrated in a survey of routine cannabis users in Italy and Spain conducted by Pacifici and colleagues (2003). Through analyzing blood drawn from these participants over the course of 6 months, self-reported cannabis use was associated with reduced numbers of natural killer cells as well as general suppressed activity among various immune system cells. This included a reduction in proinflammatory cytokines, as well as an increase in anti-inflammatory cytokines. Thus, cannabis may be effective medicinally for autoimmune inflammation, but cannabis use may also enhance one's risk of infection.

One example of this is multiple sclerosis (Ayoglu et al., 2016). Both Δ^9-THC and cannabidiol reduced spasticity (i.e., continuous muscle contractions) and general motor function in animal models (Feliu et al. 2015). In clinical trials, **Sativex**, a one-to-one ratio of cannabidiol and Δ^9-THC, reduced spasticity among multiple sclerosis patients, although Δ^9-THC alone did not. Overall, we find a general consensus that Sativex and Δ^9-THC have some efficacy for multiple sclerosis (Alexander, 2016; Koppel et al., 2014). Sativex is currently approved in the United Kingdom, Spain, and Canada for the treatment of muscle spasms and stiffness in multiple sclerosis. Canada also approved Sativex for the treatment of pain in cancer. Patients indicate that Sativex is generally well tolerated (Barnes, 2006; Wade, 2012).

Sativex
Cannabinoid medication that consists of a one-to-one ratio of cannabidiol and Δ^9-THC

⚙ *Drug Profile:* Cannabidiol and Δ^9-THC (1:1 Ratio)	
Trade name	Sativex
Properties	Agonist for cannabinoid CB and CB_2 receptors
Uses	Cannabinoid medication for the treatment of multiple sclerosis and cancer pain

The preceding studies provide evidence for using cannabis and its constituents or synthetic analogs as treatments for certain medical conditions. These findings also suggest that FDA-approved cannabinoid medications may serve in place of medicinal marijuana. However, medical marijuana may provide greater tolerability than Δ^9-THC, partly because of variability in absorption and metabolism among different individuals (Joerger et al., 2012). Thus, by smoking cannabis, users can self-regulate the amount used to achieve a desired effect.

Other components in cannabis may limit negative subjective or other behavioral effects of Δ^9-THC. A study by Vann and colleagues (2008) assessed the effects of Δ^9-THC in a conditioned place preference model using rats (**Figure 11.9**). After completing pairing sessions with Δ^9-THC or placebo, a test session revealed that rats avoided the chamber paired with Δ^9-THC. In other words, Δ^9-THC produced a *conditioned place aversion*. In a subsequent experiment, these researchers conducted the same procedure using a combination of Δ^9-THC and cannabidiol as a treatment condition versus placebo. This time, a test session revealed neither an aversion nor a preference, suggesting that cannabidiol canceled out the aversive effects of Δ^9-THC.

FIGURE 11.9 ● In a study by Vann and colleagues (2008), THC (Δ⁹-THC) in the absence of cannabidiol (CBD) (noted by 0:10 in figure) produced a conditioned place aversion in rats. However, when cannabidiol was also administered, noted by the 1:10 and 10:10 ratios, a conditioned place aversion did not occur. The *y*-axis indicates the amount of time spent in the drug side of the compartment compared to pretraining sessions. Negative time values represent avoidance of the compartment.

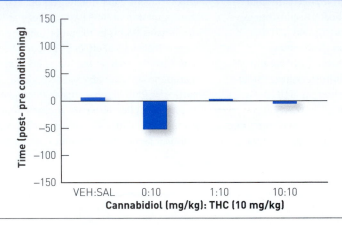

SOURCE: Vann et al., 2008. Reprinted with permission.

We find generally, at present, weak support for using cannabis to treat other disorders. One of the more anecdotally reported uses of cannabis involves its use for treating epilepsy. In a review of studies published as recently as 2013, Gloss and Vickey (2014) found that studies so far conducted on the use of cannabinoids for treating epilepsy were of too low a quality to draw any reliable conclusions.

STOP & CHECK

1. What is the FDA-approved use for dronabinol?

2. How might cannabis relieve glaucoma?

3. Why might cannabis users prefer smoking cannabis as opposed to taking dronabinol for medicinal purposes?

1. The FDA approved dronabinol for the reduction of nausea and vomiting during chemotherapy. 2. CB₁ receptors in the eye may have a direct role in liquid pressure, a contributor to optic nerve damage in glaucoma. Δ⁹-THC in cannabis may relieve this pressure by activating these CB₁ receptors. 3. First, smoking cannabis allows patients to adjust drug levels to achieve and maintain a desired effect. Second, other components in cannabis may counteract some of the negative subjective effects of dronabinol.

Chapter Summary

Cannabinoids represent a class of drugs that produce psychoactive effects by acting on cannabinoid receptors in the nervous system. Cannabinoids exist in cannabis plants, are produced as synthetic drugs, and occur as endogenous neurotransmitters. Cannabis plants produce psychoactive effects through Δ^9-THC, their main psychoactive constituent. With the exception of prescription Δ^9-THC (dronabinol), the DEA lists cannabinoid compounds as schedule I controlled substances. Users smoke or orally administer cannabinoid compounds. Once in the body, Δ^9-THC has a long elimination rate, which increases during chronic cannabis use. Cannabinoid compounds engender pharmacological actions by acting on the endocannabinoid system, which involves neurotransmitters called *anandamide* and *2-AG* that bind to CB_1 and CB_2 cannabinoid receptors. Cannabis use increases heart rate, enhances appetite, produces deficits in memory, and impairs motor coordination. The subjective effects include euphoria, relaxation, and overestimation of time passage. Regular use of cannabis results in tolerance to many of its pharmacological effects. There has been extensive research on the use of medical marijuana and cannabinoid compounds. In particular, cannabinoids may reduce adverse effects from chemotherapy, promote weight gain, relieve pain, reduce intraocular pressure, and treat certain autoimmune diseases.

Key Terms

Cannabinoids 330
Cannabis 330
Phytocannabinoids 330
Δ^9-tetrahydrocannabinol (Δ^9-THC) 330
Marijuana (or marihuana) 330
Dabbing 331
Hashish 332
Herbal marijuana alternatives (or synthetic marijuana) 332

Herbal incense 332
Liquid incense (or cannabinoid-enhanced electronic liquid) 332
Contact high 336
Endocannabinoids 338
Anandamide 338
2-arachidonoyl-glycerol (2-AG) 338
Cannabinoid receptors 339
Amotivational syndrome 345

Accelerated time (cannabis use) 346
Cannabis use disorder 349
Cannabis withdrawal disorder 349
Medicinal cannabis 350
Sativex 352

Visit the Student Study Site at **study.sagepub.com/prus2e** to access additional study tools, including eFlashcards, web quizzes, video resources, web resources, SAGE journal articles, and more.

12

Psychedelic Drugs

DID HOFMANN TAKE A "TRIP"?

While mixing chemicals at Sandoz Laboratories in Switzerland on the afternoon of April 16, 1943, Dr. Albert Hofmann acquired a sudden illness. He went home and journaled his experience, noting his initial symptoms as a "great restlessness and mild dizziness." He entered a pleasant delirium containing "extremely excited fantasies" along with "fantastic visions of extraordinary realness and with an intense kaleidoscopic play of colors."

As a seasoned chemist, Hofmann deliberated on the ergot fungi derivatives he made that day and wondered about accidental ingestion. After recovering, Hofmann returned to work and took a tiny amount of one of the derivatives. This time his experience was stronger and different. It took hours to recover, and when he did, Hofmann wrote of his experience:

As far as I can remember, the following were the most outstanding symptoms:

(Continued)

(Continued)

vertigo, visual disturbances, the faces of those around me appeared as grotesque, colored masks; marked motoric unrest, alternating with paralysis; an intermittent feeling in the head, limbs, and the entire body, as if they were filled with lead; dry, constricted sensation in the throat; feeling of choking; clear recognition of my condition, in which state I sometimes observed, in the manner of an independent neutral observer, that I shouted half insanely or babbled incoherent words. Occasionally I felt as if I were out of my body. . . . Especially noteworthy was the fact that sounds were transposed into visual sensations so that from each tone or noise a comparable colored picture was evoked, changing in form and color kaleidoscopically.

Hofmann provided the first account of a popular recreational substance, the 25th compound of Sandoz Laboratories' lysergic acid series, LSD (Brecher, 1972).

Psychedelic drugs
Drugs that induce a reality-altering experience consisting of hallucinations, sensory distortions, or delusions.

Psychedelic drugs induce a reality-altering experience consisting of hallucinations, sensory distortions, or delusions. The term *psychedelic* means "mind expanding." Within this definition, we find a wide variety of pharmacological effects among the psychedelic drugs. Thus, we further classify psychedelic drugs into three general categories: *hallucinogens, mixed stimulant–psychedelics,* and *dissociative anesthetics*. This chapter will focus on the representative drugs for each category, including the hallucinogen LSD (*acid*), the mixed stimulant–psychedelic MDMA (*Ecstasy*), and the dissociative anesthetic *phencyclidine* (*PCP*) (Abraham, McCann, & Ricaurte, 2002).

Hallucinogens

Hallucinogens
Large class of psychedelic drugs that produce hallucinations as their main pharmacological effects

Lysergic acid diethylamide (LSD)
Hallucinogen known as acid, window pane, and blotter

Hallucinogens represent a large class of psychedelic drugs that produce hallucinations as their main pharmacological effects. The most representative drug of this class is **lysergic acid diethylamide (LSD)**, which goes by a variety of streets names such as *acid, window pane,* and *blotter,* among other street names. Other hallucinogens include psilocybin, mescaline, and dimethyltryptamine. LSD is synthesized from lysergic acid using any number of preparation methods (Soine, 1986). In response to these measures, the Drug Enforcement Administration (DEA) not only classified LSD as a schedule I substance but also classified its precursor, lysergic acid, as a schedule I controlled substance (Drug Enforcement Administration, 2012b).

Drug Profile: lysergic acid diethylamide (LSD)

Street name	Acid, window pane, and blotter, among others
Subjective Effects:	Visual hallucinations

Psilocybin is the main psychoactive constituent in hallucinogenic mushrooms belonging to the genus *Psilocybe* (Schultes, 1969). User refers to these mushrooms by different street names such as *magic mushrooms* or *shrooms*. After oral administration, psilocybin rapidly converts to its active metabolite psilocin, a hallucinogenic substance that likely accounts for most of psilocybin's effects (Hasler, Bourquin, Brenneisen, Bar, & Vollenweider, 1997).

Psilocybin Main psychoactive constituent in hallucinogenic mushrooms belonging to the genus *Psilocybe*

Drug Profile: psilocybin (and psilocin)

Street name	Magic mushrooms or shrooms
Subjective Effect:	Visual hallucinations; produced mostly from active metabolite, psilocin

---

Mescaline is found in *peyote*, a small, spineless cactus native to southern North America (**Figure 12.1**). Users obtain mescaline by chewing disk-shaped buttons within the cactus crown (Schultes, 1969). Street names for mescaline include peyote (in reference to the plant), buttons, and mesc, among others. As noted in the next section, mescaline is used in some religious practices.

Drug Profile: mescaline

Street name:	Peyote, buttons, and mesc
Subjective Effects:	Visual hallucinations; used in some religious ceremonies

---

Another hallucinogen is *dimethyltryptamine* (DMT). We find **DMT** in *Mimosa hostilis, Virola calophylla,* and other hallucinogenic South American plants (Agurell, Holmstedt, Lindgren, & Schultes, 1969). Plants containing DMT may be brewed to make a drink called *ayahuasca*. Unlike other hallucinogens, the body also produces small amounts of DMT. The function of endogenous DMT remains largely unknown, although it appears to serve as an agonist for sigma-1 receptor (Angrist et al., 1976; Axelrod, 1961; Fontanilla et al., 2009; Frecska, Szabo, Windelman, Luna, & McKenna, 2013). The sigma-1 receptor was once considered a receptor for opioids, but subsequent research found

Dimethyltryptamine (DMT) Hallucinogenic compound found in certain South American plants and produced endogenously

FIGURE 12.1 ●   The peyote cactus contains the hallucinogen mescaline. Mescaline is concentrated in the "button" shaped feature on the crown of the cactus.

SOURCE: Copyright iStockphoto/bob cheung.

sigma-1 as a site on the endoplasmic reticulum (Hayashi and Su 2007). Further DMT may act on the serotonin system, but these potential interactions have yet to be sorted out (Frecska et al., 2013).

💊 *Drug Profile:* dimethyltryptamine (DMT)	
Street name	DMT, DET, AMT, business man's special, among others
Action	Unknown, but may activate sigma-1 receptors and may act on the serotonin system
Subjective effects	Visual hallucinations; small amounts produced in the body

A newer class of hallucinogens is called *NBOMe drugs,* a reference to their chemical structure as N-methoxybenzyl molecular analogs of different families of phenethyl-amine compounds. Users typically refer to NBOMe drugs as "n-bombs." Their use

mainly began in 2010, and many countries still have yet to regulate their use. They produce pharmacological actions and effects similar to other hallucinogens.

Close to 40 million U.S. residents had ever used a hallucinogenic substance, according to surveys conducted in 2014. Women make up approximately 37 percent of those ever trying a hallucinogenic substance, again by their broad definition. Approximately 25 million U.S. residents have specifically used LSD in their lifetimes (Center for Behavioral Health Statistics, 2015). We also find hallucinogen use prevalent on college campuses. In surveys of undergraduate college students, approximately 15 percent reported using LSD, and nearly 25 percent had used hallucinogenic mushrooms (Substance Abuse and Mental Health Services Administration, 2010).

STOP & CHECK

1. What are the three main types of psychedelic drugs?

2. What is the representative drug for hallucinogens?

3. What is the hallucinogenic compound found in peyote?

1. Hallucinogens, mixed stimulants–psychedelics, and dissociative anesthetics 2. Lysergic acid diethylamide (LSD) 3. Mescaline

Origins of LSD and Other Hallucinogens

Primitive cultures used hallucinogenic plants as psychic medicines to treat maladies, communicate with gods, and perform magic. The Aztecs used peyote and similar hallucinogens in religious ceremonies. In addition to rich visual hallucinations, peyote granted perceptions of great insight and altered realities, providing the integral experience of communicating with gods. The Spanish conquistadors banned these practices, but neither the Inquisitors nor military authorities eliminated peyote's ceremonial use (Schultes, 1969).

In the mid-18th century, peyote use was adopted by Native American cultures and was used in religious ceremonies by the Comanche, Kiowa, Cheyenne, and many other tribes. Comanche chief **Quanah Parker** stated that the Great Spirit Within communicated with him through a peyote experience to make peace with the white man and seek spiritual communion and wisdom.

When Oklahoma outlawed peyote in 1899, Quanah Parker helped persuade the state legislature to overturn the law, which it did in 1908. Peyote's legal status continued largely because of its importance to the Native American Church of North America. As the use of peyote continued in native American tribes, peyote use spread among U.S. college campuses during the 1950s and 1960s (Brecher, 1972). Today,

Quanah Parker
Comanche chief who advocated using peyote in religious ceremonies

peyote and its primary psychoactive ingredient mescaline are schedule I controlled substances, although this act exempts peyote use for religious purposes by the Native American Church of North America (American Indian Religious Freedom Act Amendments, 1994).

Although hallucinogenic substances have existed in plants for as long as humans have existed. In fact, Caporael (1976) wrote a convincing case that the infamous Salem witchcraft trials occurred because of accidental exposure to ergot fungus among the residents. As described in the opening of this chapter, Swiss chemist **Albert Hofmann** accidentally discovered LSD's hallucinogenic effects at Sandoz Laboratories in 1943 while synthesizing derivatives from ergot.

Hofmann learned two key things from his self-experiment with LSD. The first was dosage. He took only one-quarter milligram of LSD, which to his surprise produced a strong effect. The second thing was that LSD is a powerful hallucinogenic drug. Hofmann's second "trip" lasted hours, providing the experience described at the beginning of this chapter.

After LSD's hallucinogenic effects were discovered, the substance was tested for a variety of uses. The U.S. Army tested LSD as an aid for inducing captured enemy prisoners to talk more freely. The army also tested LSD as a chemical weapon. During the psychoanalysis era, psychiatrists used LSD to gain access to supposedly unconscious thoughts in their patients (Brecher, 1972). Antony Busch and Warren Johnson (1950) published the first paper for LSD use in psychiatric patients, stating that LSD "may offer a means of more readily gaining access to the chronically withdrawn patients" and that its use might shorten psychotherapy. Other studies supported these claims (Chandler & Hartman, 1960; Natale, Kowitt, Dahlberg, & Jaffe, 1978).

In 1960, Sidney Cohen reported on a LSD survey returned by 44 researchers and therapists. These respondents reported administering LSD to nearly 5,000 men and women, equating to more than 25,000 total administrations. The volume of LSD therapeutic use declined, however, as published reports and conference proceedings noted negative psychological experiences, referred to as *bad trips*, emerging in many patients. Many practitioners especially feared producing prolonged bad trips, lasting as long as 48 hours. Occasionally, bad trips led to suicides.

Psychologist Timothy Leary became a well-known figure among hallucinogen users, after leading studies alongside Richard Alpert, on the effects of psilocybin in human volunteers at Harvard University for what was referred to as the **Harvard Psilocybin Project** from 1960 to 1962. One of the founding board members included Aldous Huxley, who later became famous for the novel *Brave New World* (1932) and his nonfiction accounts of his experiences taking mescaline in *The Doors of Perception* (1954). One of the Harvard Psilocybin Project studies, referred to as the *Concord Prison Experiment*, reported lower recidivism rates among paroled former inmates because of combined psilocybin treatment with psychotherapy (Leary et al., 1965). However, a reassessment of these data by Ralph Metzner, a coauthor of the original study, reported a fabrication of these data (Metzner, 1998). Another experiment, called the *Marsh Chapel Experiment*, found that psilocybin induced profound religious experiences among divinity students (Pahnke & Richards, 1966). Follow-up studies reported similar findings (Doblin, 1991).

Albert Hofmann Swiss chemist who discovered LSD

Harvard Psilocybin Project Studies led by Timothy Leary and Richard Alpert to examine effects of psilocybin in human volunteers

State and federal regulations for LSD increased as therapeutic use of LSD decreased (Brecher, 1972). Eventually, LSD and other hallucinogens became schedule I controlled substances, precluding therapeutic use. Research on LSD and other hallucinogens in humans continues in order to learn about their pharmacological actions and in some cases to examine potential therapeutic uses.

STOP & CHECK

1. Who discovered LSD's hallucinogenic effects?

2. Aside from recreation, what were the other historical uses of LSD?

1. Albert Hofmann, a chemist who worked for Sandoz Laboratories 2. LSD was tested by the U.S. military to aid in prisoner interrogation and to use as a chemical weapon. The drug was also used in psychotherapy.

LSD Ingestion and Effects

LSD and most other hallucinogens are normally orally administered. This was the administration route used by Albert Hofmann's accidental LSD ingestion and self-experimentation described previously. LSD is potent, with effective amounts beginning at only 0.025 mg. Researchers consider 0.075 to 0.15 mg a moderate dose range capable of achieving a significantly altered state of consciousness (Passie, Halpern, Stichtenoth, Emrich, & Hintzen, 2008). Given these doses, an amount of LSD the size of an aspirin tablet would affect 3,000 people!

The high potency of LSD requires a different method for drug preparation. A common preparation method involves applying drops of a solution of LSD onto small squares of blotter paper or the glue sides of postage stamps. In either case, LSD sticks to the paper, and recreational users ingest the drug by licking the paper.

Through the oral administration route, LSD reaches peak absorption after 60 minutes. Cells in the liver metabolize LSD, producing *2-oxo-3-hydroxy-LSD*. LSD's elimination half-life is approximately 3 hours, which facilitates pharmacological effects lasting as long as 8 hours (Passie et al., 2008).

LSD and the Serotonin Neurotransmitter System

The chemical structure of LSD resembles serotonin's chemical structure, allowing LSD to act on serotonin receptors (**Figure 12.2**). Specifically, LSD functions as a receptor agonist with a high binding affinity for 5-HT_{1A}, 5-HT_{2A}, 5-HT_6, and 5-HT_7 receptors. In particular, LSD activates serotonin receptors located postsynaptically on other neurotransmitter neurons, such as glutamate and GABA neurons (Passie et al., 2008).

Serotonin

LSD

These neurotransmission effects affect many sensory-processing systems in the brain. In the visual cortex, LSD activates both 5-HT_{1A} and 5-HT_{2A} receptors, which can modify any number of visual processes (**Table 12.1**). For example, these actions can interfere with modal object completion for objects like those shown in **Figure 12.3**. **Modal object completion** is a perception of object boundaries inferred from incomplete representations of the object. According to electroencephalogram (EEG) recordings, the N170 waveform is strongly associated with modal object completion. In a study by Kometer et al. (2011) using human volunteers, the LSD-like hallucinogen psilocybin inhibited both modal object completion and weakened N170 waveform amplitudes in specific areas of the visual cortex. The objects viewed by participants consisted of *Kaniza* objects, the perception of objects despite their lacking complete borders. Moreover, these reduced N170 waveform amplitudes correlated with overall decreased activity in the occipital lobe.

Modal object completion
Perception of object boundaries inferred from incomplete representations of the object

TABLE 12.1 ● **Effects of Hallucinogens on Structures in the Brain**

Structure	Effects of Hallucinogen
Visual cortex	Alters visual processes, including modal object completion
Temporomedial cortex	Increases activity of this area, which is involved in complex visual processing
Cerebral cortex	Increases sensory signals to prefrontal cortex
Locus coeruleus	Decreases spontaneous activity, thereby sending normally suppressed sensory information to the cerebral cortex
Prefrontal cortex	Increases activity of the prefrontal cortex, the central sensory integration area of the cerebral cortex

FIGURE 12.3 ● 12.3a LSD and other hallucinogens disrupt the ability to perceive nonexistent borders, a process called *modal object completion*, of Kanizsa objects, shown with a dark line (responses to non-Kanizsa objects shown by the red line). 12.3b During these tasks, hallucinogens impair the N170 waveform (the *N* stands for negative and the 170 refers to the location of the negative peak in milliseconds [ms]) in the occipital lobe on EEG recordings.

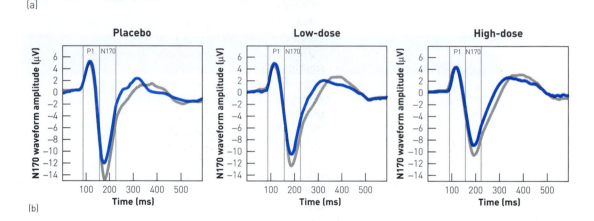

(a)

(b)

SOURCE: Kometer et al., 2011. Reprinted with permission.

Hallucinogens also alter functioning in the locus coeruleus. In the locus coeruleus, LSD's activation of postsynaptic 5-HT$_{2A}$ receptors increases the activity of both glutamate and GABA neurons. Enhanced glutamate release increases sensory signals to the cerebral cortex. At the same time, GABA release decreases spontaneous activity in the locus coeruleus, causing greater refinement of sensory signals sent to the cerebral cortex. In essence, LSD causes normally suppressed sensory information from the locus coeruleus to become more refined and salient.

In the prefrontal cortex, the central integration area for processed sensory information, activation of 5-HT$_{2A}$ receptors by LSD also causes increased glutamate release. Enhanced glutamate release, in turn, increases activity in the prefrontal cortex. These findings correlate with human drug imaging data. In a positron emission tomography (PET) imaging study conducted by Vollenweider and colleagues (1997), the LSD-like hallucinogen psilocybin produced a significant increase in the metabolism of labeled glucose, an index of neuronal activity, in the prefrontal cortex. In addition, psilocybin elicited enhanced activity in the temporomedial cortex, a region involved

in complex visual processing. These enhanced activity levels in the prefrontal cortex and temporomedial cortex also occurred while participants experienced visual hallucinations.

Chronic use of hallucinogens may cause structural changes to parts of the cerebral cortex. Bouso and colleagues (2015) found that long-term use of DMT correlated with a thinning of the posterior cingulate cortex. Further, those who self-reported more intense experiences of psychedelic effects from DMT were more likely to have thinner tissue in the posterior cingulate cortex. The researchers found this structure of particular interest because of its involvement the brain's *default mode network*. The **default mode network** consists of activity occurring in a series of brain structures during times of non-goal directed activity or inattention. When an individual disengages from a task—or said another way, a person's mind wanders—we find the activity of brain structures switch to those part of the default mode network, the apparent default mode of the brain.

Default mode network Activity occurring in a series of brain structure during times of non-goal-directed activity or inattention

STOP & CHECK

1. What is the most common administration route for LSD and other hallucinogens?

2. Although LSD activates many types of serotonin receptors, which receptor is most associated with visual hallucinations?

1. Oral administration 2. The 5-HT$_{2A}$ receptor

LSD's Mild Physiological Effects and Profound Hallucinogenic Effects

LSD and many other serotonin-like hallucinogens primarily elicit subjective pharmacological effects. Even the LSD megadose taken by Hofmann—0.25 mg—produced few noticeable physiological effects. In his account of the trip, Hofmann said that his physician "found a rather weak pulse, but an otherwise normal circulation," and Hofmann felt fine the next day. At normally used doses, a person may exhibit only modest increases in heart rate, increases in pupil diameter, slight dizziness, mild nausea, diarrhea, or stomach ache. The physiological safety of this drug is indicated by a human lethal dose of 14 mg, far above the doses capable of producing hallucinogenic effects (Brecher, 1972).

Although few, if any, physiological effects occur with normally used amounts, LSD and other serotonin-like hallucinogens exhibit pronounced subjective experiences. However, the term *hallucination* needs qualification. A **true hallucination** is a perception of images or sounds that are not real. Drugs such as LSD, on the other hand, normally produce **pseudo-hallucinations**, the altered perception of things that *are* real. Normal LSD doses cause distorted, waiving, or kaleidoscopic forms of real images in a visual field (El-Mallakh & Walker, 2010). True hallucinations can occur with LSD, but they are considered rare (Passie et al., 2008).

True hallucination Perception of images or sounds that are not real

Pseudo-hallucinations Altered perception of things that are real

As previously mentioned, the overall hallucinogenic experience is called a **trip**, and a trip can be good or bad. **Good trips** occur as highly pleasant sensory distortions and pseudo-hallucinations. During good trips, users may experience feelings of enhanced perception or insightfulness. A user may also experience **synesthesia**, or experiencing sensory stimuli in an incorrect sensory modality. LSD-elicited synesthesia, for example, often consists of experiencing sounds when seeing colors and vice versa (Brown, McKone, & Ward, 2010). The "From Actions to Effects" section later in this chapter describes synesthesia in greater detail. Hofmann, too, experienced synesthesia, stating that "sounds were transposed into visual sensations so that from each tone or noise a comparable colored picture was evoked, changing in form and color kaleidoscopically" (Brecher, 1972).

A **bad trip** is associated with disturbing true hallucinations, psychotic episodes, negative emotional states, altered perceptions of time, and out-of-body sensations (Eveloff, 1968). Hofmann experienced a bad trip after intentionally taking LSD. He stated that the faces of those around him "appeared as grotesque, colored masks" and that "I sometimes observed, in the manner of an independent neutral observer, that I shouted half insanely or babbled incoherent words." He reported that this experience was as if "I were out of my body" (Brecher, 1972).

A person's expectations and previous experiences affect LSD's subjective effects. Factors that affect a person's trip can include physical surroundings, current emotional state, comments made by friends, and many other factors. In fact, Eveloff (1968) states that profound skepticism about LSD's effects largely suppress the LSD experience. LSD also causes **hypersuggestibility**, a state of easy influence by suggestions that can jeopardize reality testing. Eveloff (1968) reported that during some trips, users have jumped off buildings in the belief they could fly or stepped in front of traveling cars in the belief they lacked material substance.

The nature of hallucinogenic experiences presents an important challenge for hallucinogen research in animals. Even if an animal experienced something like a hallucinogenic trip, how could we tell? Rather than attempt to model such an experience, animal researchers instead study other features of hallucinogens such as their behavioral stimulus properties.

Winter and colleagues (2007) conducted a drug-discrimination study using the hallucinogen psilocybin as the training drug in rats. After training rats in this task, the researchers conducted tests to determine the similarity between psilocybin's stimulus effects and those of other hallucinogenic drugs. As shown in **Figure 12.4,** rats exhibited stimulus generalization from mescaline to the hallucinogens LSD, psilocin, and DMT, demonstrating similar subjective effects between psilocybin and these compounds. Also recall that psilocin serves as the active metabolite for psilocybin.

Hallucinogens and Flashbacks

The primary adverse effects of hallucinogens consist of negative subjective experiences, such as those experienced during a bad trip. Occasionally, users may randomly experience a striking memory of the previous trip. Such an experience is referred to as a flashback or as a symptom of hallucinogen persisting perception disorder. These terms are used somewhat synonymously, but there are key differences in how the terms are applied. **Flashback** usually refers to a short, non-distressing recurrence of a previous

Trip Hallucinogenic experience

Good trip Highly pleasant sensory distortions and pseudo-hallucinations

Synesthesia Experiencing sensory stimuli in an incorrect sensory modality

Bad trip Disturbing true hallucinations, psychotic episodes, negative emotional states, altered perceptions of time, and out-of-body sensations

Hypersuggestibility A state of easy influence by suggestions that can jeopardize reality testing

Flashback Random, short, and nondistressing memory of a previous hallucinogenic experience

FIGURE 12.4 ● In a mescaline drug-discrimination study, stimulus generalization occurred from mescaline to the hallucinogenic drugs LSD, psilocybin, and DMT. Said another way, these drugs served a substitutes for the training drug psilocybin, causing rats to respond as if there were treated with psilocybin. The *y*-axis shows the percentage of responses occuring on the psilocybin lever, and the *x*-axis shows the doses of each drug tested.

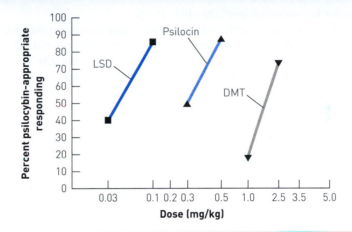

SOURCE: Winter et al., 2007. Reprinted with permission.

Hallucinogen persisting perception disorder Recurring, lengthy, and unpleasant memory from a previous hallucinogenic experience

trip. On the other hand, **hallucinogen persisting perception disorder** is characterized by recurring, longer-term, and unpleasant experiences that are difficult to reverse (Lerner et al., 2002). For example, a case study on hallucinogen persisting perception disorder described a patient who reported seeing afterimages. These included motions occurring in her peripheral field, halo effects flickering from objects that had a pattern on them, misperceiving the size of objects, and random spots of bright light (Hermle, Simon, Ruchsow, & Geppert, 2012).

STOP & CHECK

1. How does a true hallucination differ from a pseudo-hallucination?

2. How does a good trip differ from a bad trip?

1. A true hallucination is a perception of something not really there, whereas a pseudo-hallucination is an altered perception of something that really is there. 2. A good trip elicits a pleasurable psychedelic drug experience, whereas a bad trip elicits a distressful and disturbing experience.

Mixed Stimulant–Psychedelic Drugs

Beyond the hallucinogens, other psychedelic drugs exhibit broader pharmacological effects. In particular, a **mixed stimulant–psychedelic drug** refers to a substance that exhibits both psychostimulant effects and hallucinations. One such drug is 3,4-methylenedioxymethamphetamine, better known by its common abbreviation **MDMA** or street name *Ecstasy*. Ecstasy, however, does not always refer to MDMA. Instead, Ecstasy can refer to any number of stimulant or psychedelic preparations that may contain only small amounts, or even no amount, of MDMA. In an analysis of Ecstasy tablets collected by England's Forensic Science Service, a number of tablets contained the MDMA-like drug MDEA (3,4-methylenedioxyethamphetamine) instead of MDMA (Cole, Bailey, Sumnall, Wagstaff, & King, 2002). Other studies report Ecstasy pills containing methamphetamine, dextromethorphan, ketamine, and cocaine.

Mixed stimulant–psychedelic drug Substance that exhibits both psychostimulant effects and hallucinations

MDMA A mixed stimulant-psychedelic drug

🔎 *Drug Profile:* MDMA (3,4-methylenedioxyethamphetamine)

Street name	Ecstasy (although the term does not always refer to MDMA)
Subjective effects	Produces stimulant effects, hallucinations, and enhances feelings of empathy and closeness with others

---

Although MDMA is best known for its psychedelic and psychostimulant effects, it is also known as an **entactogen**, meaning "touching within," or as an **empathogen**, referring to "enhanced empathy." These terms synonymously refer to effects observed in early MDMA studies that users become friendlier, exhibit a closeness with others, and perceive greater insight into their thoughts and emotions (Nichols & Oberlender, 1990). Like LSD, these features made MDMA an attractive adjunctive medication for use in psychoanalysis (Rochester & Kirchner, 1999).

MDMA shares a similar chemical structure with amphetamine and possesses many of amphetamine's psychostimulant effects. Yet MDMA also produces LSD-like hallucinations, so it fits into the mixed psychedelic–stimulant class of drugs. This class also includes the drugs AMT and 5-MeO-DIPT (Abraham et al., 2002). MDMA is frequently used in **raves**, large organized parties held in dance clubs or warehouses where electronic dance music is played with accompanying light displays. MDMA and other psychedelic drugs enhance this club experience (Miller & Schwartz, 1997).

MDMA users mainly consist of high school and college-age individuals. According to the National Institute on Drug Abuse, approximately 3.0 million high school students 12 and older used MDMA in 2014 (Center for Behavioral Health Statistics and Quality, 2015). MDMA use is higher among college-age students. From surveys given to U.S. college students in the mid-Atlantic region, 9 percent reported using MDMA in their lifetime. For close to half of those college students reporting MDMA use, polydrug use was common, particularly including marijuana, inhalants, LSD, and cocaine (Wish, Fitzelle, O'Grady, Hsu, & Arria, 2006).

Entactogen "Touching within;" usually in reference to mixed stimulant-psychedelic drugs

Empathogen "Enhanced empathy, usually in reference to mixed stimulant-psychedelic drugs

Rave Large organized party held in a dance club or warehouse where electronic dance music is played with a light show

MDMA Therapeutic and Recreational Use

MDMA was discovered in 1914 by Merck (the same company that had patented and distributed cocaine) during research efforts to develop amphetamine derivatives. Although studied for a time by the U.S. Army, experimental psychopharmacologist Alexander Shulgin popularized the drug for recreational use in the 1970s (McDowell & Kleber, 1994).

Shulgin's career walked a unique path between traditional laboratory scientist and club drug enthusiast. Shulgin was a chemist who had been educated at Harvard and Berkeley and had extensive training in pharmacology. He developed industrial chemicals for Bio-Rad Laboratories and Dow Chemical Company. At Dow, Shulgin developed *Zectran*, the first biodegradable pesticide. Shulgin also had a private laboratory at home, where he developed various psychedelic drugs, which he sampled himself and provided to his friends (Gems, 1999).

Shulgin played an important role in developing and promoting MDMA. After being introduced to the drug, Shulgin developed an easier synthesis method and reported the method to other psychedelic drug enthusiasts, allowing them to make it themselves. In 1976, Shulgin described MDMA's effects to Leo Zeff, a psychoanalyst who had used LSD on patients in the 1960s. Intrigued by Shulgin's account, Leo Zeff administered MDMA to several patients. Believing many of MDMA's subjective effects beneficial as a psychoanalytical agent, Zeff reported these accounts to colleagues, spurring an interest in MDMA for psychoanalysis that lasted until the 1980s (Pentney, 2001).

Beginning in the late 1970s, MDMA emerged as a recreational drug. People sought it for spiritual enlightenment, improving sensuality in relationships, and pure enjoyment. In humans, MDMA-related medical problems were rare, with only eight MDMA-related emergency room visits between 1977 and 1981. In laboratory animals, however, the occurrence of both acute and chronic adverse effects led to MDMA being labeled a dangerous drug. In 1985, despite opposition by therapists and recreational MDMA users, the DEA temporarily listed MDMA as a schedule I controlled substance, indicating high abuse potential and no therapeutic usefulness (Pentney, 2001; Rochester & Kirchner, 1999). The schedule I status was made permanent in 1988. The first clinical trial for MDMA in psychotherapy was published relatively recently, in 2011. The study, conducted by Mithoefer and colleagues (2011) (described later), reported that MDMA assisted therapy for patients with posttraumatic stress disorder (PTSD).

STOP & CHECK

1. Why is MDMA called an empathogen?

2. Although MDMA was developed decades earlier, who popularized MDMA in the 1970s?

1. Empathogen is derived from the tendency of MDMA to induce friendliness, closeness with others, and greater insight into one's thoughts and emotions. 2. Psychopharmacologist Alexander Shulgin

MDMA Metabolism and the Length of Psychedelic Drug Effects

MDMA users prefer to administer MDMA orally, usually through swallowing an MDMA-containing tablet. After they swallow the tablet, MDMA readily absorbs through the gastrointestinal tract, reaching peak blood plasma levels after approximately 2 hours. MDMA's elimination half-life is approximately 9 hours (De La Torre, Farré, Roset, et al., 2000) (see **Figure 12.5**).

MDMA is metabolized in the liver primarily by CYP2D6 enzymes and to a lesser extent by other enzymes such as CYP1A2. CYP1A2 converts MDMA to methylenedioxyamphetamine (MDA). Like MDMA, MDA exhibits psychedelic drug effects. Its users thus experience specific MDMA effects and then, after metabolic transformation, effects elicited by MDA as well.

Deficiencies in the CYP2D6 enzyme lead to accumulation of MDMA in the body. Approximately 10 percent of Caucasians exhibit these deficiencies. Accumulated MDMA leads to prolonged drug effects and an increased probability of adverse effects occurring at low to moderate doses. For example, certain *selective serotonin reuptake inhibitors* (SSRIs) such as *fluoxetine (Prozac)* inhibit CYP2D6 activity. These actions inhibit MDMA metabolism, leading to effects similar to those with inherent CYP2D6 deficiencies (Yang et al., 2006).

Inhibition of MDMA metabolism also can occur in people with fully functional CYP2D6 enzymes. De la Torre and colleagues (2000) studied the blood plasma levels of MDMA to determine MDMA's degradation rate. During this study, the researchers

FIGURE 12.5 ●   MDMA (Ecstasy) remains in the body well beyond 24 hours, as shown for both a low dose (1.0 mg/kg) and high dose (1.6 mg/kg). The *y*-axis refers to the amount of MDMA in the blood, and the *x*-axis refers to time since MDMA administration.

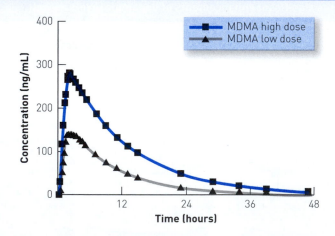

SOURCE: Kolbrich, E. A., Goodwin, R. S., Gorelick, D. A., Hayes, R. J., Stein, E. A., & Huestis, M. A. (2008). Physiological and subjective responses to controlled oral 3,4- methylenedioxymethamphetamine administration. *J Clin Psychopharmacol*, *28*(4), 432–440. doi:, p. 9. Reprinted with permission.

found that the MDMA's elimination rate was not constant. Rather, MDMA metabolism slowed down over time. Based on these findings, taking further MDMA doses contributes to stronger and longer-lasting pharmacological effects than may otherwise be expected.

MDMA and Serotonin and Dopamine Neurotransmission

1. Serotonin Antagonist ~~Inhibitor~~ (prevent storage)

2. Serotonin Agonist (prevent reuptake)

Acute administration of MDMA alters serotonin neurotransmission at axon terminals through two mechanisms (**Figure 12.6**). First, MDMA inhibits serotonin transportation into synaptic storage vesicles. In doing so, MDMA prevents serotonin storage. Second, MDMA causes the reversal of serotonin membrane transporters. By reversing serotonin membrane transporters, MDMA expels any unstored serotonin (that wasn't catabolized by MAO) out into the synaptic cleft. Through these two mechanisms, MDMA produces an increase in extracellular brain serotonin levels. These increased serotonin levels lead in turn to increased activation of serotonin receptors (Rudnick & Wall, 1992).

Like amphetamine, MDMA produces similar actions at dopamine axon terminals, leading to enhanced extracellular levels of dopamine in the brain (Figure 12.6). However, MDMA's effects on dopamine axonal terminals are weaker than its effects on

FIGURE 12.6 ● MDMA produces dose-dependent effects on serotonin (5-HT) and dopamine (DA) neurotransmission. At lower doses (left), MDMA effectively inhibits serotonin entry into vesicles and reverses the serotonin reuptake transporter direction. These actions cause large enhancements in serotonin release. Few effects occur at dopamine axon terminals at low doses, producing minimal changes in dopamine release. At higher doses (right), MDMA remains effective at enhancing serotonin levels. Yet, we also find inhibited entry of dopamine into vesicles and a reversal of the dopamine membrane transporter direction. This combination of actions causes significant enhancements of dopamine levels as well.

Low dose

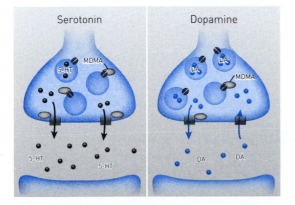

High dose

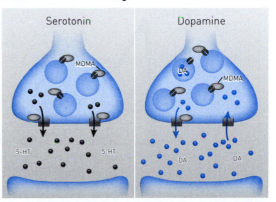

SOURCE: © Cengage Learning 2014.

serotonin axonal terminals. As a result, higher MDMA doses are necessary to enhance dopamine levels (Abraham et al., 2002; Steele, Nichols, & Yim, 1987).

Chronic administration of MDMA can produce severe damage to serotonin neurons. This damage appears according to every standard measure of serotonin neurons, including loss of brain serotonin, the serotonin metabolite 5-hydroxyindolacetic acid (5-HIAA), tryptophan hydroxylase, and the serotonin membrane transporter. Hatzidimitriou and colleagues (1999) provided a striking example of MDMA-induced neuronal loss in monkeys.

In this study, researchers treated monkeys with MDMA daily over 4 days. Two weeks after treatment ended, MDMA-treated monkeys had a dramatic decline in serotonin neuron axons, as shown in the middle panels of **Figure 12.7.** Serotonin neuron loss remained low in a monkey assessed 7 years after this experiment, as shown in the right panel of Figure 12.7. This finding suggests a severe neurotoxic effect from repeated MDMA use and a dismal likelihood of neuronal recovery.

FIGURE 12.7 ● Four days of MDMA administration led to a significant reduction in cortical serotonin neurons 2 weeks after treatment (middle panels) and 7 years after treatment (right panels) compared to a monkey treated with placebo (left panels). The top row of panels (A, B, and C) were dark-field photomicrograph sagittal sections from the frontal cortex. The middle panels (D, E, and H) were taken from the parietal cortex, and the bottom panels (G, H, and I) were taken from the primary visual cortex.

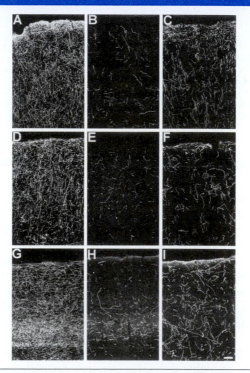

SOURCE: Hatzidimitriou et al., 1999.

Because the cellular techniques used in animals cannot be used in living humans, we lack precise indices of MDMA-induced neurotoxic function in humans. However, the limited data available, in concert with extensive animal data, suggest that serotonin neuron loss occurs in human MDMA users as well. First, heavy MDMA users have lower 5-HIAA levels in cerebrospinal fluid, suggesting less serotonin production in their nervous systems (McCann, Ridenour, Shaham, & Ricaurte, 1994). Second, PET imaging techniques reveal lower levels of serotonin membrane transporters in routine MDMA users. For example, Erritzoe and colleagues (2011) found reduced serotonin membrane transporter levels in routine MDMA users. Particularly striking, frequent hallucinogen use, such as LSD or mescaline, did not have reductions in serotonin membrane transporter levels in users. However, MDMA-induced reduction in serotonin membrane transporter levels may not be permanent. Selvaraj and colleagues (2009) failed to find serotonin membrane transporter reductions in heavy MDMA users who had refrained from MDMA use for more than 1 year.

STOP & CHECK

1. How might a drug that inhibits CYP2D6 activity, such as fluoxetine, affect the pharmacokinetics of MDMA?

2. What are the key differences in pharmacological actions between low and high MDMA doses?

3. What effect does sustained MDMA use have on serotonin neurons?

1. The CYP2D6 enzyme metabolizes MDMA. Any drug that inhibits CYP2D6 activity will slow down MDMA metabolism, causing prolonged MDMA effects. 2. Lower MDMA doses primarily enhance serotonin neurotransmission, whereas higher MDMA doses enhance both serotonin and dopamine neurotransmission. 3. Heavy, sustained MDMA use destroys serotonin neurons.

MDMA's Psychedelic and Psychostimulant Effects

The effects that MDMA has in a party setting may differ from those reported under carefully controlled laboratory conditions. These differences occur for multiple reasons. First, as stated earlier in this chapter, the term *Ecstasy* inconsistently refers to MDMA. A so-called Ecstasy tablet may include MDMA, but it also may contain other drugs (Cole et al., 2002). Second, MDMA is seldom taken alone. For example, many club goers take MDMA while consuming alcohol (Mohamed, Hamida, Pereira de Vasconcelos, Cassel, & Jones, 2009). Third, an individual may take MDMA while also taking prescribed psychoactive medications. For example, an individual taking certain antidepressant drugs may have an exaggerated reaction to MDMA's effects (Mohamed, Ben Hamida, Cassel, de Vasconcelos, & Jones, 2011). Fourth, MDMA's effects vary depending on the dose administered (Abraham et al., 2002).

MDMA's physiological effects resemble those of psychostimulant drugs such as amphetamine at higher doses. For example, Kolbrich and colleagues (2008) assessed

the effects of low (1.0 mg/kg) and high (1.6 mg/kg) doses of MDMA in occasional MDMA users (**Figure 12.8**). In these volunteers, only the high MDMA dose produced an increase in heart rate and blood pressure.

Review! Psychostimulant drugs activate the sympathetic nervous system. (Chapter 6.)

Low MDMA doses elicit few physiological effects. However, both low and high MDMA doses elicit significant subjective effects. In the same study, Kolbrich and colleagues (2008) found that low MDMA doses produced feelings or sensations of heightened senses, racing thoughts, and euphoric effects. The high MDMA dose included these effects as well as perceptions of increased energy and feelings of closeness to others (figure 12.8).

FIGURE 12.8   ●   In human volunteers, a high MDMA dose increases sympathetic nervous system effects such as heart rate (a) and sense of energy (b), whereas low doses create perceptions of heightened senses (c).

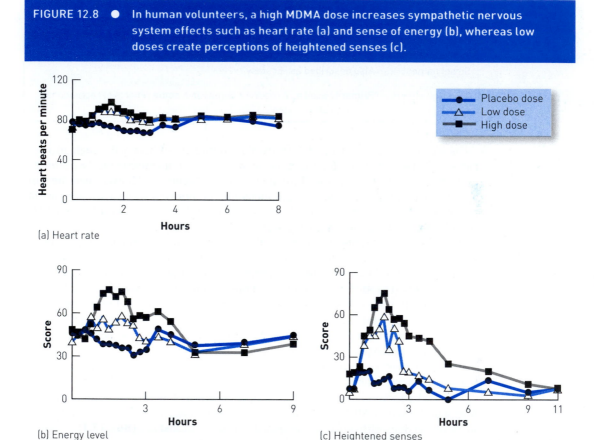

(a) Heart rate

(b) Energy level

(c) Heightened senses

SOURCE: Kolbrich, E. A., Goodwin, R. S., Gorelick, D. A., Hayes, R. J., Stein, E. A., & Huestis, M. A. (2008). Physiological and subjective responses to controlled oral 3,4- methylenedioxymethamphetamine administration. *J Clin Psychopharmacol*, *28*(4), 432–440. doi: p. 9. Reprinted with permission.

The subjective effects of MDMA relate to both psychostimulants and hallucinogenic drugs. Tancer and Johanson (2003) recruited human volunteers to assess the effects of MDMA compared to the psychostimulant d-amphetamine and the hallucinogen metachlorophenylpiperazine (mCPP). *mCPP* binds to all serotonin receptors and acts as agonist; in addition, mCPP inhibits serotonin reuptake through serotonin transporters (Baumann, Ayestas, Dersch, & Rothman, 2001; Hamik & Peroutka, 1989). mCPP has mostly been used as a study compound by researchers, but we now find mCPP used recreationally as another psychedelic drug with purported hallucinogen-like effects (Bossong et al., 2010). Like d-amphetamine, MDMA produced increases in a scale for drug "liking," an indication of reinforcing effects. Similar to mCPP, MDMA produced increases in perception and hallucinogen-like effects. There were also shared traits among these drugs. MDMA, d-amphetamine, and mCPP increased ratings of friendliness and talkativeness. Each drug also increased a sense of improved cognition (Tancer & Johanson, 2003).

⌀ *Drug Profile:* **metachlorophenylpiperazine (mCPP)**	
Street name	Also described as "Ecstasy"
Uses and effects	Primarily used as a research compound; some reports of recreational use as a hallucinogen

Based on animal models, MDMA exhibits reinforcing effects, although in comparison, conventional reinforcing drugs such as methamphetamine produce stronger reinforcing effects. For example, Fantegrossi and colleagues (2002) examined the reinforcing effects of MDMA and methamphetamine in monkeys using a self-administration model. Across a range of doses, subjects self-administered significantly less MDMA compared to methamphetamine (**Figure 12.9**).

Beyond reinforcing effects, MDMA is also the representative drug for empathogens, which, as stated earlier, refer to enhanced empathy. Women appear more sensitive to MDMA's psychedelic and empathogenic properties than men. In fact, Leicht and colleagues (2001) found that women exhibited a greater sensitivity to nearly every measure of MDMA's effects, including overall improved mood, feelings of depersonalization, time-perception changes, and emotional sensitivity. Moreover, women experienced more frequent and profound visual perception changes such as visual hallucinations (pseudo), synesthesia, and memories.

As stated previously, animals poorly model the psychedelic effects experienced by humans. However, animal models *can* provide indexes of sociability. Morley and McGregor (2000) used a social interaction test to compare relatively low MDMA doses to placebo. After administration, MDMA-treated rats exhibited fewer aggressive behaviors and greater social interactions with other rats compared to placebo-treated rats (**Box 12.1**).

MDMA's Adverse Effects

Like the pharmacological effects already described, elevated dopamine and serotonin levels account for MDMA's adverse effects. Like the hallucinogens, MDMA also can

FIGURE 12.9 ● Rhesus monkeys self-administered methamphetamine more readily compared to MDMA. The *y*-axis shows the number of drug injections the monkeys earned during a session, and the *x*-axis shows the number of doses of self-administered drugs.

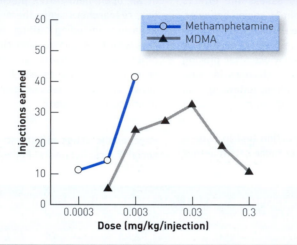

SOURCE: With kind permission from Springer Science+Business Media: Fantegrossi, W. E., Ullrich, T., Rice, K. C., Woods, J. H., & Winger, G. (2002). 3,4- Methylenedioxymethamphetamine (MDMA, "ecstasy") and its stereoisomers as reinforcers in rhesus monkeys: serotonergic involvement. *Psychopharmacology (Berl), 161*(4), 356–3, p. 9.

lead to flashbacks and hallucinogen persisting perception disorder likely due to its actions on serotonin neurotransmission (Litjens, Brunt, Alderliefste, & Westerink, 2014). MDMA shares adverse effects with many psychostimulant drugs such as methamphetamine. Physiologically, higher doses of MDMA, which are achieved by taking two or more standard MDMA doses, such as 1.6 mg/kg, can substantially activate the sympathetic nervous system, leading to significant increases in heart rate, breathing rate, blood pressure, and body temperature (De La Torre, Farré, Roset, et al., 2000; Kolbrich et al., 2008). This is one of the most common causes of unconsciousness from MDMA use. Other serious problems include brain hemorrhaging and chaotic heartbeat (Kolbrich et al., 2008).

In raves, where dancing occurs in crowded conditions, MDMA use can lead to severe overheating and dehydration, increasing the risk of multiple organ failure. **Multiple organ failure** from MDMA use is a serious medical event that, in addition to hyperthermia and dehydration, is associated with seizures, muscle breakdown, kidney failure, and blood vessel blockade. Liver damage may also occur because of contaminants produced during MDMA synthesis (Abraham et al., 2002; McDowell & Kleber, 1994).

Psychologically, MDMA doses may cause adverse effects, including paranoia, true hallucinations, panic, and delirium. Moreover, MDMA overdose can cause impulsive

Multiple organ failure Occurs due to hyperthermia from MDMA use, resulting in seizures, muscle breakdown, kidney failure, and blood vessel blockade

BOX 12.1 SOCIAL INTERACTION TESTS

Social interaction tests assess the effects that drugs have on animal social behavior. These assessments use naturally social species, such as rats, and involve observing any of several key social behaviors after placing animals together. Social behaviors in rats, for example, include sniffing, following, and crawling over or under each other.

In a typical social interaction test in rats, a researcher places two or more rats together in an open field. After placing rats in the box, researchers score the number of social behaviors, including sniffing, nudging another rats with their snouts, and closely following other rats. To ensure accurate behavioral recording, multiple researchers may score a social interaction test session and compare their scores afterward.

Psychedelic drugs affect rodent behavior in social interaction tests. For example, Morley

FIGURE 1 ● **In a social interaction test, rats treated with the 5.0 mg/kg dose of MDMA spent significantly more time interacting with other rats compared to saline-treated rats. The y-axis shows time spent interacting with other rats, and the x-axis refers to the dose of MDMA. The zero (0) dose refers to saline.**

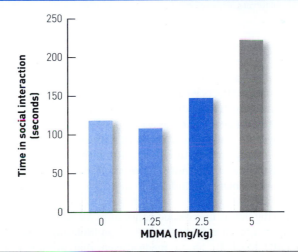

SOURCE: Morley & McGregor, 2000. Reprinted with permission.

and McGregor (2000) tested the stimulant–psychedelic drug MDMA in rats using this test. This study found that MDMA-treated rats spent significantly more time interacting with other rats compared to saline-treated rats **(Figure 1)**. Using a different psychedelic drug, Sams-Dodd (1998) evaluated the effects of the dissociative anesthetic phencyclidine (PCP) on social behavior in rats. After conducting a social interaction test, PCP-treated rats exhibited reduced social interactions compared to saline-treated rats **(Figure 2)**. In other words, PCP-treated rats appeared socially withdrawn.

FIGURE 2 ● Phencyclidine-treated rats exhibited significantly reduced social interactions compared to vehicle-treated rats in a social interaction test. The y-axis refers to time spent interacting with other rats, and the x-axis shows the PCP dose. The zero (0) dose refers to vehicle.

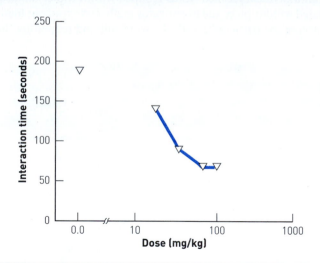

SOURCE: Adapted with permission from Macmillan Publishers Ltd: Nature, Sams-Dodd, F. (1998). Effects of continuous D-amphetamine and phencyclidine administration on social behaviour, stereotyped behaviour, and locomotor activity in rats. *Neuropsychopharmacology, 19*(1), 18–25. doi: S0893133X97002005 [pii]. Copyright © 1998.

irrational behavior such as walking into the middle of street traffic or attempting to jump from buildings several stories high (Hooft & van de Voorde, 1994; Kaye, Darke, & Duflou, 2009; McDowell & Kleber, 1994).

Rebound effects occur from normal MDMA use. Rebound normally occurs after 24 hours from MDMA use and primarily consists of depression and lethargy. These effects are related to MDMA's pharmacological actions at dopamine and serotonin axon terminals. As described previously, MDMA empties stored serotonin and dopamine from axon terminals and prevents serotonin and dopamine reuptake. These actions leave serotonin and dopamine stores temporarily depleted. Replenishing these stores requires synthesizing new serotonin and dopamine molecules, a process that can take several days for full recovery (**Figure 12.10**) (Parrott, 2001).

Cognitive deficits occur from repeated MDMA use. These deficits particularly affect verbal working memory. During verbal working memory tasks, where a participant recalls words given minutes earlier, former heavy MDMA users perform poorer compared to nonrecreational drug users or non-MDMA polydrug users (Schilt et al., 2010). In particular, MDMA users do more poorly on complex verbal memory tasks.

For example, Brown and colleagues (2010) studied verbal working memory in long-term MDMA users and compared their results to those of long-term cannabis users and non-recreational drug users. The researchers conducted several tasks ranging from simple tasks, in which an individual freely recalled words from a list, to complex tasks, in which an individual recalled words grouped within triplets of associated words. In the associated word triplets, the investigator might have read out loud *frog–chair–apple*, later prompting the participant with the word *frog* and requesting the remaining two

FIGURE 12.10 ● Acute administration of sufficiently high MDMA doses (left) produces an increase in serotonin and dopamine release. A rebound effect occurs after the stores of dopamine and serotonin have emptied (right), resulting in diminished serotonin and dopamine levels.

Acute Administration

Rebound

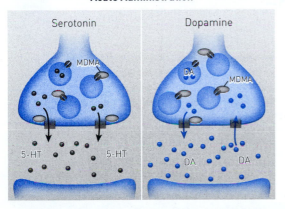

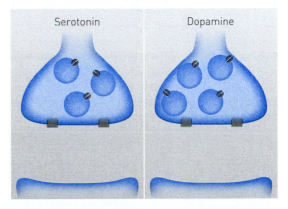

words. The results? MDMA users performed well on the simple free-word recall task, but not on the difficult triplet-word association task. Given these results, MDMA users appear to have sustained deficits in complex verbal working memory that may fail to improve over time.

STOP & CHECK

1. How do low-dose MDMA subjective effects differ from high-dose MDMA subjective effects?

2. Why might taking MDMA and dancing at a party be a bad idea?

3. Why do rebound effects occur after MDMA use?

1. Low MDMA doses produce feelings or sensations of heightened senses, racing thoughts, and reinforcing effects. High MDMA doses include these effects—and perceptions of increased energy levels and feelings of closeness to others. **2.** MDMA enhances sympathetic nervous system activity, making an individual prone to hyperthermia, increased heart rate, and hyperventilation. Engaging in physically exerting activities in this state can lead to unconsciousness, brain hemorrhaging, and chaotic heartbeat. **3.** Rebound effects are the result of emptied serotonin and dopamine synaptic pools. The diminished neurotransmitter levels account for depression and lethargy.

MDMA Use in Psychotherapy

As previously noted, psychotherapists administered MDMA to patients during psychoanalysis therapy in the past, providing anecdotal reports of positive results. This continued until the DEA classified MDMA as a schedule I controlled substance in the mid-1980s. The DEA scheduling not only eliminated all therapeutic MDMA use but also for practical purposes precluded clinical studies with MDMA.

The first clinical study on MDMA was reported in 2008 and conducted in Spain. Bouso and colleagues (2008) administered four women with PTSD a single low dose of MDMA, followed by 6 hours of psychotherapy. Two women with PTSD in the study received placebo. A post-treatment assessment found improvements in three out of four women treated with MDMA, compared to the two women treated with placebo. The study had intended to include more participants as well as more assessments, but political and media pressure led to an abrupt halt to study, leaving them with only six study participants who had completed at least a portion of the study.

The first complete clinical trial with MDMA was reported in 2011. In this study, Mithoefer and colleagues (2011) assessed low-dose MDMA treatment in conjunction with psychotherapy in patients with PTSD. During the course of the study, patients either received one or two treatments with MDMA or a placebo. Overall, MDMA-treated patients exhibited an 83 percent reduction in PTSD symptoms, whereas placebo-treated PTSD patients exhibited only a 25 percent reduction in PTSD symptoms (**Figure 12.11**). The MDMA doses used produced few physiological or adverse effects.

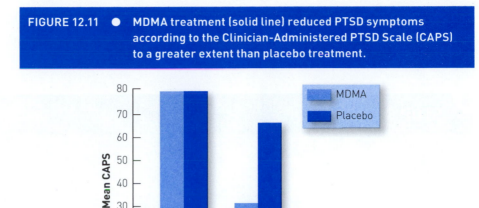

FIGURE 12.11 ● MDMA treatment (solid line) reduced PTSD symptoms according to the Clinician-Administered PTSD Scale (CAPS) to a greater extent than placebo treatment.

SOURCE: Michael C Mithoefer, Mark T Wagner, Ann T Mithoefer, Lisa Jerome, and Rick Doblin. The safety and efficacy of ±3,4-methylenedioxymethamphetamine-assisted psychotherapy in subjects with chronic, treatment-resistant posttraumatic stress disorder: the first randomized controlled pilot study *J Psychopharmacol* April 2011 25: 439–452, first published on July 19, 2010 doi: 10.1177/0269881110378371, p. 13. Copyright © 2010 by SAGE. Reprinted by Permission of SAGE.

A follow-up of these same study participants 17 to 74 months after the completion of the study revealed all but two participants maintained clinical improvements in PTSD (Mithoefer et al., 2013).

In a later study on using MDMA for treating PTSD, Oehen and colleagues (2013) found that patients self-reported improvements in PTSD, but that improvements were not seen on the same measure used by the study shown in Figure 12.11. These researchers did agree with this early report that MDMA appeared safe to use when administered by medical practitioners and again for a limited number of treatments.

During therapy for PTSD, patients resist thinking about a traumatic experience that led to the disorder. Psychotherapy becomes particularly ineffective for patients unable to tolerate strong feelings or circumvent emotional numbing about the traumatic event. Clinicians who study MDMA's empathogenic effects find that MDMA may reduce resistance to thinking about an event or facilitate emotions surrounding the effect. In psychotherapy, reducing such barriers provides a therapist access to the root psychic causes of a psychological disorder. Thus, the apparent success of MDMA-assisted psychotherapy for PTSD in this first clinical study supports previous anecdotal claims from therapists who employed MDMA during the years before the DEA's schedule I categorization. However, clinical study researchers today benefit

FIGURE 12.12 ● Phencyclidine enhances serotonin neurotransmission (left) by inhibiting serotonin reuptake transporters and activating 5-HT$_{2A}$ receptors. Activating 5-HT$_{2A}$ receptors stimulates associated G proteins. Phencyclidine enhances dopamine neurotransmission (right) through inhibiting dopamine membrane transporters and by functioning as a partial agonist for dopamine D$_2$ receptors. As a partial agonist, phencyclidine activates some D$_2$ receptors while failing to activate others. PCP = phencyclidine, 5-HT = serotonin, DA = dopamine, G = G protein.

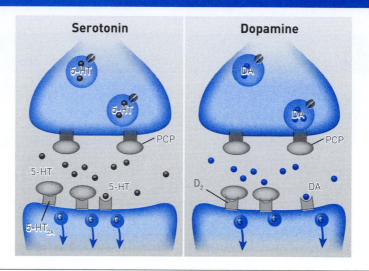

SOURCE: © Cengage Learning 2014.

from knowledge of MDMA neurotoxic effects and seem to have chosen lower doses in response to this evidence. Still, other reports caution on the use of MDMA as a pharmacotherapy, citing resemblances to the effects of MDMA with LSD, potential negative subjective effects occurring from MDMA, rebound effects that occur, and the risk of neurotoxicity (Parrott, 2014).

Tolerance and Dependence During Chronic MDMA Use

Shulgin, the psychopharmacologist who promoted MDMA, reported that MDMA's positive effects declined after the first seven uses, anecdotally describing tolerance to MDMA's effects. Novice users soon increase the number of MDMA tablets consumed in order to continue achieving positive subjective effects. Experienced MDMA users may take as many as 10–20 tablets in a single occasion. However, a potential confounder in this reporting is that, according to MDMA users, MDMA tablets are steadily getting weaker (Parrott, 2001).

A characterization of withdrawal symptoms depends on whether or not to consider *rebound* as a sign of dependence. Rebound fails to meet the classical view on

withdrawal symptoms, which normally develop after long-term use. Rebound, instead, could occur after first-time use. When excluding rebound from consideration as withdrawal, researchers seldom find withdrawal symptoms, including any indications of physical dependence or psychological dependence such as drug craving (Parrott, 2001).

Despite a lack of dependence by the typical definition, Cottler and colleagues (2001) found that close to half of MDMA users surveyed met the DSM criteria for a substance use disorder. Sixty-three percent of those surveyed indicated using MDMA despite having knowledge of its harmful effects. Furthermore, 43 percent reported using MDMA in hazardous situations such as driving a vehicle or having unprotected sex. Thirty-nine percent spent a lot of time trying to obtain and use MDMA.

STOP & CHECK

1. Why might MDMA aid PTSD therapy?

2. Although somewhat controversial, what are the main arguments that MDMA is an addictive substance?

1. Some therapists contend that MDMA's empathogenic effects enable clients to more readily think about and emotionally engage in events surrounding PTSD's causative traumatic event. 2. First, MDMA exhibits tolerance to subjective effects. Second, many recreational users continue taking MDMA despite knowing the drug is harmful.

Recreational Use of Dissociative Anesthetics

Dissociative anesthetics Sedative pain-relieving drugs that produce feelings of disconnectedness from the body and have depressant and stimulant effects

Phencyclidine A commonly abused dissociative anesthetic

Dissociative anesthetics are sedative pain-relieving drugs that produce feelings of disconnectedness from the body along with depressant and stimulant effects. Not all of these effects occur at the same time but instead depend on the dose taken. There are three primary dissociative anesthetics. **Phencyclidine**, also known by the street names *PCP* or *angel dust*, is the most abused dissociative anesthetic. **Ketamine**, also known as *Special K* or *K*, is another recreationally used dissociative anesthetic. Beyond these drugs, dozens of chemical analogues of phencyclidine exhibit similar pharmacological effects (Abraham et al., 2002; Soine, 1986).

 Drug Profile: phencyclidine

Street name	PCP, angel dust
Uses	Recreational purposes; most abused among dissociative anesthetics

Ketamine Recreationally used dissociative anesthetic that is used as an anesthetic for animals

 Drug Profile: ketamine

Street name	Special K, K
Uses	Recreational purposes; used in animals as an anesthetic

Like most psychedelic drugs, phencyclidine and other dissociative anesthetic use occurs in party or club settings. Phencyclidine comes in a variety of forms, including pills, powder, and liquid (Pradhan, 1984). Clandestine laboratories provide the main source of phencyclidine and other dissociated anesthetic drugs (Soine, 1986). The U.S. Drug Enforcement Administration lists phencyclidine and ketamine as schedule II substances, reflecting the DEA's view that dissociative anesthetics not only have high abuse potential but also legitimate medical uses (Drug Enforcement Administration, 2012b). This scheduling also allows for clinical investigations on other uses for dissociative anesthetics, such as evaluating ketamine as an antidepressant drug (see Chapter 13).

Development of Phencyclidine, Ketamine, and Dizocilpine

Like most psychedelic drugs, phencyclidine, ketamine, and dizocilpine were first developed by pharmaceutical companies. *Phencyclidine*, the first dissociative anesthetic drug, was discovered in 1926 by Parke, Davis, and Company during a development program for anesthetic drugs. Phencyclidine was used as a veterinary anesthetic and later used as an anesthetic in humans. In humans, however, patients reported experiencing nightmares, severe anxiety, delusional thoughts, and delirium after recovering from anesthesia. *Ketamine* was also used as an anesthetic drug in humans but was soon discontinued for adolescents and adults because of similar disturbing effects. Yet, we do not find these effects occurring in children, and therefore, ketamine may still be used for this population. Ketamine also remains a common veterinary anesthetic (Abraham et al., 2002; Domino & Luby, 2012).

After abandoning dissociative anesthetics for human anesthetic uses, dissociative anesthetic use continued in two different directions. The first was recreational use. Phencyclidine emerged as a recreational drug during the 1960s. Regarded for relaxing effects, phencyclidine was referred to as the *PeaCe Pill*, leading to the popular street name *PCP*. Users refer to its powder form as *angel dust*. Phencyclidine received a bad street reputation in San Francisco during the mid-1960s because of the disturbing effects similar to those experienced by phencyclidine anesthesia patients. However, phencyclidine use reappeared in the 1970s and remains a popular recreational substance (Lerner & Burns, 1978).

The second direction for dissociative anesthetic use was psychiatric research. As discussed later in this section, human phencyclidine or ketamine use produces a temporary psychological state remarkably similar to schizophrenia. Phencyclidine-like dissociative anesthetics exhibit hallucinations, paranoia, and other positive schizophrenia symptoms, as well as emotional affect, social withdrawal, and other negative schizophrenia symptoms. Phencyclidine and related dissociative anesthetics also elicit schizophrenia-like cognitive impairments. These pharmacological characteristics led to a new neurological model for understanding schizophrenia, which is described in greater detail in Chapter 15 (Jentsch & Roth, 1999).

Absorption and Elimination of Phencyclidine

Phencyclidine administration includes intravenous injection, inhalation, and insufflation. Phencyclidine was used orally during the 1960s, but users since then have shifted to using the powder form. With the powder form, users insufflate, intravenously inject, or smoke phencyclidine. Further, users may administer phencyclidine with other drugs, such as sprinkling phencyclidine powder onto cannabis joints (Lerner & Burns, 1978).

The administration route affects the onset time for drug effects. Smoking phencyclidine leads to psychoactive effects within 1 to 5 minutes and reaches peak effects within 5 to 30 minutes after administration. Insufflation achieves drug effects within 30 seconds to 1 minute (Lerner & Burns, 1978). After absorption, phencyclidine's elimination half-life is 18 hours, but it can be as long as 51 hours (Cook, Perez-Reyes, Jeffcoat, & Brine, 1983). Thus, a single administration of phencyclidine produces long-lasting effects.

STOP & CHECK

1. What is the key psychedelic effect of dissociative anesthetics?

2. How long does phencyclidine remain in the body?

1. Dissociative anesthetic drugs produce feelings of disconnectedness from the body. **2.** Phencyclidine, the representative drug for dissociative anesthetics, has an elimination half-life of 18 hours, which accounts for long-lasting pharmacological effects.

Phencyclidine's Effects on Dopamine and Serotonin Neurotransmission

Phencyclidine, as well as ketamine and dizocilpine, exhibit a number of pharmacological actions in the nervous system. Overall, phencyclidine affects serotonin, dopamine, acetylcholine, and glutamate neurotransmission (**Table 12.2**) (Abraham et al., 2002; Jentsch & Roth, 1999). Phencyclidine causes enhanced serotonin neurotransmission through at least two key mechanisms (See **Figure 12.12** on p. 381). First, phencyclidine causes inhibition of the serotonin membrane transporter. This action prevents serotonin reuptake and causes serotonin levels outside the neuron to increase. Greater serotonin levels cause an increase in serotonin receptor activation. Second, phencyclidine functions as an agonist at 5-HT$_{2A}$ receptors (Kapur & Seeman, 2002; Smith, Meltzer, Arora, & Davis, 1977).

Phencyclidine has similar actions on the dopamine system (See **Figure 12.12** on p. 381). On dopamine axon terminals, we also find inhibition of reuptake through dopamine membrane transporters. As with serotonin, this action causes an increase in dopamine levels outside of the neuron, which facilitates activation of dopamine receptors. Phencyclidine is also a partial agonist for dopamine D$_2$ receptors (Kapur & Seeman, 2002; Smith et al., 1977).

Review! A partial agonist is a drug that binds to a receptor but has a weaker ability, compared to full agonists, for activating the receptor. (Chapter 4.)

Phencyclidine also acts on other neurotransmitter systems. At higher concentrations, phencyclidine functions as a noncompetitive antagonist for cholinergic

TABLE 12.2 ● Effects of Phencyclidine on Neurotransmission	
Neurotransmitter	**Effects**
Serotonin	Enhances serotonin levels by inhibiting reuptake and functioning as an agonist for 5-HT$_{2A}$ receptors
Dopamine	Enhances dopamine levels by inhibiting reuptake and functioning as a partial agonist for D$_2$ receptors
Acetylcholine	Acts as a noncompetitive antagonist for nicotinic receptors at neuromuscular junctions and autonomic nervous system ganglia; also an antagonist for muscarinic receptors
Endogenous opioids	Activates opioid kappa receptors
Glutamate	Antagonist for glutamate NMDA receptors; interferes with long-term potentiation

nicotinic receptors at neuromuscular junctions and at ganglia in the peripheral nervous system. Phencyclidine's actions at neuromuscular junctions cause muscles to contract. At ganglion cells, phencyclidine alters sympathetic and parasympathetic nervous system activity (Fryer & Lukas, 1999). High concentrations of phencyclidine-like drugs also antagonize cholinergic muscarinic receptors in the central and autonomic nervous systems. Higher concentrations also activate opioid kappa receptors (Hustveit, Maurset, & Oye, 1995).

Dissociative Anesthetics and Glutamate Neurotransmission

In addition to the actions already described, phencyclidine and similar dissociative anesthetics function as antagonists for glutamate NMDA (*N*-methyl-D-aspartate) receptors. As described in Chapter 4, NMDA receptors are ionotropic and contain binding sites for many substances on the ion channel's subunits. The NMDA receptor's channel contains a binding site for phencyclidine and the other dissociative anesthetics covered in the section. When binding to this site, phencyclidine prevents positively charged ions from entering the channel. By preventing NMDA receptor activation, phencyclidine interferes with a process called long-term potentiation (Abraham et al., 2002).

Long-term potentiation is a form of synaptic plasticity critical for learning and memory. *Potentiation* means "strengthening," and *plasticity* refers to adaptive change in neural characteristics, often occurring at synapses. Long-term potentiation depends on postsynaptic glutamate AMPA and NMDA glutamate receptors and the neurotransmitter glutamate (**Figure 12.13**).

At these synapses, glutamate binds to both AMPA and NMDA receptors. Before long-term potentiation, however, glutamate only successfully activates AMPA receptors. Activation fails to occur at NMDA receptors because a Mg^{+2} ion blocks the NMDA receptor channel, preventing ions from entering the channel. Long-term potentiation occurs when the membrane depolarizes sufficiently to repel the Mg^{+2} ion from the

Long-term potentiation
Form of synaptic plasticity important for learning and memory.

FIGURE 12.13 ● Before long-term potentiation (left synapse), a magnesium ion prevents other ions from entering the NMDA receptor channel. During long-term potentiation (middle synapse), sustained activation of the AMPA receptors elicits sufficient depolarization to expel the magnesium ion from the NMDA receptor channel. The expulsion of magnesium supports a stronger synaptic connection by enabling positively charged ions to the neuron through the NMDA receptor channel. Phencyclidine and other dissociative anesthetic drugs block the NMDA receptor channel. By blocking the NMDA receptor channel, phencyclidine disables long-term potentiation. LTP = long-term potentiation, Glut = glutamate, Na⁺= sodium, Ca⁺= calcium, Mg⁺= magnesium, PCP = phencyclidine.

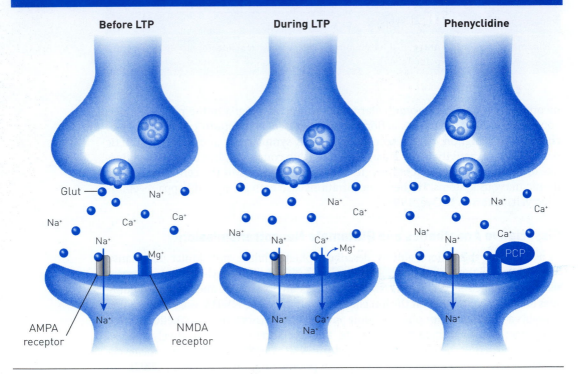

channel. Sufficient membrane depolarization occurs as a result of repeated and sustained AMPA receptor activation.

Review! Both glutamate AMPA and NMDA receptors produce excitatory postsynaptic potentials by allowing the entry of positively charged ions such as Na⁺. (Chapter 3.).

Once depolarization changes dislodge the Mg^{+2} ion from the NMDA channel, Na^+ and Ca^{2+} ions enter the NMDA channel. The entry of additional positively charged ions leads to greater membrane depolarization and facilitates neuronal excitability. Thus, by dislodging the Mg^{+2} ion from the NMDA channel, glutamate becomes more effective in exciting the neuron—that is, by creating excitatory post synaptic potentials. When phencyclidine enters the brain, it acts at NMDA receptors by blocking the receptor's channel. In doing so, phencyclidine prevents long-term potentiation from forming or disrupts currently existing long-term potentiated synapses.

Review! *Excitatory postsynaptic potentials* refers to excitatory input from other neurons that result in membrane depolarization. (Chapter 3.)

STOP & CHECK

1. What effects do dissociative anesthetic drugs have on serotonin and dopamine neurotransmission?

2. AMPA and NMDA glutamate receptors are critical for _____, a form of synaptic plasticity critical for learning and memory.

3. How does a dissociative anesthetic drug such as phencyclidine interfere with long-term potentiation?

1. Dissociative anesthetics prevent serotonin and dopamine reuptake. They also function as agonists for 5-HT$_{2A}$ receptors and as partial agonists for dopamine D$_2$ receptors. **2.** Long-term potentiation **3.** Phencyclidine binds to a site with the NMDA channel, which prevents ions from entering the neuron through the NMDA channel. This action weakens the postsynaptic neurons response to the presynaptic neuron.

The Anesthetic and Psychedelic Effects of Dissociative Anesthetics

Phencyclidine's behavioral effects change by dose. At lower doses, phencyclidine elicits a drunken-like state. These doses exhibit CNS depressant effects. Moreover, users often report a numbness in fingers and toes, an indication of anesthetic effects. At moderate doses, these drugs produce appreciable numbness throughout the body. These doses relate to an enhanced CNS depressant effect.

Phencyclidine offers unique psychedelic effects compared to LSD and MDMA. In particular, phencyclidine elicits a feeling of disconnectedness from the body. In particular, recreational dissociative anesthetic users also report **out-of-body experiences**, the sensation of floating above one's body or even viewing one's body as if one is separate from it. This property led to classifying phencyclidine and related drugs as *dissociative* anesthetics.

Moderate doses also impair memory. Thus, dissociative anesthetic users may have a rich psychedelic experience yet cannot remember it later. These memory-impairing effects likely relate to disruption of long-term potentiation. By acting like Mg^{+2} ions that

Out-of-body experience The sensation of floating above one's body or even viewing one's body as if one is separate from it

block NMDA receptors, dissociative anesthetics prevent long-term potentiation and, ultimately, the formation of memories (Abraham et al., 2002). Results from numerous studies suggest that frequent use of ketamine, and likely other dissociative anesthetics, leads to deficits in short- and long-term memory (Morgan & Curran, 2011).

In a study conducted by Morgan and colleagues (2004), human volunteers were assessed on a series of pharmacological measures during intravenous infusion of the phencyclidine-like drug ketamine. When asked to recite a message they heard played from a recorder either 10 or 80 minutes earlier, ketamine-treated patients recalled significantly fewer words compared to placebo-treated patients (**Figure 12.14**).

Whereas low and moderate doses elicit depressant effects, high phencyclidine doses produce psychostimulant effects. These include an amphetamine-like rush and other increased arousals. Peripherally, high phencyclidine doses elicit sympathetic nervous system activation, leading to increased heart rate, blood pressure, respiration rate, body temperature, and other sympathetic nervous system effects (Siegel, 1978).

Further, phencyclidine psychostimulant effects account for differences in self-administration studies compared to hallucinogens such as LSD. Unlike LSD, animals learn to self-administer phencyclidine. This phencyclidine property was first discovered in 1973 by Robert Balster and colleagues (1973). In this study, rhesus monkeys initiated lever responding in order to receive intravenous injections of phencyclidine. Data such as these strongly suggest that phencyclidine produces reinforcing effects in human as well.

FIGURE 12.14 ● In a study by Morgan and colleagues (2004), both low and high ketamine doses in humans led to significantly poorer recall of a message played either 10 minutes earlier (short delay) or 80 minutes earlier (long delay) (left figure). Ketamine also elicited agreement with the question "Want more of the drug?" (middle) and "Like effects of the drug?" (right).

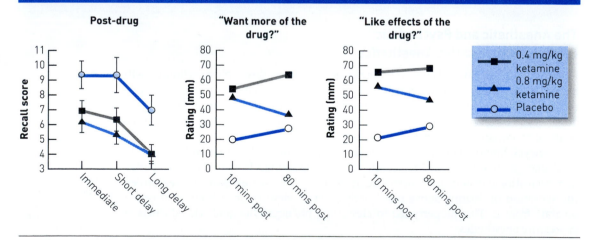

SOURCE: With kind permission from Springer Science+Business Media: Morgan, C. A., Mofeez, A., Brandner, B., Bromley, L., & Curran, H. V. (2004). Ketamine impairs response inhibition and is positively reinforcing in healthy volunteers: a dose–response study. *Psychopharmacology, 172*(3), 298–308. doi: 10.1007/s00213-003-165, p. 10.

Morgan and colleagues (2004) also found evidence of reinforcing effects with dissociative anesthetics in humans. During ketamine infusion, participants gave positive responses to reinforcer-related questions posed by the researchers, including "Want more of the drug?" and "Like effects of the drug?" Placebo-treated participants reported none of these positive responses (Figure 12.14).

Dissociative Anesthetics and Schizophrenia-Like Effects

Many of phencyclidine's severe adverse effects occur at large doses. At these doses, phencyclidine can produce cataleptic-like effects on movements. The effect is associated with antagonism of nicotinic cholinergic receptors at neuromuscular junctions.

As first described in the history of dissociative anesthetics, a schizophrenia-like state is another adverse effect. This episode of schizophrenia persists for days and even weeks. In the study conducted by Morgan and colleagues (2004) described previously, the phencyclidine-like drug ketamine produced effects that measured as schizophrenia-like symptoms on a psychiatric scale. The production of schizophrenia-like states led to the *glutamate hypothesis of schizophrenia*. The glutamate hypothesis basically states that schizophrenia symptoms manifest from diminished glutamate neurotransmission. Chapter 15 provides more information about this hypothesis for schizophrenia.

Tolerance, Dependence, and the Use of Dissociative Anesthetics

Generally, phencyclidine or ketamine users administer these drugs once a week or less. The separation of drug administrations by days or weeks prevents the development of tolerance. However, for those who take phencyclidine or ketamine on a regular basis, greater doses become necessary to achieve similar pharmacological effects, a clear indication of tolerance.

For the same dosing reasons already described, dependence on phencyclidine, ketamine, or other dissociative anesthetics seldom occurs. When it does, it manifests as psychological withdrawal symptoms. These symptoms include craving the drug or feeling lethargic and depressed. These drugs rarely produce physical dependence (Lerner & Burns, 1978).

STOP & CHECK

1. At which doses do the anesthetic effects of a dissociative anesthetic drug occur?

2. Which effects of dissociative anesthetic drugs relate to interference of long-term potentiation?

3. How do the reinforcing effects of dissociative anesthetics compare to the hallucinogen LSD?

1. Numbness occurs at low doses and become more pronounced at moderate doses. **2.** Memory disruptive effects **3.** Unlike LSD, animals learn to self-administer dissociative anesthetics. In addition, humans report enjoying the dissociative anesthetic drug ketamine. Overall, dissociative anesthetics appear to exhibit greater reinforcing effects than LSD.

Other Psychedelic Drugs

As is apparent from the drugs covered so far in this chapter, we find an ever-growing list of psychedelic drugs, including newly synthesized drugs, discovered constituents in plants, and reassessed effects of already known substances. To this end, a coverage of all psychedelic drugs is beyond the scope of this text. However, three other types of these drugs need mentioning.

Dextromethorphan
Opioid receptor drug used in cough suppressant that in large enough doses can produce psychedelic effects

The first is **dextromethorphan**, an opioid receptor drug and cough suppressant found in many over-the-counter cold medications. Because of its presence in Robitussin cough syrups, recreational dextromethorphan users, who mainly consist of adolescents, refer to consuming large amounts of cough syrup to achieve psychedelic effects as *Robo-tripping*. At cough suppressant doses, dextromethorphan functions primarily as an opioid receptor agonist, just like the prescription opioid cough suppressant codeine. At higher doses, dextromethorphan functions as a glutamate NMDA receptor antagonist, an action similar to phencyclidine. Together, these actions produce pharmacological effects similar to both opioid receptor agonists, like morphine, and NMDA receptor antagonists, like phencyclidine.

💊 *Drug Profile:* **dextromethorphan**	
Trade name	Sold as Robitussin cough syrup (and generic brand names); recreational use referred to as robo-tripping
Actions	Agonist for opioid receptors and antagonist for NMDA receptors
Effects	Suppressing cough; psychedelic effects consist of visual perceptual changes, feelings of transcendence, and mystical experiences

Users can achieve enjoyable and stimulating drug effects after ingesting 100 mg of dextromethorphan, roughly equivalent to 25 ml of over-the-counter cough syrup. Psychedelic effects, similar to those produced by dissociative anesthetics, occurs at doses near 475 mg, equivalent to about 120 ml, or one full 4-ounce bottle of cough syrup. Psychedelic effects consist of visual perceptual changes, feelings of transcendence, and mystical experiences (Reissig et al., 2012).

Salvinorin A
Psychoactive compound found in *Salvia divinorum*, referred to as *magic mint* or *diviner's sage*

The second drug is **Salvinorin A**, the psychoactive constituent in *Salvia divinorum*. *Salvia divinorum* is referred to as *magic mint* and *diviner's sage*. Recreational users administer Salvinorin A by chewing or smoking *Salvia* leaves. Unlike LSD, Salvinorin A exhibits no activity at $5\text{-}HT_{2A}$ receptors (Roth et al., 2002). It differs from LSD by also functioning as an agonist for kappa opioid receptors. The discovery of this pharmacological action suggests that kappa opioid receptors play a role in sensory perception (Chavkin et al., 2004; Roth et al., 2002). Salvinorin A also produces modest increases in dopamine levels in the nucleus accumbens in rats (Braida et al., 2008). Salvinorin A users report experiencing visions and perceptions, such as becoming objects, revisiting places from the past, depersonalization, uncontrollable laughter, and perceptions of being several places at once from amounts as low as 0.2–1.0 mg (Siebert, 1994).

🕮 Drug Profile: Salvinorin A	
Street name	Magic mint, diviner's sage
Actions	Agonist for kappa opioid receptors
Effects	Visions; perceptions of becoming objects, revisiting places from the past; depersonalization; uncontrollable laughter

Animal research findings suggest that Salvinorin A also produces reinforcing effects. Salvinorin A administration produces a conditioned place preference in zebrafish and rats (Braida et al., 2008; Braida et al., 2007). Rats self-administer lower doses of intravenously administered Salvinorin A (Braida et al., 2008).

Muscarinic receptor antagonists such as *scopolamine* and *atropine* represent another type of psychedelic drug. Both scopolamine and atropine occur naturally in plants such as *Atropa belladonna*, which is known as deadly night shade, and *Datura stramonium*, which is also known as Jamestown weed. These substances have ancient histories of human use, including medicinal and religious practices (Schultes, 1969). Scopolamine and atropine produce true visual hallucinations, delusional thinking, and disorientation about time and place by acting as antagonists for muscarinic cholinergic receptors in the central and peripheral nervous systems (Goudie et al., 2001; Watanabe et al., 1978). Scopolamine or atropine use also causes dry mouth, hypertension, and urinary retention, owing to blockade of cholinergic receptors in the parasympathetic nervous system (Shervette, Schydlower, Fearnow, & Lampe, 1979).

🕮 Drug Profile: scopolamine	
Actions	Antagonist for cholinergic muscarinic receptors
Effects	true visual hallucinations, delusional thinking, and disorientation about time and place

🕮 Drug Profile: atropine	
Actions	Antagonist for cholinergic muscarinic receptors
Effects	true visual hallucinations, delusional thinking, and disorientation about time and place

STOP & CHECK

1. What is the psychedelic compound found in over-the-counter cough syrups such as Robitussin DM?

2. Although Salvinorin A elicits hallucinogenic effects through activating 5-HT$_{2A}$ receptors, what other pharmacological action might contribute to the compound's psychedelic effects?

3. Why are scopolamine and atropine unattractive recreational psychedelic substances?

1. Dextromethorphan **2.** Salvinorin A also functions as an agonist for kappa opioid receptors. **3.** Scopolamine, atropine, and other muscarinic receptor antagonists exhibit confusion and delusional thinking. In particular, these drugs exhibit profound inhibition of memory.

From Actions to Effects: Synesthesia

Some psychedelic drug users experience a phenomenon called *synesthesia*. During **synesthesia**, the perceiving a stimulus through an incorrect sensory modality. For example, a person experiencing synesthesia may correctly see the colors of an object, but also perceive sounds radiating from those colors.

Although occurring during some hallucinogenic experiences, synesthesia commonly arises without an apparent cause. In fact, about 1 in 23 individuals routinely experience synesthesia in normal everyday situations—we refer to these individuals as *synesthetes*. Synesthetes report these experiences as normal and generally pleasant (Hubbard, 2007). Further, studies indicate no reliable association between psychiatric conditions and synesthesia.

Several neurobiological models exist to explain synesthesia. One model implicates potential abnormalities in portions of the brain where multiple sensory modalities meet. For example, the *temporo-parietal-occipital junction*, the meeting point for the parietal, occipital, and temporal lobes, may lack proper inhibitory feedback functioning during synesthesia. Improper feedback may, in turn, lead to additional sensory perceptions to a single sensory stimulus. Other models suggest that synesthesia reflects an abnormality in processes that integrate sensory information into a single multisensory scene (Hubbard, 2007).

Review! Visual processing first takes place in the occipital lobe. The parietal lobe assesses touch information and contributes to visual processing. The temporal lobe processes auditory information as well as visual processing. (Chapter 2.)

Although the neurobiology of innately occurring synesthesia remains uncertain, drug-induced synesthesia presents a clearer picture. Perception researchers Brang and Ramachandran (2008) described several lines of evidence linking 5-HT$_{2A}$ receptor activation to hallucinogen-induced synesthesia. The first line of evidence is that

5-HT$_{2A}$ receptor agonists such as LSD produce synesthesia. Second, antidepressant drugs acting as serotonin reuptake inhibitors inhibit synesthesia. The elevated serotonin levels caused by serotonin reuptake inhibitors lead to the activation of 5-HT$_{1A}$ receptors that, in turn, *reduce* 5-HT$_{2A}$ activation, a mechanism that counteracts synesthesia. Chapter 14 provides more information about the interactions between 5-HT$_{1A}$ and 5-HT$_{2A}$ receptors.

Third, antidepressant drugs acting as norepinephrine reuptake inhibitors also inhibit synesthesia. Similar to the second mechanism described already, elevated norepinephrine levels lead to greater activation of α_2 adrenoceptors, which also reduce 5-HT$_{2A}$ receptor activation. Fourth, melatonin causes synesthesia in some individuals. Melatonin inhibits serotonin levels, reducing the inhibitory influence 5-HT$_{1A}$ receptors have on 5-HT$_{2A}$ receptors. By removing the inhibitor, 5-HT$_{2A}$ receptor-induced synesthesia becomes more likely to occur. Based on these four reasons, Brang and Ramachandran (2008) suggest that 5-HT$_{2A}$ receptors, are in fact, *synesthesia receptors*.

STOP & CHECK

1. Is synesthesia a mental disorder?

2. Which receptor likely accounts for hallucinogen-induced synesthesia?

1. Synesthesia is not considered a mental disorder; it correlates poorly with psychiatric disorders, and individuals do not find synesthetic experiences disturbing or disruptive. 2. The 5-HT$_{2A}$ receptor

Chapter Summary

Psychedelic drugs include a long list of substances that vary in effects, ranging from hallucinations, sensory distortion, delusions, and dissociation. The three primary psychedelic drug classes include hallucinogens, mixed stimulant–psychedelics, and dissociative anesthetics. The representative drug for hallucinogens, LSD, closely resembles the chemical structure of neurotransmitter serotonin and subsequently functions as an agonist for many serotonin receptors. Activation of 5-HT$_{2A}$ receptors in particular leads to visual hallucinations as well as synesthesia. In addition to hallucinations, LSD

produces a suggestible state that can lead to altered perceptions of reality.

Mixed stimulant–psychedelic drugs exhibit effects similar to both psychostimulant drugs such as amphetamine and hallucinogenic drugs such as LSD. MDMA, the representative drug for mixed stimulant–psychedelic drugs, elevates sensory perceptions at lower doses by enhancing serotonin neurotransmission and produces additional psychostimulant effects at higher doses by enhancing dopamine neurotransmission.

Dissociative anesthetics such as phencyclidine and ketamine produce both

(Continued)

(Continued)

depressant and psychostimulant effects along with anesthesia, feelings of disconnectedness from the body, and memory-impairing effects. These effects arise from enhancing serotonin and dopamine neurotransmission as well as from blocking glutamate NMDA receptors, which are important for memory function.

Many other psychedelic drugs exist. Dextromethorphan found in Robitussin cough syrup elicits morphine-like euphoria and dissociative anesthetic-like psychedelic effects. Salvinorin A, found in the plant *Salvia divinorum*, produces hallucinogenic effects by serving as an opioid kappa receptor agonist. Muscarinic receptor antagonists, such as scopolamine, produce hallucinations, delirium, confusion, delusions, and poor judgment.

Key Terms

Psychedelic drugs 356
Hallucinogens 356
Lysergic acid diethylamide
  (LSD) 356
Psilocybin (and psilocin) 357
Mescaline 357
Dimethyltryptamine
  (DMT) 357
Quanah Parker 359
Albert Hofmann 360
Harvard Psilocybin
  Project 360
Modal object completion 362

Default mode network 364
True hallucination 364
Pseudo-hallucinations 364
Trip 365
Good trip 365
Synesthesia 365
Bad trip 365
Hypersuggestibility 365
Flashback 365
Hallucinogen persisting
  perception disorder 366
Mixed stimulant–psychedelic
  drugs 367

MDMA ("Ecstasy") 367
Entactogen 367
Empathogen 367
Rave 367
Multiple organ failure
  (MDMA use) 375
Dissociative anesthetics 382
Phencyclidine 382
Ketamine 382
Long-term potentiation 385
Out-of-body experience 387
Dextromethorphan 390
Salvinorin A 390

Visit the Student Study Site at **study.sagepub.com/prus2e** to access additional study tools, including eFlashcards, web quizzes, video resources, web resources, SAGE journal articles, and more.

13

Treatments for Depression and Bipolar Disorder

CHAPTER OUTLINE

- Mental Disorders
- Depression
- The Prevalence of Depressive Disorders
- Combination Strategies for Treating Depression With Antidepressant Drugs
- Combining Psychotherapy and Pharmacotherapy for Treating Depression
- Antidepressant Drugs and Monoamine Neurotransmitter Systems
- Bipolar Disorder
- From Actions to Effects: Pharmacogenetic Factors and Treatment Response in Depression
- Chapter Summary

DID RESERPINE REVOLUTIONIZE THE STUDY OF ANTIDEPRESSANT MEDICATIONS?

In 1952, reserpine was first isolated from the *Rauwolfia serpentina*, a plant known for its tranquilizing properties. In healthy volunteers, researchers not only verified reserpine's tranquilizing effects but also noticed that it produced a depressed mood. Attempts to understand this drug's actions divided opinion into two camps. On the one hand, Bernard

(Continued)

(Continued)

Brodie and others argued that serotonin depletion accounted for reserpine's effects; on the other hand, Arvid Carlsson and others argued that dopamine and norepinephrine accounted for its effects. This debate sparked important discoveries about the production, release, and reuptake of monoamine neurotransmitters. When a drug was serendipitously found reducing depression in humans, researchers saw that these first antidepressant drugs reversed reserpine-induced depression in animals. Moreover, the wealth of research centered on reserpine convinced researchers that monoamine neurotransmitters were central to the actions of antidepressant drugs.

Despite the important discoveries resulting from studies on reserpine, it appears to be a part of forgotten history. As psychopharmacologist Silvio Garattini (2006) noted, "The new pharmacology texts no longer even mention this drug that was so instrumental in the generation of new knowledge about the chemical mediators in the brain that gave rise to the field of psychopharmacology."

The preceding chapters of this text concerned changes in brain function and behavior caused by psychoactive substances. Thus, normal behavior became abnormal after a drug was administered. For mental illness, we have the opposite. Behavior may appear abnormal before treatment, but the goal of drug treatment is for behavior to become normal. The subsequent chapters of this text shift from drugs of abuse to those used for treating mental disorders, which we refer to as *therapeutic drugs* or *pharmacotherapeutic drugs*.

Mental Disorders

Mental disorder
Impairment in normal behavioral, cognitive, or emotional functioning

Just as we have referred to the *Diagnostic and Statistical Manual* (DSM) for defining substance dependencies, we can also refer to the DSM for defining different types of mental disorders. We consider a mental disorder as an impairment in normal behavioral, cognitive, or emotional functioning. Mental disorders are highly prevalent throughout the world and occur across all demographics. According to the World Health Organization (WHO), an estimated 450 million people qualify for a mental disorder diagnosis, whereas many others have various symptoms associated with mental disorders. Based on 2002 estimates, WHO reported that 154 million individuals have depression, and 877,000 commit suicide annually. WHO also found that despite the tremendous impact that poor mental health has on a society, only 1 percent of health costs are devoted to mental health in low- to middle-income countries (World Health Organization, 2016).

To diagnose a mental disorder, the DSM generally requires that an individual experience significant dysfunction and stress from the disorder and that the disorder does not arise from a medical condition with a clear physiological cause. For example, the DSM does not qualify Alzheimer's disease as a mental disorder, despite clear changes in mental functioning, because Alzheimer's disease derives from clear organic cause. This distinction makes sense less today than years past, when neuroscience technology had not advanced sufficiently to glean physiological causes for mental disorders. We will learn much about the neurobiology of DSM mental disorders in these remaining chapters and focus on how therapeutic drugs alter biological processes to improve mental functioning. The subsequent chapters cover the following major mental disorders: depression, bipolar disorder, anxiety, and schizophrenia.

Depression

According to the DSM-5, **major depressive disorder** is characterized by at least five symptoms occurring within the same 2-week period. These symptoms can include a depressed mood, lack of interest or pleasure in activities once enjoyable, change in body weight, change in sleep patterns, fatigue, feelings of worthlessness, difficulties in thinking or in concentrating, and thoughts of suicide (**Table 13.1**). Moreover, these symptoms significantly interfere with normal everyday activities such as going to work, doing daily chores, and socializing with family and friends (American Psychiatric Association, 2013).

Depression also may occur in a milder form called **persistent depressive disorder** (or **dysthymia**). The primary symptoms for persistent depressive disorder include a depressed mood that occurs nearly every day for at least 2 years. In addition, individuals diagnosed with dysthymic disorder must have at least two symptoms listed for major depressive disorder.

Nonspecific descriptions may be used for some symptoms of depressive disorders. For example, "changes in body weight" doesn't specify whether this consists of weight loss or weight gain. In depression, we might find either of these changes occurring. A severely depressed individual may eat excessively, possibly because eating provides temporary improvements in mood, or may eat too little, possibly because the individual lacks an appetite. The same may be true for sleeping; an individual may sleep most of the day or suffer long bouts of insomnia.

Clinicians also recognize that many other dimensions of depression exist, something that the DSM classifies as *specifiers*. A clinician, for example, might find significant features of anxiety accompanying a clear diagnosis of major depressive disorder. In this instance, the clinician would diagnose the patient with major depressive disorder, along with the specifier "with anxious distress." Adding this specifier may inform treatment directions. For example, the patient may receive medications for both depression and anxiety.

Major depressive disorder Disorder characterized by at least five depressive symptoms that last 2 weeks or longer

Persistent depressive disorder (or **dysthymia**) A disorder that includes a depressed mood that occurs nearly every day for at least 2 years

TABLE 13.1 ● Symptoms of Depressive Disorders	
Disorder	**Symptoms May Include . . .**
Major depressive disorder	Depressed mood occurring daily and for most of the day
	Anhedonia (lack of pleasure) and disinterest
	Changes in body weight (gain or loss)
	Changes in sleep patterns (insomnia or hypersomnia)
	Fatigue and loss of energy
	Feelings of worthlessness and guilt
	Difficulty thinking and making decisions
	Recurrent thoughts of suicide
Persistent depressive disorder	Same as those for major depressive disorder
Specifiers	Additional symptoms to those for depression, depending on the specifier. For example, the specifier "with anxious distress" includes anxiety symptoms and the specifier "with psychotic features" includes hallucinations and delusions.

In addition to a specifier for anxiety, we also find that some depressed individuals exhibit delusions or hallucinations. In this context, a clinician would add the specifier "with psychotic features." When we find psychosis present in depression, hallucinations and delusions tend to relate to depressed mood and negative thoughts. For example, an individual may have delusions that she has cancer all throughout her body or that no one wants her to live. An individual may hear voices stating the same types of things. Those with psychosis and depression may benefit from medications to treat both types of symptoms (Spiker et al., 1985). There are many other types and specifiers for depression, but these go beyond the scope of this text.

We also find a degree of cognitive dysfunction in depression. The degree and types of cognitive impairment tend to vary across studies, owing in large part to the age of participants, severity of depression, and other population differences. In general, individuals with depression tend to exhibit impairments in episodic memory, an ability to explicitly describe one's memory of certain past experiences (Goodwin, 1997; Zakzanis, Leach, & Kaplan, 1998). Further, those with major depressive disorder also exhibit reduced ability to sustain attention (Zakzanis et al., 1998). Cognitive function normalizes when depressive symptoms subside (Paelecke-Habermann, Pohl, & Leplow, 2005).

STOP & CHECK

1. What is the major distinction between a neurological disorder and a mental disorder?

2. How is major depressive disorder different from persistent depressive disorder?

1. If the condition causing abnormal behavior has a clear organic cause, then it is a neurological disorder. Otherwise, it is a mental disorder that can be diagnosed by the DSM. 2. Major depressive disorder requires more diagnosis symptoms than dysthymic disorder, and the symptoms for major depressive disorder need only last 2 weeks, whereas a depressed mood for dysthymic disorder must consistently occur for 2 years.

The Prevalence of Depressive Disorders

Depression is the fourth leading cause of disability worldwide because of its prevalence and dramatic effects on quality of life (Murray & Lopez, 1997). According to a U.S. national survey conducted by Kessler, Petukhova, Sampson, Zaslavsky, and Wittchen (2012), the prevalence of major depressive disorder during a lifetime is 16.6 percent (**Figure 13.1**). Yet among university students we find a much higher rate. In a review of published reports on depression among university students, Ibrahim and

FIGURE 13.1 ● **The lifetime likelihood of experiencing depression is approximately 16 percent.**

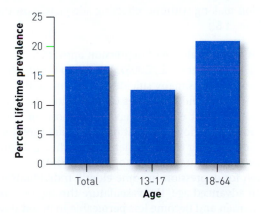

SOURCE: Data from Kessler et al., 2012.

colleagues (2013) found that an average of approximately 30 percent of students met the DSM criteria for a depressive disorder.

Women are twice as likely to be diagnosed with major depressive disorder as men. Yet these differences in the prevalence of depression between men and women may derive from different depressive symptoms occurring in men than those in women. Depressed men tend to exhibit greater irritability, over-reactivity, impulsivity, anger, aggression, and substance abuse as symptoms more often than women. Women are more likely to exhibit feelings of heavy, leaden feelings in arms or legs (known as *lead paralysis*) and greater fatigue (Winkler, Pjrek, & Kasper, 2005). These differences may result in women meeting the standard definitions of major depressive disorder more often than men. To determine whether this might be a factor, Martin, Neighbors, and Griffith (2013) examined rates of depression by comparing more conventional diagnostic criteria to criteria that included certain depressive symptoms more common in men. When factoring in aggression, substance abuse, and risk-taking behavior, the researchers found no differences in rates of depression between men and women.

Approximately, one out of six individuals with major depressive disorder commit suicide, and the Centers for Disease Control and Prevention (CDC) estimates that as many as 12 to 25 suicide attempts are made for every suicide death. Men are nearly twice as likely to commit suicide as women. Suicide is the third-highest cause of death in teenagers, but it is far more likely to occur in male adolescents and young adults than in female adolescents and young adults. One-third of those who commit suicide test positive for alcohol (Centers for Disease Control and Prevention, 2015). As we learned in Chapter 8, alcohol produces disinhibition, which, in this case can result in a shift from someone considering suicide to actually going through with it. This obviously makes alcohol consumption among those struggling with depression especially concerning.

Review! Disinhibition consists of a weakening of behavioral control that manifests as poor risk assessment, engagement in dangerous behavior, and impulsivity. Impulsivity consists of decision making without reflecting adequately on the consequences of those decisions. (Chapter 8.)

Across age groups, the prevalence of depression appears to be relatively balanced, as shown in Figure 13.1 (Kessler et al., 2005). Yet we do find high rates of depression among the elderly, and twice as many suicides occur among the elderly compared to other adult groups. We also find high rates of depression, 17 percent, among those with Alzheimer's disease. Most elderly receive a diagnosis of depression from their primary doctors. Studies find, however, that most primary care doctors fail to make a diagnosis of depression for their elderly patients, and when a diagnosis is made, their doctors prescribe incorrect treatments (Alexopoulos, 2005).

A potential reason for depression in some elderly individuals may be poor blood flow to the brain. In advanced age, the vasculature throughout the body, including the brain, tends to harden and become less permeable to blood flow, which is critical for maintaining brain activity. In such a state, reduced brain activity may contribute to a depressed mood. The term for depressed symptoms associated with poor blood flow in the brain is called **vascular depression** (Alexopoulos et al., 1997).

Just as we find a high prevalence of depression, we also find a high number of antidepressant prescriptions. In fact, the CDC states that antidepressants are the third most prescribed drugs among those 12 and older in the United States and the most prescribed drug among those between 18 and 44 years of age. Women are more than twice as likely to take antidepressant drugs than men, and more than one in five women ages 40 to 59 take antidepressant medications. In addition to the high frequency of being prescribed antidepressant drugs, most patients take these medications for at least 2 years (Pratt, Brody, & Gu, 2011).

Vascular depression
Depressed symptoms associated with poor blood flow in the brain

STOP & CHECK

1. Women are more likely to be diagnosed with major depressive disorder, but men are more likely to commit _____.

2. Despite a high prevalence of depression and a greater likelihood to successfully commit suicide, _____ individuals seldom receive a depression diagnosis from a mental health professional.

3. _____ depression refers to depressed symptoms associated with poor blood flow in the brain.

1. suicide 2. elderly 3. Vascular

Neuroimaging Techniques and Functional Differences in Depression

The development of advanced neuroimaging equipment has significantly aided our understanding of depression. The structural abnormalities in depression involve many structures, including the amygdala, hippocampus, prefrontal cortex, and nucleus accumbens (**Table 13.2**). The *amygdala*, a brain structure that mediates feelings of fear and aggression, appears overactive in depression. Using positron emission tomography (PET), Drevets and colleagues showed that individuals with depression exhibit increased cerebral blood flow in the left amygdala (Drevets et al., 1992). This same research group later found increased glucose uptake, a further indication that neuronal activity also occurs in the amygdala during depression (Drevets, Bogers, & Raichle, 2002).

Magnetic resonance imaging (MRI) studies also reveal volume reductions in the hippocampus in depression. In an extensive review of imaging studies among depressed patients, Campbell, Marriott, Nahmias, and MacQueen (2004) found that

TABLE 13.2 ● Structures Implicated in Depression

Structure	Function in Depression
Amygdala	Increased activity
Hippocampus	Reduced volume
Prefrontal cortex	Reduced activity
Nucleus accumbens	Reduced volume; Decreased activity
Basal ganglia	Reduced volume

the majority of studies reported these reductions in depressed individuals compared to nondepressed individuals. As presented later in this chapter, researchers have an interest in the hippocampus because of the ability of antidepressant drugs to promote neuron growth in this structure.

Although the amygdala appears overactive in depression, studies indicate underactivity in the left dorsal prefrontal cortex during depression (Savitz & Drevets, 2009). For example, in a study conducted by Drevets and colleagues (2002), PET assessments using F-18-fluorodeoxyglucose in unmedicated patients with unipolar depression consistently revealed decreased metabolism in the dorsal prefrontal cortex. The volume of gray and white matter also appears reduced in the left and right dorsal prefrontal cortex in depression and seems to be related to the severity of depression (Chen et al., 2007).

Volume reductions also suggest irregularities in the basal ganglia. The basal ganglia includes the nucleus accumbens, found in the ventral portion of the basal ganglia, and the other basal ganglia structures that facilitate movement. Although movement disorders are not a feature of depression, approximately half of all Parkinson's disease patients report a major depressive episode before the first occurrence of Parkinson's symptoms (Santamaria, Tolosa, & Valles, 1986).

Experimental deep brain stimulation treatments for depression also suggest that the nucleus accumbens is underactive in depression. In one such procedure, Schlaepfer and colleagues (2008) implanted brain electrodes into the nucleus accumbens of three patients. After surgery, activating the electrode led to improvements in depression. In addition to these improvements, the patients spontaneously remarked about interests in doing something novel or something they had not done in many years. One patient, for example, said that she wanted to take up bowling again, and another patient wished to visit the Cologne Cathedral because it was nearby and he had never done so before.

Antidepressant Drugs

The first antidepressant drugs emerged during the 1950s when pharmacological treatments for mental illness were virtually unknown. The first antidepressant drug,

STOP & CHECK

1. The _____, a structure important for anxiety, is overactive in depression.

2. In depression, the left _____ appears to be underactive and to have reduced gray and white matter volume.

3. The volume reduction in the _____ is of particular interest because antidepressant drugs increase proliferation in this structure.

1. amygdala 2. dorsal prefrontal cortex 3. hippocampus

iproniazid (Marsilid), was developed for the treatment of tuberculosis in 1953 (Fox & Gibas, 1953). Loomer, Saunders, and Kline (1957) were the first to report a reduction in depressive symptoms among patients treated with iproniazid. Experimental animal findings showed that iproniazid reversed sedation and miosis produced by a drug called *reserpine*. (See **Box 13.1** for information on the use of animal behavior models to identify antidepressant drugs.)

As was learned later, reserpine served to deplete the brain of monoamine neurotransmitters by irreversibly blocking transporters for synaptic vesicles (Carlsson, Lindqvist, Magnusson, 1957; Holzbauer & Vogt, 1956; Viveros, Arqueros, Connett, & Kirshner, 1969). This action subsequently leads to catabolism (i.e., enzymatic breakdown of a molecule) of these neurotransmitters. The irreversiible blockage of transporters on synaptic vesicles prevents the storage of any newly synthesized neurotransmitters. As a result, newly synthesized neurotransmitters largely become catabolized before escaping the axon terminal (Pletscher, Shore, & Brodie, 1955). Early case reports in fact described a mental depression occurring from long-term treatment with reserpine (Freis, 1954). Thus, as noted earlier, reserpine served as an early model that helped to discover some of the first antidepressant drugs.

Another critical development stemming from studies on reserpine involved understanding the role that monoamine depletion played in Parkinson's disease (a disorder we now link directly to dopamine depletion). During studies in the 1950s, researchers found that reserpine depleted norepinephrine in the brain (Carlsson, 2001; Holzbauer & Vogt, 1956). To determine if norepinephrine depletion might account for the sedation and loss of muscle movement caused by reserpine, Carlsson and colleagues administered a precursor for norepinephrine synthesis: levodopa. They reported their findings in 1957, stating that sedated rabbits woke up after treatment with levodopa and linked these effects to norepinephrine (recall that dopamine had yet to be identified as a neurotransmitter in the brain at this time) (Carlsson et al., 1957) (**Figure 13.2**). Oliver Sacks famously wrote of levodopa treatment in patients exhibiting catatonic-like behavior from encephalitis lethargica in his book *Awakenings* (1973), and you can see these accounts dramatized in the 1990 movie of the same title. Thus, studies on reserpine led to a greater understanding

BOX 13.1 ANIMAL BEHAVIORAL MODELS FOR IDENTIFYING ANTIDEPRESSANT DRUGS

An important challenge during drug development is an ability to behaviorally identify effective medications. Researchers have developed animal behavioral procedures that, although not resembling depression in a human, predict antidepressant efficacy. The primary models used include the forced swim test, tail suspension test, and differential reinforcement of a low-rate, 72-second task.

The *forced swim test* is an animal behavioral model of depression that measures the length of time a small animal, usually a rat or mouse, will swim in a cylinder of water (**Figure 1**). When the animal determines escape is impossible, it assumes a floating posture and only commits movements necessary to keeps its head above water. Antidepressant researchers coin this floating posture as *behavioral despair*. The test arose from studies by Porsolt, Le Pichon, and Jalfre (1977) showing the successful identification of clinically proven antidepressant drugs. The *tail suspension test* is an animal behavioral model of depression

FIGURE 1 ● Periods of immobility during a forced swim test (left) or tail suspension task (right) are used as indexes of antidepressant response.

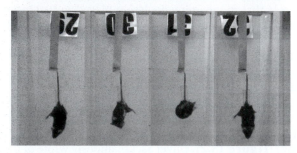

SOURCE: Photo courtesy of Adem Can, PhD, and Todd D. Gould, MD, Department of Psychiatry, University of Maryland School of Medicine, Baltimore MD.

that measures the length of time a mouse will struggle to escape while being suspended by its tail (Figure 1). In this model, antidepressant treatments reduces the amount of time an animal gives up struggling, or despairs (Cryan, Mombereau, & Vassout, 2005).

A *differential reinforcement of low-rate reinforcement schedule (DRL-72 sec)* requires a rat to withhold lever presses for food in an operant chamber until after 72 seconds have elapsed. If a rat presses the lever too soon, the 72-second counter resets. Only responses occurring after the full 72 seconds have passed result in food pellets. Thus, withholding responses for a period of time results in earning reinforcers. Antidepressant drugs, in this procedure, cause an increase in the reinforcement rate, defined as the number of food pellets earned over time, meaning that animals tend to wait

FIGURE 2 ● **Antidepressant drugs improve the efficiency of responding in rats trained on a differential reinforcement of low-rate 72-second operant schedule. Specifically, antidepressant drugs increase the reinforcement rate (shown by the solid symbols) and reduce the response rates (open symbols) compared to a control test (i.e., saline test). The data are graphed as percentages of control in order to easily show how each value can be compared to the control tests.**

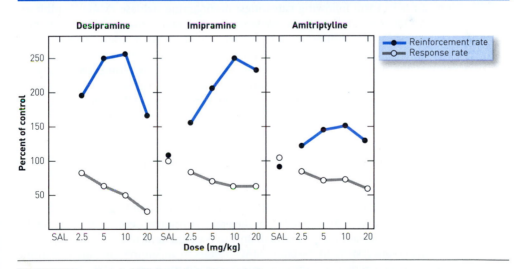

SOURCE: O'Donnell et al., 2005. Reprinted with permission.

(Continued)

(Continued)

longer before responding. In addition, response rates, defined as the number of responses that occur over a period of time, either increase or remain unchanged after acute administration of an antidepressant drug. We certainly many other drug classes capable of reducing responses in this procedure, but not without reducing overall response rates. Instead, antidepressant drugs enhance the likelihood of a rat waiting to respond until the right time, but they do not reduce responding overall. For example, benzodiazepine anxiolytic drugs (often referred to as tranquilizers) generally decrease both reinforcement and response rates. **Figure 2** shows the effects of several tricyclic antidepressant effects on reinforcement and response rates in this task (O'Donnell, Marek, & Seiden, 2005).

of neurotransmission in the brain and helped to form theories about the causes of mental and neurological disorders.

Since these early days of the psychopharmacology era, the pharmaceutical industry has developed dozens of different antidepressant medications that vary in their pharmacological actions, clinical efficacy, and adverse effects. We classify antidepressant drugs according to their pharmacological actions and chemical structures, which has led to the following categories: monoamine oxidase (MAO) inhibitors, tricyclic antidepressant drugs, selective serotonin reuptake inhibitors, serotonin–norepinephrine reuptake inhibitors, and atypical antidepressant drugs (**Table 13.3**). Largely because of the actions of reserpine and early MAO inhibitors, researchers developed the monoamine hypothesis of depression. The **monoamine hypothesis of depression** states that a monoamine deficiency causes depressive mood. Although more than half a century of research has passed since these first drugs came out, we still develop antidepressant drugs largely based on this hypothesis (Skolnick & Basile, 2006).

Monoamine hypothesis of depression
Hypothesis stating that a monoamine neurotransmitter deficiency causes depressive mood

Review! Monoamine neurotransmitters consist of dopamine, norepinephrine, and serotonin. (Chapter 3.)

Monoamine Oxidase Inhibitors Researchers have discovered and named two types of MAO: MAO_A and MAO_B. We find MAO_A in the brain, peripheral nervous system, and the intestinal tract, whereas MAO_B is found mainly in the brain and, to a lesser extent, in the peripheral nervous system. In the brain, MAO_A resides in dopamine and norepinephrine neurons, and MAO_B resides in serotonin and norepinephrine neurons (Mills, 1997).

Iproniazid became known as the first clinically used antidepressant drug among the MAO inhibitors. **MAO inhibitors** produce antidepressant effects by binding to MAO and preventing it from breaking down monoamine neurotransmitters, including

MAO inhibitors
Produce antidepressant effects by binding to MAO and preventing it from breaking down monoamine neurotransmitters

> **FIGURE 13.2 ●** The top panel shows two rabbits treated with reserpine, a monoamine neurotransmitter depleter. The lower panel shows these same rabbits after treatment with levodopa. These findings helped to stimulate research into understanding the role of neurotransmitters in mental and neurological disorders.

SOURCE: Carlsson, A. (1960). Zur Frage der wirkungsweise einiger psychopharmaka. *Psychiatric Neurology* 140:220–222.

serotonin, dopamine, and norepinephrine, as well as other monoamine compounds such as tyramine (**Table 13.4**). Depending on the particular drug, an MAO inhibitor may bind irreversibly or reversibly to MAO. For **irreversible MAO inhibitors**, the drug never releases from MAO. To make up for the loss of functional MAO enzymes, neurons synthesize more MAO. For **reversible MAO inhibitors**, the drug either temporarily binds to MAO or other compounds such as tyramine to displace the drug from MAO.

An adverse effect termed the *cheese reaction* limited the use of the first MAO inhibitors for treating depression. Clinicians characterize the **cheese reaction** as overactivation of the sympathetic nervous system because of MAO inhibition causing increased

Irreversible MAO inhibitors
Antidepressant drugs that irreversibly inhibit MAO

Reversible MAO inhibitors
Antidepressant drugs that either temporarily bind to MAO or allow other compounds to displace the drug from MAO

Cheese reaction
Overactivated sympathetic nervous system functioning because of MAO inhibition that leads to increased heart rate, hypertension, sweating, and inhibited digestion

TABLE 13.3 ● Selected Antidepressant Drugs				
Monoamine Oxidase Inhibitors	**Tricyclic Antidepressant Drugs**	**Selective Serotonin Reuptake Inhibitors**	**Serotonin-Norepinephrine Reuptake Inhibitors**	**Atypical Antidepressant Drugs**
Iproniazid (Marsilid)	Amitriptyline (Elavil)	Citalopram (Celexa)	Duloxetine (Cymbalta)	Agomelatine (Valdoxan or Thymanax)
Moclobemide (Aurorix)	Clomipramine (Anafranil)	Dapoxetine (Priligy)	Milnacipran (Ixel, Savella)	Bupropion (Wellbutrin)
Phenelzine (Nardil)	Desipramine (Pertofrane)	Escitalopram (Lexapro)	Venlafaxine (Effexor)	Mirtazapine (Remeron)
Selegiline (Emsam)	Imipramine (Tofranil)	Fluoxetine (Prozac)		Vortioxetine (Brintellix or Trintellix)
Tranylcypromine (Parnate)		Fluvoxamine (Luvox)		
		Indalpine (Upstene)		
		Paroxetine (Paxil)		
		Sertraline (Zoloft)		

SOURCE: © Cengage Learning 2014.

heart rate, hypertension (high blood pressure), sweating, and inhibited digestion. In fact, when severe enough, we refer to the high degree of hypertension occurring here as a *hypertensive crisis*. This reaction occurs when MAO inhibition increases the levels of norepinephrine and tyramine. Norepinephrine activates β_1 adrenoceptors on cardiac tissue, causing increased heart rate and strength of muscle contractions. Tyramine, which does not cross the blood-brain barrier, likely enhances these effects by displacing stored norepinephrine in sympathetic nervous system neurons, causing some norepinephrine to leak from axon terminals and contribute to the activation of β_1 adrenoceptors (Axelrod, Gordon, Hertting, Kopin, & Potter, 1962; Graefe, Bossle, Wolfel, & Burger, 1999).

Modern MAO inhibitors reduce, but do not eliminate, the risk of a cheese reaction. The first type of modern MAO inhibitors were selective inhibitors of MAO_B. **Selective MAO_B inhibitors**, such as *selegiline (Emsam)*, have a greater affinity for MAO_B than MAO_A, thereby engendering most of their effects through acting in the brain. Selegiline also can be administered through a skin patch, allowing the drug to bypass the intestinal tract, where it would otherwise cause some build-up of tyramine.

The second type of modern MAO inhibitors are reversible inhibitors of MAO_A (abbreviated as RIMA). **RIMA drugs** selectively inhibit MAO_A but allow for displacement

Selective MAO_B inhibitors Antidepressant drugs that primarily inhibit MAO_B enzymes and exhibit weaker inhibition of MAO_A enzymes

RIMA drugs (reversible inhibitors of MAO_A) Antidepressant drugs that selectively inhibit MAO_A but allow for displacement from MAO_A by tyramine

TABLE 13.4 ● Pharmacological Actions of Antidepressant Drugs		
Antidepressant Drug Class	**Pharmacological Actions**	**Neurotransmitter Levels**
MAO inhibitors	Inhibit MAO, preventing catabolism of monoamine neurotransmitters	Increase dopamine, norepinephrine, and serotonin
Tricyclic antidepressant drugs	Inhibit reuptake of serotonin and norepinephrine; binds to various receptors	Increase serotonin and norepinephrine levels
Selective serotonin reuptake inhibitors (SSRIs)	Inhibit reuptake of serotonin	Increase serotonin levels
Serotonin-norepinephrine reuptake inhibitors (SNRIs)	Inhibit reuptake of serotonin and norepinephrine	Increase serotonin and norepinephrine levels
Atypical antidepressant drugs	Vary depending on the particular drug	Generally increase one or more monoamine neurotransmitters

from MAO_A by tyramine. By allowing MAO_A to break down tyramine, RIMA provides patients with a lower risk of a cheese reaction. *Moclobemide (Aurorix, Manerix)* is a RIMA clinically available for depression in Canada and Europe, but the weak efficacy of the drug failed to gain it FDA approval in the United States (Youdim, 2006).

STOP & CHECK

1. What was the first antidepressant drug, iproniazid, actually developed for?

2. A deficiency of dopamine, norepinephrine, or serotonin is the basis for the _____ hypothesis of depression.

3. MAO_A is found in the intestinal tract, peripheral nervous system, and the brain, whereas MAO_B is primarily found in the _____.

4. Why might a reversible MAO_A inhibitor be preferable to an irreversible MAO inhibitor to treat depression?

1. tuberculosis 2. monoamine 3. brain 4. A reversible MAO_A inhibitor enhances levels of the monoamines dopamine, norepinephrine, and serotonin, but has a low cheese reaction risk because it can be displaced by tyramine. An irreversible MAO inhibitor causes a build-up of tyramine, which contributes to sympathetic nervous system activation and the subsequent cheese reaction.

Tricyclic Antidepressant Drugs **Tricyclic antidepressant drugs** inhibit reuptake of norepinephrine and serotonin and function as antagonists for various receptors, often including muscarinic acetylcholine receptors (Table 13.4) (Lenox & Frazer, 2002).

Tricyclic antidepressant drugs Antidepressant drugs that inhibit the reuptake of norepinephrine and serotonin and function as antagonists for various receptors

Tricyclic refers to three connected benzene rings shared by drugs in this category. Chemists developed the first drug tricyclic antidepressant drug, imipramine, in an attempt to produce drugs similar to the first antipsychotic drug *chlorpromazine (Thorazine)* for the purpose of treating schizophrenia (Davis, 2006). Although failing to effectively treat schizophrenia, clinicians noticed improvements in mood, prompting clinical testing for depression instead (Kuhn, 1958).

Tricyclic antidepressant drugs provide certain pharmacological actions similar to MAO, but do so through a different mechanism. Tricyclic antidepressants achieve elevations in serotonin and norepinephrine levels by inhibiting reuptake at membrane transporters, rather than through inhibiting catabolism of neurotransmitters as MAO inhibitors do. This also avoids a cheese reaction from occurring with tricyclic antidepressant drugs, although these drugs have unique adverse effects of their own.

A number of adverse effects occur from tricyclic antidepressant drugs binding to various receptors in the nervous system. Most tricyclic antidepressant drugs serve as antagonists for cholinergic muscarinic receptors. In the parasympathetic nervous system, blocking muscarinic receptors causes dry mouth, dry eyes, constipation, urinary retention (from a lack of bladder relaxation), and various other effects related to blocking neurotransmission in this system. As a result of dry eyes, blurred vision also may occur. In the brain, blocking muscarinic receptors can also lead to impairments in memory and cognitive functioning (Lenox & Frazer, 2002).

Many tricyclic antidepressants also block α_1 adrenoceptors, causing vasodilation and effects similar to orthostatic *hypotension*, low blood pressure typically noted by an individual feeling lightheaded or dizzy when suddenly standing up. Greater blood flow to the head resulting from vasodilation may also cause headaches and the feeling of a "head rush." Many of these drugs act as histamine H_1 receptor antagonists, which cause sedative effects just as antihistamine cold medicines do. In addition, tricyclic antidepressants are known to cause weight gain, which can lead to a variety of health concerns, including type II diabetes (Brown, Majumdar, & Johnson, 2008; Lenox & Frazer, 2002). Taking all of these adverse effects in mind, it's not surprising that patients prescribed tricyclic antidepressants report feeling "drug laden," which can reduce *patient compliance* (i.e., the likelihood of a patient continuing to take the prescribed medication) (Lenox & Frazer, 2002).

STOP & CHECK

1. Tricyclic antidepressants reduce depressive symptoms by preventing the reuptake of _____ and _____.

2. What effect might the adverse effects of tricyclic antidepressant drugs have on patient compliance?

1. serotonin and norepinephrine **2.** These adverse effects decrease the likelihood of patients reliably taking these medications. Parasympathetic nervous system inhibition can cause a number of bothersome effects, including dry mouth, blurred vision, constipation, cognitive disruption, and urinary retention. In particular, weight gain often deters patient compliance.

Review! Adrenoceptors are the receptors for the neurotransmitter norepinephrine. (Chapter 3.)

Selective Serotonin Reuptake Inhibitors (SSRIs) The pharmacological actions of tricyclic antidepressant drugs established a directed effort to develop drugs that selectively inhibited the reuptake of serotonin or norepinephrine. Based on these pharmacological actions and other experimental support for the specific influence of serotonin on mood, Arvid Carlsson worked with Astra Pharmaceuticals to develop *zimelidine (Zelmid)* for the treatment of depression (Shorter, 1997). Thus, zimelidine was the first selective serotonin reuptake inhibitor. A **selective serotonin reuptake inhibitor (SSRI)** elevates serotonin levels by blocking reuptake through serotonin membrane transporters (Table 13.4). Beginning in 1981, zimelidine was marketed in Europe for a limited time, but was abruptly withdrawn from the market because it damaged myelin sheathing around central and peripheral nervous system axons.

Researchers at Eli Lilly discovered a safer SSRI—*fluoxetine*—which is best known by its trade name *Prozac*. Fluoxetine met FDA approval for the treatment of depression in 1987. It was found to be generally safer than MAO inhibitors and tricyclic antidepressant drugs, and fluoxetine became one of the most prescribed drugs in history (Shorter, 1997).

Because of their perceived safety, SSRIs have been prescribed for depression in teens and children. However, in 2005 the FDA issued a **black box warning** (or **boxed warning**), a warning on the package insert given a black border around to draw special attention to it, that SSRIs increased suicide risk in teens and children (Food and Drug Administration, 2005). This warning was based on a review of published clinical studies in teens that together indicated a higher suicide rate (4 percent) compared to placebo-treated patients (2 percent). This warning does not ban the use of these medications in children and teens, but rather, indicates that physicians must carefully monitor suicidal tendencies after prescribing these medications.

We find other significant concerns for SSRIs as well. They may cause a **serotonin syndrome**, a life-threatening condition characterized by agitation, restlessness, disturbances in cognitive functioning, and possibly hallucinations. This syndrome is usually avoided by taking low or moderate doses of an SSRI, although a drug reaction with another serotonin compound, such as a different antidepressant drug or lithium can increase the risk of serotonin syndrome (Sternbach, 1991).

Just as taking SSRIs might lead to a serotonin syndrome, abrupt withdrawal from SSRI treatment may cause a serotonin *discontinuation* syndrome. The **serotonin discontinuation syndrome** is characterized by sensory disturbances, sleeping disturbances, disequilibrium, flulike symptoms, and gastrointestinal effects. Those seeking to discontinue SSRI use must slowly wean themselves from the medication by reducing the amount taken over time (Sternbach, 1991).

Elevations in serotonin levels are likely to cause **sexual side effects**, including erectile dysfunction, inability to achieve orgasm, and loss of sexual drive. In a survey asking patients taking SSRIs to determine how they felt compared to their usual state, the majority of those surveyed reported far less interest in having sex and less pleasure during sex (Opbroek et al., 2002; see Figure 13.2). These side effects negatively affect one's quality of life and contribute to poor patient compliance with these medications.

Selective serotonin reuptake inhibitor (SSRI) Antidepressant drug that elevates serotonin levels by blocking reuptake through serotonin membrane transporters

Black box warning (or boxed warning) A warning on a drug's package insert given a black border around to draw special attention to it

Serotonin syndrome Antidepressant-drug-induced life-threatening condition characterized by agitation, restlessness, disturbances in cognitive functioning, and possibly hallucinations

Serotonin discontinuation syndrome Syndrome caused by abrupt withdrawal of an antidepressant drug, resulting in sensory disturbances, sleeping disturbances, disequilibrium, flu-like symptoms, and gastrointestinal effects

Sexual side effects Sexual dysfunction, including erectile dysfunction, inability to achieve orgasm, and loss of sexual drive caused by antidepressant drugs

Emotional blunting (or affective blunting) Feelings of emotional detachment along with experiencing reduced positive and negative emotions

An often overlooked adverse effect of SSRIs is a condition referred to as *emotional blunting*. **Emotional blunting** (or **affective blunting**) consists of feelings of emotional detachment along with experiencing reduced positive and negative emotions. Patients describing these reduced emotional feelings insist that they result from the medication, rather than depression, and use labels such as "dulled," "flattened," or "numbed" to express how they feel (Price, Cole, & Goodwin, 2009). Thus, a person with emotional blunting may not seem particularly sad or happy, just neutral.

We gain some insight into emotional blunting among patients treated with SSRIs from a survey conducted by Opbroek and colleagues (2002). The patients studied consisted of those reporting sexual dysfunction and in the course of evaluation were surveyed on other items to determine how they felt compared to their "usual"

FIGURE 13.3 ● Average scores on a questionnaire asking SSRI-treated patients how they currently felt compared to their "usual" state.

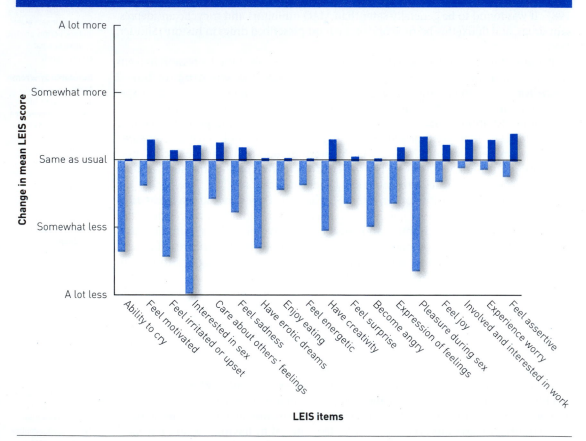

SOURCE: Opbroek, A., Delgado, P. L., Laukes, C., McGahuey, C., Katsanis, J., Moreno, F. A., & Manber, R. (2002). Emotional blunting associated with SSRI-induced sexual dysfunction. Do SSRIs inhibit emotional responses?. *International Journal of Neuropsychopharmacology*, 5(02), 147–151.

state. **Figure 13.3** provides their average responses. In particular, we find a substantial reduction in sexual interest and enjoyment, as reported above, and many of the participants reporting a lower ability to cry, become angry, care about the feelings of others, and feel creative.

STOP & CHECK

1. SSRIs enhance serotonin levels by blocking _____.

2. High doses of an SSRI may cause a _____, which is characterized by agitation, restlessness, cognitive disruption, and hallucinations.

3. Abrupt withdrawal from SSRI treatment causes a _____.

1. serotonin transporters **2.** serotonin syndrome **3.** serotonin discontinuation syndrome

---

Serotonin–Norepinephrine Reuptake Inhibitors (SNRIs) **Serotonin–norepinephrine reuptake inhibitors (SNRIs)**, which are also called **dual serotonin and norepinephrine reuptake inhibitors**, enhance levels of serotonin and norepinephrine by blocking serotonin and norepinephrine membrane transporters. The push for a new antidepressant drugs led to the development of *venlafaxine (Effexor)*, the first of the class of SNRIs. Venlafaxine (Effexor) received FDA approval for the treatment of depression in 1993. Venlafaxine and other SNRIs, such as *duloxetine (Cymbalta)*, are at least as effective as SSRIs for the treatment of depression, and some studies conclude that SNRIs are more effective. As inhibitors of serotonin reuptake, they share the same adverse effects as SSRIs.

Papakostas, Thase, Fava, Nelson, and Shelton (2007) conducted a meta-analysis on clinical depression studies that used either an SSRI or an SNRI to determine which class was the most effective. The literature review was extensive, including more than 90 trials and more than 17,000 patients. In each comparison, an SNRI produced a slightly greater improvement than an SSRI. The effects were modest, but consistent (**Figure 13.4**).

Another disorder linked, at least in part, to stress is fibromyalgia. **Fibromyalgia syndrome** is a musculoskeletal disorder characterized by widespread pain occurring as muscle tenderness in addition to other symptoms including fatigue, disrupted sleep, and depressed mood (Abeles, Pillinger, Solitar, & Abeles, 2007). The disorder occurs in among 3.4 percent of women and 0.5 percent of men in the United States (Wolfe, Ross, Anderson, Russell, & Herbert, 1995). The cause of fibromyalgia remains unknown but likely involves multiple interaction mechanisms including sensitization of pain pathways, reduced neurotransmission of monoamine neurotransmitters, and a current or previous mental disorder, such as depression or anxiety (Abeles et al., 2007). Pain levels, which fluctuate throughout the day, are particularly worsened by stress (Fischer et al., 2016).

Serotonin–norepinephrine reuptake inhibitors (SNRIs) (or dual serotonin and norepinephrine reuptake inhibitors) Antidepressant drugs that enhance levels of serotonin and norepinephrine by blocking serotonin and norepinephrine membrane transporters

Fibromyalgia syndrome A musculoskeletal disorder characterized by widespread pain occurring as muscle tenderness as well as other symptoms including fatigue, disrupted sleep, and depressed mood

FIGURE 13.4 ● According to a review of antidepressant clinical trials, SNRIs (shown in light blue) consistently reveal greater improvements in depressive symptoms than SSRIs (shown in dark blue). However, these differences were seldom robust. The particular SNRI studied is noted on the x-axis, and the "combined" label refers to all studies combined.

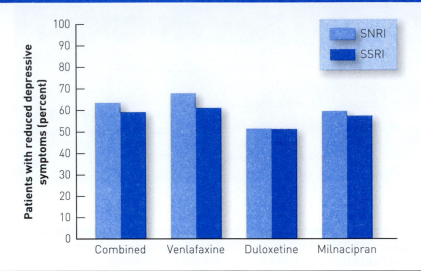

SOURCE: Papakostas et al., 2007. Reprinted with permission.

Both norepinephrine and serotonin, among many other neurotransmitters, have been shown to modulate pain signaling (Millan, 2002). The notion that diminished norepinephrine and serotonin levels in fibromyalgia may contribute to increased pain sensitivity led to testing different types of antidepressant drugs. Arnold and colleagues (2004) reported one of the major findings in this area—that the SNRI duloxetine reduced pain and other features of fibromyalgia in both depressed and non-depressed patients. Antidepressant drugs, especially those of the SNRI class, have become the first-line pharmacological treatments for fibromyalgia. Aside from antidepressant drugs, the drug *pregabalin (Lyrica)* also is used (Crofford et al., 2005). Unlike the antidepressant drugs, pregabalin facilitates GABA neurotransmission, thereby attenuating pain signals to the brain as well as potentially reducing stress. Non-pharmacological treatment strategies include physical therapy, relaxation techniques, cognitive–behavioral therapy, and exercise (Rossy et al., 1999).

Atypical antidepressant drugs (or multimodal antidepressant drugs)
Antidepressant drugs that reduce depression through mechanisms that differ from those of other antidepressant classifications

Atypical Antidepressant Drugs **Atypical antidepressant drugs** (or **multimodal antidepressant drugs**) reduce depression through mechanisms that differ from those of other antidepressant classifications. They are neither MAO inhibitors nor tricyclic antidepressants. Nor do atypical antidepressant drugs selectively block either serotonin reuptake, norepinephrine reuptake, or both. Thus, this category is a bit of a catch-all for antidepressant drugs that do not fit into other antidepressant drug categories. All atypical antidepressants drugs currently available alter neurotransmission for one or more monoamine neurotransmitters.

One of the most prescribed atypical antidepressant drugs is *bupropion (Wellbutrin)*. Bupropion is a reuptake inhibitor for norepinephrine and dopamine and therefore is unique among the antidepressants for its lack of serotonin elevation. Given the lack of serotonin effects, bupropion does not carry a risk for serotonin syndrome, and it does not have a risk of sexual side effects (Ascher et al., 1995).

Controversy surrounds the atypical antidepressant drug *reboxetine*, which functions as a selective norepinephrine reuptake inhibitor. Clinical study data released in the 1990s indicated superior, long-term antidepressant effects and a low rate of adverse effects compared to placebo (Burrows, Maguire, & Norman, 1998). Such findings allowed approval of reboxetine for use in Europe, but the FDA denied approval based on unpublished clinical data that reboxetine's drug maker, Pfizer, was required to release under U.S. law (but not required to release in Europe) (Szalavitz, 2010). A study examining these unpublished data together with published data concluded that reboxetine not only lacked clinical efficacy for depression, but that the unpublished data revealed greater adverse effects from the drug than published data had indicated (Eyding et al., 2010).

A recently developed atypical antidepressant drug is *vortioxetine (Brintellix, Trintellix)*, which met FDA approval in 2013. Like SNRIs, vortioxetine inhibits serotonin reuptake, and to a more modest extent, also inhibits norepinephrine reuptake (Bang-Andersen et al., 2011). Researchers classified vortioxetine as an atypical antidepressant because of its additional effects at a host of serotonin receptors, serving as an antagonist for some serotonin receptors (e.g., 5-HT$_3$) and an agonist for other receptors (e.g.,. 5-HT$_{1A}$) (Sanchez, Asin, & Artigas, 2015).

Another atypical antidepressant drug is *agomelatine (Valdoxan* or *Thymanax)*, a drug approved for use in Europe but not currently approved by the FDA for use in the United States. Agomelatine acts as an agonist for melatonin receptors and an antagonist for serotonin 5-HT$_{2C}$ receptors. Studies find that agomelatine restores sleep patterns among study participants with major depressive disorder, likely by acting on melatonin receptors. Researchers also report reduced depression among agomelatine-treated patients compared to those treated with placebo. While not serving as a reuptake inhibitor for monoamine neurotransmitters, antagonism of 5-HT$_{2C}$ receptors may produce increased levels of dopamine, as discussed later in this chapter. Consistent with these pharmacological actions, clinical trials with agomelatine did not find increased rates of sexual dysfunction (Sansone & Sansone, 2011).

STOP & CHECK

1. How does the efficacy and safety of SNRIs compare to SSRIs?

2. What is atypical about atypical antidepressant drugs?

1. SNRIs are at least as effective for depression as SSRIs, and many clinical studies indicate a modestly greater efficacy by SNRIs. Both SNRIs and SSRIs have similar adverse effects. 2. The mechanisms of action for atypical antidepressant drugs differ from those of other antidepressant drug classes.

Review! Melatonin is a sleep inducing hormone that plays an important role in circadian rhythm, our natural sleep cycle. (Chapter 3.)

Limitations in Antidepressant Drug Effectiveness and Development

Although antidepressant drug classes differ pharmacologically and have unique adverse effects, they share many of the same limitations for treating depression. We consider three issues in this section: length of response time, treatment resistance, and strong placebo effects in clinical trials. The "From Actions to Effects" section later in this chapter also considers pharmacogenetic factors in antidepressant response.

Length of Response Time   All antidepressant drugs have a lengthy response time. For those who eventually respond to antidepressant drugs, clinically significant effects occur after 2 weeks of treatment and generally show full effects after 4 weeks. If patients fail to respond sufficiently after 4 weeks, then the likelihood of successful treatment with the drug diminishes. The long response time is particularly concerning when treating patients with a high risk of suicide (Nierenberg et al., 2000).

Treatment Resistance   Many patients may fail to respond adequately to antidepressant treatment. Fava and Davidson (1996) estimated that between 29 and 46 percent of patients fail to fully recover with antidepressant drug treatment. In these cases, clinicians may increase the dose of the SSRI, add another medication (see following), or switch altogether to a different antidepressant drug. We identify an individual as having **treatment-resistant depression** after successive failed attempts to significantly reduce depressive symptoms by antidepressant medication, including a treatment course with an SSRI (Trivedi et al., 2006).

Treatment-resistant depression Diagnosis made after successive failed attempts to significantly reduce depressive symptoms

Placebo Effects in Clinical Studies   Placebo effects present an important issue for drug developers during clinical trials for antidepressant drugs. To gain governmental approval, novel antidepressant drugs must be tested in clinical trials that compare the novel drug to placebo. When conducting clinical trials with antidepressant drugs, a clinically significant improvement often occurs in placebo-treated patients. This requires a novel antidepressant drug to produce clinical effects that significantly exceed those found with placebo. Given these strong placebo effects combined with the cautious nature of clinical drug testing, researchers may fail to find clinically significant antidepressant drug effects.

The placebo effect is a criticism of antidepressant efficacy. As raised by Kirsch (2014) and many others, the placebo effect indicates a lack of clinical efficacy by many antidepressant drugs brought to clinical trials. According to analysis conducted of FDA clinical trials, only 43 percent reported clinical improvements beyond those observed from placebo. Moreover, the observation that non-antidepressant drugs occasionally produced supposedly antidepressant effects over placebo in some trials has led to the criticism that perhaps any perceived drug effect by a study participant interpreted an antidepressant effect, thus resulting in reduced rates of depression. Said another way, an antidepressant drug might actually be a placebo (Kirsch, 2014).

In an unexpected way, the lack of efficacy by reboxetine (mentioned earlier) might serve as a counterargument to claims that antidepressant drugs are simply placebos. As noted earlier, unpublished clinical data revealed a lack of efficacy for depression, but also higher rates of adverse effects. Thus, study participants found a lack of antidepressant efficacy despite experiencing clear drug effects (Szalavitz, 2010).

STOP & CHECK

1. How many weeks does it take for antidepressant drugs to become effective?

2. Treatment-resistant depression is often identified after failed treatment with a(n) _____.

3. A particular challenge in antidepressant clinical trials is that patients often improve when taking a(n) _____.

1. At least two to four weeks 2. SSRI 3. placebo

Combination Strategies for Treating Depression With Antidepressant Drugs

Recent years have seen an emergence of combination strategies for antidepressant treatments. The purpose of a **combination drug strategy** is to administer a medication to adjust the effects of another medication. We find a number of different terms used to describe these approaches. For drugs intended to boost the therapeutic effects of a medication, we use the term **augmentation strategy** (or **adjunctive treatment or adjunctive therapy**). **Add-on treatments** simply imply an adjustment of a medication's effects by another drug, in this case identical to the term *combination drug strategy* referred to earlier. Yet, most times we find "add-on treatment" regarded as synonymous with "augmentation strategy." Unfortunately, the imprecise usage of these common terms for describing combined treatment strategies leaves one guessing as to the purposes of a combined drug strategy.

We find the use of *antipsychotic* drugs—drugs developed for treating schizophrenia—as adjunctive treatments (i.e., to strengthen antidepressant effects in this context) for patients who do not respond adequately to antidepressant drugs. Normally, these patients meet the criteria for treatment resistance, as described earlier. Chapter 15 covers antipsychotic drugs in detail, but in general we find that antipsychotic drugs act at dopamine and serotonin receptors, usually as antagonists.

The antipsychotic drugs most commonly used as adjunctive medications, as well as meeting FDA approval for this purpose, are *aripiprazole (Abilify), quetiapine (Seroquel),* and *olanzapine (Zeprexa)*. We also find *risperidone (Risperdal)* used **off-label** (that is, a nongovernment approved use of a clinically available drug) for this purpose. Olanzapine is approved for use only in combination with fluoxetine; in fact, we find a combined olanzapine and fluoxetine pill marketed under the trade name *Symbyax*. These antipsychotic drugs fall under the *atypical* class of antipsychotic drugs, which differ in

Combination drug strategy The administration of a medication to adjust the effects of another medication

Augmentation strategy (or adjunctive treatment/therapy) Administration of a drug intended to boost the therapeutic effects of a medication

Add-on treatment The administration of a medication to adjust the effects of another medication; often used to describe a drug boosting the therapeutic effects of a medication

Off-label A nongovernment approved use of a clinically available drug

their therapeutic and adverse effects in some ways compared to many older antipsychotic drugs, termed *typical* antipsychotic drugs (again, more on this in Chapter 15).

Drug Profile: sildenafil	
Trade name	Viagra
Properties	Inhibit phosphodiesterase isozymes
Uses	Used for treating erectile dysfunction
Similar drugs	Tadalafil (Cialis)

In a review of clinical studies that examined the efficacy of atypical antipsychotic drugs as adjunctive treatments for depression, Speilmans and colleagues (2013) found that atypical antipsychotic drugs do provide improvements, albeit modest, in depression symptoms, quality of life, and functional outcomes (e.g., improvements in social and occupational functioning). The study authors also noted that a lack of long-term studies on antipsychotic drugs used adjunctively with antidepressant drugs left them uncertain as to whether potential adverse effects might offset the minimal therapeutic benefits derived from these adjunctive treatment approaches.

We also find drugs used as combination treatments to remedy certain adverse effects brought on by antidepressant medications. A typical example of this is bupropion (Wellbutrin) as an add-on medication for treating sexual dysfunction produced by antidepressant drugs, particularly for drugs that inhibit serotonin reuptake (e.g., SSRIs and SNRIs). While used off-label for this purpose, practitioners have for years prescribed bupropion as an add-on therapy to address this particular adverse effect. In reviews of published studies evaluating bupropion for reducing sexual dysfunction from SSRIs or SNRIs, bupropion appears to reduce sexual dysfunction from a moderate to substantial degree. These improvements mostly occur in women. Among men, medications that treat erectile dysfunction (i.e., impotence), such as *sildenafil (Viagra)* and *tadalafil (Cialis)*, instead appear more effective than bupropion as add-on treatments for treating sexual dysfunction from antidepressants drugs (Taylor et al., 2013). These drugs treat erectile dysfunction by inhibiting phosphodiesterase isozymes that diminish the duration and rigidity of an erection (Boolell et al., 1996; Brock et al., 2002).

Combining Psychotherapy and Pharmacotherapy for Treating Depression

The general consensus reached from clinical studies is that a combination of psychotherapy and antidepressant drugs is superior to using antidepressant drugs alone. One of the more common psychotherapies evaluated in combination studies consists of cognitive therapy. Cognitive therapy attempts to adjust one's depressive thoughts (e.g., "I'll never be happy" or "I fail at everything") as a means for improving mood. Combining a cognitive therapy with an SSRI, SNRI, or atypical antidepressant drug has been shown to produce greater efficacy for major depressive disorder than using an antidepressant alone or cognitive therapy alone (Hollon et al., 2014; Keller et al., 2000; Thase et al., 1997). Yet a combination of a tricyclic antidepressant drug with psychotherapy does not appear more effective than psychotherapy alone (Blackburn, Bishop, Glen, Whalley, & Christie, 1981; Hollon et al., 1992).

The benefits derived from a combined approach versus using an antidepressant drug or psychotherapy alone may also depend on the severity of depression. In one study, those with milder depressive symptoms benefited just as well with psychotherapy alone as they did with a combination of psychotherapy with an antidepressant drug. Yet in severe cases of depression, the combination appeared most effective (Thase et al., 1997).

STOP & CHECK

1. What terms describe a drug used to boost the therapeutic effects of a medication?

2. What type of drug is used to boost the antidepressant effects of an antidepressant drug?

3. Which particular adverse effect might bupropion or a drug like Viagra be prescribed as an add-on for an antidepressant drug?

4. Aside from another medication, what might be combined with an antidepressant drug to improve a patient's response to treatment?

1. One of these terms is "augmentation strategy," but we also find the terms "adjunctive treatment" and occasionally "add-on treatment," used as well. 2. Antipsychotic drug, nearly always an *atypical antipsy-chotic drug* 3. Sexual dysfunction. 4. Psychotherapy, such as cognitive therapy.

Antidepressant Drugs and Monoamine Neurotransmitter Systems

Although imaging procedures conducted in depressed patients help us to identify brain regions involved in depression, these techniques tell us nothing about the neurochemical abnormalities found in depression. Thus, we are largely left to study the actions of antidepressant drugs as a means to infer potential neurochemical abnormalities in depression. Although this approach is not ideal, it has led to the development of many therapeutic psychoactive drugs on the market today.

Antidepressant Drugs and Serotonin Neurotransmission One of the mechanisms important for producing antidepressant effects concerns altering serotonin neurotransmission. We find that most antidepressant drugs increase serotonin levels after administration, either through reducing catabolism of serotonin (as with the MAO inhibitors) or by preventing reuptake of serotonin (as with SSRIs, SNRIs, and many tricyclic antidepressant drugs). As a result, greater activation of serotonin receptors occurs. Some antidepressant drugs also directly bind to serotonin receptors, which helps researchers to understand which serotonin receptors may be most important for treating depression.

The serotonin receptor most studied for a role in depression and as a target for treating depression is the 5-HT_{2C} receptor. We find 5-HT_{2C} receptors activated when antidepressants drugs increase serotonin levels. Yet we also find that many antidepressant drugs directly bind to and serve as *antagonists* for these receptors. Antidepressant drugs serving as antagonists for 5-HT_{2C} receptors include the tricyclic antidepressant drugs imipramine and clomipramine and the SSRI fluoxetine (Millan, 2005; Ni & Miledi, 1997). Further, drugs acting as selective antagonists for 5-HT_{2C} receptors produce antidepressant effects in animal models. Antagonism of 5-HT_{2C} receptors appears to increase dopamine levels in the brain (see following), which may contribute to antidepressant effects. To account for antidepressant drugs that produce an activation of 5-HT_{2C} receptors (i.e., through increasing serotonin levels), researchers generally agree that chronic treatment with an antidepressant drug will eventually *desensitize* 5-HT_{2C} receptors. The desensitization of 5-HT_{2C} receptors results in a state similar to one achieved by an antagonist acting at these receptors (Martin, Hamon, Lanfumey, & Mongeau, 2014).

The 5-HT_{1A} receptor is another receptor implicated in depression and the actions of antidepressant drugs. In people with major depressive disorder who were never treated with an antidepressant drug, PET imaging studies reveal greater 5-HT_{1A} receptors levels compared to those without depression (Parsey et al., 2006; Parsey et al., 2010; Kaufman, DeLorenzo, Choudhury, & Parsey, 2016). In mice bred to exhibit helplessness as a model of depression, researchers found increased levels of 5-HT_{1A} receptors in structures thought important for depression, including the prefrontal cortex, amygdala, and hippocampus (Naudon, El Yacoubi, Vaugeois, Leroux-Nicollet, & Costentin, 2002). This study further found that chronic administration with an SSRI reduced both depression-like behavior in these mice and 5-HT_{1A} receptor levels. 5-HT_{1A} receptors may also account for depression observed among some individuals treated with the medication *isotretinoin (Accutane)* for acne (Hull & D'Arcy, 2003). A study examining this medication and receptor expression found that isotretinoin increased 5-HT_{1A} receptor levels on cell lines, providing a potential explanation for greater rates of depression among those treated with isotretinoin (O'Reilly, Trent, Bailey, and Lane, 2007; Kaufman et al., 2016).

The black box warning noted earlier for SSRIs concerned a potential increased risk of suicide in teens. This increased risk likely occurs from a potential *reduction* in serotonin during the first days of treatment. After these first days, serotonin should increase as desensitization of receptors that would otherwise inhibit the activity of serotonin neurons occurs. We address the model and precise receptors that may be responsible for diminished serotonin levels in the next chapter (Chapter 14, "From Actions to Effects").

The hypothesis that diminished serotonin levels initially caused by antidepressants may increase risk of suicide coincides with studies examining serotonin metabolite levels in the cerobrospinal fluid of suicide attempters. Many studies have examined metabolite levels in cerebrospinal fluid among suicide attemptors in order to infer the level of serotonin neurotransmission occurring in the central nervous system. Low metabolite levels suggest diminished production of serotonin in the central nervous system. Researchers consistently find diminished serotonin metabolite levels among depressed patients who attempt suicide compared to depressed patients who do not attempt suicide, irrespective of treatment type (Åsberg, Träskman, & Thorén, 1976; Mann, & Malone, 1997; Nordström et al., 1994).

Antidepressant Drugs and Dopamine Neurotransmission Several lines of evidence also suggest that dopamine is critical for antidepressant effects. We begin by noting that acute administration of most antidepressant drugs fails to increase dopamine release or cause other changes in dopamine neurotransmission within the limbic system (Pozzi, Invernizzi, Garavaglia, & Samanin, 1999). Yet during the course of chronic administration with antidepressant drugs, including the tricyclic antidepressant drugs tianeptine, imipramine, and the SSRI fluoxetine, dopamine levels increase in the nucleus accumbens (D'Aquila, Collu, Gessa, & Serra, 2000). These actions in the nucleus accumbens may treat *anhedonia* (a lack of joy) in depression.

Chronic administration with fluoxetine also increases the availability of dopamine D_2 receptors in the limbic system. In a study by Maj, Dziedzicka-Wasylewska, Rogoz, Rogoz, and Skuza (1996), a greater density of limbic system D_2 receptors was found in rats chronically treated with fluoxetine compared to rats treated with vehicle (i.e., placebo). In another study, chronic administration with fluoxetine, the tricyclic antidepressant drug desipramine, or the MAO inhibitor tranylcypromine, produced increases in nucleus accumbens levels of mRNA that encode for the synthesis of D_2 receptors (Ainsworth, Smith, & Sharp, 1998). Given that increases in dopamine release and dopamine D_2 receptors occur in the limbic system after chronic administration, many researchers suspect that these changes, in part, account for the lengthy response time for antidepressant drugs (Skolnick & Basile, 2006).

Elevations in dopamine levels in the prefrontal cortex may occur after acute or chronic administration of an antidepressant drug, depending on the particular drug. For example, Bymaster and colleagues (2002) found that among the SSRI drugs they studied after acute administration, only fluoxetine produced increases in prefrontal cortex dopamine levels as assessed using microdialysis in rats. The researchers noted that fluoxetine was the only drug in their study that served as an antagonist for 5-HT_{2C} receptors. Selective antagonism of 5-HT_{2C} has been shown to increase dopamine concentrations in the frontal cortex, suggesting a potential mechanism for some antidepressant drugs to increase dopamine levels in the prefrontal cortex after acute administration (Gobert et al., 2000). Otherwise, antidepressant drugs increase dopamine levels in the prefrontal cortex after chronic administration (Carlson, Visker, Nielsen, Keller, & Glick, 1996; Tanda, Frau, & Di Chiara, 1996).

A potential link between prefrontal cortical dopamine levels and antidepressant effects may account for observations of antidepressant efficacy from the dissociative anesthetic drug ketamine. Ketamine's antidepressant effects were first reported by Berman and colleagues (2000), who assessed intravenous infusion of a low ketamine dose to seven volunteers with major depressive disorder. Patients exhibited an immediate reduction in depressive symptoms that lasted as long as 3 days after treatment. A subsequent study found that ketamine's antidepressant effects lasted as long as 1 week (Zarate et al., 2006).

Review! Ketamine is an NMDA noncompetitive receptor antagonist and dissociative anesthetic that causes visual hallucinations, out-of-body experiences, cognitive impairment, and psychosis. (Chapter 12.)

These antidepressant effects appear to result from ketamine's actions in the prefrontal cortex. In laboratory rats, ketamine administration increases both dopamine and glutamate concentrations in the prefrontal cortex (Lorrain, Baccei, Bristow, Anderson, & Varney, 2003). Moreover, Li and colleagues (2010) revealed rapid prefrontal cortical synaptic changes, including dendritic spine growth and increased proteins used for intracellular signaling, after acute administration. In particular, ketamine activated a protein kinase called *mammalian target of rapamycin*, which is normally abbreviated as mTOR. The effects of ketamine also may alter dopamine levels in the limbic system, based on the finding that a direct administration of the NMDA receptor antagonist called CPP (an abbreviation of its chemical name[1]) into the prefrontal cortex causes increased dopamine levels in the nucleus accumbens (Del Arco, Segovia, & Mora, 2008) (**Figure 13.5**). It remains to be seen if ketamine will someday be used as an antidepressant drug itself or instead if ketamine will remain a compound for research purposes, perhaps paving the way for a new class of antidepressant drugs (Hillhouse & Porter, 2015; Krystal, Sanacora, & Duman, 2013).

Recent studies have also evaluated cholinergic muscarinic receptor antagonists as antidepressant drugs. In particular, the drug *scopolamine*, which is known as a psychedelic drug used for recreational purposes (see Chapter 12), has been tested in multiple clinical trials for treating depression. Furey and Drevets (2006) first demonstrated that scopolamine produces a rapid antidepressant effect lasting several days after a single intravenous infusion. A subsequent study found sustained antidepressants by administering scopolamine every 3 to 4 days to patients with major depressive disorder (Drevets & Furey, 2010).

These results with scopolamine suggest that cholinergic muscarinic receptor antagonism may contribute the antidepressant effects of many tricyclic antidepressant drugs. Yet tricyclic antidepressant drugs do not produce the rapid antidepressant effects observed after scopolamine infusion. These considerations led Voleti and colleagues (2013) to examine further the potential mechanisms responsible for scopolamine antidepressant effects. They found that scopolamine, like ketamine, stimulates intracellular signaling involving mTOR as well as increasing the number and activity of dendritic spines in the prefrontal cortex. Thus, at present, researchers believe that scopolamine engenders antidepressant effects through a mechanism similar to ketamine.

Neuronal Growth Occurs During Antidepressant Treatment Chronic administration of antidepressant drugs causes neuronal growth and production in the hippocampus (Dranovsky & Hen, 2006; Duman, Malberg, & Thome, 1999; Sahay & Hen, 2007). Because an increase in neuron density occurs over weeks during chronic administration,

---

1 3-[(R)-2-carboxypiperazin-4-yl]-propyl-1- phophonic acid.

FIGURE 13.5 ● In rats, direct administration of the NMDA receptor antagonist CPP into the prefrontal cortex (the downward arrow shows when the injection occurred) caused a significant elevation of dopamine levels in the nucleus accumbens. Dopamine was sampled from the nucleus accumbens using a microdialysis probe. The drug was administered into the prefrontal cortex through a cannula.

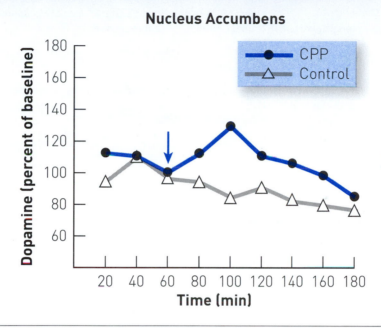

Nucleus Accumbens

SOURCE: With kind permission from Springer Science+Business Media: Del Arco, A. (2008). Blockade of NMDA receptors in the prefrontal cortex increases dopamine and acetylcholine release in the nucleus accumbens and motor activity. *Psychopharmacology (Berl)*, *201*(3), 325–38, fig. 2. doi: 10.1007/s00213-008-1288-3.

researchers suspect a link between these changes and the response delay for antidepressant effects (Santarelli et al., 2003). Thus, learning how antidepressant drugs increase proliferation in the hippocampus may aid in developing ways to shorten the response time to these drugs.

The SSRI fluoxetine (Prozac) has been shown to increase the activation of TrkB receptors, which are activated by BDNF. In turn, activation of TrkB receptors has been shown to increase the production of neurons in the hippocampus (Li et al., 2008). Together, these findings suggest that SSRIs may produce new cells in the hippocampus via the BDNF system.

Review! Brain-derived neurotrophic factor (BDNF) is a neurotrophin, which facilitates neurogrowth and neuroconnectivity. (Chapter 3.)

Bipolar Disorder

Bipolar disorder Mental disorder characterized by abnormal changes between depressive and manic mood states

Mania Consists of an abnormal elevation or irritation in mood along with increased arousal or energy levels

Euthymia A stable mood state

Type I bipolar disorder Type of bipolar disorder that exhibits depression and episodes of severe mania

Bipolar disorder is a mental disorder characterized by abnormal changes between depressive and manic mood states, representing two "poles" of mood. Depression in bipolar disorder exhibits the same features of depression characterized earlier in this chapter. In many ways, mania exhibits opposite features of depression. **Mania** consists of an abnormal elevation or irritation in mood along with increased arousal or energy levels. Manic behavior may occur as fast speaking, rapidly changing ideas and impulsive decision making. During a manic episode, individuals may engage in excessive spending, reckless behaviors, drastic decision making, drug abuse and hypersexuality. We use the term **euthymia** to refer to a stable mood state; in bipolar disorders, we characterize euthymia as expressing neither manic nor depressed symptoms.

We also find cognitive dysfunction as a feature of bipolar disorder. Martínez-Arán and colleagues (2004) sought to examine cognitive functioning in bipolar disorder by examining participants during a euthymic state and comparing test results to healthy control participants. In these comparisons, those with bipolar disorder exhibited poorer performance on tests for problem solving and working memory. In other studies, those with bipolar disorder tested during a euthymic state have shown deficits in sustained attention (Clark, Iversen, & Goodwin, 2002; Bora, Vahip, & Akdeniz, 2006). The appearance of cognitive deficits during a euthymic state shows that they are likely inherent to the disorder rather than something shown only during depressive or manic state.

The DSM-5 defines two types of bipolar disorder that differ primarily by the severity of mania. **Type I bipolar disorder** consists of exhibiting depression and episodes of severe mania. When presented with a severe manic episode, a mental health professional need not require evidence of depression to make a type I diagnosis. **Type II bipolar disorder** consists of exhibiting depression along with episodes of less-severe mania. We also use the term *hypomania* to refer to this form of mania.

Some researchers propose a type III bipolar disorder. This suggestion comes from evidence that antidepressant drugs cause some patients to shift into a manic state. Because this occurs in only a subpopulation of patients, this may represent a distinct type of bipolar disorder. Currently, the DSM does not recognize a third type of this disorder (Akiskal & Pinto, 1999).

Many patients with bipolar disorder receive an incorrect diagnosis when first presenting to a clinician. According to a study conducted by Hirschfeld, Lewis, and Vornik (2003), nearly 70 percent of individuals with bipolar disorder receive a misdiagnosis, and many of these misdiagnosed patients required seeing an average of four physicians and require more than 10 years or longer to receive a correct diagnosis. Reasons cited for misdiagnosis include gathering limited or incorrect clinical histories from patients and a lack of understanding about bipolar disorder among physicians making the misdiagnosis. The most common incorrect diagnosis is *depression*, which tends to occur most frequently in bipolar disorder. Further, individuals in manic states seldom see a reason to seek help, feeling that nothing is wrong with them. Thus, an individual may be more likely seek help while feeling depressed (Bowden, 2001).

Bipolar disorder is far less prevalent than major depressive disorder. According to a national survey conducted by the National Institute of Mental Health, the lifetime prevalence of any type of bipolar disorder in the United States is 4.4 percent. The average age for the first diagnosis of a bipolar disorder is 20.8 years old (Merikangas et al., 2007).

Neurobiology of Bipolar Disorder

Neuroimaging studies have revealed that areas of reduced activity in the frontal and temporal lobes of the right hemisphere have a tendency to produce manic episodes, whereas those occurring in the left hemisphere have a tendency to produce depressive episodes. Several studies have shown that the volume of the basal ganglia and thalamus tends to be larger in patients with bipolar disorder.

Functional MRI in bipolar disorder reveals areas of excessive activity in cortical white matter areas from unknown causes. Subsequently, these areas of activity are called *unidentified bright objects* (UBOs). The occurrence of UBOs in bipolar disorder reportedly ranges between 5 to 50 percent. The presence of UBOs in white matter areas might interfere with interconnectivity between the frontal and temporal cortex, which may relate to reduced activity in these regions as previously noted (Berns & Nemeroff, 2003).

Diffusion tensor MRI reveals diminished integrity and damage of axons in white matter in the cingulate cortex among those with bipolar disorder. This same imaging method has shown abnormalities in neurons connecting the amygdala to the cingulate cortex and connecting the lateral prefrontal cortex with the orbitofrontal cortex, a structure that closely communicates with the amygdala. Taken together, the altered connections between these structures in bipolar disorder may account for poor regulation of mood (Benedetti et al., 2011).

Type II bipolar disorder Type of bipolar disorder that exhibits depression along with episodes of less-severe mania

STOP & CHECK

1. How do type I and type II bipolar disorders differ?

2. What effects might antidepressant drugs have on bipolar disorder?

3. In bipolar disorder, mania is associated with reduced activity in the frontal and temporal lobes, whereas depressive symptoms are associated with reduced activity in the _____.

4. _____ may interfere with frontal and temporal lobe interconnectivity, possibly mediating mania in bipolar dipolar disorder.

1. Severe mania is observed in type I bipolar disorder, whereas hypomania occurs in type II bipolar disorder. 2. Although the depressive symptoms of bipolar disorder can improve, antidepressant drugs can cause some patients to switch from a depressed state to a manic state. For this reason, some researchers propose a third type of bipolar disorder for this subpopulation. 3. left hemisphere 4. UBOs

Mood Stabilizers, Anticonvulsants, Antipsychotics, and Antidepressants for Bipolar Disorder

Mood stabilizer
Drug that reduces both depressive and manic symptoms

Many of the treatments for bipolar disorder were first developed and approved for the treatment of other mental disorders. Thus, we have few drugs that are considered purely **mood stabilizers**—that is, drugs that reduce both depressive and manic symptoms. Beyond mood stabilizers, other treatments include anticonvulsant drugs and antipsychotic drugs. Although clinicians may also prescribe antidepressant drugs to bipolar disorder patients, they seldom administered antidepressant drugs alone, instead preferring to combine them with another bipolar treatment.

Lithium Mood stabilizer used for treating bipolar disorder

Lithium Is One of the Oldest and Most Effective Treatments for Bipolar Disorder

Lithium was the first mood stabilizer found effective for bipolar disorder. We find some uses of lithium by early neurologists and psychiatrists, including Silas Weir Mitchell, who referred to using lithium bromide for epilepsy and as a calming agent in 1870, and William Hammond, who administered lithium bromide for acute mania in 1871. Yet we see references to "bromide" as attributable to the effects of lithium bromide, perhaps more than "lithium" (Cade, 1949; Shorter, 2009). We do find, however, the Danish psychiatrist Frederik Lange using lithium *carbonite* for treating depression in 1894 (Shorter, 2009).

Its effectiveness for mania was later evaluated in 1949 by John Cade, who is most often credited with reintroducing lithium as a medicine for modern psychiatry. Cade served as a physician and superintendent of a hospital in Australia, a position he assumed after spending three years in a Japanese prisoner-of-war camp. After noticing that lithium chloride appeared to calm down guinea pigs, he administered the compound to several manic patients, finding striking reductions in mania. After other investigators validated these findings in Europe and the United States, lithium became a primary treatment for bipolar disorder (Cade, 1949; Shorter, 1997).

💊 **Drug Profile: lithium**	
Trade name	Camcolit, Eskalith, Lithobid, Lithonate, among others
Properties	Intracellular actions, including second messengers and gene expression; may have neuroprotective effects; may inhibit GSK-3
Uses	Used for treating bipolar disorder; appears more effective for mania than depression

Since this discovery, hundreds of studies have reported on the mood-stabilizing effects of lithium in bipolar disorder. We can determine the general consensus of lithium's efficacy by reviewing randomized double-blind, placebo-controlled trials conducted in patients with bipolar disorder. Geddes and colleagues (2004) conducted an assessment of five studies that used this design. They found that lithium overall proved consistently more effective than placebo for preventing manic symptoms. However, they failed to see substantial reductions in depressive symptoms. Thus, we find that lithium provides greater efficacy for mania than for depression.

Lithium treatment poses a risk of serious adverse effects. The risk for these adverse effects accompany a narrow therapeutic index and narrow therapeutic dose range. For these reasons, blood monitoring is used to carefully adjust lithium dosing (**Figure 13.6**). When first beginning lithium therapy, therapeutically effective concentrations fall within a range of 0.8 to 1.2 milliequivalents per liter (mEq/l) of blood. After lithium has accumulated in the body over the course of approximately 2 weeks, the concentration must be reduced to 0.6 to 0.8 mEq/l to avoid adverse effects. At this stage, these lower concentrations sufficiently maintain therapeutic effects (Ferrier, Tyrer, & Bell, 1995).

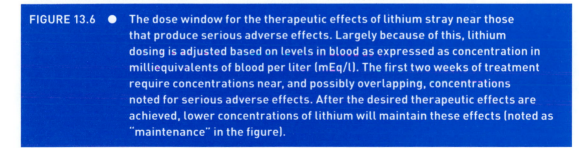

FIGURE 13.6 ● The dose window for the therapeutic effects of lithium stray near those that produce serious adverse effects. Largely because of this, lithium dosing is adjusted based on levels in blood as expressed as concentration in milliequivalents of blood per liter (mEq/l). The first two weeks of treatment require concentrations near, and possibly overlapping, concentrations noted for serious adverse effects. After the desired therapeutic effects are achieved, lower concentrations of lithium will maintain these effects (noted as "maintenance" in the figure).

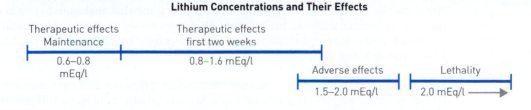

Lithium Concentrations and Their Effects

Therapeutic effects
Maintenance
0.6–0.8 mEq/l

Therapeutic effects
first two weeks
0.8–1.6 mEq/l

Adverse effects
1.5–2.0 mEq/l

Lethality
2.0 mEq/l ⟶

Review! A therapeutic index represents the difference between lethal and therapeutic drug doses. (Chapter 1.)

At lithium blood concentrations of 1.5 to 2.0 mEq/l, gastrointestinal effects become prominent, including nausea, vomiting, and diarrhea. Adverse effects may occur at therapeutic blood concentrations as well, including thirst and increased urination, largely because of lithium-induced inhibition of kidney function. Lithium may also produce tremor at therapeutic doses. Higher lithium concentrations, beginning at approximately 2.0 to 2.5 mEq/l, may produce renal failure and muscle rigidity. Moreover, these concentrations pose a serious risk of coma and death. Taken together, even an accidental second ingestion of lithium might increase blood concentrations to near fatal levels.

Lithium's Mechanisms of Action   Lithium (Li^+) is element number 3 on the periodic table and is part of the same grouping as sodium (Na^+, atomic number = 11) and potassium (K^+, atomic number = 19). As you may recall from Chapter 3, Na^+ and K^+ play important roles in generating action potentials. Lithium enters neurons through Na^+ channels. Once inside a neuron, lithium takes part in a large variety of intracellular actions, including second-messenger actions and gene expression. This presents a great challenge to researchers who are endeavoring to unravel the pharmacological actions important for lithium's mood-stabilizing properties. Based on such studies, the current general consensus among researchers is that lithium's efficacy for bipolar disorder derives from neuroprotective effects against neurodegeneration (Chiu & Chuang, 2010).

We find these neuroprotective effects in preclinical studies. In particular, lithium promotes the survival of neurons during *excitotoxicity*. Lithium also protects neurons during detrimental conditions, including the absence of growth factor, heat shock, and high doses of anticonvulsant drugs. A key action for lithium's neuroprotective effects may involve inhibition of the enzyme *glycogen synthase kinase 3* (Chiu & Chuang, 2010).

Review! Excitotoxicity consists of neuronal damage and death caused by overstimulation by glutamate. (Chapter 3.)

Glycogen synthase kinase 3 (GSK-3) Protein kinase that promotes apoptosis and regulates inflammation

Apoptosis A programmed cell death important for normal brain development; also triggered by excitotoxicity

Although involved in many processes, **glycogen synthase kinase 3 (GSK-3)** is a protein kinase that promotes apoptosis and regulates inflammation. **Apoptosis** is referred to as a programmed cell death, a process important for normal brain development. Excitotoxicity also produces apoptosis. In mice, overexpression of the GSK-3 gene causes an increase in behavioral activity, whereas inhibition of GSK-3 enzyme activity decreases behavioral activity (O'Brien et al., 2004). These results suggest that GSK-3 inhibition may lead to decreases in hyperactivity, which is somewhat analogous to mania in humans. In another study, an inhibitor of GSK-3 enzymes led to decreased immobility time in a forced swim test, an indication of antidepressant effects (**Figure 13.7**) (Gould, Einat, Bhat, & Manji, 2004).

Anticonvulsant Drugs   Clinicians also use anticonvulsant drugs to treat bipolar disorder, including *carbamazepine (Tegretol)*, *valproic acid* (or *valproate*; trade name is *Depakote*), *oxcarbazepine (Trileptal)*, and *lamotrigine (Lamictal)*. Most anticonvulsant drugs serve as positive modulators for $GABA_A$ receptors, although we find that other $GABA_A$ positive modulators such as barbiturates appear ineffective for treatment of bipolar disorder.

FIGURE 13.7 ● **Lithium may reduce depressive and manic symptoms, at least in part, through inhibition of GSK-3, an enzyme that promotes apoptosis and regulates inflammation. A selective inhibitor of GSK-3 activity called *AR-A014418* has been shown to decrease immobility time in rats in a forced swim task, suggesting an antidepressant effect (left figure). In this figure, dimethyl sulfoxide (DMSO) was the vehicle for AR-A014418 and was tested alone to provide a control group. AR-A014418 also reduced hyperactivity induced by amphetamine (right figure).**

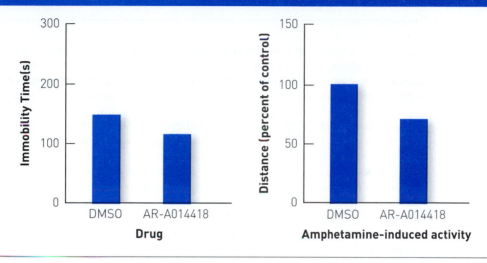

SOURCE: Gould, T. D., Einat, H., Bhat, R., & Manji, H. K. (2004). AR-A014418, a selective GSK-3 inhibitor, produces antidepressant-like effects in the forced swim test. *The International Journal of Neuropsychopharmacology, 7*(04), 387–390. doi: doi:10.1017/S146114, p. 4. Reproduced with permission.

STOP & CHECK

1. Although effective for bipolar disorder, lithium's adverse effects are coupled with a narrow _____ index, requiring careful monitoring of blood concentrations.

2. How does lithium enter neurons?

3. Although lithium has many neurobiological effects, perhaps the most implicated action for treating bipolar disorder is inhibition of the _____ enzyme.

1. therapeutic 2. Lithium enters neurons through sodium channels. 3. GSK-3

Instead, other actions produced by anticonvulsant drugs may account for reduced symptoms in bipolar disorder.

Beyond facilitating GABA neurotransmission, anticonvulsant drugs produce a variety of other effects on neurons. First, many of the anticonvulsant drugs for bipolar disorder inhibit Na⁺ channel functioning. At therapeutic doses, Na⁺ channel inhibition largely

🔧 **Drug Profile: carbamazepine**	
Trade name	Tegretol
Properties	Positive modulator for $GABA_A$ receptors
Uses:	Used for treating epileptic seizures; stabilizing mood in bipolar disorder
Similar drugs	Valproic acid (Depakote), oxcarbazepine (Trileptal), & lamotrigine (Lamictal)

affects high-frequency action potentials. This action not only likely plays a role in their antiseizure effects, but also may reduce manic symptoms in bipolar disorder. Second, many of these anticonvulsant drugs inhibit GSK-3 activity, a mechanism of action comparable to the effects of lithium (Chiu & Chuang, 2010; Keck, McElroy, & Nemeroff, 1992).

Atypical Antipsychotic Drugs Although clinicians use antipsychotic drugs for the treatment of schizophrenia, antipsychotic drugs are also used for the treatment of bipolar disorder. In particular, the *atypical* antipsychotic drugs have become safer first-line treatments compared to lithium. These drugs include *quetiapine (Seroquel), aripiprazole (Abilify), olanzapine (Zeprexa)*, and r*isperidone (Risperdal)*, among others. The compounds serve to reduce and prevent mania from occurring in this disorder (Pae, Serretti, Patkar, & Masand, 2008; Tohen & Zarate, 1998).

One of the most common treatment approaches involves a combination of both an atypical antidepressant drugs and an antidepressant drug. One of the first treatment combinations reported for bipolar disorder consisted of the atypical antipsychotic drug olanzapine and the SSRI antidepressant drug fluoxetine (as noted earlier, this combination is now sold as Symbyax). During the course of 8 weeks, Tohen and colleagues (2003) administered placebo, olanzapine alone, or a treatment combination of olanzapine and fluoxetine in patients with type I bipolar disorder. They found significantly reduced depression scores after treatment with the drug combination compared to either placebo or olanzapine given alone. Manic symptoms occurred too infrequently in the placebo-treated patients to allow for studying treatment effects on mania in this study.

Treatment time course serves as the most clinically important finding in this study. After 3 weeks of treatment, 50 percent of participants were responsive to the olanzapine and fluoxetine combination compared to only 30 percent of olanzapine-treated patients. Thus, the addition of fluoxetine decreased the amount of time it took for a reduction in depressive symptoms to occur (**Figure 13.8**).

This study provided an important shift in treatment strategies for bipolar disorder. In an extensive review of clinical studies evaluating antipsychotic drugs and other traditional medications for depressive symptoms in bipolar disorder, the fluoxetine–olanzapine combination provided the greatest effects. The atypical antipsychotic drug quetiapine was shown to be the second most effective for depressive symptoms, whereas other antipsychotic drugs and the more traditional treatments for bipolar disorder were inconsistently effective for depressive symptoms (Vieta et al., 2010).

The ability of quetiapine alone to be effective for depressive symptoms is a bit of mystery because, after all, the receptor binding profile for quetiapine is very similar

FIGURE 13.8 ● The percentage of patients with bipolar disorder with a substantial improvement in depressive scores during the course of treatment with either placebo, olanzapine alone, or a combination of olanzapine and fluoxetine. More patients in the combination group found improvements in depression sooner compared to the other groups (note the strong placebo effect). *Final* refers to the last assessment, occurring between days 59 and 65 of treatment.

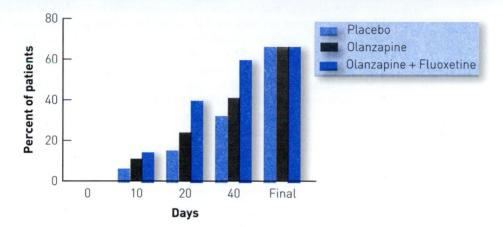

to other atypical antipsychotic drugs, including olanzapine. The unique efficacy quetiapine has for depression may not actually be a result of the quetiapine molecule but of *N-desalkylquetiapine*, one of the metabolites for quetiapine. N-desalkylquetiapine chemically resembles a tetracyclic antidepressant drug (like a tricyclic antidepressant, except with four rings), and pharmacological studies reveal that N-desalkylquetiapine inhibits reuptake of serotonin and norepinephrine (Jensen et al., 2008). In this way, quetiapine treatment may functionally serve like a combination of an atypical antipsychotic drug and an antidepressant drug.

STOP & CHECK

1. Like lithium, anticonvulsant drugs effective for bipolar disorder inhibit the _____ enzyme.

2. Another common bipolar treatment is a combination of an atypical antipsychotic drug and a(n) _____ drug.

3. How might the effects of quetiapine be similar to those produced by a combination of olanzapine and fluoxetine?

1. GSK3 **2.** antidepressant drug **3.** Quetiapine is an atypical antipsychotic drug, but the active metabolite for quetiapine, N-desalkylquetiapine, may have antidepressant effects.

From Actions to Effects: Pharmacogenetic Factors and Treatment Response in Depression

Earlier in this chapter, we presented significant limitations for the efficacy of antidepressant mediations. Another limitation involves pharmacogenetic differences, which may inhibit a patient's response to antidepressant drugs. For example, genetic differences may alter the ability of an antidepressant drug to cross the blood–brain barrier. In a study conducted by Uhr and colleagues (2008), variations in the ABCB1 gene were examined because this gene encodes for P-glycoprotein, a transporter important for the ability of certain antidepressants drugs to cross the blood–brain barrier. In patients who had a polymorphism in the ABCB1 gene, full recovery from depression was less likely if they were treated with a drug transported by P-glycoprotein, such as the tricyclic antidepressant drug *amitriptyline (Elavil)*, the SSRIs *paroxetine (Paxil)* and *citalopram (Celexa)*, or the SNRI *venlafaxine (Effexor)* (**Table 13.5**). They did not find a correlation with the antidepressant drug *mirtazapine (Remeron)*, which does not rely on P-glycoprotein to cross the blood–brain barrier.

Pharmacogenetic factors may also alter serotonin transporter function, an important site of action for many antidepressant drugs. The gene for the serotonin transporter is *SLC6A4*, and it includes a region important for serotonin transporter function called the *serotonin transporter-gene–linked polymorphic region*. Clinicians find a poorer treatment response and shorter time until depressive symptoms return in patients who have a short variation of this region (Horstmann & Binder, 2009; Serretti, Kato, De Ronchi, & Kinoshita, 2007). These effects may be due to a reduced levels of serotonin transporters among individuals with this polymorphism, leading to few sites for antidepressant drugs to act on (Lesch et al., 1996; Smeraldi et al., 1998).

Finally, genetic expression of neurotrophins may affect antidepressant treatment response. These investigations stem from findings that chronic antidepressant drug

TABLE 13.5 ● Selected Pharmacogenetic Factors for Antidepressant Response

Pharmacogenetic Factor	Function	Impact on Antidepressant Response
ABCB1 gene polymorphism	Affects P-glycoprotein transporter function in blood-brain barrier	Inhibits passage of certain antidepressant drugs from entering the brain through the blood–brain barrier, reducing antidepressant effects
Short variation of serotonin transporter-gene–linked polymorphic region	Affects function of the serotonin membrane transporter; may find fewer serotonin transporters in those with this polymorphism	Reduced antidepressant effects possibly by having fewer transporters to bind to
Val66Met polymorphism on the gene for BDNF	May reduce BDNF levels and levels of TrkB receptors	Reduced ability of antidepressant drugs to promote neurogenesis and proliferation

administration promotes neural proliferation in the hippocampus. In particular, several studies have focused on the polymorphism called *Val66Met* existing on the gene for BDNF. This polymorphism reduces BDNF levels and may subsequently lead to reduced density of TrkB receptors (Bath et al., 2008; Egan et al., 2003). As noted previously, antidepressant drugs may promote proliferation by indirectly activating TrkB receptors. Patients with this polymorphism tend to have poorer treatment response to antidepressant drugs (Horstmann & Binder, 2009; Shimizu, Hashimoto, & Iyo, 2004).

Review! Neurotrophins are a family of molecules that promote the survival and plasticity of neurons during development and in adulthood. BDNF binds selectively to TrkB receptors. (Chapter 3.)

STOP & CHECK

1. How might a short variation of the serotonin-transporter-gene–linked polymorphic region impact the effectiveness of antidepressant drugs?

2. Two pharmacokinetic factors important for antidepressant drugs that are affected by pharmacogenetic factors are _____.

3. Gene polymorphisms for neurotrophins may diminish the effects on antidepressant drugs on _____.

1. An individual with this polymorphism may have fewer functional serotonin reuptake transporters. Fewer serotonin reuptake transporters are fewer targets for SSRIs or other antidepressant drugs that block serotonin reuptake. 2. the ability to cross the blood–brain barrier (P-glycoprotein activity) and drug metabolism (CYP2D6 polymorphisms) 3. proliferation in the hippocampus

Chapter Summary

A major depressive disorder is characterized by feelings of sadness, worthlessness, and other symptoms that persist for 2 weeks. Persistent depressive disorder consists of fewer symptoms, but these symptoms persist for at least 2 years. Depression is highly prevalent across age groups and carries a significant risk of suicide.

Neurobiologically, depression appears to be associated with overactivity in the amygdala, reduced activity in the left dorsal prefrontal cortex, and reduced volume of the hippocampus. The classes of antidepressant drugs include MAO inhibitors, tricyclic antidepressant drugs, SSRIs, SNRIs, and atypical antidepressant drugs. Important challenges to using antidepressant drugs to treat depression include a lengthy response time, treatment resistance, large placebo effects in clinical trials, and pharmacogenetic differences.

(Continued)

(Continued)

Bipolar disorder is a mental disorder that is characterized by abnormal changes between depressive and manic mood states. Mania is most severe in type I bipolar disorder and less severe in type II disorder. Bipolar disorder is associated with a larger basal ganglia and thalamus and disruptions of normal cortical processing. A long-used and still common treatment for bipolar disorder is lithium, which is effective for reducing manic symptoms and, to a lesser extent, depressive symptoms. However, lithium's severe adverse effects coupled with a small therapeutic index makes lithium less desirable if other effective treatments are available. Subsequently, bipolar disorder may be treated with anticonvulsant drugs or antipsychotic drugs. In particular, combined treatment with an antipsychotic drug and an antidepressant drug may be effective for improving depression in bipolar disorder.

Key Terms

Mental disorder 396
Major depressive disorder 397
Persistent depressive disorder (or dysthymia) 397
Vascular depression 401
Monoamine hypothesis of depression 406
MAO inhibitors 406
Irreversible MAO inhibitors 407
Reversible MAO inhibitors 407
Cheese reaction 407
Selective MAO_B inhibitors 408
Reversible inhibitor of MAO_A (RIMA) 408
Tricyclic antidepressant drugs 409
Selective serotonin reuptake inhibitor (SSRI) 411

Black box warning (or boxed warning) 411
Serotonin syndrome 411
Serotonin discontinuation syndrome 411
Sexual side effects 411
Emotional blunting (or affective blunting) 412
Serotonin norepinephrine reuptake inhibitors (SNRIs) (or dual serotonin and norepinephrine reuptake inhibitors) 413
Fibromyalgia syndrome 413
Atypical antidepressant drugs 414
Treatment-resistant depression 416

Combination drug strategy 417
Augmentation strategy (or adjunctive treatment/therapy) 417
Add-on treatment 417
Off-label 417
Bipolar disorder 424
Mania 424
Euthymia 424
Type I bipolar disorder 424
Type II bipolar disorder 425
Mood stabilizer 426
Lithium 426
Glycogen synthase kinase 3 (GSK-3) 428
Apoptosis 428

Visit the Student Study Site at **study.sagepub.com/prus2e** to access additional study tools, including eFlashcards, web quizzes, video resources, web resources, SAGE journal articles, and more.

14

Treatments for Anxiety Disorders

WAS MILTOWN TOO GOOD TO BE TRUE?

In the first half of the 20th century, barbiturate drugs served as prescription medications for relieving anxiety. Yet by the 1950s, the dangers of barbiturates gained widespread attention. This decade saw a dramatic increase in both accidental and suicidal deaths from barbiturate use. In 1951, the addictive properties of barbiturates led the *New York Times* to declare them more dangerous than heroin or cocaine (Lopez-Munoz, Ucha-Udabe, & Alamo, 2005).

The world was ready for safer barbiturate-like drugs when *meprobamate (Miltown)* hit the market. Wallace Laboratories sold meprobamate

(Continued)

(Continued)

as a tranquilizer to rid anxiousness, but the company falsely claimed there was no risk of addiction. Tone (2005) describes meprobamate use as an "overnight sensation," accounting for 57 million prescriptions to Americans in 1957 alone. Convinced of its safety, physicians freely prescribed meprobamate to relieve everyday tensions. When pharmacies ran out of meprobamate, they posted signs to alert their customers. Television comic Milton Berle once told viewers that they were only addicted to Miltown if they took more than their doctors. The popularity of meprobamate soon faded; by the mid-1960s, most patients had switched to a somewhat safer alternative: the benzodiazepines (Tone, 2005).

Anxiety Disorders

Fear A negative emotion caused by a real or perceived imminent danger or threat

Anxiety Worry and distress concerning potential events or outcomes

We all experience periods of fear and anxiety. We define **fear** as a negative emotion caused by a real or perceived imminent danger or threat. Fear promotes our safety, allowing us to avoid or attempt to handle dangerous situations we may face.

Anxiety differs from fear in regard to the likelihood of dangerous situations. We can define **anxiety** as worry and distress concerning potential events or outcomes. Anxiety occurs around events that have yet to happen or that may not even be real. That is, we can think of fear as an emotion occurring in the moment, whereas anxiety is worry about real or perceived events yet to come. Like fear, anxiety too promotes our safety by helping us prepare for such events, potentially limiting their potential for harm or allowing us to avoid the event altogether. Yet we also find many who become preoccupied with worry or apprehension, to the extent that anxiety disrupts their everyday lives. In these cases, we may define someone as having an *anxiety disorder*.

The *Diagnostic and Statistical Manual of Mental Disorders,* 5th edition (DSM-5) considers a number of different types of anxiety disorders. These include separation anxiety disorders (more common in children), selective mutism (also most common in children), specific phobia (e.g., fear of heights, fear of spiders, etc.), panic disorder, agoraphobia, social anxiety disorder, and generalized anxiety disorder (American Psychiatric Association, 2013). We cover some of these types briefly here.

Specific phobias Significant anxiety provoked by exposure to specific feared objects or situations

Specific phobias occur as intense fear or anxiety from a specific object or situation. A *phobia* is something far more severe than a general dislike for something. Instead, a phobia manifests as a strong repulsion to such situations—that is, an arachnophobic (i.e., one who has a fear of spiders) may entirely avoid a room after once encountering a spider there. Depending on the type, a phobia may cause significant disruptions in normal daily living activities.

Panic disorder consists of repeat occurrences of **panic attacks**. Panic attacks are an abrupt and possibly unexpected strong physiological reaction accompanied by intense apprehension, fearfulness, or terror. Many individuals mistake their first panic attack as a heart attack, providing us a glimpse into the severity of a panic attack. A panic attack may actually occur in most anxiety disorders, but this the primary symptom seen in panic disorder.

Another disorder listed in the DSM is **agoraphobia**, defined as a profound fear of being in a situation from which escape is difficult or embarrassing, particularly if a panic attack occurs. **Social anxiety disorder** is a fear of being in or performing in social or public situations. These situations provoke an immediate anxiety response, one that may be severe enough to elicit a panic attack. Although these disorders appear similar, they have important differences. Those with social anxiety disorder fear negative attention from others, but can be quite calm when left entirely alone in social situations. Yet, they do fear the negative scrutiny they'll receive if they show anxiety in social situations. Those will agoraphobia avoid these situations out of fear of having a panic attack if they are unable to escape the event or receive any help (American Psychiatric Association, 2013).

Generalized anxiety disorder is characterized by chronic, excessive worry about events, individuals, or activities. Individuals with generalized anxiety disorder may feel worried continually and subsequently exhausted. This worry often generalizes to various perceived physical ailments, often leading to unnecessary medical care.

Beyond these anxiety disorder types found in the DSM-5, two other disorders traditionally considered anxiety disorders are obsessive-compulsive disorder and posttraumatic stress disorder. The previous DSM (the DSM-IV Text Revision) included these disorders as types of anxiety disorder, but the DSM-5 places them in different categories of mental disorders. Because the pharmacological treatments we consider in this chapter have been used to treat obsessive-compulsive disorder and posttraumatic stress disorder, describe them here and particularly focus on their anxiety features.

Obsessive–compulsive disorder (OCD) consists of distress arising from obsessions, with compulsive behavior endeavoring to reduce distress by addressing the obsessions. Obsessions can include thoughts about germs or other contaminations, unresolved doubts (such as whether doors have been left open or home appliances have been left on), and not having objects in a precise order. Because of these anxiety-causing obsessions, individuals with OCD engage in compulsive behaviors that reduce this anxiety. Thus, common compulsions include excessive hand washing, checking doors or appliances, and organizing objects, respectively. The DSM-5 includes OCD in the category "obsessive-compulsive and related disorders," with related disorders including *hoarding disorder, body dysmorphic disorder, excoriation (skin-picking) disorder,* among others.

Posttraumatic stress disorder now finds itself in a new category titled "trauma- and stressor-related disorders," which also includes *acute stress disorder, reactive attachment disorders,* and *attachment disorders,* among others. **Posttraumatic stress disorder (PTSD)** is characterized by a persistent state of physiological arousal or

Panic disorder Repeat occurrences of panic attacks

Panic attacks An abrupt and possibly unexpected strong physiological reaction accompanied by intense apprehension, fearfulness, or terror

Agoraphobia Anxiety about being in situations from which escape is difficult or embarrassing

Social anxiety disorder Fear of being in or performing in social or public situations

Generalized anxiety disorder Chronic, excessive worry about events, individuals, or activities

Obsessive–compulsive disorder (OCD) Distress arising over obsessions; accompanied by compulsive behavior that endeavors to reduce this distress

Posttraumatic stress disorder (PTSD) Persistent state of physiological arousal or exaggerated response to certain stimuli, particularly those associated with a traumatic event

exaggerated response to certain stimuli, particularly those associated with a traumatic event. These symptoms appear as great fear, feelings of helpless and even horror concerning the causative event. Individuals with PTSD often have moments of recall of the traumatic event, possibly occurring in dreams. Some individuals may experience flashbacks in which reality temporarily gives way to a reliving of the traumatic event (American Psychiatric Association, 2013). The symptoms of PTSD appear to be long lasting. In a study among Vietnam War veterans conducted 40 years after completion of the war, 8.5 percent of female veterans and 12.2 percent of male veterans were found to have PTSD symptoms related to the war (Marmar et al., 2015).

Anxiety disorders are highly prevalent. The current prevalence rate of any anxiety disorder, including PTSD and OCD, is estimated to be 7.3 percent worldwide. In total, anxiety disorders are twice as common among females than males and appear equally prevalent across different age groups (Baxter, Scott, Vos, & Whiteford, 2013). In an evaluation of lifetime prevalence in the United States, Kessler and colleagues (2012) estimated that 33.7 percent had an anxiety disorder, again including PTSD and OCD (**Figure 14.1**). The majority of these individuals experienced either some type of specific phobia or social phobia. A fourth of those experiencing an anxiety disorder reported having PTSD.

Anxiety disorders may develop as a result of both environmental and genetic factors. Childhood physical and sexual abuse correlates highly with having an anxiety

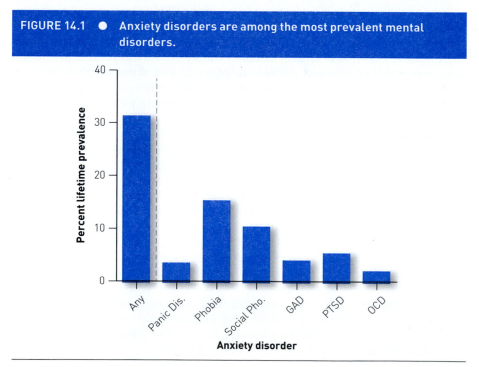

FIGURE 14.1 ● **Anxiety disorders are among the most prevalent mental disorders.**

SOURCE: Data from Kessler et al., 2012.

disorder in adulthood (Cougle, Timpano, Sachs-Ericsson, Keough, & Riccardi, 2010). Overall, genetic risk accounts for 30 percent to 40 percent of anxiety disorder diagnoses (Norrholm & Ressler, 2009). In particular, genetics accounts for 47 percent of the likelihood of developing PTSD after experiencing a traumatic event (Sartor et al., 2012). Given their prevalence, anxiety disorders have a significant economic burden on society. For example, Greenberg and colleagues (1999) reported that the annual cost of treating anxiety disorders in 1990 was approximately $42.3 billion. The economic cost models for anxiety disorders not only assess direct psychiatric care but also prescription costs, unnecessary medical care, and various other factors. This study also estimated that anxiety disorders account for approximately $4.1 billion per year in lost workplace productivity. Using similar consideration of direct medical care and indirect costs (e.g., lost work productivity), Olesen and colleagues (2012) estimated that anxiety disorders in Europe cost €74.4 billion (approximately $55.9 billion at the time study was conducted) per year.

STOP & CHECK

1. An anxiety about being in situations where escape is difficult or embarrassing is called _____.

2. A profound fear of something such as heights, spiders, or confined spaces is defined as a(n) _____, according to the DSM.

1. agoraphobia 2. specific phobia

Structures Involved in Fear and Anxiety

As presented in Chapter 4, studies identify the amygdala as a critical structure for fear and anxiety. Increased activity in this structure is associated with fear, anxiety, and aggression in numerous animal and human studies. In humans, increased activity in the amygdala causes states of fear and anxiety, and amygdala dysfunction occurs in every type of anxiety disorder as well as PTSD (Davis & Whalen, 2001; Shin & Liberzon, 2010). Yet the amygdala may be less involved in OCD. Rather, researchers associate OCD with abnormal functioning in the thalamus, cingulate cortex, prefrontal cortex, orbitofrontal cortex, basal ganglia, and nucleus accumbens (Graybiel & Rauch, 2000; Laplane et al., 1989).

The amygdala appears responsible for relating stimuli or events to fear and for mediating the physiological and psychological reactions to fear. Studies in both animals and humans consistently reveal increased activity in the amygdala during fear conditioning, a process in which a stimulus is associated with an aversive event such as a shock. Moreover, increases in amygdala activity occur when receiving oral warnings, watching videos of humans being fear conditioned, and seeing pictures of faces with frightened expressions. Researchers find associations between deficient amygdala functioning in humans, which may result from infections, injury, or parasites, with placid reactions to aversive stimuli and self-inflicted injury (Shin & Liberzon, 2010).

The amygdala receives information from many parts of the brain (**Figure 14.2**). The nervous system sends sensory information, including visual, auditory, touch, and pain, from the thalamus to the amygdala via two pathways. First, the thalamo-amygdala pathway sends crude and unprocessed sensory information directly from the thalamus to the amygdala. We refer to this as the *short route* for sensory information from the thalamus. As largely unprocessed information, this pathway provides the

FIGURE 14.2 ● **The amygdala receives sensory inputs from the body and sends information to the prefrontal cortex, hypothalamus, and other areas important for anxiety responses.**

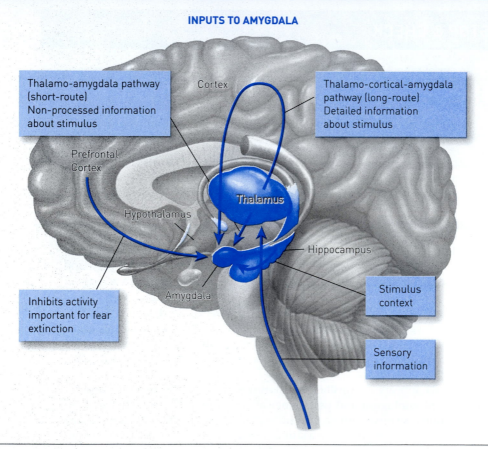

INPUTS TO AMYGDALA

amygdala only basic features of a stimulus, such as a loud noise, but does not indicate what the stimulus actually is (Davis & Whalen, 2001).

Second, the thalamo-cortical-amygdala pathway sends sensory information to the amygdala after processing in the cerebral cortex. We refer to this as the *long route* for sensory information from the thalamus because it requires a slightly longer amount of time to reach the amygdala. Because the sensory information is processed in the cortex, the information contains information about what the stimulus is. For example, instead of a "loud noise" as the short pathway may communicate, a person may afterward discern a "dog's bark" as the long pathway may communicate (Davis & Whalen, 2001).

The hippocampus sends information on the context surrounding the stimulus to the amygdala. Thus, if the context of the environment is important for the amygdala's response to the stimulus, then information sent from the hippocampus will modify this response. Thus, a person may have a weak fear response when seeing a large dog—the stimulus in this example—behind a large fence—the stimulus context. Inputs to the amygdala from the prefrontal cortex act to reduce amygdala activity, resulting in an inhibited reaction to fearful stimuli. We also find the prefrontal cortex important for extinction of fear conditioning or, in other words, unlearning that particular stimuli are fearful (Davis & Whalen, 2001). We cover the role the amygdala and other structures play in how we experience fear or anxiety in the next section.

An elegant demonstration of the hippocampus's role in pairing a context with fearful stimuli was conducted using optogenetic techniques (see **Box 14.1** for an overview of optogenetics) by Liu and colleagues (2012). These researchers sought to activate only neurons in the *dentate gyrus* of the hippocampus, a region of the hippocampus particularly important for discriminating between different contexts that were activated when mice underwent a fear conditioning procedure (see **Box 14.2** for a description of fear conditioning). The objective of this study was to use light to activate channelrhodopsin proteins only on those neurons in the dentate gyrus activated during fear conditioning.

To select only these neurons presumably active during conditioning of an environmental context with fearful stimuli, Liu and colleagues (2012) used transgenic techniques to cause neurons expressing *c-fos* in the dentate gyrus to also produce channelrhodopsin. We described c-fos as a transcription factor in Chapter 2. We also described c-fos as an **early immediate gene**, a gene rapidly activated in response to stimuli. C-fos, in particular, becomes activated in response to stimuli, making it useful to target in this study.

Early immediate gene A gene rapidly activated in response to stimuli

With all of this set up, Liu and colleagues placed these mice in a chamber and emitted a tone while the mice received intermittent electrical shocks to the chamber's grid floor. In procedures like this, mice quickly learn that the context is associated with aversive stimulation, which depends upon the activation of specific neurons in the dentate gyrus of the hippocampus. Those neurons activated during conditioning triggered c-fos, as neurons activated by stimuli typically do, and they also triggered genetic instructions to begin synthesized channelrhodopsin. Once the conditioning session ended, the researchers also administered the animals a substance to prevent any other activated neurons from synthesizing channelrhodopsin. This last step helped to narrow

BOX 14.1 OPTOGENETICS

Optogenetics is a research technique that uses light to alter the firing rate of specific types of neurons (**Figure 1**). The process relies on ion channels that open when a particular frequency of light (i.e., color) reaches them. Thus, these channels serve as *light-gated*

FIGURE 1

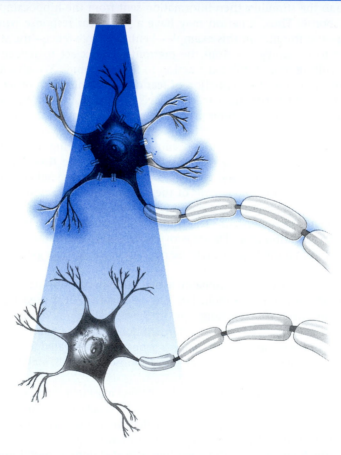

Researchers use optogenetic techniques to selectively change the activity of one type of neuron (top neuron in this example) by shining light through fiber optic cables onto light-gated ion channels. Neurons lacking light-gated ion channels do have a change in activity when light is shown upon them (bottom neuron).

ion channels, in contrast to the voltage-gated ion channels and ligand-gated ion channels referred to in Chapter 3.

Optogenetics presently utilizes three different types of ion channels: (1) *channelrhodopsin*, (2) *halorhodopsin*, and (3) *archaerhodopsin* (Zhang et al., 2011). Channelrhodopsin responds best to blue light, which we state specifically as a 480 nanometer wavelength. Positively charged Na+ ions flow through this channel when opened, leading to activation of the neuron. Functionally, these activated channels produce an effect similar to an excitatory postsynaptic potential (EPSP). Thus, the activation of channelrhodopsin by blue light leads a neuron to increase its rate of action potentials (i.e., the firing rate).

Halorhodopsin and archaerhodopsin both produce inhibitory effects when activated. Halorhodopsin responds to green/yellow light (best at 570 nanometer wavelength) and causes the influx of negatively charged Cl- ions. Archaerhodopsin responds to green light (550–576 nanometer wavelength) and causes positively charged H+ ions to leave the neuron (Han et al., 2011; Zhang et al., 2011). In this way, activation of archaerhodopsin produces inhibitory effects on a neuron.

Optogenetics is used in genetically modified organisms (see **Box 2.1** in Chapter 2 for review) to study the nervous system and behavior. Genes that cause the production of light-gated ion channels may be added to an organism's DNA by injecting the organism with an engineered virus. The virus inserts itself into an organism's DNA, where in this case, the new DNA serves as a gene that will instruct neurons to synthesize these light-gated ion channels.

Linking particular neurotransmitter systems to behavior has become one the main approaches for optogenetics. As noted in **Box 3.1** in Chapter 3, one of the main techniques prior to the invention of optogentics was the use of electrical stimulation of certain structures in the brain in animals. Yet no structure in the brain has purely one type of neuron. Even stimulating the ventral tegmental area leads to the activation of more than dopamine neurons.

Yet with optogenetics, researchers can cause only one type of neuron to express light-gated ion channels. To aim a greater selectivity, a researcher may opt to have only dopamine neurons express channelrhodopsin, for example. Doing so would lead blue light, applied by optical fibers implanted in the brain, to selectively activate dopamine neurons.

Steidl and Veverka (2015) performed a behavioral experiment in which optogenetic techniques allowed them to draw conclusions about the role of a structure called the *laterodorsal tegmental nucleus* in regulating the activity of the ventral tegmental area neurons. They reasoned laterodorsal tegmental nucleus neurons may activate mesolimbic dopamine neurons. If so, greater dopamine release should occur in the nucleus accumbens, the brain's reward center.

To perform this experiment, the researchers injected a virus containing the encoding

(Continued)

(Continued)

for channelrhodopsin into the laterodorsal tegmental nucleus in rats. They then emitted a blue light only in the ventral tegmental area, reasoning that axons from laterodorsal tegmental nucleus should be activated. If this were the case, then behaviors linked to enhanced mesolimbic dopamine activity (e.g., rewarding effects) should occur.

To test this, rats were placed in an operant chamber (i.e., a Skinner box) containing two levers—pressing one lever caused the activation of the blue-light fiber optic cable implanted in the ventral tegmental area, whereas the other did nothing. The result? Rats were willing to work (i.e., press a lever) to activate the blue light, whereas little lever pressing occurred on the inactive lever (**Figure 2**). The researchers concluded that the blue light caused laterodorsal tegmental nucleus neurons to activate mesolimbic dopamine neurons, which in turn produced rewarding effects.

FIGURE 2 ● Pressing a lever led to either the light-induced activation of laterodorsal tegmental nucleus neurons terminating in the ventral tegmental area (square symbols) or no activation (triangles). The vertical axis shows the number of lever presses, whereas the horizontal axis shows the number of each testing session that was conducted. The symbols provide the average number of lever presses for the group of rats. We infer from these findings that the rats found the activating lever to produce rewarding effects.

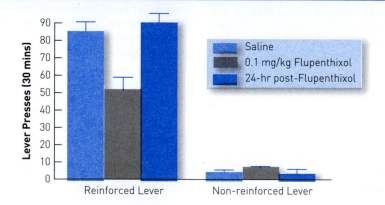

down expression of channelrhodopsin to only those neurons in the dentate gyrus of the hippocampus that were activated during the conditioning session.

After carrying out these procedures, Liu and colleagues then placed these mice in a different context and watched for freezing responses, a typical fear response in mice. When the optical fiber light was kept off, few freezing responses were observed in this different environment. Thus, none of the environmental stimuli seemed similar enough to those stimuli present during the conditioning session when mice received the aversive stimulation to cause fear responses. Yet when the optical fiber was turned on, emitting blue light over neurons in the dentate gyrus, mice froze. The researchers found, therefore, a way to trigger the *memory* of contexts associated with fear. The memory, in turn, led mice to emit a fear response.

STOP & CHECK

1. A key structure mediating fear and anxiety is the _____.

2. Of the two loops for routing sensory information from the thalamus to the amygdala, which is most likely to facilitate a fear caused by a sudden, loud noise?

1. amygdala **2.** The short loop, which routes crude, unprocessed information from the thalamus directly to the amygdala.

Anxious Feelings, the Amygdala, and the Sympathetic Nervous System

Just as the amygdala receives fear-related stimuli, the amygdala also sends information for fear-related responses (**Figure 14.3**). After receiving fear-related stimulus information, the amygdala sends output signals to the prefrontal cortex, hypothalamus, and locus coeruleus, among other structures. The prefrontal cortex plays a role in determining how we behave in a fearful situation—that is, whether we should approach or avoid a fearful stimulus. The hypothalamus and locus coeruleus facilitate physiological reactions to fear.

The physiological response to fear largely manifests from an activated sympathetic nervous system. Signals from the amygdala and the hypothalamus travel to the locus coeruleus, and the locus coeruleus ultimately causes the release of epinephrine (also referred to as *adrenaline*) and norepinephrine (also referred to as *noradrenaline*) from the adrenal gland. If the sympathetic nervous system is active enough, then respiration, heartbeat, blood pressure, and sweating increase (Davis & Whalen, 2001).

Many anxiety sufferers report having a fear of panic attacks, which consist of strong physiological responses noted by trembling, rapid forceful beating of the heart, restricted breathing, sweating, and dampening of visual or auditory sensations.

BOX 14.2 ANIMAL MODELS FOR SCREENING ANXIETY TREATMENTS

As with other classes of drugs, *anxiolytics*—drugs that reduce anxiety—are identified in animal behavioral models before they are tested in humans. Many of these models are developed for face validity and thus use tasks that can produce behaviors indicative of stress, fear, or anxiety.

The activity of rodents in an open field provides a simple assessment of anxiety. After being placed in the field, rodents spend much of their time running along the walls or edge of the space rather than the open center. We refer to this as *thigmotaxis*, and it is indicative of fear or anxiety. Drugs effective for

FIGURE 1 ● An elevated plus maze is a common model for screening anti-anxiety compounds. An elevated plus maze has two closed arms and two open arms. Anxiety is shown when an animal avoids the open arms of the maze.

SOURCE: Adapted from Stoelting Co.

anxiety increase the time spent in the center area of the field (Hall, 1934).

The *elevated plus maze* is perhaps the most commonly used model because of its ease, speed, simplicity of equipment, and screening quality (**Figure 1**). An elevated plus maze has four arms connected in the shape of a plus symbol, and as the name further implies, the maze is elevated above the ground by about 3 feet. Two of the four arms have tall walls, whereas the other two arms are open. After placing an animal, usually a rat or mouse, in the center of the maze, researchers measure anxiety according to how long the animal spends in the arms with walls compared to the arms without walls. A drug's anxiolytic effects

are demonstrated when treated animals spend more time in the arms without walls (Pellow & File, 1986). Although benzodiazepines generally increase the time spent within open arms, SSRIs do not always show this effect (Takeuchi, Owa, Nishino, & Kamei, 2010).

In the *Vogel conflict test,* an animal, usually a rat or mouse, learns to press a lever to earn a lick of water (**Figure 2a**). At times during this task, a lick will result in a brief, mild electric shock. This presents a conflict: A drink to relieve thirst also causes an aversive shock. The stress or anxiety caused in this task is relieved by anxiolytic drugs—that is, the drugs result in animals taking more licks (Vogel, Beer, & Clody, 1971).

FIGURE 2 ● (a) The Vogel conflict test involves an animal receiving a periodic shock for receiving a lick of water as a reinforcer. (b) Fear conditioning involves an organism learning to associate a stimulus with an aversive stimulus, such as electric shock. (c) Schedule-induced polydipsia consists of excessive water consumption occurring during periods between reinforcer delivery for a particular reinforcement schedule.

(Continued)

(Continued)

b

Conditioning involves
pairing a stimulus with
aversive stimulation

Freezing response does not occur
in the same context when the
conditioned stimulus is absent

A freezing response can occur in a
different context as long as the
conditioned stimulus is present

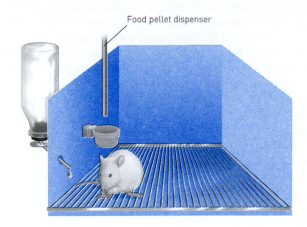

Food pellet dispenser

c

Fear conditioning is a process in which animals learn to associate stimuli with an aversive stimulus (**Figure 2b**). In a human version of this task, researchers deliver a mild electric shock to a participant's skin while the participant observes a stimulus. During subsequent sessions, the participant demonstrates fear conditioning by startling whenever researchers present the stimulus. Despite the known role of the amygdala in fear conditioning, benzodiazepines seldom inhibit fear responses in this task (Baas et al., 2009; Grillon, 2008).

The *schedule-induced polydipsia paradigm* consists of excessive water consumption occurring during periods between reinforcer delivery for a particular reinforcement schedule (**Figure 2c**). In a typical experimental design schedule-induced polydipsia paradigm, experiments are conducted in animals seeking food pellets in an operant chamber that contains a water bottle. Generally, the food pellets are delivered after set intervals of time, such as every 60 seconds; a sipper tube for a water bottle is always available in the test chamber. Rats are hungry before these sessions but not thirsty. During the intervals between food pellet deliveries, rats tend to drink water from the water bottle. Over time, water consumption in this task develops into excessive drinking, or *polydipsia*. Rats may consume more water during a 30-minute test session than they do throughout an entire day. Schedule-induced polydipsia may be mediated by anxiety, and chronic administration of antidepressant drugs reduces polydipsia.

Objective assessments confirm the physiological effects associated with panic attacks. For example, in a study conducted by Hoehn-Saric and colleagues (2004), individuals with panic disorder or generalized anxiety disorder self-reported anxiety levels at regular intervals throughout the course of several days. These individuals also wore portable physiological recording equipment in an effort to link objective physiological measures with subjective reports of anxiety as they went about their normal daily lives. This study found that physiological measures of increased heart rate and perspiration confirmed self-reports of these events.

These real-life assessments validate experimentally induced methods of producing panic, including hyperventilation-induced panic and CO_2-induced panic. Both methods produce increases in a participant's reported level of panic and physiological responses to panic. Anxiety studies have also reported that individuals with panic disorder appear more sensitive to CO_2-induced panic than individuals with other anxiety disorders (Papp et al., 1993; Welkowitz, Papp, Martinez, Browne, & Gorman, 1999). Anxiety medication use or prior cognitive behavioral therapy reduces CO_2-induced panic severity (Gorman, Martinez, Coplan, Kent, & Kleber, 2004).

Stress and the HPA Axis

General adaptation syndrome Stress syndrome occurring in three progressive phases: alarm stage, resistance, and exhaustion

We can consider our reactions to short- and long-term stress according to the **general adaptation syndrome** proposed by Selye (1950) (**Table 14.1**). This syndrome has three stages. The first stage is called *alarm* and is characterized by increased physiological arousal in preparation for an emergency situation. The alarm stage consists of the acute reactions to fearful stimuli, including activation of the sympathetic nervous system.

The second stage of the general adaptation syndrome is called *resistance* and is characterized by a sustained level of physiological arousal in response to prolonged stress. During this stage, the hypothalamus releases corticotrophin releasing factor, which in turn elicits the release of *adrenocorticotropic hormone (ACTH)* from the pituitary

TABLE 14.1 ● General Adaptation Syndrome		
Stage	**Characteristics**	**Physiology**
1: Alarm	Increased physiological arousal in preparation for an emergency situation	Hypothalamus activates sympathetic nervous system
2: Resistance	Sustained level of physiological arousal	Hypothalamus elicits the release of ACTH from pituitary gland; adrenal gland releases cortisol
3: Exhaustion	Fatigue, susceptibility to disease	Immune system and metabolic activity of organs throughout the body are underactive

SOURCE: © Cengage Learning 2014.

FIGURE 14.3 ● Outputs from the amygdala go to the prefrontal cortex, hypothalamus, and locus coeruleus. Although the prefrontal cortex is important for approach and avoidance behaviors, the hypothalamus and locus coeruleus are important for sympathetic nervous system activation.

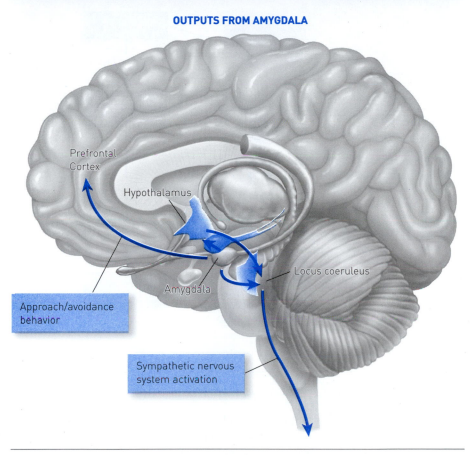

OUTPUTS FROM AMYGDALA

SOURCE: © Cengage Learning 2014.

gland. ACTH causes the adrenal gland to release **cortisol**, a stress-related hormone that causes several other effects in the body, including increases in metabolic activity, immune system activity, and glucose and other nutrients. Given their combined distinct role in stress responses, these structures are referred to as the **hypothalamic–pituitary–adrenal (HPA) axis** (**Figure 14.4**).

Cortisol Hormone released from the adrenal gland during stress

Hypothalamic–pituitary–adrenal axis (HPA) A system involved in physiological responses to stress

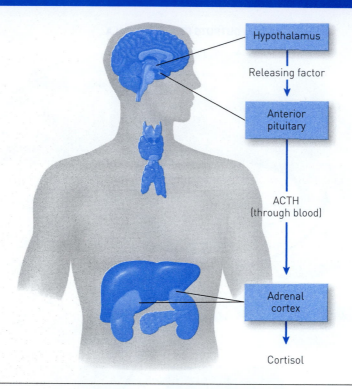

FIGURE 14.4 ● The HPA axis includes the hypothalamus, pituitary gland, and adrenal gland. In response to sustained stress, the hypothalamus elicits the anterior pituitary gland to release ACTH, which in turn causes the adrenal cortex to release cortisol.

SOURCE: © Cengage Learning 2014.

The third and final stage of the general adaptation syndrome is *exhaustion*. In this stage, the body can no longer maintain the high, sustained levels of physiological arousal that occurred during the second stage. This leads to impaired immune system function and reduced metabolic activity of organs throughout the body. An individual who is in the exhaustion phase is susceptible to disease and feels fatigued.

Prolonged increases in cortisol levels are associated with damage to the hippocampus. In this structure, high levels of cortisol are associated with damaged and destroyed neurons, decreased hippocampal size, and memory impairments (Sapolsky, 1992). Further, chronic stress conditions are related to reduced dendrite sizes on neurons and cause memory impairments in rats (Kleen, Sitomer, Killeen, & Conrad, 2006).

For these reasons, researchers consider cortisol a *stress hormone* and have heavily studied its potential role in disorders associated with prolonged stress such as PTSD. Yet changes in cortisol levels in PTSD are inconsistent. Thus compared to healthy controls, some studies find increased levels of cortisol (*hypercortisolism*) in PTSD, while other studies find decreased levels of cortisol (*hypocortisolism*).

When referring to changes in hormone or neurochemical levels, researchers often categorize these changes in two phases. A *tonic phase* is generally a baseline state; for PTSD, this might be altered cortisol levels before a traumatic event or altered cortisol levels during a normal day after being diagnosed with PTSD. A *phasic phase* occurs during a stressful event, which for PTSD might have been the actual traumatic event that led to PTSD or the presence of stimuli that might trigger reminders about the traumatic event.

Several studies found consistently lower tonic cortisol levels in individuals with PTSD (Mason, Giller, Kosten, Ostroff, & Podd, 1986; Yehuda et al., 1990). Other studies, however, have shown increased tonic cortisol levels in individuals with PTSD (De Bellis et al., 1999; Pitman & Orr, 1990). Phasic levels of cortisol in PTSD are more consistent across studies. Researchers find high phasic cortisol levels immediately after traumatic events, including military battles and rape (Howard, Olney, Frawley, Peterson, & Guerra, 1955; Resnick, Yehuda, Pitman, & Foy, 1995). Moreover, phasic cortisol levels increase when an individual is exposed to reminders about the traumatic event (Elzinga, Schmahl, Vermetten, van Dyck, & Bremner, 2003).

According to Mouthaan and colleagues (2014), many studies attempting to link PTSD to phasic cortisol levels differ according to how soon after a traumatic event cortisol levels are taken, severity of injury, time of the event, how the samples are taken (e.g., saliva or urine), the number of participants studied, imbalance of male or female participants in a sample, and other methodological factors. To determine whether factors such as these might explain inconsistencies between studies, this group recruited a sample of nearly 400 participants who had blood samples taken within 72 hours of an injury from a traumatic event. The researchers took additional blood samples 6 weeks and 6 months later. The large sample size allowed them to have a suitable balance of demographic characteristics among the study participants. They found that low cortisol levels sampled at both 6 weeks and 6 months after the traumatic event served to predict the onset of PTSD symptoms. This study provides strong evidence that corticol levels may actually be diminished in PTSD once other factors are taken into account.

STOP & CHECK

1. Panic attacks can be experimentally induced through hyperventilation or exposure to _____.

2. During a fear-provoking situation, the approach–avoidance behavior is mediated by the _____.

3. Feelings of fear, such as increased heart rate and faster breathing, result from activation of the _____.

4. The _____ plays an important role in the body's reaction to stress.

1. CO_2 gas 2. prefrontal cortex 3. sympathetic nervous system 4. HPA axis

Anxiolytic and Antidepressant Drugs and the Treatment of Anxiety

Barbiturates

Anxiolytic drugs
Drugs prescribed
to treat anxiety

Drugs prescribed to treat anxiety are called **anxiolytic drugs**. The first anxiolytic drugs consisted of sedative barbiturates introduced in the early 1900s after German chemists Emil Fischer and Josef von Mering developed barbital (Fischer & von Mering, 1903; Shorter, 1997). Barbital served as the first known sedative barbiturate. Barbital was synthesized as a derivative of an earlier compound, barbituric acid, discovered years earlier by Adolf von Baeyer, who may have named it after his girlfriend, Barbara. Von Baeyer also became the founder of Bayer Pharmaceuticals, which developed many of the 50 known therapeutic barbiturate compounds (Lopez-Munoz et al., 2005). Soon after their discovery, barbiturates were commonly used in psychiatric hospitals and prescribed by general family physicians for sleep, nervousness, and other purposes (Shorter, 1997).

We classify barbiturates by time course. Long-acting barbiturates generally take at least 1 hour to take effect, but produce these effects for 10 to 12 hours. These barbiturates have poor lipid solubility and slow metabolism. Ultrashort-acting barbiturates produce effects within 10 to 20 seconds and maintain drug effects for approximately 30 minutes. These barbiturates are highly soluble in lipids, quickly store in fats, and rapidly metabolize. We classify barbiturates falling between these time courses as short- or intermediate-acting barbiturates (**Table 14.2**).

Other uses for barbiturates include anesthesia and reduced seizures. Phenobarbital and other barbiturates at the time also were used to aid a general anesthetic, such as *ether*, to induce full anesthesia. In the early 1930s, a new barbiturate called *hexobarbital* (*Evipal* from Bayer Pharmaceuticals) became the first barbiturate capable of producing general anesthesia (Lopez-Munoz et al., 2005; Weese & Scharpff, 1932). Barbiturates were also the first drugs capable of reducing the frequency and severity of epileptic seizures.

TABLE 14.2 ● Barbiturates Classified by Duration for Onset and Duration of Drug Action

Class of Barbiturate	Selected Barbiturates	Lipid Solubility	Duration for Onset	Duration of Action
Ultrashort-acting	Thiopental (Pentothal) Methohexital (Brevital)	High	A few minutes	~30 min
Short- or intermediate-acting	Secobarbital (Seconal) Pentobarbital (Nembutal)	Medium	~30 min	~8 hr
Long-acting	Phenobarbital (Luminol) Mephobarbitaol (Mebaral)	Low	~1hr	~12 hr

SOURCE: © Cengage Learning 2014

💊 *Drug Profile:* ether	
Other names	Diethyl ether, ethyl ether, ethoxyethane
Properties	Activates GABA$_A$ receptors
Uses	Once used as a general anesthetic; some modern anesthetics (below), called halogenated ethers, have similar chemical structure (but are non-flammable)
Similar drugs	Isoflurane (Forane)
	Halothane (Fluothane)

STOP & CHECK

1. A drug prescribed specifically for the treatment of anxiety is a called a(n) _____.

2. Why are some barbiturates, like phenobarbital, longer acting than other barbiturates?

1. anxiolytic drug. 2. Longer-acting barbiturates tend to have lower lipid solubility and a longer metabolism process than shorter-acting barbiturates.

Barbiturates Serve as Drugs of Abuse During the decades that preceded the introduction of benzodiazepines in the 1960s, short-acting barbiturates were commonly abused. Users referred to barbiturates as *downers*, among other names. Along with reduced anxiety, barbiturates produced feelings of well-being and lowered inhibitions.

Barbiturates also appear to have positive reinforcing effects. Nonhuman primates readily self-administer barbiturates. Further, barbiturates increase the breaking points on progressive ratio schedules (Griffiths, Findley, Brady, Dolan-Gutcher, & Robinson, 1975; Morgan, 1990). In human laboratory studies, participants prefer barbiturates just as well as morphine (McClane & Martin, 1976) and short-acting barbiturates more than longer-lasting barbiturates (Morgan, 1990).

Review! A break point refers to the number of responses an organism will emit to earn a drug injection. (Chapter 5.)

Griffiths and colleagues (1980) asked human participants to rate how much they "liked" the effects produced by the barbiturate pentobarbital compared to the benzodiazepine diazepam. Consistent with other studies, they reported pentobarbital to be well liked, particularly when compared to diazepam. At the same time, they reported diazepam as somewhat liked, but this liking did not increase as the doses of diazepam increased. Thus, the effects of barbiturates appear more rewarding than the effects of benzodiazepines.

Chronic Barbiturate Administration Increases the Risk of Respiratory Depression   Most deaths occurring from barbiturate overdose result from respiratory depression. Many accidental overdoses likely occurred for those prescribed a barbiturate because of barbiturates' memory-impairing effects, resulting in an individual taking a barbiturate after forgetting that one had been taken earlier (Lopez-Munoz et al., 2005).

The risk of accidental overdose increases during long-term usage because of a shrinking therapeutic index. Initially, we find a barbiturate's therapeutic dose range far lower than its lethal dose range. However, chronic use causes tolerance to therapeutic effects but not to respiratory depressant effects. As a result, the therapeutic doses shift dangerously close to lethal doses. At this point, even an accidental second administration of a barbiturate might lead to severe respiratory depression.

Abrupt Withdrawal Causes a Barbiturate Abstinence Syndrome   Abrupt cessation from chronic barbiturate administration can lead to a **barbiturate abstinence syndrome** that is characterized by anxiety, muscle weakness, and abdominal pain. Moreover, in severe cases, seizures may develop, particularly for individuals taking higher doses of barbiturates. Thus, abrupt cessation from barbiturate treatment is dangerous, so users must gradually reduce the amount of a barbiturate administered or switch to a medication that will offset the effects of this abstinence syndrome (Westgate & Stiebler, 1964).

Barbiturates Produce Pharmacological Effects Through Facilitating GABA Neurotransmission   GABA, the most common inhibitory neurotransmitter in the nervous system, is key for therapeutic and aversive effects of barbiturates. Barbiturates selectively bind to a site, referred to as the *barbiturate site*, on $GABA_A$ receptors (**Figure 14.5**). Through this site, barbiturates function as a positive modulator, which enhances the inhibitory effects of GABA.

We find $GABA_A$ receptors throughout the brain, but structures of interest here include the amygdala, thalamus, cerebral cortex, and medulla as illustrated in **Figure 14.6**. The anxiolytic effects of barbiturates derive from inhibition of amygdala activity. Inhibition of thalamic and cortical activity accounts for the effects of barbiturates on seizures, memory, attention, and other cognitive functions. The sedative-hypnotic effects of barbiturates occur by suppressing cortical functioning and structures important for cortical arousal. The term **sedative-hypnotic** is used to describe drugs that are calming

Barbiturate abstinence syndrome Anxiety, muscle weakness, and abdominal pain caused by abrupt cessation of barbiturate use

Sedative-hypnotic A drug that produces both calming (sedative) and sleep-inducing (hypnotic) effects

STOP & CHECK

1. In humans, the rewarding effects of barbiturates appear equivalent to those of the opioid _____.

2. The major cause of overdose death with barbiturates is _____.

3. The primary mechanism of action for barbiturates is the facilitation of _____ receptor activation by GABA.

1. morphine 2. respiratory depression 3. $GABA_A$

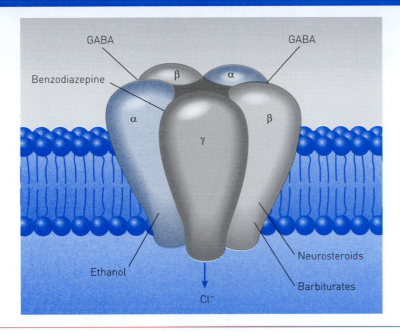

FIGURE 14.5 ● The GABA$_A$ receptor contains a binding site for barbiturates. Binding to this site facilitates the binding of GABA to the GABA receptor.

SOURCE: © Cengage Learning 2014.

(i.e., sedative) and sleep inducing (i.e., hypnotic). The effects of barbiturates on respiratory function result from inhibition of the medulla (Ito, Suzuki, Wellman, & Ho, 1996; Meldrum, 1982).

Benzodiazepines

Benzodiazepines became available in the 1960s amid the growing illicit barbiturate use and increased occurrence of barbiturate overdose. The potential for such medications was realized after non-barbiturate tranquilizers such as Miltown became popular in the 1950s; however, these medications also provided abuse potential and other adverse effects. In 1960, *chlordiazepoxide*, better known by its trade name *Librium*, became the first benzodiazepine drug to reach the market (Tone, 2005).

During this decade, Librium became the most commonly prescribed drug in the United States, only to be surpassed soon after by *diazepam (Valium)*. We attribute the discoveries of Librium and Valium to Leo Sternbach, a chemist working for Roche Pharmaceuticals. These and the dozens of benzodiazepines to follow produced less sedation than barbiturates, making them far more appealing for outpatient treatment. In 1981, the Upjohn Company produced *alprazolam (Xanax)*, which remains a

FIGURE 14.6 ● The doses of a CNS depressant such as a barbiturate decrease consciousness as the dose is increased. Alertness is affected first and is linked to suppression of cortical functioning, particularly the prefrontal cortex. A higher dose will provide anxiety relief, resulting from an inhibition of functioning in the amygdala. Even higher doses will affect brain-stem areas, resulting in sedation and sleep. If doses are high enough, the medulla will no longer elicit breathing.

INPUTS TO AMYGDALA

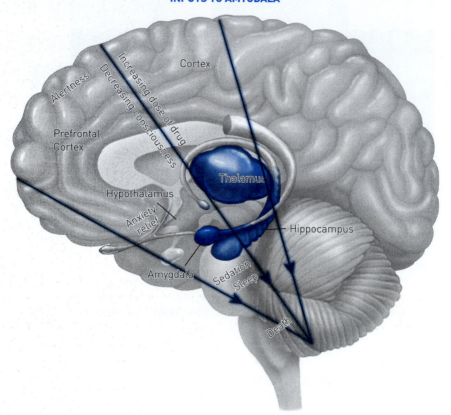

SOURCE: © Cengage Learning 2014.

commonly prescribed benzodiazepine today. Roche Pharmaceuticals discovered *clonazepam (Klonopin)*, which also remains a frequently prescribed drug (Shorter, 1997). Today, we find benzodiazepines to be relatively common drugs; in 2008, an estimated 5.2 percent of adults had used a benzodiazepine for either short-term or long-term use. The majority of benzodiazepine prescriptions came from general practitioners (Olfson, King, & Schoenbaum, 2015).

Physicians may prescribe a benzodiazepine as a chronic treatment or for use on an "as needed" basis. Depending on these uses, certain benzodiazepines serve better than others. Short-acting benzodiazepines such as alprazolam and clonazepam take 1 to 2 hours for full effect and have a 12- to 24-hour elimination half-life. Physicians may prescribe these drugs to take as needed for anxiety. Thus, a patient may take these medications when experiencing anxiety or when expecting anxiety. Physicians may also prescribe short-lasting benzodiazepines for insomnia, although newer non-benzodiazepine medications such as Ambien serve as first-line treatments for insomnia today. We find intermediate- and long-lasting benzodiazepines used chronically to relieve or prevent generalized anxiety disorder, seizures, and other conditions where long-lasting minor effects are desired.

Metabolism accounts for the differences in length of drug action among the benzodiazepines. Unlike short-acting benzodiazepines, intermediate- and long-lasting benzodiazepines produce other benzodiazepines as active metabolites (**Figure 14.7**). In particular, the benzodiazepine drug *nordiazepam* serves as an active metabolite for many benzodiazepines. Thus, nordiazepam and other active benzodiazepine metabolites produce further benzodiazepine effects. Moreover, enzymes convert nordiazepam to *oxazepam (Serax)*, a short-acting benzodiazepine with no active metabolites (Marin, Coles, Merrell, & McMillin, 2008; Tobin, Lorenz, Brousseau, & Conner, 1964).

FIGURE 14.7 ● The duration of action for benzodiazepines depends on the process of metabolism. The two long-lasting benzodiazepines shown here are metabolized into nordiazepam by the CYP3A4 enzyme. Nordiazepam also has benzodiazepine effects, as does its metabolite oxazepam. Oxazepam is also prescribed as a short-lasting benzodiazepine and does not have an active metabolite.

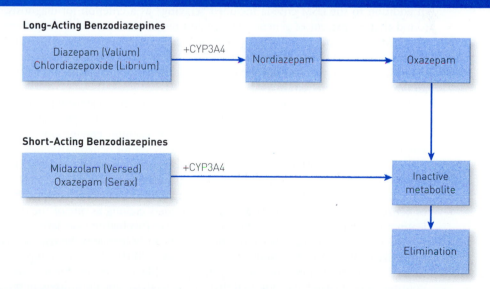

SOURCE: Data from Marin et al., 1964.

Pharmacogenetic factors also play a role in benzodiazepine metabolism. Benzodiazepines are broken down (i.e., oxidized) primarily by the cytochrome P450 (CYP) enzyme subfamilies CYP-2C19 and CYP-3A4. However, a polymorphism of the CYP-2C19 gene, specifically a CYP2C19*2 polymorphism, causes poor metabolism of benzodiazepines. As a result, patients with this polymorphism exhibit a stronger and longer-lasting treatment response likely because of greater levels of non-metabolized benzodiazepines in the body. Polymorphisms of the CYP-3A4 gene have not revealed differences in the ability to metabolize benzodiazepines.

The CYP3A5 enzyme is uniquely involved in metabolism of the benzodiazepines alprazolam and midazolam. Researchers associate a CYP3A5*3 polymorphism with poor metabolism of alprazolam and subsequently higher levels of alprazolam in blood plasma. This particular polymorphism occurs in approximately 85–98 percent of Europeans, but in only 55–64 percent of African Americans (Tiwari, Souza, & Muller, 2009).

Risks of Benzodiazepine Use Like barbiturate drugs, benzodiazepines are generally considered by physicians to be substances of abuse. This determination results partly from the development of a **benzodiazepine withdrawal syndrome** characterized by depression, anxiety, mania, suicidality, and convulsions occurring after abrupt withdrawal of a chronically used benzodiazepine. The physiological withdrawal symptoms of benzodiazepines may last for several months. A lower probability of this withdrawal syndrome occurs after gradually reducing the dose of a benzodiazepine over time. The appearance of physical dependence along with inferences that benzodiazepine act similarly to barbiturates supports a notion that benzodiazepine has abuse potential.

Kan, Breteler, and Zitman (1997) sought to determine the prevalence of an addiction to benzodiazepines among general practice or psychiatric out-patients taking benzodiazepines at least once a week. The researchers surveyed for features of a benzodiazepine use disorder using both the DSM (at this time, the DSM-III) and the ICD-10, which in addition to the DSM criteria included "craving" as a criterion for diagnosis. They found that 51 percent of general practice and 69 percent of psychiatric patients met the DSM criteria for benzodiazepine dependence at some point in their lifetimes. The rates were similarly high when using ICD-10 criteria. When looking at specific features of these diagnoses, the majority of patients had experienced withdrawal symptoms and an impaired ability to reduce use.

Craving was especially high in this study with 85 percent of general practice and 94 percent of psychiatric patients describing a craving for benzodiazepines at some point in their lives. A later study conducted to specifically examine craving among benzodiazepine users found that those who experience craving for benzodiazepines generally had a greater severity of benzodiazepine use disorder symptoms and a greater negative mood (Mol et al., 2005). Together these findings indicate that craving occurs for many individuals during long-term use, especially when an individual develops other signs of benzodiazepine abuse. The DSM-5 now considers craving as one of the diagnostic features of a benzodiazepine use disorder (American Psychiatric Association, 2013).

One's history of using other substances significantly increases the risk of misusing benzodiazepines (Brunette, Noordsy, Xie, & Drake, 2003). We can attempt to study these risks by rating how much study participants like the effects of benzodiazepines. Routine users of GHB have indicated that the benzodiazepine flunitrazepam produced

Benzodiazepine withdrawal syndrome A physiological form of dependence characterized by anxiety, mania, suicidality, and convulsions that occurs after abrupt withdrawal of a chronically used benzodiazepine

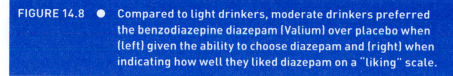

FIGURE 14.8 ● Compared to light drinkers, moderate drinkers preferred the benzodiazepine diazepam (Valium) over placebo when (left) given the ability to choose diazepam and (right) when indicating how well they liked diazepam on a "liking" scale.

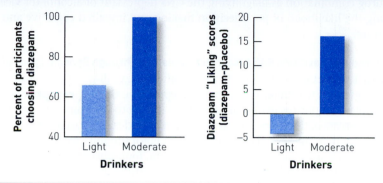

SOURCE: Data from deWit et al., 1989.

rewarding subjective effects (Abanades et al., 2007). Further, moderate alcohol drinkers, far more than light alcohol drinkers, prefer the effects of benzodiazepine pills compared to placebo and report liking these effects (deWit, Pierri, & Johanson, 1989) (**Figure 14.8**).

Other risks of benzodiazepines occur from accidental injury, poor decision making, or consuming other drugs when under the effects of a benzodiazepine. We find an increased likelihood of emergency room visits and hospital admissions due to accidental injuries while taking benzodiazepines (Oster, Huse, Adams, Imbimbo, and Russell, 1990). Researchers find increased traffic accidents, as well as injuries from these accidents, occurring in people who had taken a benzodiazepine prior to driving (Neutel, 1995).

STOP & CHECK

1. Like barbiturates, _____ also are characterized by their time of onset and duration of their drug effects.

2. Polymorphism of the CYP-2C19 gene affects the _____ of benzodiazepines, accounting partly for individual differences in sensitivity to benzodiazepine drug effects.

3. A history of using substances of abuse increase the likelihood of misuse with a _____.

1. benzodiazepines 2. metabolism 3. benzodiazepine

Among potential drug combinations with benzodiazepines, we find most misuse occurring from combining a benzodiazepine with alcohol. The combined use of these substances, in particular, corresponds to greater rates of drug-induced death, harm caused by drug overdose, and higher rates of accidental injury, including major traffic accidents (Chan, 1984). As noted in the chapter on alcohol (Chapter 8), we can think of this drug combination as magnifying the CNS depressant of alcohol (or vice versa) increasing the likelihood of poor decision making and impaired cognitive and motor functioning.

Benzodiazepines Facilitate GABA Neurotransmission Through Specific Types of GABA$_A$ Receptors Like barbiturates, benzodiazepines affect the GABA$_A$ receptor. However, this class of drugs binds to different sites on the receptor. The **GABA$_A$ receptor** is an ionotropic receptor comprising five subunits (Figure 14.5). Of the five subunits, two are of the α type and two are of the β type. The fifth is a bit of a wildcard: It can be a γ, ρ, δ, or ε subunit. Although there are several types of GABA$_A$ receptor subunits, each subunit has multiple subtypes. There are six subtypes of the α subunit, four subtypes of the β subunit, and six subunits of the γ subunit currently known. We identify these different subtypes using subscript numbers, such as α_2 or β_3.

The GABA$_A$ receptor provides two binding sites for the neurotransmitter GABA. These sites exist in regions formed where an α subunit joins a β subunit. GABA must occupy both sites to open the GABA$_A$ receptor. Benzodiazepines serve as GABA$_A$ positive modulators by binding to a site, referred to as a *benzodiazepine site*, on specific α subunits (Amin & Weiss, 1993; Sigel & Buhr, 1997).

Benzodiazepines have a high affinity for a benzodiazepine site contained within an α_1 subunit (Sigel & Buhr, 1997). However, benzodiazepines have a lower affinity for the benzodiazepine sites contained within α_2, α_3, or α_5 subunits (Klepner, Lippa, Benson, Sano, & Beer, 1979; Pritchett, Luddens, & Seeburg, 1989). Benzodiazepines bind poorly to α_4 and α_6 subunits (Derry, Dunn, & Davies, 2004; Pritchett et al., 1989). Putting this all together, we essentially have two different types of benzodiazepine sites. We refer to the *high-affinity site*, contained on the α_1 subunit, as the **BZ I site**; we refer to the *low-affinity site*, contained in α_2, α_3, or α_5 subunits, as the **BZ II site**.

As shown in **Figure 14.9**, the locations of these receptors in the brain help explain the behavioral effects of benzodiazepines. We find BZ I sites highly expressed in the cerebellum, substantia nigra, and thalamus (Wisden, Laurie, Monyer, & Seeburg, 1992). Although they are not structures implicated in anxiety, they explain why benzodiazepines disrupt balance and coordination (cerebellum), reduce seizure activity, and produce hypnotic effects by inhibiting cortical arousal (substantia nigra and thalamus) (Veliskova, Velisek, Nunes, & Moshe, 1996; Veliskova, Velisek, & Moshe, 1996).

At the same time, we find BZ II sites highly expressed in the amygdala and hypothalamus, two areas traditionally important for anxiety and stress, and various parts of the cerebral cortex (Wisden et al., 1992). During benzodiazepine treatment for anxiety, benzodiazepines produce behavioral effects by acting at both types of BZ sites. These actions lead to their anxiolytic effects as well as undesirable effects, including hypnotic effects and a potential for physical dependence.

Are There Endogenous Benzodiazepines? Given that sites exist on GABA$_A$ receptors for benzodiazepines, researchers have looked for **endozepines**, endogenous substances

---

GABA$_A$ receptor
Ionotropic receptor comprised of five subunits and activated to the neurotransmitter GABA

BZ I site Allosteric site on the GABA$_A$ receptor α_1 subunit that a benzodiazepine can bind to; also referred to as the high affinity site

BZ II site Allosteric site on the GABA$_A$ receptor α_2, α_3, or α_5 subunits that that a benzodiazepine can bind to; also referred to as the low affinity site

Endozepines
Endogenous substances that bind to benzodiazepine sites

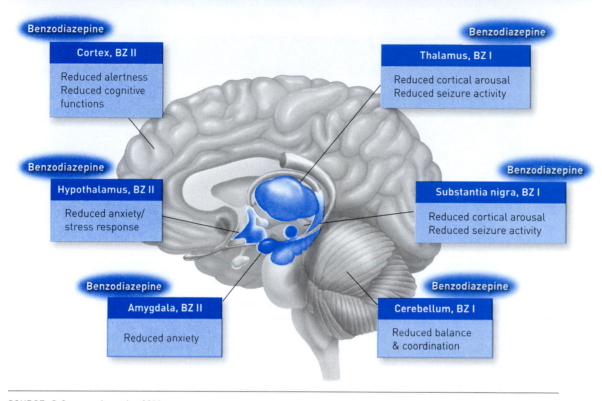

FIGURE 14.9 ● **The behavioral effects of benzodiazepines depend on the location of BZ I or BZ II sites in structures throughout the brain.**

Benzodiazepine

Cortex, BZ II

Reduced alertness
Reduced cognitive
functions

Benzodiazepine

Thalamus, BZ I

Reduced cortical arousal
Reduced seizure activity

Benzodiazepine

Hypothalamus, BZ II

Reduced anxiety/
stress response

Benzodiazepine

Substantia nigra, BZ I

Reduced cortical arousal
Reduced seizure activity

Benzodiazepine

Amygdala, BZ II

Reduced anxiety

Benzodiazepine

Cerebellum, BZ I

Reduced balance
& coordination

SOURCE: © Cengage Learning 2014.

that bind to benzodiazepine sites. Endozepines include the protein *diazepam-binding inhibitor* and a family of neuropeptide fragments cleaved from diazepam-binding inhibitor, including *octadecaneuropeptide* and *triakontatetraneuropeptide* (Guidotti et al., 1983; Slobodyansky, Guidotti, Wambebe, Berkovich, Costa, 1989). In addition, there are a number of endogenous ligands, called β-*carbolines*, which also bind to benzodiazepine sites (Robinson, Anderson, Crosby, Nutt, & Hudson, 2003).

We find endozepines released from astrocytes, and they serve as negative modulators when binding to benzodiazepine sites on $GABA_A$ receptors (Gach et al., 2015; Lamacz et al., 1996; Qian, Bilderback, & Barmack, 2008). In this regard, we can refer to endozepines as **gliotransmitters**, chemical transmitters released from glial cells. The functional significance of endozepines has yet to firmly determined, but they may have a role in promoting neuronal proliferation by preventing GABA-induced inhibition of neuronal proliferation in the subventricular zone (Alfonso, Le Magueresse, Zuccotti, Khodosevich, & Monyer, 2012). In addition, endozepines may inhibit food intake (Gach et al., 2015; Lanfray et al., 2013). We also find benzodiazepine sites outside of the

Gliotransmitters
Chemical
transmitters
released from
glial cells

nervous system, located on mitochondria, where they appear to enhance immune system response (Clavier et al., 2014; Krueger, 1995). A number of studies have also shown that β-carboline compounds produce anxiogenic effects (i.e., anxiety-inducing effects) in animal models (Novas, Wolfman, Medina, & Robertis, 1988).

STOP & CHECK

1. Benzodiazepines have a greater affinity for the BZ I site, which is found on α_1 subunits, and have a lower affinity for the _____ site, which is contained on α_2, α_3, or α_5 subunits.

2. Benzodiazepines reduce seizure activity by binding to BZ I sites on GABA$_A$ receptors in the substantia nigra and _____.

3. What actions to endozepines display for GABA$_A$ receptors?

1. BZ II 2. thalamus 3. They serve as negative modulators.

Z-drugs

Z-drugs (or **non-benzodiazepine hypnotics**) consist of sleep aids that act by binding to BZ I sites. The name *Z-drug* refers to the generic names of drugs in this class that typically begin with a *z*. These drugs include *zolpidem (Ambien), zopiclone (Zimovane), eszopiclone (Lunesta)*, and *zaleplon (Sonata)*. We also refer to these drugs as non-benzodiazepine hypnotics to indicate a difference in the chemical structures from benzodiazepines, while also emphasizing their hypnotic effects. Z-drugs have become the most widely prescribed sleep aids in the world (Huedo-Medina, Kirsch, Middlemass, Klonizakis, Siriwardena, 2012).

Z-drugs all exhibit a high binding affinity for GABA$_A$ receptors that include the α_1 subunit (again, referred to as the BZ I site). Some of the Z-drugs also bind with an appreciable affinity for other subunits characterized as the BZ II site. For example, zolpidem,

🔹 *Drug Profile: zolpidem*	
Trade name	Ambien
Properties	Serves as positive modulator for BZ I site GABA$_A$ receptors
Uses	Prescribed as a sleep aid
Similar drugs	Zopiclone (Zimovane)
	Eszopiclone (Lunesta)
	Zaleplon (Sonata)

one of the most selective Z-drugs for $\alpha_1\beta_2\gamma_2$ GABA$_A$ receptor, exhibits a moderate affinity for $\alpha_2\beta_1\gamma_2$ and $\alpha_3\beta_3\gamma_2$ GABA$_A$ receptors. Zopiclone, however, exhibits an appreciable affinity for $\alpha_1\beta_2\gamma_2$ and $\alpha_2\beta_1\gamma_2$ GABA$_A$ receptors and a moderate affinity for $\alpha_3\beta_3\gamma_2$, $\alpha_3\beta_3\gamma_3$, $\alpha_5\beta_3\gamma_2$, and $\alpha_5\beta_3\gamma_3$ GABA$_A$ receptors. Thus, we can expect hypnotic effects from positive modulation of α_1-subunit containing GABA$_A$ receptors, and we can also expect other effects from BZ-II sites (i.e., α_2, α_3, or α_5-subunit) (Dämgen & Lüddens, 1999).

Hypnotic effects represent the primary pharmacological effects of Z-drugs. Yet, we find a number of other effects from Z-drugs as well. Z-drugs provide a risk, albeit low, of producing **sleep-related complex behaviors** while sleeping. These complex behaviors include walking, driving, cooking, eating, and carrying on conversations all while asleep. The likelihood of these sleep-related complex behaviors increases with Z-drug use (Dolder & Nelson, 2012; Hoque & Chasson, 2009). Z-drugs also can cause imbalance, impair memory, and impair driving. These considerations present a hazard for those who set an alarm to wake up before the effects of the Z-drug wears off, which is why drug manufacturers recommend at least 8 hour allotted for sleep (Gunja, 2013).

Sleep-related complex behaviors Complex behaviors that occur while sleeping, including walking, driving, cooking, eating, and carrying on conversations

Anticonvulsant Drugs for Treating Anxiety Disorders

Anticonvulsant drugs, which are used for the treatment of seizures, facilitate the neurotransmission of GABA. As barbiturates and benzodiazepines also facilitate GABAergic neurotransmission, anticonvulsants also appear to exhibit anti-anxiety effects. A variety of anticonvulsants have been found effective for treating anxiety, including valproic acid, carbamazepine, gabapentin, lamotrigine, vigabatrin, and pregabalin. In general, anticonvulsant drugs have shown promising results in case studies and clinical trials for the treatment of anxiety, but we need further studies to determine their safety and efficacy compared to benzodiazepines and antidepressant compounds (Gorman, Kent, & Coplan, 2002).

STOP & CHECK

1. Which benzodiazepine site appears most important for the pharmacological effects of "Z-drugs"?

2. Z-drugs present a risk for _____ behaviors, which can include sleep walking or sleep driving.

3. Why might anticonvulsant drugs effectively treat anxiety?

1. The BZ I site. 2. sleep-related complex 3. Anticonvulsant drugs such as benzodiazepines and barbiturates facilitate the activation of GABA$_A$ receptors.

Antidepressant Drugs and the Treatment of Anxiety Disorders

Although this chapter has so far focused on the anxiolytic drugs barbiturates and benzodiazepines, the first-line treatments for anxiety disorders have shifted from these medications to antidepressant drugs. Among the antidepressant drugs, we find the selective serotonin reuptake inhibitors (SSRIs) and the serotonin–norepinephrine reuptake inhibitors (SNRIs) most used for treating anxiety.

SSRIs and SNRIs Reduce and Prevent Anxiety SSRIs and SNRIs have become the first-line treatments for anxiety disorders. As described in Chapter 13, SSRIs and SNRIs both prevent the reuptake of serotonin through serotonin membrane transporters, and SNRIs also prevent the reuptake of norepinephrine through norepinephrine membrane transporters. Serotonin membrane transporters are of particular interest in anxiety disorders, based on genetic studies linking serotonin transporter gene polymorphisms to anxiety. In particular, individuals found to have a short allele, expressed homozygously or even heterozygously, in the serotonin transporter gene are more likely to exhibit anxiety as a personality trait (Lesch et al., 1996; Sen, Burmeister, & Ghosh, 2004). Those with the short allele of the serotonin transporter also exhibit greater activity in the amygdala based on fMRI studies (Hariri et al., 2002).

The SSRIs *paroxetine (Paxil)* and *fluoxetine (Prozac)* have both demonstrated an efficacy in clinical trials for panic disorder, social phobia, generalized anxiety disorder, and posttraumatic disorder (Gorman et al., 2002). Moreover, researchers have found paroxetine effective versus placebo for the treatment of specific phobia (Benjamin, Ben-Zion, Karbofsky, & Dannon, 2000). Clinical studies also find SNRIs effective for anxiety disorders. *Duloxetine (Cymbalta)* met approval by the Food and Drug Administration (FDA) in 2008 for the treatment of general anxiety, based on a series of positive clinical studies (Carter & McCormack, 2009). *Venlafaxine (Effexor)* also has proven effective, and has been approved by the FDA for generalized anxiety disorder and social phobia (Altamurar, Pioli, Vitto, & Mannu, 1999; Davidson, DuPont, Hedges, & Haskins, 1999). As in the treatment of depression, SSRI and SNRIs require at least 2 weeks to relieve the symptoms of anxiety.

Clinical studies generally find SSRIs and SNRIs effective for the treatment of OCD, but the response time appears longer than for other anxiety disorders, often ranging up to 10–12 weeks. The SSRI *fluvoxamine (Luvox)* has long been considered the first-line treatment of OCD as well as impulse control disorders, eating disorders, and Tourette's syndrome (Goodman, Ward, Kablinger, & Murphy, 1997). Antipsychotic drugs may also augment the effects of SSRIs for treating OCD. Diniz and colleagues (2010) found that the atypical antipsychotic drug *quetiapine (Seroquel)* improved the response to an SSRI in OCD patients who failed to respond SSRI treatment alone.

Although SSRIs and SNRIs have become the first-line treatments for anxiety, approximately one-third of patients do not respond adequately. This failure rate is found in depression as well. **Table 14.3** compares antidepressant drugs to benzodiazepines for the treatment of anxiety.

Buspirone and the Treatment of Anxiety Disorders

Buspirone (BuSpar) is a partial agonist for the serotonin (5-HT)$_{1A}$ receptor that produces anxiolytic effects. Although generally not considered effective for panic disorder or social phobia, buspirone appears as effective as benzodiazepines for the treatment of

TABLE 14.3 ● SSRIs/SNRIs Versus Benzodiazepines for the Treatment of Anxiety		
	SSRI/SNRI	**Benzodiazepine**
Abuse potential	Unlikely	Possible, especially in former or current illicit drug users
Physical dependence	Serotonin discontinuation syndrome when withdrawal is abrupt	Physiological withdrawal symptoms with abrupt discontinuation
Efficacy	Effective for all types of anxiety; approximately 1/3 of patients are unresponsive	Not effective for OCD; most patients responsive
Response time	2–4 weeks (8–10 weeks for OCD)	Immediate

SOURCE: © Cengage Learning 2014.

generalized anxiety disorder. Unlike benzodiazepines, buspirone neither exhibits abuse potential nor potentiates the effects of depressant drugs (DeMartinis, Rynn, Rickels, & Mandos, 2000; van Vliet, den Boer, Westenberg, & Pian, 1997). Similar to SSRI and SNRIs, buspirone takes several weeks to become effective.

✏ *Drug Profile:* buspirone	
Trade name	BuSpar
Properties	Serves as a partial agonist for 5-HT_{1A} receptors
Uses	Treatment of anxiety disorders

Absorption issues have also limit the bioavailability of buspirone. Buspirone rapidly breaks down in the stomach by CYP-3A4 enzymes, reducing the amount of buspirone for absorption by up 90 percent (Sakr & Andheria, 2013). This has led to as little as 4 percent of the drug available for reaching the brain (Gannu et al., 2009). To address this limitation, researchers have developed extended release tablets, which appear to improve clinical efficacy likely by providing greater protection of buspirone from stomach enzymes (Sakr & Andheria, 2013). Studies continue to develop improved methods of extended release tablets for buspirone as well as other delivery methods, such as intranasal administration, to improve the bioavailability of buspirone (Kassem, ElMeshad, & Fares, 2014; Khan, Patil, Yeole, & Gaikwad, 2009).

STOP & CHECK

1. Antidepressant drugs such as SSRI and SNRIs have become first-line treatments for _____.

2. Unlike the response time for other anxiety disorders, the response time for _____ often ranges from 10 to 12 weeks.

3. Although effective for anxiety in animal models, poor _____ of buspirone in humans severely limits its clinical uses.

1. anxiety disorders 2. OCD 3. bioavailability

From Actions to Effects: How Do Antidepressant Drugs Reduce Anxiety?

As presented in Chapter 13, a key pharmacological action of most antidepressant drugs consists of increased concentrations of serotonin. These concentrations increase during chronic administration of antidepressant drugs. Given that a delayed response to antidepressant drugs occurs for both the treatment of depression and the treatment of anxiety, researchers have focused on potential mechanisms that may lead to greater increases in serotonin concentrations over the course chronic administration. These mechanisms include serotonin transporters, 5-HT_{1A} receptors, and α_2 heteroceptors as shown in **Figure 14.10**.

Figure 14.10 labels these processes occurring in an arrangement of serotonin and norepinephrine neurons. First, we find that an SSRI (as well as a SNRI) blocks serotonin membrane transporters, preventing reuptake of serotonin and therefore increasing levels of serotonin outside of the neuron. Yet these increases must be too low to achieve anxiolytic and antidepressants effects if a drug is only given acutely. Second, we also note a SNRI will also inhibit reuptake of norepinephrine through norepinephrine membrane transporters. We can find some norepinephrine axon terminals near serotonin synapses; in this way, released norepinephrine can bind to α_2 heteroceptors located on serotonin axon terminals.

Third, evidence suggests that postsynaptic 5-HT_{1A} receptors serve a critical function for serotonin's effects on anxiety. We find postsynaptic 5-HT_{1A} receptors in the cerebral cortex, hippocampus, hypothalamus, and amygdala (Aznar, Qian, Shah, Rahbek, & Knudsen, 2003). 5-HT_{1A} receptor knock-out mice exhibit greater levels of anxiety compared to normal mice (Gross, Santarelli, Brunner, Zhuang, & Hen, 2000; Olivier et al., 2001). In rats, direct injection of the 5-HT_{1A} receptor partial agonist 8-OH-DPAT into the amygdala decreases anxiety in an **elevated plus maze** (Zangrossi, Viana, & Graeff, 1999). Box 14.2 describes the elevated plus maze procedure and other models used for screening treatments for anxiety. Prolonged activation of postsynaptic 5-HT_{1A} receptors causes *sensitization* of these receptors. Sensitized postsynaptic 5-HT_{1A} receptors may enhance serotonin's inhibitory effects on those neurons and ultimately reduce activity in those structures, thereby producing anxiolytic effects. Activation of inhibitory postsynaptic 5-HT_{2A} receptors in these structures may serve a similar role.

Elevated plus maze Anxiety model consisting of a two arms with walls and two arms without wall connected in the shape of a plus symbol elevated above the ground; anxiety is shown when animals avoid the open arms

FIGURE 14.10 ● SSRIs and SNRIs produce desensitization at presynaptic 5-HT$_{1A}$ autorreceptors on serotonin (5-HT) neurons, and SNRIs also produce desensitization of presynaptic α_2 adrenoceptors (acting as heteroceptors) on serotonin axon terminals. Desensitization, in turn, enhances the release of 5-HT, possibly accounting for the effects of SSRIs and SNRIs on anxiety.

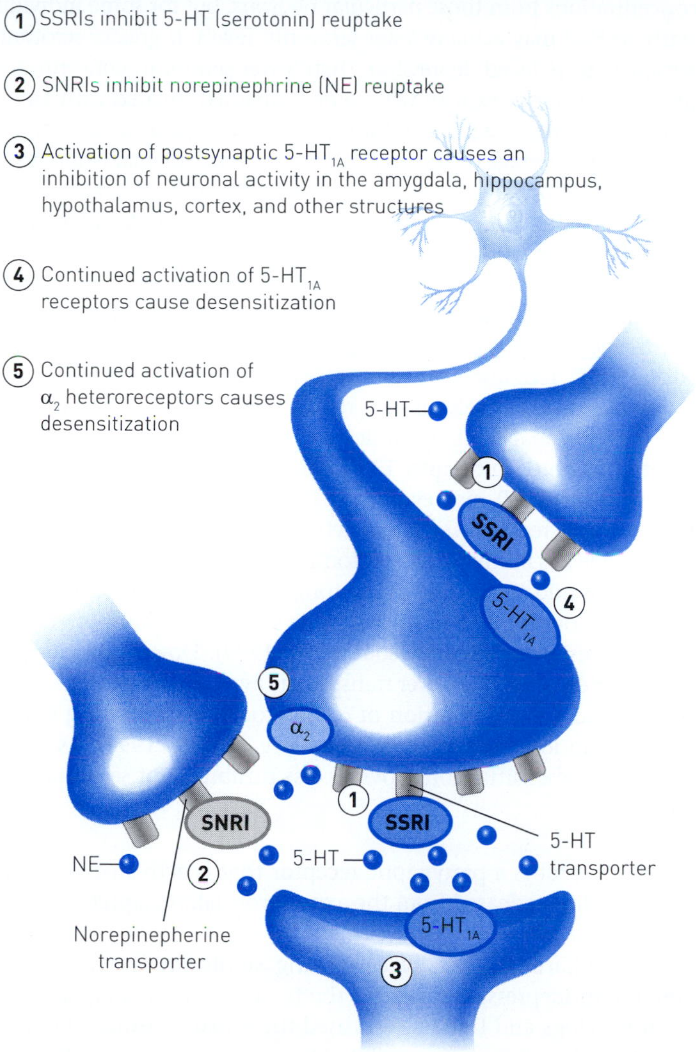

1 SSRIs inhibit 5-HT (serotonin) reuptake
2 SNRIs inhibit norepinephrine (NE) reuptake
3 Activation of postsynaptic 5-HT$_{1A}$ receptor causes an inhibition of neuronal activity in the amygdala, hippocampus, hypothalamus, cortex, and other structures
4 Continued activation of 5-HT$_{1A}$ receptors cause desensitization
5 Continued activation of α_2 heteroreceptors causes desensitization
5-HT
1
SSRI
5-HT$_{1A}$
4
5
α_2
1
SNRI
SSRI
NE
2
5-HT
5-HT transporter
Norepinepherine transporter
5-HT$_{1A}$
3

SOURCE: © Cengage Learning 2014.

Fourth, to understand why serotonin levels may not be high enough to achieve therapeutic effects, we can look to both presynaptic 5-HT$_{1A}$ receptors and α_2 heteroceptors. We find 5-HT$_{1A}$ receptors located presynaptically on serotonin neurons and acting as autoreceptors, serving to inhibit serotonin release from the neuron. Rather than finding these receptors at the axon terminal, we instead find them on the somas and dendrites of serotonin neurons. Thus, we refer to these types of receptors as *somatodendritic autoreceptors*. During acute administration, increased serotonin concentrations activate somatodendritic 5-HT$_{1A}$ receptors, causing inhibition of serotonin neurons these receptors are found on. Not only does this diminish the ability of SSRIs (and SNRIs) to increase serotonin concentrations from those particular neurons, but for some individuals, initial treatment with an SSRI may actually *lower* serotonin levels. If greater serotonin concentrations associate with reduced depression, then lower serotonin concentrations should *increase* depression. This may explain why some individuals treated with antidepressants for depression become *more* depressed during the early days of treatment. As noted in Chapter 13, a small percentage of adolescents may become suicidal when first beginning treatment with an SSRI or SNRI. 5-HT$_{1A}$ receptors levels, in particular, have been investigated using PET imaging among those with major depressive disorder who attempted suicide compared to those who did not. 5-HT$_{1A}$ receptors were higher in brainstem raphe nuclei, a structure where somatodendritic 5-HT$_{1A}$ receptors are found, among suicide attempters compared to non-suicide attempters (Sullivan et al., 2015). Connecting these findings with the actions of somatodendritic 5-HT$_{1A}$ receptors described earlier, greater somatodendritic 5-HT$_{1A}$ receptor levels may cause greater inhibition of serotonin neurons, and lead to lower serotonin levels. In fact, researchers also find lower serotonin metabolite levels in cerebrospinal fluid, an indicated of lower serotonin production, among suicide attempters, as noted in Chapter 13. Continuing the fourth point, chronic administration of an SSRI (or SNRI) may eventually cause desensitization of somatodendritic 5-HT$_{1A}$ receptors due to reduced G-protein activity (Hensler, 2002). Desensitized 5-HT$_{1A}$ autoreceptors provide less inhibition of serotonin neurons, thereby increasing the activity of serotonin neurons and the release of serotonin (Blier & Abbott, 2001). Contributing to these effects is a downregulation of serotonin membrane transporters also resulting from chronic administration (Benmansour et al., 1999). Downregulation of serotonin membrane transporters leads to a fewer transporters available for reuptake of serotonin.

Fifth, we also find a desensitization of α_2 heteroceptors occurring over the course of chronic administration (Mongeau, de Montigny, & Blier, 1994). As these receptors are inhibitory, their desensitization provides less inhibition of serotonin release from serotonin neurons.

Review! A heteroceptor is a presynaptic receptor that is activated by neurotransmitters different from those released from the axon terminal. (Chapter 3.)

Given all this, pharmacologically enhancing serotonin levels may shorten the response time for antidepressant drugs for the treatment of anxiety as well as depression. For example, Hogg and Dalvi (2004) used the schedule-induced polydipsia paradigm (a model used for screening anxiolytic drugs) to evaluate the effects of repeated administration with the SSRI fluoxetine to reduce water intake over the course of 6 days of administration in rats (**Figure 14.11**). Adding the 5-HT$_{1A}$ receptor antagonist WAY100635 (WAY) with fluoxetine treatment significantly reduced the number of

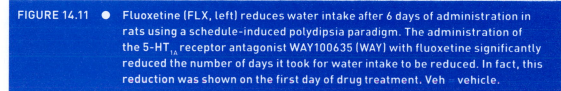

FIGURE 14.11 ● Fluoxetine (FLX, left) reduces water intake after 6 days of administration in rats using a schedule-induced polydipsia paradigm. The administration of the 5-HT$_{1A}$ receptor antagonist WAY100635 (WAY) with fluoxetine significantly reduced the number of days it took for water intake to be reduced. In fact, this reduction was shown on the first day of drug treatment. Veh = vehicle.

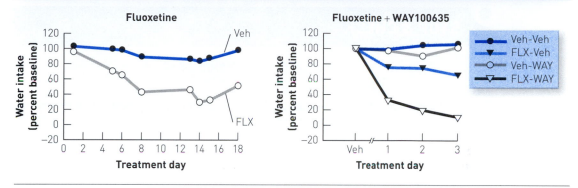

SOURCE: Hogg & Dalvi, 2004. Reprinted with permission.

days it took for water intake to be reduced (an anxiolytic effect). In fact, this reduction was shown on the first day of drug treatment.

We find a similar result reported by Prus and colleagues (2015), who tested an α_2 adrenoceptor antagonist using the schedule-induced polydipsia paradigm. In this study, the α_2 adrenoceptor antagonist yohimbine increased the suppression of drinking produced by fluoxetine. The researchers concluded that antagonism of α_2 adrenoceptors may have prevented inhibition of serotonin release, thereby causing an increase in serotonin levels. In human patients with major depressive disorder, treatment with yohimbine also has shortened the time needed for antidepressant effects to occur (Sanacora et al., 2004).

Fifth, postsynaptic receptors for norepinephrine may also contribute to reductions in anxiety. Norepinephrine neurons from the locus coeruleus elicit sympathetic nervous activity that, as described earlier, may account for the physiological effects of fear, anxiety, and acute stress. Norepinephrine neurons from the locus coeruleus also project to the amygdala, and the activation of postsynaptic norepinephrine β_1 adrenoceptors in the amygdala enhances anxiety. Again, the ability of SNRIs, which increase norepinephrine levels, to treat anxiety seems counterintuitive. But, just as desensitization of 5-HT$_{1A}$ autoreceptors ultimately facilitates reductions in anxiety, so do does desensitization of β_1 adrenoceptors. Eventually, fewer active β_1 adrenoceptors result in a weaker activation of the amygdala, and subsequently, a reduction in anxiety (Duncan et al., 1989; Ordway et al., 1991).

As a final note, while 5-HT$_{1A}$ receptors might be implicated in the effects of antidepressant drugs for the treatment of anxiety, we must also keep in mind human genetic studies showing links between reduced serotonin membrane transporter functioning (the short allele discussed earlier in this chapter) and anxiety traits. Based on what we find from the pharmacological model for anxiolytic effects discussed in this section, one would expect *reduced* anxiety for those with reduced serotonin transporter function, since less reuptake should mean greater serotonin levels. Yet genetic studies in mice lacking serotonin transporters suggests this is not the case. In serotonin transporter null mice, the activity of serotonin neurons appears to be diminished, despite these mice having lower levels of somatodendritic 5-HT$_{1A}$ receptors, which should mean less inhibition of serotonin neurons (Fabre et al., 2000; Gobbi, Murphy, Lesch, & Blier, 2001). Findings such as these remind us that models to help explain the pharmacological actions drugs may be different from mechanisms mediating the actual disorder.

STOP & CHECK

1. Long-term administration with an SSRI or SNRI can desensitize 5-HT$_{1A}$ receptors, resulting in a(n) _____ in serotonin levels.

2. Long-term administration of an SNRI can desensitize α_2 heteroceptors on serotonin neurons, resulting in a(n) _____ in serotonin levels.

3. Long-term administration of a SNRI can desensitize β_1 adrenoceptors in the amygdala, resulting in a(n) _____ in anxiety.

1. increase 2. increase 3. decrease

Chapter Summary

Anxiety disorders, which include specific phobias, panic disorder, agoraphobia, social anxiety disorder, and generalized anxiety disorder, and related disorders, including PTSD and OCD, are highly prevalent. The amygdala plays an important role in anxiety disorders. Other limbic system structures, including the hippocampus and cingulate cortex, might also play a role in anxiety disorders as demonstrated in studies using fear conditioning. The hypothalamic-pituitary-adrenal (HPA) axis mediates the feelings associated with panic attacks and mediates the body's response to long-term stress. Sustained stress leads to activation of the HPA axis and increased levels of cortisol, the body's stress hormone. Drugs effective for anxiety include anxiolytic drugs, antidepressant drugs, and 5-HT$_{1A}$ receptor agonists. Barbiturates, the first anxiolytic drugs, caused CNS depressant effects, carried a risk for respiratory failure, and had a high abuse liability. Barbiturates facilitated the effects of the inhibitory neurotransmitter GABA by

binding to barbiturate sites on GABA$_A$ receptors. Benzodiazepines replaced barbiturates for the treatment of anxiety and are still used today. Benzodiazepines also are CNS depressants, but carry less risk of respiratory suppression and have a lower risk of abuse. Benzodiazepines facilitate the effects of GABA through binding to either BZ I or BZ II sites on GABA$_A$ receptors. Z-drugs, which include sleep-aids, function primarily by binding to BZ I sites on GABA$_A$ receptors, making them effective for sleep but not for treating anxiety.

Antidepressant drugs have become the first-line treatments for anxiety disorders largely because of their efficacy and low abuse liability. The 5-HT$_{1A}$ receptor agonist buspirone has shown promise in many animal studies; clinically, however, bioavailability issues limit its therapeutic effects. The desensitization of somatodendritic 5-HT$_{1A}$ autoreceptors play an important role in anxiety and may be important for the efficacy of SSRIs and SNRIs for the treatment of anxiety.

Key Terms

Fear 436
Anxiety 436
Specific phobias 436
Panic disorder 437
Panic attacks 437
Agoraphobia 437
Social anxiety disorder 437
Generalized anxiety
 disorder 437
Obsessive–compulsive
 disorder 437
Post-traumatic stress
 disorder (PTSD) 437

Early immediate gene 441
General adaptation
 syndrome 450
Cortisol 451
Hypothalamic–pituitary–
 adrenal axis 451
Anxiolytic drugs 454
Barbiturate abstinence
 syndrome 456
Sedative-hypnotic 456
Benzodiazepine withdrawal
 syndrome 460
$GABA_A$ receptor 462

BZ I site 462
BZ II site 462
Endozepines 462
Gliotransmitters 463
Z-drugs 464
Sleep-related complex
 behaviors 465
Elevated plus maze 468

Visit the Student Study Site at **study.sagepub.com/prus2e** to access additional study tools, including eFlashcards, web quizzes, video resources, web resources, SAGE journal articles, and more.

Antipsychotic Drugs

KRAEPELIN'S INFLUENCE IN DISTINGUISHING NEUROLOGICAL FROM MENTAL DISORDERS

As the chair of psychiatry at the University of Munich from 1903 to 1922, Emil Kraepelin worked with his colleagues in researching mental deterioration. From studying patients in the hospital ward, Kraepelin determined that major distinctions existed for dementia occurring in the young compared to the elderly. One of Kraepelin's colleagues, Alois Alzheimer, revealed that dementia in many elderly patients corresponded to degeneration of the cerebral cortex, hippocampus, and other parts of the brain. However, dementia occurring in young adults, which Kraepelin described as *dementia praecox*—and which was later named *schizophrenia*—appeared to reveal no neuro-anatomical signs of decline. In his textbooks on psychiatric disorders, Kraepelin categorized all mental disorders stemming from a clear biological cause (e.g., the later-named Alzheimer's disease) as *neurological disorders* while categorizing those without clear biological causes as *psychiatric disorders* (e.g., dementia praecox). This distinction, among other important works on the classification of mental disorders, played a foundational role in the creation of the American Psychiatric Association's *Diagnostic and Statistical Manual of Mental Disorders* (DSM), beginning with the third edition, as well as the International Classification of Diseases, the two primary classification systems for mental disorders used today.

SOURCE: Shorter, 1997, and Hippius and Müller, 2008.

Schizophrenia

Schizophrenia is a severe, lifelong mental illness consisting of disturbed thinking, abnormal behavior, an inability to understand what is real, and impaired processing of emotions. The symptoms of schizophrenia consist of either **positive symptoms** or **negative symptoms**. The terms *positive* and *negative* refer to the presence of abnormal behaviors or the reduction in normal behaviors, respectively. Examples of positive symptoms include hallucinations, delusions, and thoughts of persecution, whereas negative symptoms include reduced emotional responsiveness, social withdrawal, reduced movement, and lack of motivation.

The DSM-5 includes schizophrenia in the category "Schizophrenia Spectrum and Other Psychotic Disorders," which overall refers to disorders defined by delusions, hallucinations, disorganized speech and thinking, disorganized behavior, abnormal motor behavior, and/or negative symptoms (American Psychiatric Association, 2013a). Schizophrenia consists of the most severe of these disorders and has at least two of the features listed in this category (with at least consisting of delusions, hallucinations, or disorganized speech and thinking). The symptoms expressed must be highly disruptive for a period of at least 6 months.

Past versions of the DSM described five types of schizophrenia: (1) a *paranoid* type characterized by prominent positive symptoms; (2) a *catatonic* type characterized by predominantly negative symptoms, including immobility; (3) a *disorganized* type characterized by disorganized behaviors and silly or immature emotional expression; (4) an *undifferentiated* type that does not appropriately fit these other categories; and (5) a *residual* type for patients who now exhibit less prominent symptoms of schizophrenia, but did so in the past. Those who wrote the DSM-5 removed these distinctions because they believed that defining subtypes did not add value to making an overall schizophrenia diagnosis (American Psychiatric Association, 2013b).

Schizophrenia
Severe, lifelong mental illness consisting of disturbed thinking, abnormal behavior, an inability to understand what is real, and impaired processing of emotions

Positive symptoms
Addition of abnormal behaviors such as hallucinations, delusions, and thoughts of persecution in schizophrenia

Negative symptoms
Reduction of normal behaviors such as reduced emotional responsiveness, social withdrawal, reduced movement, and lack of motivation in schizophrenia

Longitudinal studies find that 50–70 percent of individuals diagnosed with schizophrenia exhibit chronic symptoms; the remaining 30–50 percent of patients tend to exhibit residual features of schizophrenia (Bota, Munro, Nguyen, & Preda, 2011). Moreover, we find that approximately one-third of those with schizophrenia qualify as treatment-resistant patients. Those defined as having **treatment resistant schizophrenia** exhibit no or minimal improvements after two trials with either a typical or an atypical antipsychotic drug, two types of antipsychotic drugs described later in this chapter.

For patients with catatonic schizophrenia who do not respond to antipsychotic medication, physicians may prescribe benzodiazepines, which tend to show some efficacy for reducing catatonia (Ungvari, Kau, Wai-Kwong, & Shing, 2001). In addition to schizophrenia, other disorders in which catatonia may occur include depression, alcohol withdrawal, and acquired immunodeficiency syndrome (most often referred to as AIDS; occurs from infection by the human immunodeficiency virus, HIV) (Geoffroy, Rolland, & Cottencin, 2012; Starkstein et al., 1996; Volkow, Harper, Munnisteri, & Clother, 1987). AIDS can lead to inflammation in the brain, which in turn can cause a number of behavioral, cognitive, and physiological effects. In fact, those with AIDS can exhibit psychotic symptoms, which may be treated by antipsychotic medications (Lera & Zirulnik, 1999). In a study examining treatments for catatonia, Ungvari, Leung, Wong, and Lau (1994) evaluated the effects of either the benzodiazepines lorazepam or diazepam in 18 patients found with catatonia. Some of the patients had catatonic schizophrenia, while other patients exhibited catatonia from depression, bipolar depression, or other mental disorders. In all but two of the patients, 2 days of benzodiazepine treatment led to reductions in catatonia.

Although clinicians diagnose schizophrenia based on the presence of positive and negative symptoms, researchers find striking and consistent impairments in cognitive functioning (Silver, Feldman, Bilker, & Gur, 2003). Nearly all individuals with schizophrenia have moderate to severe deficits in cognitive functioning, including working memory, reference memory, attention, and executive functioning, compared to the general population (Green, Kern, & Heaton, 2004; Keefe & Fenton, 2007; Wilk et al., 2004) (see **Figure 15.1**). Cognitive impairment may be present before the first episode of schizophrenia (Keefe & Fenton, 2007). Researchers find that cognitive impairment contributes to poor functional outcomes. **Functional outcomes** consist of a patient's inclusion into a community, behaving normally in social situations, and successfully employing psychosocial skills. Examples of functional outcomes in schizophrenia include employability, ability to conduct daily living activities, and the ability to form friendships (Green, 1996; Green, Kern, Braff, & Mintz, 2000).

Many patients with schizophrenia demonstrate a **sensory-gating deficit** that is characterized by a diminished capacity to filter out unimportant stimuli in their environment. Attendance to these unimportant stimuli may lead to misperceptions of their environment, possibly facilitating delusional behavior (Adler et al., 1998). Researchers assess sensory-gating deficits in schizophrenia by using a prepulse inhibition procedure as described in **Box 15.1**.

Treatment-resistant schizophrenia Patients with schizophrenia who exhibit minimal or no improvements after two trials with either typical or atypical antipsychotic drugs

Functional outcomes (schizophrenia) A patient's inclusion into a community, behaving normally in social situations, and successfully employing psychosocial skills

Sensory-gating deficit A schizophrenic's diminished capacity to filter out unimportant stimuli in his or her environment

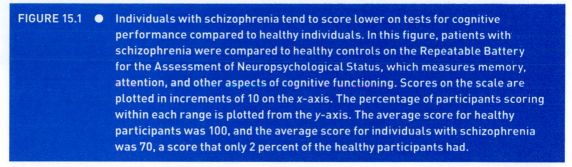

FIGURE 15.1 ● Individuals with schizophrenia tend to score lower on tests for cognitive performance compared to healthy individuals. In this figure, patients with schizophrenia were compared to healthy controls on the Repeatable Battery for the Assessment of Neuropsychological Status, which measures memory, attention, and other aspects of cognitive functioning. Scores on the scale are plotted in increments of 10 on the *x*-axis. The percentage of participants scoring within each range is plotted from the *y*-axis. The average score for healthy participants was 100, and the average score for individuals with schizophrenia was 70, a score that only 2 percent of the healthy participants had.

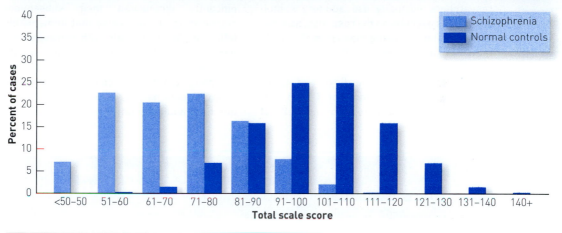

SOURCE: Keefe, R. S., & Fenton, W. S. (2007). How should DSM-5 criteria for schizophrenia include cognitive impairment? *Schizophr Bull*, *33*(4), 912–920. doi: sbm046 [pii] 10.1093/schbul/sbm046, p.8. By permission of Oxford University Press.

A theory known as cognitive dysmetria attempts to link facets of sensory processing with cognitive functioning and the manifestation of positive and negative symptoms. **Cognitive dysmetria** consists of abnormalities in processing, coordinating, and responding to information. As a result of cognitive dysmetria, one may perceive hallucinations, form delusions, exhibit odd or disorganized speech, incorrectly respond to emotional stimuli, have impaired attention, and exhibit other characteristics found in schizophrenia (Andreasen, Paradiso, & O-Leary, 1998).

A first diagnosis for schizophrenia is usually found in one's late teens or early 20s. We seldom find schizophrenia occurring before puberty or after age 40 (Lewis & Lieberman, 2000). Schizophrenia is relatively prominent among psychiatric disorders, affecting 1 percent of the world's population. This equates to approximately 3 million individuals in the United States (Regier et al., 1993). The prevalence of schizophrenia occurs equally in males and females, although males may develop this disorder 2–4 years earlier than females and exhibit more severe

Cognitive dysmetria
Abnormalities in processing, coordinating, and responding to information

BOX 15.1 PREPULSE INHIBITION

The prepulse inhibition procedure consists of determining one's ability to demonstrate a weaker reflexive response to a sudden stimulus after exposure to a weaker form of the stimulus immediately before. In humans, researchers normally use auditory stimuli and assess eyeblink as the response, as measured in intensity using measures of muscle movement around the eye.

For example, Braff, Swerdlow, and Geyer (1999) assessed the effects of a brief 112-decibel blast of white noise on intensity of eyeblink startle response (**Figure 1**). Then during selected trials, a quieter pulse of white noise occurred 40 milliseconds before the 112-decibel white noise. For those without schizophrenia, the preceded noise significantly diminished their subsequent startle to the louder noise that immediately followed. Yet individuals with schizophrenia had a significantly poorer reduction in startle response under these same circumstances. We infer from these findings that those with schizophrenia have a weaker ability to filter out these auditory stimuli.

FIGURE 1 ● **Individuals with schizophrenia demonstrated a diminished ability to inhibit a startle response compared to normal controls in a prepulse inhibition test.**

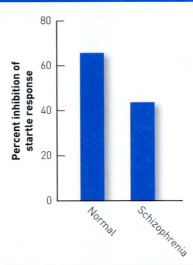

SOURCE: Data from Braff et al., 1999.

symptoms. A modestly increased prevalence of schizophrenia occurs in northern geographic regions and for individuals born during winter months, the latter possibly related to winter diseases such as influenza (Davies, Welham, Chant, Torrey, & McGrath, 2003).

Schizophrenia provides a significant societal impact, with no more than 73 percent of individuals able to find any employment and only 14.5 percent of individuals finding competitive employment (Rosenheck et al., 2006). Depression rates among individuals with schizophrenia are high, with as many as 10 percent committing suicide each year (Caldwell & Gottesman, 1990; Miles, 1977; Pompili et al., 2007). In general, researchers find a 16–18-year shorter life span among those with schizophrenia compared to the general population (Laursen, 2011).

Schizophrenia clearly has a genetic basis, although this is not the only determining factor. In the general population, as noted above, we find a 1 percent rate of prevalence. This risk factor increases slightly to about 2–4 percent when there is a cousin, uncle or aunt, or nephew or niece with schizophrenia. However, having one parent with schizophrenia increases the risk to 13 percent and having both parents with schizophrenia increases the risk to about 50 percent. Having an identical twin with schizophrenia also provides a 50-percent chance of developing schizophrenia (**Figure 15.2**). The remaining risks for developing schizophrenia come from the environment, which may consist of responses to stress, life events, or other factors (Tsuang, 2000; van Os, Kenis, & Rutten, 2010).

In the years before a first diagnosis of schizophrenia, patients usually exhibit subtle, early signs of schizophrenia. These pre-schizophrenia signs are collectively referred to as the **prodromal phase of schizophrenia,** which is characterized by schizophrenia-like symptoms that occur less frequently and with less severity than the symptoms found in schizophrenia. These include, in particular, deficits in working memory, attention, sensory gating, and sociability. Of these, attention impairments appear most predictive of the prodromal phase. In addition to these behavioral and cognitive features, those identified with prodromal phase characteristics also exhibit reduced volume of cortical gray matter (Stone et al., 2009).

Prodromal phase of schizophrenia Schizophrenia-like symptoms that occur less frequently and with less severity than the symptoms found in schizophrenia

STOP & CHECK

1. Reduced emotional expression and social isolation are both examples of _____ symptoms of schizophrenia.

2. Although not considered part of the diagnosis criteria, impairments in _____ functioning are commonly found in patients with schizophrenia.

1. negative 2. cognitive

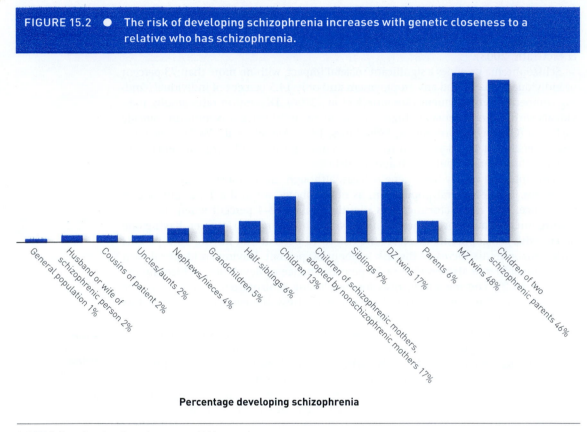

FIGURE 15.2 ● The risk of developing schizophrenia increases with genetic closeness to a relative who has schizophrenia.

Percentage developing schizophrenia

SOURCE: Based on data from Gottesman, 1991.

Schizophrenia's Complex Neurobiological Profile

Schizophrenia derives from a complexity of neurobiological traits, including genetic abnormalities, reduced volume of brain structures, and abnormal connectivity among brain structures (Lewis & Lieberman, 2000; Ross, Margolis, Reading, Pletnikov, & Coyle, 2006). Yet most of these characteristics remain to be fully understood (Ross et al., 2006).

Among the many genes studied for a risk of schizophrenia, we find perhaps the most evidence implicating the *disrupted in schizophrenia 1* (DISC1) gene (Hodgkinson et al., 2004; Roberts, 2007). Associations occur between abnormal DISC1 genes and occurrence of schizophrenia in Scottish and Finnish individuals (Ekelund et al., 2001; Millar et al., 2000). The DISC1 gene encodes for the DISC1 protein, which plays an important role in a cascade of signaling events that take place within neurons, as well as the development of neurons (Mao et al., 2009). In particular, DISC1 genes may affect cell migration, which can lead to architectural abnormalities in cellular networks (Wong & Van Tol, 2003).

Although monozygotic twins have, by definition, identical genetic makeups, epigenetic factors may explain why one twin may develop schizophrenia while the other twin does not. Castellani, Melka, Gui, O'Reilly, and Singh (2015) examined monozygotic twins among whom only one twin had schizophrenia. They found many instances of in the expression of genes of the twin with schizophrenia. These differences in expression were found for DISC1 as well as a host of other genes potentially implicated in schizophrenia (which are beyond the scope of this textbook to cover).

Review! Epigenetics is the study of mechanisms of gene expression not involving alterations to DNA sequences. (Chapter 2.)

Structural differences in schizophrenia may vary across patients as shown through inconsistent findings across neuroimaging studies. The most consistent observations suggest reduced volume sizes of structures in the left hemisphere and temporal lobe. Studies also find reduced volume of the frontal lobe, including the prefrontal cortex, and the thalamus in the left hemisphere, and reduced connectivity from the thalamus to the cerebellum (Byne, Hazlett, Buchsbaum, & Kemether, 2009; Ross et al., 2006). The cognitive dysmetria theory, in particular, refers to dysfunctions in connectivity between the thalamus and the cerebellum and the thalamus and cerebral cortex as contributing to abnormal sensory processing, timing functions, and error processing, which may lead to many of the symptoms and cognitive disturbances described earlier (Andreasen et al., 1998; Barch, 2014). Furthermore, imaging and postmortem studies tend to reveal a modest volume reduction of the hippocampus in both hemispheres (Lewis & Lieberman, 2000). Functional imaging studies also reveal abnormal levels of activity in the hippocampus during auditory hallucinations, memory tasks, and rest (Heckers, 2001).

Volume reductions may arise from altered circuitry within these structures. Postmortem studies find a possible disorganization of axons in cortical white matter (Akbarian et al., 1996; Arnold, Talbot, & Hahn, 2005). Individuals with schizophrenia also appear to have fewer projections from the thalamus going to the prefrontal cortex (Lewis & Lieberman, 2000). The result of these or other possible altered circuitry may cause differences in neurotransmission, which we consider in the context of antipsychotic drug actions later in this chapter.

Taken together, researchers see the many different abnormalities described above as support for the neurodevelopmental hypothesis for schizophrenia. The **neurodevelopmental hypothesis** for schizophrenia states that abnormal nervous system development leads to irregular neuronal signaling in the brain, resulting in the characteristics of schizophrenia (Weinberger, 1996). As Lewis and Lieberman (2000) describe, genetics causes alterations in neuronal growth and development, which likely impacts synaptogenesis and myelination, before and after birth. Recent studies, as noted earlier, indicate that epigenetic factors may be critical in the expression of genes leading to such potential abnormalities in

Neurodevelopmental hypothesis Hypothesis for schizophrenia stating that abnormal nervous system development leads to irregular neuronal signaling in the brain, resulting in the characteristics of schizophrenia

neuronal growth and development (Castellani et al., 2015). These abnormalities might eventually cause the prodromal phase of schizophrenia, as described earlier, during adolescence. The transition from a prodromal phase to the full onset of schizophrenia may later arise in reaction to environmental factors, such as involvement in prolonged stressful situations or using substances of abuse (**Figure 15.3**).

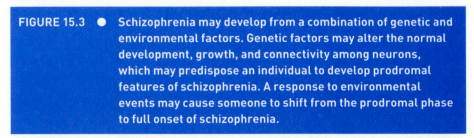

FIGURE 15.3 ● Schizophrenia may develop from a combination of genetic and environmental factors. Genetic factors may alter the normal development, growth, and connectivity among neurons, which may predispose an individual to develop prodromal features of schizophrenia. A response to environmental events may cause someone to shift from the prodromal phase to full onset of schizophrenia.

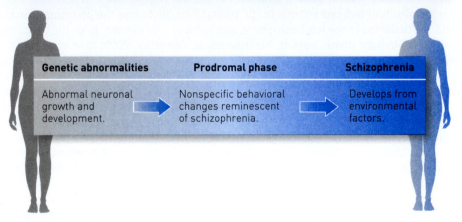

Genetic abnormalities	Prodromal phase	Schizophrenia
Abnormal neuronal growth and development.	Nonspecific behavioral changes reminiscent of schizophrenia.	Develops from environmental factors.

SOURCE: Adapted from Lewis and Lieberman, 2000.

A Brief History of Schizophrenia and Its Treatment

Stories of madness have been documented throughout human history, but the first clinical diagnosis for schizophrenia was made only in 1871 by Ewald Hecker in Görlitz, Germany. Hecker gave several psychotic young patients a diagnosis of *hebephrenia*, a term coined by his clinical director, Karl Kahlbaum. In 1893, Kraepelin first named this disorder *dementia praecox*, noting the striking cognitive decline by relatively young individuals, particularly compared to dementias he studied in the elderly. Some years later, in 1911, Dr. Eugen Bleuler coined the term *schizophrenia* because of what he saw as a "splitting of psychic functions" in this disorder and a consistent lack of increasing cognitive decline like that seen in Alzheimer's disease (Shorter, 1997). Lacking a clear biological cause coupled with the rise of psychoanalysis in psychiatry, we the psychiatric community in the early to mid-20th century were seeking causes of schizophrenia in one's upbringing. One of most notorious of these now-abandoned notions was the *schizophrenogenic mother* concept—that is, bad mothering causes schizophrenia (Hartwell, 1996; Neill, 1990).

Early attempts to treat schizophrenia appear cruel by today's standards. During the early 20th century, psychiatric staff often employed confinement methods as purported treatments, which often included the use of an isolation cell or straitjacket. Staff members also restrained patients in ice baths for hours or days at a time. Some psychiatrists induced fevers in their patients, which resulted in a temporary abatement of symptoms afterward. By the 1930s, convulsive shock therapies, using either insulin or electricity, sometimes offered real gains in symptom remission, although only temporarily and with significant risk to the patient (Shorter, 1997).

Also during this time, the first of a series of techniques, collectively referred to as *frontal lobotomies*, began to be offered as a long-lasting treatment for schizophrenia, although they provided no symptom improvements and were made at great cost to the patient's health, assuming the patient even survived the procedure (Freeman & Watts, 1945; Shorter, 1997). There were several different ways developed to produce frontal lobotomies, but all of these methods involved penetrating the frontal lobe with an instrument, often simply a rod, and then moving the instrument around to destroy brain tissue. The result was often described as a state of drowsiness and disorientation. There also was significant risk of death from these procedures from hemorrhaging in the brain. Dr. Walter Freeman is most noted for promoting frontal lobotomy techniques for treating schizophrenia, and he is particularly known for the *transorbital leucotomy*. The first procedures involved the use of ordinary ice picks, thus leading to so-called icepick lobotomies (**Figure 15.4**). During this procedure, Freeman punched the instrument up into the frontal lobe through the inner corner of the eye socket. He then moved it around within the frontal lobe to destroy brain tissue (Kucharski, 1984; Shorter, 1997).

Some years later, in 1952, Dr. Henri Laborit administered a preanesthetic agent called *chlorpromazine* to manic patients at St. Anne's Hospital in Paris in hopes that it might calm his patients. He indeed found them calmer, yet he also noticed an abatement of symptoms among those with psychosis as well. The efficacy of chlorpromazine specifically for schizophrenia was soon studied by Drs. Jean Delay, Pierre Deniker, and Jean-Marie Harl, who published their findings on the effects of chlorpromazine in psychotic patients in that same year (Delay, Deniker, & Harl, 1952). Without question this discovery revolutionized the treatment for mental illnesses and might very well have led to a Nobel Prize for its discoverers. Yet a bitter dispute erupted between those claiming to have made the discovery first—Laborit claimed first to find a reduction psychosis while Delay and Deniker claimed first to formally study it. In fact, between Delay and Deniker, Deniker was widely recognized as the clinician evaluating chlorpromazine's antipsychotic effects. We find this demonstrated when the Lasker Prize for Clinical Medical Research—often considered the prelude to the Nobel Prize—was given to Laborit and Deniker in 1957, excluding Delay. We do not find Jean-Marie

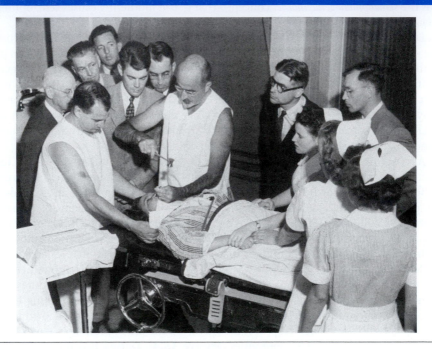

SOURCE: Getty Images/Bettmann.

Harl mentioned in these disputes because he was primarily a trainee at the time, but also because he died soon after from a climbing accident (science prizes tend not to be given posthumously). Unfortunately, as a clinical trainee, Harl likely did most of the study's clinical work (Healy, 2002).

Yet neither Laborit nor Deniker received a Nobel Prize. We're left to speculate a bit why this might be. Edward Kunz (2014), who knew and collaborated with Laborit on unrelated projects, suggested that French clinicians disagreed with Laborit's various medical theories and helped to dissuade the nominating committee from granting Laborit a Nobel Prize. Adding to this, according to Healy (2002), Delay served on the Nobel Prize nominating committee and likely sought to prevent awarding the prize to Laborit. If Laborit were not to get it, then it's unlikely that they would have given the prize to Deniker instead, whom the Lasker Prize committee had considered a co-discoverer.

Chlorpromazine and therapeutically similar drugs that followed revolutionized the treatment of schizophrenia. Of the procedures predating the antipsychotic drugs, only electroconvulsive shock therapy remains, although it is a substantially improved version compared to the 1930s and 1940s and is used as a last resort for those patients who fail to improve with antipsychotic drug treatment (Chanpattana & Sackeim, 2010).

Neurotransmission Hypotheses for Schizophrenia

Most theories concerning the neuropathology of schizophrenia consider abnormalities in dopamine and glutamate neurotransmission. Much of what we know about these irregularities comes from studying the actions of antipsychotic drugs and experimentally inducing temporary psychotic states in healthy human volunteers with dopaminergic and glutamatergic drugs.

The first well-established hypothesis for schizophrenia is the **dopamine hypothesis**, which states that positive symptoms arise from excessive dopamine release in the limbic

Dopamine hypothesis (for schizophrenia) Hypothesis for schizophrenia stating that positive symptoms arise from excessive dopamine release in the limbic system

FIGURE 15.5 ● According to the dopamine hypothesis for schizophrenia, increased dopamine release from mesolimbic dopamine neurons causes the positive symptoms of schizophrenia. Mesolimbic dopamine neurons terminate in structures of the limbic system such as the nucleus accumbens shown here.

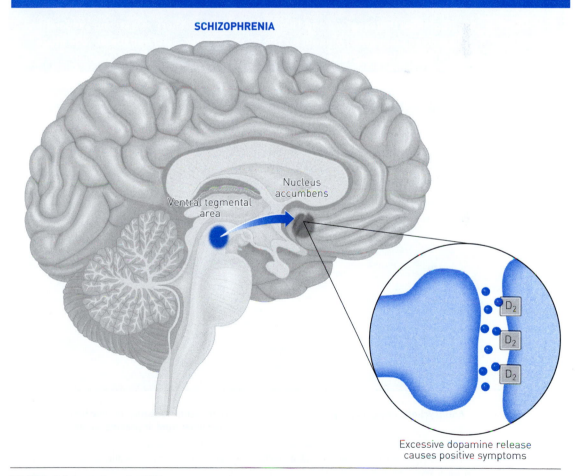

SCHIZOPHRENIA

Nucleus accumbens

Ventral tegmental area

Excessive dopamine release causes positive symptoms

SOURCE: © Cengage Learning 2014.

system (Meltzer & Stahl, 1976) (**Figure 15.5**). The hypothesis derives from the discovery that antipsychotic drugs act as antagonists for D_2 receptors and that amphetamine, through increasing dopamine release, causes psychotic symptoms (Seeman & Lee, 1975; Wallis, McHarg, & Scott, 1949). As shown in **Figure 15.6**, antipsychotic drug doses effective for schizophrenia correlate highly to their strength of binding to D_2 receptors (Seeman, 2005; Seeman & Lee, 1975).

Although we still find the dopamine hypothesis useful for understanding antipsychotic drug actions, we also find glutamate dysregulated in schizophrenia. According to the **glutamate hypothesis** for schizophrenia, diminished levels of glutamate release throughout the cerebral cortex and limbic system may lead to the symptoms of schizophrenia (Paz, Tardito, Atzori, & Tseng, 2008; Sesack, Carr, Omelchenko, & Pinto, 2003). Support for this hypothesis comes from human drug overdose cases and experimental studies with the dissociative anesthetics phencyclidine and ketamine

Glutamate hypothesis (for schizophrenia)
Hypothesis for schizophrenia stating that diminished levels of glutamate release throughout the cerebral cortex and limbic system may lead to the symptoms of schizophrenia

FIGURE 15.6 ● Dopamine D_2 Receptors and Therapeutic Efficacy. There is a strong association between strength of binding for the D2 receptor (y-axis) and the dosage of an antipsychotic drug necessary to produce antipsychotic effects (x-axis).

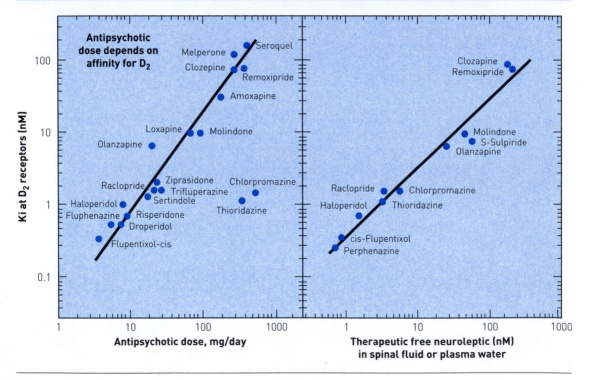

SOURCE: Adapted by permission from Macmillan Publishers Ltd: "Antipsychotic drug doses and neuroleptic/dopamine receptors," by P. Seeman, T. Lee, M. Chau-Wong, and K. Wong, *Nature*, 261, 1976, pp. 717–719.

(Jacob, Carlen, Marshman, & Sellers, 1981; Krystal et al., 1994). An appealing feature of this hypothesis is that ketamine and phencyclidine cause users to exhibit behaviors similar to negative symptoms and cognitive impairment, as well as positive symptoms, in schizophrenia. We show how the glutamate and dopamine hypotheses can be integrated in complementary ways in the "From Actions to Effects" section at the end of this chapter.

Review! The dissociative anesthetic drugs ketamine and phencyclidine function as antagonists for glutamate NMDA receptors. (Chapter 12.).

STOP & CHECK

1. The first antipsychotic drug was _____, which Laborit first provided to manic patients, and Delay, Deniker, and Harl formally evaluated in patients with schizophrenia.

2. The hypothesis for positive symptoms in schizophrenia states elevated concentrations of _____ are found in the limbic system.

1. chlorpromazine 2. dopamine

Typical and Atypical Antipsychotic Drugs

We divide the wide variety of antipsychotic drugs into two broad categories: typical antipsychotic drugs and atypical antipsychotic drugs (**Table 15.1**). However, many different names are used to describe these categories. Researchers and clinicians may instead refer to typical antipsychotic drugs as *first-generation* or *classical* antipsychotic drugs. We also find the term *neuroleptic* synonymous with a typical antipsychotic drug, although many people misapply this term to describe all types of antipsychotic drugs. Atypical antipsychotic drugs may be called *second-generation* or *novel* antipsychotic drugs. Finally, some researchers describe a third class of antipsychotic drugs, generally referred to as *third-generation* antipsychotic drugs, to describe newer agents that may differ pharmacologically from drugs in these other categories (Meltzer, 2002). This chapter will first describe the development and pharmacology of typical antipsychotic drugs and then those of atypical antipsychotic drugs. Finally, it follows with a discussion about possible third-generation antipsychotic drugs.

Typical Antipsychotic Drugs: The First Medications for Schizophrenia

As noted previously, the first of the typical antipsychotic drugs was chlorpromazine. A number of chlorpromazine-like drugs followed, including the typical antipsychotic

TABLE 15.1 ● Selected Antipsychotic Drugs	
Typical Antipsychotic Drugs	**Atypical Antipsychotic Drugs**
Chlorpromazine (Thorazine)	Amisulpride (Solian)
Droperidol (Inapsine)	Aripiprazole (Abilify)*
Fluphenazine (Prolixin)	Asenapine (Saphris)
Haloperidol (Haldol)	Cariprazine (Vraylar)
Loxapine (Loxitane)	Clozapine (Clozaril)
Molindone (Moban)	Iloperidone (Fanapt)
Perazine (Taxilan)	Lurasidone (Latuda)
Perphenazine (Trilafon)	Olanzapine (Zyprexa)
Pimozide (Orap)	Paliperidone (Invega)
Prochlorperazine (Compazine)	Quetiapine (Seroquel)
Thiothixene (Navane)	Risperidone (Risperdal)
Thioridazine (Mellaril)	Ziprasidone (Geodon)
Trifluoperazine (Stelazine)	

*Sometimes referred to as a "third-generation" antipsychotic drug.

Typical antipsychotic drugs (or first-generation or classical antipsychotic drugs) Class of antipsychotic drugs that reduce the positive symptoms of schizophrenia, have weak efficacy for negative symptoms and cognitive impairment, and produce extrapyramidal side effects at therapeutic doses

Extrapyramidal side effects (EPS) Adverse effects consisting of tremor, muscle rigidity, and involuntary movements associated with antipsychotic drugs

haloperidol, a butyrophenone compound synthesized in 1958. As a class, **typical antipsychotic drugs** reduce the positive symptoms of schizophrenia, have weak efficacy for negative symptoms and cognitive impairment, and produce extrapyramidal side effects at therapeutic doses (**Table 15.2**). The pharmacological actions of antipsychotic drugs derive from antagonism of dopamine D_2 receptors. Typical antipsychotic drugs may require as long as 6–8 weeks to produce full efficacy (Agid, Kapur, Arenovich, & Zipursky, 2003; Emsley, Rabinowitz, & Medori, 2006).

Figure 15.7 shows these actions using the dopamine hypothesis of schizophrenia. As previously noted, this hypothesis consists of elevated levels of dopamine and its subsequent activation of dopamine D_2 receptors. Typical antipsychotic drugs reduce positive symptoms by counteracting elevated dopamine release through antagonism of D_2 receptors. These actions also account for extrapyramidal side effects (Meltzer & Stahl, 1976).

Extrapyramidal side effects (EPS) consist of tremor, muscle rigidity, and involuntary movements (Owens, 1999). As we see in Figure 15.7, the nigrostriatal dopamine pathway, which terminates in the basal ganglia, likely functions normally in schizophrenia. D_2 receptor antagonism reduces dopamine neurotransmission in this pathway, causing diminished control of movement. In many ways, EPS resembles the

TABLE 15.2 ● Typical Versus Atypical Antipsychotic Drug Effects and Mechanisms

Typical Antipsychotic		Atypical Antipsychotic
Positive symptoms	Effective	Effective
Negative symptoms	Generally ineffective	Modestly effective
Cognitive impairment	Generally ineffective	Modestly effective
Extrapyramidal side effects	Occur at therapeutically effective doses. Generally requires treatment with an anticholinergic drug.	Unlikely to occur at minimally therapeutically effective doses
Tardive dyskinesia	Likely to develop after long-term use	Very unlikely
Mechanism of action	Mainly through blockade of dopamine D_2 receptors	Through blockade of D_2 receptors and serotonin $(5\text{-HT})_{2A}$ receptors. However, many other receptors implicated in these effects.

SOURCE: © Cengage Learning 2014.

features of Parkinson's disease, which also derive from disrupted dopamine neuro-transmission in this pathway.

Today, physicians seldom prescribe typical antipsychotic drugs for schizophrenia, but the low costs of these medications make them more readily available in economically impoverished parts of the world. For patients who are treated with a typical antipsychotic drug, physicians usually also prescribe a muscarinic receptor antagonist such as *benztropine* to reduce EPS severity (e.g., Brune et al., 1962). Unfortunately, muscarinic receptor antagonists further impair cognitive functioning in schizophrenia (Spohn & Strauss, 1989; Veselinović et al., 2015). Long-term usage with a typical antipsychotic drug, even when also prescribed with an anticholinergic drug, may result in an EPS-related condition called *tardive dyskinesia*.

Drug Profile: benztropine (or benzatropine)

Trade name	Cogentin
Properties	Antagonist for cholinergic muscarinic receptors
Uses	Used to reduce extrapyramidal side effects from antipsychotic drugs
Similar drugs for treating EPS	Trihexyphenidyl (Artane)

Tardive dyskinesia is a motor disorder that affects muscles primarily around the mouth and other parts of the face. Characteristic features of tardive dyskinesia include facial tics and rhythmic, involuntary movements of the jaw such as chewing or teeth

Tardive dyskinesia Motor disorder primarily affecting muscles of the face that may occur after long-term antipsychotic drug use

FIGURE 15.7 ● Antipsychotic drugs reduce the positive symptoms of schizophrenia (top) by acting as an antagonist for D_2 receptors, which counteracts the activity of mesolimbic dopamine neurons. Yet antagonism of D_2 receptors impairs normal dopamine neurotransmission in the basal ganglia, leading to extrapyramidal side effects.

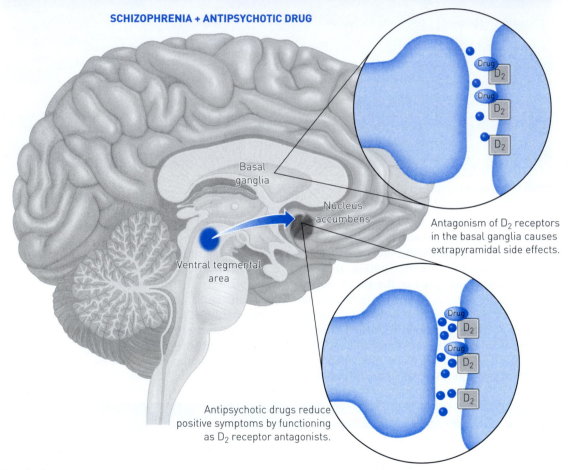

SCHIZOPHRENIA + ANTIPSYCHOTIC DRUG

Basal ganglia

Nucleus accumbens

Ventral tegmental area

Antagonism of D_2 receptors in the basal ganglia causes extrapyramidal side effects.

Antipsychotic drugs reduce positive symptoms by functioning as D_2 receptor antagonists.

Neuroleptic malignant syndrome Flu-like symptoms such as sweating, fever, and other symptoms such as blood pressure changes and autonomic nervous system irregularities induced by antipsychotic drugs

grinding, involuntary use of the tongue such as in lip licking, or excessive lip smacking and pursing. These adverse effects may not occur until after a patient stops taking the medication. In fact, tardive dyskinesia can persist for months and even years after cessation from typical antipsychotic treatment (Owens, 1999).

Typical antipsychotic drugs also may produce neuroleptic malignant syndrome. Some of the symptoms of **neuroleptic malignant syndrome** resemble those of influenza, including sweating and fever, whereas other symptoms include blood pressure changes, autonomic nervous system irregularities such as changes in heart and breathing rate, and muscle rigidity (Caroff, 1980). These symptoms are severe and life threatening; any appearance tends to occur during the first few weeks of treatment. In nearly all cases, EPS also occurs with neuroleptic malignant syndrome (Addonizio, Susman, & Roth, 1987).

Typical antipsychotic drugs also are noted for **hyperprolactinemia**, which occurs from abnormally high blood levels of prolactin over prolonged periods of time. The symptoms of hyperprolactinemia include reduced lactation, loss of libido, disruptions in menstrual cycles, erectile dysfunction, and hypogonadism. Dopamine D_2 receptors regulate the release of prolactin from the anterior hypothalamus (Meltzer, Koenig, Nash, & Gudelsky, 1989).

In addition to the effects of typical antipsychotic in schizophrenia, many of the typical antipsychotic drugs produce *antiemetic* effects. **Antiemetics** are drugs that reduce nausea and vomiting. Given these properties, typical antipsychotic drugs might be given with general anesthetics, to prevent vomiting during surgery, or be given to cancer patients on chemotherapy, which commonly produces nausea and vomiting. Nausea and vomiting occur from activation of the **chemoreceptor trigger zone**, an area in the medulla unprotected by the blood–brain barrier that receives inputs from substances in the blood. The chemoreceptor trigger zone sends signals, involving in part dopamine neurotransmission mediated by dopamine D_2 receptors, to the **area postrema** in the medulla, which elicits vomiting. Many typical antipsychotics drugs, which again serve as dopamine D_2 receptor antagonists, may block signals from the chemoreceptor trigger zone to area postrema, thereby preventing vomiting. Some typical antipsychotic drugs also act as antagonists for $5-HT_3$ receptors, a receptor action particularly linked to antiemetic effects (Jordan, Gralla, Jahn, & Molassiotis, 2014).

Hyperprolactinemia Disorder characterized by abnormally high blood levels of prolactin over prolonged periods of time, resulting in reduced lactation, loss of libido, disruptions in menstrual cycles, erectile dysfunction, and hypogonadism

Antiemetic Drugs that reduce nausea and vomiting

Chemoreceptor trigger zone Area in the medulla unprotected by the blood–brain barrier receptive to substances in the blood or cerebrospinal fluid that when activated sends inputs to the area postrema to produce vomiting

Area postrema Area in the medulla that produces vomiting

STOP & CHECK

1. The primary pharmacological action thought responsible for the therapeutic effects of typical antipsychotic drugs consists of antagonism of _____ receptors.

2. In addition to primarily treating positive symptoms of schizophrenia, typical antipsychotic drugs also produce _____ at therapeutic doses.

3. A severe condition known as _____ syndrome consists of flu-like and other symptoms that can occur from treatment with antipsychotic drugs.

4. Typical antipsychotic drugs might produce antiemetic effects through antagonism of D2 receptors, which reduces neurotransmission from the chemoreceptor trigger zone to the _____ .

1. dopamine D2 **2.** extrapyramidal side effects **3.** neuroleptic malignant **4.** area postrema

Atypical Antipsychotic Drugs: First-Line Treatments for Schizophrenia

Clozapine (Clozaril) was the first atypical antipsychotic drug. It was synthesized in 1959 only a few years after the discovery of chlorpromazine. Yet researchers disregarded clozapine as an antipsychotic drug at first because of a lack of EPS in animal models. In other words, because all known antipsychotic drugs at the time produced EPS in humans, researchers identified potential antipsychotic drugs by their ability to produce EPS in animals. Thus, we do not find clozapine used clinically for schizophrenia until the 1970s and 1980s (Hippius, 1989; Matz, Rick, Thompson, & Gershon, 1974). The remarkable efficacy of clozapine led to the development of many other atypical antipsychotic drugs, including *olanzapine (Zyprexa)* and *risperidone (Risperdal)* (Table 15.1). As a class, **atypical antipsychotic drugs** reduce positive and negative symptoms and carry a low risk of EPS at therapeutic doses. Like typical antipsychotic drugs, atypical antipsychotic drugs may also require as long as 6–8 weeks to produce full efficacy (Agid et al., 2003; Emsley et al., 2006).

From clinical studies, we find that atypical antipsychotic drugs produce modest to moderate gains in negative symptoms. Moreover, clinical studies find consistent, albeit also modest, gains in cognitive functioning (Meltzer & McGurk, 1999; Woodward, Purdon, Meltzer, & Zald, 2005). Thus, we find some improvement in functional outcomes after atypical antipsychotic drug treatment, although these are less than desired (Green, Kern, Braff, & Mintz, 2000; Kaneda, Jayathilak, & Meltzer, 2010). Atypical antipsychotic drugs may also reduce depression in schizophrenia, and clinical studies find that clozapine, olanzapine, and risperidone reduce suicide risk among individuals with schizophrenia (Barak, Mirecki, Knobler, Natan, & Aizenberg, 2004; Meltzer, 2001). We also find improvements from some atypical antipsychotic drugs for *treatment-resistant* schizophrenia. Clozapine, for example, provides significant clinical improvement in 70 percent of treatment-resistant patients (Kane, Honigfeld, Singer, & Meltzer, 1988).

Atypical antipsychotic drugs carry the risk of serious adverse effects. As already noted, atypical antipsychotic drugs are capable of treating schizophrenia at doses that do not produce EPS. However, most atypical antipsychotic drugs will produce EPS at a sufficiently high dose. Atypical antipsychotic drugs also carry a risk of neuroleptic malignant syndrome (Trollor, Chen, & Sachdev, 2009). Although having lower risk than typical antipsychotic drugs, atypical antipsychotic drugs may produce hyperprolactinemia. Thus, when compared to typical antipsychotic drugs, atypical antipsychotic drugs have a lower risk, but not a complete absence of these adverse effects.

Clinicians carefully monitor for three other types of adverse effects. First, many atypical antipsychotic drugs produce significant increases in body weight (Kroeze et al., 2003; Wirshing et al., 1999). Increases in body weight accompany a substantial risk of type II diabetes (Gonçalves, Araújo, & Martel, 2015; Tschoner et al., 2009). Second, many atypical antipsychotic drugs produce a cardiovascular effect called **QT interval prolongation**. The QT interval refers to readings found on an electrocardiogram, which is used to monitor the components of heartbeat. Although prolonging the QT intervals appears safe in itself, this condition can degenerate into a more serious condition called *torsades de pointes*, which may lead to cardiac arrest (Ray, Chung, Murray, Hall, & Stein, 2009; Stollberger, Huber, & Finsterer, 2005).

Atypical antipsychotic drugs (or second-generation or novel antipsychotic drugs) Antipsychotic drugs that reduce positive and negative symptoms and carry a low risk of EPS at therapeutic doses

QT interval prolongation Prolonged heartbeat as revealed from the QT interval of an electrocardiogram

Third, some atypical antipsychotic drugs pose a slight risk of producing **agranulocytosis**, a disorder characterized by reduced white blood cell counts in the immune system. Clozapine is most noted for this adverse effect. As a result, patients prescribed clozapine must have weekly or monthly blood draws to monitor white blood cell counts (Amsler, Teerenhovi, Barth, Harjula, & Vuopio, 1977).

As noted for the typical antipsychotic, we also find atypical antipsychotic drugs used as antiemetics. In fact, concerns over side effects found for the typical antipsychotic drugs tend to make atypical antipsychotic drugs preferred for antiemetic effects if effective. Olanzapine, in particular, is used as an effective antiemetic, which is likely due to its antagonist actions at D_2 and 5-HT$_3$ receptors (Jordan et al., 2014).

> **Agranulocytosis**
> Disorder characterized by reduced white blood cell counts in the immune system

STOP & CHECK

1. We characterize _____ antipsychotic drugs as having an efficacy for both positive and negative symptoms, as well as cognitive impairment

2. Clozapine and potentially other atypical antipsychotic drugs carry a risk of _____, a condition noted by reduced white blood cell counts.

1. atypical 2. agranulocytosis

Pharmacological Actions of Atypical Antipsychotic Drugs

As noted earlier, the principal mechanism of action for typical antipsychotic drugs consists of dopamine D_2 receptor blockade. We find more complex mechanisms of actions in atypical antipsychotic drugs. These mechanisms fall largely into two hypotheses for atypical antipsychotic drugs.

The first hypothesis, referred to as **serotonin-dopamine** (or **5-HT$_{2A}$-D$_2$ receptor**) **hypothesis**, states that atypical antipsychotic drug effects derive from preferential antagonism of serotonin$_{2A}$(5-HT)$_{2A}$ receptors compared to dopamine D_2 receptors. As shown in **Table 15.3**, receptor binding studies support this hypothesis by finding that the vast majority of atypical antipsychotic drugs fit this profile (Meltzer, Matsubara, & Lee, 1989; Schotte et al., 1996). Note that for the atypical antipsychotic drugs shown, greater affinities, expressed as K_i's, occur for the 5-HT$_{2A}$ receptor compared to the D_2 receptor.

The second hypothesis, referred to as the **fast D$_2$-off** hypothesis, states that atypical antipsychotic effects derive from a rapid dissociation of the antipsychotic drug from the D_2 receptor. Typical antipsychotic drugs, on the other hand, slowly dissociate from the D_2 receptor (Kapur & Seeman, 2000). In other words, atypical antipsychotic drugs do not block D_2 receptors for as long a time as typical antipsychotic drugs. While we find support for both hypotheses, at present we find pharmaceutical companies most often following the 5-HT$_{2A}$-D$_2$ receptor hypothesis for developing new atypical antipsychotic drugs (Carpenter & Davis, 2012).

> **Serotonin-dopamine (or 5-HT$_{2A}$-D$_2$ receptor) hypothesis**
> Hypothesis stating that atypical antipsychotic drug effects derive from preferential antagonism of serotonin 5-HT$_{2A}$ receptors compared to dopamine D_2 receptors
>
> **Fast D$_2$-off**
> Hypothesis stating that atypical antipsychotic effects derive from a rapid dissociation of the antipsychotic drug from the D_2 receptor

TABLE 15.3 ● Receptor Binding Affinities for Haloperidol and Clozapine		
Receptor	Haloperidol	Clozapine
D_2	1.4	150
Serotonin (5-HT)$_{2A}$	25	3.3
5-HT$_{2C}$	> 5,000	13
Muscarinic cholinergic receptors (M_1–M_5)	4,670	34
α_1 adrenoceptors	19	23
α_2 adrenoceptors	> 5,000	160

NOTE: The numbers in the table represent the binding affinity (K_i values in nM) of haloperidol and clozapine for certain receptors in the brain. The lower the number on the table, the greater the binding affinity (i.e., the greater strength of binding) the drug has for the receptor. For example, haloperidol has a greater affinity for the D_2 receptor than it does for the 5-HT$_{2A}$ receptor, whereas the opposite is true for clozapine. Clozapine has a greater affinity for muscarinic receptors and for noradrenergic α_2 adrenoceptors than haloperidol does, and both drugs have a similar affinity for the alpha$_1$ adrenoceptor.

SOURCE: Data from Schotte et al., 1996.

Pharmacological Effects Generated From Other Receptor Actions   As shown in Table 15.3, antipsychotic drugs bind to more than dopamine and serotonin receptors. Although the primary hypotheses for antipsychotic drugs concern the role of dopamine and serotonin receptors, other receptors may contribute to either antipsychotic effects or side effects. The α_2 adrenoceptor for norepinephrine, for example, provides an important example of other receptor actions contributing to antipsychotic efficacy. In a preclinical study by Hertel, Fagerquist, and Svensson (1999), combined administration of an α_2 adrenoceptor antagonist with a dopamine D_2 receptor antagonist led to atypical antipsychotic drug-like effects on conditioned avoidance responding without producing catalepsy (see **Box 15.2**). Thus, for atypical antipsychotic drugs, such as clozapine, which block α_2 adrenoceptors, α_2 adrenoceptor antagonism may contribute to atypical antipsychotic drug effects (**see Table 15.4**).

For some atypical antipsychotic drugs, muscarinic receptor antagonism causes dry eyes, dry mouth, and other anticholinergic effects. Clozapine's antagonism of histamine H_1 receptors causes drowsiness, similar to how an antihistamine causes drowsiness, during the first several days of treatment (Ahnaou, Megens, & Drinkenburg, 2003). Receptor binding studies also implicate H_1 receptors, as well as 5-HT$_{2C}$ receptors, in antipsychotic drug-induced weight gain and subsequent risk of type II diabetes (Table 15.4; Kroeze et al., 2003; Reynolds, Hill, & Kirk, 2006).

Third-Generation Antipsychotic Drugs

Third-generation antipsychotic drugs produce antipsychotic effects through a mechanism(s) of action different from those of typical and atypical antipsychotic

Third-generation antipsychotic drugs Drugs that produce antipsychotic effects through a mechanism(s) of action different from those of typical and atypical antipsychotic drugs

TABLE 15.4 ● Receptors and Antipsychotic Effects

Receptor (neurotransmitter)	Antipsychotic Receptor Action	Effects
α_2 adrenoceptor (norepinephrine)	Antagonism	May contribute to atypical antipsychotic effects when combined with D_2 receptor antagonism
D_2 receptor (dopamine)	Antagonism	Antipsychotic effects; EPS
H_1 receptor (histamine)	Antagonism	Drowsiness; weight gain and risk of type II diabetes
Muscarinic receptor (acetylcholine)	Antagonism	Dry eyes, dry mouth, and other anticholinergic effects
5-HT$_{2A}$ receptors	Antagonism	Atypical antipsychotic effects when combined with D_2 receptor antagonism
5-HT$_{2C}$ receptors	Antagonism	Weight gain and risk of type II diabetes

drugs. In particular, potential third-generation antipsychotic drugs have deviated from the pharmacological actions found among typical and atypical antipsychotic drugs, rather than having unique therapeutic effects. Currently, the only clinically available compound that might qualify as a third-generation antipsychotic drug is *aripiprazole (Abilify)*.

Unlike typical and atypical antipsychotic drugs, aripiprazole functions as a weak partial agonist for dopamine D_2 receptors at therapeutic doses. Yet aripiprazole shares antagonist effects at 5-HT$_{2A}$ receptors, making this drug some what similar to atypical antipsychotic drugs (Burris et al., 2002). Clinically, aripiprazole exhibits atypical antipsychotic effects because it is unlikely to produce EPS at therapeutically effective dosages. Aripiprazole appears slightly less effective than the atypical antipsychotic drug olanzapine for treating schizophrenia, but might offer less risk of type II diabetes (Fleischhacker et al., 2009).

Administration Forms for Antipsychotic Drugs

Pharmaceutical companies provide all typical and atypical antipsychotic drugs in pill form, allowing for oral administration. However, patient compliance considerations lead companies to develop other administration routes as well. In a hospital, patients, out of possible mistrust of health care staff, may refuse to take a medication or attempt to hide medication under their tongues. During in-patient care, patients may receive intramuscular injections of antipsychotic drugs instead. Drug developers have sought to provide antipsychotic drugs in dissolvable pill or nasal spray form (Miller, Ashford, Archer, Rudy, & Wermeling, 2008; Potkin, Cohen, & Panagides, 2007). We also find many antipsychotic drugs available in *depot* administration

BOX 15.2 ANIMAL MODELS FOR IDENTIFYING TYPICAL AND ATYPICAL ANTIPSYCHOTIC DRUGS: CONDITIONED AVOIDANCE AND CATALEPSY

As noted previously, researchers find difficulty in identifying treatments in animals for uniquely human disorders. For finding treatments for schizophrenia, researchers tend to avoid modeling the entire disorder, but instead model some distinct feature of the disorder. Another strategy involves characterizing the distinct changes in animal behavior, whatever they may be, after administration of clinically proven antipsychotic drugs. After identifying these behaviors, we then screen experimental compounds by determining if they elicit similar behaviors. From these perspectives on antipsychotic drug development, we find two procedures highly effective for screening atypical antipsychotic drugs: conditioned avoidance responding and catalepsy.

Conditioned avoidance responding consists of a learning model that requires animals, usually rats or mice, to associate a warning stimulus with an impending aversive stimulus

FIGURE 1 ● During a conditioned avoidance response task, an organism learns to emit an avoidance response upon the activation of a warning stimulus (left). Failure to do emit an avoidance response will result in the organism receiving an aversive stimulus, such as an electric shock. We can measure catalepsy in rodents using an inclined grid (right) where researchers record the amount of time taken for a rodent to move on the grid. Cataleptic rats or mice tend to take on a frozen posture on the grid. Other catalepsy models also examine lack of movement as an index of catalepsy.

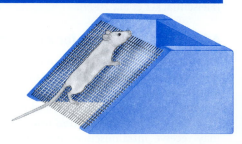

FIGURE 2 ● Both the atypical antipsychotic drug clozapine (left) and the typical antipsychotic drug haloperidol (right) decrease the percentage of trials a laboratory rat avoided aversive stimulation (top panels). Haloperidol, but not clozapine, increased scores divided in time increments during a catalepsy assessment. The *x*-axis for all graphs shows the dose of each drug expressed in mg/kg.

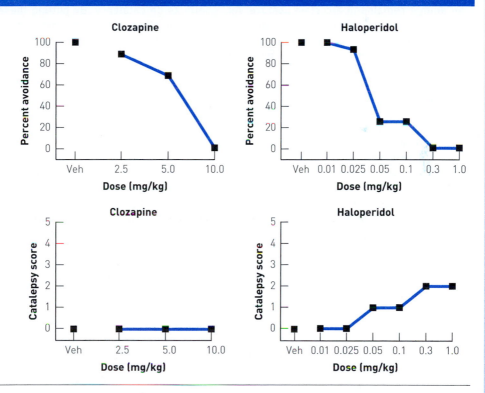

SOURCE: Holly et al., 2011.

(Continued)

(Continued)

such as mild electric shock. An animal then learns to avoid the aversive stimulus by emitting some type of response, such as pressing a lever or crossing into a different compartment (**Figure 1**). All known clinically effective typical and atypical antipsychotic drugs inhibit conditioned avoidance responding. Thus, antipsychotic effects manifest as poor avoidance of aversive stimulation.

Because the conditioned avoidance procedure fails to separate typical from atypical antipsychotic drugs, we add an assessment of *catalepsy* in these experiments. Catalepsy assessments consist of recording how long an animal remains in a certain posture. As presented in this chapter, typical—but not atypical—antipsychotic drugs produce EPS at therapeutically effective doses. By using

catalepsy as an index of EPS in animals, researchers can determine if EPS occurs at doses effective in reducing accuracy in the conditioned avoidance response task.

For example, Holly, Ebrecht, and Prus (2011) evaluated the atypical antipsychotic drug clozapine and the typical antipsychotic drug haloperidol using these two procedures. As shown in **Figure 2**, both clozapine and haloperidol led to significant decreases in avoidance of the aversive stimulation. Haloperidol, however, produced these decreases in avoidance at doses that significantly increased catalepsy, whereas clozapine produced no effects on catalepsy. By putting these findings together, clozapine produces antipsychotic effects without producing EPS, a key feature of atypical antipsychotic effects.

forms. **Antipsychotic depot injections** (or **long-acting antipsychotic injections**) provide a slow release of antipsychotic drug, over the course of weeks, after a single injection. A depot administration circumvents concerns over patient compliance and provides for a steady state of drug effects.

Many antipsychotic drugs produce active metabolites. For example, the active metabolite of risperidone, called *paliperidone (Invega)*, was recently developed as an atypical antipsychotic drug (Dlugosz & Nasrallah, 2007). Although this is the first active metabolite approved clinically as an atypical antipsychotic drug, the active metabolite of clozapine, N-desmethylclozapine (Pimavanserin), has also shown promising antipsychotic effects in animal models (Lameh et al., 2007; Philibin et al., 2009).

Antipsychotic depot injections (or long-acting antipsychotic injections) Drug formulation that provides a slow release of antipsychotic drug, over the course of weeks, after a single injection

Autism spectrum disorder (or autism) Neurodevelopmental disorder consisting of social impairments, verbal and nonverbal language difficulties, irritability (e.g., emotional outbursts, tantrums), and repetitive behaviors

STOP & CHECK

1. An important pharmacological distinction between atypical and typical antipsychotic drugs is that atypical antipsychotic drugs act as an antagonist for both D$_2$ receptors and _____ receptors.

2. The _____ hypothesis states that *atypical* antipsychotic drug effects derive from a quick dissociation from the dopamine D$_2$ receptor.

3. A _____ injection of antipsychotic provides for a slow release of antipsychotic after a single injection.

1. 5-HT$_{2a}$ 2. fast D$_2$-off 3. Depot

Antipsychotic Drugs and Autism

Autism spectrum disorder (often referred to as simply **autism**) is a neurodevelopmental disorder consisting of social impairments, verbal and nonverbal language difficulties, irritability (e.g., emotional outbursts, tantrums) and repetitive behaviors typically occurring before age 3. The general worldwide estimate of autism is 1 percent (American Psychiatric Association, 2013). Yet we find a number of studies reporting dramatic increases in autism diagnoses. For example, the U.S. Centers for Disease Control reported a 78 percent increase in autism diagnoses from 2002 to 2008 (Baio, 2012). A fivefold increase in autism diagnoses occurred in the United Kingdom in the 1990s, but rates plateaued in the 2000s (Taylor, Jick, & MacLaughlin, 2013). We find a 4-times greater prevalence of autism in males than in females (Chakrabarti & Fombonne, 2005).

Numerous hypotheses exist for the causes of autism. Researchers and clinicians agree on genetic links to this disorder, which began with twin studies showing that autism occurring in one monozygotic twin will likely occur in the other monozygotic twin (Bailey et al., 1995; Greenberg, Hodge, Sowinski, & Nicoll, 2001). In fact, one study found that in 92 percent of cases in which a monozygotic twin received an autism diagnosis, the other twin either had autism or exhibited features related to autism (Bailey et al., 1995). Studies have mostly linked genetic abnormalities to multiple chromosomes, including 4 and 7 (Alarcón et al., 2002; Schellenberg et al., 2006). From affected chromosomes, numerous genetic changes could lead to neurodevelopmental effects (Szatmari et al., 2007). We find general consensus relating to abnormal connectivity in the prefrontal cortex, which may have implications in a host of cognitive, social, and emotional features in this disorder (Courchesne et al., 2011; Just, Cherkassky, Teller, & Minshew, 2004). Another emerging concept is that activity in the visual system may be out of sync with activity in the motor system, perhaps leading to an individual not visually perceiving or processing the consequences of motor responses. This might account for the difficulty those with autism have for imitating gestures (Nebel et al., 2016).

The management of autism often includes *applied behavior analysis* therapy or psychoactive medications. An applied behavior analyst normally provides therapy for autistic children with the goal of correcting problem social, communicative, and adaptive behaviors. One of the primary psychoactive drug approaches involves prescribing antipsychotic drugs. Those currently approved by the U.S. FDA for use in autism include *aripiprazole* and *risperidone*. Antipsychotics primarily manage certain features of autism. Both aripiprazole and risperidone reduce autism-related irritability, and in fact, are specifically approved by the FDA for this purpose. For example, McCracken and colleagues (2002) reported that 8 weeks of risperidone treatment to children and adolescents with autism led to greater reductions in irritability than placebo in about two-thirds of their patients. Owen and colleagues (2009) later reported similar findings after 8 weeks of aripiprazole treatment. Yet these studies also demonstrated similar adverse effects as seen in those with schizophrenia, including risks of weight gain, fatigue, and EPS. In fact, the likelihood of these adverse effects occurring appears higher in children and adolescents than in adults (Correll, 2008).

STOP & CHECK

1. Studies in monozygotic _____ first suggested a genetic cause for autism.

2. Abnormal connectivity in the _____ may contribute to many of the symptoms of autism.

3. Antipsychotic drugs are specifically approved to treat _____ in autism.

1. twins **2.** prefrontal cortex **3.** irritability

From Actions to Effects: Antipsychotic Drug Actions and Neurotransmission in Schizophrenia

Beyond differences in receptor actions between typical and atypical antipsychotic drugs, microdialysis studies reveal important differences in dopamine neurotransmission between these drug classes. Moreover, these neurotransmission differences correspond to the role of dopamine in the glutamate hypothesis of schizophrenia. As shown in **Figure 15.8**, the glutamate hypothesis, together with other evidence, reveals diminished cortical levels of dopamine and enhanced limbic system levels of dopamine in schizophrenia. Figure 15.8 focuses on the prefrontal cortex and nucleus accumbens for these regions, respectively. Researchers relate diminished dopamine levels in the prefrontal cortex to cognitive impairment and negative symptoms. The different effects that atypical and typical antipsychotic drugs have on dopamine levels in the prefrontal cortex relate to their general clinical effects for cognitive impairment and negative symptoms.

Microdialysis studies find that atypical, but not typical, antipsychotic drugs increase dopamine concentrations in the prefrontal cortex. For example, in a study by Kuroki, Meltzer, and Ichikawa (1999), the atypical antipsychotic drugs clozapine and risperidone significantly increased dopamine concentrations in the rat medial prefrontal cortex. However, the typical antipsychotic drug haloperidol failed to increase dopamine concentrations in the prefrontal cortex (**Figure 15.9**).

FIGURE 15.8 ● In schizophrenia, disruption in neurotransmission occurs for glutamate and dopamine. In this image we find underactive mesocortical dopamine neurons that originate in the ventral tegmental area and terminate in prefrontal cortex and other parts of the cortex. Thus, dopamine levels in the prefrontal cortex may be too low. Diminished dopamine activity in the prefrontal cortex causes less activation of glutamate neurons that innervate the ventral tegmental area and facilitate a positive feedback loop. Lower activity of glutamate neurons from the prefrontal cortex to the nucleus accumbens may result in less activation of GABA neurons that terminate in the ventral tegmental area. Diminished GABA neuron activity may disinhibit mesolimbic dopamine neurons, leading to increased dopamine release in the nucleus accumbens and perhaps other parts of the limbic system. Thus, overall this model demonstrates how dopamine levels in the prefrontal cortex may be low, while dopamine levels in the limbic system may be high. The "+" symbols represent excitatory effects, and the "−" symbols represent inhibitory effects.

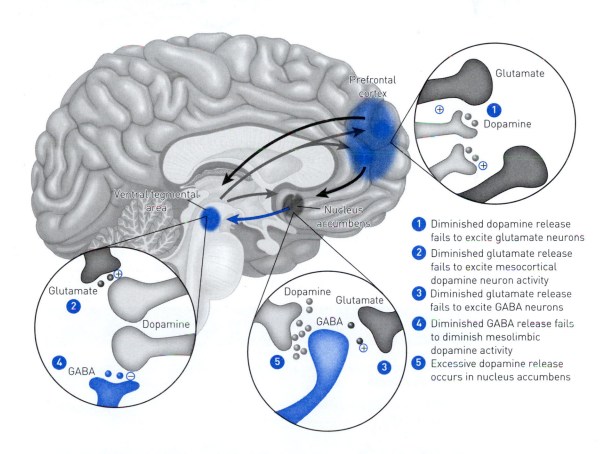

1 Diminished dopamine release fails to excite glutamate neurons
2 Diminished glutamate release fails to excite mesocortical dopamine neuron activity
3 Diminished glutamate release fails to excite GABA neurons
4 Diminished GABA release fails to diminish mesolimbic dopamine activity
5 Excessive dopamine release occurs in nucleus accumbens

FIGURE 15.9 ● Microdialysis procedures reveal that atypical antipsychotic drugs such as clozapine (left) produce increased dopamine concentrations in the prefrontal cortex, although typical antipsychotic drugs such as haloperidol tend to have minimal effects on dopamine concentrations in the prefrontal cortex (right). The arrow indicates when the injection of clozapine or haloperidol was given. The *y*-axis shows the percentage of dopamine level change compared to baseline plotted at the 100 percent level. The *x*-axis shows the time before (with minus signs) and after drug injection.

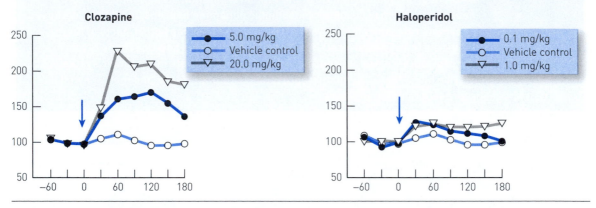

SOURCE: Kuroki, T., Meltzer, H. Y., & Ichikawa, J. (1999). Effects of antipsychotic drugs on extracellular dopamine levels in rat medial prefrontal cortex and nucleus accumbens. *J Pharmacol Exp Ther*, 288(2), 774–781. Used with permission.

To determine why atypical antipsychotic drugs elevated prefrontal cortical dopamine levels, Liegeois, Ichikawa, and Meltzer (2002) assessed the effects of drugs selective for 5-HT$_{2A}$ receptors and D$_2$ receptors on prefrontal cortical dopamine concentrations. They found that neither the 5-HT$_{2A}$ receptor antagonist M100907 nor haloperidol, a D$_2$ receptor antagonist, significantly increased dopamine concentrations in the prefrontal cortex. After combining the two drugs, however, these researchers found significant increases in dopamine concentrations in the prefrontal cortex. Based on these findings, the actions of atypical antipsychotic drugs on 5-HT$_{2A}$ and D$_2$ receptors may account for their effects on cortical dopamine neurotransmission and possibly their ability to improve cognitive impairment and negative symptoms in schizophrenia.

STOP & CHECK

1. How do dopamine levels in the prefrontal cortex relate to cognitive impairment in schizophrenia?

2. How might atypical antipsychotic drugs—but not typical antipsychotic drugs—increase prefrontal cortical dopamine levels?

1. Diminished prefrontal cortical dopamine levels may lead to cognitive impairment in schizophrenia. 2. Combined actions of 5-HT$_{2A}$ and D$_2$ receptor antagonism appear to increase prefrontal cortical dopamine concentrations.

Chapter Summary

Schizophrenia is a severe thought disorder diagnosed by the presence of positive symptoms and negative symptoms. In addition, many patients exhibit deficits in cognitive functioning, which is an important predictor of functional outcomes. Schizophrenia occurs from genetic and environmental factors. The main treatments for schizophrenia consist of typical and atypical antipsychotic drugs. Typical antipsychotic drugs reduce positive symptoms of schizophrenia and produce extrapyramidal side effects at therapeutically effective doses. They produce antipsychotic effects by serving as antagonists for D_2 receptors. Atypical antipsychotic drugs are effective for positive symptoms and, to some degree, negative symptoms and cognitive impairment. They

are also capable of producing these therapeutic effects at doses that do not produce EPS. The therapeutic effects of atypical antipsychotic drugs are produced through preferential antagonism of 5-HT_{2A} receptors compared to D_2 receptors or they are produced by quicker dissociation from D_2 receptors. In either case, an important factor in the clinical effects of atypical antipsychotic drugs may be there ability to enhance dopamine levels in the prefrontal cortex while reducing dopamine levels in the limbic system. Many antipsychotic drugs produce significant weight gain and subsequently carry the risk of type II diabetes. For the management of autism spectrum disorder, antipsychotic drugs can reduce autism-related irritability.

Key Terms

Visit the Student Study Site at **study.sagepub.com/prus2e** to access additional study tools, including eFlashcards, web quizzes, video resources, web resources, SAGE journal articles, and more.

• References •

AAALAC. (2012). What is AAALAC? Retrieved from www.aaalac.org/about/index.cfm

Abanades, S., Farré, M., Barral, D., Torrens, M., Closas, N., Langohr, K. . . . & De la Torre, R. (2007). Relative abuse liability of γ-hydroxybutyric acid, flunitrazepam, and ethanol in club drug users. *Journal of Clinical Psychopharmacology, 27*(6), 625–638 10.1097/jcp.1090b1013e31815a32542

Abanades, S., Farré, M., Segura, M., Pichini, S., Barral, D., Pacifici, R., . . . & De La Torre, R. (2006). Gamma-hydroxybutyrate (GHB) in humans: Pharmacodynamics and pharmacokinetics. *Annals of the New York Academy of Sciences, 1074*, 559–576. doi: 1074/1/559 [pii]

Abeles, A. M., Pillinger, M. H., Solitar, B. M., & Abeles, M. (2007). Narrative review: The pathophysiology of fibromyalgia. *Annals of Internal Medicine, 146*(10), 726–734. doi: 10.7326/0003-4819-146-10-200705150-00006

Abood, M. E., & Martin, B. R. (1992). Neurobiology of marijuana abuse. *Trends in Pharmacological Sciences, 13*, 201–206.H

Abraham, H. D., McCann, U. D., & Ricaurte, G. A. (2002). Psychedelic drugs. *Neuropsychopharmacology: The fifth generation of progress* (pp. 1545–1556). Brentwood, NJ: American College of Neuropsychopharmacology.

Adams, I. B., & Martin, B. R. (1996). Cannabis: Pharmacology and toxicology in animals and humans. *Addiction, 91*, 1585–1614. doi: 10.1046/j.1360-0443.1996.911115852.x

Addolorato, G., Balducci, G., Capristo, E., Attilia, M. L., Taggi, F., Gasbarrini, G., & Ceccanti, M. (1999). Gamma-hydroxybutyric acid (GHB) in the treatment of alcohol withdrawal syndrome: A randomized comparative study versus benzodiazepine. *Alcoholism: Clinical and Experimental Research, 23*(10), 1596–1604. doi: 10.1111/j.1530-0277.1999.tb04049.x

Addonizio, G., Susman, V. L., & Roth, S. D. (1987). Neuroleptic malignant syndrome: Review and analysis of 115 cases. *Biological Psychiatry, 22*(8), 1004–1020.

Adinoff, B., Bone, G. H., & Linnoila, M. (1988). Acute ethanol poisoning and the ethanol withdrawal syndrome. *Medical Toxicology and Adverse Drug Experience, 3*(3), 172–196.

Adler, L. E., Olincy, A., Waldo, M., Harris, J. G., Griffith, J., Stevens, K. . . . & Freedman, R. (1998). Schizophrenia, sensory gating, and nicotinic receptors. *Schizophrenia Bulletin, 24*(2), 189–202.

Agar, M. (1974). Talking about doing: Lexicon and event. *Language in Society, 3*, 83–89.

Aggarwal, S. K., Carter, G. T., Sullivan, M. D., ZumBrunnen, C., Morrill, R., & Mayer, J. D. (2009). Medicinal use of cannabis in the United States: Historical perspectives, current trends, and future directions. *Journal of Opioid Management, 5*, 153–168.

Agid, O., Kapur, S., Arenovich, T., & Zipursky, R. B. (2003). Delayed-onset hypothesis of antipsychotic action: A hypothesis tested and rejected. *Archives of General Psychiatry, 60*(12), 1228–1235. doi: 10.1001/archpsyc.60.12.1228

Agurell, S., Holmstedt, B., Lindgren, J. E., & Schultes, R. E. (1969).

Alkaloids in certain species of Virol and other South American plants of the ethnopharmacologic interest. *Acta Chemica Scandinavica, 23*, 903–916.

Ahmed, B., Jacob, P. III, Allen, F., & Benowitz, N. (2011). Attitudes and practices of hookah smokers in the San Francisco Bay Area. *Journal of Psychoactive Drugs, 43*(2), 146–152.

Ahnaou, A., Megens, A. A., & Drinkenburg, W. H. (2003). The atypical antipsychotics risperidone, clozapine and olanzapine differ regarding their sedative potency in rats. *Neuropsychobiology, 48*(1), 47–54. doi: 10.1159/000071829

Ainsworth, K., Smith, S. E., & Sharp, T. (1998). Repeated administration of fluoxetine, desipramine and tranylcypromine increases dopamine D_2-like but not D_1-like receptor function in the rat. *Journal of Psychopharmacology, 12*(3), 252–257.

Akiskal, H. S., & Pinto, O. (1999). The evolving bipolar spectrum: prototypes I, II, III, and IV. *Psychiatric Clinics of North America, 22*, 517–534.

Akbarian, S., Kim, J. J., Potkin, S. G., Hetrick, W. P., Bunney, W. E., & Jones, E. G. (1996). Maldistribution of interstitial neurons in prefrontal white matter of the brains of schizophrenic patients. *Archives of General Psychiatry, 53*, 425–436.

Alarcón, M., Cantor, R. M., Liu, J., Gilliam, T. C., Geschwind, D. H., & Autism Genetic Resource Exchange Consortium. (2002). Evidence for a language quantitative trait locus on chromosome 7q in multiplex autism families. *American Journal of Human Genetics, 70*(1), 60–71. doi: 10.1086/338241

Alcoholics Anonymous. (2012). AA fact file. Retrieved from www.aa.org/pdf/products/m-24_aafactfile

Alexander, S.P.H. (2016). Therapeutic potential of cannabis-related drugs. *Progress in Neuro-Psychopharmacology & Biological Psychiatry, 64*, 157–166. doi: 10.1016/j.pnpbp.2015.07.001

Alexopoulos, G. S. (2005). Depression in the elderly. *The Lancet, 365*(9475), 1961–1970. doi: 10.1016/S0140-6736(05)66665-2

Alexopoulos, G. S., Meyers, B. S., Young, R. C., Campbell, S., Silbersweig, D., & Charlson, M. (1997). "Vascular depression" hypothesis. *Archives of General Psychiatry, 54*(10), 915–922. doi: 10.1001/ archpsyc.1997.01830220033006

Alfonso, J., Le Magueresse, C., Zuccotti, A., Khodosevich, K., & Monyer, H. (2012). Diazepam binding inhibitor promotes progenitor proliferation in the postnatal SVZ by reducing GABA signaling. *Cell Stem Cell, 10*(1), 76–87. doi: 10.1016/j.stem.2011.11.011

Al-Hebshi, N. N., & Skaug, N. (2005). Khat (Catha edulis): An updated review. *Addiction Biology, 10*(4), 299–307. doi: 10.1080/13556210500353020

Allen S. S., Allen, A. M., Lunos, S., Hatsukami, D. K. (2009). Patterns of self-selected smoking cessation attempts and relapse by menstrual phase. *Addiction Behavior, 34*, 928–931. doi: 10.1016/j.addbeh.2009.05.013

Alper, A. T., Akyol, A., Hasdemir, H., Nurkalem, Z., Guler, O., Guvenc, T. S. . . . & Gurkan, K. (2008). Glue (toluene) abuse: Increased QT dispersion and relation with unexplained syncope. *Inhalation Toxicology, 20*(1), 37–41. doi: 10.1080/08958370701758304

Altamura, A. C., Pioli, R., Vitto, M., & Mannu, P. (1999). Venlafaxine in social phobia: A study in selective serotonin reuptake inhibitor non-responders. *International Clinical Psychopharmacology, 14*(4), 239–245.

American Dental Association. (2005). For the dental patient: Methamphetamine use and oral health. *Journal of the American Dental Association, 136*, 1491.

American Psychiatric Association. (2000). *Diagnostic and statistical manual of mental disorders* (4th ed.). Arlington, VA: Author.

American Psychiatric Association. (2012). R10 cannabis withdrawal. Retrieved from www.dsm5.org/ProposedRevision/Pages/proposedrevision.aspx?rid=430

American Psychiatric Association. (2013a). *Diagnostic and statistical manual of mental disorders* (5th ed.). Washington, DC: American Psychiatric Publishing.

American Psychiatric Association. (2013a). *Highlights of changes from DSM-IV-TR to DSM-5.* Washington, DC: American Psychiatric Publishing. Retrieved from http://www.dsm5.org/documents/changes%20from%20dsm-iv-tr%20to%20dsm-5.pdf

Amin, J., & Weiss, D. S (1993). GABA receptor needs two homologous domains of the beta-subunit for activation by GABA but not by pentobarbital. *Nature, 366*(6455), 565–569. doi: 10.1038/366565a0

Amsler, H. A., Teerenhovi, L., Barth, E., Harjula, K., & Vuopio, P. (1977). Agranulocytosis in patients treated with clozapine. *Acta Psychiatrica Scandinavoca Supplement, 56*(4), 241–248. doi: 10.1111/j.1600-0447.1977.tb00224.x

Anderson, A. L., Reid, M. S., Li, S. H., Holmes, T., Shemanski, L., Slee, A. . . . & Elkashef, A. M. (2009). Modafinil for the treatment of cocaine dependence. *Drug and Alcohol Dependence, 104*(1–2), 133–139. doi: 10.1016/j.drugalcdep.2009.04.015

Anderson, B. L., Dang, E. P., Floyd, R. L., Sokol, R., Mahoney, J., & Schulkin, J. (2010). Knowledge, opinions, and practice patterns of obstetrician-gynecologists regarding their patients' use of alcohol. *Journal of Addiction Medicine, 4*(2), 114–121. 10.1002/dta.254

Andreasen, N. C., Paradiso, S., & O'Leary, D. S. (1998). "Cognitive dysmetria" as an integrative theory of schizophrenia: A dysfunction in cortical-subcortical-cerebellar circuitry? *Schizophrenia Bulletin, 24*(2), 203–218.

Andréasson, S., Engström, A., Allebeck, P., & Rydberg, U. (1987). Cannabis and schizophrenia: A longitudinal study of Swedish conscripts. *The Lancet,* *330*(8574), 1483–1486. doi: 10.1016/S0140-6736(87)92620-1

Andresen, H., Aydin, B. E., Mueller, A., & Iwersen-Bergmann, S. (2011). An overview of gamma-hydroxybutyric acid: Pharmacodynamics, pharmacokinetics, toxic effects, addiction, analytical methods, and interpretation of results. *Drug Testing and Analysis.* doi: 10.1002/dta.254

Angrist, B., Gershon, S., Sathananthan, G., Walker, R. W., Lopez-Ramos, B., Mandel, L. R., & Vandenheuvel, W. J. (1976). Dimethyltryptamine levels in blood of schizophrenic patients and control subjects. *Psychopharmacology (Berl), 47*, 29–32.

Anonymous. (1966). Concentration camp for dogs. *Life, 60*(5), p. 7.

Anonymous. (2009). Marching for science. *Nature Neuroscience, 12*, 523. 10.1038/nn0509-523

Arango, C. (2015). Present and future of developmental neuropsychopharmacology. *European Neuropsychopharmacology, 25*, 703–712. doi: 10.1016/j.euroneuro.2014.11.003

Arinaminpathy, Y., Sansom, M.S.P., & Biggin, P. C. (2002). Molecular dynamics simulations of the ligand-binding domain of the ionotropic glutamate receptor GluR2. *Biophysical Journal, 82*(2), 676–683. doi: 10.1016/s00063495(02)75430–1

Ariyoshi, N., Miyamoto, M., Umetsu, Y., Kunitoh, H., Dosaka-Akita, H., Sawamura, Y.-i., . . . & Kamataki, T. (2002). Genetic polymorphism of CYP2A6 gene and tobacco-induced lung cancer risk in male smokers. *Cancer Epidemiology, Biomarkers, and Prevention, 11*(9), 890–894.

Armitage, A. K., & Turner, D. M. (1970). Absorption of nicotine in cigarette and cigar smoke through the oral mucosa. *Nature, 226*(5252), 1231–1232.

Armstrong, N., & Gouaux, E. (2000). Mechanisms for activation and antagonism of an AMPA-sensitive glutamate receptor: Crystal structures of the GluR2 ligand binding core. *Neuron, 28*(1), 165–181. doi: 10.1016/s08966273(00)00094–5

Arnér, S., & Meyerson, B. A. (1988). Lack of analgesic effect of opioids on neuropathic and idiopathic forms of pain. *Pain, 33*(1), 11–23. doi: 10.1016/03043959(88)90198–4

Arnold, L. M., Lu, Y., Crofford, L. J., Wohlreich, M., Detke, M. J., Iyengar, S., & Goldstein, D. J. (2004). A double-blind, multicenter trial comparing duloxetine with placebo in the treatment of fibromyalgia patients with or without major depressive disorder. *Arthritis and Rheumatism, 50*(9), 2974–2984. doi: 10.1002/art.20485

Arnold, S. E., Talbot, K., & Hahn, C. G. (2005). Neurodevelopment, neuroplasticity, and new genes for schizophrenia. *Progress in Brain Research, 147*, 319–345.

Arria, A. M., & O'Brien, M. C. (2011). The "high" risk of energy drinks. *Journal of the American Medical Association, 305*(6), 600–601. doi: jama.2011.109 [pii]

Åsberg, M., Träskman, L., & Thorén, P. (1976). 5-HIAA in the cerebrospinal fluid: A biochemical suicide predictor? *Archives of General Psychiatry, 33*(10), 1193–1197.

Ascher, J. A., Cole, J. O., Jean-Noel, C., Feighner, J. P., Ferris, R. M., Fibiger, H. C., . . . & Richelson, E. (1995). Bupropion: A review of its mechanism of antidepressant activity. *Journal of Clinical Psychiatry, 56*, 395–401.

Ashton, C. H. (2001). Pharmacology and effects of cannabis: A brief review. *British Journal of Psychiatry, 178*(2), 101–106. doi: 10.1192/bjp.178.2.101

Auld, D. S., & Robitaille, R. (2003). Glial cells and neurotransmission: an inclusive view of synaptic function. *Neuron, 40*, 389–400. doi: 10.1016/S0896–6273(03)00607–X

Aura, J., & Riekkinen, P. Jr. (1999). Blockade of NMDA receptors located at the dorsomedial prefrontal cortex impairs spatial working memory in rats. *Neuroreport, 10*(2), 243–248.

Austin, G. A. (1985). *Alcohol in Western society from antiquity to 1800: A chronological history.* Santa Barbara, CA: ABC-Clio Information Services.

Axelrod, J. (1961). Enzymatic formation of psychotomimetic metabolites from normally occurring compounds. *Science, 134*, 343.

Axelrod, J., Gordon, E., Hertting, G., Kopin, I. J., & Potter, L. T. (1962). On the mechanism of tachyphylaxis to tyramine in the isolated rat heart. *British Journal of Pharmacology and Chemotherapy, 19*, 56–63.

Ayoglu, B., Mitsios, N., Kockum, I., Khademi, M., Zandian, A., Sjöberg, R. . . . & Grönlund, H. (2016). Anoctamin 2 identified as an autoimmune target in multiple sclerosis. *Proceedings of the National Academy of Sciences, 113*(8), 2188–2193. doi: 10.1073/pnas.1518553113

Aznar, S., Qian, Z., Shah, R., Rahbek, B., & Knudsen, G. M. (2003). The 5-HT$_{1A}$ serotonin receptor is located on calbindin- and parvalbumin-containing neurons in the rat brain. *Brain Research, 959*(1), 58–67.

Baas, J. M., Mol, N., Kenemans, J. L., Prinssen, E. P., Niklson, I., Xia-Chen, C., . . . & van Gerven, J. (2009). Validating a human model for anxiety using startle potentiated by cue and context: The effects of alprazolam, pregabalin, and diphenhydramine. *Psychopharmacology (Berl), 205*(1), 73–84. doi: 10.1007/ s00213–009–1516–5

Back, S. E., Brady, K. T., Jackson, J. L., Salstrom, S., & Zinzow, H. (2005). Gender differences in stress reactivity among cocaine-dependent individuals. *Psychopharmacology, 180*, 169–176.

Bahl, V., Weng, N. J.-H., Schick, S. F., Sleiman, M., Whitehead, J., Ibarra, A., & Talbot, P. (2016). Cytotoxicity of thirdhand smoke and identification of acrolein as a volatile thirdhand smoke chemical that inhibits cell proliferation. *Toxicological Sciences, 150*(1), 234–246. doi: 10.1093/toxsci/kfv327

Baker, F., Ainsworth, S. R., Dye, J. T., Crammer, C., Thun, M. J., Hoffmann, D., . . . & Shopland, D. R. (2000). Health risks associated with cigar smoking. *Journal of the American Medical Association, 284*(6), 735–740. doi: 10.1001/jama.284.6.735

Baker, J. R., Jatlow, P., & McCance-Katz, E. F. (2007). Disulfiram effects on responses to intravenous cocaine administration. *Drug and Alcohol Dependence, 87*(2–3), 202–209. doi: 10.1016/j. drugalcdep.2006.08.016

Baker, L. E., Searcy, G. D., Pynnonen, D. M., & Poling, A. (2008). Differentiating the discriminative stimulus effects of

gammahydroxybutyrate and ethanol in a three-choice drug discrimination procedure in rats. *Pharmacology Biochemistry and Behavior, 89*(4), 598–607. doi: 10.1016/j. pbb.2008.02.016

Bale, A. S., Tu, Y., Carpenter-Hyland, E. P., Chandler, L. J., & Woodward, J. J. (2005). Alterations in glutamatergic and gabaergic ion channel activity in hippocampal neurons following exposure to the abused inhalant toluene. *Neuroscience, 130*(1), 197–206. doi: 10.1016/j. neuroscience.2004.08.040

Ballenger, J. C., & Post, R. M. (1978). Kindling as a model for alcohol withdrawal syndromes. *British Journal of Psychiatry, 133*, 1–14.

Balster, R. L. (1998). Neural basis of inhalant abuse. *Drug and Alcohol Dependence, 51*(1–2), 207–214.

Balster, R. L., Johanson, C. E., Harris, R. T., & Schuster, C. R. (1973). Phencyclidine self-administration in the rhesus monkey. *Pharmacology Biochemistry and Behavior, 1*(2), 167–172. doi: 10.1016/00913057(73)90094–4

Bang-Andersen, B., Ruhland, T., Jørgensen, M., Smith, G., Frederiksen, K., Jensen, K. G., . . . & Stensbøl, T. B. (2011). Discovery of 1-[2-(2, 4-dimethylphenylsulfanyl) phenyl] piperazine (Lu AA21004): A novel multimodal compound for the treatment of major depressive disorder. *Journal of Medicinal Chemistry, 54*, 3206–3221. doi: 10.1021/jm101459g

Bailey, A., Le Couteur, A., Gottesman, I., Bolton, P., Simonoff, E., Yuzda, E., & Rutter, M. (1995). Autism as a strongly genetic disorder: Evidence from a British twin study. *Psychological Medicine, 25*(01), 63–77. doi: http://dx.doi.org/10.1017/S0033291700028099

Baio, J. (2012). Prevalence of autism spectrum disorders: Autism and Developmental Disabilities Monitoring Network, 14 Sites, United States, 2008. Morbidity and Mortality Weekly Report. Surveillance Summaries. Vol. 61, Num. 3. *Centers for Disease Control and Prevention.* Retrieved from http://www.cdc.gov/mmwr/preview/mmwrhtml/ss6103a1.htm?sacidbss6103a1aw

Barak, Y., Mirecki, I., Knobler, H. Y., Natan, Z., & Aizenberg, D. (2004). Suicidality and second generation antipsychotics in schizophrenia patients: A case-controlled retrospective study during a 5-year period. *Psychopharmacology (Berl), 175*(2), 215–219. doi: 10.1007/ s00213–004–1801–2

Barch, D. M. (2014). Cerebellar-thalamic connectivity in schizophrenia. *Schizophrenia Bulletin, 40*(6), 1200–1203. doi: 10.1093/schbul/sbu076

Barnes, M. P. (2006). Sativex: Clinical efficacy and tolerability in the treatment of symptoms of multiple sclerosis and neuropathic pain. *Expert Opinion on Pharmacotherapy, 7*(5), 607–615. doi: 10.1517/14656566.7.5.607

Barrett, R. J., White, D. K., & Caul, W. F. (1992). Tolerance, withdrawal, and supersensitivity to dopamine mediated cues in a drug-drug discrimination. *Psychopharmacology (Berl), 109*(1–2), 63–67.

Bass, M. (1970). Sudden sniffing death. *Journal of the American Medical Association, 212*(12), 2075–2079.

Bath, K. G., Mandairon, N., Jing, D., Rajagopal, R., Kapoor, R., Chen, Z.-Y., . . . Lee, F. S. (2008). Variant brain-derived neurotrophic factor (Val66Met) alters adult olfactory bulb neurogenesis and spontaneous olfactory discrimination. *Journal of Neuroscience, 28*(10), 2383–2393. doi: 10.1523/jneurosci.4387–07.2008

Battista, N., Di Tommaso, M., Bari, M., & Maccarone, M. (2012). The endocannabinoid system: An overview. *Frontiers in Behavioral Neuroscience, 6*, 1–7.

Baumann, M. H., Ayestas, M. A., Dersch, C. M., & Rothman, R. B. (2001). 1-(m-Chlorophenyl) piperazine (mCPP) dissociates in vivo serotonin release from long-term serotonin depletion in rat brain. *Neuropsychopharmacology, 24*(5), 492–501. doi: 10.1016/S0893–133X(00)00221–9

Baumann, M. H., Ayestas, M. A., Jr., Partilla, J. S., Sink, J. R., Shulgin, A. T., Daley, P. F., . . . & Cozzi, N. V. (2012). The designer methcathinone analogs, mephedrone and methylone, are substrates for monoamine transporters in brain tissue. *Neuropsychopharmacology, 37*(5), 1192–1203. doi: 10.1038/ npp.2011.304

Baxter, A. J., Scott, K. M., Vos, T., & Whiteford, H. A. (2013). Global prevalence of anxiety disorders: A systematic review and meta-regression. *Psychological Medicine, 43*(05), 897–910. doi: 10.1017/S003329171200147X

Becker, J. B., & Hu, M. (2008). Sex differences in drug abuse. *Frontiers in neuroendocrinology, 29*(1), 36-47. doi: 10.1016/j.yfrne.2007.07.003

Beckstead, M. J., Weiner, J. L., Eger, E. I., Gong, D. H., & Mihic, S. J. (2000). Glycine and gammaaminobutryic acid(A) recepor function is enhanced by inhaled drugs of abuse. *Molecular Pharmacology, 57*, 1199–1205.

Begas, E., Kouvaras, E., Tsakalof, A., Papakosta, S., & Asprodini, E. K. (2007). In vivo evaluation of CYP1A2, CYP2A6, NAT-2 and xanthine oxidase activities in a Greek population sample by the RP-HPLC monitoring of caffeine metabolic ratios. *Biomedical Chromatography, 21*(2), 190–200. doi: 10.1002/bmc.736

Beltramo, M., Stella, N., Calignano, A., Lin, S. Y., Makriyannis, A., & Piomelli, D. (1997). Functional role of high-affinity anandamide transport, as revealed by selective inhibition. *Science, 277*(5329), 1094–1097. doi: 10.1126/science.277.5329.1094

Belujon, P., Jakobowski, N. L., Dollish, H. K., & Grace, A. A. (2016). Withdrawal from acute amphetamine induces an amygdala-driven attenuation of dopamine neuron activity: Reversal by ketamine. *Neuropsychopharmacology, 41*, 619–627. doi: 10.1038/npp.2015.191

Benedetti, F., Absinta, M., Rocca, M. A., Radaelli, D., Poletti, S., Bernasconi, A., . . . & Colombo, C. (2011). Tract-specific white matter structural disruption in patients with bipolar disorder. *Bipolar Disorders, 13*(4), 414–424. doi: 10.1111/j.1399–5618.2011.00938.x

Benjamin, J., Ben-Zion, I. Z., Karbofsky, E., & Dannon, P. (2000). Double-blind placebo-controlled pilot study of paroxetine for specific phobia. *Psychopharmacology (Berl), 149*(2), 194–196.

Benmansour, S., Cecchi, M., Morilak, D. A., Gerhardt, G. A., Javors, M. A., Gould, G. G., & Frazer, A. (1999). Effects of chronic antidepressant treatments on serotonin transporter function, density, and mRNA level. *Journal of Neuroscience, 19*(23), 10494–10501.

Benowitz, N. L., Herrera, B., & Jacob, P. (2004). Mentholated cigarette smoking inhibits nicotine metabolism. *Journal of Pharmacology and Experimental Therapeutics, 310*, 1208–1215. doi: 10.1124/jpet.104.066902

Berman, R. M., Cappiello, A., Anand, A., Oren, D. A., Heninger, G. R., Charney, D. S., & Krystal, J. H. (2000). Antidepressant effects of ketamine in depressed patients. *Biological Psychiatry, 47*(4), 351–354. doi: 10.1016/s00063223(99)00230–9

Berns, G. S., & Nemeroff, C. B. (2003). The neurobiology of bipolar disorder. *Seminars in Medical Genetics, 123C*, 76–84.

Bernstein, G. A., Carroll, M. E., Thuras, P. D., Cosgrove, K. P., & Roth, M. E. (2002). Caffeine dependence in teenagers. *Drug and Alcohol Dependence, 66*(1), 1–6.

Beseler, C. L., & Hasin, D. S. (2010). Cannabis dimensionality: Dependence, abuse, and consumption. *Addictive Behaviors, 35*, 961–969.

Beyton, C. M., Sumnall, H. R., McVeigh, J., Cole, J. C., & Bellis, M. A. (2006). The ability of two commercially available quick test kits to detect drug-facilitated sexual assault drugs in beverages. *Addiction, 101*, 1413–1420. doi: 10.1111/j.1360–0443.2006.01420.x

Bjork, J. M., Hommer, D. W., Grant, S. J., & Danube, C. (2004). Impulsivity in abstinent alcohol-dependent patients: Relation to control subjects and type 1-/type 2-like traits. *Alcohol, 34*(2–3), 133–150.

Blackburn, I. M., Bishop, S., Glen, A. I., Whalley, L. J., & Christie, J. E. (1981). The efficacy of cognitive therapy in depression: A treatment trial using cognitive therapy and pharmacotherapy, each alone and in combination. *British Journal of Psychiatry, 139*(3), 181–189. doi: 10.1192/bjp.139.3.181

Blake, C. A., Barker, K. L., & Sobel, B. E. (2006). The role of modern biology and medicine in drug development in academia and industry. *Experimental Biology and Medicine, 231*(11), 1680–1681.

Blanchard, J., & Sawers, S. J. (1983). The absolute bioavailability of caffeine in man. *European Journal of Clinical Pharmacology, 24*(1), 93–98.

Blankman, J. L., Simon, G. M., & Cravatt, B. F. (2007). A comprehensive profile of brain enzymes that hydrolyze the endocannabinoid 2-arachidonoylglycerol. *Chemistry and Biology, 14*(12), 1347–1356. doi: S10745521(07)00399–7 [pii]

Blier, P., & Abbott, F. V. (2001). Putative mechanisms of action of antidepressant drugs in affective and anxiety disorders and pain. *Journal of Psychiatry and Neuroscience, 26*, 37–43.

Bolser, D. C. (2006). Cough suppressant and pharmacologic protussive therapy. *Chest, 129*(1 suppl), 238S–249S. doi: 10.1378/ chest.129.1_suppl.238S

Boolell, M., Allen, M. J., Ballard, S. A., Gepi-Attee, S., Muirhead, G. J., Naylor, A. M., . . . & Gingell, C. (1996). Sildenafil: An orally active type 5 cyclic GMP-specific phosphodiesterase inhibitor for the treatment of penile erectile dysfunction. *International Journal of Impotence Research, 8*(2), 47–52.

Booth, M. (1998). *Opium: A history.* New York, NY: St. Martin's Press.

Booth, M. (2005). *Cannabis: A history.* New York, NY: Picador.

Bora, E., Vahip, S., & Akdeniz, F. (2006). Sustained attention deficits in manic and euthymic patients with bipolar disorder. *Progress in Neuro-Psychopharmacology and Biological Psychiatry, 30*(6), 1097–1102. doi: 10.1016/j.pnpbp.2006.04.016

Bossong, M., Brunt, T., Van Dijk, J., Rigter, S., Hoek, J., Goldschmidt, H., & Niesink, R. (2010). mCPP: An undesired addition to the ecstasy market. *Journal of Psychopharmacology, 24*(9), 1395–1401. doi: 10.1177/0269881109102541

Bota, R. G., Munro, S., Nguyen, C., & Preda, A. (2011). Course of schizophrenia: What has been learned from longitudinal studies? In M. Ritsner (Ed.), *Handbook of schizophrenia spectrum disorders* (Vol. II., pp. 281–300). Netherlands: Springer.

Boules, M., Oliveros, A., Liang, Y., Williams, K., Shaw, A., Robinson, J., . . . & Richelson, E. (2011). A neurotensin analog, NT69L, attenuates intravenous nicotine self-administration in rats. *Neuropeptides, 45*(1), 9–16. doi: 10.1016/j.npep.2010.09.003

Bouso, J. C., Doblin, R., Farré, M., Alcázar, M. Á., & Gómez-Jarabo, G. (2008). MDMA-assisted psychotherapy using low doses in a small sample of women with chronic posttraumatic stress disorder. *Journal of Psychoactive Drugs, 40*(3), 225–236. doi: 10.1080/02791072.2008.10400637

Bouso, J. C., Palhano-Fontes, F., Rodríguez-Fornells, A., Ribeiro, S., Sanches, R., Crippa, J.A.S., . . . & Riba, J. (2015). Long-term use of psychedelic drugs is associated with differences in brain structure and personality in humans. *European Neuropsychopharmacology, 25*(4), 483–492. doi: 10.1016/j.euroneuro.2015.01.008

Bowden, C. L. (2001). Strategies to reduce misdiagnosis of bipolar depression. *Psychiatric Services, 52*(1), 51–55. doi: 10.1176/appi.ps.52.1.51

Bowen, S. E., & Balster, R. L. (1998). A direct comparison of inhalant effects on locomotor activity and schedule-controlled behavior in mice. *Experimental and Clinical Psychopharmacology, 6*, 235–247. doi: 10.1037/1064–1297.6.3.235

Brabant, C., Guarnieri, D. J., & Quertemont, E. (2014). Simulant and motivational effects of alcohol: lessons from rodent and primate models. *Pharmacology Biochemistry and Behavior, 122*, 37–52. doi: 10.1016/j.pbb.2014.03.006

Bradberry, C. W., Nobiletti, J. B., Elsworth, J. D., Murphy, B., Jatlow, P., & Roth, R. H. (1993). Cocaine and cocaethylene: Microdialysis comparison of brain drug levels and effects on dopamine and serotonin. *Journal of Neurochemistry, 60*(4), 1429–1435.

Bradley, C. (1937), Behavior of children receiving benzedrine. *American Journal of Psychiatry, 94*, 577–585.

Bradstreet, M. P., Higgins, S. T., McClernon, F. J., Kozink, R. V., Skelly, J. M., Washio, Y., Lopez, A. A., & Parry, M. A. (2014). Examining the effects of initial smoking abstinence on response to smoking-related stimuli and response inhibition in a human laboratory model. *Psychopharmacology, 231*, 2145–2158. doi: 10.1007/s00213–013–3360-x

Brady, K. T., Lydiard, R. B., Malcolm, R., & Ballenger, J. C. (1991). Cocaine-induced psychosis. *Journal of Clinical Psychiatry, 52*(12), 509–512.

Braff, D. L., Swerdlow, N. R., & Geyer, M. A. (1999). Symptom correlates of prepulse inhibition deficits in male schizophrenic patients. *American Journal of Psychiatry, 156*(4), 596–602.

Braida, D., Limonta, V., Capurro, V., Fadda, P., Rubino, T., Mascia, P., . . . & Sala, M. (2008). Involvement of κ-opioid and endocannabinoid system on Salvinorin A-induced reward. *Biological Psychiatry, 63*(3), 286–292. doi: 10.1016/j.biopsych.2007.07.020

Braida, D., Limonta, V., Pegorini, S., Zani, A., Guerini-Rocco, C., Gori, E., & Sala, M. (2007). Hallucinatory and rewarding effect of salvinorin A in zebrafish: κ-opioid and CB1cannabinoid receptor involvement. *Psychopharmacology, 190*(4), 441–448. doi: 10.1007/s00213006–0639–1

Brang, D., & Ramachandran, V. S. (2008). Psychopharmacology of synesthesia: The role of serotonin S2a receptor activation. *Medical Hypotheses, 70*(4), 903–904. doi: S0306–9877(07)00580–4 [pii]

Brauer, L. H., Hatsukami, D., Hanson, K., & Shiffman, S. (1996). Smoking topography in tobacco chippers and dependent smokers. *Addictive Behaviors, 21*(2), 233–238. doi: 0306–4603 (95)00054–2 [pii]

Brecher, E. M. (1972). *Licit and illicit drugs.* Mount Vernon, NY: Consumers Union of the United States.

Brents, L. K., Gallus-Zawada, A., Radominska-Pandya, A., Vasiljevik, T., Prisinzano, T. E., Fantegrossi, W. E., . . . & Prather, P. L. (2012). Monohydroxylated metabolites of the K2 synthetic cannabinoid JWH-073 retain intermediate to high cannabinoid 1 receptor (CB1R) affinity and exhibit neutral antagonist to partial agonist activity. *Biochemical Pharmacology, 83*(7), 952–961. doi: 10.1016/j.bcp.2012.01.004

Brents, L. K., Reichard, E. E., Zimmerman, S. M., Moran, J. H., Fantegrossi, W. E., & Prather, P. L. (2011). Phase I hydroxylated metabolites of the K2 synthetic cannabinoid JWH-018 retain in vitro and in vivo cannabinoid 1 receptor affinity and activity. *PloS one, 6*(7), e21917. doi: 10.1371/journal.pone.0021917

Brill, H., & Hirose, T. (1969). The rise and fall of the methamphetamine epidemic in Japan, 1945–1955. *Seminars in Psychiatry, 1973*, 179–194.

Brink, C.B., Harvey, B.H., Bodenstein, J., Venter, D.P., & Oliver, D.W. (2004). Recent advances in drug action and therapeutics: Relevance of novel concepts in G-proteincoupled receptor and signal transduction pharmacology. *British Journal of Clinical Pharmacology, 57*, 373–387. doi 10.1007/ s00213–012–2680–6

Brock, G. B., McMahon, C. G., Chen, K. K., Costigan, T., Shen, W., Watkins, V., . . . & Whitaker, S. (2002). Efficacy and safety of tadalafil for the treatment of erectile dysfunction: Results of integrated analyses. *Journal of Urology, 168*(4), 1332–1336. doi: 10.1016/S0022–5347(05)64442–4

Brown, A. J. (2007). Novel cannabinoid receptors. *British Journal of Pharmacology, 152*(5), 567–575. doi: 10.1038/sj.bjp.0707481

Brown, J., McKone, E., & Ward, J. (2010). Deficits of long-term memory in ecstasy users are related to cognitive complexity of the task. *Psychopharmacology, 209*(1), 51–67. doi: 10.1007/ s00213–009–1766–2

Brown, J. M., Hanson, G. R., & Fleckenstein, A. E. (2001). Regulation of the vesicular monoamine transporter-2: A novel mechanism for cocaine and other psychostimulants. *Journal of Pharmacology and Experimental Therapeutics, 296*, 762–767.

Brown, L. C., Majumdar, S. R., & Johnson, J. A. (2008). Type of antidepressant therapy and risk of type 2 diabetes in people with depression. *Diabetes Research and Clinical Practice, 79*(1), 61–67. doi: 10.1016/j.diabres.2007.07.009

Bruci, Z., Papoutsis, I., Athanaselis, S., Nikolaou, P., Pazari, E., Spiliopoulou, C., & Vyshka, G. (2012). First systematic evaluation of the potency of *Cannabis sativa* plants grown in Albania. *Forensic Science International, 222*(1), 40–46. doi: 10.1016/j.forsciint.2012.04.032

Brune, G. G., Morpurgo, C., Bielkus, A., Kobayashi, T., Tourlentes, T. T., & Himwich, H. E. (1962). Relevance of drug-induced extrapyramidal reactions to behavioral changes during neuroleptic treatment. I. Treatment with trifluoperazine singly and in combination with trihexyphenidyl. *Comprehensive Psychiatry, 3*, 227–234.

Brunette, M. F., Noordsy, D. L., Xie, H., & Drake, R. E. (2003). Benzodiazepine use and abuse among patients with severe mental illness and co-occurring substance use disorders. *Psychiatric Services, 54*, 1395–1401.

Brunzell, D. H. (2012). Preclinical evidence that activation of mesolimbic alpha 6 subunit containing nicotinic acetylcholine receptors supports nicotine addiction phenotype. *Nicotine and Tobacco Research, 14*, 1258–1269. doi: 10.1093/ntr/nts089

Bunnell, R. E., Agaku, I. T., Arrazola, R., Apelberg, B. J., Caraballo, R. S., Corey, C. G., . . . & King, B. A. (2014). Intentions to smoke cigarettes among never-smoking US middle and high school electronic cigarette users, National Youth Tobacco Survey, 2011-2013. *Nicotine and Tobacco Research, 17*, 228–235. doi: 10.1093/ntr/ntu166

Burris, K. D., Molski, T. F., Xu, C., Ryan, E., Tottori, K., Kikuchi, T., . . . & Molinoff, P. B. (2002). Aripiprazole, a novel antipsychotic, is a high-affinity partial agonist at human dopamine D2 receptors. *Journal of Pharmacology and Experimental Therapeutics, 302*(1), 381–389.

Burrows, G. D., Maguire, K. P., & Norman, T. R. (1998). Antidepressant efficacy and tolerability of the selective norepinephrine reuptake inhibitor reboxetine: A review. *Journal of Clinical Psychiatry, 59*(Suppl. 14), 4–7.

Busch, A. K., & Johnson, W. C. (1950). L.S.D. 25 as an aid in psychotherapy: Preliminary report of a new drug. *Diseases of the Nervous System, 11*(8), 241–243.

Butt, A. M., Jones, H. C., & Abbott, N. J. (1990). Electrical resistance across the blood-brain barrier in anaesthetized rats: A developmental study. *Journal of Physiology, 429*(1), 47–62. doi: 10.1113/jphysiol.1990.sp018243

Buysse, D., Bate, G., & Kirkpatrick, P. (2005). Fresh from the pipeline: Ramelteon. *Nature Reviews Drug Discovery, 4*(11), 881–882. doi: 10.1038/nrd1881

Byck, R. (Ed.). (1974). *Cocaine papers by Sigmund Freud.* New York, NY: New American Library.

Bymaster, F. P., Zhang, W., Carter, P. A., Shaw, J., Chernet, E., Phebus, L., . . . & Perry, K. W. (2002). Fluoxetine, but not other selective serotonin uptake inhibitors, increases norepinephrine and dopamine extracellular levels in prefrontal cortex. *Psychopharmacology, 160*(4), 353–361. doi: 10.1007/s00213-001-0986-x

Byne, W., Hazlett, E., Buchsbaum, M., & Kemether, E. (2009). The thalamus and schizophrenia: Current status of research. *Acta Neuropathologica, 117*(4), 347–368. doi: 10.1007/s00401-0080404-0

Cade, J.F.J. (1949). Lithium salts in the treatment of psychotic excitement. *Medical Journal of Australia, 2*(10), 349–351.

Cadet, J. L., & Krasnova, I. N. (2007). Interactions of HIV and methamphetamine: Cellular and molecular mechanisms of toxicity potentiation. *Neurotoxicity Research, 12*(3), 181–204.

Caine, S. B., Thomsen, M., Gabriel, K. I., Berkowitz, J. S., Gold, L. H., Koob, G. F., . . . & Xu, M. (2007). Lack of self-administration of cocaine in dopamine D1 receptor knock-out mice. *Journal of Neuroscience, 27*(48), 13140–13150. doi: 10.1523/ jneurosci.2284–07.2007

Cairney, S., Maruff, P., Burns, C., & Currie, B. (2002). The neurobehavioural consequences of petrol (gasoline) sniffing. *Neuroscience and Biobehavioral Reviews, 26*(1), 81–89. doi: 10.1016/ s0149-7634(01)00040-9

Caldwell, C. B., & Gottesman, II. (1990). Schizophrenics kill themselves too: A review of risk factors for suicide. *Schizophrenia Bulletin, 16*(4), 571–589.

Campbell, A. D., & McBride, W. J. (1995). Serotonin-3 receptor and ethanol-stimulated dopamine release in the nucleus accumbens. *Pharmacology Biochemistry and Behavior, 51*(4), 835–842.

Campbell, S., Marriott, M., Nahmias, C., & MacQueen, G. M. (2004). Lower hippocampal volume in patients suffering from depression: A meta-analysis. *American Journal of Psychiatry, 161*, 598–607.

Caporael, L. R. (1976). Ergotism: The satan loosed in Salem? *Science, 192*, 21–26.

Carai, M.A.M., Colombo, G., Reali, R., Serra, S., Mocci, I., Castelli, M. P., Cignarella, G., & Gessa, G. L. (2002). Central effects of 1,4-butanediol are mediated by GABA$_B$ receptors via its conversion into γ-hydroxybutyric acid. *European Journal of Pharmacology, 441*, 157–163. doi: http://dx.doi.org/10.1016/S0014-2999(02)01502-9

Carbone, L. (2000). Justification for the use of animals. In J. Silverman, M. A. Suckow, & S. Murthy (Eds.), *The IACUC handbook* (2nd ed., pp. 157–174). Boca Raton, FL: Taylor & Francis Group.

Carboni, E., Imperato, A., Perezzani, L., & Di Chiara, G. (1989). Amphetamine, cocaine, phencyclidine, and nomifensine increase extracellular dopamine concentrations preferentially in the nucleus accumbens of freely moving rats. *Neuroscience, 28*(3), 653–661.

Carlson, J. N., Visker, K. E., Nielsen, D. M., Keller, R. W., & Glick, S. D. (1996). Chronic antidepressant drug treatment reduces turning behavior and increases dopamine levels in the medial prefrontal cortex. *Brain Research, 707*, 122–126. doi: 10.1016/0006-8993(95)01341-5

Carlsson, A. (2001). A paradigm shift in brain research. *Science, 294*(5544), 1021–1024. doi: 10.1126/science.1066969

Carlsson, A., Lindqvist, M., & Magnusson, T.O.R. (1957). 3, 4-Dihydroxyphenylalanine and 5-hydroxytryptophan as reserpine antagonists. *Nature, 180*, 1200.

Carlsson, A., Lindqvist, M., Magnusson, T., & Waldeck, B. (1958). On the presence of 3-hydroxytyramine in brain. *Science, 127*(3296), 471.

Carmona, R. H. (2005). A 2005 message to women from the U.S. Surgeon General: Advisory on alcohol use in pregnancy. Retrieved from www.surgeongeneral.gov/news/2005/02/sg02222005.html

Caroff, S. N. (1980). The neuroleptic malignant syndrome. *Journal of Clinical Psychiatry, 41*(3), 79–83.

Carpenter, W. T., & Davis, J. M. (2012). Another view of the history of antipsychotic drug discovery and development. *Molecular Psychiatry, 17*(12), 1168–1173. doi: 10.1038/mp.2012.121

Carson-Dewitt, R. (Ed.). (2003). *Drugs, alcohol, and tobacco: Learning about addictive behavior*, Vol. 1. New York, NY: Macmillan.

Carter, L., Griffiths, R., & Mintzer, M. (2009). Cognitive, psychomotor, and subjective effects of sodium oxybate and triazolam in healthy volunteers. *Psychopharmacology (Berl), 206*(1), 141–154. doi: 10.1007/ s00213-009-1589-1

Carter, L. P., Pardi, D., Gorsline, J., & Griffiths, R. R. (2009). Illicit gamma-hydroxybutyrate (GHB) and pharmaceutical sodium oxybate (Xyrem®): Differences in characteristics and misuse. *Drug and Alcohol Dependence, 104*, 1–10. doi: 10.1016/j.drugalcdep.2009.04.012

Carter, N. J., & McCormack, P. L. (2009). Duloxetine: A review of its use in the treatment of generalized anxiety disorder. *CNS Drugs, 23*(6), 523–541. 10.2165/00023210–20092306000006.

Casale, J. F., & Klein, R.F.X. (1993). Illicit production of cocaine. *Forensic Science Review, 5*, 95–107.

Cascini, F., Aiello, C., & Di Tanna, G. (2012). Increasing delta-9-tetrahydrocannabinol (Δ-9-THC) content in herbal cannabis over time: Systematic review and meta-analysis. *Current Drug Abuse Reviews, 5*, 32–40.

Castellani, C. A., Melka, M. G., Gui, J. L., O'Reilly, R. L., & Singh, S. M. (2015). Integration of DNA sequence and DNA methylation changes in monozygotic twin pairs discordant for schizophrenia. *Schizophrenia Research, 169*(1), 433–440. doi: 10.1016/j.schres.2015.09.021

Center for Behavioral Health Statistics and Quality. (2014a). Results from the 2013 National Survey on Drug Use and Health: Summary of National Findings. *NSDUH Series H-48*, HHS Publication No. (SMA) 14–4863. Rockville, MD: Substance Abuse and Mental Health Services Administration.

Center for Behavioral Health Statistics and Quality. (2014b). *National survey on Drug Use and Health, 2013 and 2014*. Rockville, MD: Substance Abuse and Mental Health Services Administration.

from http://www.samhsa.gov/data/sites/default/files/NSDUH-DetTabs2014/NSDUH-DetTabs2014.htm

Center for Behavioral Health Statistics and Quality. (2015). 2014 National Survey on Drug Use and Health: Detailed Tables. *Substance Abuse and Mental Health Services Administration* Rockville, MD:Author.

Centers for Disease Control and Prevention (CDC). (2008). *National Ambulatory Medical Care Survey.* Retrieved from www.cdc.gov/nchs/data/ahcd/namcs_summary/ namcssum2008.pdf

Centers for Disease Control and Prevention (CDC). (2008). Smoking-attributable mortality, years of potential life lost, and productivity losses—United States 2000–2004. *Morbidity and Mortality Weekly Report, 57*, 1226–1228.

Centers for Disease Control and Prevention (CDC). (2010). Traumatic brain injury in the United States: Emergency department visits, hospitalizations, and deaths 2002–2006. Retrieved from www.cdc.gov/TraumaticBrainInjury/

Centers for Disease Control and Prevention (CDC). (2011a). Effects of blood alcohol concentration. Retrieved from http://www.cdc.gov/Motorvehiclesafety/Impaired_ Driving/bac.html

Centers for Disease Control and Prevention (CDC). (2011b). Emergency department visits after use of a drug sold as "Bath Salts"—Michigan, November 13, 2010–March 3, 2011.

Centers for Disease Control and Prevention (CDC). (2011c). Washington, DC: U.S. Government Printing Office.

Centers for Disease Control and Prevention (CDC). (2011d). Summary health statistics for U.S. adults: National health interview survey, 2010. *Vital and Health Statistics, 10*(252). Retrieved from http://www.cdc.gov/nchs/data/series/sr_10/sr10_260.pdf

Centers for Disease Control and Prevention. (2013, February 15). Acute kidney injury associated with synthetic cannabinoid use—multiple states, 2012. *Morbidity and Mortality Weekly Report, 62*(6), 93–98.

Centers for Disease Control and Prevention. (2015). Suicide: Facts at a glance. Retrieved from http://www .cdc.gov/violenceprevention/pdf/suicide-datasheet-a.pdf

Chakrabarti, S., & Fombonne, E. (2005). Pervasive developmental disorders in preschool children: Confirmation of high prevalence. *American Journal of Psychiatry, 162*(6), 1133–1141. doi: http:// dx.doi .org/10.1176/appi.ajp.162.6.1133

Chan, A. W. (1984). Effects of combined alcohol and benzodiazepine: a review. *Drug and Alcohol Dependence, 13*(4), 315–341.

Chandler, A. L., & Hartman, M. A. (1960). Lysergic acid diethylamide (LSD-25) as a facilitating agent in psychotherapy. *Archives of General Psychiatry, 2*, 286–299.

Chanpattana, W., & Sackeim, H. A. (2010). Electroconvulsive therapy in treatment-resistant schizophrenia: Prediction of response and the nature of symptomatic improvement. *Journal of ECT, 26*(4), 289–298.

Chapman, L. F. (1970). Experimental induction of hangover. *Quarterly Journal of Studies on Alcohol, 5*, 67–86.

Chavkin, C., James, I., & Goldstein, A. (1982). Dynorphin is a specific endogenous ligand of the kappa opioid receptor. *Science, 215*(4531), 413–415. doi: 10.1126/ science .6120570

Chavkin, C., Sud, S., Jin, W., Stewart, J., Zjawiony, J. K., Siebert, D. J., . . . Roth, B. L. (2004). Salvinorin A, an active component of the hallucinogenic sage *Salvia divinorum* is a highly efficacious κ-opioid receptor agonist: Structural and functional considerations. *Journal of Pharmacology and Experimental Therapeutics, 308*(3), 1197–1203. doi: 10.1124/ jpet.103.059394

Chen, C.-H., Ridler, K., Suckling, J., Williams, S., Fu, C.H.Y., Merlo-Pich, E., & Bullmore, E. (2007). Brain imaging correlates of depressive symptom severity and predictors of symptom improvement after antidepressant treatment. *Biological Psychiatry, 62*(5), 407–414. doi: 10.1016/j. biopsych.2006.09.018

Chen, J. G., Sachpatzidis, A., & Rudnick, G. (1997). The third transmembrane domain of the serotonin transporter contains residues associated with substrate and cocaine binding. *Journal of Biological Chemistry, 272*(45), 28321–28327.

Chen, K., & Kandel, D. (2002). Relationship between extent of cocaine use and dependence among adolescents and adults in the United States. *Drug and Alcohol Dependence, 68*, 65–85. doi: dx.doi.org/10.1016/S0376–8716(02)00086–8

Chen, Y., & Sommer, C. (2006). Nociceptin and its receptor in rat dorsal root ganglion neurons in neuropathic and inflammatory pain models: Implications on pain processing. *Journal of the Peripheral Nervous System, 11*(3), 232–240. doi: 10.1111/j.15298027.2006.0093.x

Chesher, G. B., Bird, K. D., Jackson, D. M., Perrignon, A., & Starmer, G. A. (1990). The effects of orally administered Δ9-tetrahydrocannabinol in man on mood and performance measures: A dose-response study. *Pharmacology Biochemistry and Behavior, 35*(4), 861–864. doi: 10.1016/0091–3057(90)90371-n

Childress, A. C., Sallee, F. R., & Berry, S. A. (2011). Single-dose pharmacokinetics of NWP06, an extended-release methylphenidate suspension, in children and adolescents with ADHD. *Postgraduate Medicine, 123*(5), 80–88. doi: 10.3810/ pgm.2011.09.2462

Chin, R. L., Sporer, K. A., Cullison, B., Dyer, J. E., & Wu, T. D. (1998). Clinical course of gammahydroxybutyrate overdose. *Annals of Emergency Medicine, 31*(6), 716–722.

Chinnawirotpisan, P., Theeragool, G., Limtong, S., Toyama, H., Adachi, O. O., & Matsushita, K. (2003). Quinoprotein alcohol dehydrogenase is involved in catabolic acetate production, while NAD-dependent alcohol dehydrogenase in ethanol assimilation in *Acetobacter pasteurianus* SKU1108. *Journal of Bioscience and Bioengineering, 96*(6), 564–571. doi: S13891723(04)70150–4 [pii]

Chiu, C.-T., & Chuang, D.-M. (2010). Molecular actions and therapeutic potential of lithium in preclinical and clinical studies of CNS disorders.

Pharmacology and Therapeutics, 128(2): 281–304. doi: 10.1016/j. pharmthera.2010.07.006

Christrup, L. L. (1997). Morphine metabolites. *Acta Anaesthesiologica Scandinavica, 41*(1), 116–122. doi: 10.1111/j.1399–6576.1997. tb04625.x

Cicero, T. J., Ellis, M. S., Surratt, H. L., & Kurtz, S. P. (2014). The changing face of heroin use in the United States: A retrospective analysis of the past 50 years. *JAMA Psychiatry, 71*, 821–826. doi: 10.1001/jamapsychiatry.2014.366

Clark, L., Iversen, S. D., & Goodwin, G. M. (2002). Sustained attention deficit in bipolar disorder. *British Journal of Psychiatry, 180*(4), 313–319. doi: 10.1192/ bjp.180.4.313

Clark, P. A., Capuzzi, K., & Fick, C. (2011). Medical marijuana: Medical necessity versus political agenda. *Medical Science Monitor, 17*, 249–261.

Clavier, T., Tonon, M. C., Foutel, A., Besnier, E., Lefevre-Scelles, A., Morin, F., . . . & Dureuil, B. (2014). Increased plasma levels of endozepines, endogenous ligands of benzodiazepine receptors, during systemic inflammation: A prospective observational study. *Critical Care, 18*(6), 1–8. doi: 10. 1186/ s13054–014–0633–7

Cloninger, C. R. (1987). Neurogenetic adaptive mechanisms in alcoholism. *Science, 236*(4800), 410–416.

Coe, J. W., Brooks, P. R., Vetelino, M. G., Wirtz, M. C., Arnold, E. P., Huang, J., . . . O'Neill, B. T. (2005). Varenicline: An alpha4beta2 nicotinic receptor partial agonist for smoking cessation. *Journal of Medicinal Chemistry, 48*(10), 3474–3477. doi: 10.1021/jm050069n

Coffey, C., Carlin, J. B., Degenhardt, L., Lynskey, M., Sanci, L., & Patton, G. C. (2002). Cannabis dependence in young adults: An Australian population study. *Addiction, 97*(2), 187–194.

Cogliano, V. J., Baan, R., Straif, K., Grosse, Y., Lauby-Secretan, B., El Ghissassi, F., . . . & Galichet, L. (2011). Preventable exposures associated with human cancers. *Journal of the National Cancer Institute, 103*(24), 1827–1839. doi: 10.1093/jnci/djr483

Cohen, C., Perrault, G., Voltz, C., Steinberg, R., & Soubrie, P. (2002).

SR141716, a central cannabinoid (CB[1]) receptor antagonist, blocks the motivational and dopamine-releasing effects of nicotine in rats. *Behavioural Pharmacology, 13*(5–6), 451–463.

Cohen, S. (1977). Inhalant abuse: An overview of the problem. *NIDA Research Monograph, 15,* 2–11.

Cole, J. C., Bailey, M., Sumnall, H. R., Wagstaff, G. F., & King, L. A. (2002). The content of ecstasy tablets: Implications for the study of their long-term effects. *Addiction, 97*(12), 1531–1536. doi: 10.1046/j. 1360–0443.2002.00222.x

Comb, M., Seeburg, P. H., Adelman, J., Eiden, L., & Herbert, E. (1982). Primary structure of the human Met- and Leu-enkephalin precursor and its mRNA. *Nature, 295*(5851), 663–666.

Comer, S. D., Collins, E. D., & Fischman, M. W. (2001). Buprenorphine sublingual tablets: Effects on IV heroin self-administration by humans. *Psychopharmacology, 154*(1), 28–37. doi: 10.1007/s002130000623

Cone, E. J., & Johnson, R. E. (1986). Contact highs and urinary cannabinoid excretion after passive exposure to marijuana smoke. *Clinical Pharmacology and Therapy, 40,* 247–256.

Conger, J. J. (1956). Reinforcement theory and the dynamics of alcoholism. *Quarterly Journal of Studies on Alcohol, 17,* 296–305.

Connolly, G. N., Richter, P., Aleguas, A., Jr, Pechacek, T. F., Stanfill, S. B., & Alpert, H. R. (2010). Unintentional child poisonings through ingestion of conventional and novel tobacco products. *Pediatrics, 125*(5), 896–899. doi: 10.1542/peds .2009-2835

Cook, C., Biddlestone, L., Coop, A., & Beardsley, P. (2006). Effects of combining ethanol (EtOH) with gamma-hydroxybutyrate (GHB) on the discriminative stimulus, locomotor, and motor-impairing functions of GHB in mice. *Psychopharmacology (Berl), 185*(1), 112–122. doi: 10.1007/s00213005-0276-0

Cook, C. E., Perez-Reyes, M., Jeffcoat, A. R., & Brine, D. R. (1983). Phencyclidine disposition in humans after small doses of radiolabeled drug. *Federation Proceedings, 42*(9), 2566–2569.

Cook, R., & Calabrese, E. J. (2006). The importance of hormesis to public health. *Environmental Health Perspectives, 114,* 1631–1635. doi:10.1289/ehp.8606.

Correll, C. U. (2008). Assessing and maximizing the safety and tolerability of antipsychotics used in the treatment of children and adolescents. *Journal of Clinical Psychiatry 69*(Suppl 4), 26–36.

Cosgrove, K. P., Esterlis, I., McKee, S. A., Bois, F., Seibyl, J. P., Mazure, C. M., . . . & O'Malley, S. S. (2012). Sex differences in availability of β2*-nicotinic acetylcholine receptors in recently abstinent tobacco smokers. *Archives of General Psychiatry, 69*(4), 418–427. doi: 0.1001/archgenpsychiatry.2011.1465

Cottler, L. B., Womack, S. B., Compton, W. M., & Ben-Abdallah, A. (2001). Ecstasy abuse and dependence among adolescents and young adults: Applicability and reliability of DSM-IV criteria. *Human Psychopharmacology: Clinical and Experimental, 16*(8), 599–606. doi: 10.1002/hup.343

Cougle, J. R., Timpano, K. R., Sachs-Ericsson, N., Keough, M. E., & Riccardi, C. J. (2010). Examining the unique relationships between anxiety disorders and childhood physical and sexual abuse in the National Comorbidity Survey-Replication. *Psychiatry Research, 177*(1–2), 150–155. doi: S01651781(09)00108–5 [pii]

Courchesne, E., Mouton, P. R., Calhoun, M. E., Semendeferi, K., Ahrens-Barbeau, C., Hallet, M. J., . . . & Pierce, K. (2011). Neuron number and size in prefrontal cortex of children with autism. *Journal of the American Medical Association, 306*(18), 2001–2010. doi: 10.1001/jama.2011.1638

Coutelle, C., Hohn, B., Benesova, M., Oneta, C. M., Quattrochi, P., Roth, H.-J., Schmidt-Gayk, H., Schneeweiss, A., Bastert, G., & Seitz, H. K. (2004). Risk factors in alcohol associated breast cancer: Alcohol dehydrogenase polymorphism and estrogens. *International Journal of Oncology, 25,* 1127–1159. doi: 10.3892/ijo.25.4.1127

Cravatt, B. F., Giang, D. K., Mayfield, S. P., Boger, D. L., Lerner, R. A., & Gilula, N. B. (1996). Molecular characterization of an enzyme that degrades neuromodulatory fatty-acid amides. *Nature, 384*(6604), 83–87. doi: 10.1038/384083a0

Crawford, P. (2005). Best practice guidelines for the management of women with epilepsy. *Epilepsia, 46*(s9), 117–124. doi: 10.1111/j.1528-1167.2005.00323.x

Crofford, L. J., Rowbotham, M. C., Mease, P. J., Russell, I. J., Dworkin, R. H., Corbin, A. E., ... & Sharma, U. (2005). Pregabalin for the treatment of fibromyalgia syndrome: Results of a randomized, double-blind, placebo-controlled trial. *Arthritis & Rheumatism, 52*(4), 1264–1273. doi: 10.1002/art.20983

Cruz, S. L., & Dominguez, M. (2011). Misusing volatile substances for their hallucinatory effects: A qualitative pilot study with Mexican teenagers and a pharmacological discussion of their hallucinations. *Substance Use and Misuse, 46*(Suppl. 1), 84–94. doi: 10.3109/10826084.2011.580222

Cruz, S. L., Mirshahi, T., Thomas, B., Balster, R. L., & Woodward, J. J. (1998). Effects of the abused solvent toluene on r 10.1111/j.1528-1167.2005.00323. xecombinant N-methyl-d-aspartate and nonN-methyl-d-aspartate receptors expressed in *Xenopus* oocytes. *Journal of Pharmacology and Experimental Therapeutics, 286*(1), 334–340.

Cryan, J. F., Mombereau, C., & Vassout, A. (2005). The tail suspension test as a model for assessing antidepressant activity: Review of pharmacological and genetic studies in mice. *Neuroscience and Biobehavioral Reviews, 29*(4–5), 571–625. doi: 10.1016/j.neubiorev.2005.03.009

Cui, D., & Morris, M. E. (2009). The drug of abuse γ-hydroxybutyrate is a substrate for sodium-coupled monocarboxylate transporter (SMCT) 1 (SLC5A8): Characterization of SMCT-mediated uptake and inhibition. *Drug Metabolism and Disposition, 37*(7), 1404–1410. doi: 10.1124/dmd.109.027169

Curran, V., Brignell, C., Fletcher, S., Middleton, P., & Henry, J. (2002). Cognitive and subjective dose-response effects of acute oral Δ⁹tetrahydrocannabinol (THC) in infrequent cannabis users. *Psychopharmacology, 164*(1), 61–70. doi: 10.1007/s00213-002-1169-0

Dackis, C. A., Kampman, K. M., Lynch, K. G., Pettinati, H. M., & O'Brien, C. P. (2004). A double-blind, placebo-controlled trial of modafinil for cocaine dependence. *Neuropsychopharmacology, 30*(1), 205–211.

Dahan, A., Yassen, A., Romberg, R., Sarton, E., Teppema, L., Olofsen, E., & Danhof, M. (2006). Buprenorphine induces ceiling in respiratory depression but not in analgesia. *British Journal of Anaesthesiology, 96*(5), 627–632. doi: 10.1093/bja/ael051

Dämgen, K., & Lüddens, H. (1999). Zaleplon displays a selectivity to recombinant GABAA receptors different from zolipdem, zopiclone and benzodiazepines. *Neuroscience Research Communications, 25*(3), 139-148. doi: 10.1002/(SICI)1520-6769(199911/12)25:3<139::AID-NRC3>3.0.CO;2-W

D'Aquila, P. S., Collu, M., Gessa, G. L., & Serra, G. (2000). The role of dopamine in the mechanism of action of antidepressant drugs. *European Journal of Pharmacology, 405*(1–3), 365–373. doi: S0014299900005665 [pii]

Darke, S., Williamson, A., Ross, J., Teesson, M., & Lynskey, M. (2004). Borderline personality disorder, antisocial personality disorder and risk-taking among heroin users: Findings from the Australian Treatment Outcome Study (ATOS). *Drug and Alcohol Dependence, 74*, 77–83. doi: 10.1016/j.drugalcdep.2003.12.002

Davidson, J. R., DuPont, R. L., & Haskins, J. T. (1999). Efficacy, safety, and tolerability of venlafaxine extended release and buspirone in outpatients with generalized anxiety disorder. *Journal of Clinical Psychiatry, 60*(8), 1–478.

Davies, G., Welham, J., Chant, D., Torrey, E. F., & McGrath, J. (2003). A systematic review and meta-analysis of Northern Hemisphere season of birth studies in schizophrenia. *Schizophrenia Bulletin, 29*(3), 587–593.

Davis, B., Dang, M., Kim, J., & Talbot, P. (2015). Nicotine concentrations in electronic cigarette refill and do-it-yourself fluids. *Nicotine and Tobacco Research, 17*, 134–141. doi: 10.1093/ntr/ntu080

Davis, C., Curtis, C., Levitan, R. D., Carter, J. C., Kaplan, A. S., & Kennedy, J. L. (2011). Evidence that "food addiction" is a valid phenotype of obesity.

Appetite, 57(3), 711–717. doi: 10.1016/j.appet.2011.08.017

Davis, J. M. (2006). Tricyclic antidepressants, neurotransmitters, and neuropsychopharmacology. In T. A. Ban & R. U. Udabe (Eds.), *The neurotransmitter era in neuropsychopharmacology*, 141–152. Buenos Aires, Argentina: Editorial Polemos.

Davis, M., & Whalen, P. J. (2001). The amygdala: Vigilance and emotion. *Molecular Psychiatry, 6*(1), 13–34.

De Bellis, M. D., Baum, A. S., Birmaher, B., Keshavan, M. S., Eccard, C. H., Boring, A. M., . . . & Ryan, N. D. (1999). A.E. Bennett Research Award. Developmental traumatology. Part I: Biological stress systems. *Biological Psychiatry, 45*(10), 1259–1270. doi: S000632239900044X [pii]

de Boer, J. Z., Hale, J. R., & Chanton, J. (2001). New evidence for the geological origins of the ancient Delphic oracle (Greece). *Geology, 29*, 707–710.

Del Arco, A., Segovia, G., & Mora, F. (2008). Blockade of NMDA receptors in the prefrontal cortex increases dopamine and acetylcholine release in the nucleus accumbens and motor activity. *Psychopharmacology, 201*(3), 325–338. doi: 10.1007/s00213008-1288–3

de la Garza, R., & Johanson, C. E. (1985). Discriminative stimulus properties of cocaine in pigeons. *Psychopharmacology (Berl), 85*(1), 23–30.

De La Torre, R., Farré, M., Ortuño, J., Mas, M., Brenneisen, R., Roset, P. N., . . . & Camí, J. (2000). Non-linear pharmacokinetics of MDMA ("ecstasy") in humans. *British Journal of Clinical Pharmacology, 49*(2), 104–109. doi: 10.1046/j.13652125.2000.00121.x

De La Torre, R., Farré, M., Roset, P. N., López, C. H., Mas, M., Ortuño, J.,. . .& Camí, J. (2000). Pharmacology of MDMA in humans. *Annals of the New York Academy of Sciences, 914*(1), 225–237. doi: 10.1111/j.17496632.2000.tb05199.x

Delay, J., Deniker, P., & Harl, J. M. (1952). Therapeutic use in psychiatry of phenothiazine of central elective action (4560 RP). *Annals of Medicine and Psychology (Paris), 110*(2 1), 112–117.

De Leonibus, E., Verheij, M.M.M., Mele, A., & Cools, A. (2006). Distinct kinds of novelty processing differentially increase extracellular dopamine in different brain regions. *European Journal of Neuroscience, 23*(5), 1332–1340. doi: 10.1111/j.14609568.2006.04658.x

DeMartinis, N., Rynn, M., Rickels, K., & Mandos, L. (2000). Prior benzodiazepine use and buspirone response in the treatment of generalized anxiety disorder. *Journal of Clinical Psychiatry, 61*(2), 91–94.

Deng, J., Shen, C., Wang, Y. J., Zhang, M., Li, J., Xu, Z. Q., . . . & Zhou, H. D. (2010). Nicotine exacerbates tau phosphorylation and cognitive impairment induced by amyloid-beta 25–35 in rats. *European Journal of Pharmacology, 637*(1–3), 83–88. doi: S0014-2999(10)00226–8 [pii]

De Petrocellis, L., Melck, D., Bisogno, T., Milone, A., & Di Marzo, V. (1999). Finding of the endocannabinoid signalling system in Hydra, a very primitive organism: Possible role in the feeding response. *Neuroscience, 92*(1), 377–387. doi: 10.1016/s03064522(98)00749–0

Derry, J.M.C., Dunn, S.M.J., & Davies, M. (2004). Identification of a residue in the gammaaminobutyric acid type A receptor alpha subunit that differentially affects diazepam-sensitive and -insensitive benzodiazepine site binding. *Journal of Neurochemistry, 88*(6), 1431–1438.

De Schepper, H. U., Cremonini, F., Park, M. I., & Camilleri, M. (2004). Opioids and the gut: Pharmacology and current clinical experience. *Neurogastroenterology and Motility, 16*(4), 383–394. doi: 10.1111/j.13652982.2004.00513.x

DeWire, S. M., Yamashita, D. S., Rominger, D. H., Liu, G., Cowan, C. L., Graczyk, T. M., . . . & Koblish, M. (2013). AG protein-biased ligand at the μ-opioid receptor is potently analgesic with reduced gastrointestinal and respiratory dysfunction compared with morphine. *Journal of Pharmacology and Experimental Therapeutics, 344*, 708–717. doi: 10.1124/jpet.112.201616

De Wit, H., Pierri, J., & Johanson, C. E. (1989). Reinforcing and subjective effects of diazepam in nondrug-abusing volunteers. *Pharmacology Biochemistry and Behavior, 33*(1), 205–213.

de Wit, S., & Dickinson, A. (2009). Associative theories of goal-directed behaviour: A case for animal-human translational models. *Psychological Research, 73*(4), 463–476. doi: 10.1007/ s00426009–0230–6

Diana, M., Mereu, G., Mura, A., Fadda, F., Passino, N., & Gessa, G. (1991). Low doses of gamma-hydroxybutyric acid stimulate the firing rate of dopaminergic neurons in unanesthetized rats. *Brain Research, 566*(1–2), 208–211.

DiFranza, J. R., Svageau, J. A., Rigotti, N. A., Ockene, J. K., McNeill, A. D., Coleman, M., & Wood, C. (2004). Trait anxiety and nicotine dependence in adolescents: A report from the DANDY study. *Addictive Behaviors, 29*, 911–919. doi: 10.1016/j. addbeh.2004.02.021

Di Marzo, V., Goparaju, S. K., Wang, L., Liu, J., Bátkai, S., Járai, Z., . . . & Kunos, G. (2001). Leptin-regulated endocannabinoids are involved in maintaining food intake. *Nature, 410*(6830), 822–825. doi: 10.1038/35071088

Ding, Z.-M., Oster, S., Hall, S., Engleman, E., Hauser, S., McBride, W., & Rodd, Z. (2011). The stimulating effects of ethanol on ventral tegmental area dopamine neurons projecting to the ventral pallidum and medial prefrontal cortex in female Wistar rats: Regional difference and involvement of serotonin-3 receptors. *Psychopharmacologia, 216*(2), 245–255. doi: 10.1007/ s00213–011–2208–5

Ding, Z. M., Toalston, J. E., Oster, S. M., McBride, W. J., & Rodd, Z. A. (2009). Involvement of local serotonin-2A but not serotonin-1B receptors in the reinforcing effects of ethanol within the posterior ventral tegmental area of female Wistar rats. *Psychopharmacology, 204*(3), 381–390. doi: 10.1007/ s00213–009–1468–9

Dingemanse, J., & Appel-Dingemanse, S. (2007). Integrated pharmacokinetics and pharmacodynamics in drug development. *Clinical Pharmacokinetics, 46*(9), 713–737.

Diniz, J. B., Shavitt, R. G., Pereira, C. A., Hounie, A. G., Pimentel, I., Koran, L. M., . . . & Miguel, E. C. (2010). Quetiapine versus clomipramine in the augmentation of selective serotonin reuptake inhibitors for the treatment of obsessive-compulsive disorder: A randomized, open-label trial. *Journal of Psychopharmacology, 24*(3), 297–307. doi: 0269881108099423 [pii]

Djordjevic, M. V., Hoffman, D., Glynn, T., & Connolly, G. N. (1995). U.S. commercial brands of moist snuff, 1994: I. Assessment of nicotine, moisture, and pH. *Tobacco Control, 4*, 62–66.

Dlugosz, H., & Nasrallah, H. A. (2007). Paliperidone: A new extended-release oral atypical antipsychotic. *Expert Opinion on Pharmacotherapy, 8*(14), 2307–2313.

Doblin, R. (1991). Pahnke's "Good Friday Experiment": A long-term follow-up and methodological critique. *Journal of Transpersonal Psychology, 23*, 1–28.

Doherty, J. D., Stout, R. W., & Roth, R. H. (1975). Metabolism of (1–14C)gamma-hydroxybutyric acid by rat brain after intraventricular injection. *Biochemical Pharmacology, 24*(4), 469–474.

Dolder, C. R., & Nelson, M. H. (2008). Hypnosedative-induced complex behaviours. *CNS Drugs, 22*(12), 1021–1036. doi: 10.2165/0023210– 200822120–00005

Domino, E. F., & Luby, E. D. (2012). Phencyclidine/schizophrenia: One view toward the past, the other to the future. *Schizophrenia Bulletin, 38*: 914–919.

Donjacour, C.E.H. M., Aziz, N. A., Roelfsema, F., Frölich, M., Overeem, S., Lammers, G. J., & Pijl, H. (2011). Effect of sodium oxybate on growth hormone secretion in narcolepsy patients and healthy controls. *American Journal of Physiology—Endocrinology and Metabolism, 300*(6), E1069–E1075. doi: 10.1152/ajpendo.00623.2010

dos Reis, A. Jr. (2009). Sigmund Freud (1856–1939) and Karl Koller (1857–1944) and the discovery of local anesthesia. *Revista Brasileira Anestesiologia, 59*(2), 244–257.

Doyon, S. (2001). The many faces of ecstasy. *Current Opinion in Pediatrics, 13*(2), 170–176.

Dranovsky, A., & Hen, R. (2006). Hippocampal neurogenesis: Regulation by stress and antidepressants. *Biological Psychiatry, 59*(12), 1136–1143. doi: S0006–3223(06)00581–6 [pii]

Drdla, R., Gassner, M., Gingl, E., & Sandkuhler, J. (2009). Induction of synaptic long-term potentiation after opioid withdrawal. *Science, 325*(5937), 207–210. doi: 10.1126/ science.1171759

Drevets, W., Videen, T., Price, J., Preskorn, S., Carmichael, S., & Raichle, M. (1992). A functional anatomical study of unipolar depression. *Journal of Neuroscience, 12*(9), 3628–3641.

Drevets, W. C., Bogers, W., & Raichle, M. E. (2002). Functional anatomical correlates of antidepressant drug treatment assessed using PET measures of regional glucose metabolism. *European Neuropsychopharmacology, 12*(6), 527–544. doi: 10.1016/ s0924– 977x(02)00102–5

Drevets, W. C., & Furey, M. L. (2010). Replication of scopolamine's antidepressant efficacy in major depressive disorder: A randomized, placebo-controlled clinical trial. *Biological Psychiatry, 67*(5), 432–438. doi: 10.1016/j.biopsych.2009.11.021

Drevets, W. C., Price, J. L., Bardgett, M. E., Reich, T., Todd, R. D., & Raichle, M. E. (2002). Glucose metabolism in the amygdala in depression: Relationship to diagnostic subtype and plasma cortisol levels. *Pharmacology Biochemistry and Behavior, 71*(3), 431–447. doi: 10.1016/ s00913057(01)00687–6

Drug Enforcement Administration (DEA), Justice. (2010). Exempt chemical mixtures containing gamma-butyrolactone. Final rule. *Federal register, 75*(124), 37301.

Drug Enforcement Administration. (2011). *3–4-methylenedioxy-pyrovalerone (MDPV)*. Washington, DC: United States Department of Justice.

Drug Enforcement Administration. (2012a). Gamma hydrobutyric acid. U.S. Department of Justice. Retrieved from www.deadiversion.usdoj.gov/ drugs_concern/ghb/ghb.htm

Drug Enforcement Administration. (2012b). Scheduling actions. Washington, DC: U.S. Department of Justice. Retrieved from www. deadiversion.usdoj.gov/schedules/ orangebook/a_sched_alpha.pdf

Drug Enforcement Administration. (2012c). *Salvia divinorum*. Washington,

DC: U.S. Department of Justice. Retrieved from www.justice.gov/dea/concern/salvia_divinorum.html

Duarte, D. F. (2005). Una breve história do ópio e dos opióides. *Revista Brasileira de Anestesiologia, 55*, 135–146.

Dubowski, K. M. (1985). Absorption, distribution and elimination of alcohol: Highway safety aspects. *Journal of Studies on Alcohol* (Suppl 10), 98–108.

Dufour, M. C. (1999). What is moderate drinking? Defining "drinks" and drinking levels. *Alcohol Research and Health, 23*, 5–14.

Duman, R. S., Malberg, J., & Thome, J. (1999). Neural plasticity to stress and antidepressant treatment. *Biological Psychiatry, 46*(9), 1181–1191. doi: S00063223(99)00177–8 [pii]

Duncan, G. E., Paul, I. A., Powell, K. R., Fassberg, J. B., Stumpf, W. E., & Breese, G. R. (1989). Neuroanatomically selective down-regulation of beta adrenergic receptors by chronic imipramine treatment: Relationships to the topography of [3H]imipramine and [3H]desipramine binding sites. *Journal of Pharmacology and Experimental Therapeutics, 248*(1), 470–477.

Dupont, H. L., Sanchez, J. F., Ericcson, C. D., Gomez, J. M., Dupont, M. W., Luna, A. C., & Mathewson, J. J. (1990). Comparative efficacy of loperamide hydrocholoride and bismuth subsalicylate in the management of acute diarrhea. *The American Journal of Medicine, 88*(6), S15–S19.

Duvauchelle, C. L., Ikegami, A., Asami, S., Robens, J., Kressin, K., & Castaneda, E. (2000). Effects of cocaine context on NAcc dopamine and behavioral activity after repeated intravenous cocaine administration. *Brain Research, 862*(1–2), 49–58.

Duvauchelle, C. L., Ikegami, A., & Castaneda, E. (2000). Conditioned increases in behavioral activity and accumbens dopamine levels produced by intravenous cocaine. *Behavioral Neuroscience, 114*(6), 1156–1166.

Eccles, J. C. (1948). Conduction and synaptic transmission in the nervous system. *Annual Reviews in Physiology, 10*, 93–116.

Eccles, J. C., Fatt, P., & Koketsu, K. (1954). Cholinergic and inhibitory synapses in a pathway from motor-axon collaterals to motoneurones. *Journal of Physiology, 126*, 524–562.

Egan, M. F., Kojima, M., Callicott, J. H., Goldberg, T. E., Kolachana, B. S., Bertolino, A., . . . & Weinberger, D. R. (2003). The BDNF val66met polymorphism affects activity-dependent secretion of BDNF and human memory and hippocampal function. *Cell, 112*(2), 257–269. doi: 10.1016/s0092–8674(03)00035–7

Ekelund, J., Hovatta, I., Parker, A., Paunio, T., Varilo, T., Martin, R., . . . & Peltonen, L. (2001). Chromosome 1 loci in Finnish schizophrenia families. *Human Molecular Genetics, 10*, 1611–1617.

Ellinwood, E. H., King, G., & Lee, T. H. (2000). Chronic amphetamine use and abuse. In F. E. Bloom & D. J. Kupfer (Eds.), *Psychopharmacology: The fourth generation of progress.* Brentwood, TN: American College of Neuropsychopharmacology.

Elliott, S., & Burgess, V. (2005). The presence of gamma-hydroxybutyric acid (GHB) and gammabutyrolactone (GBL) in alcoholic and non-alcoholic beverages. *Forensic Science International, 151*(2–3), 289–292. doi: 10.1016/j.forsciint.2005.02.014

Ellis, R. J., Toperoff, W., Vaida, F., van den Brande, G., Gonzales, J., Gouaux, B., . . . & Atkinson, J. H. (2009). Smoked medicinal cannabis for neuropathic pain in HIV: A randomized, crossover clinical trial. *Neuropsychopharmacology, 34*(3), 672–680. doi: 10.1038/npp.2008.120

El-Mallakh, R. S., & Walker, K. L. (2010). Hallucinations, pseudohallucinations, and parahallucinations. *Psychiatry: Interpersonal and Biological Processes, 73*, 34–42.

Elmes, D. G., Kantowitz, B. H., & Roediger, H. L. (2006). *Research methods in psychology* (8th ed.). New York, NY: Cengage Learning.

ElSohly, M. A., & Salamone, S. J. (1999). Prevalence of drugs used in cases of alleged sexual assault. *Journal of Analytical Toxicology, 23*(3), 141–146. doi: 10.1093/jat/23.3.141

Elzinga, B. M., Schmahl, C. G., Vermetten, E., van Dyck, R., & Bremner, J. D. (2003). Higher cortisol levels following exposure to traumatic reminders in abuse-related PTSD. *Neuropsychopharmacology, 28*(9), 1656–1665.

Emboden, W. A. (1972). Ritual use of *Cannabis sativa L.*: A historical-ethnographic survey. In P. T. Furst (Ed.), *Flesh of the gods: The ritual use of hallucinogens.* New York, NY: Praeger.

Emerson, T. S., & Cisek, J. E. (1993). Methcathinone: A Russian designer amphetamine infiltrates the rural Midwest. *Annals of Emergency Medicine, 22*(12), 1897–1903.

Emsley, R., Rabinowitz, J., & Medori, R. (2006). Time course for antipsychotic treatment response in first-episode schizophrenia. *American Journal of Psychiatry, 163*(4), 743–745. doi: 10.1176/appi.ajp.163.4.743

Ernst, M., Matochik, J. A., Heishman, S. J., Van Horn, J. D., Jons, P. H., Henningfield, J. E., & London, E. D. (2001). Effect of nicotine on brain activation during performance of a working memory task. *Proceedings of the National Academy of Sciences of the United States of America, 98*(8), 4728–4733. doi: 10.1073/pnas.061369098

Erritzoe, D., Frokjaer, V. G., Holst, K. K., Christoffersen, M., Johansen, S. S., Svarer, C., . . . & Knudsen, G. M. (2011). In vivo imaging of cerebral serotonin transporter and serotonin2A receptor binding in 3,4-Me thylenedioxymethamphetamine (MDMA or "Ecstasy") and hallucinogen users. *Archives of General Psychiatry, 68*(6), 562–576. doi: 68/6/562 [pii]

Ervin, G. N., & Nemeroff, C. B. (1988). Interactions of neurotensin with dopamine-containing neurons in the central nervous system. *Progress in Neuropsychopharmacology and Biological Psychiatry* (12 Suppl), S53–S69.

Etches, R. C., Sandler, A. N., & Daley, M. D. (1989). Respiratory depression and spinal opioids. *Canadian Journal of Anaesthesiology, 36*(2), 165–185. doi: 10.1007/ BF03011441

European Monitoring Centre for Drugs and Drug Addiction. (2009). *Annual report*

2009: The state of the drugs problem in Europe. Luxembourg: Publications Office of the European Union.

Eveloff, H. H. (1968). The LSD syndrome: A review. *California Medicine, 109*(5), 368–373.

Everett, G. M. (1972). Effects of amyl nitrite ("poppers") on sexual experience. *Medical Aspects of Human Sexuality, 6,* 146–151.

Every-Palmer, S. (2011). Synthetic cannabinoid JWH-018 and psychosis: An explorative study. *Drug and Alcohol Dependence, 117*(2), 152–157. doi: 10.1016/j.drugalcdep.2011.01.012

Eyding, D., Lelgemann, M., Grouven, U., Härter, M., Kromp, M., Kaiser, T., . . . & Wieseler, B. (2010). Reboxetine for acute treatment of major depression: Systematic review and meta-analysis of published and unpublished placebo and selective serotonin reuptake inhibitor controlled trials. *The BMJ, 341,* c4737. doi: 10.1136/bmj.c4737

Fabre, V., Beaufour, C., Evrard, A., Rioux, A., Hanoun, N., Lesch, K. P., . . . & Martres, M. P. (2000). Altered expression and functions of serotonin 5-HT1A and 5-HT1B receptors in knock-out mice lacking the 5-HT transporter. *European Journal of Neuroscience, 12*(7), 2299–2310. doi: 10.1046/j.1460-9568.2000.00126.x

Fagerstrom, K., Etter, J-F., & Unger, J. B. (2015). E-cigarettes: A disruptive technology that revolutionizes our field? *Nicotine and Tobacco Research, 17,* 125–126. doi: 10.1093/ntr/ntu240

Fantegrossi, W. E., Ullrich, T., Rice, K. C., Woods, J. H., & Winger, G. (2002). 3,4-Me thylenedioxymethamphetamine (MDMA, "Ecstasy") and its stereoisomers as reinforcers in rhesus monkeys: Serotonergic involvement. *Psychopharmacology (Berl), 161*(4), 356–364. doi: 10.1007/s00213-002-1021-6

Farré, M., & Camí, J. (1991). Pharmacokinetic considerations in abuse liability evaluation. *British Journal of Addiction, 86*(12), 1601–1606. doi: 10.1111/j.13600443.1991.tb01754.x

Farsalinos, K. E., Spyrou, A., Tsimopoulou, K., Stefopoulos, C., Romagna, G., & Voudris, V. (2014). Nicotine absorption from electronic cigarette use: Comparison between first and new-generation devices. *Scientific Reports, 4,* 1–7. doi: 10.1038/srep04133

Fava, M., & Davidson, K. G. (1996). Definition and epidemiology of treatment-resistant depression. *Psychiatric Clinics of North America, 19*(2), 179–200.

FDA-approved labeling for Xyrem oral solution. (2005). Palo Alto, CA: Jazz Pharmaceuticals. Retrieved from www.fda.gov/downloads/Drugs/DrugSafety/ucm089830.pdf

Felder, C. C., Briley, E. M., Axel-rod, J., Simpson, J. T., Mackie, K., & Devane, W. A. (1993). Anandamide, an endogenous cannabimimetic eicosanoid, binds to the cloned human cannabinoid receptor and stimulates receptor-mediated signal transduction. *Proceedings of the National Academy of Sciences, 90,* 7656–7660.

Feliú, A., Moreno-Martet, M., Mecha, M., Carrillo-Salinas, F. J., de Lago, E., Fernández-Ruiz, J. & Guaza, C. (2015). A Sativex®-like combination of phytocannabinoids as a disease-modifying therapy in a viral model of multiple sclerosis. *British Journal of Pharmacology, 172:* 3579–3595. doi: 10.1111/bph.13159

Fenster, C. P., Rains, M., Noerager, B., Quick, M. W., & Lester, R.A.J. (1997). Influence of subunit composition on desensitization of neuronal acetylcholine receptors at low concentrations of nicotine. *Journal of Neuroscience, 17,* 5747–5759.

Ferraguti, F., & Shigemoto, R. (2006). Metabotropic glutamate receptors. *Cell Tissue Research, 326,* 483–504. doi: 10.1007/s00441-006-0266-5

Ferrier, I. N., Tyrer, S. P., & Bell, A. J. (1995) Lithium therapy. *Advances in Psychiatric Treatment, 1,* 102–108. 10.1192/apt.1.4.102

Fillmore, M. T., Marczinski, C. A., & Bowman, A. M. (2005). Acute tolerance to alcohol effects on inhibitory and activational mechanisms of behavioral control. *Journal of Studies on Alcohol and Drugs, 66*(5), 663–672.

Fischer, E., & von Mering, J. (1903). Uber eine neue Klasse von Schlafmitteln. *Therapie der Gegenwart, 44,* 97–101.

Fischer, S., Doerr, J. M., Strahler, J., Mewes, R., Thieme, K., & Nater, U. M. (2016). Stress exacerbates pain in the everyday lives of women with fibromyalgia syndrome: The role of cortisol and alpha-amylase. *Psychoneuroendocrinology, 63,* 68–77. doi: 10.1016/j.psyneuen.2015.09.018

Fish, E., DeBold, J., & Miczek, K. (2002). Repeated alcohol: Behavioral sensitization and alcohol-heightened aggression in mice. *Psychopharmacology, 160*(1), 39–48. doi: 10.1007/s00213-0010934-9

Fisone, G., Borgkvist, A., & Usiello, A. (2004). Caffeine as a psychomotor stimulant: Mechanism of action. *Cellular and Molecular Life Sciences, 61*(7), 857–872. doi: 10.1007/s00018-003-3269-3

Fleischhacker, W. W., McQuade, R. D., Marcus, R. N., Archibald, D., Swanink, R., & Carson, W. H. (2009). A double-blind, randomized comparative study of aripiprazole and olanzapine in patients with schizophrenia. *Biological Psychiatry, 65*(6), 510–517. doi: 10.1016/j.biopsych.2008.07.033

Fiore, M. C., Novotny, T. E., Pierce, J. P., Hatziandreu, E. J, Patel, K. M., & Davis, R. M. (1989). Trends in cigarette smoking in the United States: The changing influence of gender and race. *Journal of the American Medical Association, 261,* 49–55.

Foltin, R. W., Fischman, M. W., Brady, J. V., Bernstein, D. J., Capriotti, R. M., Nellis, M. J., & Kelly, T. H. (1990). Motivational effects of smoked marijuana: Behavioral contingencies and low-probability activities. *Journal of Experimental Analysis of Behavior, 53*(1), 5–19. doi: 10.1901/ jeab.1990.53-5

Fontanilla, D., Johannessen, M., Hajipour, A. R., Cozzi, N. V., Jackson, M. B., & Ruoho, A. E. (2009). The hallucinogen N, N-dimethyltryptamine (DMT) is an endogenous sigma-1 receptor regulator. *Science, 323*(5916), 934–937. doi: 10.1126/science.1166127

Food and Drug Administration (FDA). (2002). New drug and biological drug products: Evidence needed to demonstrate effectiveness of new drugs when human efficacy studies are not ethical or feasible. *Federal Register, 67*(105).

Food and Drug Administration. (2005, June 30). Suicidality in adults being treated with antidepressant medications. *FDA Public Health Advisory*.

Food and Drug Administration. (2007). Adderall labeling information. Application number NDA 011522. Washington, DC: Author.

Fowler, J. S., Volkow, N. D., Wang, G. J., Pappas, N., Logan, J., MacGregor, R., . . . & Cilento, R. (1996a). Inhibition of monoamine oxidase B in the brains of smokers. *Nature, 379*(6567), 733–736. doi: 10.1038/379733a0

Fowler, J. S., Volkow, N. D., Wang, G. J., Pappa, N., Logan, J., MacGregor, R., . . . Wolf, A. P. (1996b). Brain monoamine oxidase A inhibition in cigarette smokers. *Proceedings of the National Academy of Sciences, 93,* 14065–14069.

Fox, H. H., & Gibas, J. T. (1953). Synthetic tuberculostats: VII Monoalkyl derivatives of isonicotinylhydrazine. *Journal of Organic Chemistry, 18,* 994–1002.

Frary, C. D., Johnson, R. K., & Wang, M. Q. (2005). Food sources and intakes of caffeine in the diets of persons in the United States. *Journal of the American Dietetic Association, 105,* 110–113.

Frecska, E., Szabo, A., Winkelman, M. J., Luna, L. E., & McKenna, D. J. (2013). A possibly sigma-1 receptor mediated role of dimethyltryptamine in tissue protection, regeneration, and immunity. *Journal of Neural Transmission,* 1295–1303. doi: 10.1007/s00702-013-1024-y

Frederiksen, L. W., Martin, J. E., & Webster, J. S. (1979). Assessment of smoking behavior. *Journal of Applied Behavioral Analysis, 12*(4), 653–664. doi: 10.1901/ jaba.1979.12-653

Fredholm, B. B. (2011). Notes on the history of caffeine use. *Methylxanthines* (Vol. 200, pp. 1–9). Berlin: Springer.

Fredholm, B. B., & Arnaud, M. J. (2011). Pharmacokinetics and metabolism of natural methylxanthines in animal and man. *Methylxanthines* (Vol. 200, pp. 33–91). Berlin: Springer.

Freeman, W., & Watts, J. W. (1945). Prefrontal lobotomy the problem of schizophrenia. *American Journal of Psychiatry, 101,* 739–748.

Freeman, D., Dunn, G., Murray, R. M., Evans, N., Lister, R., Antley, A. . . . & Di Simplicio, M. (2014). How cannabis causes paranoia: Using the intravenous administration of Δ⁹-tetrahydrocannabinol (THC) to identify key cognitive mechanisms leading to paranoia. *Schizophrenia Bulletin, 41,* 391–399. doi: 10.1093/schbul/sbu098

Freis, E. D. (1954). Mental depression in hypertensive patients treated for long periods with large doses of reserpine. *New England Journal of Medicine, 251*(25), 1006–1008.

Freud, S. (1974). *The cocaine papers.* New York, NY: Stonehill Publishing and Robert Byck.

Frezza, M., diPadova, C., Pozzato, G., Terpin, M., Baraona, E., & Lieber, C. S. (1990). High blood alcohol levels in women: The role of decreased gastric alcohol dehydrogenase activity and first-pass metabolism. *New England Journal of Medicine, 322,* 95–99.

Fryer, J. D., & Lukas, R. J. (1999). Noncompetitive functional inhibition at diverse, human nicotinic acetylcholine receptor subtypes by bupropion, phencyclidine, and ibogaine. *Journal of Pharmacology and Experimental Therapeutics, 288*(1), 88–92.

Fudala, P. J., & Woody, G. E. (2002). Current and experimental therapeutics for the treatment of opioid addiction. In K. L. Davis, D. Charney, J. T. Coyle, & C. Nemeroff (Eds.), *Neuropsychopharmacology: The fifth generation of progress* (pp. 1507–1518). Philadelphia: Lippincott, Williams, & Wilkins.

Fujioka, K. & Shibamoto, T. (2008). Chlorogenic acid and caffeine contents in various commercial brewed coffees. *Food Chemistry, 106*(1), 217–221. doi: 10.1016/j.foodchem.2007.05.091

Furey, M. L., & Drevets, W. C. (2006). Antidepressant efficacy of the antimuscarinic drug scopolamine: A randomized, placebo-controlled clinical trial. *Archives of General Psychiatry, 63*(10), 1121–1129.

Gach, K., Belkacemi, O., Lefranc, B., Perlikowski, P., Masson, J., Walet-Balieu, M. L., . . & Tonon, M. C. (2015). Detection, characterization and biological activities of [bisphospho-thr

3, 9] ODN, an endogenous molecular form of ODN released by astrocytes. *Neuroscience, 290,* 472–484. doi: 10.1016/j.neuroscience.2015.01.045

Gallimberti, L., Gentile, N., Cibin, M., Fadda, F., Canton, G., Ferri, M., Ferrara, S. D., & Gessa, G. L. (1989). Gamma-hydroxybutyric acid for treatment of alcohol withdrawal syndrome. *Lancet, 30,* 787–789. doi: 10.1016/S0140-6736(89)90842-8

Galloway, G. P., Newmeyer, J., Knapp, T., Stalcup, S. A., & Smith, D. (1996). A controlled trial of imipramine for the treatment of methamphetamine dependence. *Journal of Substance Abuse Treatment, 13*(6), 493–497. doi: 10.1016/s0740-5472(96)00154-7

Ganesan, K., Raza, S. K., & Vijayaraghavan, R. (2010). Chemical warfare agents. *Journal of Pharmacy and Bioallied Sciences, 2*(3), 166–178. doi: 10.4103/0975-7406.68498

Gannu, R., Yamsani, S. K., Palem, C. R., Yamsani, V. V., Kotagiri, H., & Yamsani, M. R. (2009). Development of high performance liquid chromatography method for buspirone in rabbit serum: Application to pharmacokinetic study. *Analytica chimica acta, 647*(2), 226–230. doi: 10.1016/j.aca.2009.06.005

Garattini, S. (2006) Reserpine and the opening of the neurotransmitter era in neuropsychopharmacology. In T. A. Ban & R. U. Udabe (Eds.), *The neurotransmitter era in neuropsychopharmacology* (pp. 127–138). Buenos Aires, Argentina: Editorial Polemos.

Garcia, J., Kimeldorf, D. J., & Koellino, R. A. (1955). Conditioned aversion to saccharin resulting from exposure to gamma radiation. *Science, 122*(3160), 157–158.

Garrett, B. (2015). *Brain and behavior: An introduction to biological psychology* (4th ed.). Thousand Oaks, CA: Sage.

Garrett, M. D., Walton, M. I., McDonald, E., Judson, I., & Workman, P. (2003). The contemporary drug development process: Advances and challenges in preclinical and clinical development. *Progress in Cell Cycle Research, 5,* 145–158.

Gately, I. (2001) *La diva nicotina: The story of how tobacco seduced the world.* London, England: Simon and Schuster.

Gebissa, E. (2010). Khat in the Horn of Africa: Historical perspectives and current trends. *Journal of Ethnopharmacology, 132*(3), 607–614. doi: 10.1016/j. jep.2010.01.063

Geddes, J. R., Burgess, S., Hawton, K., Jamison, K., & Goodwin, G. M. (2004). Long-term lithium therapy for bipolar disorder: Systematic review and meta-analysis of randomized controlled trials. *American Journal of Psychiatry, 161*(2), 217–222. doi: 10.1176/ appi.ajp.161.2.217

Gems, D. (1999). Alexander Shulgin and Ann Shulgin, PIHKAL, a chemical love story. Alexander Shulgin and Ann Shulgin, TIHKAL, the continuation. *Theoretical Medicine and Bioethics, 20,* 477–479.

Geoffroy, P. A., Rolland, B., & Cottencin, O. (2012). Catatonia and alcohol withdrawal: A complex and underestimated syndrome. *Alcohol and Alcoholism, 47*(3), 288–290. doi: 10.1093/ alcalc/agr170

Georgotas, A., & Zeidenberg, P. (1979). Observations on the effects of four weeks of heavy marihuana smoking on group interaction and individual behavior. *Comprehensive Psychiatry, 20*(5), 427–432. doi: 0010440X(79)90027–0 [pii]

Gerasimov, M. R. (2004). Brain uptake and biodistribution of [11C] toluene in nonhuman primates and mice. In P. M. Conn (Ed.), *Methods in enzymology* (Vol. 385, pp. 334–349). San Diego, CA: Academic Press.

Gerasimov, M. R., Schiffer, W. K., Marsteller, D., Ferrieri, R., Alexoff, D., & Dewey, S. L. (2002). Toluene inhalation produces regionally specific changes in extracellular dopamine. *Drug and Alcohol Dependence, 65*(3), 243–251. doi: 10.1016/s0376–8716(01)00166–1

Gerber, G. J., & Stretch, R. (1975). Drug-induced reinstatement of extinguished self-administration behavior in monkeys. *Pharmacology Biochemistry and Behavior, 3*(6), 1055–1061.

Gertsch, J., Pertwee, R. G., & Di Marzo, V. (2010). Phytocannabinoids beyond the *Cannabis* plant: Do they exist? *British Journal of Pharmacology, 160*(3), 523–529. doi: BPH745 [pii]

Ginsburg, B. C., Pinkston, J. W., & Lamb, R. J. (2011). Reinforcement magnitude modulation of rate dependent effects in pigeons and rats. *Experimental and Clinical Psychopharmacology, 19*(4), 285–294. doi: 10.1037/a0024311

Giroud, C., de Cesare, M., Berthet, A., Varlet, V., Concha-Lozano, N., & Favrat, B. (2015). E-cigarettes: A review of new trends in cannabis use. *International Journal of Environmental Research and Public Health, 12,* 9988–10008. doi: 10.3390/ijerph120809988

Glaser, H. H., & Massengale, O. N. (1962). Glue-sniffing in children. *Journal of the American Medical Association, 181,* 301.

Glennon, R. A. (2014). *Cathinone.* Retrieved from www.pharmacy.vcu .edu/medchem/articles/cat/cat.html

Glennon, R. A. (2014). Bath salts, mephedrone, and methylenedioxypyrovalerone as emerging illicit drugs that will need targeted therapeutic intervention. *Advances in Pharmacology, 69,* 581–620. doi: 10.1016/B978–0–12–420118–7.00015–9

Gloss, D., & Vickrey, B. (2014). Cannabinoids for epilepsy. *Cochrane Library.* doi: 0.1002/14651858.CD009270. pub3

Gobbi, G., Murphy, D. L., Lesch, K. P., & Blier, P. (2001). Modifications of the serotonergic system in mice lacking serotonin transporters: An *in vivo* electrophysiological study. *Journal of Pharmacology and Experimental Therapeutics, 296*(3), 987–995.

Gobert, A., Rivet, J. M., Lejeune, F., Newman-Tancredi, A., Adhumeau-Auclair, A., Nicolas, J. P., . . . & Millan, M. J. (2000). Serotonin$_{2C}$ receptors tonically suppress the activity of mesocortical dopaminergic and adrenergic, but not serotonergic, pathways: A combined dialysis and electrophysiological analysis in the rat. *Synapse, 36,* 205–221. doi: 10.1002/(SICI)1098–2396(20000601)36:3<205::AID-SYN5>3.0.CO;2-D

Goldman, D. A. (2001). Thalidomide use: Past history and current implications for practice. *Oncology Nursing Forum, 28*(3), 471–477, 478–479.

Gomes, T., Juurlink, D. N., Dhalla, I. A., Mailis-Gagnon, A., Paterson, J. M., & Mamdani, M. M. (2011). Trends in opioid use and dosing among socio-economically disadvantaged patients. *Open Medicine, 5,* e12–e22.

Gonçalves, P., Araújo, J. R., & Martel, F. (2015). Antipsychotics-induced metabolic alterations: Focus on adipose tissue and molecular mechanisms. *European Neuropsychopharmacology, 25*(1), 1–16. doi: 10.1016/j. euroneuro.2014.11.008

Gonzales, D., Rennard, S. I., Nides, M., Oncken, C., Azoulay, S., Billing, C. B., . . . & Reeves, K. R. (2006). Varenicline, an alpha4beta2 nicotinic acetylcholine receptor partial agonist, vs sustained-release bupropion and placebo for smoking cessation: A randomized controlled trial. *Journal of the American Medical Association, 296*(1), 47–55. doi: 10.1001/jama.296.1.47

Gonzales, R. A., & Weiss, F. (1998). Suppression of ethanol-reinforced behavior by naltrexone is associated with attenuation of the ethanol-induced increase in dialysate dopamine levels in the nucleus accumbens. *Journal of Neuroscience, 18*(24), 10663–10671.

Goodman, W. K., Ward, H., Kablinger, A., & Murphy, T. (1997). Fluvoxamine in the treatment of obsessive-compulsive disorder and related conditions. *Journal of Clinical Psychiatry, 58*(Suppl. 5), 32–49.

Goodwin, D. W., Powell, B., & Stern, J. (1971). Behavioral tolerance to alcohol in moderate drinkers. *American Journal of Psychiatry, 127*(12), 1651–1653. doi: 10.1176/ appi.ajp.127.12.1651

Goodwin, G. M. (1997). Neuropsychological and neuroimaging evidence for the involvement of the frontal lobes in depression. *Journal of Psychopharmacology, 11,* 115–122. doi: 10.1177/026988119701100204

Gorman, J. M., Kent, J. M., & Coplan, J. D. (2002). Current and emerging therapeutics of anxiety and stress disorders. In K. L. Davis, D. Charney, J. T. Coyle, & C. Nemeroff (Eds.), *Neuropsychopharmacology: The fifth generation of progess* (pp. 967–980). Brentwood, TN: American College of Neuropsychopharmacology.

Gorman, J. M., Martinez, J., Coplan, J. D., Kent, J., & Kleber, M. (2004). The effect of successful treatment on the emotional and physiological response to carbon dioxide inhalation in patients with panic disorder. *Biological Psychiatry, 56*(11), 862–867.

Gossop, M., Bradley, B., & Phillips, G. T. (1987). An investigation of withdrawal symptoms shown by opiate addicts during and subsequent to a 21-day in-patient methadone detoxification procedure. *Addictive Behaviors, 12*(1), 1–6. doi: 10.1016/03064603(87)90002-5

Goto, Y., & Grace, A. A. (2005). Dopaminergic modulation of limbic and cortical drive of nucleus accumbens in goal-directed behavior. *Nature Neuroscience, 8*(6), 805–812. doi: 10.1038/nn1471

Goudie, A. J., Baker, L. E., Smith, J. A., Prus, A. J., Svensson, K. A., Cortes-Burgos, L. A., . . . & Haadsma-Svensson, S. (2001). Common discriminative stimulus properties in rats of muscarinic antagonists, clozapine and the D 3 preferring antagonist PNU99194A: An analysis of possible mechanisms. *Behavioural Pharmacology, 12*(5), 303–315.

Gould, T. D., Einat, H., Bhat, R., & Manji, H. K. (2004). ARA014418, a selective GSK-3 inhibitor, produces antidepressant-like effects in the forced swim test. *International Journal of Neuropsychopharmacology, 7*(04), 387–390. doi: 10.1017/ S1461145704004535

Graefe, K. H., Bossle, F., Wolfel, R., & Burger, A. (1999). Sympathomimetic effects of MIBG: Comparison with tyramine. *Journal of Nuclear Medicine, 40*(8), 1342.

Grant, B. F., & Harford, T. C. (1990). Concurrent and simultaneous use of alcohol with cocaine: Results of national survey. *Drug and Alcohol Dependence, 25*(1), 97–104.

Grant, K. A., Valverius, P., Hudspith, M., & Tabakoff, B. (1990). Ethanol withdrawal seizures and the NMDA receptor complex. *European Journal of Pharmacology, 176*(3), 289–296.

Grattan-Miscio, K., & Vogel-Sprott, M. (2005). Effects of alcohol and performance incentives on immediate working memory. *Psychopharmacology, 181*(1), 188–196. doi: 10.1007/s00213-005-2226-2

Graybiel, A. M., & Rauch, S. L. (2000). Toward a neurobiology of obsessive-compulsive disorder. *Neuron, 28*(2), 343–347. doi: S0896–6273(00)00113–6 [pii]

Green, M. F. (1996). What are the functional consequences of neurocognitive deficits in schizophrenia? *American Journal of Psychiatry, 153*(3), 321–330.

Green, M. F., Kern, R. S., Braff, D. L., & Mintz, J. (2000). Neurocognitive deficits and functional outcome in schizophrenia: Are we measuring the "right stuff"? *Schizophrenia Bulletin, 26*(1), 119–136.

Green, M. F., Kern, R. S., & Heaton, R. K. (2004). Longitudinal studies of cognition and functional outcome in schizophrenia: Implications for MATRICS. *Schizophrenia Research, 72*(1), 41–51. doi: S0920–9964(04)00344–5 [pii]

Greenberg, D. A., Hodge, S. E., Sowinski, J., & Nicoll, D. (2001). Excess of twins among affected sibling pairs with autism: Implications for the etiology of autism. *American Journal of Human Genetics, 69*(5), 1062–1067. doi: 10.1086/324191

Greenberg, P. E., Sisitsky, T., Kessler, R. C., Finkelstein, S. N., Berndt, E. R., Davidson, J. R., . . . & Fyer, A. J. (1999). The economic burden of anxiety disorders in the 1990s. *Journal of Clinical Psychiatry, 60*(7), 427–435.

Grella, C. E., Hser, Y. I., & Hsieh, S. C. (2003). Predictors of drug treatment re-entry following relapse to cocaine use in DATOS. *Journal of Substance Abuse Treatment, 25*(3), 145–154.

Griffin, M. L., Weiss, R. D., & Lange, U. (1989). A comparison of male and female cocaine abuse. *Archives of General Psychiatry, 46*, 122–126. doi:10.1001/archpsyc.1989.01810020024005

Griffiths, R. R., Bigelow, G. E., Liebson, I., & Kaliszak, J. E. (1980). Drug preference in humans: Double-blind choice comparison of pentobarbital, diazepam and placebo. *Journal of Pharmacology and Experimental Therapeutics, 215*(3), 649–661.

Griffiths, R. R., & Chausmer, A. L. (2000). Caffeine as a model drug of dependence: Recent developments in understanding caffeine withdrawal, the caffeine dependence syndrome, and caffeine negative reinforcement. *Nihon Shinkei Seishin Yakurigaku Zasshi, 20*(5), 223–231.

Griffiths, R. R., Findley, J. D., Brady, J. V., Dolan-Gutcher, K., & Robinson, W. W. (1975). Comparison of progressive-ratio performance maintained by cocaine, methylphenidate and secobarbital. *Psychopharmacologia, 43*(1), 81–83.

Grillon, C. (2008). Models and mechanisms of anxiety: Evidence from startle studies. *Psychopharmacology (Berl), 199*(3), 421–437. doi: 10.1007/s00213-007-1019-1

Gross, C., Santarelli, L., Brunner, D., Zhuang, X., & Hen, R. (2000). Altered fear circuits in 5-HT(1A) receptor KO mice. *Biological Psychiatry, 48*(12), 1157–1163. doi: S0006322300010416 [pii]

Greiner, T., Burch, N. R., & Edelberg, R. (1958). Psychopathology and psychophysiology of minimal LSD-25 dosage: a preliminary dosage-response spectrum. *AMA Archives of Neurology & Psychiatry, 79*, 208–210. doi: 10.1001/archneurpsyc.1958.02340020088016

Grund, J-P. C., Laypov. A., & Harris, M. (2013). Breaking worse: The emergence of krokodil and excessive injuries among people who inject drugs in Eurasia. *International Journal of Drug Policy, 24*, 265–274. doi: 10.1016/j.drugpo.2013.04.007

Guidotti, A., Forchetti, C. M., Corda, M. G., Konkel, D., Bennett, C. D., & Costa, E. (1983). Isolation, characterization, and purification to homogeneity of an endogenous polypeptide with agonistic action on benzodiazepine receptors. *Proceedings of the National Academy of Sciences, 80*(11), 3531–3535.

Guillem, K., Vouillac, C., Azar, M. R., Parsons, L. H., Koob, G. F., Cador, M., & Stinus, L. (2005). Monoamine oxidase inhibition dramatically increases the motivation to self-administer nicotine in rats. *Journal of Neuroscience, 25*(38), 8593–8600. doi: 10.1523/jneurosci.2139-05.2005

Guillon, J. M. (2010). Place and role of safety pharmacology in drug development. *Annales pharmaceutiques françaises, 68*(5), 291–300.

Gulya, K., Grant, K. A., Valverius, P., Hoffman, P. L., & Tabakoff, B. (1991). Brain regional specificity and time-course of changes in the NMDA receptor-ionophore complex during ethanol withdrawal. *Brain*

Research, 547(1), 129–134. doi: 0006-8993(91)90583-H [pii]

Gundersen, H., Specht, K., Grüner, R., Ersland, L., & Hugdahl, K. (2008). Separating the effects of alcohol and expectancy on brain activation: An fMRI working memory study. *NeuroImage, 42*(4), 1587–1596. doi: 10.1016/j.neuroimage.2008.05.037

Gunja, N. (2013). In the Zzz zone: The effects of Z-drugs on human performance and driving. *Journal of Medical Toxicology, 9*(2), 163–171. doi: 10.1007/s13181-013-0294-y

Guttman, M., Leger, G., Reches, A., Evans, A., Kuwabara, H., Cedarbaum, J. M., & Gjedde, A. (1993). Administration of the new COMT inhibitor OR611 increases striatal uptake of fluorodopa. *Movement Disorders, 8*(3), 298–304. doi: 10.1002/ mds.870080308

Guzman, M., Duarte, M. J., Blazquez, C., Ravina, J., Rosa, M. C., Galve-Roperh, I., . . . & Gonzalez-Feria, L. (2006). A pilot clinical study of Δ9-tetrahydrocannabinol in patients with recurrent glioblastoma multiforme. *British Journal of Cancer, 95*(2), 197–203. doi: 10.1038/sj.bjc.6603236

Hadad, N. A., & Knackstedt, L. A. (2014). Addicted to palatable foods: Comparing the neurobiology of Bulimia Nervosa to that of drug addiction. *Psychopharmacology, 231*, 1897–1912. doi: 10.1007/s00213-014-3461-1

Haile, C. N., Kosten, T. R., & Kosten, T. A. (2009). Pharmacogenetic treatments for drug addiction: Cocaine, amphetamine, and methamphetamine. *American Journal of Drug and Alcohol Abuse, 35*(3), 161–177. doi: 911581221 [pii] 10.1080/00952 990902825447

Hajnal, A., Smith, G. P., & Norgren, R. (2004). Oral sucrose stimulation increases accumbens dopamine in the rat. *American Journal of Physiology—Regulatory, Integrative and Comparative Physiology, 286*(1), R31–R37. doi: 10.1152/ajpregu.00282.2003

Hall, W. (2010). What are the policy lessons of national alcohol prohibition in the United States, 1920–1933? *Addiction, 105*(7), 1164–1173. doi: 10.1111/j.13600443.2010.02926.x

Hall, W., & Zador, D. (1997). The alcohol withdrawal syndrome. *The Lancet,* 349(9069), 1897–1900. doi: 10.1016/s01406736(97)04572-8

Hameedi, F. A., Rosen, M. I., McCance-Katz, E. F., McMahon, T. J., Price, L. H., Jatlow, P. I., . . . & Kosten, T. R. (1995). Behavioral, physiological, and pharmacological interaction of cocaine and disulfiram in humans. *Biological Psychiatry, 37*(8), 560–563. doi: 10.1016/0006-3223(94)00361-6

Hamik, A., & Peroutka, S. J. (1989). 1-(m-Chlorophenyl) piperazine (mCPP) interactions with neurotransmitter receptors in the human brain. *Biological Psychiatry, 25*, 569–575. doi: 10.1016/0006-3223(89)90217-5

Han, X., Chow, B. Y., Zhou, H., Klapoetke, N. C., Chuong, A., Rajimehr, R., . . . & Boyden, E. S. (2011). A high-light sensitivity optical neural silencer: Development and application to optogenetic control of non-human primate cortex. *Frontiers in System Neuroscience, 5*, 18. doi: 10.3389/fnsys.2011.00018

Haney, M., Gunderson, E. W., Rabkin, J., Hart, C. L., Vosburg, S. K., Comer, S. D., & Foltin, R. W. (2007). Dronabinol and marijuana in HIV-positive marijuana smokers. Caloric intake, mood, and sleep. *Journal of Acquired Immune Deficiency Syndrome, 45*(5), 545–554. doi: 10.1097/ QAI.0b013e31811ed205

Harburg, E. (1981). Negative affect, alcohol consumption and hangover symptoms among normal drinkers in a small community. *Journal of Studies on Alcohol and Drugs, 42*, 998–1012.

Hariri, A. R., Mattay, V. S., Tessitore, A., Kolachana, B., Fera, F., Goldman, D., . . . & Weinberger, D. R. (2002). Serotonin transporter genetic variation and the response of the human amygdala. *Science, 297*(5580), 400–403. doi: 10.1126/science.1071829

Harlow, J. M. (1868). Recovery from the passage of an iron bar through the head. *Publications of the Massachusetts Medical Society, 2*(3), 327–246.

Hart, C. L., Ward, A. S., Haney, M., Comer, S. D., Foltin, R. W., & Fischman, M. W. (2002). Comparison of smoked marijuana and oral Δ⁹-tetrahydrocannabinol in humans. *Psychopharmacology (Berl), 164*(4), 407–415. doi: 10.1007/s00213-002-1231-y

Hartwell, C. E. (1996). The schizophrenogenic mother concept in American psychiatry. *Psychiatry, 59*, 274–297.

Hashibe, M., Straif, K., Tashkin, D. P., Morgenstern, H., Greenland, S., & Zhang, Z.-F. (2005). Epidemiologic review of marijuana use and cancer risk. *Alcohol, 35*(3), 265–275. doi: 10.1016/j.alcohol.2005.04.008

Hasler, F., Bourquin, D., Brenneisen, R., Bar, T., & Vollenweider, F. X. (1997). Determination of psilocin and 4-hydroxyindole-3-acetic acid in plasma by HPLC-ECD and pharmacokinetic profiles of oral and intravenous psilocybin in man. *Pharmaceutica Acta Helvetiae, 72*(3), 175–184.

Hassan, M. (2014). Governor Hassan declares state of emergency as a result of overdoses from synthetic cannabinoid. The Office of Governor Maggie Hassan. Retrieved from http://governor.nh.gov/media/news/2014/pr-2014-08-14-emergency.htm

Hatsukami, D. K., & Fischman, M. W. (1996). Crack cocaine and cocaine hydrochloride. *Journal of the American Medical Association, 276*(19), 1580–1588. doi: 10.1001/jama.1996.03540190052029

Hatzidimitriou, G., McCann, U. D., & Ricaurte, G. A. (1999). Altered serotonin innervation patterns in the forebrain of monkeys treated with (±)3,4-methylenedioxymethamphetamine seven years previously: Factors influencing abnormal recovery. *Journal of Neuroscience, 19*(12), 5096–5107.

Hauptmann, N., & Shih, J. C. (2001). 2-Naphthylamine, a compound found in cigarette smoke, decreases both monoamine oxidase A and B catalytic activity, *Life Science, 68*, 1231–1241.

Hayashi, T., & Su, T. P. (2007). Sigma-1 receptor chaperones at the ER-mitochondrion interface regulate Ca(2+) signaling and cell survival. *Cell, 131*, 596–610. doi: 10.1016/j.cell.2007.08.036

Hazekamp, A., Bastola, K., Rashidi, H., Bender, J., & Verpoorte, R. (2007). Cannabis tea revisited: A systematic evaluation of the cannabinoid composition of cannabis tea. *Journal of Ethnopharmacology, 113*(1), 85–90.

Healy, D. (2002). *The creation of psychopharmacology.* Cambridge, MA: Harvard University Press.

Heather, N. (1989). Disulfiram treatment for alcoholism. *British Medical Journal, 299*(6697), 471–472. doi: 10.1136/ bmj.299.6697.471

Hebert, L. E., Scherr, P. A., Bienias, J. L., Bennett, D. A., & Evans, D. A. (2003). Alzheimer disease in the U.S. population: Prevalence estimates using the 2000 census. *Archives of Neurology, 60*(8), 1119–1122.

Heckers, S. (2001). Neuroimaging studies of the hippocampus in schizophrenia. *Hippocampus, 11*(5), 520–528. doi: 10.1002/ hipo.1068

Henningfield, J. E., Fant, R. V., Radzius, A., & Frost, S. (1999). Nicotine concentration, smoke pH, and whole tobacco aqueous pH of some cigar brands and types popular in the United States. *Nicotine and Tobacco Research, 1*(2), 163–168. doi: 10.1080/14622299050011271

Henningfield, J. E., & Keenan, R. M. (1993). Nicotine delivery kinetics and abuse liability. *Journal of Consulting and Clinical Psychology, 61*(5), 743–750.

Henningfield, J. E., Radzius, A., & Cone, E. J. (1995). Estimation of available nicotine content of six smokeless tobacco products. *Tobacco Control, 4,* 57–61.

Hensler, J. G. (2002). Differential regulation of 5-HT 1A Receptor-G protein interactions in brain following chronic antidepressant administration. *Neuropsychopharmacology, 26*(5), 565–573. doi: 10.1016/S0893-133X(01)00395–5

Hepler, R. S., & Frank, I. R. (1971). Marihuana smoking and intraocular pressure. *Journal of the American Medical Association, 217,* 1392.

Herculano-Houzel, S. (2009). The human brain in numbers: A linearly scaled-up primate brain. *Frontiers in Human Neuroscience, 3.* doi: 10.3389/ neuro.09.031.2009

Herculano-Houzel, S. (2012). The remarkable, yet not extraordinary, human brain as a scaled-up primate brain and its associated cost. *Proceedings of the National Academy of*

Sciences, 109(Supplement 1), 10661–10668. doi:10.1073/ pnas.1201895109

Herkenham, M., Lynn, A. B., Little, M. D., Johnson, M. R., Melvin, L. S., de Costa, B. R., & Rice, K. C. (1990). Cannabinoid receptor localization in brain. *Proceedings of the National Academy of Sciences of the USA, 87*(5), 1932–1936.

Hermle, L., Simon, M., Ruchsow, M., & Geppert, M. (2012). Hallucinogen-persisting perception disorder. *Therapeutic Advances in Psychopharmacology, 2,* 199–205. doi: 10.1177/ 2045125312451270

Herraiz, T., & Chaparro, C. (2005). Human monoamine oxidase is inhibited by tobacco smoke: β-carboline alkaloids act as potent and reversible inhibitors *Biochemical and Biophysical Research Communications, 326,* 378–386. doi: 10.1016/j.bbrc.2004.11.033

Hertel, P., Fagerquist, M. V., & Svensson, T. H. (1999). Enhanced cortical dopamine output and anti-psychotic-like effects of raclopride by alpha2 adrenoceptor blockade. *Science, 286*(5437), 105–107.

Hillbom, M., Pieninkeroinen, I., & Leone, M. (2003). Seizures in alcohol-dependent patients: Epidemiology, pathophysiology, and management. *CNS Drugs, 17*(14), 1013–1030.

Hillhouse, T. M., & Porter, J. H. (2015). A brief history of the development of antidepressant drugs: From monoamines to glutamate. *Experimental and Clinical Psychopharmacology, 23*(1), 1–21. doi: 10.1037/a0038550

Hillig, K. W., & Mahlberg, P. G. (2004). A chemotaxonomic analysis of cannabinoid variation in *Cannabis* (Cannabaceae). *American Journal of Botany, 91*(6), 966–975. doi: 10.3732/ ajb.91.6.966

Hines, L. M., Stampfer, M. J., Ma, J., Gaziano, J. M., Ridker, P. M., Hankinson, S. E., . . . & Hunter, D. J. (2001). Genetic variation in alcohol dehydrogenase and the beneficial effect of moderate alcohol consumption on myocardial infarction. *New England Journal of Medicine, 344*(8), 549–555. doi: 10.1056/ NEJM200102223440802

Hippius, H. (1989). The history of clozapine. *Psychopharmacology, 99,* S3–S5.

Hippius, H., & Müller, N. (2008). The work of Emil Kraepelin and his research group in München. *European Archives of Psychiatry and Clinical Neuroscience, 258* (Suppl. 2): 3–11.

Hirschfeld, R. M., Lewis, L., & Vornik L. A. (2003). Perceptions and impact of bipolar disorder: How far have we really come? Results of the National Depressive and Manic-Depressive Association 2000 survey of individuals with bipolar disorder. *Journal of Clinical Psychiatry, 64,* 161–174. doi: 10.4088/ JCP.v64n0209

Hodgkinson, C. A., Goldman, D., Jaeger, J., Persaud, S., Kane, J. M., Lipsky, R. H., & Malhotra, A. K. (2004). Disrupted in schizophrenia 1 (DISC1): Association with schizophrenia, schizoaffective disorder, and bipolar disorder. *American Journal of Human Genetics, 75*(5), 862–872.

Hoehn-Saric, R., McLeod, D. R., Funderburk, F., & Kowalski, P. (2004). Somatic symptoms and physiologic responses in generalized anxiety disorder and panic disorder: An ambulatory monitor study. *Archives in General Psychiatry, 61,* 913–921.

Hogg, S., & Dalvi, A. (2004). Acceleration of onset of action in schedule-induced polydipsia: Combinations of SSRI and 5-HT1A and 5-HT1B receptor antagonists. *Pharmacology Biochemistry and Behavior, 77*(1), 69–75. doi: S0091305703002971 [pii]

Hollon, S. D., DeRubeis, R. J., Evans, M. D., Wiemer, M. J., Garvey, M. J., Grove, W. M., & Tuason, V. B. (1992). Cognitive therapy and pharmacotherapy for depression: Singly and in combination. *Archives of General Psychiatry, 49*(10), 774–781. doi: 10.1001/ archpsyc.1992.01820100018004

Hollon, S. D., DeRubeis, R. J., Fawcett, J., Amsterdam, J. D., Shelton, R. C., Zajecka, J., . . . & Gallop, R. (2014). Effect of cognitive therapy with antidepressant medications vs antidepressants alone on the rate of recovery in major depressive disorder: A randomized clinical trial. *Journal of the American Medical Association*

Psychiatry, 71(10), 1157–1164. doi: 10.1001/jamapsychiatry.2014.1054

Holly, E. N., Ebrecht, B., & Prus, A. J. (2011). The neurotensin-1 receptor agonist PD149163 inhibits conditioned avoidance responding without producing catalepsy in rats. *European Neuropsychopharmacology, 21*(7), 526–531. doi: S0924–977X (10)00280–4 [pii]

Holly, E. N., Shimamoto, A., DeBold, J. F., & Miczek, K. A. (2012). Sex differences in behavioral and neural cross-sensitization and escalated cocaine taking as a result of episodic social defeat stress in rats. *Psychopharmacology, 224*(1), 179-188. doi: 10.1007/s00213-012-2846-2

Holmes, A., Li, Q., Murphy, D. L., Gold, E., & Crawley, J. N. (2003). Abnormal anxiety-related behavior in serotonin transporter null mutant mice: The influence of genetic background. *Genes, Brain, and Behavior, 2*(6), 365–380. doi: 10.1046/j.16011848.2003.00050.x

Holzbauer, M., & Vogt, M. (1956). Depression by reserpine of the noradrenaline concentration in the hypothalamus of the cat. *Journal of Neurochemistry, 1*(1), 8–11.

Homberg, J., De Boer, S., Raasø, H., Olivier, J., Verheul, M., Ronken, E., . . . & Cuppen, E. (2008). Adaptations in pre- and post-synaptic 5-HT1A receptor function and cocaine supersensitivity in serotonin transporter knockout rats. *Psychopharmacology, 200*(3), 367–380. doi: 10.1007/s00213008–1212-x

Hooft, P. J., & van de Voorde, H. P. (1994). Reckless behaviour related to the use of 3,4-methylenedioxy methamphetamine (Ecstasy): Apropos of a fatal accident during car-surfing. *International Journal of Legal Medicine, 106*(6), 328–329. doi: 10.1007/bf01224781

Hoque, R., & Chesson Jr, A. L. (2009). Zolpidem-induced sleepwalking, sleep related eating disorder, and sleep-driving: Fluorine-18-flourodeoxyglucose positron emission tomography analysis, and a literature review of other unexpected clinical effects of zolpidem. *Journal of Clinical Sleep Medicine, 5*(5), 471-476.

Horlocker, T. T., Burton, A. W., Connis, R. T., Hughes, S. C., Nickinovich, D. G., Palmer, C. M., . . . & Wu, C. L. (2009). Practice guidelines for the prevention, detection, and management of respiratory depression associated with neuraxial opioid administration. *Anesthesiology, 110*(2), 218–230. doi: 10.1097/ ALN.0b013e31818ec946

Hormes, J. T., Filley, C. M., & Rosenberg, N. L. (1986). Neurologic sequelae of chronic solvent vapor abuse. *Neurology, 36*(5), 698–702.

Horstmann, S., & Binder, E. B. (2009). Pharmacogenomics of antidepressant drugs. *Pharmacology and Therapeutics, 124*(1), 57–73. doi: S0163–7258(09)00132–6 [pii]

Hosztafi, S. (2001). The history of heroin. *Acta Pharmaceutica Hungarica, 71*(2), 233–242.

Howard, J. M., Olney, J. M., Frawley, J. P., Peterson, R. E., & Guerra, S. (1955). Adrenal function in the combat casualty. *American Medical Association Archives of Surgery, 71*(1), 47–58.

Howard, O., & Perron, B. E. (2009). Nitrous oxide inhalation among adolescents: Prevalence, correlates, and co-occurrence with volatile solvent inhalation. *Journal of Psychoactive Drugs, 41*, 337–347.

Howland, J., Rohsenow, D. J., Bliss, C. A., Almeida, A. B., Calise, T. V., Heeren, T., & Winter, M. (2010). Hangover predicts residual alcohol effects on psychomotor vigilance the morning after intoxication. *Journal of Addiction Research & Therapy, 1*(101). doi: 1000101 [pii]

Hser, Y. I., Hoffman, V., Grella, C. E., & Anglin, M. D. (2001). A 33-year follow-up of narcotics addicts. *Archives of General Psychiatry, 58*(5), 503–508.

Hsu, Y. N., Amin, J., Weiss, D. S., & Wecker, L. (1996). Sustained nicotine exposure differentially affects α3β2 and α4β2 neuronal nicotinic receptors expressed in Xenopus oocytes. *Journal of Neurochemistry, 66*(2), 667–675. doi: 10.1046/j.1471–4159.1996.66020667.x

Hu, X., Primack, B. A., Barnett, T. E., & Cook, R. L. (2011). College students and use of K2: An emerging drug of abuse in young persons. *Substance Abuse Treatment, Prevention, and Policy, 6*(16). doi: 10.1186/1747-597X-6-16

Hubbard, E. M. (2007). Neurophysiology of synesthesia. *Current Psychiatry Reports, 9*(3), 193–199.

Hubbard, R. L., Craddock, S. G., & Anderson, J. (2003). Overview of 5-year follow-up outcomes in the drug abuse treatment outcome studies (DATOS). *Journal of Substance Abuse Treatment, 25*(3), 125–134.

Hubert, G. W., Jones, D. C., Moffett, M. C., Rogge, G., & Kuhar, M. J. (2008). CART peptides as modulators of dopamine and psycho-stimulants and interactions with the mesolimbic dopaminergic system. *Biochemical Pharmacology, 75*(1), 57–62. doi: 10.1016/j. bcp.2007.07.028

Huedo-Medina, T. B., Kirsch, I., Middlemass, J., Klonizakis, M., & Siriwardena, A. N. (2012). Effectiveness of non-benzodiazepine hypnotics in treatment of adult insomnia: Meta-analysis of data submitted to the Food and Drug Administration. *BMJ, 345*, e8343. doi: http://dx.doi.org/10.1136/bmj.e8343

Hughes, J., Kosterlitz, H. W., & Leslie, F. M. (1975). Effect of morphine on adrenergic transmission in the mouse vas deferens: Assessment of agonist and antagonist potencies of narcotic analgesics. *British Journal of Pharmacology, 53*, 371–381.

Hughes, J., Smith, T., Morgan, B., & Fothergill, L. (1975). Purification and properties of enkephalin: The possible endogenous ligand for the morphine receptor. *Life Sciences, 16*(12), 1753–1758.

Hughes, J. R., Oliveto, A. H., Liguori, A., Carpenter, J., & Howard, T. (1998). Endorsement of DSMIV dependence criteria among caffeine users. *Drug and Alcohol Dependence, 52*(2), 99–107.

Hughes, T. (2015). Feds ask Supreme Court to stay out of lawsuit over Colorado marijuana. *USA Today*, December 17, 2015. Retrieved from http://www.usatoday.com/story/news/2015/12/16/feds-ask-supreme-court-stay-out-lawsuit-over-colorado-marijuana/77457652/

Hull, P. R., & D'Arcy, C. (2003). Isotretinoin use and subsequent depression and suicide. *American Journal of Clinical Dermatology, 4*(7), 493–505. doi: 10.2165/00128071–200304070–00005

Hungund, B. L., Szakall, I., Adam, A., Basavarajappa, B. S., & Vadasz,

C. (2003). Cannabinoid CB1 receptor knockout mice exhibit markedly reduced voluntary alcohol consumption and lack alcohol-induced dopamine release in the nucleus accumbens. *Journal of Neurochemistry, 84*(4), 698–704. doi: 10.1046/j.14714159.2003.01576.x

Hustveit, O., Maurset, A., & Oye, I. (1995). Interaction of the chiral forms of ketamine with opioid, phencyclidine, sigma, and muscarinic receptors. *Pharmacology and Toxicology, 77*(6), 355–359.

Ibrahim, A. K., Kelly, S. J., Adams, C. E., & Glazebrook, C. (2013). A systematic review of studies of depression prevalence in university students. *Journal of Psychiatric Research, 47*(3), 391–400. doi: 10.1016/j.jpsychires.2012.11.015

Ifland, J. R., Preuss, H. G., Marcus, M. T., Rourke, K. M., Taylor, W. C., Burau, K., . . . & Manso, G. (2009). Refined food addiction: A classic substance use disorder. *Medical Hypotheses, 72*(5), 518–526. doi: 10.1016/j. mehy.2008.11.035

Ikeda, H., Stark, J., Fischer, H., Wagner, M., Drdla, R., Jager, T., & Sandkuhler, J. (2006). Synaptic amplifier of inflammatory pain in the spinal dorsal horn. *Science, 312*(5780), 1659–1662. doi: 10.1126/science.1127233

International Conference on Harmonization. (1996). Guideline for industry: Structure and content of clinical study reports (Vol. 61FR37320). *Federal Register*. International Conference on Harmonisation of Technical Requirements for Registration of Pharmaceuticals for Human Use.

Ishida, K., Murata, M., Katagiri, N., Ishikawa, M., Abe, K., Kato, M., . . . & Taguchi, K. (2005). Effects of Î²-phenylethylamine on dopaminergic neurons of the ventral tegmental area in the rat: A combined electrophysiological and microdialysis study. *Journal of Pharmacology and Experimental Therapeutics, 314*(2), 916–922. doi: 10.1124/jpet.105.084764

Israel, Y., Khanna, J. M., Orrego, H., Rachamin, G., Wahid, S., Britton, R., . . . & Kalant, H. (1979). Studies on metabolic tolerance to alcohol, hepatomegaly, and alcoholic liver disease. *Drug and Alcohol Dependence, 4*(1–2), 109–118.

Ito, T., Suzuki, T., Wellman, S. E., & Ho, I. K. (1996). Pharmacology of barbiturate tolerance/dependence: GABAA receptors and molecular aspects. *Life Sciences, 59*(3), 169–195.

Jacob, M. S., Carlen, P. L., Marshman, J. A., & Sellers, E. M. (1981). Phencyclidine ingestion: Drug abuse and psychosis. *International Journal of Addiction, 16*(4), 749–758.

Jacob, P. III, Abu Raddaha, A. H., Dempsey, D., Havel, C., Peng, M., Yu, L., & Benowitz, N. L. (2011). Nicotine, carbon monoxide, and carcinogen exposure after a single use of a water pipe. *Cancer Epidemiology, Biomarkers, and Prevention, 20*(11), 2345–2353. doi: 10.1158/1055-9965.EPI-11-0545

Jacobson, S. W., Jacobson, J. L., & Sokol, R. J. (1994). Effects of fetal alcohol exposure on infant reaction time. *Alcoholism: Clinical and Experimental Research, 18*(5), 1125–1132. doi: 10.1111/j.1530-0277.1994.tb00092.x

Jager, G., Kahn, R. S., Van Den Brink, W., Van Ree, J. M., & Ramsey, N. F. (2006). Long-term effects of frequent cannabis use on working memory and attention: An fMRI study. *Psychopharmacology, 185*(3), 358–368. doi: 10.1016/j.euroneuro.2006.10.003

James, D., Adams, R. D., Spears, R., Cooper, G., Lupton, D. J., Thompson, J. P., & Thomas, S. H. (2011). Clinical characteristics of mephedrone toxicity reported to the U.K. National Poisons Information Service. *Emergency Medicine Journal, 28*(8), 686–689. doi: 10.1136/emj.2010.096636

James, J., & Rogers, P. (2005). Effects of caffeine on performance and mood: Withdrawal reversal is the most plausible explanation. *Psychopharmacology, 182*(1), 1–8. doi: 10.1007/s00213-005-0084-6

Janzer, R. C., & Raff, M. C. (1987). Astrocytes induce blood–brain barrier properties in endothelial cells. *Nature, 325*(6101), 253–257. doi: 10.1038/325253a0

Jaworski, J. N., Kozel, M. A., Philpot, K. B., & Kuhar, M. J. (2003). Intra-accumbal injection of CART (cocaine-amphetamine regulated transcript) peptide reduces cocaine-induced locomotor activity. *Journal of Pharmacology and Experimental Therapeutics, 307*, 1038–1044. doi: 10.1124/jpet.103.052332

Jayadev, S., Smith, C. O., & Bird, T. D. (2011). Neurogenetics: Five new things. *Neurology: Clinical Practice, 1*, 41–48. doi: 10.1212/CPJ.0b013e31823c0f5f

Jayaram-Lindström, N., Hammarberg, A., Beck, O., & Frank, J. (2008). Naltrexone for the treatment of amphetamine-dependence: A randomized, placebo-controlled trial. *American Journal of Psychiatry, 11*, 1442–1448. doi: 10.1176/appi.ajp.2008.08020304

Jenkins, J., & Hubbard, S. (1991). History of clinical trials. *Seminars in Oncology Nursing, 7*(4), 228–234.

Jensen, N. H., Rodriguiz, R. M., Caron, M. G., Wetsel, W. C., Rothman, R. B., & Roth, B. L. (2008). N-desalkylquetiapine, a potent norepinephrine reuptake inhibitor and partial 5-HT1A agonist, as a putative mediator of quetiapine's antidepressant activity. *Neuropsychopharmacology, 33*(10), 2303–2312. doi: 1301646 [pii]

Jentsch, J. D., & Roth, R. H. (1999). The neuropsychopharmacology of phencyclidine: From NMDA receptor hypofunction to the dopamine hypothesis of schizophrenia. *Neuropsychopharmacology, 20*(3), 201–225. doi: 10.1016/ S0893-133X(98)00060-8

Joeres, R., Klinker, H., Heusler, H., Epping, J., Zilly, W., & Richter, E. (1988). Influence of smoking on caffeine elimination in healthy volunteers and in patients with alcoholic liver cirrhosis. *Hepatology, 8*(3), 575–579.

Joerger, M., Wilkins, J., Fagagnini, S., Baldinger, R., Brenneisen, R., Schneider, U., . . . & Weber, M. (2012). Single-dose pharmacokinetics and tolerability of oral delta-9-tetrahydrocannabinol in patients with amyotrophic lateral sclerosis. *Drug Metabolism Letters, 6*(2), 102–108. doi: 10.2174/1872312811206020102

Johanson, C. E., Lundahl, L. H., Lockhart, N., & Schubiner, H. (2006). Intravenous cocaine discrimination in humans. *Experimental and Clinical Psychopharmacology, 14*(2), 99–108. doi: 2006-07129-001 [pii]

Johnson, C. L., & Sansone, R. A. (1993). Integrating the twelve-step approach with traditional psychotherapy for the treatment of eating disorders. *International Journal of Eating Disorders, 14*(2), 121–134.

Johnston, G. A. (2013). Advantages of an antagonist: Bicuculline and other GABA antagonists. *British Journal of Pharmacology, 169*, 328–336. doi: 10.1111/bph.12127

Johnston, I. R. (1982). The role of alcohol in road crashes. *Ergonomics, 25*(10), 941–946.

Johnston, L. D., O'Malley, P. M., & Bachman, J. G. (2003). *Monitoring the future national survey results on drug use, 1975–2002. Vol. I: Secondary school students.* Bethesda, MD: National Institute on Drug Abuse.

Jones, E. (1953). *The life and work of Sigmund Freud* (Vol. 1). New York, NY: Basic Books.

Jones, S. R., Garris, P. A., & Wightman, R. M. (1995). Different effects of cocaine and nomifensine on dopamine uptake in the caudate-putamen and nucleus accumbens. *Journal of Pharmacology and Experimental Therapeutics, 274*(1), 396–403.

Jordan, K., Gralla, R., Jahn, F., & Molassiotis, A. (2014). International antiemetic guidelines on chemotherapy induced nausea and vomiting (CINV): content and implementation in daily routine practice. *European journal of pharmacology, 722*, 197–202. doi: 10.1016/j.ejphar.2013.09.073

Jordan, K., Sippel, C., & Schmoll, H. J. (2007). Guidelines for antiemetic treatment of chemotherapy-induced nausea and vomiting: Past, present, and future recommendations. *The Oncologist, 12*(9), 1143–1150. doi: 10.1634/theoncologist.12–9–1143

Juliano, L. M., Evatt, D. P., Richards, B. D., & Griffiths, R. R. (2012). Characterization of individuals seeking treatment for caffeine dependence. *Psychology of Addictive Behaviors, 26*(4), 948. doi: 10.1037/a0027246

Juliano, L. M., Fucito, L. M., & Harrell, P. T. (2011). The influence of nicotine dose and nicotine dose expectancy on the cognitive and subjective effects of cigarette smoking. *Experimental and Clinical Psychopharmacology, 19*(2), 105–115. doi: 10.1037/ a0022937

Just, M. A., Cherkassky, V. L., Keller, T. A., & Minshew, N. J. (2004). Cortical activation and synchronization during sentence comprehension in high-functioning autism: Evidence of underconnectivity. *Brain, 127*(8), 1811–1821. doi: http://dx.doi.org/10.1093/brain/awh199

Kalant, H. (2001). Medicinal use of cannabis: History and current status. *Medicinal Use of Cannabis, 6*, 80–91.

Kalayasiri, R., Sughondhabirom, A., Gueorguieva, R., Coric, V., Lynch, W. J., Lappalainen, J., . . . & Malison, R. T. (2007). Dopamine β-hydroxylase gene (DβH) -1021C→T influences self-reported paranoia during cocaine self-administration. *Biological Psychiatry, 61*(11), 1310–1313. doi: 10.1016/j.biopsych.2006.08.012

Kalivas, P. W. (2002). Neurocircuitry of addiction. In K. L. Davis, D. Charney, J. T. Coyle, & C. Nemeroff (Eds.), *Neuropsychopharmacology: The fifth generation of progress* (pp. 1357–1366). Brentwood, NJ: American College of Neuropsychopharmacology.

Kalivas, P. W. (2009). The glutamate homeostasis hypothesis of addiction. *Nature Revews Neuroscience, 10*(8), 561–572. doi: 10.1038/nrn2515

Kalivas, P. W., Churchill, L., & Klitenick, M. A. (1993). GABA and enkephalin projection from the nucleus accumbens and ventral pallidum to the ventral tegmental area. *Neuroscience, 57*(4), 1047–1060.

Kampman, K. M. (2010). What's new in the treatment of cocaine addiction? *Current Psychiatry Reports, 12*(5), 441–447. doi: 10.1007/s11920–010–0143–5

Kampman, K. M., Pettinati, H., Lynch, K. G., Dackis, C., Sparkman, T., Weigley, C., & O'Brien, C. P. (2004). A pilot trial of topiramate for the treatment of cocaine dependence. *Drug and Alcohol Dependence, 75*(3), 233–240. doi: 10.1016/j.drugalcdep.2004.03.008

Kan, C. C., Breteler, M. H. M., & Zitman, F. G. (1997). High prevalence of benzodiazepine dependence in out-patient users, based on the DSM-III-R and ICD-10 criteria. *Acta Psychiatrica Scandinavica, 96*(2), 85–93. doi: 10.1111/j.1600-0447.1997.tb09911.x

Kane, J., Honigfeld, G., Singer, J., & Meltzer, H. (1988). Clozapine for the treatment-resistant schizophrenic: A double-blind comparison with chlorpromazine. *Archives of General Psychiatry, 45*(9), 789–796.

Kaneda, Y., Jayathilak, K., & Meltzer, H. (2010). Determinants of work outcome in neuroleptic-resistant schizophrenia and schizoaffective disorder: Cognitive impairment and clozapine treatment. *Psychiatry Research, 178*, 57–62.

Kapur, S., & Seeman, P. (2000). Antipsychotic agents differ in how fast they come off the dopamine D2 receptors: Implications for atypical antipsychotic action. *Journal of Psychiatry and Neuroscience, 25*(2), 161–166.

Kapur, S., & Seeman, P. (2002). NMDA receptor antagonists ketamine and PCP have direct effects on the dopamine D(2) and serotonin 5-HT(2) receptors-implications for models of schizophrenia. *Molecular Psychiatry, 7*(8), 837–844. doi: 10.1038/ sj.mp.4001093

Karhunen, T., Tilgmann, C., Ulmanen, I., & Panul, P. (1995). Catechol-O-methyltransferase (COMT) in rat brain: Immunoelectron microscopic study with an antiserum against rat recombinant COMT protein. *Neuroscience Letters, 187*(1), 57–60. doi: 10.1016/0304–3940(95)11337-V

Kassem, M. A., ElMeshad, A. N., & Fares, A. R. (2014). Enhanced bioavailability of buspirone hydrochloride via cup and core buccal tablets: Formulation and in vitro/in vivo evaluation. *International Journal of Pharmaceutics. 463*(1), 68–80. doi: 10.1016/j.ijpharm.2014.01.003

Kaufman, J., DeLorenzo, C., Choudhury, S., & Parsey, R. V. (2016). The 5-HT$_{1A}$ receptor in major depressive disorder. *European Neuropsychopharmacology, 26*, 397–410. doi: 10.1016/j.euroneuro.2015.12.039

Kaye, S., Darke, S., & Duflou, J. (2009). Methylene-dioxymethamphetamine(MDMA)-related fatalities in Australia: Demographics, circumstances, toxicology and major organ pathology. *Drug and Alcohol Dependence, 104*(3), 254–261. doi: 10.1016/j. drugalcdep.2009.05.016

Keck, P. E., McElroy, S. L., & Nemeroff, C. B. (1992). Anticonvulsants in the treatment of bipolar disorder. *Journal of Neuropsychiatry and Clinical Neurosciences, 4*, 395–405.

Keefe, R. S., & Fenton, W. S. (2007). How should DSM-V criteria for schizophrenia include cognitive impairment? *Schizophrenia Bulletin, 33*(4), 912–920. doi: sbm046 [pii]

Keller, M. B., McCullough, J. P., Klein, D. N., Arnow, B., Dunner, D. L., Gelenberg, A. J., . . . & Trivedi, M. H. (2000). A comparison of nefazodone, the cognitive behavioral-analysis system of psychotherapy, and their combination for the treatment of chronic depression. *New England Journal of Medicine, 342*(20), 1462–1470. doi: 10.1056/NEJM200005183422001

Kenford, S. L., Fiore, M. C., Jorenby, D. E., Smith, S. S., Wetter, D., & Baker T. B. (1994). Predicting smoking cessation: Who will quit with and without the nicotine patch. *Journal of the American Medical Association, 271*, 589–594. doi: 10.1001/jama.1994.03510320029025

Ker, K., Edwards, P. J., Felix, L. M., Blackhall, K., & Roberts, I. (2010). Caffeine for the prevention of injuries and errors in shift workers. *Cochrane Database Systems Review* (5), CD008508. doi: 10.1002/14651858.CD00 8508

Kerner, K. (1988). Current topics in inhalant abuse. In R. A. Crider & B. A. Rouse (Eds.), *Epidemiology of inhalant abuse* (pp. 8–29). Rockville, MD: National Institute on Drug Abuse.

Kessler, R. C., Berglund, P., Demler, O., Jin, R., Merikangas, K. R., & Walters, E. E. (2005). Lifetime prevalence and age-of-onset distributions of DSM-IV disorders in the National Comorbidity Survey Replication. *Archives of General Psychiatry, 62*(6), 593–602. doi: 62/6/593 [pii]

Kessler, R. C., Petukhova, M., Sampson, N. A., Zaslavsky, A. M., Wittchen, H.-U. (2012). Twelve-month and lifetime prevalence and lifetime morbid risk of anxiety and mood disorders in the United States. *International Journal of Methods in Psychiatric Research, 21*, 169–184. doi: 10.1002/mpr.1359

Khalil, A. A., Steyn, S., & Castagnoli, N. (2000). Isolation and characterization of a monoamine oxidase inhibitor from tobacco leaves. *Chemical Research in Toxicology, 13*(1), 31–35. doi: 10.1021/tx990146f

Khan, S., Patil, K., Yeole, P., & Gaikwad, R. (2009). Brain targeting studies on buspirone hydrochloride after intranasal administration of mucoadhesive formulation in rats. *Journal of Pharmacy and Pharmacology, 61*(5), 669–675. doi: 10.1211/ jpp/61.05.0017

King, A. C., Cao, D., O'Malley, S. S., Kranzler, H. R., & Cai, X. (2012). Effects of naltrexone on smoking cessation outcomes and weight gain in nicotine-dependent men and women. *Journal of Clinical Psychopharmacology, 32*(5), 630. doi: 10.1097/JCP.0b013e3182676956

King, B. A., Patel, R., Nguyen, K., & Dube, S. R. (2014). Trends in awareness and use of electronic cigarettes among US adults, 2010-2013. *Nicotine and Tobacco Research*, ntu191. doi: 10.1093/ntr/ntu191

Kirsch, I. (2014). Antidepressants and the placebo effect. *Zeitschrift für Psychologie, 222*(3), 128.

Klasser, G. D., & Epstein, J. (2005). Methamphetamine and its impact on dental care. *Journal of the Canadian Dental Association, 71*(10), 759–762.

Kleen, J. K., Sitomer, M. T., Killeen, P. R., & Conrad, C. D. (2006). Chronic stress impairs spatial memory and motivation for reward without disrupting motor ability and motivation to explore. *Behavioral Neuroscience, 120*, 842–851.

Klepner, C. A., Lippa, A. S., Benson, D. I., Sano, M. C., & Beer, B. (1979). Resolution of two biochemically and pharmacologically distinct benzodiazepine receptors. *Pharmacology Biochemistry and Behavior, 11*(4), 457–462.

Kleykamp, B. A., Griffiths, R. R., & Mintzer, M. Z. (2010). Dose effects of triazolam and alcohol on cognitive performance in healthy volunteers. *Experimental and Clinical Psychopharmacology, 18*(1), 1–16. doi: 2010–02775001 [pii]

Kolbrich, E. A., Goodwin, R. S., Gorelick, D. A., Hayes, R. J., Stein, E. A., & Huestis, M. A. (2008). Physiological and subjective responses to controlled oral 3,4-methylenedioxymethamphetamine administration. *Journal of Clinical Psychopharmacology, 28*(4), 432–440. doi: 10.1097/ JCP.0b013e31817ef470

Kometer, M., Cahn, B. R., Andel, D., Carter, O. L., & Vollenweider, F. X. (2011). The 5-HT2A/1A agonist psilocybin disrupts modal object completion associated with visual hallucinations. *Biological Psychiatry, 69*(5), 399–406. doi: 10.1016/j.biopsych.2010.10.002

Koob, G. F., & Volkow, N. D. (2009). Neurocircuitry of addiction. *Neuropsychopharmacology, 35*(1), 217–238.

Kopelman, M. D., Thomson, A. D., Guerrini, I., & Marshall, E. J. (2009). The Korsakoff syndrome: Clinical aspects, psychology, and treatment. *Alcohol and Alcoholism, 44*(2), 148–154. doi: 10.1093/alcalc/agn118

Koppel, B. S., Brust, J. C., Fife, T., Bronstein, J., Youssof, S., Gronseth, G., & Gloss, D. (2014). Systematic review: Efficacy and safety of medical marijuana in selected neurologic disorders. Report of the Guideline Development Subcommittee of the American Academy of Neurology. *Neurology, 82*(17), 1556–1563. doi: 10. 1212/WNL.0000000000000363

Kosten, T. R., Domingo, C. B., Shorter, D., Orson, F., Green, C., Somoza, E., . . . & Tompkins, D. A. (2014). Vaccine for cocaine dependence: a randomized double-blind placebo-controlled efficacy trial. *Drug and Alcohol Dependence, 140*, 42–47. doi: 10.1016/j.drugalcdep.2014.04.003

Krabbendam, L., Visser, P. J., Derix, M.M.A., Verhey, F., Hofman, P., Verhoeven, W., Tuinier, S., & Jolles, J. (2000). Normal cognitive performance in patients with chronic alcoholism in contrast to patients with Korsakoff's syndrome. *Journal of Neuropsychiatry and Clinical Neuroscience, 12*, 44–50.

Kroeze, W. K., Hufeisen, S. J., Popadak, B. A., Renock, S. M., Steinberg, S., Ernsberger, P., . . . & Roth, B. L. (2003). H1-histamine receptor affinity predicts short-term weight gain for typical and atypical antipsychotic drugs. *Neuropsychopharmacology, 28*(3), 519–526.

Krueger, K. E. (1995). Molecular and functional properties of mitochondrial benzodiazepine receptors. *Biochimica* et Biophysica Acta (BBA)-Reviews on Biomembranes, 1241(3), 453–470.

Krystal, J. H., Cramer, J. A., Krol, W. F., Kirk, G. F., & Rosenheck, R. A. (2001). Naltrexone in the treatment of alcohol dependence. New England Journal of Medicine, 345(24), 1734–1739. doi: 10.1056/NEJMoa011127

Krystal, J. H., Karper, L. P., Seibyl, J. P., Freeman, G. K., Delaney, R., Bremner, J. D., . . . Charney, D. S. (1994). Subanesthetic effects of the noncompetitive NMDA antagonist, ketamine, in humans: Psychotomimetic, perceptual, cognitive, and neuroendocrine responses. Archives of General Psychiatry, 51(3), 199–214.

Krystal, J. H., Petrakis, I. L., Mason, G., Trevisan, L., & D'Souza, D. C. (2003). N-methyl-Daspartate glutamate receptors and alcoholism: Reward, dependence, treatment, and vulnerability. Pharmacology and Therapeutics, 99(1), 79–94.

Krystal, J. H., Sanacora, G., & Duman, R. S. (2013). Rapid-acting glutamatergic antidepressants: The path to ketamine and beyond. Biological Psychiatry, 73(12), 1133–1141. doi: 10.1016/j.biopsych.2013.03.026

Kucharski, A. (1984). History of frontal lobotomy in the United States, 1935–1955. Neurosurgery, 14(6), 765–772.

Kuhn, R. (1958). The treatment of depressive states with G-22355 (imipramine hydrochloride). American Journal of Psychiatry, 115, 459–464.

Kunz, E. (2014). Henri Laborit and the inhibition of action. Dialogues in Clinical Neuroscience, 16(1), 113.

Kuroki, T., Meltzer, H. Y., & Ichikawa, J. (1999). Effects of antipsychotic drugs on extracellular dopamine levels in rat medial prefrontal cortex and nucleus accumbens. Journal of Pharmacology and Experimental Therapeutics, 288(2), 774–781.

Kurtzman, T. L., Otsuka, K. N., & Wahl, R. A. (2001). Inhalant abuse by adolescents. Journal of Adolescent Health, 28(3), 170–180. doi: 10.1016/s1054139x(00)00159-2

LaLumiere, R. T., & Kalivas, P. W. (2008). Glutamate release in the nucleus accumbens core is necessary for heroin

seeking. Journal of Neuroscience, 28(12), 3170–3177. doi: 10.1523/jneurosci.5129–07.2008

Lamacz, M., Tonon, M. C., Smih-Rouet, F., Patte, C., Gasque, P., Fontaine, M., & Vaudry, H. (1996). The endogenous benzodiazepine receptor ligand ODN increases cytosolic calcium in cultured rat astrocytes. Molecular Brain Research, 37(1), 290–296. doi: 10.1016/0169-328X(95)00330-U

Lameh, J., Burstein, E. S., Taylor, E., Weiner, D. M., Vanover, K. E., & Bonhaus, D. W. (2007). Pharmacology of N-desmethylclozapine. Pharmacology and Therapeutics, 115(2), 223–231.

Lanfray, D., Arthaud, S., Ouellet, J., Compère, V., Do Rego, J. L., Leprince, J., . . . & Richard, D. (2013). Gliotransmission and brain glucose sensing critical role of endozepines. Diabetes, 62(3), 801–810.

Lansbergen, M. M. & Kenemans, J. L. (2008). Stroop interference and the timing of selective response activation. Clinical Neurophysiology, 119, 2247–2254. doi: 10.1016/j.clinph.2008.07.218

Laplane, D., Levasseur, M., Pillon, B., Dubois, B., Baulac, M., Mazoyer, B., . . . Baron, J. C. (1989). Obsessive-compulsive and other behavioural changes with bilateral basal ganglia lesions: A neuropsychological, magnetic resonance imaging, and positron tomography study. Brain, 112 (Part 3), 699–725.

Laursen, T. M. (2011). Life expectancy among persons with schizophrenia or bipolar disorder. Schizophrenia Research, 131, 101–104.

Leary, T., Metzner, R., Presnell, M., Weil, G., Schwitzgebel, R., & Kinne, S. (1965). A new behavior change program using psilocybin. Psychotherapy, 2, 61–72.

LeBeau, M., Andollo, W., Hearn, W. L., Baselt, R., Cone, E., Finkle, B., . . . & Saady, J. (1999). Recommendations for toxicological investigations of drug-facilitated sexual assaults. Journal of Forensic Science, 44(1), 227–230.

Leicht, M. E., Gamma, A., & Vollenweider, F. X. (2001). Gender differences in the subjective effects of MDMA. Psychopharmacology, 154, 161–168.

Lenox, R. H., & Frazer, A. (2002). Mechanisms of action of antidepressants and mood stabilizers. In K. L. Davis, D. Charney, J. T. Coyle & C. Nemeroff (Eds.), Neuropsychopharmacology: The fifth generation of progress (pp. 1139-1163). Brentwood, TN: American College of Neuropsychopharmacology.

Leonhart, M. M. (2011). Denial of petition to initiate proceedings to reschedule marijuana. (DEA-352N). Federal Register, 76(131).

Lera, G., & Zirulnik, J. (1999). Pilot study with clozapine in patients with HIV-associated psychosis and drug-induced Parkinsonism. Movement Disorders, 14(1), 128–131.

Lerner, A. G., Gelkopf, M., Skladman, I., Oyffe, I., Finkel, B., Sigal, M., & Weizman, A. (2002). Flashback and hallucinogen persisting perception disorder: Clinical aspects and pharmacological treatment approach. Israel Journal of Psychiatry and Related Sciences, 39, 92–99.

Lerner, S. E., & Burns, S. R. (1978). Phencyclidine use among youth: History, epidemiology, and acute and chronic intoxication. NIDA Research Monographs, 21, 66–118.

Lesch, K. P., Bengel, D., Heils, A., Sabol, S. Z., Greenberg, B. D., Petri, S., . . . & Murphy, D. L. (1996). Association of anxiety-related traits with a polymorphism in the serotonin transporter gene regulatory region. Science, 274(5292), 1527–1531. doi: 10.1126/science.274.5292.1527

Lewis, D. A., & Lieberman, J. A. (2000). Catching up on schizophrenia: Natural history and neurobiology. Neuron, 28, 325–334.

Lewis, J. E. (2005). Testimony at United States Senate Committee on Environment and Public Works. Retrieved from www.fbi.gov/news/testimony/investigatingand-preventing-animal-rightsextremism

Li, N., Lee, B., Liu, R. J., Banasr, M., Dwyer, J. M., Iwata, M., . . . & Duman, R. S. (2010). mTORdependent synapse formation underlies the rapid antidepressant effects of NMDA antagonists. Science, 329(5994), 959–964. doi: 329/5994/959 [pii]

Li, Y.-F., LaCroix, C., & Freeling, J. (2009). Specific subtypes of nicotinic cholinergic receptors involved in sympathetic and parasympathetic cardiovascular responses. *Neuroscience Letters, 462*(1), 20–23. doi: 10.1016/j.neulet.2009.06.081

Lieber, C. S. (1997). Ethanol metabolism, cirrhosis, and alcoholism. *Clinica Chimica Acta, 257*(1), 59–84.

Liechti, M. E., Kunz, I., Greminger, P., Speich, R., & Kupferschmidt, H. (2006). Clinical features of gamma-hydroxybutyrate and gamma-butyrolactone toxicity and concomitant drug and alcohol use. *Drug and Alcohol Dependence, 81*, 323–326. doi: 10.1016/j.drugalcdep.2005.07.010

Liegeois, J. F., Ichikawa, J., & Meltzer, H. Y. (2002). 5-HT(2A) receptor antagonism potentiates haloperidol-induced dopamine release in rat medial prefrontal cortex and inhibits that in the nucleus accumbens in a dose-dependent manner. *Brain Research, 947*(2), 157–165.

Liguori, A., D'Agostino, R. B., Dworkin, S. I., Edwards, D., & Robinson, J. H. (1999). Alcohol effects on mood, equilibrium, and simulated driving. *Alcoholism: Clinical & Experimental Research, 23*(5), 815–821. doi: 10.1111/j.1530-0277.1999.tb04188.x

Liguori, A., Hughes, J. R., & Grass, J. A. (1997). Absorption of subjective effects of caffeine from coffee, cola and capsules. *Pharmacology Biochemistry and Behavior, 58*, 721–726. doi: 10.1016/S0091-3057(97)00003-8

Lile, J. A., Kelly, T. H., Pinsky, D. J., & Hays, L. R. (2009). Substitution profile of Δ9-tetrahydrocannabinol, triazolam, hydromorphone, and methylphenidate in humans discriminating Δ9-tetrahydrocannabinol. *Psychopharmacology (Berl), 203*(2), 241–250. doi: 10.1007/s00213008-1393-3

Lineberry, T. W., & Bostwick, J. M. (2006). Methamphetamine abuse: A perfect storm of complications. *Mayo Clinic Proceedings, 81*(1), 77–84. doi: 10.4065/81.1.77

Lipari, R.N., & Hughes, A. (2015). The NSDUH Report: Trends in heroin use in the United States: 2002 to 2013. *The CBHSQ Report: April 23, 2015.* Rockville,

MD: Substance Abuse and Mental Health Services Administration, Center for Behavioral Health Statistics and Quality.

Lisko, J. G., Tran, H., Stanfill, S. B., Blount, B. C., & Watson, C. H. (2015). Chemical composition and evaluation of nicotine, tobacco alkaloids, pH, and selected flavors in e-cigarette cartridges and refill solutions. *Nicotine and Tobacco Research, 17*, 1270–1278. doi: 10.1093/ntr/ntu279

Litjens, R. P., Brunt, T. M., Alderliefste, G. J., & Westerink, R. H. (2014). Hallucinogen persisting perception disorder and the serotonergic system: A comprehensive review including new MDMA-related clinical cases. *European Neuropsychopharmacology, 24*(8), 1309–1323. doi: 10.1016/j.euroneuro.2014.05.008

Littleton, J. (1995). Acamprosate in alcohol dependence: How does it work? *Addiction, 90*, 1179–1188.

Liu, X., Ramirez, S., Pang, P. T., Puryear, C. B., Govindarajan, A., Deisseroth, K., & Tonegawa, S. (2012). Optogenetic stimulation of a hippocampal engram activates fear memory recall. *Nature, 484*(7394), 381–385. doi: 10.1038/nature11028

Loewi, O., & Navratil, E. (1926). Über humorale übertragbarkeit der herznervenwirkung. *Pflüger's Archiv European Journal of Physiology, 214*, 678–688.

Logan, B. K., Reinhold, L. E., Xu, A., & Diamond, F. X. (2012). Identification of synthetic cannabinoids in herbal incense blends in the United States. *Journal of Forensic Sciences, 57*(5), 1168–1180. doi: 10.1111/j.1556-4029.2012.02207.x

Loflin, M., & Earleywine, M. (2014). A new method of cannabis ingestion: The dangers of dabs? *Addictive Behaviors, 39*(10), 1430–1433. doi: 10.1016/j.addbeh.2014.05.013

Loimer, N., Schmid, R. W., Presslich, O., & Lenz, K. (1989). Continuous naloxone administration suppresses opiate withdrawal symptoms in human opiate addicts during detoxification treatment. *Journal of Psychiatric Research, 23*(1), 81–86. doi: 10.1016/00223956(89)90020-4

Longabaugh, R., & Morgenstern, J. (1999). Cognitive–behavioral coping-

skills therapy for alcohol dependence: Current status and future directions. *Alcohol Research and Health, 23*(2), 78–85.

Loomer, H. P., Saunders, J. C., & Kline, N. S. (1957). A clinical and pharmacodynamic evaluation of iproniazid as a psychic energizer. *Psychiatric Research, 8*, 129–141.

Lopez-Muñoz, F., Ucha-Udabe, R., & Alamo, C. (2005). The history of barbiturates a century after their clinical introduction. *Neuropsychiatric Disease Treatment, 1*(4), 329–343.

Lopreato, G. F., Phelan, R., Borghese, C. M., Beckstead, M. J., & Mihic, S. J. (2003). Inhaled drugs of abuse enhance serotonin-3 receptor function. *Drug and Alcohol Dependence, 70*, 11–15.

Lorrain, D. S., Baccei, C. S., Bristow, L. J., Anderson, J. J., & Varney, M. A. (2003). Effects of ketamine and N-methyl-D-aspartate on glutamate and dopamine release in the rat prefrontal cortex: Modulation by a group II selective metabotropic glutamate receptor agonist LY379268. *Neuroscience, 117*(3), 697–706. doi: 10.1016/S0306-4522(02)00652-8

Lotfipour, S., Arnold, M. M., Hogenkamp, D. J., Gee, K. W., Belluzzi, J. D., & Leslie, F. M. (2011). The monoamine oxidase (MAO) inhibitor tranylcypromine enhances nicotine self-administration in rats through a mechanism independent of MAO inhibition. *Neuropharmacology, 61*, 95–104. doi: 10.1016/j.neuropharm.2011.03.007

Loyola Marymount University. (2006). Blood Alcohol Content. Retrieved November 25, 2012, from http://www.lmu.edu/Page25066.aspx

Lubman, D. I., Hides, L., & Yucel, M. (2006). Inhalant misuse in youth: The need for a coordinated response. *Medical Journal of Australia, 185*, 327–330.

Lubman, D. I., Yucel, M., & Lawrence, A. J. (2008). Inhalant abuse among adolescents: Neurobiological considerations. *British Journal of Pharmacology, 154*(2), 316–326. doi: 10.1038/bjp.2008.76

Lufty, K., & Cowan, A. (2004). Buprenorphine: A unique drug with complex pharmacology. *Current Neuropharmacology, 2*, 395–402.

Lussier, J. P., Higgins, S. T., & Badger, G. J. (2005). Influence of the duration of abstinence on the relative reinforcing effects of cigarette smoking. *Psychopharmacology, 181,* 486–495. doi: 10.1007/s00213-005-0008-5

Lynne-Landsman, S. D., Livingston, M. D., & Wagenaar, A. C. (2013). Effects of state medical marijuana laws on adolescent marijuana use. *American Journal of Public Health, 103,* 1500–1506. doi: 10.2105/AJPH.2012.301117

Machu, T. K., & Harris, R. A. (1994). Alcohols and anesthetics enhance the function of 5-hydroxytryptamine3 receptors expressed in Xenopus laevis oocytes. *Journal of Pharmacology and Experimental Therapeutics, 271*(2), 898–905.

Mackay, J., & Eriksen, M. (2002). *The tobacco atlas.* World Health Organization. Old Steine, Brighton, England: Myriad Editions.

MacMillan, M. (2008). Phineas Gage: Unraveling the myth. *Psychologist, 21,* 836–839.

MacPhail, R. C., & Gollub, L. R. (1975). Separating the effects of response rate and reinforcement frequency in the rate-dependent effects of amphetamine and scopolamine on the schedule-controlled performance of rats and pigeons. *Journal of Pharmacology and Experimental Therapeutics, 194*(2), 332–342.

Madden, J. A., Konkol, R. J., Keller, P. A., & Alvarez, T. A. (1995). Cocaine and benzoylecgonine constrict cerebral arteries by different mechanisms. *Life Sciences, 56*(9), 679–686.

Maitre, M. (1997). The γ-hydroxybutyrate signalling system in brain: Organization and functional implications. *Progress in Neurobiology, 51*(3), 337–361. doi: 10.1016/s03010082(96)00064-0

Mahler, S. V., Hensley-Simon, M., Tahsili-Fahadan, P., LaLumiere, R. T., Thomas, C., Fallon, R. V., Kalivas, P. W., & Aston-Jones, G. (2014). Modafinil attenuates reinstatement of cocaine seeking: Role for cystine-glutamate exchange and metabotropic glutamate receptors. *Addiction Biology, 19,* 49–60. doi: 10.1111/j.1369-1600.2012.00506.x

Maj, J., Dziedzicka-Wasylewska, M., Rogoz, R., Rogoz, Z., & Skuza, G. (1996).

Antidepressant drugs given repeatedly change the binding of the dopamine D2 receptor agonist, [3H]N-0437, to dopamine D2 receptors in the rat brain. *European Journal of Pharmacology, 304*(1–3), 49–54.

Malinauskas, B. M., Aeby, V. G., Overton, R. F., Carpenter-Aeby, T., & Barber-Heidal, K. (2007). A survey of energy drink consumption patterns among college students. *Nutrition Journal, 6,* 35. doi: 10.1186/1475-2891-6-35

Malit, L. A., Johnstone, R. E., Bourke, D. I., Kulp, R. A., Klein, V., & Smith, T. C. (1975). Intravenous delta9-tetrahydrocannabinol: Effects on ventilatory control and cardiovascular dynamics. *Anesthesiology, 42,* 666–673.

Mamelak, M. (1989). Gammahydroxybutyrate: An endogenous regulator of energy metabolisms. *Neuroscience and Biobehavioral Reviews, 13,* 187–198.

Mann, J. J., & Malone, K. M. (1997). Cerebrospinal fluid amines and higher-lethality suicide attempts in depressed inpatients. *Biological Psychiatry, 41*(2), 162–171.

Manrique-Garcia, E., Zammit, S., Dalman, C., Hemmingsson, T., Andreasson, S., & Allebeck, P. (2012). Cannabis, schizophrenia and other non-affective psychoses: 35 years of follow-up of a population-based cohort. *Psychological Medicine, 42*(06), 1321–1328. doi: 10.1017/S0033291711002078

Mansour, A., Hoversten, M. T., Taylor, L. P., Watson, S. J., & Akil, H. (1995). The cloned μ, δ and κ receptors and their endogenous ligands: Evidence for two opioid peptide recognition cores. *Brain Research, 700,* 89–98. doi: 10.1016/0006-8993(95)00928-J

Mao, Y., Ge, X., Frank, C. L., Madison, J. M., Koehler, A. N., Doud, M. K., . . . & Tsai, L. H. (2009). Disrupted in schizophrenia 1 regulates neuronal progenitor proliferation via modulation of GSK3beta/betacatenin signaling. *Cell, 136*(6), 1017–1031. doi: S0092-8674 (09)00021-X [pii]

Mao, Z. M., Arnsten, A. F., & Li, B. M. (1999). Local infusion of an alpha-1 adrenergic agonist into the prefrontal cortex impairs spatial working memory performance in monkeys. *Biological Psychiatry, 46*(9), 1259–1265.

Marczynski, T. J., Yamaguchi, N., Ling, G. M., & Grodzinska, L. (1964). Sleep induced by the administration of melatonin (5-methoxyn-acetyltryptamine) to the hypothalamus in unrestrained cats. *Experientia, 20*(8), 435–437.

Maric, T., Sedki, F., Ronfard, B., Chafetz, D., & Shalev, U. (2012). A limited role for ghrelin in heroin self-administration and food deprivation-induced reinstatement of heroin seeking in rats. *Addiction Biology, 17*(3), 613–622. doi: 10.1111/j.13691600.2011.00396.x

Marin, S. J., Coles, R., Merrell, M., & McMillin, G. A. (2008). Quantitation of benzodiazepines in urine, serum, plasma, and meconium by LC-MS-MS. *Journal of Analytical Toxicology, 32*(7), 491–498.

Marmar, C. R., Schlenger, W., Henn-Haase, C., Qian, M., Purchia, E., Li, M., . . . & Karstoft, K. I. (2015). Course of posttraumatic stress disorder 40 years after the Vietnam War: Findings from the National Vietnam Veterans Longitudinal Study. *Journal of the American Association Psychiatry, 72*(9), 875–881. doi: 10.1001/jamapsychiatry.2015.0803

Marmor, J. B. (1998). Medical marijuana. *Western Journal of Medicine, 168,* 540–543.

Martell, B. A., Orson, F. M., Poling, J., Mitchell, E., Rossen, R. D., Gardner, T., & Kosten, T. R. (2009). Cocaine vaccine for the treatment of cocaine dependence in methadone-maintained patients: A randomized, double-blind, placebo-controlled efficacy trial. *Archives of General Psychiatry, 66*(10), 1116–1123. doi: 10.1001/archgenpsychiatry.2009.128

Martin, C. B., Hamon, M., Lanfumey, L., & Mongeau, R. (2014) Controversies on the role of 5-HT 2C receptors in the mechanisms of action of antidepressant drugs. *Neuroscience & Biobehavioral Reviews, 42,* 208-223. doi: 10.1016/j.neubiorev.2014.03.001

Martin, L. A., Neighbors, H. W., & Griffith, D. M. (2013). The experience of symptoms of depression in men vs women: Analysis of the National Comorbidity Survey Replication. *JAMA Psychiatry, 70*(10), 1100–1106. doi: 10.1001/jamapsychiatry.2013.1985

Martínez-Arán, A., Vieta, E., Colom, F., Torrent, C., Sánchez-Moreno, J.,

Reinares, M., . . . & Salamero, M. (2004). Cognitive impairment in euthymic bipolar patients: Implications for clinical and functional outcome. *Bipolar Disorders, 6*(3), 224–232. doi: 10.1111/j.1399-5618.2004.00111.x

Mason, B. J. (2001). Treatment of alcohol-dependent outpatients with acamprosate: A clinical review. *Journal of Clinical Psychiatry, 62*(Suppl.), 42–48.

Mason, J. W., Giller, E. L., Kosten, T. R., Ostroff, R. B., & Podd, L. (1986). Urinary free-cortisol levels in posttraumatic stress disorder patients. *Journal of Nervous and Mental Disease, 174*(3), 145–149.

Mason, P. E., & Kerns, W. P., II. (2002). Gamma hydroxybutyric acid (GHB) intoxication. *Academic Emergency Medicine, 9*(7), 730–739.

Massi, P., Solinas, M., Cinquina, V., & Parolaro, D. (2013). Cannabidiol as potential anticancer drug. *British Journal of Clinical Pharmacology, 75*(2), 303–312. doi: 10.1111/j.1365-2125.2012.04298.x

Mathew, R. J., Wilson, W. H., Turkington, T. G., & Coleman, R. E. (1998). Cerebellar activity and disturbed time sense after THC. *Brain Research, 797*(2), 183–189. doi: 10.1016/s00068993(98)00375-8

Matz, R., Rick, W., Thompson, H., & Gershon, S. (1974). Clozapine—a potential antipsychotic agent without extrapyramidal manifestations. *Current Therapeutic Research, Clinical and Experimental, 16*(7), 687–695.

Maxwell, C. R., Spangenberg, R. J., Hoek, J. B., Silberstein, S. D., & Oshinsky, M. L. (2010). Acetate causes alcohol hangover headache in rats. *PLoS One, 5*(12), e15963. doi: 10.1371/journal.pone.0015963

Mayes, R., Bagwell, C., & Erkulwater, J. (2008). ADHD and the rise in stimulant use among children. *Harvard Review of Psychiatry, 16*(3), 151–166. doi: 10.1080/10673220802167782

Mayo Foundation. (2011). Caffeine content for coffee, tea, soda, and more. Retrieved from www.webcitation.org/67XR8IBJQ

Mayser, P., Fromme, S., Leitzmann, G., & Gründer, K. (1995). The yeast spectrum of the "tea fungus Kombucha." *Mycoses, 38*(7-8), 289–295.

McBride, W. J., Murphy, J. M., & Ikemoto, S. (1999). Localization of brain reinforcement mechanisms: Intracranial self-administration and intracranial place-conditioning studies. *Behavioural Brain Research, 101*(2), 129–152. doi: 10.1016/s01664328(99)00022-4

McCance, E. F., Price, L. H., Kosten, T. R., & Jatlow, P. I. (1995). Cocaethylene: Pharmacology, physiology, and behavioral effects in humans. *Journal of Pharmacology and Experimental Therapeutics, 274*(1), 215–223.

McCance-Katz, E. F., Carroll, K. M., & Rounsaville, B. J. (1999). Gender differences in treatment-seeking cocaine abusers: Implications for treatment and prognosis. *American Journal of Addiction, 8*, 300–311. doi: 10.1080/105504999305703

McCann, U. D., Ridenour, A., Shaham, Y., & Ricaurte, G. A. (1994). Serotonin neurotoxicity after (+/–)3,4-methylenedioxy methamphetamine (MDMA; "Ecstasy"): A controlled study in humans. *Neuropsychopharmacology, 10*(2), 129–138.

McClane, T. K., & Martin, W. R. (1976). Subjective and physiologic effects of morphine, pentobarbital, and meprobamate. *Clinical Pharmacology and Therapy, 20*(2), 192–198. doi: 0009-9236(76)90049-7 [pii]

McCracken, J. T., McGough, J., Shah, B., Cronin, P., Hong, D., Aman, M. G., . . . & McDougle, C. J. (2002). Risperidone in children with autism and serious behavioral problems. *New England Journal of Medicine, 347*(5), 314–321. doi: 10.1056/NEJMoa013171

McDowell, D. M., & Kleber, H. D. (1994). MDMA: Its history and pharmacology. *Psychiatric Annals, 24*, 127–130.

McGlothlin, W. H., & West, L. J. (1968). The marihuana problem: An overview. *American Journal of Psychiatry, 125*(3), 126–134.

McNair, D. M., Lor, M., & Doppleman, L.F. (1971). *Educational and Industrial Testing Service*. San Diego, CA: Educational and Industrial Testing Service.

McShane, R., Areosa Sastre, A., & Minakaran, N. (2006). Memantine for dementia. *Cochrane Database of Systematic Reviews* (Online)(2), CD003154.

Mehra, R., Moore, B. A., Crothers, K., Tetrault, J., & Fiellin, D. A. (2006). The association between marijuana smoking and lung cancer: A systematic review. *Archives of Internal Medicine, 166*(13), 1359–1367. doi: 10.1001/archinte.166.13.1359

Meier, K. E., & Mendoza, S. A. (1976). Effect of ethanol on the water permeability and short-circuit current of the urinary bladder of the toad and the response to vasopressin, adenosine-39,59-monophosphate and theophylline. [In Vitro Research Support, U.S. Gov't, P.H.S.]. *Journal of Pharmacology and Experimental Therapeutics, 196*(1), 231–237.

Melamede, R. (2005). Cannabis and tobacco are not equally carcinogenic. *Harm Reduction Journal, 2*(21).

Meldrum, B. (1982). Pharmacology of GABA. *Clinical Neuropharmacology, 5*(3), 293–316.

Meltzer, H. Y. (2001). Treatment of suicidality in schizophrenia. *Annals of the New York Academy of Sciences, 932*, 44–58, 58–60.

Meltzer, H. Y. (2002). Mechanism of action of atypical antipsychotic drugs. In K. L. Davis & American College of Neuropsychopharmacology (Eds.), *Neuropsychopharmacology: The fifth generation of progress* (p. xxi). Philadelphia, PA: Lippincott Williams & Wilkins.

Meltzer, H. Y., Koenig, J. I., Nash, J. F., & Gudelsky, G. A. (1989). Melperone and clozapine: Neuroendocrine effects of atypical neuroleptic drugs. *Acta Psychiatrica Scandinavica Supplement, 352*, 24–29.

Meltzer, H. Y., Matsubara, S., & Lee, J. C. (1989). Classification of typical and atypical antipsychotic drugs on the basis of dopamine D-1, D-2 and serotonin2 pKi values. *Journal of Pharmacology and Experimental Therapeutics, 251*(1), 238–246.

Meltzer, H. Y., & McGurk, S. R. (1999). The effects of clozapine, risperidone, and olanzapine on cognitive function in schizophrenia. *Schizophrenia Bulletin, 25*(2), 233–255.

Meltzer, H. Y., & Prus, A. J. (2006). NK3 receptor antagonists for the treatment of schizophrenia. *Drug Discovery Today: Therapeutic Strategies, 3,* 555–560.

Meltzer, H. Y., & Stahl, S. M. (1976). The dopamine hypothesis of schizophrenia: A review. *Schizophrenia Bulletin, 2*(1), 19–76.

Mendelson, J. H., Mello., N. K., Sholar, M. B., Seigel, A. J., Kaufman, M. J., Leven, J. M., Renshaw, P. F., & Cohen, B. M. (1999). Cocaine pharmacokinetics in men and in women during the follicular and luteal phases of the menstrual cycle. *Neuropsychopharmacology, 21,* 294–303. doi: 10.1016/S0893-133X(99)00020-2

Merikangas, K. R., Akiskal, H. S., Angst, J., Greenberg, P. E., Hirschfeld, R.M.A., Petukhova, M., & Kessler, R. C. (2007). Lifetime and 12-month prevalence of bipolar spectrum disorder in the National Comorbidity Survey replication. *Archives of General Psychiatry, 64*(5), 543–552. doi: 10.1001/archpsyc.64.5.543

Merritt, J. C., Crawford, W. J., Alexander, P. C., Anduze, A. L., & Gelbart, S. S. (1980). Effect of marijuana on intraocular and blood pressure in glaucoma. *Ophthalmology, 87,* 222–228.

Metcalf, D. R., Emde, R. N., & Stripe, J. T. (1966). An EEG-behavioral study of sodium hydroxybutyrate in humans. *Electroencephalography and Clinical Neurophysiology, 20*(5), 506–512. doi: 10.1016/0013-4694(66)90107-6

Metzner, R. (1998). Reflections on the Concord Prison project and the follow-up study. *Journal of Psychoactive Drugs, 30*(4), 427-428. doi: 10.1080/02791072.1998.10399716

Meunier, J.-C. (1997). Nociceptin/orphanin FQ and the opioid receptor-like ORL1 receptor. *European Journal of Pharmacology, 340*(1), 1–15. doi: 10.1016/s00142999(97)01411-8

Mihic, S. J., Ye, Q., Wick, M. J., Koltchine, V. V., Krasowski, M. D., Finn, S. E., . . . & Harrison, N. L. (1997). Sites of alcohol and volatile anaesthetic action on GABA(A) and glycine receptors. *Nature, 389*(6649), 385–389. doi: 10.1038/38738

Miles, C. P. (1977). Conditions predisposing to suicide: A review. *Journal of Nervous and Mental Disease, 164*(4), 231–246.

Millan, M. J. (2002). Descending control of pain. *Progress in Neurobiology, 66*(6), 355–474. doi: 10.1016/S0301-0082(02)00009-6

Millan, M. J. (2005). Serotonin 5-HT2C receptors as a target for the treatment of depressive and anxious states: Focus on novel therapeutic strategies. *Therapie, 60*(5), 441–460. doi: 10.2515/therapie:2005065

Millar, J. K., Wilson-Annan, J. C., Anderson, S., Christie, S., Taylor, M. S., Semple, C. A., . . . & Porteous, D. J. (2000). Disruption of two novel genes by a translocation cosegregating with schizophrenia. *Human Molecular Genetics, 9,* 1415–1523.

Miller, J. L., Ashford, J. W., Archer, S. M., Rudy, A. C., & Wermeling, D. P. (2008). Comparison of intranasal administration of haloperidol with intravenous and intramuscular administration: A pilot pharmacokinetic study. *Pharmacotherapy, 28*(7), 875–882. doi: 10.1592/phco.28.7.875

Miller, K. E. (2008). Wired: Energy drinks, jock identity, masculine norms, and risk taking. *Journal of American College Health, 56*(5), 481–489. doi: 10.3200/JACH.56.5.481–490

Miller, N. S., & Schwartz, R. H. (1997). MDMA (Ecstasy) and the rave: A review. *Pediatrics, 100,* 705–708.

Miller, W. R., Walters, S. T., & Bennett, M. E. (2001). How effective is alcoholism treatment in the United States? *Journal of Studies on Alcohol, 62,* 221–220.

Mills, K. C. (1997). Serotonin syndrome: A clinical update. *Critical Care Clinics, 13*(4), 763–783. doi: 10.1016/s07490704(05)70368–7

Minematsu, N., Nakamura, H., Furuuchi, M., Nakajima, T., Takahashi, S., Tateno, H., & Ishizaka, A. (2006). Limitation of cigarette consumption by CYP2A6*4, *7 and *9 polymorphisms. *European Respiratory Journal, 27*(2), 289–292. doi: 10.1183/09031936.06.00056305

Miotto, K., Darakjian, J., Basch, J., Murray, S., Zogg, J., & Rawson, R. (2001). Gamma-hydroxybutyric acid: Patterns of use, effects, and withdrawal. *American Journal on Addictions, 10*(3), 232–241.

Mithoefer, M. C., Wagner, M. T., Mithoefer, A. T., Jerome, L., & Doblin, R. (2011). The safety and efficacy of ±3,4-methylenedioxy methamphetamine-assisted psychotherapy in subjects with chronic, treatment-resistant posttraumatic stress disorder: The first randomized controlled pilot study. *Journal of Psychopharmacology, 25*(4), 439–452. doi: 10.1177/0269881110378371

Mithoefer, M. C., Wagner, M. T., Mithoefer, A. T., Jerome, L., Martin, S. F., Yazar-Klosinski, B., . . . & Doblin, R. (2013). Durability of improvement in post-traumatic stress disorder symptoms and absence of harmful effects or drug dependency after 3, 4-methylenedioxymetham phetamine-assisted psychotherapy: A prospective long-term follow-up study. *Journal of Psychopharmacology* (Oxford, England), *27*(1), 28–39. doi: 10.1177/0269881112456611

Miyamoto, M., Nishikawa, H., Doken, Y., Hirai, K., Uchikawa, O., & Ohkawa, S. (2004). The sleep-promoting action of ramelteon (TAK-375) in freely moving cats. [Comparative Study]. *Sleep, 27*(7), 1319–1325.

Mohamed, W. M., Ben Hamida, S., Cassel, J. C., de Vasconcelos, A. P., & Jones, B. C. (2011). MDMA: Interactions with other psychoactive drugs. *Pharmacology Biochemistry and Behavior, 99*(4), 759–774. doi: 10.1016/j.pbb.2011.06.032

Mohamed, W.M.Y., Hamida, S. B., Pereira de Vasconcelos, A., Cassel, J. C., & Jones, B. C. (2009). Interactions between 3,4-Methylenedioxymetham phetamine and ethanol in humans and rodents. *Neuropsychobiology, 60*(3–4), 188–194.

Mol, A. J., Gorgels, W. J., Voshaar, R.C.O., Breteler, M. H., van Balkom, A. J., van de Lisdonk, E. H., . . . & Zitman, F. G. (2005). Associations of benzodiazepine craving with other clinical variables in a population of general practice patients. *Comprehensive Psychiatry, 46*(5), 353–360. doi: 10.1016/j.comppsych.2005.01.002

Mongeau, R., de Montigny, C., & Blier, P. (1994). Electrophysiologic evidence for desensitization of α2-adrenoceptors on serotonin terminals following long-term treatment with drugs increasing norepinephrine synaptic concentration.

Neuropsychopharmacology, 10(1), 41–51. doi: 10.1038/npp.1994.6

Montagu, K. A. (1957). Catechol compounds in rat tissues and in brains of different animals. *Nature, 180*(4579), 244–245.

Montpied, P., Morrow, A. L., Karanian, J. W., Ginns, E. I., Martin, B. M., & Paul, S. M. (1991). Prolonged ethanol inhalation decreases gammaaminobutyric acidA receptor alpha subunit mRNAs in the rat cerebral cortex. *Molecular Pharmacology, 39*(2), 157–163.

Moreno-Gonzalez, I., Estrada, L. D., Sanchez-Mejias, E., & Soto, C. (2013). Smoking exacerbates amyloid pathology in a mouse model of Alzheimer's disease. *Nature Communications, 4*, 1–10. doi: 10.1038/ncomms2494

Morgan, C. A., Mofeez, A., Brandner, B., Bromley, L., & Curran, H. V. (2004). Ketamine impairs response inhibition and is positively reinforcing in healthy volunteers: A dose–response study. *Psychopharmacology, 172*(3), 298–308. doi: 10.1007/s00213–003–1656-y

Morgan, C. J., & Curran, H. V. (2012). Ketamine use: A review. *Addiction, 107*, 27–38. doi: 10.1111/j.1360–0443.2011.03576.x

Morgan, W. W. (1990). Abuse liability of barbiturates and other sedative-hypnotics. *Advances in Alcohol and Substance Abuse, 9*(1–2), 67–82.

Morgenstern, J., Kahler, C. W., Frey, R. M., & Labouvie, E. (1996). Modeling therapeutic response to 12-step treatment: Optimal responders, nonresponders, and partial responders. *Journal of Substance Abuse, 8*(1), 45–59.

Moriyama, Y., Mimura, M., Kato, M., & Kashima, H. (2006). Primary alcoholic dementia and alcohol-related dementia. *Psychogeriatrics, 6*(3), 114–118. doi: 10.1111/j.14798301.2006.00168.x

Morley, K. C., & McGregor, I. S. (2000). (±)-3,4-Methylenedioxy methamphetamine (MDMA, ["Ecstasy"]) increases social interaction in rats. *European Journal of Pharmacology, 408*(1), 41–49. doi: 10.1016/s00142999(00)00749–4

Morrison, P. D., Zois, V., McKeown, D. A., Lee, T. D., Holt, D. W., Powell,

J. F., . . . & Murray, R. M. (2009). The acute effects of synthetic intravenous delta9tetrahydrocannabinol on psychosis, mood and cognitive functioning. *Psychological Medicine, 39*(10), 1607–1616. doi: S0033291709005522 [pii]

Mouthaan, J., Sijbrandij, M., Luitse, J. S., Goslings, J. C., Gersons, B. P., & Olff, M. (2014). The role of acute cortisol and DHEAS in predicting acute and chronic PTSD symptoms. *Psychoneuroendocrinology, 45*, 179–186. doi: 10.1016/j.psyneuen.2014.04.001

Mucha, R. F., van der Kooy, D., O'Shaughnessy, M., & Bucenieks, P. (1982). Drug reinforcement studied by the use of place conditioning in rat. *Brain Research, 243*(1), 91–105. doi: 00068993(82)91123–4 [pii]

Mulholland, P. J., Becker, H. C., Woodward, J. J., & Chandler, L. J. (2011). SK2 channels regulate alcohol-associated plasticity of glutamatergic synapses. *Biological Psychiatry, 69*, 625–632. doi: 10.1016/j.biopsych.2010.09.025

Mullard, A. (2014). New drugs cost US$2.6 billion to develop. *Nature Reviews Drug Discovery, 13*, 877–877. doi: 10.1038/nrd4507

Muller, C., Viry, S., Miehe, M., Andriamampandry, C., Aunis, D., & Maitre, M. (2002). Evidence for a γ-hydroxybutyrate (GHB) uptake by rat brain synaptic vesicles. *Journal of Neurochemistry, 80*(5), 899–904. doi: 10.1046/j.0022– 3042.2002.00780.x

Munro, S., Thomas, K. L., & Abu-Shaar, M. (1993). Molecular characterization of a peripheral receptor for cannabinoids. *Nature, 365*(6441), 61–65. doi: 10.1038/365061a0

Murray, C.J.L., & Lopez, A. D. (1997). Global mortality, disability, and the contribution of risk factors: Global Burden of Disease study. *Lancet, 349*(9063), 1436–1442. doi: 10.1016/s01406736(96)07495–8

Muscat, J. E., Richie, J. P., & Stellman, S. D. (2002). Mentholated cigarettes and smoking habits in whites and blacks. *Tobacco Control, 11*, 368–371. doi: 10.1136/tc.11.4.368

Mützell, S. (1998). A 20-year longitudinal prospective study of 284 heroin addicts

in Stockholm County, Sweden. *Archives of Public Health, 56*, 307–316.

Myers, C. S., Taylor, R. C., Moolchan, E. T., & Heishman, S. J. (2007). Dose-related enhancement of mood and cognition in smokers administered nicotine nasal spray. *Neuropsychopharmacology, 33*(3), 588–598.

Nakagawa, Y., & Chiba, K. (2015). Diversity and plasticity of microglial cells in psychiatric and neurological disorders. *Pharmacology and Therapeutics, 154*, 21–35. doi: 10.1016/j.pharmthera.2015.06.010

Narahashi, T., Moore, J. W., & Scott, W. R. (1964). Tetrodotoxin blockage of sodium conductance increase in lobster giant axons. *Journal of General Physiology, 47*(5), 965–974. doi: 10.1085/jgp.47.5.965

Natale, M., Kowitt, M., Dahlberg, C. C., & Jaffe, J. (1978). Effect of psychotomimetic (LSD and dextroamphetamine) on the use of figurative language during psychoanalysis. *Journal of Consulting and Clinical Psychology, 46*, 157–158.

National Center for Health Statistics. (2015). Overdose death rates. CDC Wonder Database. Retrieved from https://www.drugabuse.gov/related-topics/trends-statistics/overdose-death-rates on February 29, 2016.

National Drug Intelligence Center. (2004, September). Intelligence report: GHB trafficking and abuse. (2004L0424–015). Retrieved from www.justice.gov/archive/ndic/pubs10/10331/10331t.htm

National Institute on Alcohol Abuse and Alcoholism (NIAAA). (1995). Diagnostic criteria for alcohol abuse and dependence. *Alcohol Alert, 30* (PH 359). Retrieved from http://pubs.niaaa.nih.gov/publications/aa30.htm

National Institute on Alcohol Abuse and Alcoholism. (2012). What is a standard drink? Retrieved from http://pubs.niaaa.nih.gov/publica-tions/Practitioner/PocketGuide/pocket_guide2.htm

National Institute on Drug Abuse. (2015). Synthetic cannabinoids (K2/Spice). Retrieved March 1, 2016, from https://www.drugabuse.gov/drugs-abuse/synthetic-cannabinoids-k2spice.

National Institutes of Health. (2012). Retrieved February 14, 2012, from https://www.clinicaltrials.gov/ct2/help/glossary/phase.

National Research Council. (2011). *Guide for the care and use of laboratory animals* (8th ed.). Washington, DC: National Academies Press.

Naudon, L., El Yacoubi, M., Vaugeois, J. M., Leroux-Nicollet, I., & Costentin, J. (2002). A chronic treatment with fluoxetine decreases 5-HT 1A receptors labeling in mice selected as a genetic model of helplessness. *Brain Research, 936*(1), 68–75. doi: 10.1016/S0006-8993(02)02548-9

Nebel, M. B., Eloyan, A., Nettles, C. A., Sweeney, K. L., Ament, K., Ward, R. E., . . . & Mostofsky, S. H. (2015). Intrinsic visual-motor synchrony correlates with social deficits in autism. *Biological Psychiatry.* doi: 10.1016/j.biopsych.2015.08.029

Neergaard, M. J., Singh, P., Job, J., & Montgomery, S. (2007). Waterpipe smoking and nicotine exposure: A review of the current evidence. *Nicotine and Tobacco Research, 9,* 987–994. doi: 10.1080/14622200701591591.

Neill, J. (1990). Whatever became of the schizophrenogenic mother? *American Journal of Psychotherapy, 44,* 499–505.

Neutel, C. I. (1995). Risk of traffic accident injury after a prescription for a benzodiazepine. *Annals of Epidemiology, 5*(3), 239–244. doi: 10.1016/1047-2797(94)00112-7

New York State. (2015). Governor Cuomo issues health alert: Illegal synthetic marijuana sends more than 160 New Yorkers to the hospital since April 8. Retrieved March 1, 2016, from https://www.governor.ny.gov/news/governor-cuomo-issues-health-alert-illegal-synthetic-marijuana-sends-more-160-new-yorkers

Ni, Y. G., & Miledi, R. (1997). Blockage of 5HT$_{2c}$ serotonin receptors by fluoxetine (Prozac). *Proceedings of the National Academy of Sciences, 94*(5), 2036–2040.

Nichols, D. E., & Oberlender, R. (1990). Structure-activity relationship of MDMA and related compounds: A new class of psychoactive drugs? *Annals of the New York Academy of Sciences, 600,* 613–625.

Nierenberg, A. A., Farabaugh, A. H., Alpert, J. E., Gordon, B. A., Worthington, J. J., Rosenbaum, J. F., & Fava, M. (2000). Timing of onset of antidepressant response with fluoxetine treatment. *American Journal of Psychiatry, 157,* 1423–1428.

Nisell, M., Nomikos, G. G., & Svensson, T. H. (1994). Infusion of nicotine in the ventral tegmental area or the nucleus accumbens of the rat differentially affects accumbal dopamine release. *Pharmacology and Toxicology, 75*(6), 348–352.

Nonnemaker, J. M., Crankshaw, E. C., Shive, D. R., Hussin, A. H., & Farrelly, M. C. (2011). Inhalant use initiation among U.S. adolescents: Evidence from the National Survey of Parents and Youth using discrete-time survival analysis. *Addictive Behaviors, 36*(8), 878–881. doi: 10.1016/j. addbeh.2011.03.009

Nordström, P., Samuelsson, M., Åsberg, M., Träskman-Bendz, L., Åberg-Wistedt, A., Nordin, C., & Bertilsson, L. (1994). CSF 5-HIAA predicts suicide risk after attempted suicide. *Suicide and Life-Threatening Behavior, 24*(1), 1–9.

Norrholm, S. D., & Ressler, K. J. (2009). Genetics of anxiety and trauma-related disorders. *Neuroscience, 164*(1), 272–287. doi: S0306-4522(09)01061-6 [pii]

Novas, M. L., Wolfman, C., Medina, J. H., & de Robertis, E. (1988). Proconvulsant and 'anxiogenic' effects of n-butyl β carboline-3-carboxylate, an endogenous benzodiazepine binding inhibitor from brain. *Pharmacology Biochemistry and Behavior, 30*(2), 331–336.

Nutt, D., King, L. A., Saulsbury, W., & Blakemore, C. (2007). Development of a rational scale to assess the harm of drugs of potential misuse. *Lancet, 369*(9566), 1047–1053. doi: 10.1016/s01406736(07)60464-4

Nutt, J. G., Woodward, W. R., & Anderson, J. L. (1985). The effect of carbidopa on the pharmacokinetics of intravenously administered levodopa: The mechanism of action in the treatment of Parkinsonism. *Annals of Neurology, 18*(5), 537–543. doi: 10.1002/ana.410180505

Nyman, A. L., Taylor, T. M., & Biener, L. (2002). Trends in cigar smoking and perceptions of health risks among Massachusetts adults. *Tobacco Control, 11*(Suppl. 2), ii25–ii28. doi: 10.1136/tc.11.suppl_2.ii25

O'Brien, C. C. (1964). Intensive calcium therapy as an initial approach to the psychotherapeutic relationship in the rehabilitation of the compulsive drinker. *Journal of Psychology, 57,* 125–129.

O'Brien, W. T., Harper, A. D., Jove, F., Woodgett, J. R., Maretto, S., Piccolo, S., & Klein, P. S. (2004). Glycogen synthase kinase-3{beta} haploinsufficiency mimics the behavioral and molecular effects of lithium. *Journal of Neuroscience, 24*(30), 6791–6798. doi: 10.1523/jneurosci.4753–03.2004

Ochoa, E., Li, L., & McNamee, M. (1990). Desensitization of central cholinergic mechanisms and neuroadaptation to nicotine. *Molecular Neurobiology, 4*(3), 251–287. doi: 10.1007/bf02780343

O'Donnell, J. M., Marek, G. J., & Seiden, L. S. (2005). Antidepressant effects assessed using behavior maintained under a differential-reinforcement-of-low-rate (DRL) operant schedule. *Neuroscience and Biobehavioral Reviews, 29*(4–5), 785–798. doi: S0149-7634(05)00047-3 [pii]

Oehen, P., Traber, R., Widmer, V., & Schnyder, U. (2013). A randomized, controlled pilot study of MDMA (±3, 4-Methylenedioxymethamphetamine)-assisted psychotherapy for treatment of resistant, chronic Post-Traumatic Stress Disorder (PTSD). *Journal of Psychopharmacology, 27*(1), 40–52. doi: 10.1177/0269881112464827

Okun, M. S., Boothby, L. A., Bart-field, R. B., & Doering, P. L. (2001). GHB: An important pharmacologic and clinical update. *Journal of Pharmaceutical Sciences, 4*(2), 167–175.

Oldendorf, W. H. (1974). Lipid solubility and drug penetration of the blood brain barrier. *Experimental Biology and Medicine, 147*(3), 813–816. doi: 10.3181/00379727-147-38444

Oldendorf, W. H., Hyman, S., Braun, L., & Oldendorf, S. Z. (1972). Blood–brain barrier: Penetration of morphine, codeine, heroin, and methadone after carotid injection. *Science, 178*(4064), 984–986. doi: 10.1126/science.178.4064.984

Olds, J. (1956). Pleasure center in the brain. *Scientific American, 195*, 105–116.

Olds, J., & Milner, P. (1954). Positive reinforcement produced by electrical stimulation of septal area and other regions of rat brain. *Journal of Comparative and Physiological Psychology, 47*(6), 419–427.

Olesen, J., Gustavsson, A., Svensson, M., Wittchen, H. U., & Jönsson, B. on behalf of the CDBE2010 study group and the European Brain Council. (2012). The economic cost of brain disorders in Europe. *European Journal of Neurology, 19*(1), 155–162. doi: 10.1111/j.1468-1331.2011.03590.x

Olfson, M., King, M., & Schoenbaum, M. (2015). Benzodiazepine use in the United States. *JAMA Psychiatry, 72*(2), 136–142. doi: 10.1001/jamapsychiatry.2014.1763

Oliveto, A., Gentry, W. B., Pruzinsky, R., Gonsai, K., Kosten, T. R., Martell, B., & Poling, J. (2010). Behavioral effects of gamma-hydroxybutyrate in humans. *Behavioral Pharmacology, 21*(4), 332–342. doi: 10.1097/ FBP.0b013e32833b3397

Oliveto, A., Poling, J., Mancino, M. J., Feldman, Z., Cubells, J. F., Pruzinsky, R., . . . & Kosten, T. R. (2011). Randomized, double blind, placebo-controlled trial of disulfiram for the treatment of cocaine dependence in methadone-stabilized patients. *Drug and Alcohol Dependence, 113*(2–3), 184–191. doi: 10.1016/j. drugalcdep.2010.07.022

Olivier, B., Pattij, T., Wood, S. J., Oosting, R., Sarnyai, Z., & Toth, M. (2001). The 5-HT(1A) receptor knockout mouse and anxiety. *Behavioral Pharmacolology, 12*(6–7), 439–450.

Omelchenko, N., & Sesack, S. R. (2010). Periaqueductal gray afferents synapse onto dopamine and GABA neurons in the rat ventral tegmental area. *Journal of Neuroscience Research, 88*, 981–991.

Opbroek, A., Delgado, P. L., Laukes, C., McGahuey, C., Katsanis, J., Moreno, F. A., & Manber, R. (2002). Emotional blunting associated with SSRI-induced sexual dysfunction. Do SSRIs inhibit emotional responses? *International Journal of Neuropsychopharmacology, 5*(02), 147–151. doi: 10.1017/S1461145702002870

Ordway, G. A., Gambarana, C., Tejani-Butt, S. M., Areso, P., Hauptmann, M., &

Frazer, A. (1991). Preferential reduction of binding of 125I-iodopindolol to beta-1 adrenoceptors in the amygdala of rat after antidepressant treatments. *Journal of Pharmacology and Experimental Therapeutics, 257*(2), 681–690.

O'Reilly, K. C., Trent, S., Bailey, S. J., & Lane, M. A. (2007). 13-cis-Retinoic acid alters intracellular serotonin, increases 5-HT1A receptor, and serotonin reuptake transporter levels in vitro. *Experimental Biology and Medicine, 232*(9), 1195–1203. doi: 10.3181/0703-RM-83

Ortiz de Montellano, P. R. (2013). Cytochrome P450-activated prodrugs. *Future Medicinal Chemistry, 5*, 213–228. doi: 10.4155/fmc.12.197

Oscar-Berman, M., & Marinkovic, K. (2007). Alcohol: Effects on neurobehavioral functions and the brain. *Neuropsychology Review, 17*(3), 239–257. doi: 10.1007/ s11065-007-9038-6

Ossipov, M. H., Lai, J., King, T., Vanderah, T. W., Malan, T. P., Jr., Hruby, V. J., & Porreca, F. (2004). Antinociceptive and nociceptive actions of opioids. *Journal of Neurobiology, 61*(1), 126–148. doi: 10.1002/neu.20091

Oster, G., Huse, D. M., Adams, S. F., Imbimbo, J., & Russell, M. W. (1990). Benzodiazepine tranquilizers and the risk of accidental injury. *American Journal of Public Health, 80*(12), 1467–1470. doi: 10.2105/ AJPH.80.12.1467

Ott, A., Slooter, A.J.C., Hofman, A., Van Harskamp, J.C.M., Witteman, J.C.M., & Van Broeckhoven, C. (1998). Smoking and risk of dementia and Alzheimer's disease in a population-based cohort study: The Rotterdam Study. *The Lancet, 351*, 1840–1843.

Owen, R., Sikich, L., Marcus, R. N., Corey-Lisle, P., Manos, G., McQuade, R. D., . . . & Findling, R. L. (2009). Aripiprazole in the treatment of irritability in children and adolescents with autistic disorder. *Pediatrics, 124*(6), 1533–1540.

Owens, D.G.C. (1999). *A guide to the extrapyramidal side-effects of antipsychotic drugs.* Cambridge, England: Cambridge University Press.

Pacifici, R., Zuccaro, P., Pichini, S., Roset, P. N., Poudevida, S., Farré, M., . . . & De la Torre, R. (2003). Modulation of the immune system in

cannabis users. *Journal of the American Medical Association, 289*(15), 1929–1931. doi: 10.1001/jama.289.15.1929-b

Pae, C.-U., Serretti, A., Patkar, A. A., & Masand, P. S. (2008). Aripiprazole in the treatment of depressive and anxiety disorders: A review of current evidence. *CNS Drugs, 22*, 367–388.

Paelecke-Habermann, Y., Pohl, J., & Leplow, B. (2005). Attention and executive functions in remitted major depression patients. *Journal of Affective Disorders, 89*(1), 125–135. doi: 10.1016/j. jad.2005.09.006

Pahnke, W. N., & Richards, W. A. (1966). Implications of LSD and experimental mysticism. *Journal of Religion and Health, 5*, 175–208.

Paleacu, D. (2007). Tetrabenazine in the treatment of Huntington's disease. *Neuropsychiatric Disease and Treatment, 3*, 545–551.

Pan, D., Gatley, S. J., Dewey, S. L., Chen, R., Alexoff, D. A., Ding, Y. S., & Fowler, J. S. (1994). Binding of bromine-substituted analogs of methylphenidate to monoamine transporters. *European Journal of Pharmacology, 264*(2), 177–182.

Pankow, J. F., Mader, B. T., Isabelle, L. M., Luo, W., Pavlick, A., & Liang, C. (1997). Conversion of nicotine in tobacco smoke to its volatile and available free-base from through the action of gaseous ammonia. *Environmental Science and Technology, 31*, 2428–2433.

Panlilio, L. V., & Schindler, C. W. (2000). Self-administration of remifentanil, an ultra-short acting opioid, under continuous and progressive-ratio schedules of reinforcement in rats. *Psychopharmacology, 150*(1), 61–66. doi: 10.1007/ s002130000415

Papakostas, G. I., Thase, M. E., Fava, M., Nelson, J. C., & Shelton, R. C. (2007). Are antidepressant drugs that combine serotonergic and noradrenergic mechanisms of action more effective than the selective serotonin reuptake inhibitors in treating major depressive disorder? A meta-analysis of studies of newer agents. *Biological Psychiatry, 62*(11), 1217–1227. doi: 10.1016/j. biopsych.2007.03.027

Papp, L. A., Klein, D. F., Martinez, J., Schneier, F., Cole, R., Liebowitz, M. R., . . . & Gorman, J. M. (1993). Diagnostic and substance specificity of carbon-dioxide-induced panic. *American Journal of Psychiatry, 150*(2), 250–257.

Park, S., Knopick, C., McGurk, S., & Meltzer, H. Y. (2000). Nicotine impairs spatial working memory while leaving spatial attention intact. *Neuropsychopharmacology, 22*(2), 200–209. doi: S0893133X(99)00098–6 [pii]

Parpura, V., Basarsky, T. A., Liu, F., Jeftinija, K., Jeftinija, S., & Haydon, P. G. (1994). Glutamate-mediated astrocyte-neuron signalling. *Nature, 369*, 744–747. doi: 10.1038/369744a0

Parrott, A. C. (2001). Human psychopharmacology of Ecstasy (MDMA): A review of 15 years of empirical research. *Human Psychopharmacology: Clinical and Experimental, 16*(8), 557–577. doi: 10.1002/hup.351

Parrott, A. C. (2014). The potential dangers of using MDMA for psychotherapy. *Journal of Psychoactive Drugs, 46*(1), 37–43. doi: 10.1080/02791072.2014.873690

Parsey, R. V., Olvet, D. M., Oquendo, M. A., Huang, Y. Y., Ogden, R. T., & Mann, J. J. (2006). Higher 5-HT1A receptor binding potential during a major depressive episode predicts poor treatment response: Preliminary data from a naturalistic study. *Neuropsychopharmacology, 31*(8), 1745-1749. doi: 10.1038/sj.npp.1300992

Parsey, R. V., Ogden, R. T., Miller, J. M., Tin, A., Hesselgrave, N., Goldstein, E., . . . & Oquendo, M. A. (2010). Higher serotonin 1A binding in a second major depression cohort: modeling and reference region considerations. *Biological Psychiatry, 68*(2), 170–178. doi: 10.1016/j.biopsych.2010.03.023

Passie, T., Halpern, J. H., Stichtenoth, D. O., Emrich, H. M., & Hintzen, A. (2008). The pharmacology of lysergic acid diethylamide: A review. *CNS Neuroscience and Therapeutics, 14*, 295–314.

Paulus, M. P., Tapert, S. F., Pulido, C., & Schuckit, M. A. (2006). Alcohol attenuates load-related activation during a working memory task: Relation to level of response to alcohol. *Alcoholism: Clinical and Experimental Research, 30*(8), 1363–1371. doi: 10.1111/j.1530–0277.2006.00164.x

Patridge, E., Gareiss, P., Kinch, M. S., & Hoyer, D. (2016). An analysis of FDA-approved drugs: Natural products and their derivatives. *Drug Discovery Today, 21*, 204-207. doi: 10.1016/j.drudis.2015.01.009

Pavlov, I. P., & Anrep, G. V. (1927). *Conditioned reflexes: An investigation of the physiological activity of the cerebral cortex.* London, England: Oxford University Press.

Paz, R. D., Tardito, S., Atzori, M., & Tseng, K. Y. (2008). Glutamatergic dysfunction in schizophrenia: From basic neuroscience to clinical psychopharmacology. *European Neuropsychopharmacology, 18*(11), 773–786. doi: S0924977X(08)00167–3 [pii]

Pehrson, A. L., Philibin, S. D., Gross, D., Robinson, S. E., Vann, R. E., Rosecrans, J. A., & James, J. R. (2008). The effects of acute and repeated nicotine doses on spontaneous activity in male and female Sprague Dawley rats: Analysis of brain area epibatidine binding and cotinine levels. *Pharmacology Biochemistry and Behavior, 89*(3), 424–431. doi: 10.1016/j.pbb.2008.01.018

Pellow, S., & File, S. E. (1986). Anxiolytic and anxiogenic drug effects on exploratory activity in an elevated plus-maze: A novel test of anxiety in the rat. *Pharmacology Biochemistry and Behavior, 24*(3), 525–529. doi: 00913057(86)90552–6 [pii]

Pennartz, C. M., Ito, R., Verschure, P. F., Battaglia, F. P., & Robbins, T. W. (2011). The hippocampal-striatal axis in learning, prediction, and goal-directed behavior. *Trends in Neuroscience, 34*(10), 548–559. doi: 10.1016/j.tins.2011.08.001

Pentney, A. R. (2001). An exploration of the history and controversies surrounding MDMA and MDA. *Journal of Psychoactive Drugs, 33*, 213–221.

Pérez-Stable, E. J., Herrera, B., Jacob, P., & Benowitz, N. L. (1998). Nicotine metabolism and intake in black and white smokers. *Journal of the American Medical Association, 280*(2), 152–156. doi: 10.1001/jama.280.2.152

Perkins, K., Epstein, L., Stiller, R., Fernstrom, M., Sexton, J., Jacob, R., & Solberg, R. (1991). Acute effects of nicotine on hunger and caloric intake in smokers and nonsmokers. *Psychopharmacology, 103*(1), 103–109. doi: 10.1007/ bf02244083

Perkins, K. A. (2001). Smoking cessation in women: Special considerations. *CNS Drugs, 15*, 391–411.

Perkins, K. A., Grobe, J. E., Fonte, C., Goettler, J., Caggiula, A. R., Reynolds, W. A., . . . & Jacob, R. G. (1994). Chronic and acute tolerance to subjective, behavioral and cardiovascular effects of nicotine in humans. *Journal of Pharmacology and Experimental Therapeutics, 270*(2), 628–638.

Perkins, K. A., & Scott, J. (2008). Sex differences in long-term smoking cessation rates due to nicotine patch. *Nicotine and Tobacco Research, 10*, 1245–1251. doi: 10.1080/14622200802097506

Pertwee, R. G. (2001). Cannabinoid receptors and pain. *Progress in Neurobiology, 63*(5), 569–611. doi: 10.1016/s03010082(00)00031–9

Pettibone, D. J., Totaro, J. A., & Pflueger, A. B. (1984). Tetrabenazine-induced depletion of brain monoamines: characterization and interaction with selected antidepressants. *European Journal of Pharmacology, 102*(3), 425–430. doi: 10.1016/0014–2999(84)90562–4

Picciotto, M. R., Higley, M. J., & Mineur, Y. S. (2012). Acetylcholine as a neuromodulator: Cholinergic signaling shapes nervous system function and behavior. *Neuron, 76*(1), 116–129. doi: 10.1016/j.neuron.2012.08.036

Philibin, S. D., Walentiny, D. M., Vunck, S. A., Prus, A. J., Meltzer, H. Y., & Porter, J. H. (2009). Further characterization of the discriminative stimulus properties of the atypical antipsychotic drug clozapine in C57BL/6 mice: Role of 5-HT(2A) serotonergic and alpha (1) adrenergic antagonism. *Psychopharmacology (Berl), 203*(2), 303–315. doi: 10.1007/ s00213–008–1385–3

Pifl, C., Drobny, H., Reither, H., Hornykiewicz, O., & Singer, E. A. (1995). Mechanism of the dopamine-releasing actions of amphetamine and cocaine: Plasmalemmal dopamine transporter versus vesicular monoamine transporter. *Molecular Pharmacology, 47*(2), 368–373.

Piper, M. E., Cook, J. W., Schlam, T. R., Jorenby, D. E., Smith, S. S., Bolt, D. M., & Loh, W. Y. (2010). Gender, race, and education differences in abstinence rates among participants in two randomized smoking cessation trials. *Nicotine and Tobacco Research, 12*(6), 647–657. doi: 10.1093/ntr/ntq067

Pisinger, C., & Døssing, M. (2014). A systematic review of health effects of electronic cigarettes. *Preventive Medicine, 69*, 248–260. doi: 10.1016/j.ypmed.2014.10.009

Pistis, M., Muntoni, A. L., Pillolla, G., Perra, S., Cignarella, G., Melis, M., & Gessa, G. L. (2005). Gamma-hydroxybutyric acid (GHB) and the mesoaccumbens reward circuit: Evidence for GABA(B) receptor-mediated effects. *Neuroscience, 131*(2), 465–474. doi: 10.1016/j.neuroscience.2004.11.021

Pitman, R. K., & Orr, S. P. (1990). Twenty-four hour urinary cortisol and catecholamine excretion in combat-related posttraumatic stress disorder. *Biological Psychiatry, 27*(2), 245–247. doi: 00063223(90)90654-K [pii]

Placzek, E. A., Okamoto, Y., Ueda, N., & Barker, E. L. (2008). Mechanisms for recycling and biosynthesis of endogenous cannabinoids anandamide and 2-arachidonylglycerol. *Journal of Neurochemistry, 107*(4), 987–1000.

Platt, D. M., Rowlett, J. K., Izenwasser, S., & Spealman, R. D. (2004). Opioid partial agonist effects of 3-o-methylnaltrexone in rhesus monkeys. *Journal of Pharmacology and Experimental Therapeutics, 308*(3), 1030–1039. doi: 10.1124/jpet.103.060962

Pletscher, A., Shore, P. A., & Brodie, B. B. (1955). Serotonin release as a possible mechanism of reserpine action. *Science, 122*(3165), 374–375.

Poling, A. D., & Byrne, T. (2000). *Introduction to behavioral pharmacology.* Reno, Nev: Context Press.

Polissidis, A., Galanopoulos, A., Naxakis, G., Papahatjis, D., Papadopoulou-Daifoti, Z., & Antoniou, K. (2012). The cannabinoid CB1 receptor biphasically modulates motor activity and regulates dopamine and glutamate release region dependently. *International Journal of Neuropsychopharmacology, FirstView*, 1–11. doi: 10.1017/ S1461145712000156

Polo, M. (1871). *The book of Ser Marco Polo, the Venetian: Concerning the kingdoms and marvels of the East; newly translated and edited with notes, by Colonel Henry Yule with maps and other illustrations* (H. Yule, Trans.). London, England: John Murray.

Polosa, R., & Benowitz, N. L. (2011). Treatment of nicotine addiction: Present therapeutic options and pipeline developments. *Trends in Pharmacological Sciences, 32*(5), 281–289. doi: 10.1016/j.tips.2010.12.008

Pompili, M., Amador, X. F., Girardi, P., Harkavy-Friedman, J., Harrow, M., Kaplan, K., . . . & Tatarelli, R. (2007). Suicide risk in schizophrenia: Learning from the past to change the future. *Annals of General Psychiatry, 6*, 10. doi: 1744-859X-6-10 [pii]

Popik, P., & Kolasiewicz, W. (1999). Mesolimbic NMDA receptors are implicated in the expression of conditioned morphine reward. *Naunyn-Schmiedeberg's Archives of Pharmacology, 359*(4), 288–294. doi: 10.1007/pl00005354

Porcella, A., Casellas, P., Gessa, G. L., & Pani, L. (1998). Cannabinoid receptor CB1 mRNA is highly expressed in the rat ciliary body: Implications for the antiglaucoma properties of marihuana. *Molecular Brain Research, 58*, 240–245.

Porcella, A., Maxia, C., Gessa, G. L., & Pani, L. (2000). The human eye expresses high levels of CB1 cannabinoid receptor mRNA and protein. *European Journal of Neuroscience, 12*, 1123–1127.

Porcella, A., Maxia, C., Gessa, G. L., & Pani, L. (2001). The synthetic cannabinoid WIN52212–2 decreases the intraocular pressure in human glaucoma resistant to conventional therapies. *European Journal of Neuroscience, 13*, 409–412.

Porsolt, R. D., Le Pichon, M., & Jalfre, M. (1977). Depression: A new animal model sensitive to antidepressant treatments. *Nature, 266*(5604), 730–732.

Potkin, S. G., Cohen, M., & Panagides, J. (2007). Efficacy and tolerability of asenapine in acute schizophrenia: A placebo- and risperidone-controlled trial. *Journal of Clinical Psychiatry, 68*(10), 1492–1500.

Powell, A. G., Apovian, C. M., & Aronne, L. J. (2011). New drug targets for the treatment of obesity. [Review]. *Clinical Pharmacology & Therapeutics, 90*(1), 40–51. doi: 10.1038/ clpt.2011.82

Pozzi, L., Invernizzi, R., Garavaglia, C., & Samanin, R. (1999). Fluoxetine increases extracellular dopamine in the prefrontal cortex by a mechanism not dependent on serotonin: A comparison with citalopram. *Journal of Neurochemistry, 73*(3), 1051–1057.

Pradhan, S. N. (1984). Phencyclidine (PCP): Some human studies. *Neuroscience and Biobehavioral Reviews, 8*(4), 493–501. doi: 10.1016/0149–7634(84)90006-x

Prat, G., Adan, A., & Sanchez-Turet, M. (2009). Alcohol hangover: A critical review of explanatory factors. *Human Psychopharmacology, 24*(4), 259–267. doi: 10.1002/hup.1023

Pratt, L. A., Brody, D. J., & Gu, Q. (2011). Antidepressant use in persons aged 12 and over: United States, 2005–2008. *National Center for Health Statistics Data Brief, 76.*

Preston, K. L., Bigelow, G. E., & Liebson, I. A. (1988). Buprenorphine and naloxone alone and in combination in opioid-dependent humans. *Psychopharmacology, 94*(4), 484–490. doi: 10.1007/ bf00212842

Pretlow, R. A. (2011). Addiction to highly pleasurable food as a cause of the childhood obesity epidemic: A qualitative Internet study. *Eating Disorders, 19*(4), 295–307. doi: 10.1080/ 10640266.2011.584803

Price, J., Cole, V., & Goodwin, G. M. (2009). Emotional side-effects of selective serotonin reuptake inhibitors: Qualitative study. *British Journal of Psychiatry, 195*, 211–217. doi: 10.1192/ bjp.bp.108.051110

Primeaux, S. D., Wilson, S. P., Bray, G. A., York, D. A., & Wilson, M. A. (2006). Overexpression of neuropeptide Y in the central nucleus of the amygdala decreases ethanol self-administration in "anxious" rats. *Alcoholism: Clinical and Experimental Research, 30*(5), 791–801.

Pritchett, D. B., Luddens, H., & Seeburg, P. H. (1989). Type I and type II GABAA-benzodiazepine receptors produced in transfected cells. *Science, 245*(4924), 1389–1392.

ProCon. (2016, January 7). 23 legal medical marijuana states and DC. Retrieved from http://medicalmarijuana.procon.org/view.resource.php?resourceID=000881

Prus, A. J., James, J. R., & Rosecrans, J. A. (2009). Conditioned place preference. In. Jerry J. Buccafusco (Ed.), *Methods of Behavioral Analysis in Neuroscience* (pp. 59–76). Boca Raton: CRC Press LLC/Taylor & Francis.

Prus, A. J., Maxwell, A. T., Baker, K. M., Rosecrans, J. A., & James, J. R. (2007). Acute behavioral tolerance to nicotine in the conditioned taste aversion paradigm. *Drug Development Research, 68*(8), 522–528. doi: 10.1002/ddr.20219

Public Health Service. (2002). *Public health service policy on humane care and use of laboratory animals.* Washington, DC: Department of Health and Human Services.

Purnell, W. D., & Gregg, J. M. (1975). Delta (9)-tetradydrocannabinol, euphoria, and intraocular pressure in man. *Annals of Ophthalmology, 7,* 921–923.

Qian, Z., Bilderback, T. R., & Barmack, N. H. (2008). Acyl coenzyme A-binding protein (ACBP) is phosphorylated and secreted by retinal Müller astrocytes following protein kinase C activation. *Journal of Neurochemistry, 105*(4), 1287–1299. doi: 10.1111/j.1471-4159.2008.05229.x

Rafla, F. K., & Epstein, R. L. (1979). Identification of cocaine and its metabolites in human urine in the presence of ethyl alcohol. *Journal of Analytical Toxicology, 3*(2), 59–63. doi: 10.1093/jat/3.2.59

Rainey, C. L., Conder, P. A., & Goodpaster, J. V. (2011). Chemical characterization of dissolvable tobacco products promoted to reduce harm. *Journal of Agricultural and Food Chemistry, 59*(6), 2745–2751. doi: 10.1021/ jf103295d

Ramaekers, J. G., Berghaus, G., van Laar, M., & Drummer, O. H. (2004).

Dose-related risk of motor vehicle crashes after cannabis use. *Drug and Alcohol Dependence, 73*(2), 109–119. doi: 10.1016/j. drugalcdep.2003.10.008

Ramirez-Latorre, J., Yu, C. R., Qu, X., Perin, F., Karlin, A., & Role, L. (1996). Functional contributions of [alpha]5 subunit to neuronal acetylcholine receptor channels. *Nature, 380*(6572), 347–351.

Rautio, J., Kumpulainen, H., Heimbach, T., Oliyai, R., Oh, D., Jarvinen, T., & Savolainen, J. (2008). Prodrugs: Design and clinical applications. *Nature Reviews Drug Discovery, 7*(3), 255–270. doi: 10.1038/nrd2468

Ravnborg, M., Jensen, F. M., Jensen, N.-H., & Holk, I. K. (1987). Pupillary diameter and ventilatory CO_2 sensitivity after epidural morphine and buprenorphine in volunteers. *Anesthesia and Analgesia, 66*(9), 847–851.

Ray, W. A., Chung, C. P., Murray, K. T., Hall, K., & Stein, C. M. (2009). Atypical antipsychotic drugs and the risk of sudden cardiac death. *New England Journal of Medicine, 360*(3), 225–235. doi: 10.1056/NEJMoa0806994

Rees, D. C., Knisely, J. S., Jordan, S., & Balster, R. L. (1987). Discriminative stimulus properties of toluene in the mouse. *Toxicology and Applied Pharmacology, 88*(1), 97–104.

Regier, D. A., Narrow, W. E., Rae, D. S., Manderscheid, R. W., Locke, B. Z., & Goodwin, F. K. (1993). The de facto U.S. mental and addictive disorders service system: Epidemiologic catchment area prospective 1-year prevalence rates of disorders and services. *Archives of General Psychiatry, 50*(2), 85–94.

Reissig, C. J., Carter, L. P., Johnson, M. W., Mintzer, M. Z., Klinedinst, M. A., & Griffiths, R. R. (2012). High doses of dextromethorphan, an NMDA antagonist, produce effects similar to classic hallucinogens. *Psychopharmacology (Berl), 223*(1), 1–15.

Resnick, H. S., Yehuda, R., Pitman, R. K., & Foy, D. W. (1995). Effect of previous trauma on acute plasma cortisol level following rape. *American Journal of Psychiatry, 152*(11), 1675–1677.

Reynolds, G. P., Hill, M. J., & Kirk, S. L. (2006). The 5-HT2C receptor and

antipsychoticinduced weight gain: Mechanisms and genetics. *Journal of Psychopharmacology, 20*(4 Suppl.), 15–18. doi: 10.1177/1359786806066040

Richardson, N. R., & Roberts, D. C. (1996). Progressive ratio schedules in drug self-administration studies in rats: A method to evaluate reinforcing efficacy. *Journal of Neuroscience Methods, 66*(1), 1–11. doi: 0165027095001530 [pii]

Richelson, E., & Nelson, A. (1984). Antagonism by neuroleptics of neurotransmitter receptors of normal human brain in vitro. *European Journal of Pharmacology, 103*(3–4), 197–204.

Richelson, E., & Souder, T. (2000). Binding of antipsychotic drugs to human brain receptors focus on newer generation compounds. *Life Sciences, 68*(1), 29–39.

Ridenour, T. A., Bray, B. C., & Cottler, L. B. (2007). Reliability of use, abuse, and dependence of four types of inhalants in adolescents and young adults. *Drug and Alcohol Dependence, 91*(1), 40–49. doi: 10.1016/j.drugalcdep.2007.05.004

Riegel, A. C., Zapata, A., Shippenberg, T. S., & French, E. D. (2007). The abused inhalant toluene increases dopamine release in the nucleus accumbens by directly stimulating ventral tegmental area neurons. *Neuropsychopharmacology, 32*(7), 1558–1569. doi: 1301273 [pii]

Rigotti, N. A., Harrington, K. F., Richter, K., Fellows, J. L., Sherman, S. E., Grossman, E., . . . & Ylioja, T. (2015). Increasing prevalence of electronic cigarette use among smokers hospitalized in 5 US cities, 2010–2013. *Nicotine and Tobacco Research, 17*(2), 236–244. doi: 10.1093/ntr/ntu138

Ritz, M. C., Cone, E. J., & Kuhar, M. J. (1990). Cocaine inhibition of ligand binding at dopamine, norepinephrine and serotonin transporters: A structure-activity study. *Life Sciences, 46*(9), 635–645.

Roberts, R. C. (2007). Schizophrenia in translation: Disrupted in schizophrenia (*DISC1*): Integrating clinical and basic findings. *Schizophrenia Bulletin, 33*(1), 11–15. doi: 10.1093/schbul/sbl063

Robinson, E.S.J., Anderson, N. J., Crosby, J., Nutt, D. J., & Hudson, A. L.

(2003). Endogenous β-Carbolines as Clonidine-displacing substances. *Annals of the New York Academy of Sciences, 1009*(1), 157–166. doi: 10.1196/annals.1304.018

Robinson, T. E., & Becker, J. B. (1986). Enduring changes in brain and behavior produced by chronic amphetamine administration: A review and evaluation of animal models of amphetamine psychosis. *Brain Research, 396*(2), 157–198. doi: S0006–8993(86)80193–7 [pii]

Robinson, T. E., & Berridge, K. C. (2003). Addiction. *Annual Review of Psychology, 54*, 25–53. doi: 10.1146/annurev. psych.54.101601.145237

Rochester, J. A., & Kirchner, J. T. (1999). Ecstasy (3,4-methylenedioxyamphetamine): History, neurochemistry and toxicology. *Journal of the American Board of Family Practice, 12*, 137–142.

Roiko, S. A., Felmlee, M. A., & Morris, M. E. (2012). Brain uptake of the drug of abuse gamma-hydroxybutyric acid in rats. *Drug Metabolism and Disposition, 40*(1), 212–218. doi: 10.1124/dmd.111.041749

Rook, E. J., Hillebrand, M.J.X., Rosing, H., van Ree, J. M., & Beijnen, J. H. (2005). The quantitative analysis of heroin, methadone and their metabolites and the simultaneous detection of cocaine, acetylcodeine and their metabolites in human plasma by high-performance liquid chromatography coupled with tandem mass spectrometry. *Journal of Chromatography B, 824*(1–2), 213–221. doi: 10.1016/j.jchromb.2005.05.048

Rose, A. K., & Grunsell, L. (2008). The subjective, rather than the disinhibiting, effects of alcohol are related to binge drinking. *Alcoholism: Clinical and Experimental Research, 32*(6), 1096–1104. doi: 10.1111/j.15300277.2008.00672.x

Rose, M. A., & Grant, J. E. (2010). Alcohol-induced blackout. Phenomenology, biological basis, and gender differences. *Journal of Addiction Medicine, 4*, 61–73. doi: 10.1097/ADM.0b013e3181e1299d

Rosecrans, J. A. (1995). The psychopharmacological basis of nicotine's differential effects on

behavior: Individual subject variability in the rat. *Behavioral Genetics, 25*(2), 187–196.

Rosecrans, J. A., Stimler, C. A., Hendry, J. S., & Meltzer, L. T. (1989). Nicotine-induced tolerance and dependence in rats and mice: Studies involving schedule-controlled behavior. *Progress in Brain Research, 79*, 239–248.

Rosenbaum, C. D., Carreiro, S. P., & Babu, K. M. (2012). Here today, gone tomorrow . . . and back again? A review of herbal marijuana alternatives (K2, Spice), synthetic cathinones (bath salts), kratom, *Salvia divinorum*, methoxetamine, and piperazines. *Journal of Medical Toxicology, 8*(1), 15–32. doi: 10.1007/s13181011–0202-2

Rosenberg, N. L., Grigsby, J., Dreisbach, J., Busenbark, D., & Grigsby, P. (2002). Neuropsychologic impairment and MRI abnormalities associated with chronic solvent abuse. *Journal of Toxicology—Clinical Toxicology, 40*(1), 21–34.

Rosenheck, R., Leslie, D., Keefe, R., McEvoy, J., Swartz, M., Perkins, D., . . . & Lieberman, J. (2006). Barriers to employment for people with schizophrenia. *American Journal of Psychiatry, 163*(3), 411–417. doi: 10.1176/appi. ajp.163.3.411

Ross, C. A., Margolis, R. L., Reading, S.A.J., Pletnikov, M., & Coyle, J. T. (2006). Neurobiology of schizophrenia. *Neuron, 52*, 139–153.

Rossy, L. A., Buckelew, S. P., Dorr, N., Hagglund, K. J., Thayer, J. F., McIntosh, M. J., . . . & Johnson, J. C. (1999). A meta-analysis of fibromyalgia treatment interventions. *Annals of Behavioral Medicine, 21*(2), 180–191.

Roth, B. L., Baner, K., Westkaemper, R., Siebert, D., Rice, K. C., Steinberg, S., . . . & Rothman, R. B. (2002). Salvinorin A: A potent naturally occurring nonnitrogenous kappa opioid selective agonist. *Proceedings of the National Academy of Sciences of the USA, 99*(18), 11934–11939. doi: 10.1073/pnas.182234399

Rowell, T. R., & Tarran, R. (2015). Will chronic e-cigarette use cause lung disease? *American Journal of Physiology: Lung Cellular and Molecular Physiology, 309*, L1398-L1409. doi: 10.1152/ajplung.00272.2015

Roy, S., & Loh, H. (1996). Effects of opioids on the immune system. *Neurochemical Research, 21*(11), 1375–1386. doi: 10.1007/ bf02532379

Rubin, R. P. (2007). A brief history of great discoveries in pharmacology: In celebration of the centennial anniversary of the founding of the American Society of Pharmacology and Experimental Therapeutics. *Pharmacological Reviews, 59*, 289–359. doi: 10.1124/pr.107.70102

Rudnick, G., & Wall, S. C. (1992). The molecular mechanism of "Ecstasy" [3,4-methylenedioxymethamphetamine (MDMA)]: Serotonin transporters are targets for MDMA-induced serotonin release. *Proceedings of the National Academy of Sciences of the USA, 89*(5), 1817–1821.

Rusanen, M., Kivipelto, M., Quesenberry, C. P., Jr., Zhou, J., & Whitmer, R. A. (2011). Heavy smoking in midlife and long-term risk of Alzheimer disease and vascular dementia. *Archives of Internal Medicine, 171*(4), 333–339. doi: 10.1001/archinternmed.2010.393

Russell, W.M.S., & Burch, R. L. (1959). *Principles of humane animal experimentation.* Springfield, IL: Charles C Thomas.

Russell-Mayhew, S., von Ranson, K. M., & Masson, P. C. (2010). How does Overeaters Anonymous help its members? A qualitative analysis. *European Eating Disorders Review, 18*(1), 33–42. doi: 10.1002/erv.966

Rutledge, P. C., Park, A., & Sher, K. J. (2008). Twenty-first birthday drinking: Extremely extreme. *Journal of Consulting and Clinical Psychology, 76*(3), 511–516. doi: 2008–06469-015 [pii]

Saccone, S. F., Hinrichs, A. L., Saccone, N. L., Chase, G. A., Konvicka, K., Madden, P.A.F., . . . & Bierut, L. J. (2007). Cholinergic nicotinic receptor genes implicated in a nicotine dependence association study targeting 348 candidate genes with 3713 SNPs. *Human Molecular Genetics, 16*(1), 36–49. doi: 10.1093/ hmg/ddl438

Sahay, A., & Hen, R. (2007). Adult hippocampal neurogenesis in depression. *Nature Neuroscience, 10*(9), 1110–1115. doi: nn1969 [pii]

Saitoh, F., Noma, M., & Kawashima, N. (1985). The alkaloid contents of sixty

Nicotiana species. *Phytochemistry, 24*, 477–480. doi: 10.1016/S0031-9422(00)80751-7

Sakr, A., & Andheria, M. (2001). Pharmacokinetics of buspirone extended-release tablets: A single-dose study. *Journal of Clinical Pharmacology, 41*(7), 783–789. doi: 10.1177/00912700122010582

Sams-Dodd, F. (1998). Effects of continuous D-amphetamine and phencyclidine administration on social behaviour, stereotyped behaviour, and locomotor activity in rats. *Neuropsychopharmacology, 19*(1), 18–25. doi: S0893133X9700 2005 [pii]

Sanacora, G., Berman, R. M., Cappiello, A., Oren, D. A., Kugaya, A., Liu, N., . . . & Charney, D. S. (2004). Addition of the alpha2-antagonist yohimbine to fluoxetine: Effects on rate of antidepressant response. *Neuropsychopharmacology, 29*(6), 1166–1171.

Sanchez, C., Asin, K. E., & Artigas, F. (2015). Vortioxetine, a novel antidepressant with multimodal activity: Review of preclinical and clinical data. *Pharmacology and Therapeutics, 145*, 43–57. doi: 10.1016/j.pharmthera.2014.07.001

Sansone, R. A. & Sansone, L. A. (2011). Agomelatine: A novel antidepressant. *Innovations in Clinical Neuroscience, 8*, 10–14.

Santamaria, J., Tolosa, E., & Valles, A. (1986). Parkinson's disease with depression: A possible subgroup of idiopathic Parkinsonism. *Neurology, 36*(8), 1130–1133.

Santarelli, L., Saxe, M., Gross, C., Surget, A., Battaglia, F., Dulawa, S., . . . & Belzung, C. (2003). Requirement of hippocampal neurogenesis for the behavioral effects of antidepressants. *Science, 301*(5634), 805–809. doi: 10.1126/science.1083328

Sapolsky, R. M. (1992). Cortisol concentrations and the social significance of rank instability among wild baboons. *Psychoneuroendocrinology, 17*, 702–709.

Sartor, C. E., Grant, J. D., Lynskey, M. T., McCutcheon, V. V., Waldron, M., Statham, D. J., . . . & Nelson, E. C.

(2012). Common heritable contributions to low-risk trauma, high-risk trauma, posttraumatic stress disorder, and major depression. *Archives of General Psychiatry, 69*(3), 293–299. doi: 10.1001/archgenpsychiatry.2011.1385

Satel, S. (2006). Is caffeine addictive? A review of the literature. *American Journal of Drug and Alcohol Abuse, 32*(4), 493–502. doi: 10.1080/00952990600918965

Satta, R., Dimitrijevic, N., & Manev, H. (2003). *Drosophila* metabolize 1,4-butanediol into γ-hydroxybutyric acid in vivo. *European Journal of Pharmacology, 25*, 149–152. doi: 10.1016/S0014-2999(03)01993-9

Savitz, J., & Drevets, W. C. (2009). Bipolar and major depressive disorder: Neuroimaging the developmental-degenerative divide. *Neuroscience and Biobehavioral Reviews, 33*(5), 699–771. doi: 10.1016/j.neubiorev.2009.01.004

Sayette, M. A., Shiffman, S., Tiffany, S. T., Niaura, R. S., Martin, C. S., & Shadel, W. G. (2000). The measurement of drug craving. *Addiction, 95*(Suppl. 2), S189–210.

Schellenberg, G. D., Dawson, G., Sung, Y. J., Estes, A., Munson, J., Rosenthal, E., . . . & Leong, L. (2006). Evidence for genetic linkage of autism to chromosomes 7 and 4. *Molecular Psychiatry, 11*(11). doi: http://dx.doi.org/10.1038/sj.mp.4001918

Schilt, T., Koeter, M., Smal, J., Gouwetor, M., van den Brink, W., & Schmand, B. (2010). Long-term neuropsychological effects of Ecstasy in middle-aged Ecstasy/polydrug users. *Psychopharmacology, 207*(4), 583–591. doi: 10.1007/ s00213–009–1688-z

Schlaepfer, T. E., Cohen, M. X., Frick, C., Kosel, M., Brodesser, D., Axmacher, N., . . . & Sturm, V. (2008). Deep brain stimulation to reward circuitry alleviates anhedonia in refractory major depression. *Neuropsychopharmacology, 33*(2), 368–377. doi: 1301408 [pii]

Schotte, A., Janssen, P. F., Gommeren, W., Luyten, W. H., Van Gompel, P., Lesage, A. S., . . . Leysen, J. E. (1996). Risperidone compared with new and reference antipsychotic drugs: In vitro and in vivo receptor binding. *Psychopharmacology, 124*(1–2), 57–73.

Schroeder, J. P., Cooper, D. A., Schank, J. R., Lyle, M. A., Gaval-Cruz, M., Ogbonmwan, Y. E., . . . & Weinshenker, D. (2010). Disulfiram attenuates drug-primed reinstatement of cocaine seeking via inhibition of dopamine beta-hydroxylase. *Neuropsychopharmacology, 35*(12), 2440–2449. doi: 10.1038/npp.2010.127

Schulte, T., Müller-Oehring, E. M., Strasburger, H., Warzel, H., & Sabel, B. A. (2001). Acute effects of alcohol on divided and covert attention in men. *Psychopharmacology, 154*(1), 61–69. doi: 10.1007/s002130000603

Schultes, R. E. (1969). Hallucinogens of plant origin. *Science, 163*(3864), 245–254.

Schultz, C. B. (1983). Statutory classification of cocaine as a narcotic: An illogical anachronism. *American Journal of Law and Medicine, 9*, 225–245.

Schulz, R., Wüster, M., Duka, T., & Herz, A. (1980). Acute and chronic ethanol treatment changes endorphin levels in brain and pituitary. *Psychopharmacology, 68*(3), 221–227. doi: 10.1007/ bf00428107

Schwartz, R. D., & Kellar, K. J. (1985). *In vivo* regulation of [3H] acetylcholine recognition sites in brain by nicotinic cholinergic drugs. *Journal of Neurochemistry, 45*(2), 427–433.

Schweizer, T. A., & Vogel-Sprott, M. (2008). Alcohol-impaired speed and accuracy of cognitive functions: A review of acute tolerance and recovery of cognitive performance. *Experimental and Clinical Psychopharmacology, 16*(3), 240–250. doi: 2008–06716–007 [pii]

Sdao-Jarvie, K., & Vogel-Sprott, M. (1991). Response expectancies affect the acquisition and display of behavioral tolerance to alcohol. *Alcohol, 8*(6), 491–498.

Seely, K. A., Patton, A. L., Moran, C. L., Womack, M. L., Prather, P. L., Fantegrossi, W. E., . . . & McCain, K. R. (2013). Forensic investigation of K2, Spice, and "bath salt" commercial preparations: A three-year study of new designer drug products containing synthetic cannabinoid, stimulant, and hallucinogenic compounds. *Forensic Science International, 233*(1), 416–422. doi: 10.1016/j.forsciint.2013.10.002

Seeman, P. (2001). Antipsychotic drugs, dopamine receptors, and schizophrenia. *Clinical Neuroscience Research, 1*(1–2), 53–60.

Seeman, P. (2005). An update of fast-off dopamine D2 atypical anti-psychotics. *American Journal of Psychiatry, 162*(10), 1984–1985.

Seeman, P., Chau-Wong, M., Tedesco, J., & Wong, K. (1976). Brain receptors for antipsychotic drugs and dopamine: Direct binding assays. *Proceeding of the National Academy of Sciences of the USA, 72*(11), 4376–4380.

Seeman, P., & Lee, T. (1975). Antipsychotic drugs: Direct correlation between clinical potency and presynaptic action on dopamine neurons. *Science, 188*(4194), 1217–1219.

Seidel, S., Singer, E. A., Just, H., Farhan, H., Scholze, P., Kudlacek, O., . . . & Sitte, H. H. (2005). Amphetamines take two to tango: An oligomer-based counter-transport model of neurotransmitter transport explores the amphetamine action. *Molecular Pharmacology, 67*(1), 140–151. doi: 67/1/140 [pii]

Séguéla, P., Wadiche, J., Dineley-Miller, K., Dani, J. A., & Patrick, J. W. (1993). Molecular cloning, functional properties, and distribution of rat brain α7: A nicotinic cation channel highly permiable to calcium. *Journal of Neuroscience, 13*, 596–604.

Selvaraj, S., Hoshi, R., Bhagwagar, Z., Murthy, N. V., Hinz, R., Cowen, P., . . . & Grasby, P. (2009). Brain serotonin transporter binding in former users of MDMA ("Ecstasy"). *British Journal of Psychiatry, 194*(4), 355–359. doi: 10.1192/bjp. bp.108.050344

Selye, H. (1950). Stress and the general adaptation syndrome. *British Medical Journal, 1*, 1383–1392.

Sen, S., Burmeister, M., & Ghosh, D. (2004). Meta-analysis of the association between a serotonin transporter promoter polymorphism (5-HTTLPR) and anxiety-related personality traits. *American Journal of Medical Genetics Part B: Neuropsychiatric Genetics, 127*(1), 85–89. doi: 10.1002/ajmg.b.20158

Serretti, A., Kato, M., De Ronchi, D., & Kinoshita, T. (2007). Meta-analysis of

serotonin transporter gene promotor polymorphism (5-HTTLPR) association with selective reuptake inhibitor efficacy in depressed patients. *Molecular Psychiatry, 12*, 247–257.

Sesack, S. R., Carr, D. B., Omelchenko, N., & Pinto, A. (2003). Anatomical substrates for glutamate-dopamine interactions: Evidence for specificity of connections and extrasynaptic actions. *Annals of the New York Academy of Sciences, 1003*, 36–52.

Shapatava, E., Nelson, K. E., Tsertsvadze, T., & Del Rio, C. (2006). Risk behaviors and HIV, hepatitis B, and hepatitis C seroprevalence among injection drug users in Georgia. *Drug and Alcohol Dependence, 82*, S35-S38. doi: 10.1016/S0376–8716(06)80006–2

Sharp, T., Zetterstrom, T., Ljungberg, T., & Ungerstedt, U. (1987). A direct comparison of amphetamine-induced behaviours and regional brain dopamine release in the rat using intracerebral dialysis. *Brain Research, 401*(2), 322–330.

Shelton, K. L., & Balster, R. L. (2004). Effects of abused inhalants and GABA-positive modulators in dizocilpine discriminating inbred mice. *Pharmacology Biochemistry and Behavior, 79*(2), 219–228. doi: 10.1016/j.pbb.2004.07.009

Shelton, M. K., & McCarthy, K. D. (1999). Mature hippocampal astrocytes exhibit functional metabotropic and ionotropic glutamate receptors in situ. *Glia, 26*, 1–11. doi: 10.1002/(SICI)1098–1136(199903)26:1

Shen, X. Y., Orson, F. M., & Kosten, T. R. (2012). Vaccines against drug abuse. *Clinical Pharmacology and Therapy, 91*(1), 60–70. doi: 10.1038/clpt.2011.281

Shervette, R. E., Schydlower, M., Fearnow, R. G., & Lampe, R. M. (1979). Jimson "loco" weed abuse in adolescents. *Pediatrics, 63*(4), 520–523.

Shieh, K. R. & Yang, S. C. (2008). Effects of estradiol on the stimulation of dopamine turnover in mesolimbic and nigrostriatal systems by cocaine- and amphetamine-regulated transcript peptide in female rats. *Neuroscience, 154*, 1589–1597. doi: 10.1016/j.neuroscience.2008.01.086

Shiffman, S. (1989). Tobacco "chippers": Individual differences in tobacco dependence. *Psychopharmacology (Berl), 97*(4), 539–547.

Shimizu, E., Hashimoto, K., & Iyo, M. (2004). Ethnic difference of the BDNF 196G/A (val66met) polymorphism frequencies: The possibility to explain ethnic mental traits. *American Journal of Medical Genetics Part B: Neuropsychiatric Genetics, 126B*(1), 122–123. doi: 10.1002/ajmg.b.20118

Shin, L. M., & Liberzon, I. (2010). The neurocircuitry of fear, stress, and anxiety disorders. *Neuropsychopharmacology, 35*(1), 169–191. doi: npp200983 [pii]

Shoemaker, J. L., Joseph, B. K., Ruckle, M. B., Mayeux, P. R., & Prather, P. L. (2005). The endocannabinoid noladin ether acts as a full agonist at human CB2 cannabinoid receptors. *Journal of Pharmacology and Experimental Therapeutics, 314*(2), 868–875. doi: 10.1124/jpet.105.085282

Shook, J. E., Lemcke, P. K., Gehrig, C. A., Hruby, V. J., & Burks, T. F. (1989). Antidiarrheal properties of supraspinal mu and delta and peripheral mu, delta and kappa opioid receptors: Inhibition of diarrhea without constipation. *Journal of Pharmacology and Experimental Therapeutics, 249*(1), 83–90.

Shorter, E. (1997). *A history of psychiatry: From the era of the asylum to the age of Prozac.* New York, NY: Wiley.

Shorter, E. (2009). The history of lithium therapy. *Bipolar Disorder, 11*, 4–9. doi: 10.1111/j.1399–5618.2009.00706.x

Shu, H., Hayashida, M., Arita, H., Huang, W., Zhang, H., An, K., . . . & Hanaoka, K. (2011). Pentazocine-induced antinociception is mediated mainly by μ-opioid receptors and compromised by κ-opioid receptors in mice. *Journal of Pharmacology and Experimental Therapeutics, 338*(2), 579–587. doi: 10.1124/ jpet.111.179879

Siebert, D. J. (1994). *Salvia divinorum and Salvinorin A: New pharmacologic findings. Journal of Ethnopharmacology, 43*, 53–56.

Siegel, R. K. (1978). Phencyclidine use among youth: History, epidemiology, and acute and chronic intoxication. *NIDA Research Monographs, 21*, 272–288.

Siegel, S. (1984). Pavlovian conditioning and heroin overdose: Reports by overdose victims. *Bulletin of the Psychonomic Society, 22*(5), 428–430.

Siegel, S., Hinson, R. E., Krank, M. D., & McCully, J. (1982). Heroin "overdose" death: Contribution of drug-associated environmental cues. *Science, 216*(4544), 436–437.

Sigel, E., & Buhr, A. (1997). The benzodiazepine binding site of GABAA receptors. *Trends in Pharmacological Sciences, 18*(11), 425–429.

Sigmon, S. C., Herning, R. I., Better, W., Cadet, J. L., & Griffiths, R. R. (2009). Caffeine withdrawal, acute effects, tolerance, and absence of net beneficial effects of chronic administration: Cerebral blood flow velocity, quantitative EEG, and subjective effects. *Psychopharmacology (Berl), 204*(4), 573–585. doi: 10.1007/s00213009-1489-4

Silver, H., Feldman, P., Bilker, W., & Gur, R. C. (2003). Working memory deficit as a core neuropsychological dysfunction in schizophrenia. *American Journal of Psychiatry, 160*(10), 1809–1816.

Silver, J., & Miller, J. H. (2004). Regeneration beyond the glial scar. *National Review of Neuroscience, 5*(2), 146–156. doi:10.1038/nrn1326

Simpson, D. D., & Marsh, K. L. (1986). Relapse and recovery among opioid addicts 12 years after treatment. *National Institute on Drug Abuse Research Monograph Series, 72*, 86–103.

Sinha, R., Fox H., Hong, K-L., Sofuoglu, M., Morgan, P. T., & Bergquist, K. T. (2007). Sex steroid hormones, stress response, and drug craving in cocaine-dependent women: Implications for relapse susceptibility. *Experimental and Clinical Psychopharmacology, 15*, 445–452. doi: 0.1037/1064-1297.15.5.445

Singer, P. (1975). *Animal liberation: A new ethics for our treatment of animals.* New York, NY: New York Review.

Skinner, B. F. (1938). *The behavior of organisms: An experimental analysis.* New York, NY: D. Appleton-Century.

Skolnick, P., & Basile, A. S. (2006). Triple reuptake inhibitors as antidepressants. *Drug Discovery Today: Therapeutic Strategies, 3*, 489–494.

Slobodyansky, E., Guidotti, A., Wambebe, C., Berkovich, A., & Costa, E. (1989). Isolation and characterization of a rat brain triakontatetraneuropeptide, a posttranslational product of diazepam binding inhibitor: Specific action at the Ro 5-4864 recognition site. *Journal of Neurochemistry, 53*(4), 1276–1284. doi: 10.1111/j.1471-4159.1989.tb07425.x

Smeraldi, E., Zanardi, R., Benedetti, F., Di Bella, D., Perez, J., & Catalano, M. (1998). Polymorphism within the promoter of the serotonin transporter gene and antidepressant efficacy of fluvoxamine. *Molecular Psychiatry, 3*(6).

Smith, R. C., & Davis, J. M. (1977). Comparative effects of d-amphetamine, l-amphetamine, and methylphenidate on mood in man. *Psychopharmacology, 53*(1), 1–12. doi: 10.1007/bf00426687

Smith, R. C., Meltzer, H. Y., Arora, R. C., & Davis, J. M. (1977). Effects of phencyclidine on [3H]catecholamine and [3H]serotonin uptake in synaptosomal preparations from rat brain. *Biochemical Pharmacology, 26*, 1435–1439.

Soine, W. H. (1986). Clandestine drug synthesis. *Medicinal Research Reviews, 6*, 41–74.

Sokol, R. J., Delaney-Black, V., & Nordstrom, B. (2003). Fetal alcohol spectrum disorder. *Journal of the American Medical Association, 290*(22), 2996–2999. doi: 10.1001/jama.290.22.2996

Sokoloff, P., Andrieux, M., Besancon, R., Pilon, C., Martres, M. P., Giros, B., & Schwartz, J. C. (1992). Pharmacology of human dopamine D3 receptor expressed in a mammalian cell line: Comparison with D2 receptor. *European Journal of Pharmacology, 225*(4), 331–337.

Solomon, R. L., & Corbit J. D. (1974). An opponent-process theory of motivation: 1. Temporal dynamics of affect. *Psychology Review, 81*, 119–145.

Spanagel, R., Montkowski, A., Allingham, K., Shoaib, M., Holsboer, F., & Landgraf, R. (1995). Anxiety: A potential predictor of vulnerability to the initiation of ethanol self-administration in rats. *Psychopharmacology, 122*(4), 369–373. doi: 10.1007/bf02246268

Spanagel, R., Vengeliene, V., Jandeleit, B., Fischer, W.-N., Grindstaff, K., Zhang, X., Gallop, M. A., Krstew, E. V., Lawrence, A. J., & Kiefer, F. (2014). Acamprosate produces its anti-relapse effects via calcium. *Neuropsychopharmacology, 39*, 783–791. doi: 10.1038/npp.2013.264

Speilmans, G. I., Berman, M. I., Linardatos, E., Rosenlicht, N. Z., Perry, A., & Tsai, A. C (2013). Adjunctive atypical antipsychotic treatment for major depressive disorder: A meta-analysis of depression, quality of life, and safety outcomes. *PLoS Medicine, 10*, e1001403. doi: 10.1371/journal.pmed.1001403

Spiker, D. G., Weiss, J. C., Dealy, R. S., Griffin, S. J., Hanin, I., Neil, J. F., . . . & Soloff, P. H. (1985). The pharmacological treatment of delusional depression. *American Journal of Psychiatry, 142*(4), 430–436.

Spohn, H. E., & Strauss, M. E. (1989). Relation of neuroleptic and anticholinergic medication to cognitive functions in schizophrenia. *Journal of Abnormal Psychology, 98*(4), 367–380.

Sporer, K. A. (1999). Acute heroin overdose. *Annals of Internal Medicine, 130*(7), 584–590.

Spyraki, C., Fibiger, H. C., & Phillips, A. G. (1983). Attenuation of heroin reward in rats by disruption of the mesolimbic dopamine system. *Psychopharmacology, 79*(2), 278–283. doi: 10.1007/bf00427827

Starkstein, S. E., Petracca, G., Teson, A., Chemerinski, E., Merello, M., Migliorelli, R., & Leiguarda, R. (1996). Catatonia in depression: Prevalence, clinical correlates, and validation of a scale. *Journal of Neurology, Neurosurgery and Psychiatry, 60*(3), 326–332.

Stedman, T. L. (1999). *Stedman's medical dictionary* (27th ed.). Baltimore, MA: Lippincott Williams & Wilkins.

Steele, T. D., Nichols, D. E., & Yim, G.K.W. (1987). Stereochemical effects of 3,4-methylenedioxymethamphetamine (MDMA) and related amphetamine derivatives on inhibition of uptake of [3H] monoamines into synaptosomes from different regions of rat brain. *Biochemical Pharmacology, 36*, 2297–2303.

Stefanis, C. N., Alevizos, B. H., & Papadimitriou, G. N. (1982). Antidepressant effect of Ro 11–1163, a new MAO inhibitor. *International Pharmacopsychiatry, 17*(1), 43–48.

Stefater, M. A., Wilson-Perez, H. E., Chambers, A. P., Sandoval, D. A., &

Seeley, R. J. (2012). All bariatric surgeries are not created equal: Insights from mechanistic comparisons. *Endocrine Reviews, 33*(4), 595–622. doi: 10.1210/er.2011–1044

Stein, C., Schafer, M., & Hassan, A. H. (1995). Peripheral opioid receptors. *Annals of Medicine, 27*(2), 219–221.

Steinberg, H., & Sykes, E. A. (1985). Introduction to symposium on endorphins and behavioural processes; review of literature on endorphins and exercise. *Pharmacology Biochemistry and Behavior, 23*(5), 857–862.

Sternbach, H. (1991). The serotonin syndrome. *American Journal of Psychiatry, 148*(6), 705–713.

Stolerman, I. P., Pratt, J. A., Garcha, H. S., Giardini, V., & Kumar, R. (1983). Nicotine cue in rats analysed with drugs acting on cholinergic and 5-hydroxytryptamine mechanisms. *Neuropharmacology, 22*(9), 1029–1037.

Stollberger, C., Huber, J. O., & Finsterer, J. (2005). Antipsychotic drugs and QT prolongation. *International Clinical Psychopharmacology, 20*(5), 243–251.

Stone, J. M., Day, F., Tsagaraki, H., Valli, I., McLean, M. A., Lythgoe, D. J., . . . & McGuire, P. K. (2009). Glutamate dysfunction in people with prodromal symptoms of psychosis: Relationship to gray matter volume. *Biological Psychiatry, 66*, 533–539.

Subramanya, S. B., Subramanian, V. S., & Said, H. M. (2010). Chronic alcohol consumption and intestinal thiamin absorption: Effects on physiological and molecular parameters of the uptake process. *American Journal of Physiology—Gastrointestinal and Liver Physiology, 299*(1), G23–G31. doi: 10.1152/ ajpgi.00132.2010

Substance Abuse and Mental Health Services Administration. (2010). *Results from the 2009 National Survey on Drug Use and Health: Vol. I. Summary of national findings.* Rockville, MD: Office of Applied Studies.

Sullivan, J. M. (2000). Cellular and molecular mechanisms underlying learning and memory impairments produced by cannabinoids. *Learning and Memory, 7*(3), 132–139. doi: 10.1101/ lm.7.3.132

Sullivan, G. M., Oquendo, M. A., Milak, M., Miller, J. M., Burke, A.,

Ogden, R. T., . . . & Mann, J. J. (2015). Positron emission tomography quantification of serotonin1$_a$ receptor binding in suicide attempters with major depressive disorder. *JAMA Psychiatry, 72*(2), 169–178. doi: 10.1001/ jamapsychiatry.2014.2406.

Svingos, A. L., Moriwaki, A., Wang, J. B., Uhl, G. R., & Pickel, V. M. (1997). μ-Opioid receptors are localized to extrasynaptic plasma membranes of GABAergic neurons and their targets in the rat nucleus accumbens. *Journal of Neuroscience, 17*(7), 2585–2594.

Swerdlow, P. S. (2000). Use of humans in biomedical experimentation. In F. L. Marina (Ed.), *Scientific integrity: An introductory text with cases* (2nd ed., pp. 73–100). Washington, DC: ASM Press.

Swift, R., & Davidson, D. (1998). Alcohol hangover: Mechanisms and mediators. *Alcohol Health Research World, 22*(1), 54–60.

Szalavitz, M. (2010). How a study of a failed antidepressant shows that antidepressants really work. *Time.* October 18, 2010. Retrieved from http://healthland.time.com/ 2010/10/18/how-a-failed-antidepressant-study-shows-antidepressants-actually-work/

Szatmari, P., Paterson, A. D., Zwaigenbaum, L., Roberts, W., Brian, J., Liu, X. Q., . . . & Feuk, L. (2007). Mapping autism risk loci using genetic linkage and chromosomal rearrangements. *Nature Genetics, 39*(3), 319–328. doi: 10.1038/ng1985

Szymański, P., Markowicz, M., & Mikiciuk-Olasik, E. (2012). Adaptation of high-throughput screening in drug discovery—toxicological screening tests. *International Journal of Molecular Sciences, 13*(1), 427–452. doi: 10.3390/ ijms13010427.

Takeda, S., Jiang, R., Aramaki, H., Imoto, M., Toda, A., Eyanagi, R., . . . & Watanabe, K. (2010). Δ^9-tetrahydrocannabinol and its major metabolite Δ9tetrahydrocannabinol-11-oic acid as 15-lipoxygenase inhibitors. *Journal of Pharmaceutical Sciences, 100*(3), 1206–1211. doi: 10.1002/jps.22354

Tan, W. C., Lo, C., Jong, A., Xing, L., Fitzgerald, M. J., Vollmer, W. M., . . . & Sin, D. D. (2009). Marijuana and chronic obstructive lung disease: A population-based study. *Canadian Medical*

Association Journal, 180(8), 814–820. doi: 10.1503/cmaj.081040

Tancer, M., & Johanson, C.-E. (2003). Reinforcing, subjective, and physiological effects of MDMA in humans: A comparison with d-amphetamine and mCPP. *Drug and Alcohol Dependence, 72*(1), 33–44. doi: 10.1016/s03768716(03)00172–8

Tanda, G., Frau, R., & Di Chiara, G. (1996). Chronic desipramine and fluoxetine differentially affect extracellular dopamine in the rat prefrontal cortex. *Psychopharmacology, 127*, 83–87. doi: 10.1007/BF02805978

Taylor, B., Jick, H., & MacLaughlin, D. (2013). Prevalence and incidence rates of autism in the UK: Time trend from 2004–2010 in children aged 8 years. *BMJ Open, 3*(10), e003219. doi: 10.1136/ bmjopen-2013-003219

Taylor, D. P., & Hyslop, D. K. (1991). Chronic administration of buspirone down-regulates 5-HT$_2$ receptor binding sites. *Drug Development Research, 24*(1), 93–105. doi: 10.1002/ddr.430240108

Taylor, M. J., Rudkin. L., Bullemor-Day, P., Lubin, J., Chukwujekwu, C., & Hawton, K. (2013). Strategies for managing sexual dysfunction induced by antidepressant medication. *Cochrane Database of Systematic Reviews 2013, Issue 5.* Article Number CD003382. doi: 10.1002/14651858.CD003382.pub3

Temple, J. L. (2009). Caffeine use in children: What we know, what we have left to learn, and why we should worry. *Neuroscience and Biobehavioral Reviews, 33*(6), 793–806. doi: 10.1016/j. neubiorev.2009.01.001

Thase, M. E., Greenhouse, J. B., Frank, E., Reynolds, C. F., Pilkonis, P. A., Hurley, K., . . . & Kupfer, D. J. (1997). Treatment of major depression with psychotherapy or psychotherapy-pharmacotherapy combinations. *Archives of General Psychiatry, 54*(11), 1009–1015. doi: 10.1001/archpsyc.1997.01830230043006

Thiel, C. M., Zilles, K., & Fink, G. R. (2005). Nicotine modulates reorienting of visuospatial attention and neural activity in human parietal cortex. *Neuropsychopharmacology, 30*(4), 810–820.

Thomas, B. F., Gilliam, A. F., Burch, D. F., Roche, M. J., & Seltzman, H. H.

(1998). Comparative receptor binding analyses of cannabinoid agonists and antagonists. *Journal of Pharmacology and Experimental Therapeutics, 285*(1), 285–292.

Thompson, R. F. (1999). James Olds. *Biographical Memoirs, 77*. Retrieved from www.nap.edu/html/biomems/jolds.html

Ticku, M. K., Burch, T. P., & Davis, W. C. (1983). The interactions of ethanol with the benzodiaze-pine-GABA receptor-ionophore complex. *Pharmacology Biochemistry and Behavior, 18*(Suppl. 1), 15–18.

Tiwari, A. K., Souza, R. P., & Muller, D. J. (2009). Pharmacogenetics of anxiolytic drugs. *Journal of Neural Transmission, 116*(6), 667–677. doi: 10.1007/s00702-0090229-6

Tobiansky, D. J., Will, R. G., Lominac, K. D., Turner, J. M., Hattori, T., Krishnan, K., . . . & Dominguez, J. M. (2016). Estradiol in the preoptic area regulates the dopaminergic response to cocaine in the nucleus accumbens. *Neuropsychopharmacology.* doi: 10.1038/npp.2015.360

Tobin, J. M., Lorenz, A. A., Brousseau, E. R., & Conner, W. R. (1964). Clinical evaluation of oxazepam for the management of anxiety. *Diseases of the Nervous System, 25*, 689–696.

Todaro, B. (2012). Cannabinoids in the treatment of chemotherapy-induced nausea and vomiting. *Journal of the National Comprehensive Cancer Network, 10*(4), 487–492.

Toennes, S. W., Harder, S., Schramm, M., Niess, C., & Kauert, G. F. (2003). Pharmacokinetics of cathinone, cathine, and norephedrine after the chewing of khat leaves. *British Journal of Clinical Pharmacology, 56*(1), 125–130. doi: 10.1046/j.13652125.2003.01834.x

Tohen, M., Vieta, E., Calabrese, J., Ketter, T. A., Sachs, G., Bowden, C., . . . & Breier, A. (2003). Efficacy of olanzapine and olanzapine-fluoxetine combination in the treatment of bipolar I depression. *Archives of General Psychiatry, 60*(11), 1079–1088. doi: 10.1001/archpsyc.60.11.1079

Tohen, M., & Zarate Jr, C. A. (1997). Antipsychotic agents and bipolar disorder. *Journal of Clinical Psychiatry, 59*, 38–48.

Tone, A. (2005). Listening to the past: History, psychiatry, and anxiety. *Canadian Journal of Psychiatry, 50*(7), 373–380.

Trigo, J. M., Martin-García, E., Berrendero, F., Robledo, P., & Maldonado, R. (2010). The endogenous opioid system: A common substrate in drug addiction. *Drug and Alcohol Dependence, 108*(3), 183–194. doi: 10.1016/j.drugalcdep.2009.10.011

Trivedi, M. H., Rush, A. J., Wisniewski, S. R., Nierenberg, A. A., Warden, D., Ritz, L., . . . Fava, M. (2006). Evaluation of outcomes with citalopram for depression using measurement-based care in STAR*D: Implications for clinical practice. *American Journal of Psychiatry, 163*(1), 28–40. doi: 163/1/28 [pii]

Trollor, J. N., Chen, X., & Sachdev, P. S. (2009). Neuroleptic malignant syndrome associated with atypical antipsychotic drugs. *CNS Drugs, 23*(6), 477–492. doi: 3 [pii]

Tropea, D., Caleo, M., & Maffei, L. (2003). Synergistic effects of brain-derived neurotrophic factor and chondroitinase ABC on retinal fiber sprouting after denervation of the superior colliculus in adult rats. *Journal of Neuroscience, 23*(18), 7034–7044.

Trtchounian, A., Williams, M., & Talbot, P. (2010). Conventional and electronic cigarettes (e-cigarettes) have different smoking characteristics. *Nicotine and Tobacco Research, 12*(9), 905–912. doi: 10.1093/ntr/ntq114

Tschoner, A., Engl, J., Rettenbacher, M., Edlinger, M., Kaser, S., Tatarczyk, T., . . . & Ebenbichler, C. F. (2009). Effects of six second generation antipsychotics on body weight and metabolism: Risk assessment and results from a prospective study. *Pharmacopsychiatry, 42*(1), 29–34. doi: 10.1055/s-0028-1100425

Tsuang, M. (2000). Schizophrenia: Genes and environment. *Biological Psychiatry, 47*(3), 210–220. doi: 10.1016/s00063223(99)00289-9

Turner, J. M., Sillett, R. W., & McNicol, M. W. (1977). Effect of cigar smoking on carboxyhaemoglobin and plasma nicotine concentrations in primary pipe and cigar smokers and ex-cigarette smokers. *Br Med J, 2*(6099), 1387–1389. doi: 10.1136/bmj.2.6099.1387

Uhr, M., Tontsch, A., Namendorf, C., Ripke, S., Lucae, S., Ising, M., . . . & Holsboer, F. (2008). Polymorphisms in the drug transporter gene ABCB1 predict antidepressant treatment response in depression. *Neuron, 57*(2), 203–209. doi: 10.1016/j.neuron.2007.11.017

Ulrich, J., Johannson-Locher, G., Seiler, W. O., & Stahelin, H. B. (1997). Does smoking protect from Alzheimer's disease? Alzheimer-type changes in 301 unselected brains from patients with known smoking history. *Acta Neuropathologica, 94*, 450–454.

Umhau, J. C., Schwandt, M. L., Usala, J., Geyer, C., Singley, E., George, D. T., & Heilig, M. (2011). Pharmacologically induced alcohol craving in treatment seeking alcoholics correlates with alcoholism severity, but is insensitive to acamprosate. *Neuropsychopharmacology, 36*, 1178–1186. doi: 10.1038/npp.2010.253

Ungvari, G. S., Kau, L. S., Wai-Kwong, T., & Shing, N. F. (2001). The pharmacological treatment of catatonia: an overview. *European Archives of Psychiatry and Clinical Neuroscience, 251*(1), I31-I34. doi:

Ungvari, G. S., Leung, C. M., Wong, M. K., & Lau, J. (1994). Benzodiazepines in the treatment of catatonic syndrome. *Acta Psychiatrica Scandinavica, 89*(4), 285–288.

United Nations Office of Drugs and Crime. (2010). *World drug report 2010.* New York: Author.

United Nations Office of Drugs and Crime. (2014). *Global synthetic drugs assessment: Amphetamine-type stimulants and new psychoactive substances.* Vienna: United Nations Office on Drugs and Crime.

U.S. Congress (1994). The American Indian Religious Freedom Act Amendments of 1994 (AIRFAA). *Public Law,* 103–344.

U.S. Department of Agriculture USDA. (2006). 9 CFR 1A. (Title 9, Chapter 1, Subchapter A): Animal Welfare. *Federal Register.*

U.S. Department of Health and Human Services. (2006). The health consequences of involuntary exposure to tobacco smoke: A report of the Surgeon General. Atlanta, GA: U.S.

Department of Health and Human Services, Centers for Disease Control and Prevention, Coordinating Center for Health Promotion, National Center for Chronic Disease Prevention and Health Promotion, Office on Smoking and Health.

Valzelli, L. (1980). *An approach to neuroanatomical and neurochemical psychology.* Torino, Italy: C. G. Edizioni Medico Scientifiche.

van de Waterbeemd, H., Camenisch, G., Folkers, G., Chretien, J. R., & Raevsky, O. A. (1998). Estimation of blood-brain barrier crossing of drugs using molecular size and shape, and H-bonding descriptors. *Journal of Drug Targeting, 6*(2), 151–165. doi: 10.3109/10611869808997889

van Os, J., Kenis, G., & Rutten, B.P.F. (2010). The environment and schizophrenia. *Nature, 468*(7321), 203–212.

van Vliet, I. M., den Boer, J. A., Westenberg, H. G., & Pian, K. L. (1997). Clinical effects of buspirone in social phobia: A double-blind placebo-controlled study. *Journal of Clinical Psychiatry, 58*(4), 164–168.

van Zessen, R., Phillips, J. L., Budygin, E. A., & Stuber, G. D. (2012). Activation of VTA GABA neurons disrupts reward consumption. *Neuron, 73*(6), 1184–1194. doi: 10.1016/j. neuron.2012.02.016

Vann, R. E., Gamage, T. F., Warner, J. A., Marshall, E. M., Taylor, N. L., Martin, B. R., & Wiley, J. L. (2008). Divergent effects of cannabidiol on the discriminative stimulus and place conditioning effects of Δ⁹tetrahydrocannabinol. *Drug and Alcohol Dependence, 94*(1–3), 191–198. doi: S03768716(07)00490–5 [pii]

Vansickel, A. R., Cobb, C. O., Weaver, M. F., & Eissenberg, T. E. (2010). A clinical laboratory model for evaluating the acute effects of electronic "cigarettes": Nicotine delivery profile and cardiovascular and subjective effects. *Cancer Epidemiology Biomarkers and Prevention, 19*(8), 1945–1953. doi: 10.1158/1055-9965. EPI-10-0288

Varela, M., Nogue, S., Oros, M., & Miro, O. (2004). Gamma hydroxybutirate use for sexual assault. *Emergency Medicine Journal, 21,* 255–256.

Vearrier, D., Greenberg, M. I., Miller, S. N., Okaneku, J. T., & Haggerty, D. A. (2012). Methamphetamine: History, pathophysiology, adverse health effects, current trends, and hazards associated with the clandestine manufacture of methamphetamine. *Disease-a-Month, 58*(2), 38–89. doi: 10.1016/j. disamonth.2011.09.004

Veliskova, J., Velisek, L., & Moshe, S. L. (1996). Subthalamic nucleus: A new anticonvulsant site in the brain. *Neuroreport, 7*(11), 1786–1788.

Veliskova, J., Velisek, L., Nunes, M. L., & Moshe, S. L. (1996). Developmental regulation of regional functionality of substantial nigra GABAA receptors involved in seizures. *European Journal of Pharmacology, 309*(2), 167–173. doi: 001429999600341X [pii]

Veselinović, T., Vernaleken, I., Janouschek, H., Kellermann, T., Paulzen, M., Cumming, P., & Gründer, G. (2015). Effects of anticholinergic challenge on psychopathology and cognition in drug-free patients with schizophrenia and healthy volunteers. *Psychopharmacology, 232*(9), 1607–1617. doi: 10.1007/s00213–014–3794–9

Vicentic, A., & Jones, D. C. (2007). The CART (cocaine- and amphetamine-regulated transcript) system in appetite and drug addiction. *Journal of Pharmacology and Experimental Therapeutics, 320*(2), 499–506. doi: 10.1124/jpet.105.091512

Vieta, E., Locklear, J., Günther, O., Ekman, M., Miltenburger, C., Chatterton, M. L., . . . & Paulsson, B. (2010). Treatment options for bipolar depression: A systematic review of randomized, controlled trials. *Journal of Clinical Psychopharmacology, 30*(5), 579–590. 10.1097/JCP.0b013e3181f15849

Villégier, A.-S., Lotfipour, S., McQuown, S. C., Belluzzi, J. D., & Leslie, F. M. (2007). Tranylcypromine enhancement of nicotine self-administration. *Neuropharmacology, 52*(6), 1415–1425. doi: 10.1016/j.neuropharm.2007.02.001

Virk, M. S., Arttamangkul, S., Birdsong, W. T., & Williams, J. T. (2009). Buprenorphine is a weak partial agonist that inhibits opioid receptor desensitization. *Journal of Neuroscience, 29*(22), 7341–7348. doi: 10.1523/jneurosci.3723-08.2009

Viveros, O. H., Arqueros, L., Connett, R. J., & Kirshner, N. (1969). Mechanism of secretion from the adrenal medulla IV: The fate of the storage vesicles following insulin and reserpine administration. *Molecular Pharmacology, 5*(1), 69–82.

Vogel, J. R., Beer, B., & Clody, D. E. (1971). A simple and reliable conflict procedure for testing antianxiety agents. *Psychopharmacologia, 21*(1), 1–7.

Voleti, B., Navarria, A., Liu, R. J., Banasr, M., Li, N., Terwilliger, R., . . . & Duman, R. S. (2013). Scopolamine rapidly increases mammalian target of rapamycin complex 1 signaling, synaptogenesis, and antidepressant behavioral responses. *Biological Psychiatry, 74*(10), 742–749. doi: 10.1016/j.biopsych.2013.04.025

Volkow, N. D., Harper, A., Munnisteri, D., & Clother, J.E.F.F.R.E.Y. (1987). AIDS and catatonia. *Journal of Neurology, Neurosurgery, and Psychiatry, 50*(1), 104.

Volkow, N. D., & O'Brien, C. P. (2007). Issues for DSM-V: Should obesity be included as a brain disorder? [Editorial]. *American Journal of Psychiatry, 164*(5), 708–710. doi: 10.1176/appi.ajp.164.5.708

Volkow, N. D., Wang, G. J., Fischman, M. W., Foltin, R., Fowler, J. S., Franceschi, D., . . . & Pappas, N. (2000). Effects of route of administration on cocaine induced dopamine transporter blockade in the human brain. *Life Sciences, 67*(12), 1507–1515. doi: 10.1016/ s0024-3205(00)00731–1

Volkow, N. D., Wang, G. J., Fowler, J. S., Tomasi, D., & Baler, R. (2012). Food and drug reward: Overlapping circuits in human obesity and addiction. *Current Topics in Behavioral Neurosciences, 11,* 1–24. doi: 10.1007/7854_2011_169

Volkow, N. D., & Wise, R. A. (2005). How can drug addiction help us understand obesity? [Review]. *Nature Neuroscience, 8*(5), 555–560. doi: 10.1038/nn1452

Vollenweider, F. X., Leenders, K. L., Scharfetter, C., Maguire, P., Stadelmann, O., & Angst, J. (1997). Positron emission tomography and fluorodeoxyglucose studies of metabolic hyperfrontality and psychopathology in the psilocybin model of psychosis. *Neuropsychopharmacology, 16*(5), 357–372. doi: S0893–133X(96)00246–1 [pii]

Volpi, R., Chiodera, P., Caffarra, P., Scaglioni, A., Saccani, A., & Coiro, V. (1997). Different control mechanisms of growth hormone (GH) secretion between gamma-amino- and gamma-hydroxybutyric acid: Neuroendocrine evidence in Parkinson's disease. *Psychoneuroendocrinology, 22*(7), 531–538.

Volpicelli, J. R., Alterman, A. I., Hayashida, M., & O'Brien, C. P. (1992). Naltrexone in the treatment of alcohol dependence. *Archives of General Psychiatry, 49*(11), 876–880.

Volpicelli, J. R., Sarin-Krishnan, S., & O'Malley, S. S. (2002). Alcoholism pharmacotherapy. In K. L. Davis, D. Charney, J. T. Coyle, & C. Nemeroff (Eds.), *Neuropsychopharmacology: The fifth generation of progress,* 1445–1459. Brentwood, NJ: American College of Neuropsychopharmacology.

Vos, J. W., Ufkes, J.G.R., Wilgenburg, H., Geerlings, P. J., & Brink, W. (1995). Pharmacokinetics of methadone and its primary metabolite in 20 opiate addicts. *European Journal of Clinical Pharmacology, 48*(5), 361–366. doi: 10.1007/bf00194951

Wadden, T.A., Berkowitz, R. I, Silvestry, F., Vogt, R. A., St. John Sutton, M.G., Stunkard, A. J., Foster, G. D. & Aber, J. L. (1998). The fen-phen finale: A study of weight loss and vascular heart disease. *Obesity Research, 6,* 278–284. doi: 10.1002/j.1550-8528.1998.tb00350.x

Wade, D. (2012). Evaluation of the safety and tolerability profile of Sativex: Is it reassuring enough? *Expert Review of Neurotherapeutics, 12*(4 Suppl.), 9–14. doi: 10.1586/ern.12.12

Wall, T. L., Peterson, C. M., Peterson, K. P., Johnson, M. L., Thomasson, H. R., Cole, M., & Ehlers, C. L. (1997). Alcohol metabolism in Asian-American men with genetic polymorphisms of aldehyde dehydrogenase. *Annals of Internal Medicine, 127*(5), 376–379. doi: 10.7326/0003-4819-127-5-199709010-00007

Wallis, G. G., McHarg, J. F., & Scott, O.C.A. (1949). Acute psychosis caused by dextro-amphetamine. *British Medical Journal, 2*(4641), 1394.

Walter, H. J., & Messing, R. O. (1999). Regulation of neuronal voltage-gated calcium channels by ethanol.

Neurochemistry International, 35(2), 95–101.

Warburton, D. M. (2002). Commentary on: "Effects of scopolamine and nicotine on human rapid information processing performance." *Psychopharmacology* (1984) 82: 147–150. *Psychopharmacology, 162*(4), 345–348.

Ware, M. A., Wang, T., Shapiro, S., Robinson, A., Ducruet, T., Huynh, T., . . . & Collet, J. P. (2010). Smoked cannabis for chronic neuropathic pain: A randomized controlled trial. *Canadian Medical Association Journal, 182*(14), E694–E701. doi: 10.1503/ cmaj.091414

Warzak, W. J., Evans, S., Floress, M. T., Gross, A. C., & Stoolman, S. (2011). Caffeine consumption in young children. *Journal of Pediatrics, 158*(3), 508–509. doi: 10.1016/j.jpeds.2010.11.022

Watanabe, A. M., McConnaughey, M. M., Strawbridge, R. A., Fleming, J. W., Jones, L. R., & Besch, H. R. (1978). Muscarinic cholinergic receptor modulation of beta-adrenergic receptor affinity for catecholamines. *Journal of Biological Chemistry, 253*(14), 4833–4836.

Watkins, L. R., Milligan, E. D., & Maier, S. F. (2001). Glial activation: A driving force for pathological pain. *Trends in Neuroscience, 24*(8), 450–455.

Wechsler, H., Lee, J. E., Kuo, M., Seibring, M., Nelson, T. F., & Lee, H. (2002). Trends in college binge drinking during a period of increased prevention efforts: Findings from 4 Harvard School of Public Health College Alcohol Study surveys, 1993–2001. *Journal of American College Health, 50*(5), 203–217.

Weese, H., & Scharpff, W. (1932). Evipan, ein neuartiges Einschlafmittel. *Deutsche Medizinische Wochenschrift, 58,* 1205–1207.

Weil, A. T., Zinberg, N. E., & Nelsen, J. M. (1968). Clinical and psychological effects of marihuana in man. *Science, 162*(859), 1234–1242.

Weinberger, D. R. (1996). On the plausibility of "the neurodevelopmental hypothesis" of schizophrenia. *Neuropsychopharmacology, 14*(3 Suppl.), 1S–11S. doi: 10.1016/ 0893-133X(95)00199-N

Welkowitz, L. A., Papp, L., Martinez, J., Browne, S., & Gorman, J. M. (1999). Instructional set and

physiological response to CO2 inhalation. *American Journal of Psychiatry, 156*(5), 745–748.

Wesnes, K., & Warburton, D. M. (1984). Effects of scopolamine and nicotine on human rapid information processing performance. *Psychopharmacology, 82*(3), 147–150. doi: 10.1007/bf00427761

Westgate, H. D., & Stiebler, H. J. (1964). Barbiturate abstinence syndrome. *Anesthesiology, 25,* 403–405.

White, A. M., Kraus, C. L., & Swartzwelder, H. S. (2006). Many college freshmen drink at levels far beyond the binge threshold. *Alcoholism: Clinical and Experimental Research, 30*(6), 1006–1010. doi: 10.1111/j.15300277.2006.00122.x

Wiese, J. G., Shlipak, M. G., & Browner, W. S. (2000). The alcohol hangover. *Annals of Internal Medicine, 132*(11), 897–902.

Wilk, C. M., Gold, J. M., Humber, K., Dickerson, F., Fenton, W. S., & Buchanan, R. W. (2004). Brief cognitive assessment in schizophrenia: Normative data for the Repeatable Battery for the Assessment of Neuropsychological Status. *Schizophrenia Research, 70*(2–3), 175–186. doi: 10.1016/j.schres.2003.10.009

Williams, C. M., & Kirkham, T. C. (1999). Anandamide induces overeating: Mediation by central cannabinoid (CB1) receptors. *Psychopharmacology, 143*(3), 315–317. doi: 10.1007/s002130050953

Williams, J. F., & Storck, M. (2007). Inhalant abuse. *Pediatrics, 119*(5), 1009–1017. doi: 10.1542/ peds.2007-0470

Willis, W. D., & Westlund, K. N. (1997). Neuroanatomy of the pain system and of the pathways that modulate pain. *Journal of Clinical Neurophysiology, 14*(1), 2–31.

Winickoff, J. P., Friebely, J., Tanski, S. E., Sherrod, C., Matt, G. E., Hovell, M. F., & McMillen, R. C. (2009). Beliefs about the health effects of "thirdhand" smoke and home smoking bans. *Pediatrics, 123,* e74-e79. doi: 10.1542/peds.2008-2184

Winkler, D., Pjrek, E., & Kasper, S. (2005). Anger attacks in depression–evidence for a male depressive syndrome. *Psychotherapy and*

Psychosomatics, 74(5), 303–307. doi: 10.1159/000086321

Winter, J. C., Rice, K. C., Amorosi, D. J., & Rabin, R. A. (2007). Psilocybin-induced stimulus control in the rat. *Pharmacology Biochemistry and Behavior, 87*(4), 472–480. doi: 10.1016/j. pbb.2007.06.003

Wirshing, D. A., Wirshing, W. C., Kysar, L., Berisford, M. A., Goldstein, D., Pashdag, J., . . . & Marder, S. R. (1999). Novel antipsychotics: Comparison of weight gain liabilities. *Journal of Clinical Psychiatry, 60*(6), 358–363.

Wisden, W., Laurie, D. J., Monyer, H., & Seeburg, P. H. (1992). The distribution of 13 GABAA receptor subunit mRNAs in the rat brain. I. Telencephalon, diencephalon, mesencephalon. *Journal of Neuroscience, 12*(3), 1040–1062.

Wise, R. A. (1989). Opiate reward: Sites and substrates. *Neuroscience and Biobehavioral Reviews, 13*(2–3), 129–133.

Wise, R. A., Yokel, R. A., & Wit, H. D. (1976). Both positive reinforcement and conditioned aversion from amphetamine and from apomorphine in rats. *Science, 191*(4233), 1273–1275.

Wish, E. D., Fitzelle, D. B., O'Grady, K. E., Hsu, M. H., & Arria, A. M. (2006). Evidence for significant polydrug use among Ecstasy-using college students. *Journal of American College Health, 55*(2), 99–104. doi: 10.3200/ jach.55.2.99–104

Witteman, J., Post, H., Tarvainen, M., Bruijn, A., Perna, E.S.F., Ramaekers, J. G., & Wiers, R. W. (2015). Cue reactivity and its relation to craving and relapse in alcohol dependence: A combined laboratory and field study. *Psychopharmacology, 232*, 3685–3696. doi: 10.1007/s00213–015–4027–6

Wolfe, F., Ross, K., Anderson, J., Russell, I. J., & Hebert, L. (1995). The prevalence and characteristics of fibromyalgia in the general population. *Arthritis and Rheumatism, 38*(1), 19–28.

Wong, A.H.C., & Van Tol, H.H.M. (2003). Schizophrenia: From phenomenology to neurobiology. *Neuroscience and Biobehavioral Reviews, 27*, 269–306.

Wonnacott, S. (1990). The paradox of nicotinic acetylcholine receptor upregulation by nicotine. *Trends in Pharmacological Sciences, 11*(6), 216–219.

Wood, D. M., Greene, S. L., & Dargan, P. I. (2011). Clinical pattern of toxicity associated with the novel synthetic cathinone mephedrone. *Emergency Medicine Journal, 28*(4), 280–282. doi: 10.1136/emj.2010.092288

Woodward, N. D., Purdon, S. E., Meltzer, H. Y., & Zald, D. H. (2005). A meta-analysis of neuropsychological change to clozapine, olanzapine, quetiapine, and risperidone in schizophrenia. *International Journal of Neuropsychopharmacology, 8*(3), 457–472.

Woodworth, T. (1999). Date rape drugs. DEA congressional testimony, before the House Commerce Committee, Subcommittee on Oversight and Investigations. Retrieved from www.gpo.gov/fdsys/pkg/CHRG-106hhrg55638/pdf/CHRG-106hhrg55638.pdf

Woolf, N. J. (1991). Cholinergic systems in mammalian brain and spinal cord. *Progress in Neurobiology, 37*, 475–524.

Woolverton, W. L., Kandel, D., & Schuster, C. R. (1978). Tolerance and cross-tolerance to cocaine and d-amphetamine. *Journal of Pharmacology and Experimental Therapeutics, 205*(3), 525–535.

World Health Organization. (2011). *Global status report on alcohol and health.* Geneva: Author. Retrieved from www.who.int/substance_abuse/publications/global_alcohol_report/en/index.html

World Health Organization. (2012). *Health topics: Substance abuse.* Geneva: Author. Retrieved from www.who.int/topics/substance_abuse/en/

World Health Organization. (2014). *Proportion of all DALYs attributable to alcohol (AAF; %: all ages), 2012.* Geneva: Author. Retrieved from http://gamapserver.who.int/mapLibrary/Files/Maps/Global_dalys_2012.png

World Health Organization. (2016). *WHO urges more investments, services for mental health.* Geneva: Author. Retrieved from http://www.who.int/mental_health/who_urges_investment/en/

Wu, C. Y., & Wittick, J. J. (1977). Separation of five major alkaloids in gum opium and quantitation of morphine, codeine, and thebaine by isocratic reverse phase high performance liquid chromatography. *Analytical Chemistry, 49*(3), 359–363.

Wu, H., Zink, N., Carter, L. P., Mehta, A. K., Hernandez, R. J., Ticku, M. K., . . . & Coop, A. (2003). A tertiary alcohol analog of γ-hydroxybutyric acid as a specific γ-hydroxybutyric acid receptor ligand. *Journal of Pharmacology and Experimental Therapeutics, 305*(2), 675–679. doi: 10.1124/jpet.102.046797

Wyndham, C. H. (1977). Heat stroke and hyperthermia in marathon runners. *Annals of the New York Academy of Sciences, 301*(1), 128–138. doi: 10.1111/j.17496632.1977.tb38192.x

Xiao, C., & Ye, J. H. (2008). Ethanol dually modulates GABAergic synaptic transmission onto dopaminergic neurons in ventral tegmental area: Role of [mu]-opioid receptors. *Neuroscience, 153*(1), 240–248. doi: 10.1016/j.neuroscience.2008.01.040

Xiao, C., Zhou, C., Li, K., & Ye, J.-H. (2007). Presynaptic GABAA receptors facilitate GABAergic transmission to dopaminergic neurons in the ventral tegmental area of young rats. *Journal of Physiology, 580*(3), 731–743. doi: 10.1113/jphysiol.2006.124099

Yakushiji, T., Fukuda, T., Oyama, Y., & Akaike, N. (1989). Effects of benzodiazepines and non-benzodiazepine compounds on the GABA-induced response in frog isolated sensory neurones. *British Journal of Pharmacology, 98*(3), 735–740. doi: 10.1111/j.1476–5381.1989.tb14600.x

Yanagisawa, N., Morita, H., & Nakajima, T. (2006). Sarin experiences in Japan: Acute toxicity and long-term effects. *Journal of the Neurological Sciences, 249*(1), 76–85.

Yang, J., Jamei, M., Heydari, A., Yeo, K. R., de la Torre, R., Farré, M., . . . & Rostami-Hodjegan, A. (2006). Implications of mechanism-based inhibition of CYP2D6 for the pharmacokinetics and toxicity of MDMA. *Journal of Psychopharmacology, 20*(6), 842–849. doi: 10.1177/0269881106065907

Yang, K., Buhlman, L., Khan, G. M., Nichols, R. A., Jin, G., McIntosh, J. M., . . . & Wu, J. (2011). Functional nicotinic acetylcholine receptors containing α6 subunits are on GABAergic neuronal boutons adherent to ventral tegmental area dopamine neurons. *Journal of Neuroscience, 31*(7), 2537–2548. doi: 10.1523/jneurosci.3003–10.2011

Yeh, S. Y., & Woods, L. A. (1970). Isolation of morphine-3-glucuronide from urine and bile of rats injected with codeine. *Journal of Pharmacology and Experimental Therapeutics, 175*(1), 69–74.

Yehuda, R., Southwick, S. M., Nussbaum, G., Wahby, V., Giller, E. L., Jr., & Mason, J. W. (1990). Low urinary cortisol excretion in patients with posttraumatic stress disorder. *Journal of Nervous and Mental Disease, 178*(6), 366–369.

Yoshimoto, K., McBride, W. J., Lumeng, L., & Li, T. K. (1992). Ethanol enhances the release of dopamine and serotonin in the nucleus accumbens of HAD and LAD lines of rats. *Alcoholism: Clinical and Experimental Research, 16*(4), 781–785. doi: 10.1111/j.15300277.1992.tb00678.x

Youdim, M.B.H. (2006). Monoamine oxidases, their inhibitors, and the opening of the neurotransmitter era in neuropsychopharmacology. In T. A. Ban & R. U. Udabe (Eds.), *The neurotransmitter era in neuropsychopharmacology* (pp. 107–126). Buenos Aires, Argentina: Editorial Polemos.

Yuncu, Z., Zorlu, N., Saatcioglu, H., Basay, B., Basay, O., Zorlu, P. K., Kitis, O., & Gelal, F. (2015). Abnormal white matter integrity and impairment of cognitive abilities in adolescent inhalant abusers. *Neurotoxicology and Teratology, 47*, 89–95. doi: 10.1016/j.ntt.2014.11.009

Yung, M., Sharma, R., Jablenska, L., & Yung, T. (2015). A 2-cycle audit on the feasibility, efficacy and patient acceptance of 21 emergency sphrenopalatine artery ligations under local anaesthesia: our experience. *Clinical Otolaryngology, 41*, 407–411. doi: 10.1111/coa.12528

Yusof, W., & Gan, S. H. (2009). High prevalence of CYP2A6*4 and CYP2A6*9 alleles detected among a Malaysian population. *Clinica Chimica Acta, 403*(1–2), 105–109. doi: 10.1016/j.cca.2009.01.032

Zakhari, S. (1997). Alcohol and the cardiovascular system: Molecular mechanisms for beneficial and harmful action. *Alcohol Research and Health, 21*(1), 21–29.

Zakzanis, K., Leach, L., & Kaplan, E. (1998). On the nature and pattern of neurocognitive function in major depressive disorder. *Cognitive and Behavioral Neurology, 11*(3), 111–119.

Zangrossi, H., Viana, M. B., & Graeff, F. G. (1999). Anxiolytic effect of intra-amygdala injection of midazolam and 8-hydroxy-2-(di-npropylamino)tetralin in the elevated T-maze. *European Journal of Pharmacology, 369*(3), 267–270.

Zarate, C. A., Jr., Singh, J. B., Carlson, P. J., Brutsche, N. E., Ameli, R., Luckenbaugh, D. A., . . . & Manji, H. K. (2006). A randomized trial of an N-methyl-D-aspartate antagonist in treatment-resistant major depression. *Archives of General Psychiatry, 63*(8), 856–864. doi: 10.1001/archpsyc.63.8.856

Zhang, F., Vierock, J., Yizhar, O., Fenno, L. E., Tsunoda, S., Kianianmomeni, A., . . . &

Deisseroth, K. (2011). The microbial opsin family of optogenetic tools. *Cell, 147*, 1446–1457. doi: http://dx.doi.org/10.1016/j.cell.2011.12.004

Zhao-Shea, R., Liu, L., Soll, L. G., Improgo, M. R., Meyers, E. E., McIntosh, J. M., . . . & Tapper, A. R. (2011). Nicotine-mediated activation of dopaminergic neurons in distinct regions of the ventral tegmental area. *Neuropsychopharmacology, 36*(5), 1021–1032. doi: 10.1038/npp.2010.240

Zhou, F. C., Lesch, K.-P., & Murphy, D. L. (2002). Serotonin uptake into dopamine neurons via dopamine transporters: A compensatory alternative. *Brain Research, 942*(1–2), 109–119. doi: 10.1016/ s0006–8993(02)02709–9

Zimatkin, S. M., Liopo, A. V., & Deitrich, R. A. (1998). Distribution and kinetics of ethanol metabolism in rat brain. *Alcoholism: Clinical and Experimental Research, 22*(8), 1623–1627. doi: 10.1111/j.1530–0277.1998. tb03958.x

Zolkowska, D., Jain, R., Rothman, R. B., Partilla, J. S., Roth, B. L., Setola, V., Prisinzano, T. E., & Baumann, M. H. (2009). Evidence for the involvement of dopamine transporters in behavioral stimulant effects of modafinil. *Journal of Pharmacology and Experimental Therapeutics, 329*, 738–746. doi: 10.1124/jpet.108.146142

Zvosec, D. L., & Smith, S. W. (2009). Response to "Cognitive, psychomotor and subjective effects of sodium oxybate and triazolam in healthy volunteers," *206*(1), 141–154. *Psychopharmacology (Berl), 207*(3), 509–510; author reply 511–502. doi: 10.1007/s00213009–1662–9

• Author Index •

Andresen, H., 279, 281, 289
Andriamampandry, C.
  see Muller, C.
Andrieux, M.
  see Sokoloff, P.
Anduze, A. L., 352
Anglin, M. D., 159
Angrist, B., 357
Angst, J.
  see Merikangas, K. R.;
    Vollenweider, F. X.
An, K.
  see Shu, H.
Anonymous, 506
Anrep, G. V., 143
Antley, A.
  see Freeman, D.
Antoniou, K.
  see Polissidis, A.
Apelberg, B. J.
  see Bunnell, R. E.
Apovian, C. M., 164
Appel-Dingemanse, S., 25
Aramaki, H.
  see Takeda, S.
Arango, C., 54
Araújo, J. R., 492
Archer, S. M., 107, 495
Archibald, D.
  see Fleischhacker, W. W.
Arenovich, T., 488
  see also Agid, O.
Areosa Sastre, A.
  see McShane, R.
Areso, P.
  see Ordway, G. A.
Arinaminpathy, Y., 127
Arita, H.
  see Shu, H.
Ariyoshi, N., 215
Armitage, A. K., 213
Armstrong, N., 127
Arnaud, M. J., 238
Arnér, S., 323
Arnold, E. P.
  see Coe, J. W.
Arnold, L. M., 414
Arnold, M. M.
  see Lotfipour, S.
Arnold, S. E., 481
Arnow, B.
  see Keller, M. B.
Arnsten, A. F., 156
Aronne, L. J., 164
Arora, R. C., 384
  see also Smith, R. C.
Arqueros, L., 403
Arrazola, R.
  see Bunnell, R. E.
Arria, A. M., 235, 240, 367
Arthaud, S.
  see Lanfray, D.

Artigas, F., 415
Arttamangkul, S., 311
Asami, S., 156
Åsberg, M., 421
  see also Nordström, P.
Ascher, J. A., 415
Ashford, J. W., 107, 495
Ashton, C. H., 331, 331 (table), 332, 350
Asin, K. E., 415
Asprodini, E. K., 238
  see also Begas, E.
Aston-Jones, G.
  see Mahler, S. V.
Athanaselis, S.
  see Bruci, Z.
Atkinson, J. H.
  see Ellis, R. J.
Attilia, M. L.
  see Addolorato, G.
Atzori, M., 486
Auld, D. S., 81
Aunis, D.
  see Muller, C.
Aura, J., 156
Austin, G. A., 249
Autism Genetic Resource
    Exchange Consortium
  see Alarcón, M.
Axelrod, J., 357, 408
  see also Felder, C. C.
Axmacher, N.
  see Schlaepfer, T. E.
Aydin, B. E., 279
  see also Andresen, H.
Ayestas, M. A., 174, 374
Ayestas, M. A., Jr.
  see Baumann, M. H.
Ayoglu, B., 352
Azar, M. R.
  see Guillem, K.
Aziz, N. A.
  see Donjacour, C. E. H. M.
Aznar, S., 468
Azoulay, S.
  see Gonzales, D.

Baan, R.
  see Cogliano, V. J.
Baas, J. M., 449 (figure)
Babu, K. M., 332
Baccei, C. S., 422
Bachman, J. G., 291
Back, S. E., 197
Badger, G. J.
  see Lussier, J. P.
Bagwell, C., 173
Bahl, V., 210, 211
Bailey, A., 499
Bailey, M., 367
  see also Cole, J. C.
Bailey, S. J., 420
Baio, J., 499

Baker, F., 506
Baker, J. R., 199
Baker, K. M., 225 (figure), 231 (figure)
  see also Prus, A. J.
Baker, L. E., 295, 296, 296 (figure)
  see also Goudie, A. J.
Baker, T. B.
  see Kenford, S. L.
Baldinger, R.
  see Joerger, M.
Balducci, G.
  see Addolorato, G.
Bale, A. S., 293
Baler, R., 164
Ballard, S. A.
  see Boolell, M.
Ballenger, J. C., 197, 269
Balster, R. L., 290, 293, 294, 297, 388
Banasr, M.
  see Li, N.; Voleti, B.
Baner, K.
  see Roth, B. L.
Bang-Andersen, B., 415
Barak, Y., 492
Baraona, E.
  see Frezza, M.
Barber-Heidal, K., 235
Barch, D. M., 481
Bardgett, M. E.
  see Drevets, W. C.
Bari, M., 338
  see also Battista, N.
Barker, E. L., 72
Barker, K. L., 24
  see also Blake, C. A.
Barmack, N. H., 463
Barnes, M. P., 352
Barnett, T. E., 332
  see also Hu, X.
Baron, J. C.
  see Laplane, D.
Barral, D.
  see Abanades, S.
Barrett, R. J., 194, 195 (figure)
Bar, T., 357
Bartfield, R. B., 284
  see also Okun, M. S.
Barth, E., 493
Basarsky, T. A., 81
Basavarajappa, B. S., 257
Basay, B.
  see Yuncu, Z.
Basay, O.
  see Yuncu, Z.
Basch, J.
  see Miotto, K.
Baselt, R.
  see LeBeau, M.
Basile, A. S., 406, 421
Bassel-Duby, R.
  see Li, Y.
Bass, M., 292

• Subject Index •